EXPLORING
BRITAIN'S
LOST RAILWAYS

THE TIMES EXPLORING BRITAIN'S LOST RAILWAYS

Times Books, 77-85 Fulham Palace Road, London W6 8JB

First Edition 2013

Copyright © Times Books Group Ltd 2013
Text © Julian Holland
Maps and photographs © as per credits on page 304

The Times is a registered trademark of Times Newspapers Ltd

British Library Cataloguing in Publication Data
A catalogue record for this book is available from the British Library

ISBN 978 0 00 750541 8
Imp 001

If you would like to comment on any aspect of this publication, please write to:
Times Atlases, HarperCollins Publishers, Westerhill Road, Bishopbriggs, Glasgow G64 2QT
e-mail: **timesatlas@harpercollins.co.uk**

Visit our website at: **www.harpercollins.co.uk**

Search Facebook for 'Collins Maps'

Follow us **@collinsmaps**

With special thanks to

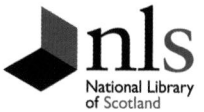

THE TIMES

EXPLORING
BRITAIN'S
LOST RAILWAYS

JULIAN HOLLAND

TIMES BOOKS
LONDON

CONTENTS

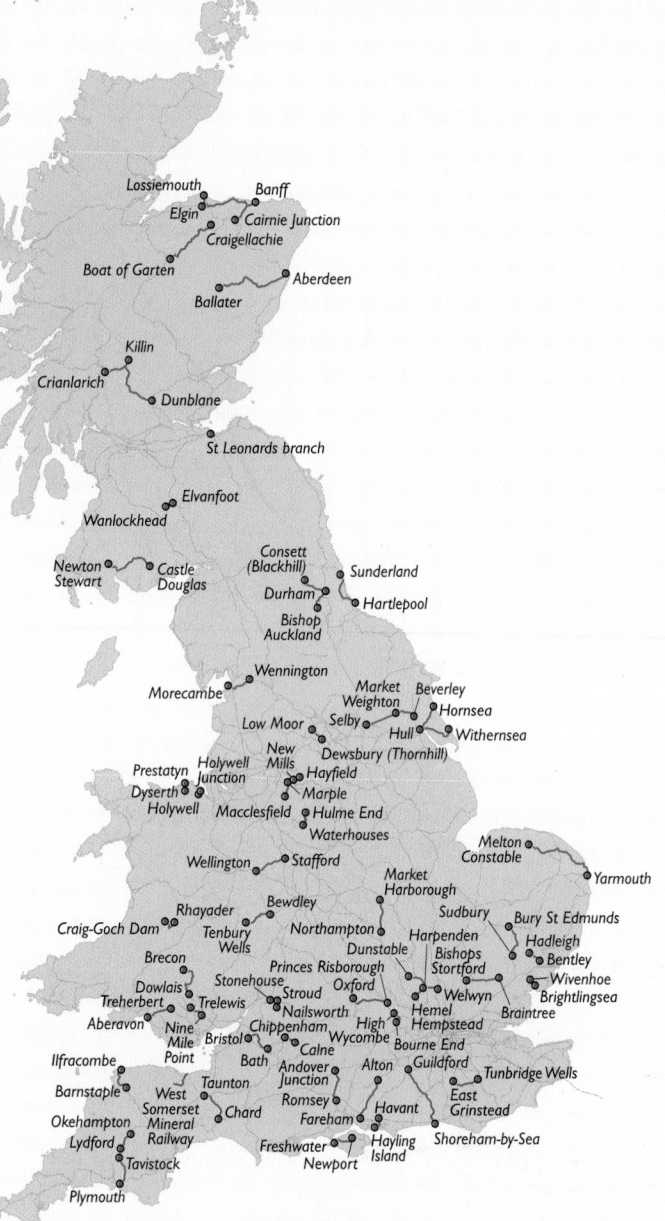

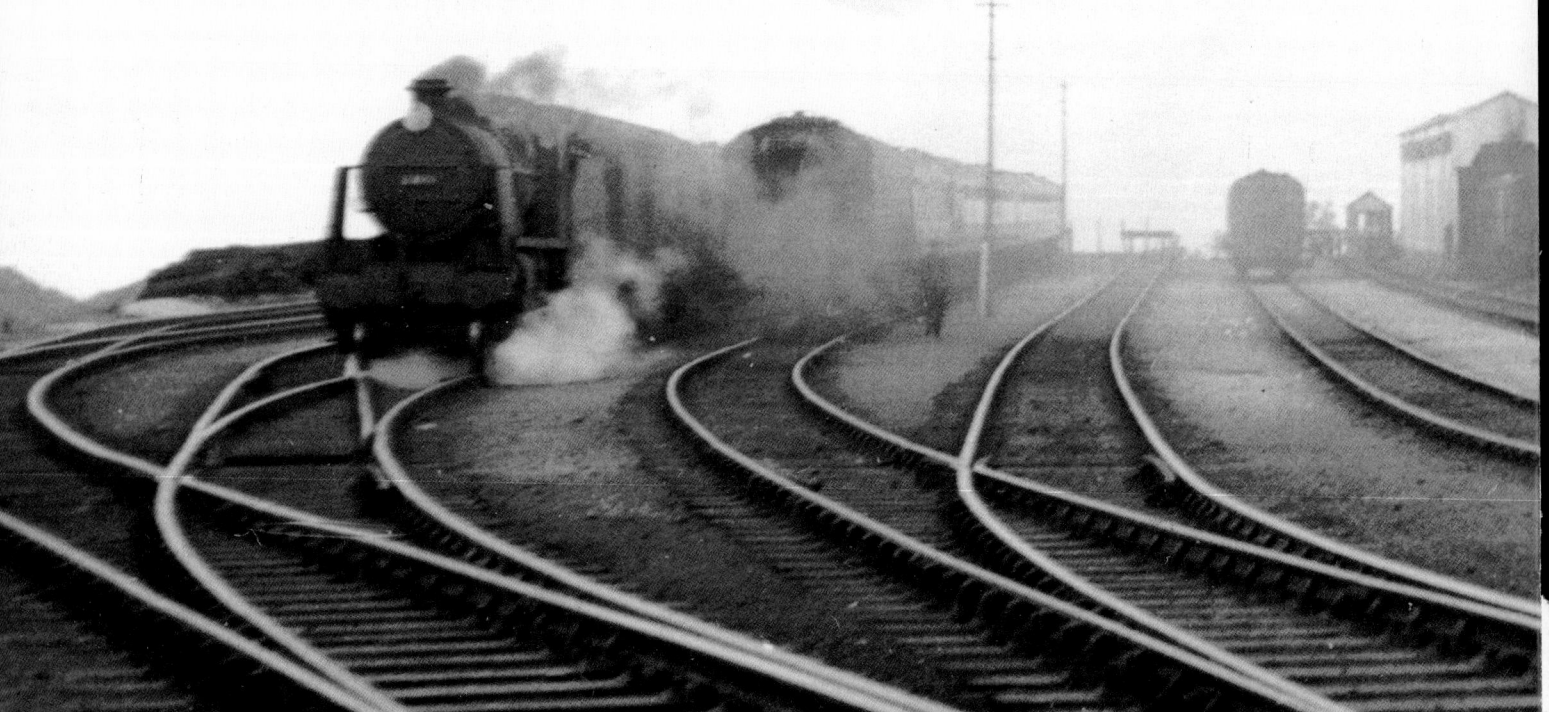

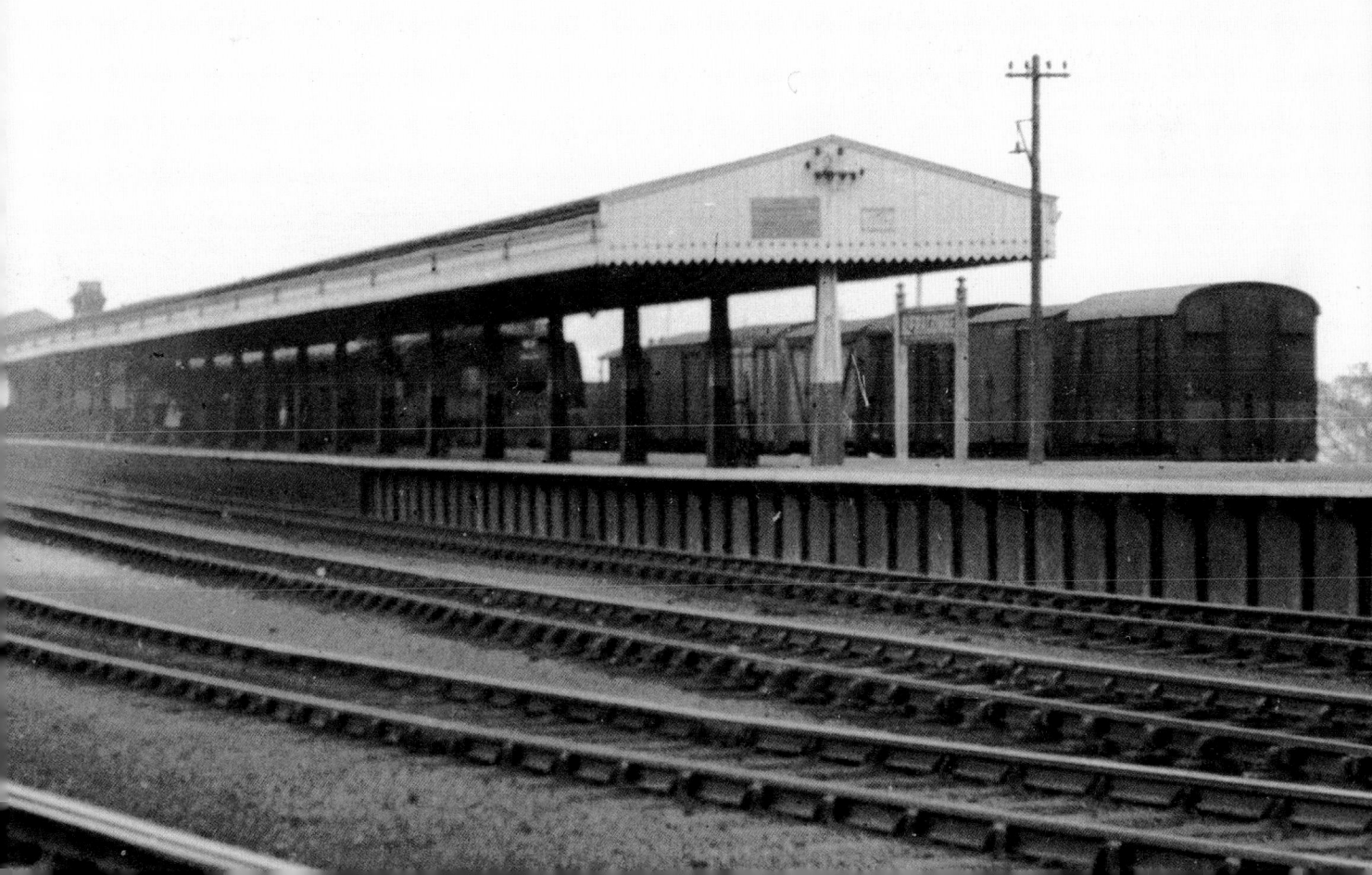

INTRODUCTION

It is now over 50 years since the publication of the infamous 'Beeching Report' (official title 'The Reshaping of British Railways') in which Dr Richard Beeching proposed the closure of around 5,000 route miles of Britain's rail network along with a third of its stations and consequently the loss of tens of thousands of railway workers' jobs. As a result around 4,500 miles of railway and 2,000 stations were closed between 1963 and the mid-1970s, much of this mileage in rural areas, leaving vast swathes of England, Wales and Scotland without a rail link to the outside world for the first time in a hundred years.

Despite this act of politically motivated vandalism railway closures in Britain were not a new phenomenon. Following nationalization of our rundown railways in 1948, the newly formed British Transport Corporation set up the Branch Lines Committee whose sole aim in life was to weed out loss-making branch lines – over 3,000

miles of these railways were subsequently closed before Dr Beeching even published his 'Report'.

Even before the bloodletting of the post-war years railway closures had already been gathering pace. The heady days of the nineteenth century had seen numerous railway companies building competing lines that eventually stood no chance when pitted against the more flexible and often cheaper alternative of road transport of the 1930s. Rural areas were particularly hard hit with the 'Big Four' railway companies closing several hundred miles of loss-making branch lines before the onset of the Second World War.

Of course, the *raison d'être* of the first railways was not to carry passengers but to carry raw materials, in particular coal, and their arrival on the scene soon put an end to the short-lived Canal Age. Years before steam haulage became the norm there were hundreds of miles of horse-drawn

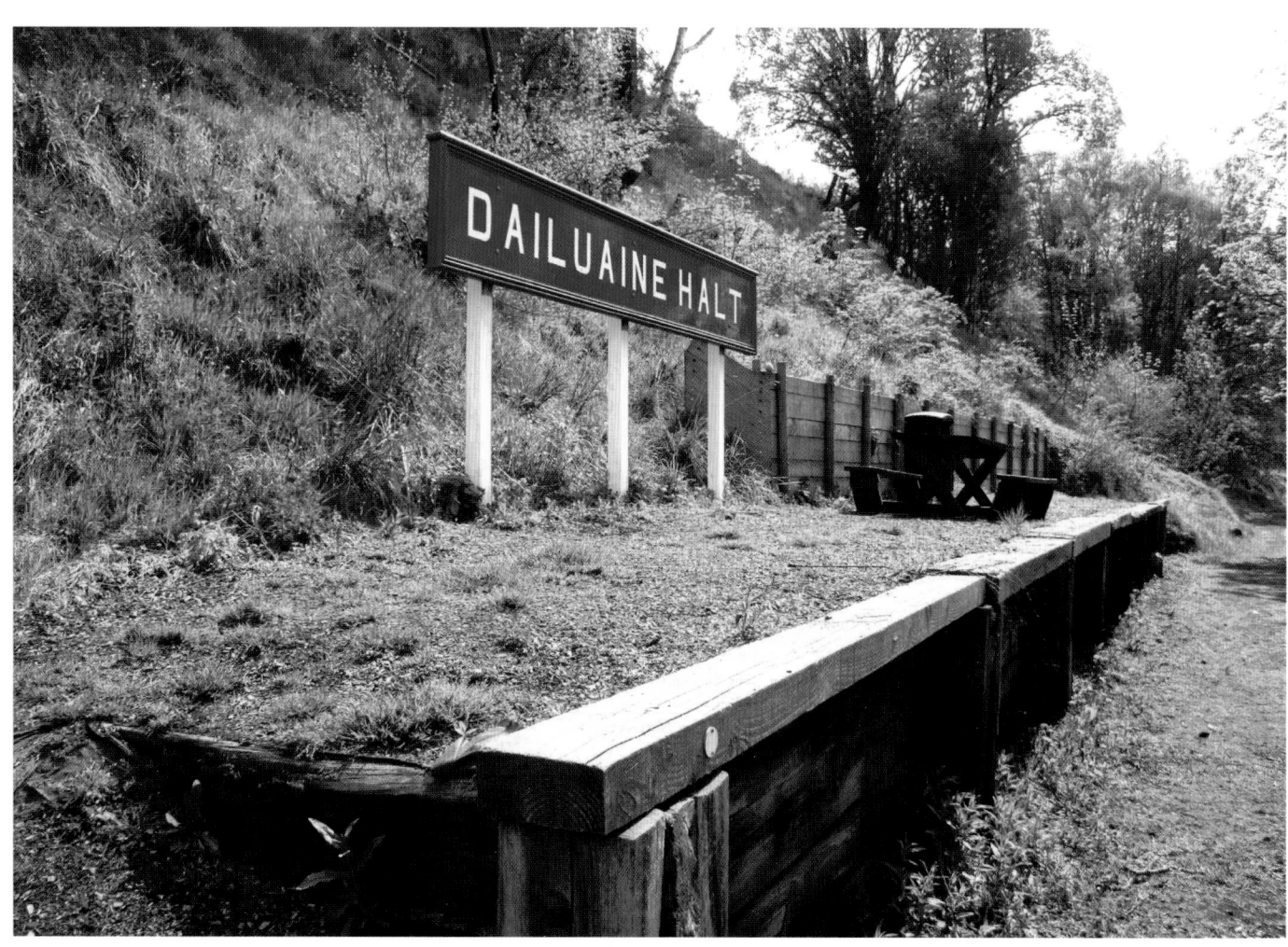

wooden waggonways linking coal mines with industrial centres and cities in South Wales, Northeast England and Central Scotland. These industrial lines were rebuilt with iron rails in the early nineteenth century at a time when the first steam locomotives were also being introduced and together they played a pivotal role in Britain's industrial revolution. However, many of these industrial railways came and went with their closure barely noticed by the travelling public.

So what happened to these thousands of miles of lost railways that once criss-crossed Britain? Many just disappeared into the landscape, the land sold off in a piecemeal fashion to farmers and many of the substantial station buildings finding a new lease of life as private residences. Nature gradually took over until the only clue to a railway's past existence was a line of trees cutting across the landscape, the occasional bridge over a flooded cutting, the stark outline of an embankment, or the bricked-up mouth of a tunnel. More substantial remains such as lofty stone viaducts striding across valleys and iron

bridges soaring across rivers remained as a striking memorial to the optimistic endeavours of their Victorian builders.

The first glimmer of hope for Britain's lost railways came in 1937 when the owners of the closed Leek & Manifold Valley Light Railway – the London Midland & Scottish Railway – gave the 8-mile trackbed to Staffordshire County Council for use as a footpath and bridleway. The Second World War then intervened before a new breed of railway preservationists took to the stage.

The world's first railway preservation scheme came in 1951 when a group of like-minded enthusiasts saved the narrow-gauge Talyllyn Railway in Wales from closure. This was followed in 1960 when the Bluebell Railway in Sussex became the first preserved standard-gauge steam-operated railway in the world to operate a public service. Since then Britain has seen an amazing renaissance in these heritage railways with over 500 miles of standard- and narrow-gauge lines – the vast majority steam-hauled – reopened to the public.

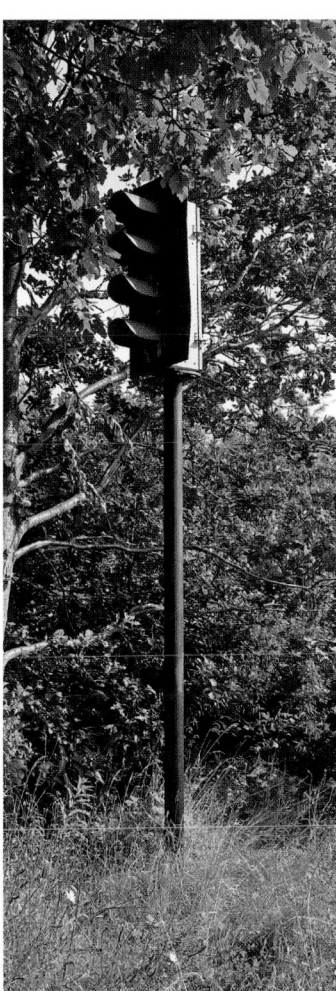

LEFT: The Speyside Way in Scotland follows much of the route of the Boat of Garten to Craigellachie railway that closed to passengers in 1965. The majority of the stations along this line have survived including the restored Dailuaine Halt – a very rudimentary affair built of sleepers, which was opened by the LNER in 1933 – midway between Carron and Aberlour.

RIGHT: Lost railway sleuths always need to keep their eyes open for a long-lost artefact – here, a modern four-aspect colour signal has surprisingly survived alongside the Spen Valley Greenway on the former railway route from Low Moor to Thornhill.

FAR RIGHT: The dank, dark and dripping Shaugh Tunnel on the former GWR route from Plymouth to Tavistock was built to accommodate Brunel's broad gauge but is now used by walkers and cyclists on Drake's Trail.

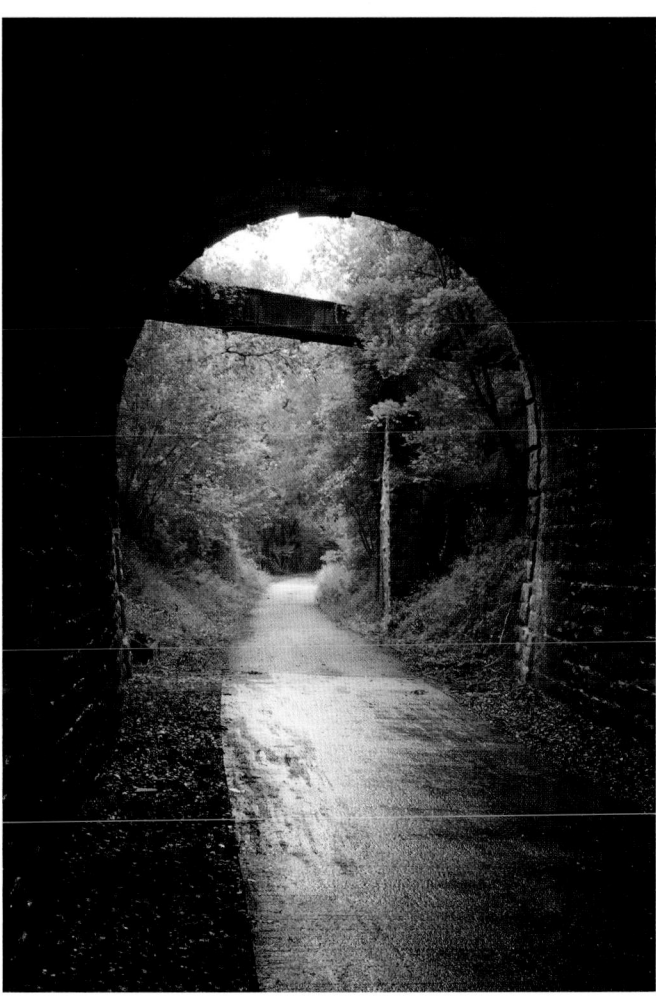

But what has happened to the other 7,000 miles or so of lost railways? While many still remain hidden away in the undergrowth or have been lost to road improvements and urban or industrial development, a growing number continue to be slowly reopened both as recreational footpaths and cycleways and as wildlife corridors. Britain's first traffic-free cycle route – the Bristol to Bath Railway Path – was opened by the fledgling sustainable transport charity Sustrans between 1979 and 1986. Since then Sustrans has opened over 10,000 miles of mainly traffic-free routes, many of them following long-closed railways, across the length and breadth of Britain. This National Cycle Network sees well over 400 million journeys taken by cyclists each year – add to this the millions of walkers and even horse riders who also use these routes and we have a truly amazing success story. While Sustrans – which does have its critics – is the leading advocate of reopening many of our closed railways as traffic-free routes, praise must also be given to the numerous local government authorities and landowners across the country and to National Lottery funding, all of which have made this possible. Some of our lost railways – for example the highly scenic route along the Spey Valley in Scotland – have also been incorporated into long-distance paths, while they all form wildlife corridors in which butterflies, birds, small mammals and wild flowers flourish.

As a young railway enthusiast and trainspotter in the early 1960s, I was fortunate to have travelled on many of these lines before they succumbed to Dr Beeching's Axe. Family summer holidays always involved a railway journey as my father did not own a car. The convoluted route from my home town of Gloucester to Lyme Regis in Dorset involved changing trains at Mangotsfield, Templecombe and Axminster, with the highlight being the Somerset & Dorset Joint Railway's route over the Mendip Hills – this was in August 1963 and the entire journey was accomplished behind steam haulage. The storm clouds were already building however, as the S&D and the Lyme

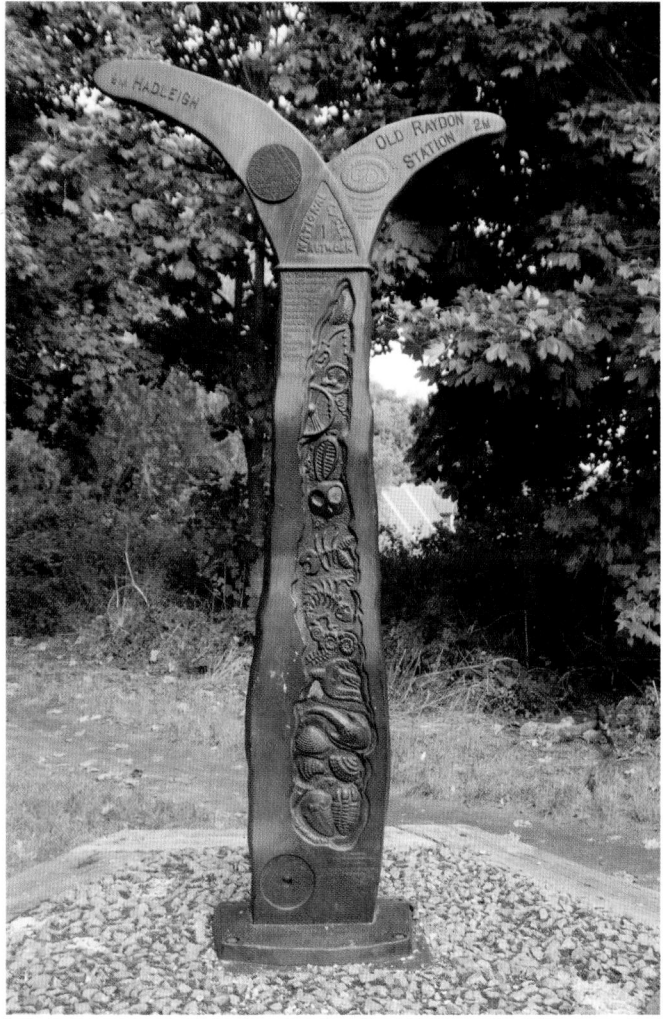

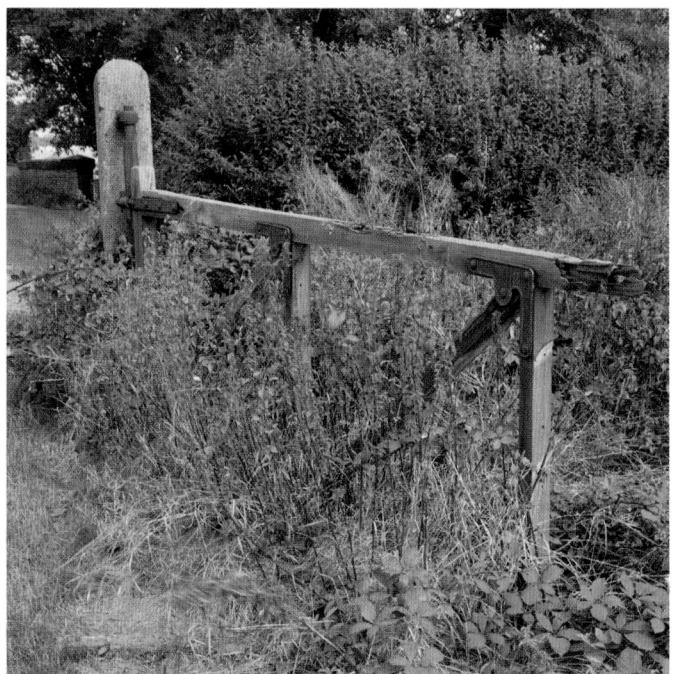

ABOVE: If you look hard enough you will discover relics of a long-lost and much-lamented period of British railway history. Still clinging to their rusted hinges, these level-crossing gates at Winestead on the Hull to Withernsea branch have survived alongside a busy road for nearly fifty years.

LEFT: This stylish Sustrans milepost at Hadleigh in Suffolk marks the distance to Raydon Wood station. The long-closed branch line now sees the passage of walkers and cyclists taking exercise along the 2-mile Hadleigh Railway Walk.

Regis branch had already been listed for closure in the 'Beeching Report' and within a few years they were consigned to the dustbin of history.

Often in the company of like-minded school friends, my trainspotting trips took me all over Britain. In between visiting dark and dirty steam engine sheds, the railway journeys across the wilds of Galloway on the 'Port Road' from Dumfries to Stranraer behind a Stanier 'Black 5' and along the Waverley Route from Carlisle to Edinburgh behind a 'Peak' diesel were just two of my many adventures in 1964. Little did I know then that nearly 50 years later I would be revisiting the routes of many of these long-lost lines to discover the hidden delights that still remain.

Exploring Britain's Lost Railways takes a nostalgic trip along over 50 of these long-closed railways, discovering their past and exploring their present role. In this book I will take you on a voyage of exploration that ranges from the long-lost West Somerset Mineral Railway, parts of which have recently been reopened by the Exmoor National Park Authority, the narrow-gauge Leek & Manifold Valley Light Railway which winds through the towering limestone crags of the Staffordshire hills and the bracing sea air of the Brightlingsea branch in Essex to the awesome splendour of the Elan Valley Railway route in Wales, the industrial landscape of the Spen Valley in Yorkshire and the 'Port Road' across the wilds of Galloway in Scotland.

This book is illustrated with many previously unpublished historical and specially commissioned present-day photographs. To complement these, the attractive period route maps give a detailed picture of how Britain looked in the golden age of railways before mass closures and motorways blighted our communities and countryside. The half-inch and one-inch to a mile Ordnance Survey maps used in this book date mainly from the 1920s while the more detailed 1:25,000 series is from the 1930s up to the 1950s. How our country has changed since then!

HOW THIS BOOK WORKS

The main text for each feature is set out in two sections. A commentary on the history of the line is followed by a description of exploring the route today.

Historical Ordnance Survey mapping has been highlighted to show the route followed by the original railway. In some cases, part of the line is still open, whether as part of the national network or as a heritage railway. Some parts are only open as freight lines or are mothballed, awaiting future investment. Other parts are no longer accessible, having been bulldozed to make way for housing or new roads, or simply taken over by nature. But many sections of these lost lines are now open to explore once more – as footpaths and cycleways.

The mapping in this book comes from 'outline' versions of the Ordnance Survey Half-Inch and One-Inch 'Popular' series, plus the 1:25,000 'Provisional' edition. Due to the age of the source material, variations in colour will occur, as well as occasional inconsistencies where sheets have been joined together.

railway line open

nearby heritage line of interest (open)

route now inaccessible

route open as a footpath/cycleway

station open

station closed

route information box

Note: By their nature nearly all the lost routes described in this book are fairly level and are perfectly adapted for walkers and in many cases for cyclists. Surfaces can vary widely from the tarmacked Bristol-to-Bath Railway Path to the muddy stretches of the Test Way. OS Landranger 1:50,000 maps are an essential companion. Many stations have survived, the majority now private residences – please respect the owners' privacy and do not trespass on private property.

WEST COUNTRY

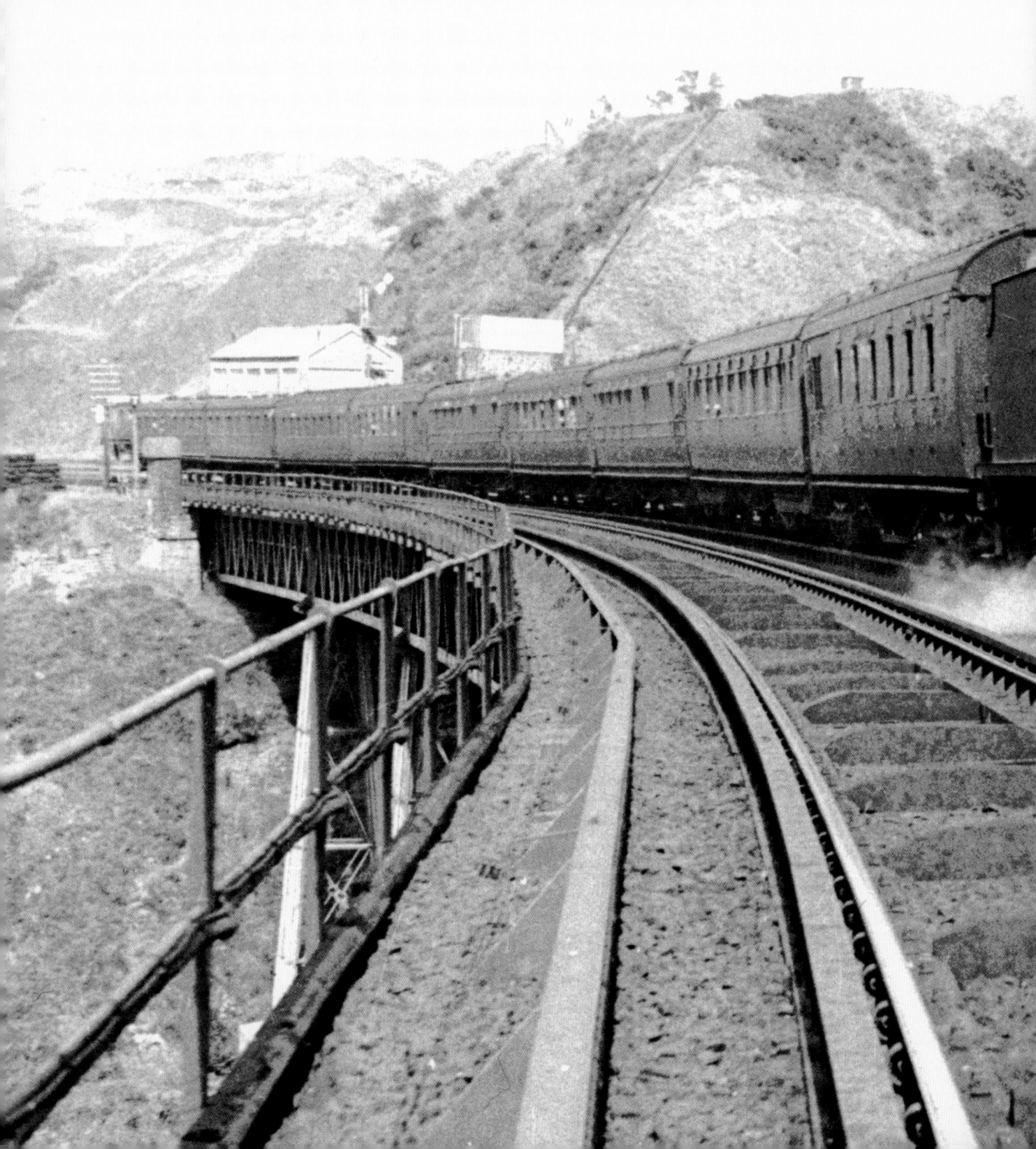

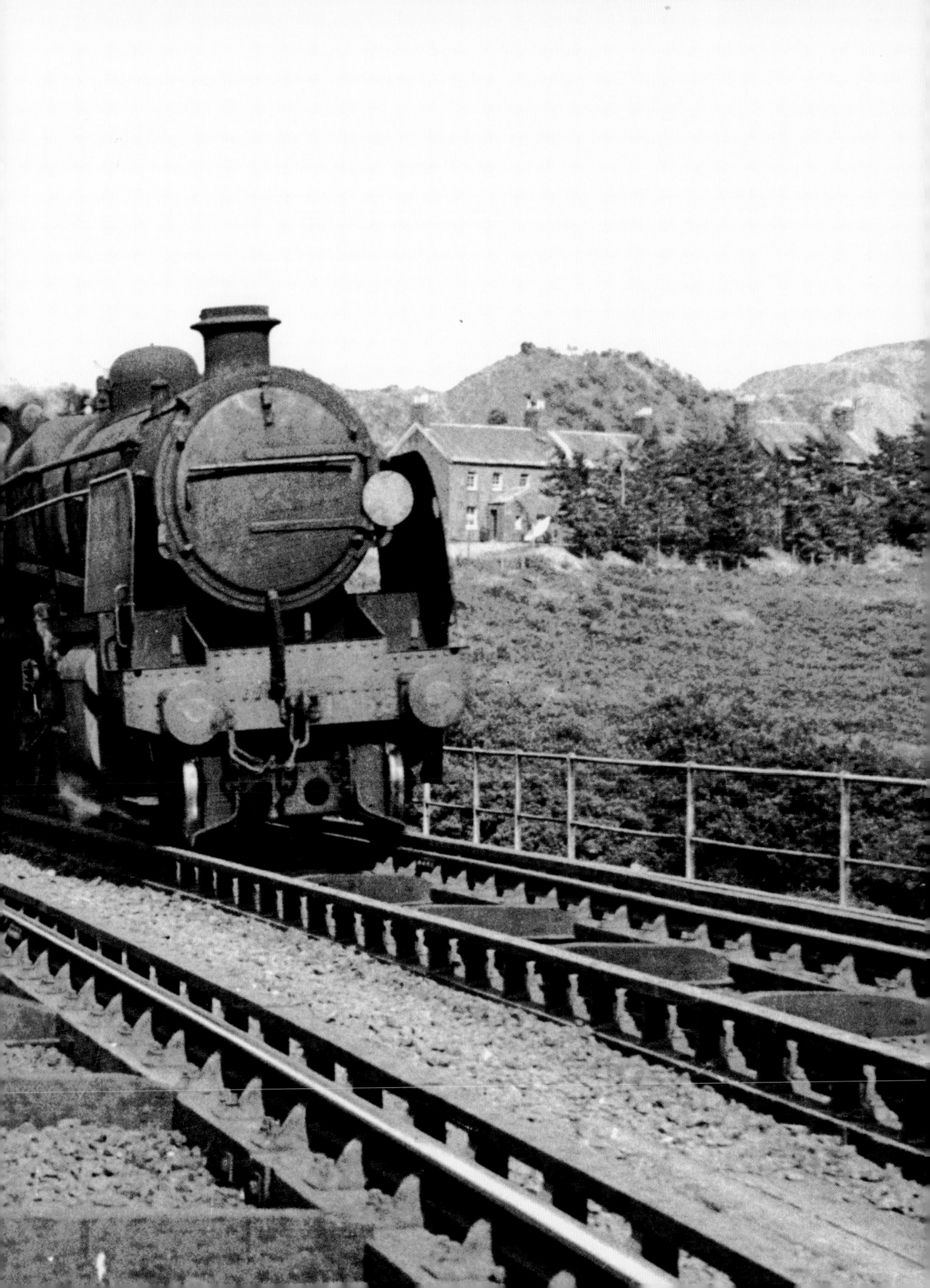

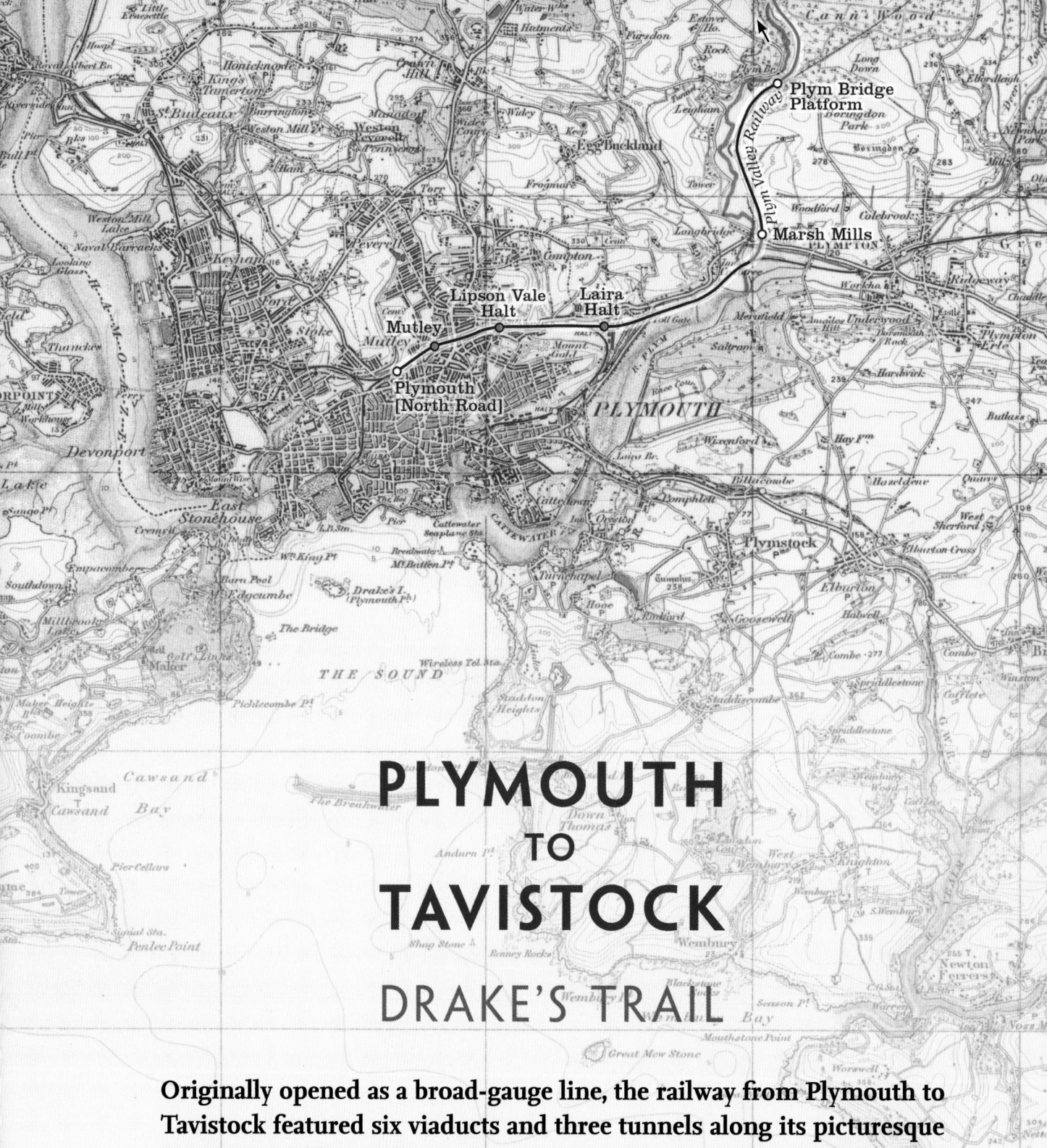

PLYMOUTH
TO
TAVISTOCK

DRAKE'S TRAIL

Originally opened as a broad-gauge line, the railway from Plymouth to Tavistock featured six viaducts and three tunnels along its picturesque route up the Plym Valley and around the edge of Dartmoor. From 1873 to 1890 the London & South Western Railway's standard-gauge trains also used the line, running along mixed-gauge track to Plymouth. Once popular with day trippers from Plymouth, the line eventually closed in a blizzard at the end of 1962 but much of it has since been reopened as a footpath and cycleway known as Drake's Trail. A short section at the southern end is now shared with the Plym Valley Railway.

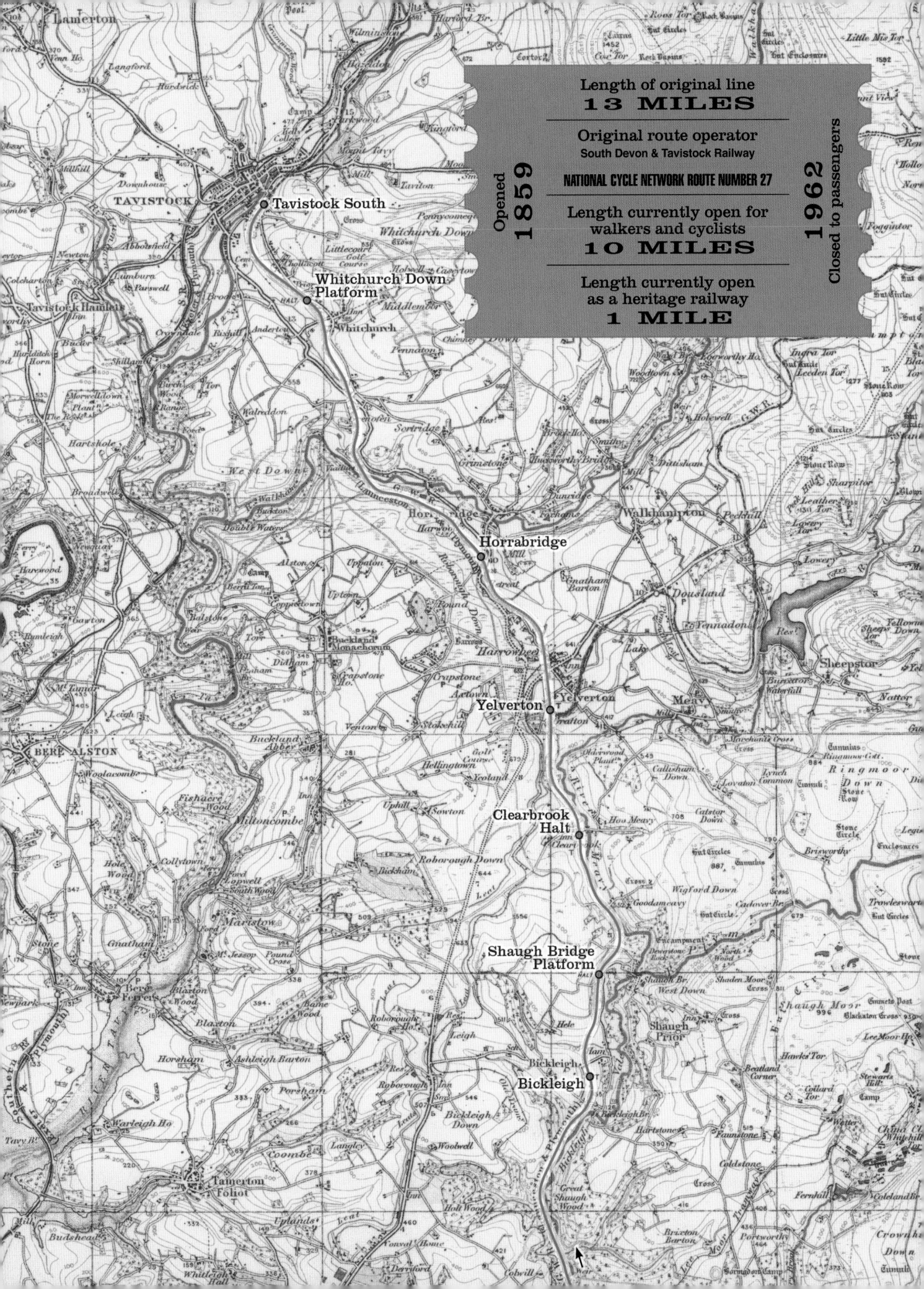

Lamerton

Tavistock South

TAVISTOCK

Whitchurch Down
Platform

Horrabridge

Yelverton

Clearbrook
Halt

Shaugh Bridge
Platform

Bickleigh

BERE ALSTON

Length of original line
13 MILES

Original route operator
South Devon & Tavistock Railway

NATIONAL CYCLE NETWORK ROUTE NUMBER 27

Length currently open for
walkers and cyclists
10 MILES

Length currently open
as a heritage railway
1 MILE

Opened **1859**

1962 Closed to passengers

Many years before the Plymouth to Tavistock railway opened, the lower reaches of the Plym Valley were a hive of industrial activity. Slate had been quarried at Cann Quarry in the Plym Valley, northeast of Plymouth, since the seventeenth century. To transport the material down river to Plymouth a 2¼-mile canal – the Cann Quarry Canal – was opened between the quarry and Marsh Mills in 1829. Beyond Marsh Mills the river was navigable down to Plymouth. Within a year a branch of Lord Morley's Plymouth & Dartmoor Tramway (later named the Lee Moor Tramway) – built to transport china clay from the southern slopes of Dartmoor – had also opened via a rope-worked incline to the Cann Quarry Canal at Plym Bridge. It was later extended northwards along the canal towpath to the quarry while a separate undertaking, the Marsh Mills Railway, opened south from Plym Bridge to china clay works at Marsh Mills in 1832.

Supported by the South Devon Railway (SDR) – famous for introducing Isambard Kingdom Brunel's short-lived atmospheric railway between Exeter and Newton Abbot – the broad-gauge South Devon & Tavistock Railway received Parliamentary approval to build a 13-mile broad-gauge single-track line from Tavistock Junction, east of Laira, to the historic market town of Tavistock in 1854. Winding its way up the Plym Valley the railway initially kept company with the tramway and redundant canal before heading up the Meavy Valley to Yelverton. From here the line continued north across the watershed before crossing the Walkham Valley and ending its journey in the Tavy Valley at Tavistock. Engineered by Brunel, the line was costly to build, requiring three tunnels and six timber viaducts to overcome these major physical obstacles.

The line opened for business on 22 June 1859, less than two months after the opening of Brunel's Royal Albert Bridge across the Tamar, and was soon amalgamated with the SDR. The Launceston & South Devon Railway opened a 19-mile extension between Tavistock and Launceston in 1865. This was amalgamated in 1873 with the SDR, which was in turn absorbed by the Great Western Railway (GWR) in 1876. In the same year the standard-gauge London & South Western Railway (LSWR) had reached Lydford, north of Tavistock, from Exeter via Okehampton (see page 20). To enable its trains to reach Plymouth the LSWR obtained

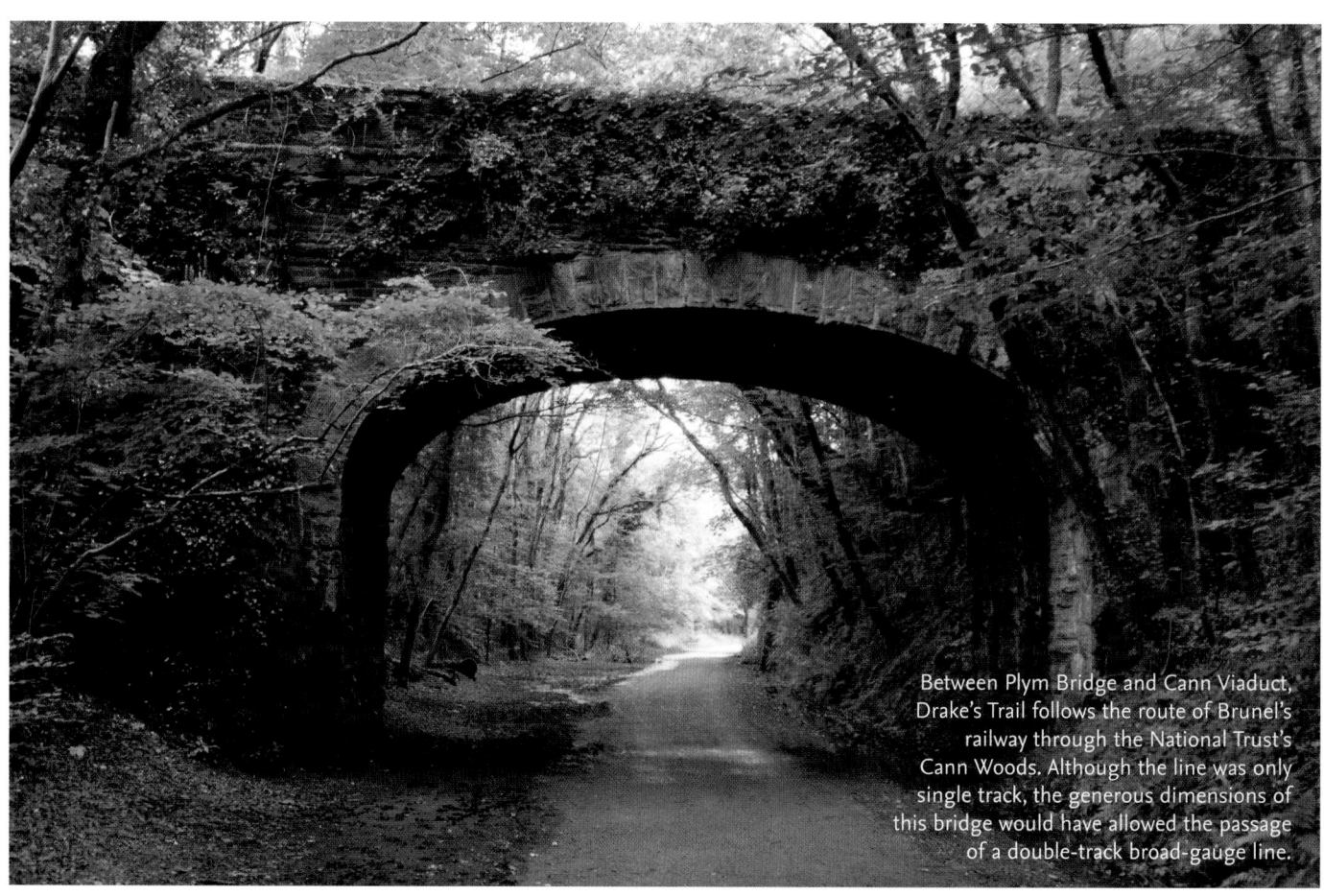

Between Plym Bridge and Cann Viaduct, Drake's Trail follows the route of Brunel's railway through the National Trust's Cann Woods. Although the line was only single track, the generous dimensions of this bridge would have allowed the passage of a double-track broad-gauge line.

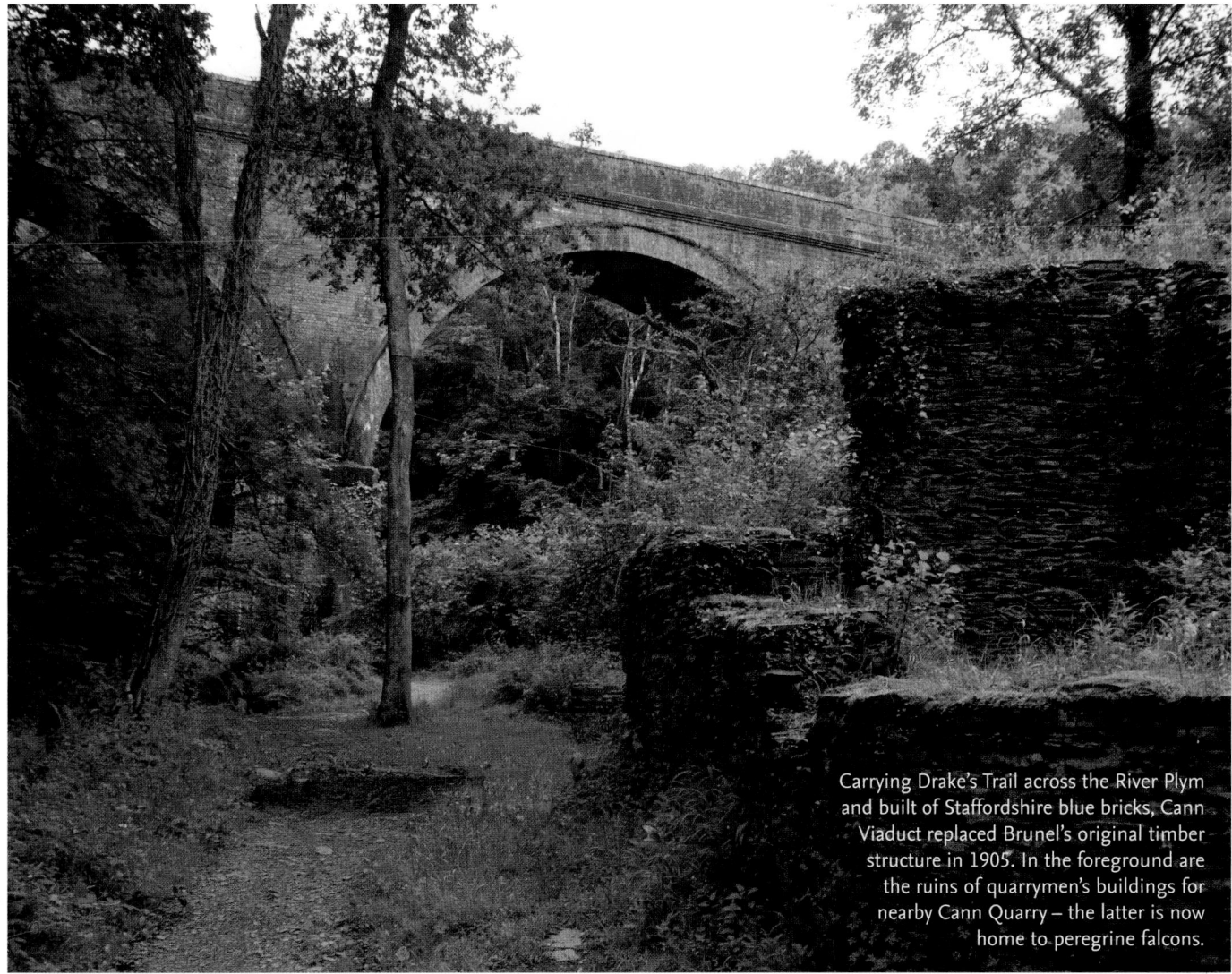

Carrying Drake's Trail across the River Plym and built of Staffordshire blue bricks, Cann Viaduct replaced Brunel's original timber structure in 1905. In the foreground are the ruins of quarrymen's buildings for nearby Cann Quarry – the latter is now home to peregrine falcons.

running powers along the GWR broad-gauge route via Tavistock. To facilitate this operation mixed-gauge track was laid and remained in use until 1890, when the LSWR was able to switch to a newly opened standard-gauge line down the Tamar Valley from Tavistock to Devonport. The GWR opened a branch line from Yelverton to Princetown, home of Dartmoor Prison, in 1883, and the company's Plymouth to Launceston route was converted to standard gauge in 1892. Brick, stone and steel structures replaced Brunel's timber-trestle viaducts around the turn of the century. One of the last to be rebuilt was Cann Viaduct, which was built of Staffordshire blue bricks in 1905.

The GWR's Tavistock line was particularly popular with day trippers from Plymouth eager to explore the scenic delights of the Plym Valley. Known as Woolworth's Specials because their fare was sixpence, special trains were run on bank holidays carrying thousands of passengers. Plym Bridge Halt was especially popular for its river and woodland walks. The Tavistock line was kept fairly busy with this traffic until the onset of the Second World War although the extension to Launceston was less well used. Tavistock had two stations served by competing GWR and Southern Railway routes to Plymouth and this duplication greatly contributed to their downfall. While the Princetown branch had already closed in 1956, the former GWR route from Plymouth to Tavistock and Launceston soldiered on until it was closed on 31 December 1962 – three months before publication of the 'Beeching Report'. The last day of services, Saturday, 29 December, saw blizzard conditions with trains abandoned or cancelled. The section from Marsh Mills to Tavistock closed completely, while the short section from Tavistock Junction to Marsh Mills continued to serve a china clay works until as recently as 2008.

The standard-gauge Plym Valley Railway now operates the short section from Marsh Mills to the beauty spot of Plym Bridge. For details of its operating days visit www.plymrail.co.uk.

Today the 13½-mile Plym Valley Trail (now also known as Drake's Trail) follows the trackbed of the GWR's Tavistock line from Plym Bridge northwards to Clearbrook. Forming part of National Cycle Network Route 27 and extremely popular with both cyclists and walkers at weekends, the Trail itself starts on the east bank of the River Plym at Point Cottage, in the grounds of the National Trust's Saltram House, and parallels the Plym Valley Railway between Marsh Mills and Plym Bridge. The Coypool Park-and-Ride car park is conveniently located close to the Trail at Marsh Mills and there is also a National Trust car park at Plym Bridge.

A good deal of time can be can be spent at Plym Bridge exploring the National Trust's woodland walks, the remains of the Cann Quarry Canal and the old tramway incline up through Cann Wood. Following the trackbed northwards up the wooded valley the Trail passes the ruins of quarry workers' cottages before crossing Cann Viaduct, where a detour can be made to the disused Cann Quarry, now home to peregrine falcons. North of the viaduct the Trail follows the valley through Great Shaugh Woods before crossing the lofty Bickleigh

Viaduct where the ivy-clad stone piers of Brunel's original timber viaduct can be seen in the valley below.

The Trail leaves the Plym Valley behind at Shaugh Bridge Platform, where the road overbridge and overgrown platform still survive as a reminder of this long-closed scenic railway. Soon the Trail enters the broad-gauge single-bore Shaugh Tunnel, its southern entrance framed by an old steel aqueduct. With water dripping from its roof this unlit and curving tunnel takes the Trail into the valley of the River Meavy before ending at the village of Clearbrook, where there is off-road parking near the popular Skylark Inn.

North of Clearbrook the newly opened Drake's Trail (NCN Route 27) follows country roads and tracks to Yelverton and then on to Horrabridge. Here the trackbed of the railway is rejoined to cross the Walkham Valley via the Gem Bridge, which was recently constructed to replace a 1910-built steel lattice truss railway viaduct that was demolished in 1965, before heading on through the dank and dripping Grenofen Tunnel to Whitchurch and Tavistock. Managed by Devon County Council, Drake's Trail is also on the route of Cycle West's Vélodyssée – a 273-mile cross-Channel link that will eventually stretch from Ilfracombe to Redon in Southern Brittany. Cycle hire shops can be found in Plymouth, Yelverton and Tavistock.

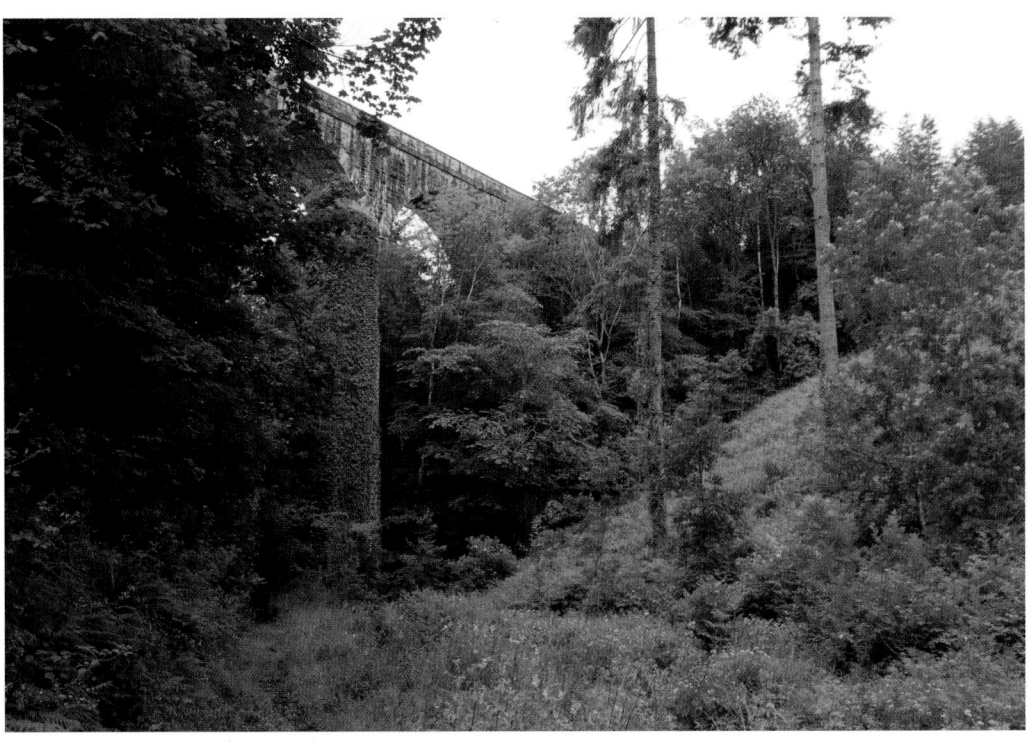

The 7-arch Bickleigh Viaduct soars gracefully over an unspoilt wooded valley, offering the Drake's Trail's walkers and cyclists magnificent views from the top. The ivy-clad stone piers of Brunel's original timber viaduct can be seen alongside.

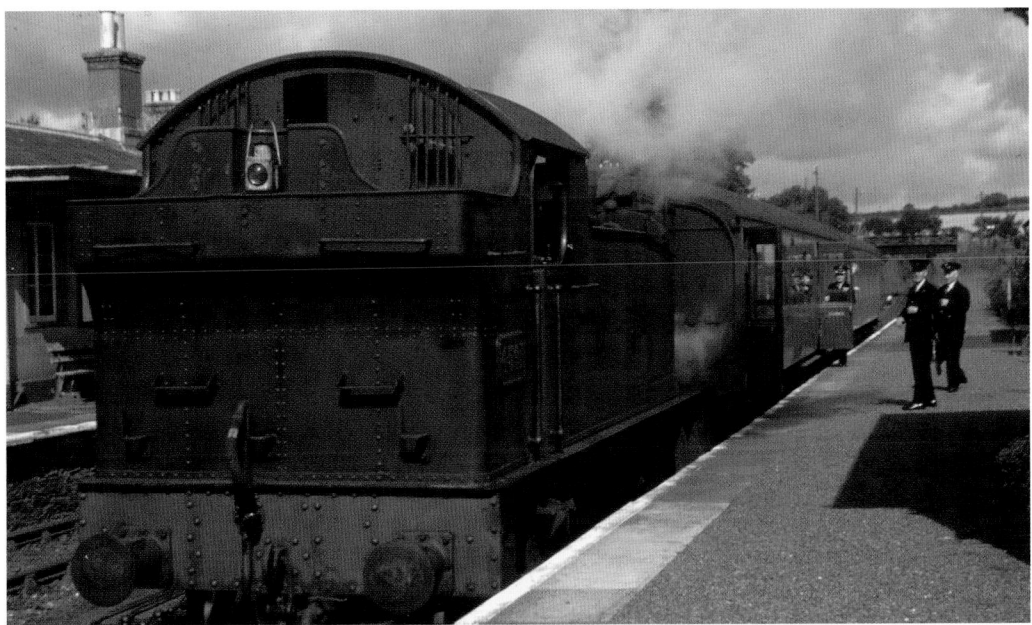

Ex-GWR '4575' Class 2-6-2T No. 4591 waits for the 'right away' from smartly dressed guard and station staff at Bickleigh station on 5 September 1962. Within four months this picturesque line up the Plym Valley had closed.

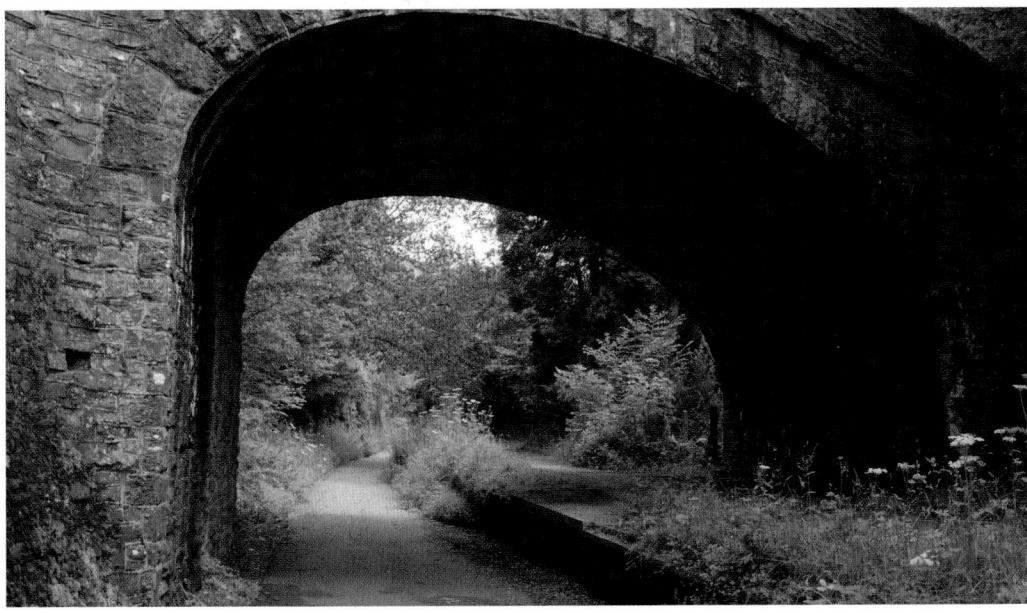

Seen alongside Drake's Trail and overshadowed by Brunel's generous broad-gauge overbridge, the platform at Shaugh Bridge was opened by the GWR in 1907 to serve the small village of Shaugh Priors, set on the opposite side of the Plym Valley.

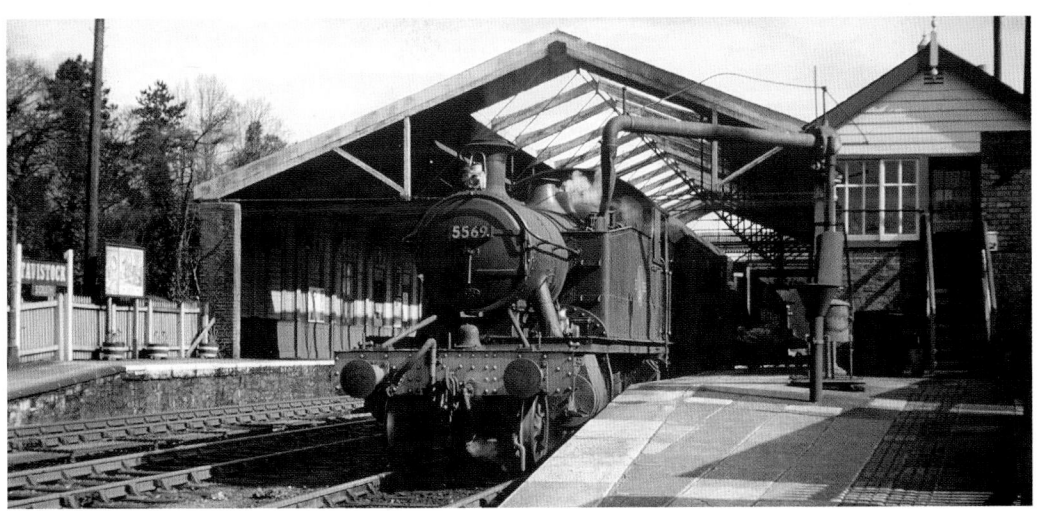

Allocated to Plymouth Laira shed, ex-GWR '4575' Class 2-6-2T No. 5569 takes on water at Tavistock South station before departing with a train for Plymouth in April 1962. Although the line closed at the end of that year, the inhabitants of the town continued to be rail-served at North station until 1968.

OKEHAMPTON
TO
LYDFORD

GRANITE WAY

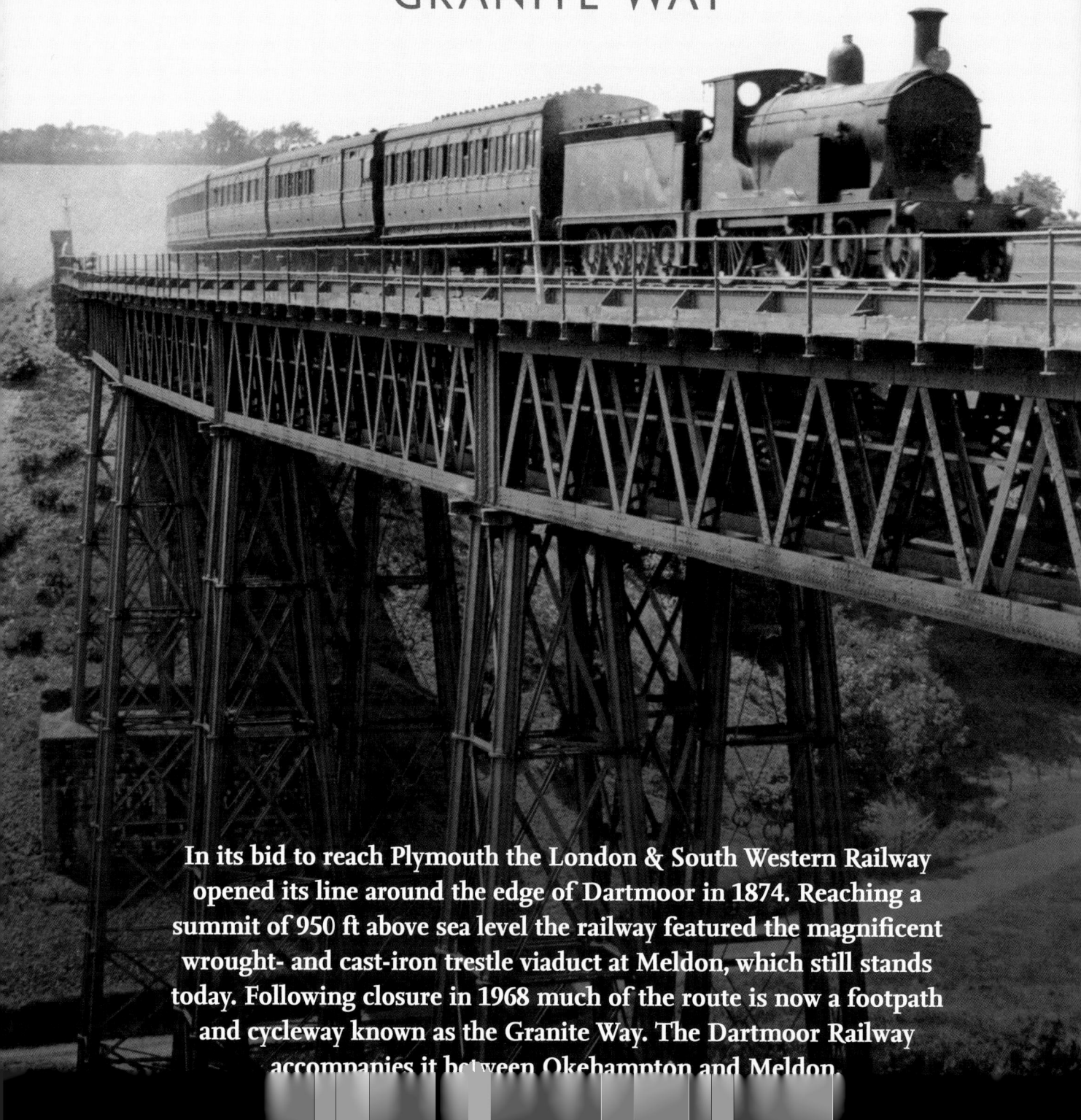

In its bid to reach Plymouth the London & South Western Railway opened its line around the edge of Dartmoor in 1874. Reaching a summit of 950 ft above sea level the railway featured the magnificent wrought- and cast-iron trestle viaduct at Meldon, which still stands today. Following closure in 1968 much of the route is now a footpath and cycleway known as the Granite Way. The Dartmoor Railway accompanies it between Okehampton and Meldon.

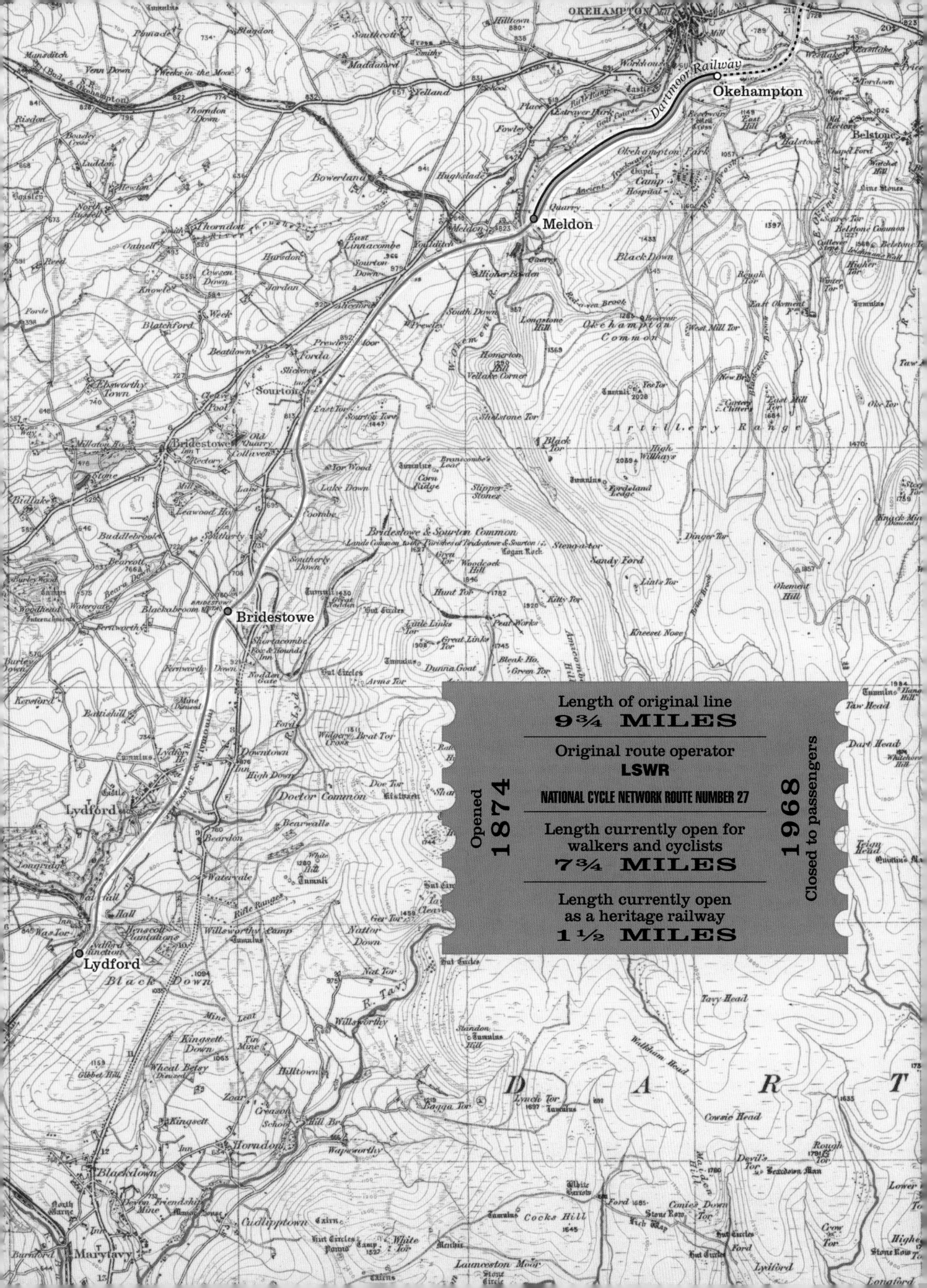

OKEHAMPTON

Dartmoor Railway

Okehampton

Meldon

Length of original line
9¾ MILES

Original route operator
LSWR

NATIONAL CYCLE NETWORK ROUTE NUMBER 27

Length currently open for
walkers and cyclists
7¾ MILES

Length currently open
as a heritage railway
1½ MILES

Opened **1874**

1968 Closed to passengers

Bridestowe

Lydford

DART

The London & South Western Railway's incursion into Devon and Cornwall took another significant step forward when they backed the Devon & Cornwall Railway's new route from Coleford Junction, north of Crediton on the Exeter to Barnstaple line, to the town of Okehampton in 1866. It opened as a single-track line in 1871 and was taken over by the LSWR the following year. However, the company had its sights on reaching Plymouth with its lucrative trans-Atlantic mail traffic and to this end extended the railway across Meldon Viaduct to a summit of 950 ft above sea level and around the edge of Dartmoor to Lydford in 1874. From here LSWR trains continued to Plymouth over mixed-gauge track along the GWR's broad-gauge Launceston branch via Tavistock and Yelverton. The entire route from Coleford Junction to Lydford was doubled in 1879 – this included widening the 120-ft-high wrought- and cast-iron Meldon Viaduct, which still stands today.

Clearly the arrangement for LSWR trains to travel over GWR mixed-gauge track from Lydford to Plymouth was unsatisfactory as a long-term solution. This state of affairs lasted until 1890 when the standard-gauge Plymouth, Devonport & South Western Junction Railway opened between Lydford and Devonport. From the outset the LSWR worked the line, which paralleled the GWR's line from Lydford to Tavistock before striking off to meet the Tamar Valley at Bere Alston and ending its journey along the eastern shore of the Tamar Estuary, entering Plymouth from the west. The LSWR and GWR stations at Lydford were side by side, while at Tavistock the LSWR station was named Tavistock North and the completely separate GWR station was renamed Tavistock South.

The LSWR now had its own route all the way from London Waterloo to Plymouth and competed with the GWR to offer the fastest journey times for the prestigious trans-Atlantic Ocean Liner traffic between the two cities. These competing routes featured some strange anomalies that lasted until the 1960s, with London-bound trains departing from Plymouth in opposite directions and meeting again at Exeter, from where they once again departed in opposite directions. The route was served by through trains to and from Waterloo and, for a short period between 1947 and 1950, by the Plymouth portion of the all-Pullman 'Devon Belle'.

1963 brought bad news for most of the former LSWR routes west of Exeter. Not only were they transferred from Southern to Western Region control but, with the exception of the Exeter to Barnstaple and Okehampton lines, they were also listed for closure in the 'Beeching Report'. In the end the line from Meldon to Bere Alston closed completely on 6 May 1968 while the section south of the latter station was singled and retained for use by Plymouth-Gunnislake local trains. Despite not being listed for closure by Beeching the line from Coleford Junction to Okehampton closed to passengers on 5 June 1972. However, it was singled and retained for stone ballast traffic from Meldon Quarry until 2011.

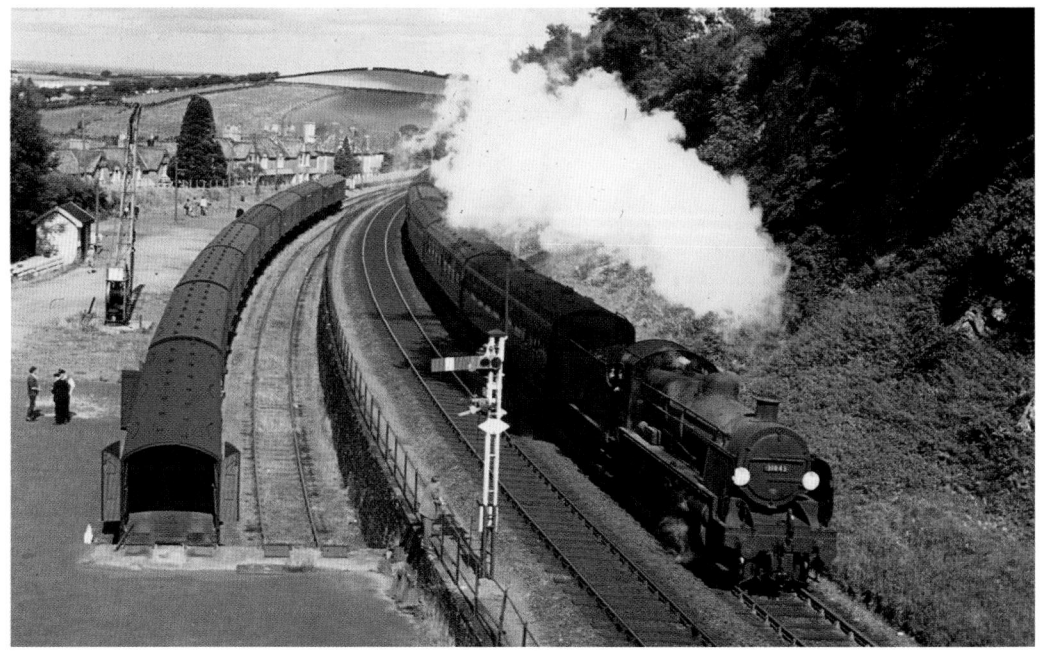

Built in 1924, ex-Southern Railway 'N' Class 2-6-0 No. 31845 passes the car dock on the approach to Okehampton station with a train from Exeter on 29 August 1964. The car transporters seen here were used on a short-lived summer weekend service to and from Surbiton in Surrey.

PREVIOUS SPREAD:
London & South Western Railway 'T9' Class 4-4-0 No. 117 crosses Meldon Viaduct with the 12.35pm from Plymouth to Exeter on 14 July 1924. This magnificent 120-ft-high wrought- and cast-iron structure still stands today, as part of the Granite Way.

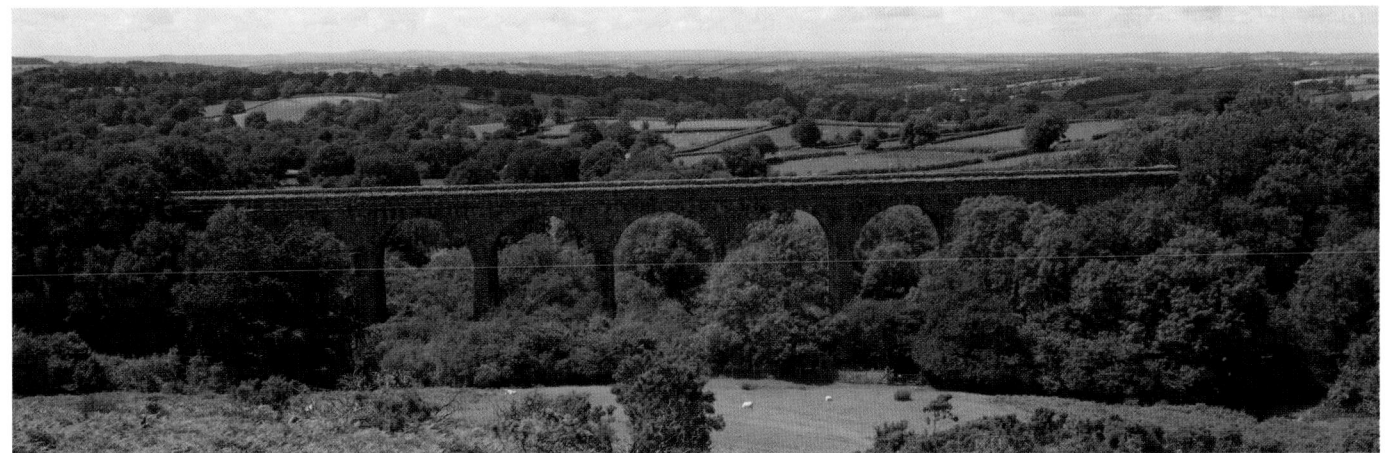

Although stone traffic is no longer carried by rail from Meldon Quarry, the line from Coleford Junction to Meldon Viaduct is intact and is currently used by heritage trains operated by the Dartmoor Railway. It is also used by a summer Sunday service operated by First Great Western from Exeter to Okehampton. In recent years Okehampton station, set high above the town it serves, has been beautifully restored by a local partnership scheme initiated by Devon County Council. A café is run by the Friends of Dartmoor Railway while the adjacent goods shed is now a Youth Hostel. Cycle hire is also available in the town. From here the 11-mile Granite Way cycleway and footpath (part of National Cycle Network Route 27) parallels the railway line as far as Meldon Viaduct where there is a café in a railway coach and a viewpoint over the valley. Here the rails end but the magnificent wrought-

and cast-iron viaduct now carries walkers and cyclists on their journey along the former railway trackbed around the edge of Dartmoor to Lydford.

En route the Granite Way passes the summit of the line, 950 ft above sea level, before crossing Lake Viaduct. Built of local stone in 1873, the viaduct offers superb views of the moor and surrounding countryside. Refreshments can be obtained by making a short detour down the valley footpath to the picturesque thatched Bearslake Inn. A short distance south of the viaduct the Granite Way temporarily leaves the railway trackbed, which involves crossing the dangerous A386 road at Beardown before following country lanes for two miles to Bridestowe, where the old railway route is rejoined for the last leg to Lydford and its welcoming Castle Inn.

TOP: Set on the very edge of Dartmoor and with far-reaching views across rolling Devon countryside, Lake Viaduct now carries walkers and cyclists on the Granite Way.

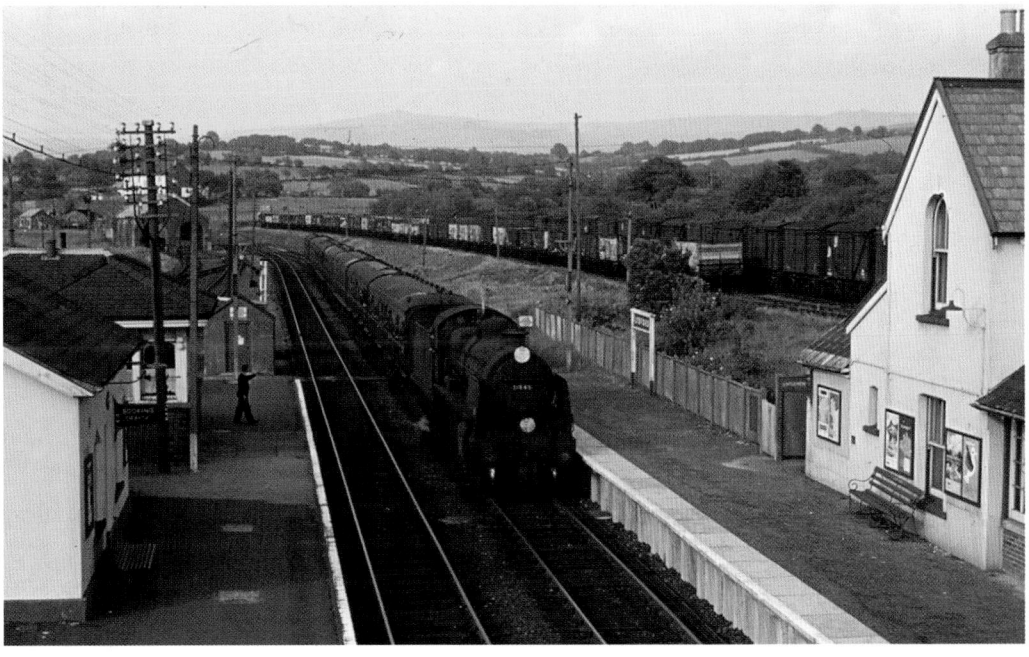

Ex-Southern Railway 'N' Class 2-6-0 No. 31849 enters Lydford station with a train for Plymouth on 17 July 1962. The ex-GWR line to Launceston is out of sight on the left while the sidings on the right appear to be filled with condemned wooden goods wagons.

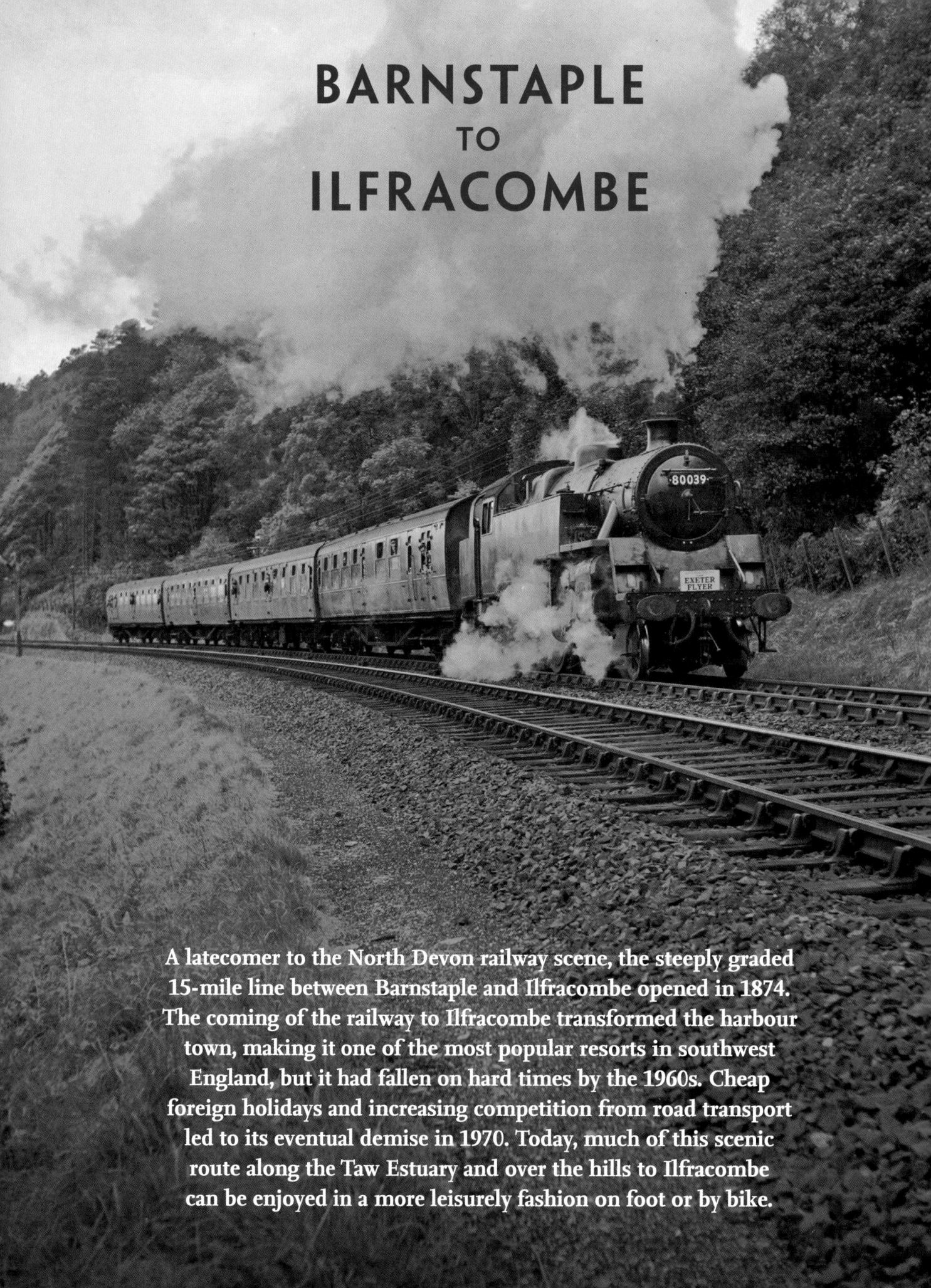

BARNSTAPLE
TO
ILFRACOMBE

A latecomer to the North Devon railway scene, the steeply graded 15-mile line between Barnstaple and Ilfracombe opened in 1874. The coming of the railway to Ilfracombe transformed the harbour town, making it one of the most popular resorts in southwest England, but it had fallen on hard times by the 1960s. Cheap foreign holidays and increasing competition from road transport led to its eventual demise in 1970. Today, much of this scenic route along the Taw Estuary and over the hills to Ilfracombe can be enjoyed in a more leisurely fashion on foot or by bike.

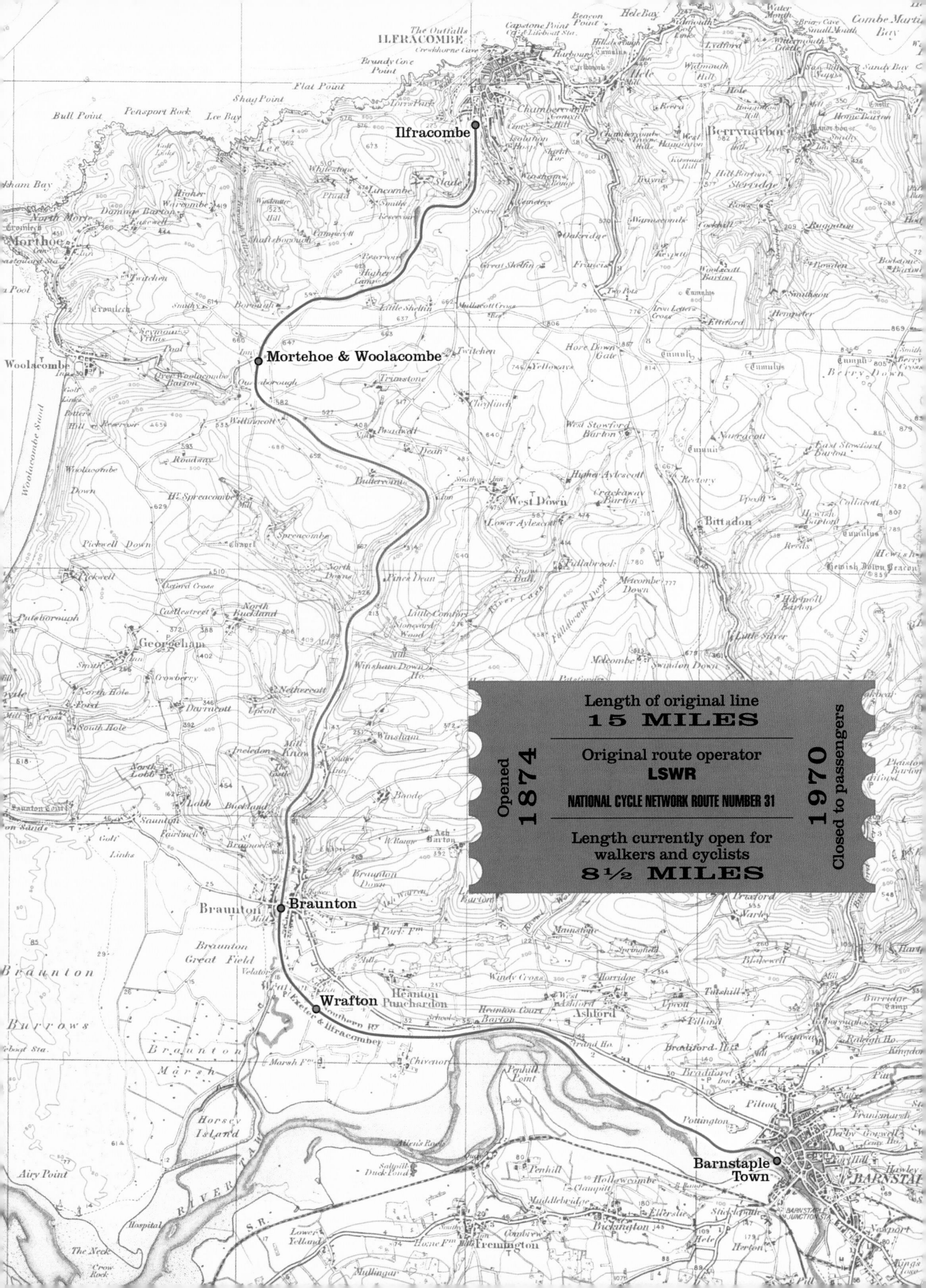

ILFRACOMBE

Ilfracombe

Mortehoe & Woolacombe

Braunton

Wrafton

Barnstaple
Town

Length of original line
15 MILES

Original route operator
LSWR

NATIONAL CYCLE NETWORK ROUTE NUMBER 31

Length currently open for
walkers and cyclists
8½ MILES

Opened
1874

1970
Closed to passengers

The first railway reached Barnstaple from the outside world in 1854, but the harbour town of Ilfracombe to the north had to wait another twenty years for its own railway connection. Several proposals, including one for a mixed-gauge line, had unsuccessfully been put forward and it took until 1870 before the London & South Western Railway (LSWR)-sponsored Barnstaple & Ilfracombe Railway received Parliamentary approval for a line to connect the two towns. By this date the country was suffering from a bout of economic woes and railway navvies were in short supply. Compounding these problems, the building of the railway also necessitated crossing the River Taw at Barnstaple, surmounting steep gradients north of Braunton and tunnelling south of Ilfracombe.

Before the coming of the railway the small town of Ilfracombe had depended mainly on farming and fishing for its economic survival. Its sheltered harbour had for centuries seen much commercial and naval activity, and by the mid-nineteenth century regular steam packet services from Swansea and Bristol were bringing an increasing number of intrepid Victorian holidaymakers to the town. The coming of the railway led to a massive increase in visitors, especially during the summer months, and by the end of the century Ilfracombe had become one of the most popular resorts in southwest England.

Meanwhile the single-track Barnstaple & Ilfracombe Railway had opened for business on 20 July 1874 and was an immediate success. By this time the railway had been amalgamated with the LSWR which also operated the line. Working the 15-mile route with its lightweight rails and steep gradients led to the line being doubled and re-laid to main-line standards by 1891. In addition to the LSWR's service from Exeter and Waterloo the Great Western Railway (GWR) also made use of the line with trains from Taunton and beyond travelling over the former Devon & Someret Railway's route via Dulverton. Summer Saturdays saw the Ilfracombe line packed to capacity, with double heading or banking of trains up the 1-in-40 gradient north of Braunton and the 1-in-36 south of Ilfracombe the order of the day until the 1960s.

Three named trains also served Ilfracombe: introduced by the LSWR in 1926, the 'Atlantic Coast Express' ('ACE') from London Waterloo carried through coaches to the town until September 1964; the shorter-lived summer weekends-only 'Devon Belle' Pullman train from Waterloo was introduced by the Southern Railway (SR) in 1947 but was withdrawn in 1954; and for a time the GWR even

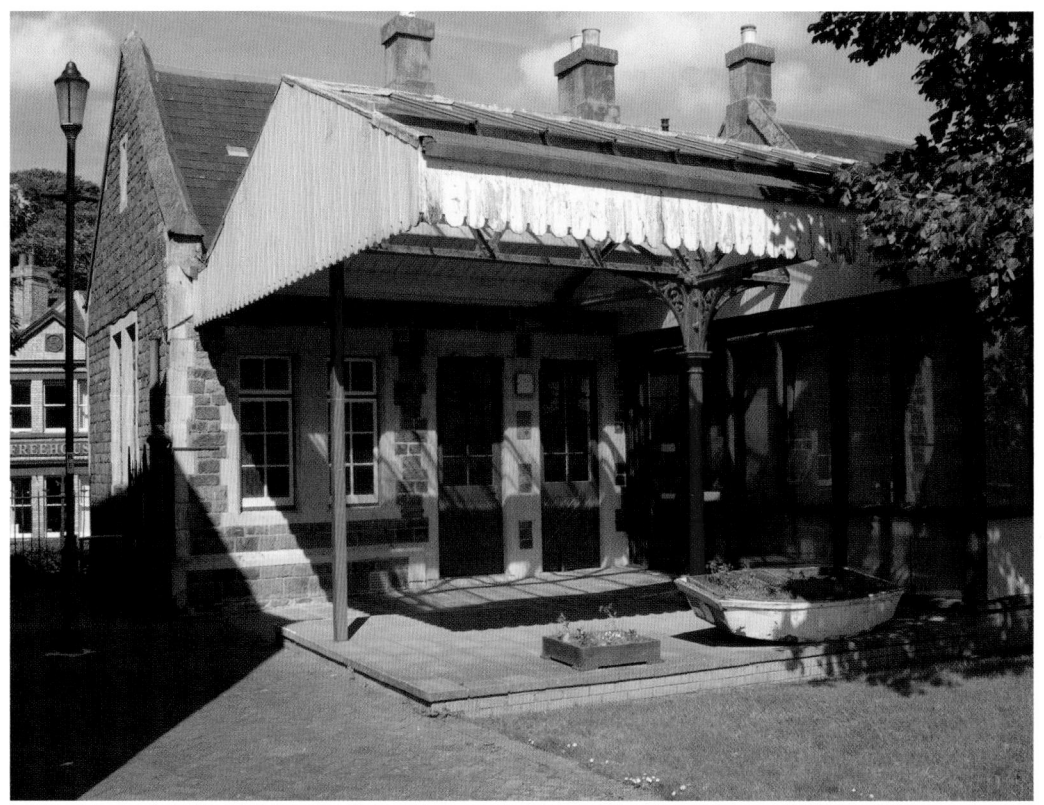

Replacing an earlier station at Barnstaple Quay, Barnstaple Town was opened in 1898 as an interchange station with the narrow-gauge Lynton & Barnstaple Railway. While the latter line closed in 1935, Town station remained open for travellers on the Ilfracombe branch until 1970. In recent years the building has seen a new lease of life as a school.

PREVIOUS SPREAD:
Smartly turned out BR Standard Class '4' 2-6-4T No. 80039 heads up the gradient past the Slade reservoirs with the return Southern Counties Touring Society's 'Exeter Flyer' enthusiasts' special on 12 September 1965. This was the penultimate steam train to work over the Ilfracombe line; the last, hauled by No. 80043, ran on 3 October of that year.

included a through coach for Ilfracombe, slipped at Taunton, in its 'Cornish Riviera Limited'.

Motive power on the Ilfracombe line needed to be powerful to cope with the extreme gradients. In the early years the LSWR introduced a special class of 0-6-0 steam locomotive built by Beyer-Peacock called, appropriately, the 'Ilfracombe Goods'. By the 1930s both SR and GWR trains were usually double-headed or banked with the line witnessing a selection of 2-6-0 locomotives from both companies. The introduction of Bulleid's air-smoothed 'Battle of Britain' and 'West Country' light Pacifics after the Second World War brought an even more varied steam extravaganza to the line on summer Saturdays which, along with the stalwart ex-GWR '4300' Class 2-6-0s on the Taunton-line trains, were a magnet for budding railway photographers as they pounded up the grades.

Despite the gloom of the 1930s Ilfracombe continued to thrive, albeit with the help of Welsh holidaymakers travelling to the town across the Bristol Channel aboard P & A Campbell's graceful White Funnel steamers. Sadly, by the early 1960s the story common to all railway-connected resorts – increased competition from car ownership and cheap holidays abroad – saw passenger numbers in serious decline on the Ilfracombe line. The transfer of all former Southern Region routes west of Salisbury into the clutches of the Western Region in 1963, coupled with the

recommendation for the line's closure in that year's 'Beeching Report', was the final nail in the coffin. September 1964 saw the end of all goods traffic and the withdrawal of the 'ACE' along with through trains from the Midlands via the former GWR route. At the same time steam was replaced by a service of diesel multiple units shuttling between Barnstaple Junction and Ilfracombe, the only exception being a well-patronized summer-Saturdays through service from London, hauled by a 'Warship' or Hymek diesel hydraulic loco, which ran until the end of the 1970 summer timetable.

Further economies were introduced in 1967 when the line was singled – by then the once-busy yard for empty coaching stock at Ilfracombe had also been lifted. Stations were left to decay and despite vociferous local protest the line closed on 5 October 1970 with the last regular train being an eight-coach diesel multiple unit filled to capacity with mourners. Despite closure the track was left in situ while a preservation group made attempts to reopen the line as a heritage railway but the high asking price set by British Railways of over £400,000 was well outside the group's capabilities and the scheme came to nothing. Hopes for reopening were raised in 1975 when the weed-infested line was paid a final visit by diesel loco No. 25063 hauling an engineers' inspection saloon up to Ilfracombe and back on 26 February, but all to no avail as the track was lifted a few months later.

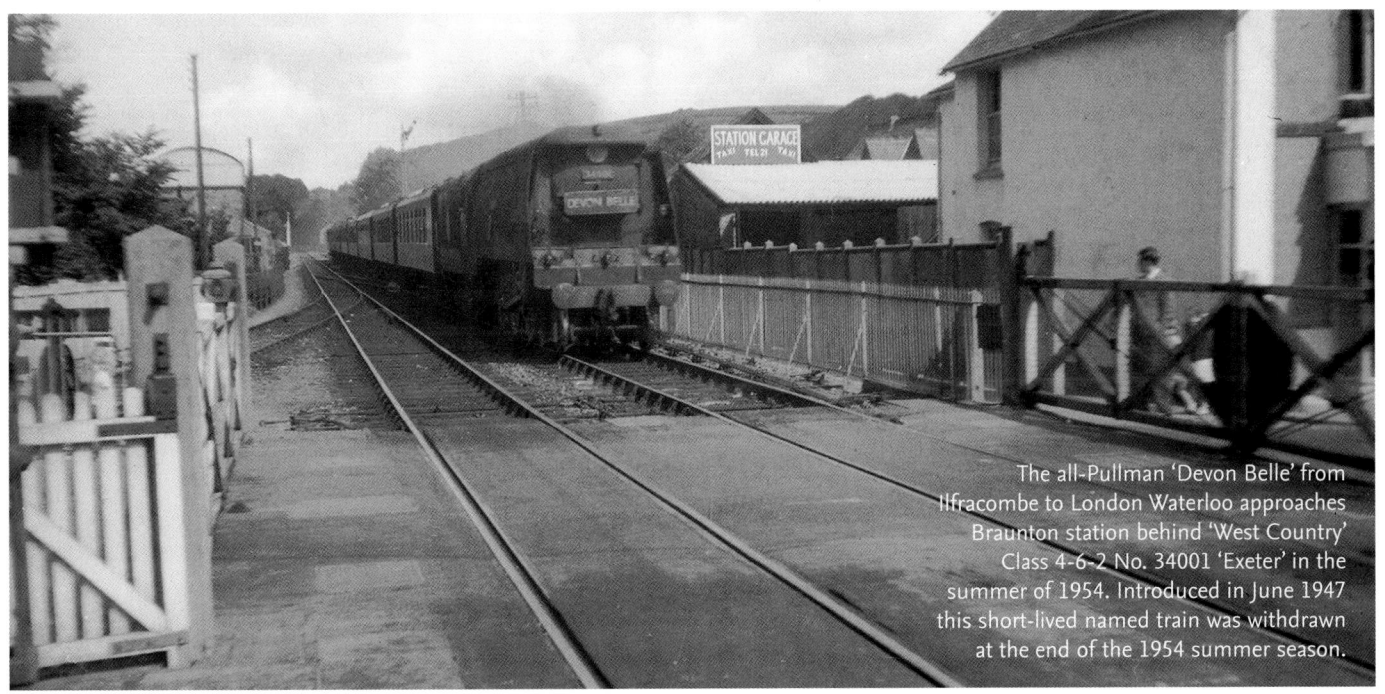

The all-Pullman 'Devon Belle' from Ilfracombe to London Waterloo approaches Braunton station behind 'West Country' Class 4-6-2 No. 34001 'Exeter' in the summer of 1954. Introduced in June 1947 this short-lived named train was withdrawn at the end of the 1954 summer season.

ollowing years of neglect the trackbed of the line between Barnstaple Quay and Braunton and between Mortehoe & Woolacombe station and Ilfracombe is now a footpath and cycleway, the southern half forming part of the popular Tarka Trail. The station buildings at Barnstaple Town, Wrafton, Braunton and Mortehoe & Woolacombe still survive, albeit with different uses. Cycle hire is available at Barnstaple station and there are convenient car parks here and at Barnstaple Quay.

Forming part of National Cycle Network Route 31 the Trail proper starts at Barnstaple Quay where the former Barnstaple Town station has been attractively restored and is now used as a nursery school. First hugging the north shore of the ever-widening Taw Estuary, the Trail heads inland behind the former RAF station at Chivenor, passing the site of Wrafton station (now a private residence) before reaching the large village of Braunton. The station building is now a shop while the goods shed is a youth club. Northwards from Braunton the Trail leaves the trackbed of the railway for a while to follow lanes to Willingcott Cross where there is a car park. Here the

path rejoins the railway trackbed to Mortehoe & Woolacombe station, now hardly recognizable in its rebuilt form of modern housing. Northwards from here the path soon reaches the summit of the line and passes the small car park at Lee Bridge before making the long descent down to Ilfracombe, past the two Slade reservoirs and through the short single-bore Slade Tunnel. Watch out en route for Southern Railway concrete permanent way shelters, an old concrete signal post and concrete fence posts. This was a stretch of line once favoured by railway photographers keen to record heavily laden steam trains struggling up the gradient out of Ilfracombe although the line-side vegetation obscures this view completely today. One of the twin bores of Slade Tunnel has been bricked up but walkers and cyclists can still head through the parallel open bore on the final approach down to Ilfracombe. Set high above this harbour town, the station site has long disappeared beneath industrial development but visitors may wish to explore the fading Victorian grandeur of the town and gaze at Damien Hirst's provocative new 66-ft-high bronze sculpture of a pregnant woman.

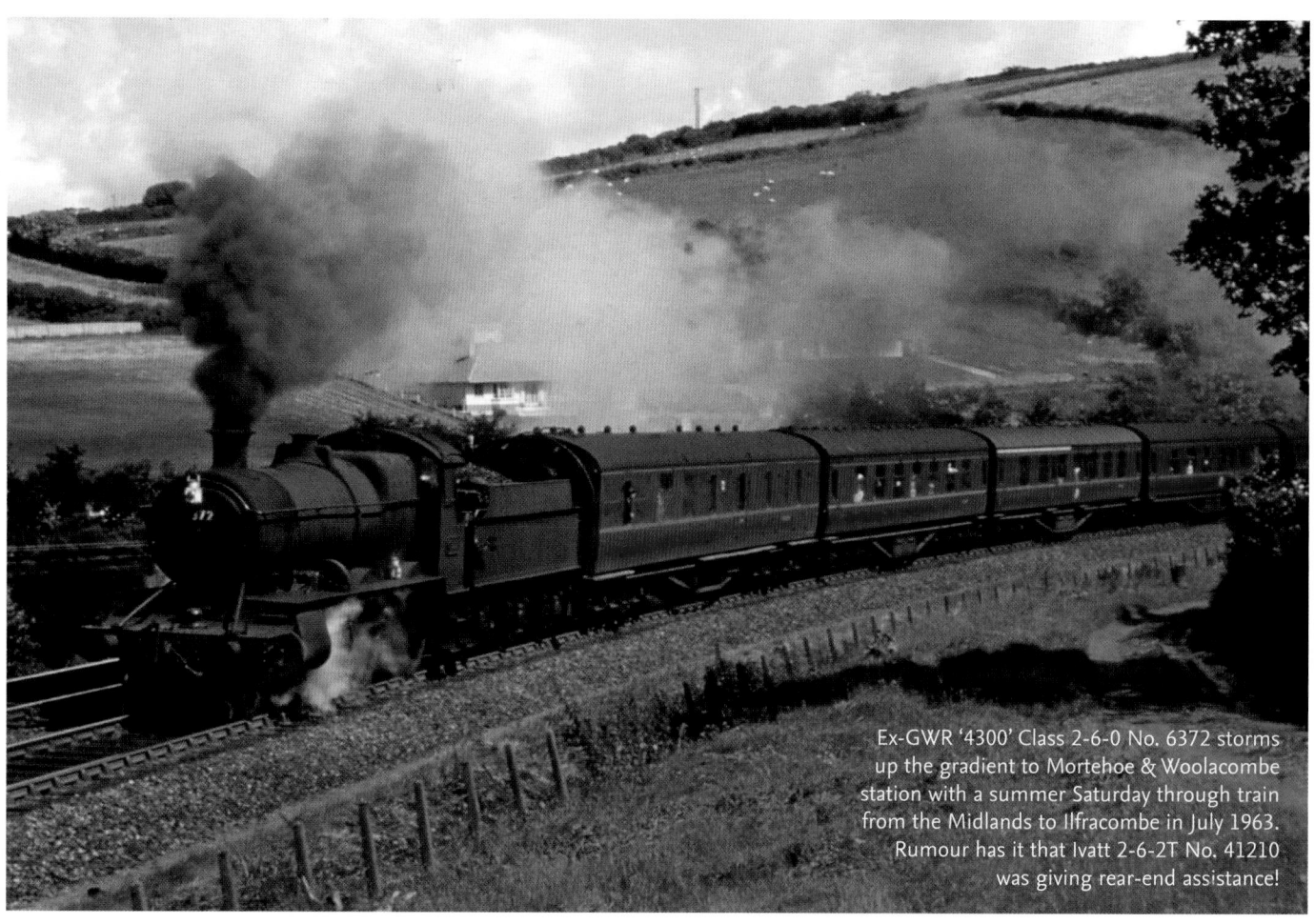

Ex-GWR '4300' Class 2-6-0 No. 6372 storms up the gradient to Mortehoe & Woolacombe station with a summer Saturday through train from the Midlands to Ilfracombe in July 1963. Rumour has it that Ivatt 2-6-2T No. 41210 was giving rear-end assistance!

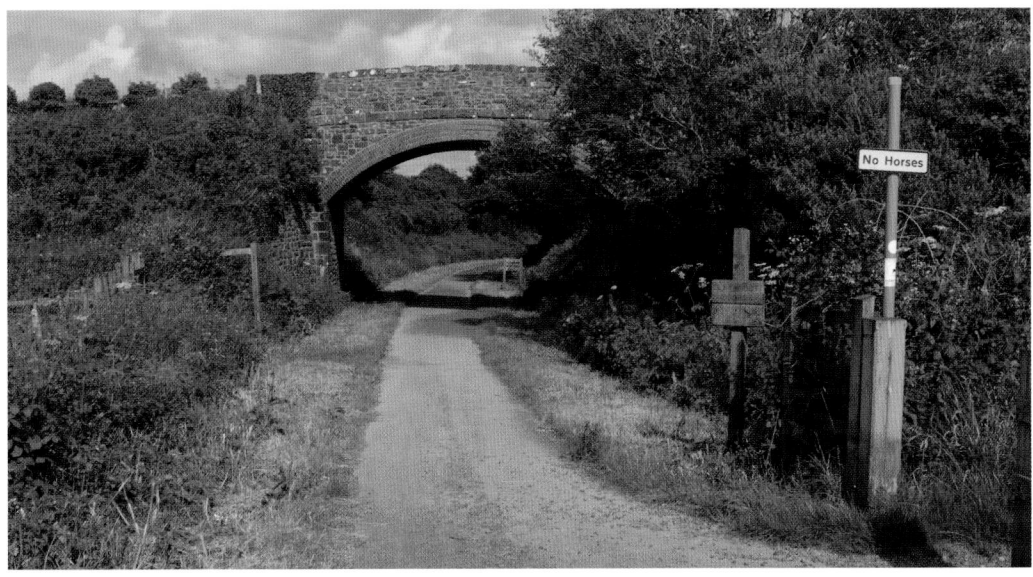

The summit of the steeply graded Ilfracombe branch was near Mortehoe & Woolacombe station and today the trackbed north of here is a popular footpath and cycleway down to Ilfracombe. Framed by this brick and stone overbridge, it is seen here near Lee Bridge car park.

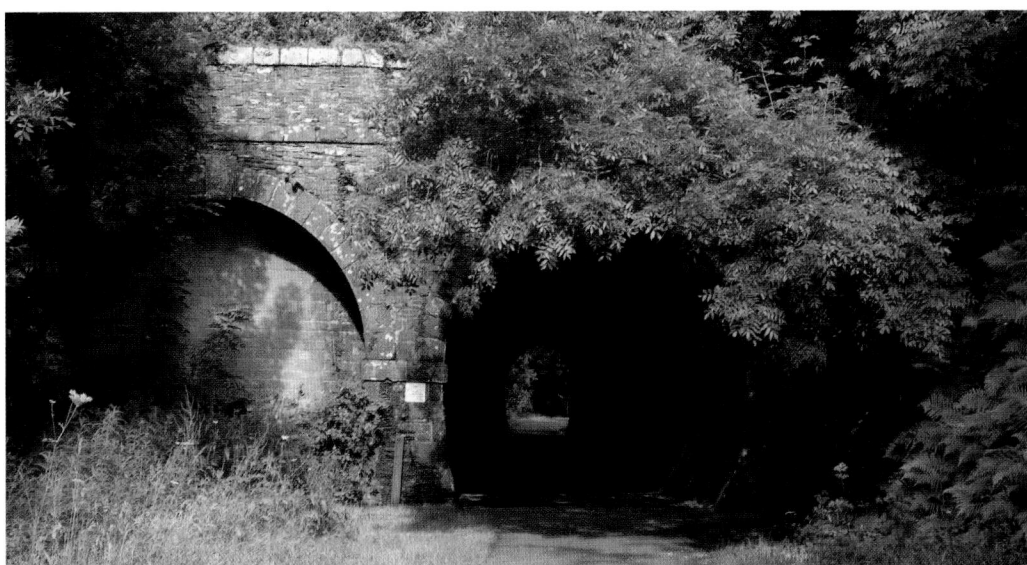

The Ilfracombe branch was built single track but was widened to double track in 1891, requiring an extra bore of Slade Tunnel, south of Ilfracombe. While the northbound bore is now bricked up and home to a colony of bats, the southbound bore is open for walkers and cyclists.

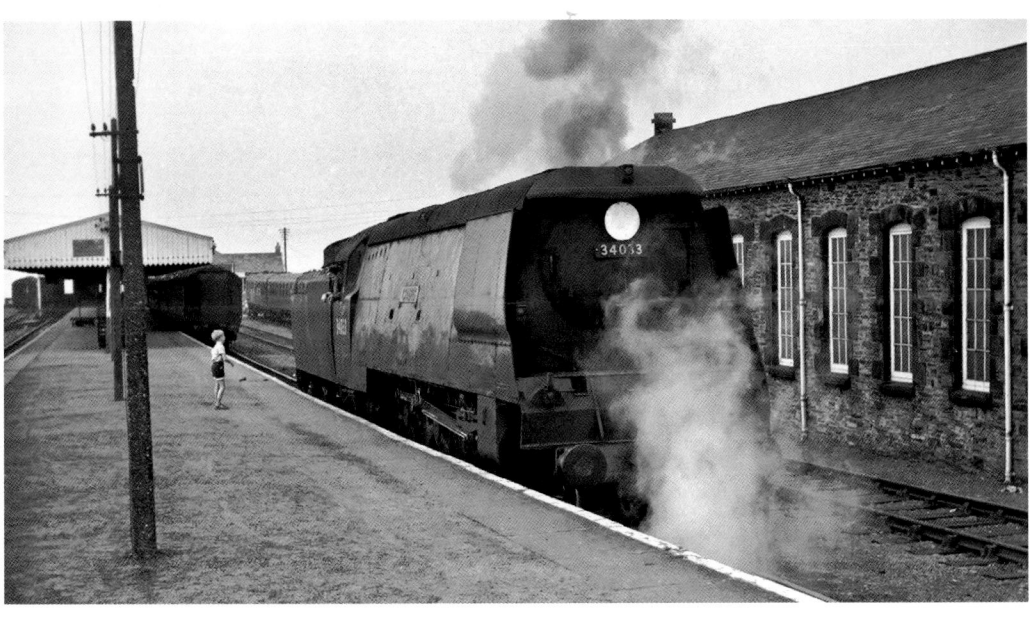

A young enthusiast has a chat with the crew of ex-SR 'Battle of Britain' Class 4-6-2 No. 34033 'Chard' at Ilfracombe station on 5 September 1959 as they await to set back into the engine shed.

WEST SOMERSET MINERAL RAILWAY

WATCHET TO THE BRENDON HILLS

Featuring an inclined plane and built to transport iron ore mined in the Brendon Hills to Watchet Harbour, the eccentric West Somerset Mineral Railway had a short and chequered life, closing twice before being sold lock, stock and barrel in an auction in 1924. Although much of the trackbed is now in private hands, the sections from Watchet to Washford and along the inclined plane have recently been reopened as footpaths by the Exmoor National Park Authority. Affording fine views over the Bristol Channel to South Wales, both the incline and the roofless winding house at the top are now Scheduled Ancient Monuments.

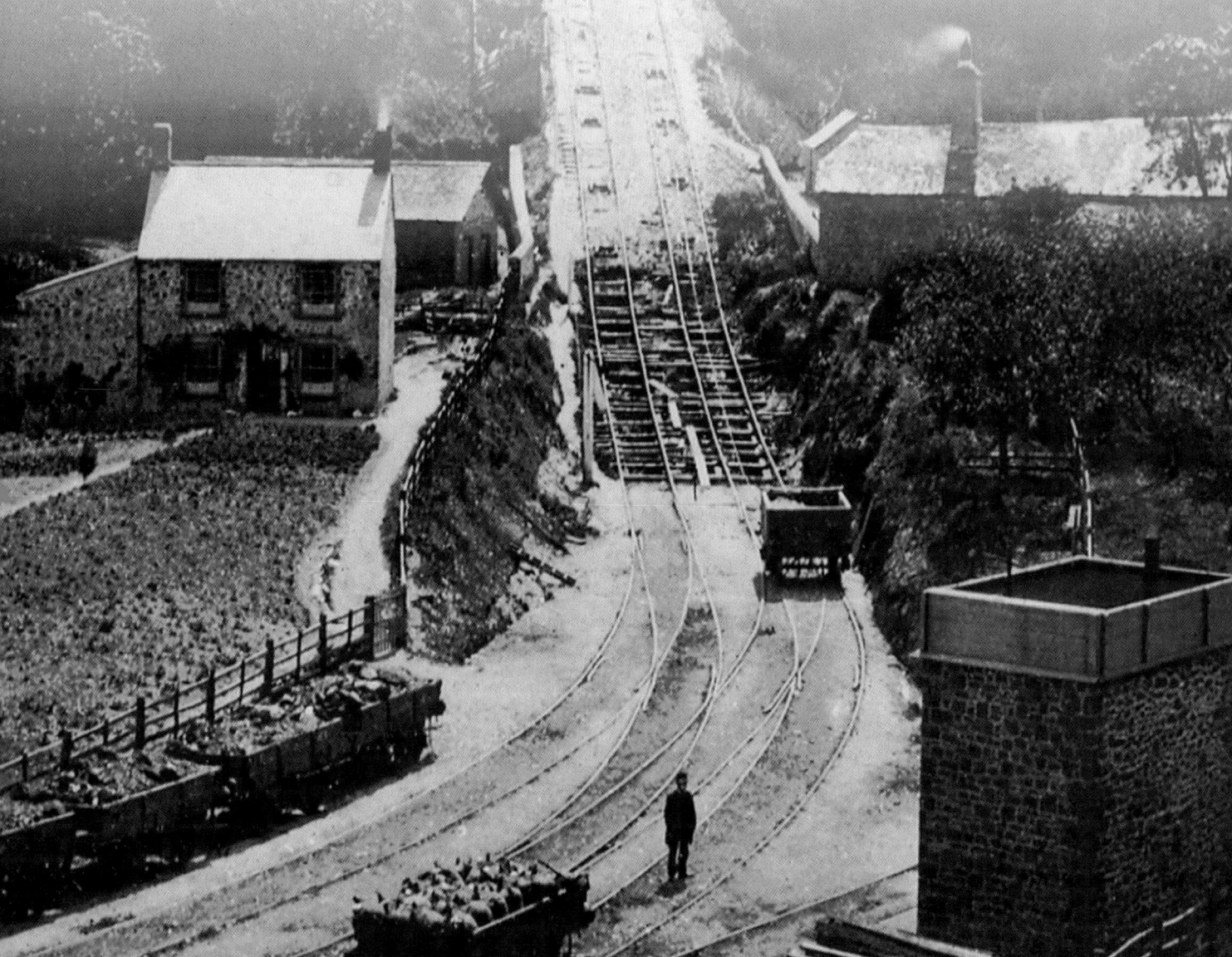

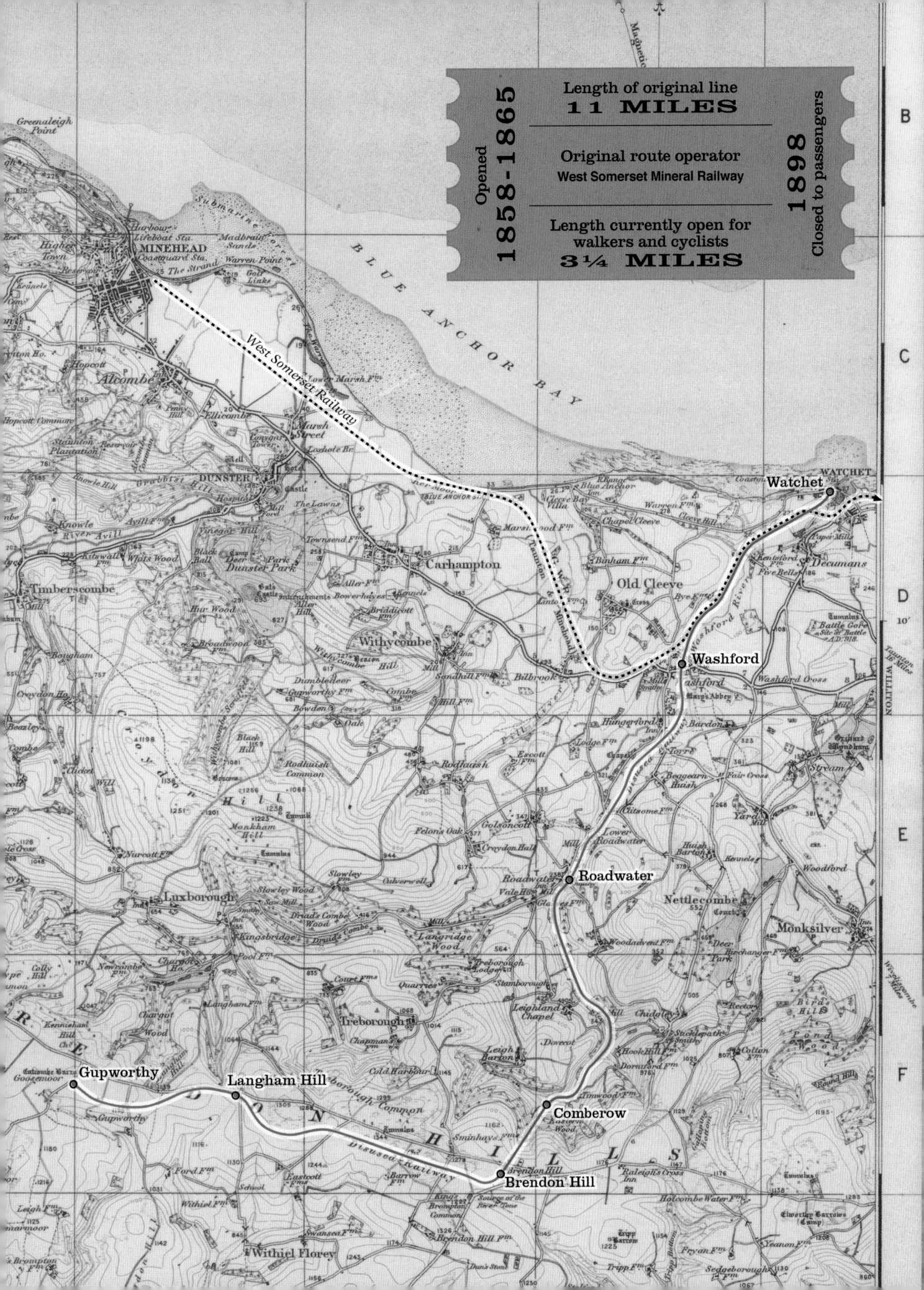

Length of original line
11 MILES

Original route operator
West Somerset Mineral Railway

Length currently open for
walkers and cyclists
3¼ MILES

Opened
1858–1865

1898
Closed to passengers

West Somerset Railway

BLUE ANCHOR BAY

MINEHEAD

Watchet

Washford

Roadwater

Comberow

Gupworthy

Langham Hill

Brendon Hill

Disused Railway

BRENDON HILLS

Rising to 1,200 ft above sea level, the Brendon Hills lie a few miles inland and parallel to the Bristol Channel. Although iron ore had been mined in the hills for centuries these operations remained fairly small scale until 1853 when two partners of the Ebbw Vale ironworks in South Wales formed the Brendon Hills Iron Ore Company. The Brendon Hills soon became a hive of industrial activity with new mines being opened up at various locations including Gupworthy, Lothbrook, Eisen Hill and Ralegh's Cross. By 1855 over 4,000 tons of ore had been mined but transporting it by horse and cart to Watchet, for onward shipment to South Wales, was a slow and expensive business. To overcome this the West Somerset Mineral Railway Act of 1855 authorized the building of a railway from Watchet Harbour to the foot of the Brendon Hills at Comberow. From here a three-quarter-mile inclined plane with a gradient of 1 in 4 would link a railway serving the Brendon mines from Ralegh's Cross in the east to the Eisen Hill in the west. The total length of the railway was to be 13½ miles and it was to be leased and worked by the Ebbw Vale Company.

Construction of the standard-gauge single-track railway commenced at Watchet in 1856 and within a year had reached Roadwater. As the nearest railway was then at Taunton, the first steam locomotive had to cover the final stretch to the terminus on a horse-hauled road carriage. By 1858 the line had been opened between Watchet and Comberow but, although the inclined plane was complete, the winding house at the top with its two 18-ft-diameter iron winding drums was not ready for use until 1861. By 1862 the output of the mines had risen to 30,000 tons annually but the westerly extension of the railway had still not been built. This was eventually completed in 1864 but only as far as Goosemoor, beyond which the cost of building a second inclined plane was considered too prohibitive for the company.

Regular passenger services between Watchet and Comberow started on 4 September 1865. One steam locomotive and three passenger coaches initially operated this lower line, joined by a second steam locomotive arriving at Watchet via the Bristol & Exeter Railway's line from Taunton in 1866. Passengers could travel at their own risk in an open wagon up the incline while, on the upper section, an open wagon fitted with planks for seats sufficed for the journey to remote Goosemoor. One steam locomotive also operated the upper section with the passenger wagon attached to mineral trains. Accidents were common!

The new Bessemer process for commercial steelmaking saw the Brendon Hill ore much in demand and by 1875 output from the mines had peaked at over 40,000 tons. The outlook was gloomy, however, with the iron and steel trade suffering a major recession and not helped by the

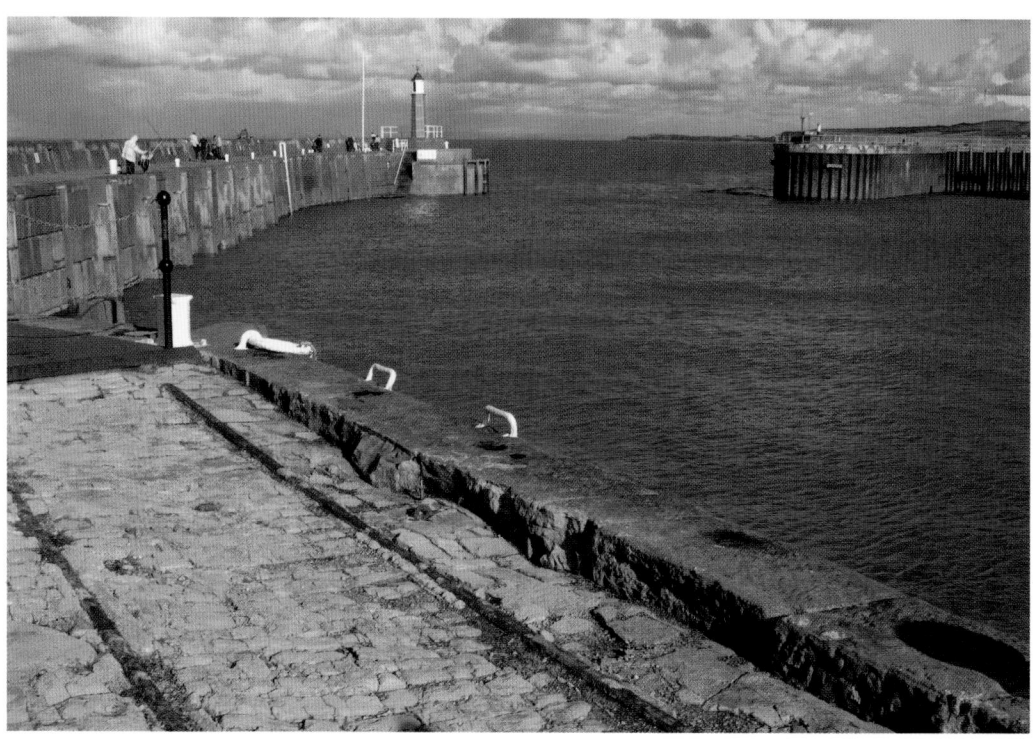

A length of original rail from the West Somerset Mineral Railway was recently uncovered during maintenance work at Watchet Harbour. It was from here that Brendon Hills' iron ore was shipped across the Bristol Channel to South Wales in the nineteenth century.

PREVIOUS SPREAD:
Here seen from Comberow, the ¾-mile 1-in-4 Brendon Incline was opened in 1861 and connected the lower and upper sections of the West Somerset Mineral Railway. It is now a Scheduled Ancient Monument with a footpath along its length offering some brisk exercise for lovers of lost railways.

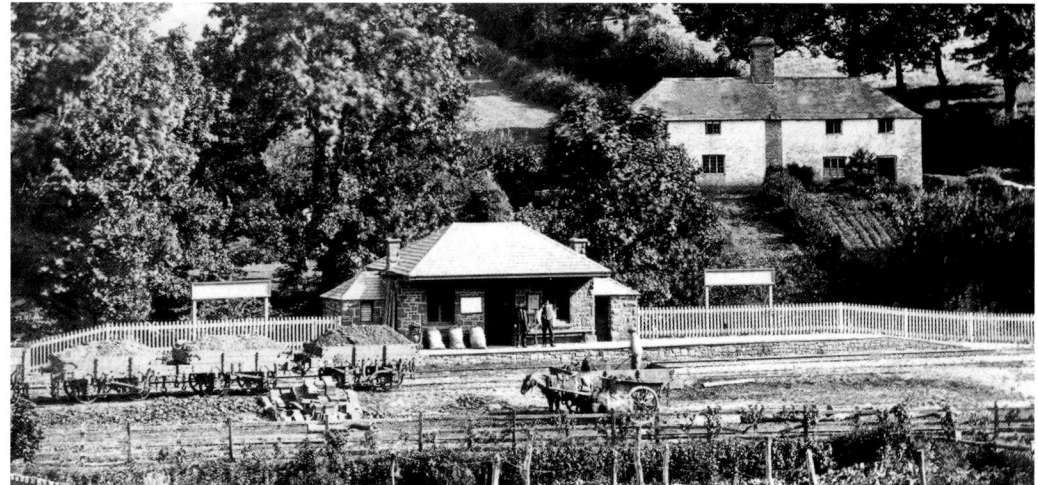

A view of Roadwater station taken in 1870. The station staff pose for the camera while wagons full of iron ore wait to be taken down to Watchet Harbour. The station and platform survive today as part of a private residence.

availability of cheap iron ore from Spain. This led to a rapid decline in demand for Brendon ore which, despite an upsurge in 1880, eventually led to the wholesale closure of the mines by 1883. Having lost its raison d'être the railway struggled on for a few more years with the troubled Ebbw Vale Company seeking to relinquish its lease. Eventually the company closed the railway completely on 7 November 1898 although it was required to maintain it and pay the rent until the end of the lease in 1919.

This was not quite the end of the West Somerset Mineral Railway, however. Formed in 1907 the Somerset Mineral Syndicate sought to reopen some of the Brendon mines along with the railway. A secondhand ex-Metropolitan Railway 4-4-0 tank engine was purchased and the railway reopened between Watchet and Brendon Hill in July. The output from the mines was small however, and by 1910 the company was bankrupt and the railway had closed again. In a further effort to honour its lease the Ebbw Vale Company rented the railway out for demonstrations of automatic train control between 1912 and 1914. When the lease came to an end in 1919 the railway was effectively abandoned and eventually put up for sale. Land and property realized just over £3,000 in the auction at the West Somerset Hotel in Watchet on 8 August 1924 and the West Somerset Mineral Railway ceased to exist.

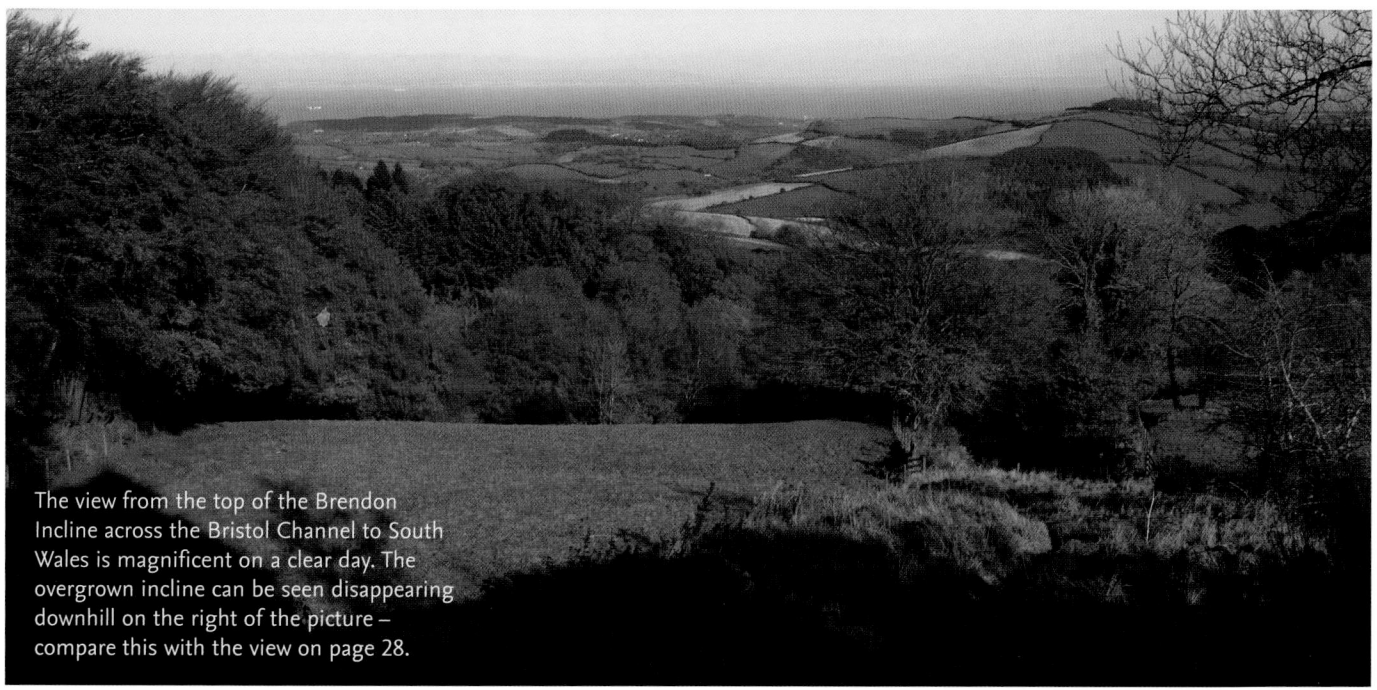

The view from the top of the Brendon Incline across the Bristol Channel to South Wales is magnificent on a clear day. The overgrown incline can be seen disappearing downhill on the right of the picture – compare this with the view on page 28.

Despite its closure over 100 years ago there is still much to be seen of the West Somerset Mineral Railway today. At Watchet the former station house is now two residential flats while the nearby goods shed is used for car repairs. On the harbour wall a section of original track is displayed, having been revealead during recent repairs and the small Watchet Market House Museum includes artefacts and a model of the railway. Paralleling the West Somerset Railway's line to Minehead, the trackbed of the mineral railway from Watchet to Washford is now a footpath.

Further up the Washford Valley the railway once passed through the grounds of ruined Cleeve Abbey but its course is now barely visible. Much remains of the railway at Roadwater, where the station and platform is now part of a private house. Nearby, the rusting bridge girders across the river and an adjacent level crossing gate have miraculously survived the ravages of time. Further up the valley to Comberow a road follows the course of the railway to the foot of the incline. Once on private land, the overgrown incline is now owned by the Exmoor National Park Authority and is a scheduled Ancient Monument. A steep path can be walked (good walking boots required) to the top where the roofless winding house has been conserved with the aid of a Heritage Lottery grant. The view from the top of the incline across the Bristol Channel to South Wales and the Brecon Beacons on a clear day is superb. There is a small area of off-road parking and on the opposite side of the B3224 from the winding house is the former Temperance Hotel, now a private residence.

Exploring the rest of the railway along the top of the Brendon Hills is best done by a combination of car or bicycle, with some locations accessible only on foot. Heading west along the B3224 from the incline winding house, the roofless engine house and chimney of Burrow Farm Mine can also be accessed on foot along the former trackbed – a permissive footpath follows the top of the beech-lined railway cutting for half a mile to the engine house. The low embankment of the railway can also be seen a short distance to the south of the road. Further west the ruins of Luxborough Road station can be spotted in woodland and a little further on lie the conserved remains of the Langham Hill Engine House. Here a large signposted car park for Chargot Woods allows access on foot to the engine house site as well as Forestry Commission trails to visit the Bearland Wood ventilation flue.

The western terminus of the mineral railway was at remote Goosemoor, where the station building is now a private residence. Explorers of the railway can find refreshment either by retracing their journey to Ralegh's Cross Inn or discovering the delights of the Royal Oak Inn in the village of Luxborough.

For guided bus trips and walks along the West Somerset Mineral Railway visit: www.westsomersetminerallineassociation.org.uk

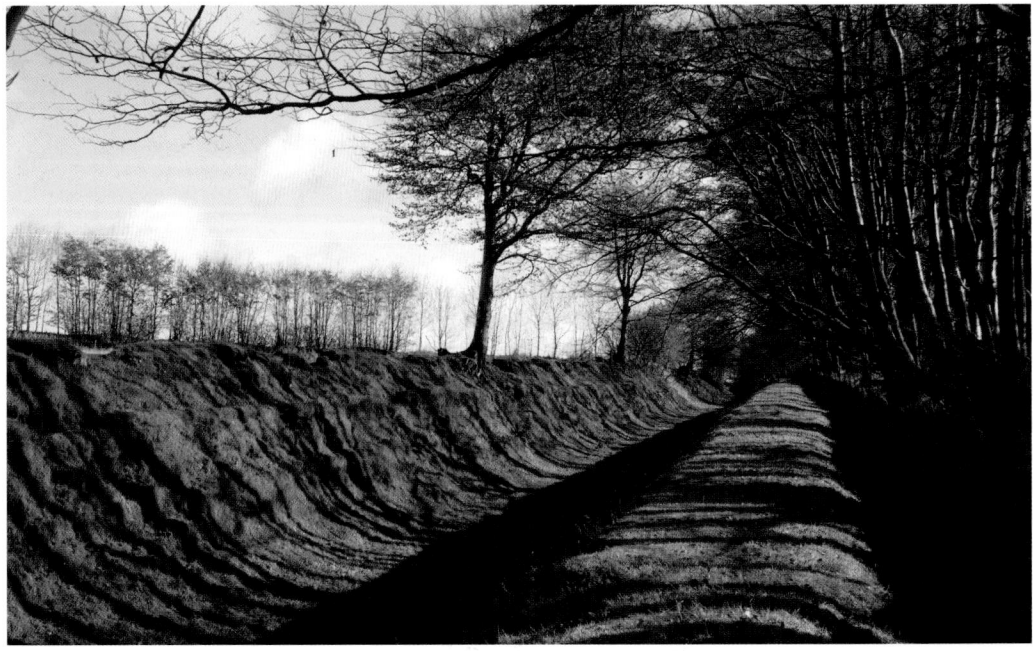

To the west of the Brendon Incline winding house, this beech-lined railway cutting can now be followed on foot by way of a permissive footpath to Burrow Farm engine house.

The engine house at Burrow Farm Mine is a rare survival of the Cornish type in Somerset and the only surviving engine house on the Brendon Hills. Conserved by the Exmoor National Park Authority in 1990, it can only be reached on foot along the trackbed of the West Somerset Mineral Line from Naked Boy's Bridge, half a mile west of the top of the Brendon Incline.

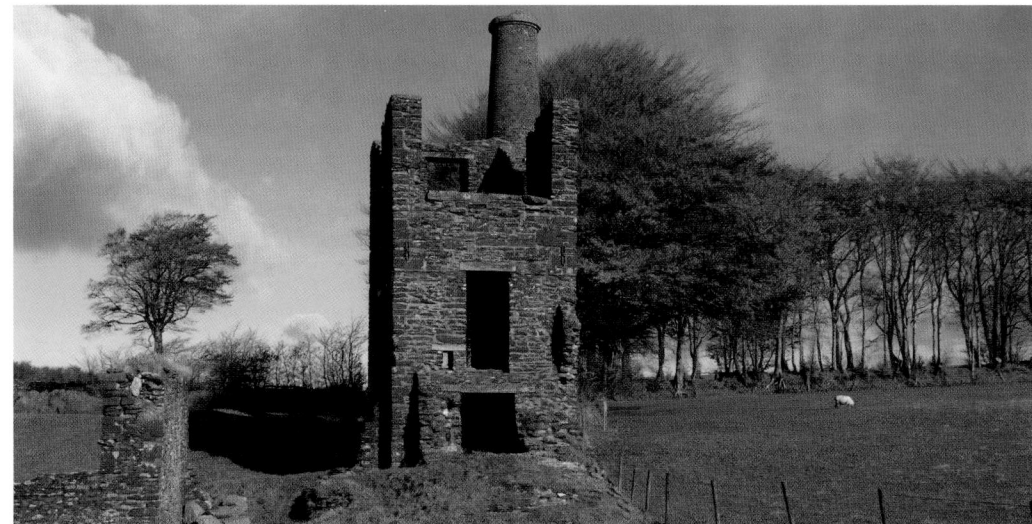

Looking more like a scene from an old Western movie, a bearded gentleman rattles along overgrown track on a hand-cranked maintenance trolley in Smith's Cutting on the upper level of the railway in 1900.

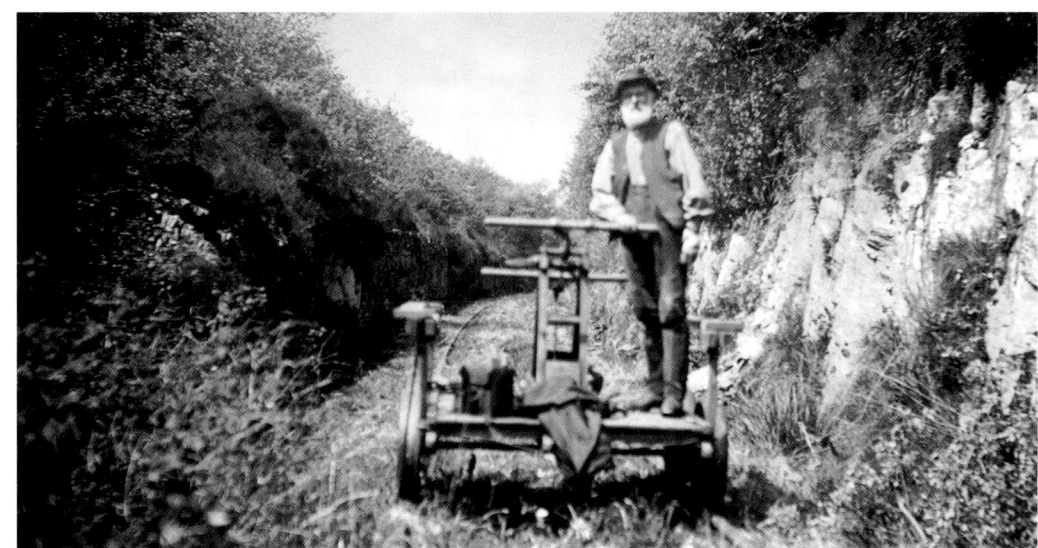

The upper level of the mineral railway terminated abruptly at isolated Goosemoor station – the building of a second inclined plane beyond was considered too costly, so the railway stopped. The station is seen here after a snowfall in November 1959, more than half a century after closure.

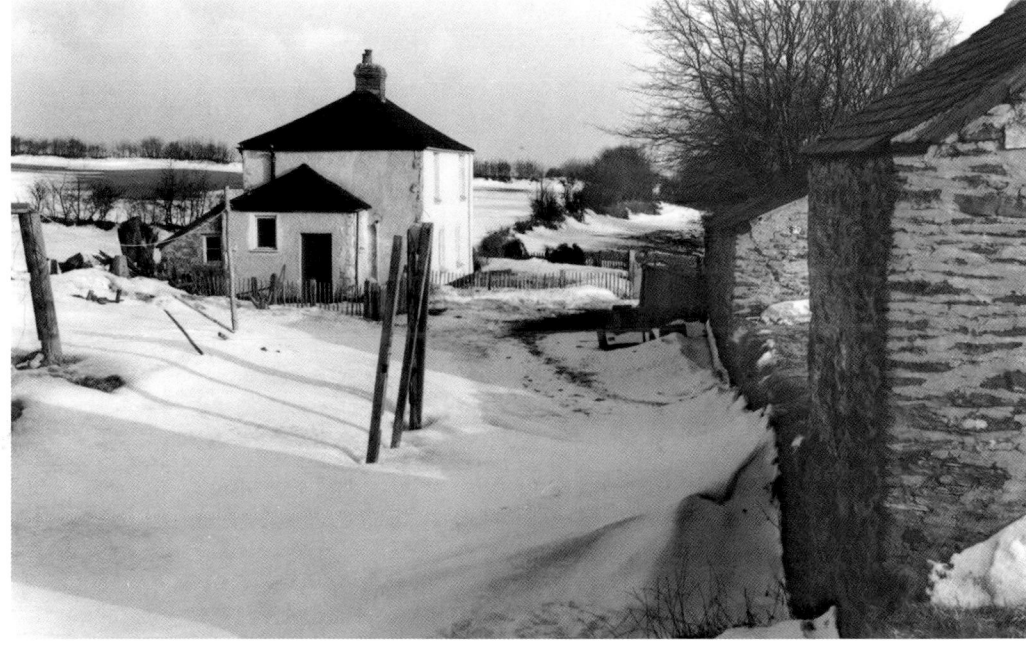

TAUNTON
TO
CHARD

THE STOP LINE WAY

Built alongside the moribund Chard Canal, the broad-gauge single-track railway from Creech Junction, east of Taunton, to the town of Chard opened in 1866. At Chard the railway met the London & South Western Railway's short branch line from Chard Junction, but although the two lines shared a joint station in the town, the companies led very separate existences until the First World War. The Ilminster to Chard section of the line is now a footpath and cycleway, although during the Second World War it formed part of the Taunton Stop Line, a continuous anti-tank obstacle designed to halt a German invasion.

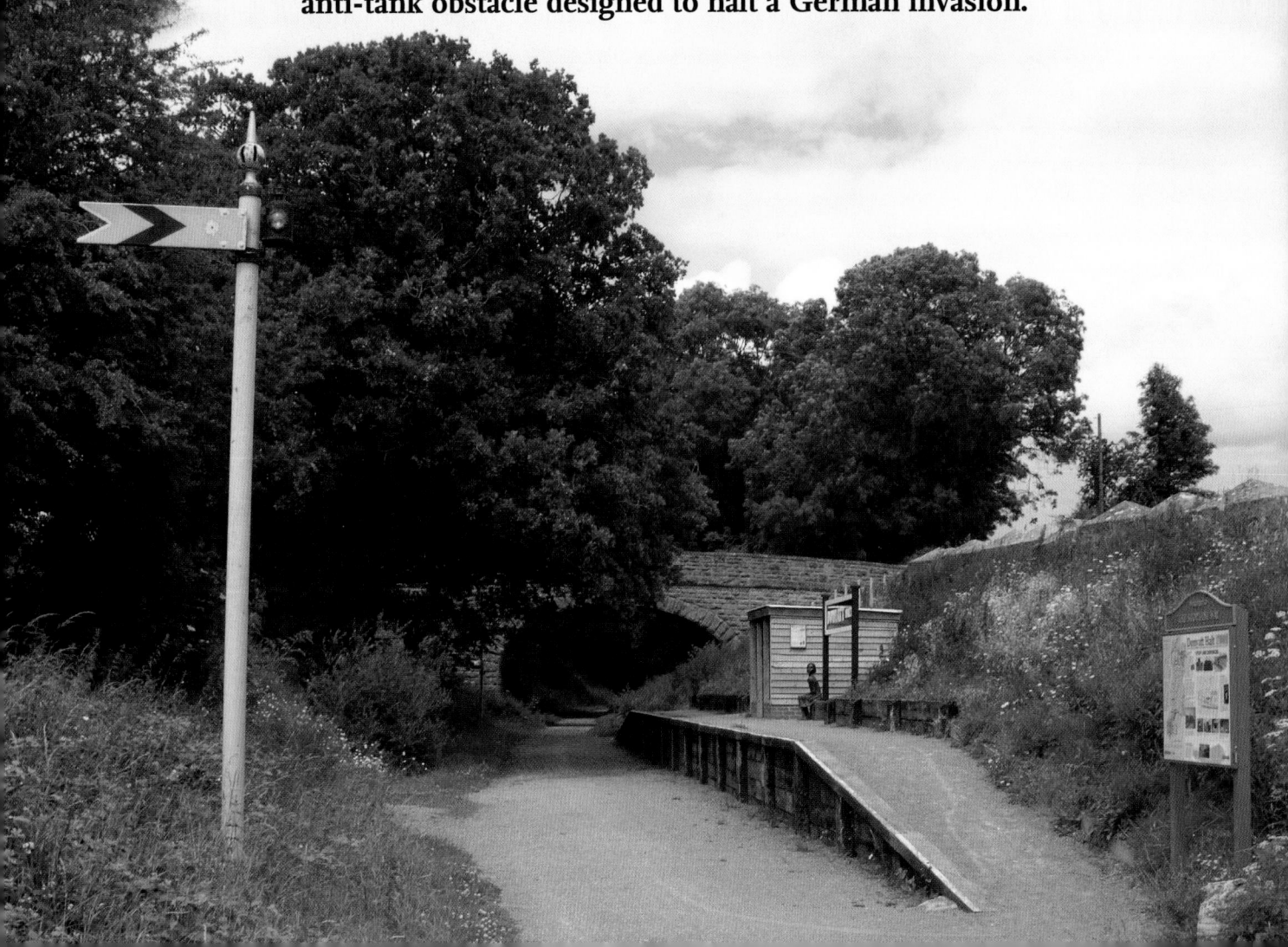

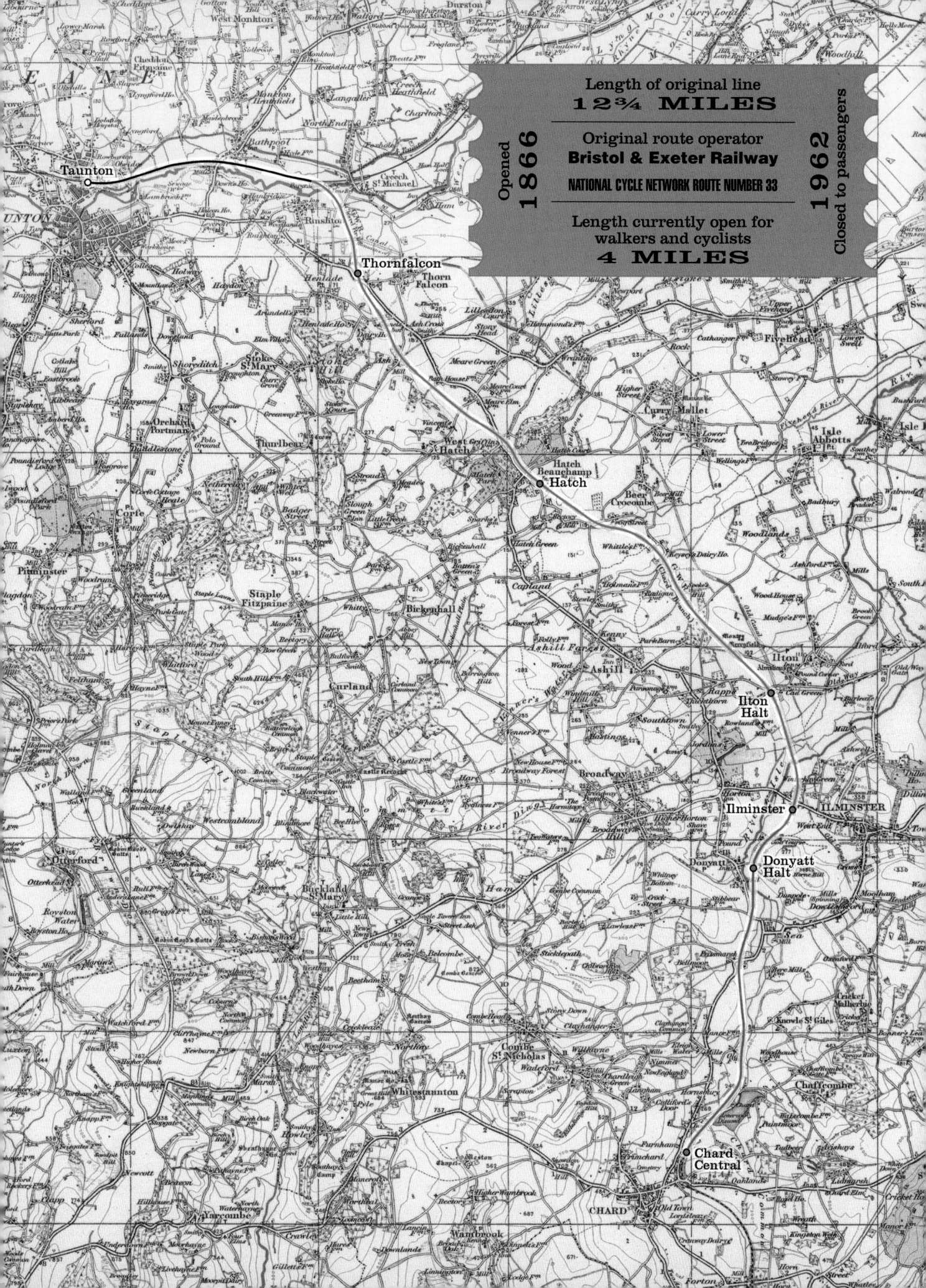

Length of original line
12¾ MILES

Original route operator
Bristol & Exeter Railway

NATIONAL CYCLE NETWORK ROUTE NUMBER 33

Length currently open for
walkers and cyclists
4 MILES

Opened
1866

Closed to passengers
1962

Taunton

Thornfalcon

Hatch
Beauchamp
Hatch

Ilton
Halt

Ilminster

Donyatt
Halt

Chard
Central

A canal had served the South Somerset town of Chard from Taunton since 1842 but the town's hopes of being placed on a grand north-south railway route linking the Bristol and English channels were dashed when the project came to nothing. Matters were made worse when the London & South Western Railway's (LSWR) main line between Exeter and Salisbury bypassed the town three miles to the south when it opened in 1860. Plans to convert the slumbering Chard Canal into a railway also failed to materialize, so the townsfolk were delighted when the Chard Railway opened a branch line from the LSWR main line at Chard Junction to Chard Town station in 1863.

Meanwhile the Chard Canal sank into obscurity. Its high construction costs – caused by the building of four aqueducts, three tunnels and four inclined planes –

guaranteed that it could never pay its way. In its early years it had carried substantial quantities of coal and stone but by 1853 it had gone into receivership. Attempts to rebuild it as a railway failed. With the LSWR having taken over the short Chard Railway the Bristol & Exeter Railway (B&ER), fearing incursion by the LSWR into its territory, bought the canal with the sole purpose of closing it!

Chard finally got a broad-gauge railway from Taunton via Ilminster, which was opened by the B&ER (amalgamated with the Great Western Railway in 1876) in 1866. It terminated in Chard at a new joint station, which later became known as Chard Central. Although built for a double-track railway – witness the existing bridges today – the route was only opened as a single-track line. Some of the LSWR's standard-gauge trains from Chard Junction continued on to the joint station via a new connecting line. Despite both companies sharing the station they both led very separate existences, with their own staff, sidings and signal boxes. Theoretically through workings became possible when the line from Taunton was converted to standard gauge by the GWR in 1891 but the intense suspicion by both

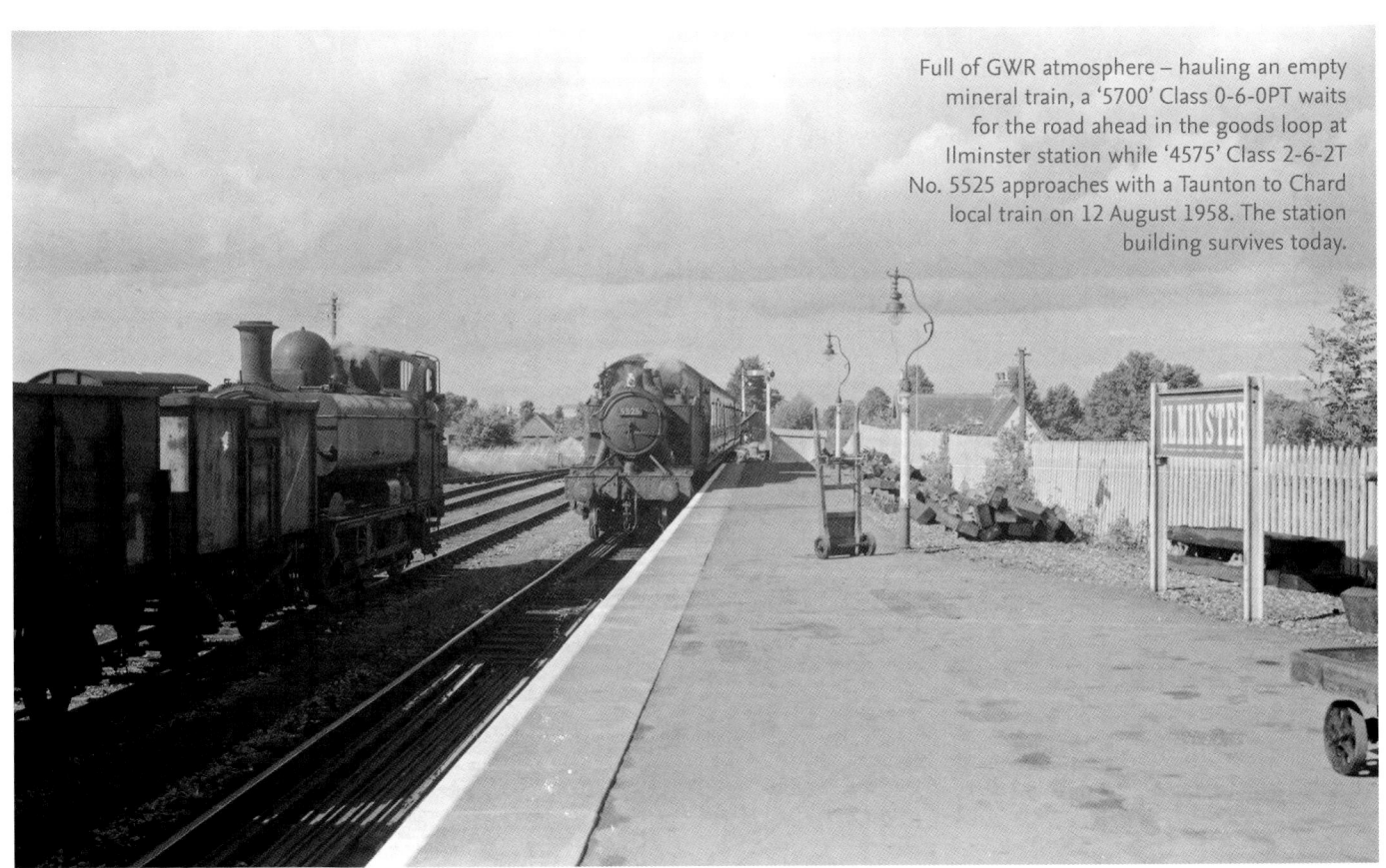

Full of GWR atmosphere – hauling an empty mineral train, a '5700' Class 0-6-0PT waits for the road ahead in the goods loop at Ilminster station while '4575' Class 2-6-2T No. 5525 approaches with a Taunton to Chard local train on 12 August 1958. The station building survives today.

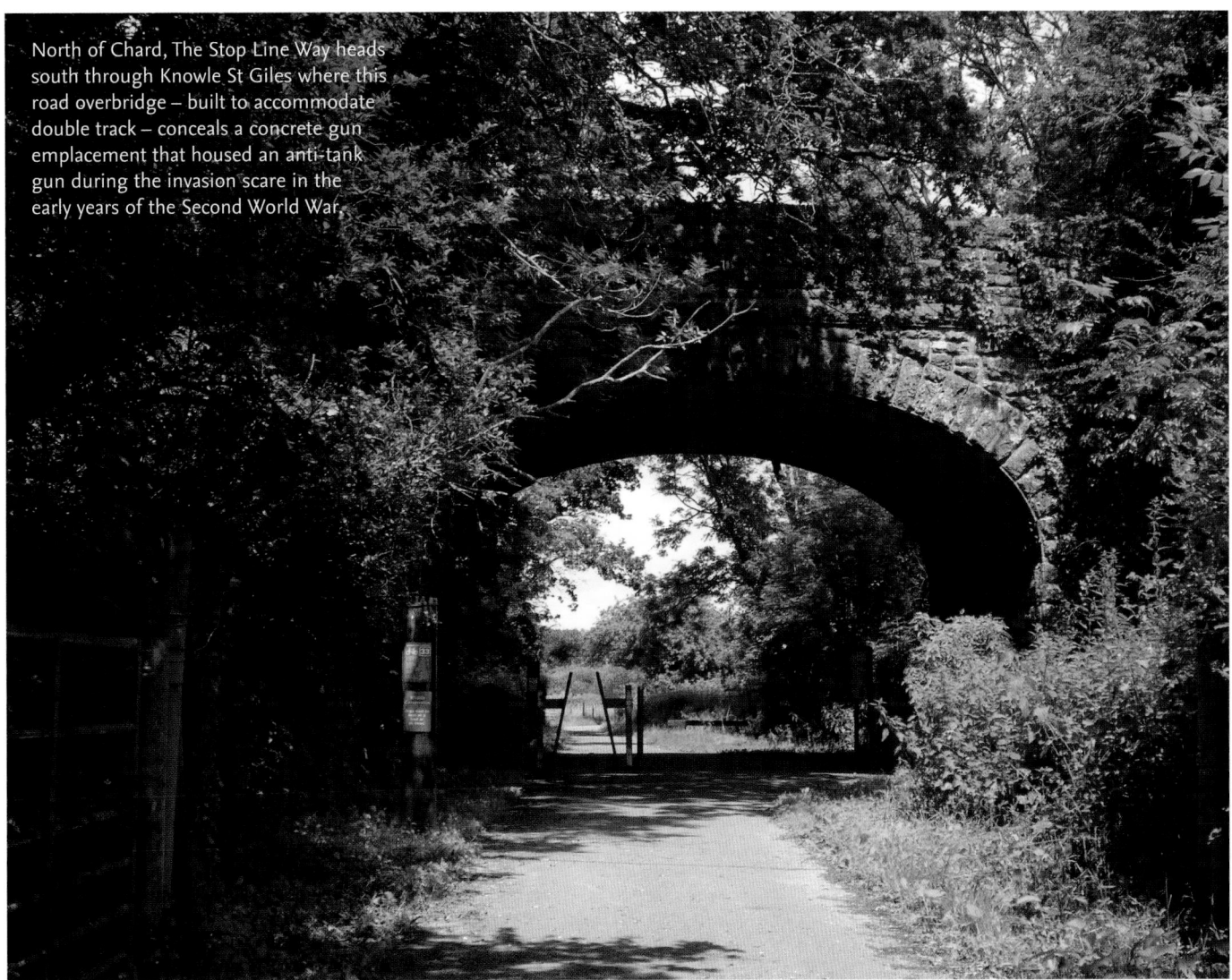

North of Chard, The Stop Line Way heads south through Knowle St Giles where this road overbridge – built to accommodate double track – conceals a concrete gun emplacement that housed an anti-tank gun during the invasion scare in the early years of the Second World War.

companies about the other's intentions precluded this. The onset of the First World War brought an urgent need for economy and the bitter rivalries between the two companies were soon forgotten when the GWR took over the operation of the branch line from Chard Junction in 1917, however the LSWR, and later the Southern Railway (SR), was still responsible for its infrastructure. Chard Town station was also closed to passengers at the same time. Further economies occurred in 1927 when the SR platform, sidings and signal box at Chard Central were removed. A new station opened at Donyatt, south of Ilminster, in 1928 – actually a single-platform halt with a waiting shelter. Donyatt Halt transformed the lives of villagers and greatly assisted the Donyatt Pottery in transporting its famous ware to distant markets. On this bucolic railway train drivers would often stop to pick up locals at unauthorized stopping places.

The Second World War brought much activity to the Ilminster to Chard section of the line because it followed the 'Taunton Stop Line', built by the Army in 1940 to contain any German invasion of southwest England. These defences ran for fifty miles from Burnham-on-Sea on the Bristol Channel to Seaton on the South Devon coast. Canals, railways and rivers were made into a continuous anti-tank obstacle with road blocks and over 380 concrete pillboxes and gun emplacements.

The post-war years saw a rapid decline in both passenger and goods traffic on country branch lines around Britain and the Taunton to Chard Junction line was no exception. Listed for closure in the 'Beeching Report', the Taunton-Chard-Chard Junction line closed to passengers on 10 September 1962. Goods services continued between Taunton and Chard until 1964 and from Chard Junction to Chard until 1966.

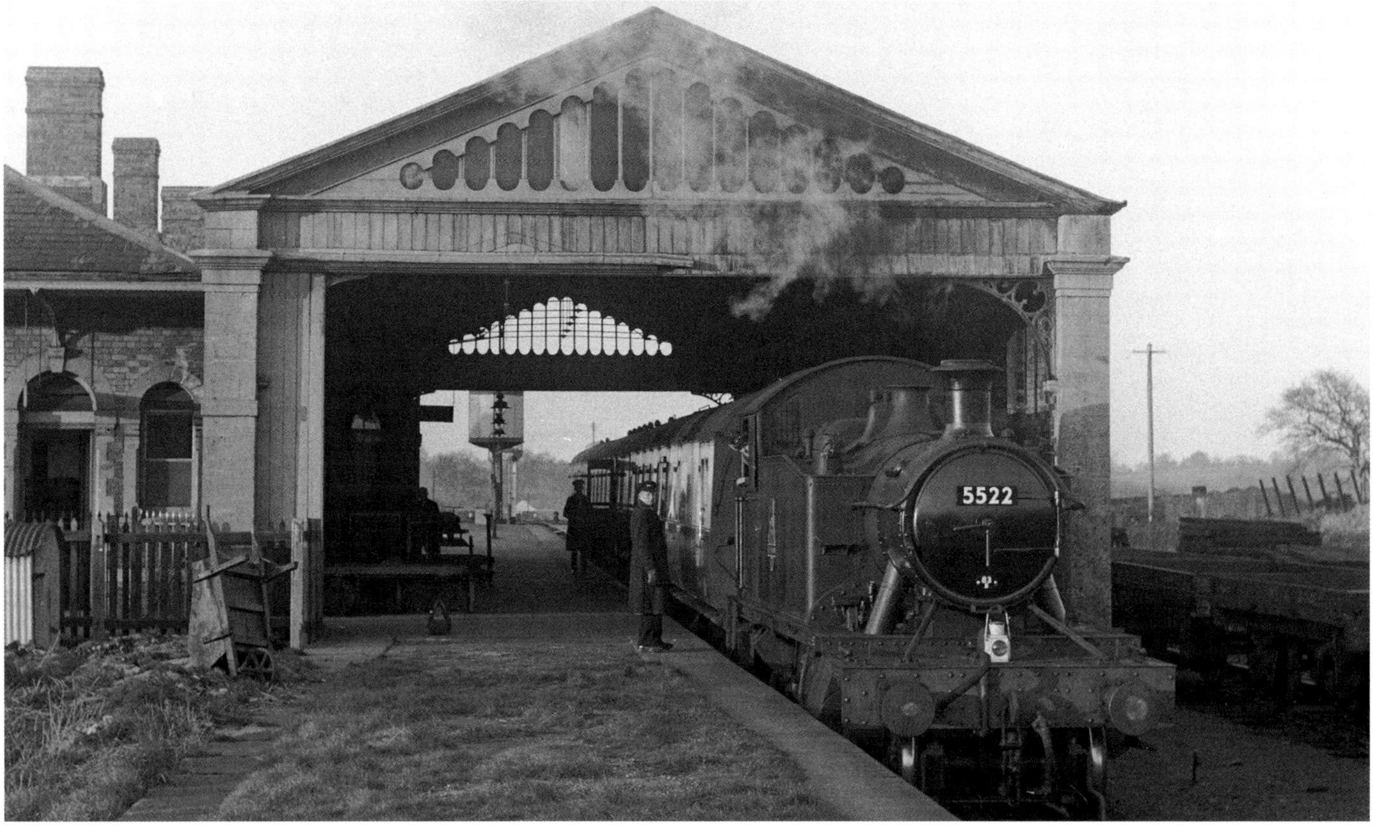

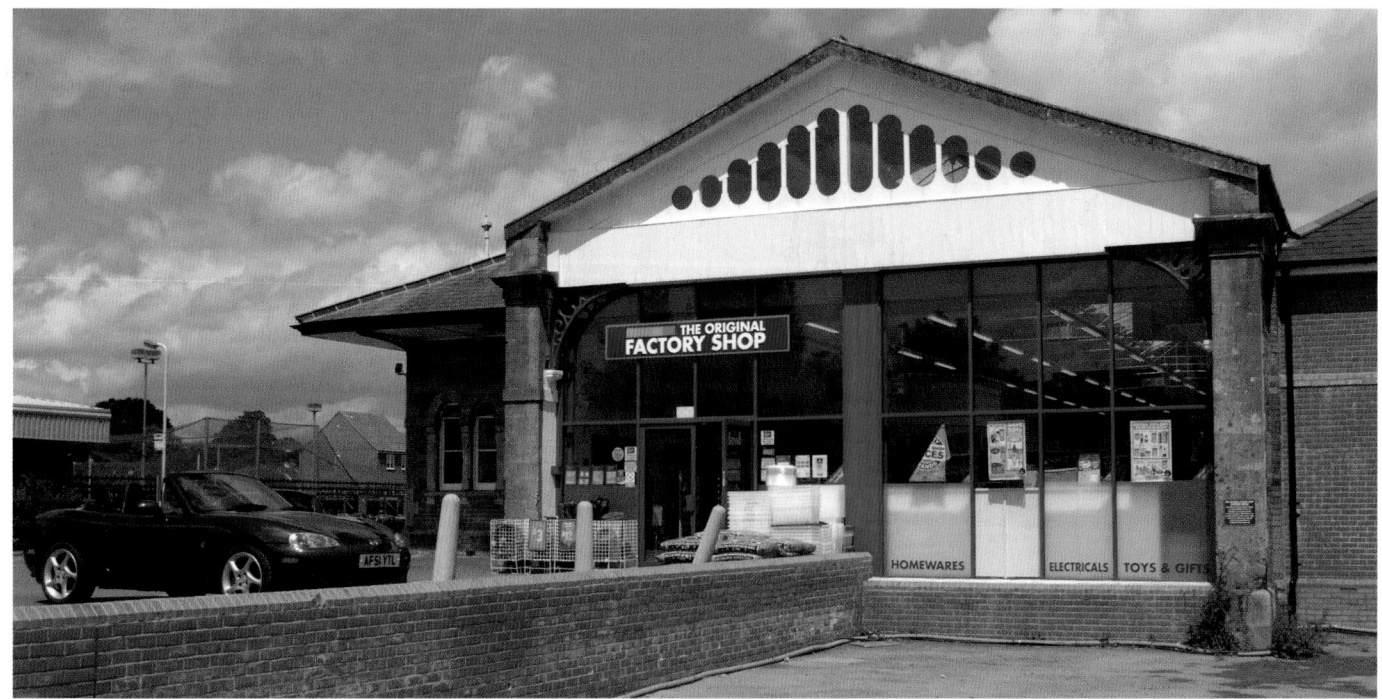

Looking remarkably clean, Taunton shed's ex-GWR '4575' Class 2-6-2T No. 5522 has just arrived at Chard Central station with a Taunton to Chard Junction train in 1958. Although the loco was withdrawn the following year the attractive overall-roofed station building has survived the ravages of time.

The scene at Chard Central station today, nearly 150 years after the line opened. The station building and its overall roof have been tastefully converted into a factory shop.

THE ORIGINAL
FACTORY SHOP

HOMEWARES   ELECTRICALS   TOYS & GIFTS

ollowing closure the trackbed between Ilminster and Chard was bought by Somerset County Council which, in 2000, in conjunction with the cycling charity Sustrans, reopened it as a footpath and cycleway known as The Stop Line Way – so named because of the anti-invasion defences built during the Second World War along the line. The trail, forming part of National Cycle Network Route 33, can be accessed at the Tesco supermarket in Ilminster or at the town's recreation ground adjacent to the route of the old Chard Canal. From here it heads west before joining the old railway route north of Donyatt Cutting. Heading south from here the trail passes under a large road bridge, built to take a double-track railway before reaching Donyatt Halt. Superbly restored with a platform, waiting shelter, nameboard, distant signal and a statue to child evacuees who arrived here from London during the Blitz, this little station also has other reminders of the wartime-invasion scare in the shape of a large number of anti-tank concrete stop blocks.

Beyond Donyatt the trail heads south through Peasmarsh to Knowle St Giles, where there is a splendid road overbridge and an adjacent large concrete gun emplacement. Manned by the Royal Artillery, this once housed a six-pounder anti-tank gun taken from a First World War tank with an effective range of 600 yds. Nearby, to the east, is another concrete pillbox that was disguised as a chicken house and beyond are the remains of the Chard Canal.

Still heading south, the trail skirts the western shore of the Chard Reservoir, which was built in 1842 to supply water for the Chard Canal. Although abandoned following the opening of the railway, this large area of water and its shoreline was given to the South Somerset District Council in 1990 and became a Local Nature Reserve.

The trail ends just south of the reservoir at the site of Chard Central station. Here, the original 1866 stone-and-brick Grade-II-listed building and its covered roof has been expertly converted into a warehouse shop. If you half close your eyes it's just possible to imagine the two-coach train from Taunton steaming in behind a GWR pannier tank!

The entire trail is well signposted, with some interesting information boards at regular intervals along the 4-mile route. Car parking is available in both Ilminster and Chard.

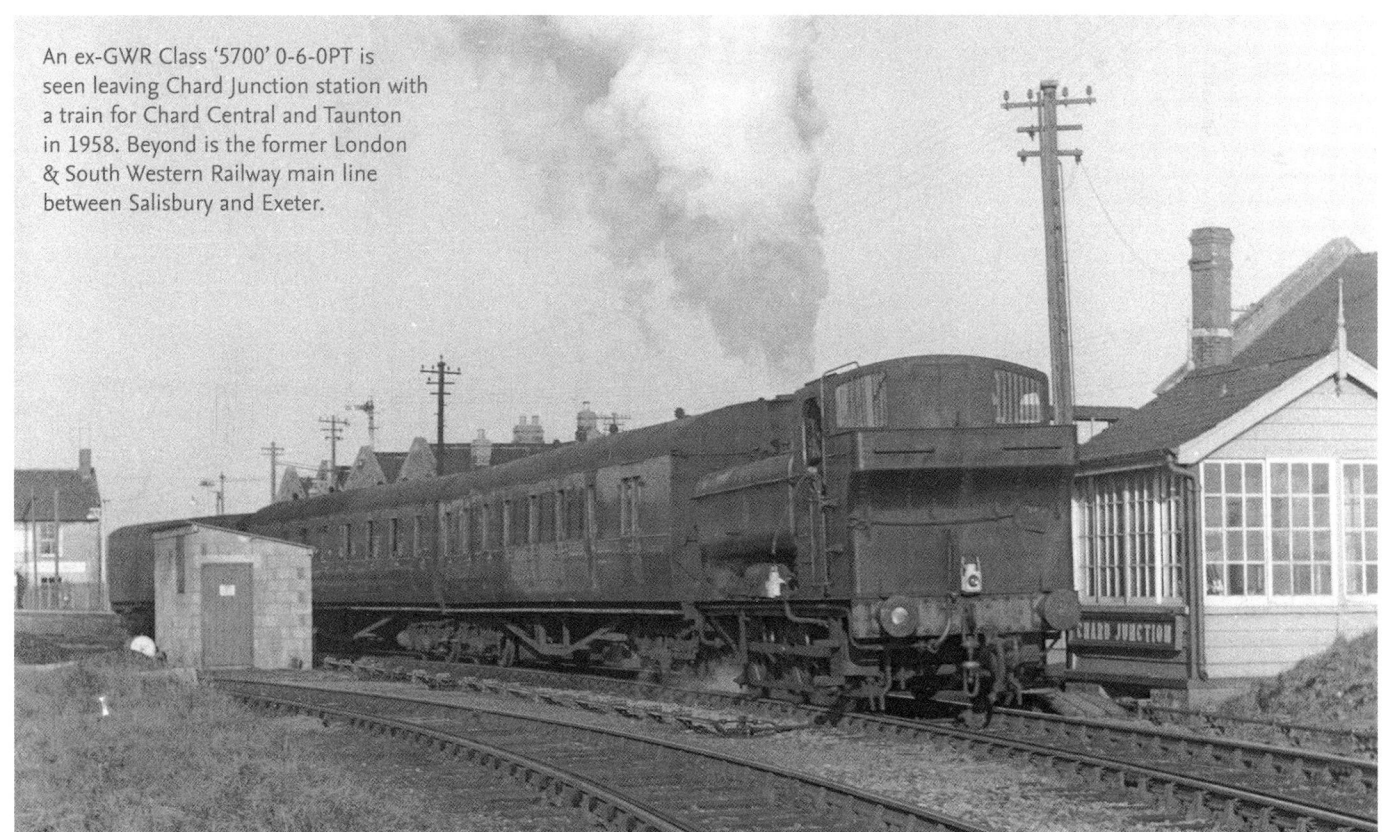

An ex-GWR Class '5700' 0-6-0PT is seen leaving Chard Junction station with a train for Chard Central and Taunton in 1958. Beyond is the former London & South Western Railway main line between Salisbury and Exeter.

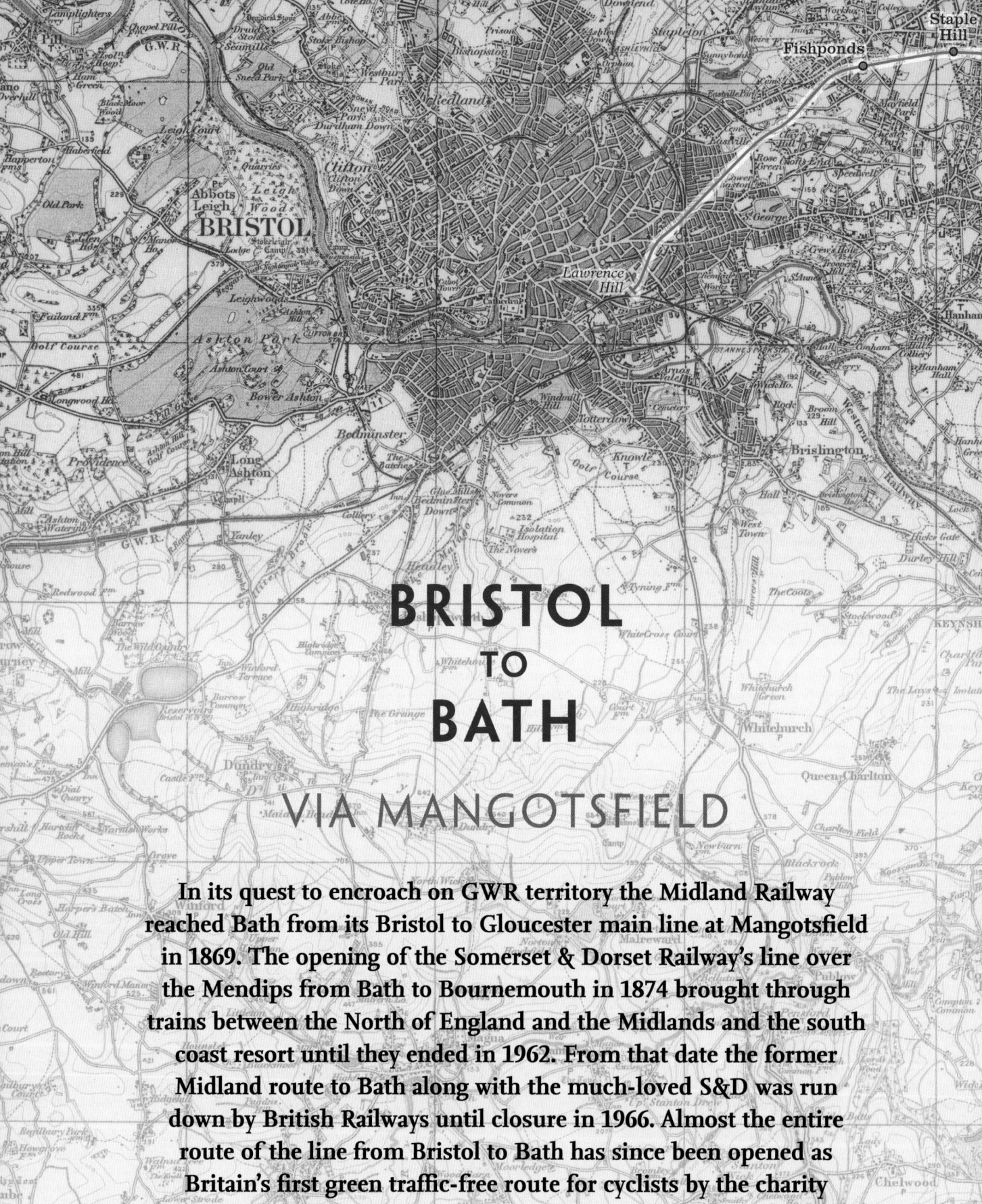

BRISTOL
TO
BATH

VIA MANGOTSFIELD

In its quest to encroach on GWR territory the Midland Railway reached Bath from its Bristol to Gloucester main line at Mangotsfield in 1869. The opening of the Somerset & Dorset Railway's line over the Mendips from Bath to Bournemouth in 1874 brought through trains between the North of England and the Midlands and the south coast resort until they ended in 1962. From that date the former Midland route to Bath along with the much-loved S&D was run down by British Railways until closure in 1966. Almost the entire route of the line from Bristol to Bath has since been opened as Britain's first green traffic-free route for cyclists by the charity Sustrans, while the section of line on either side of Bitton station has also been reopened by the Avon Valley Railway.

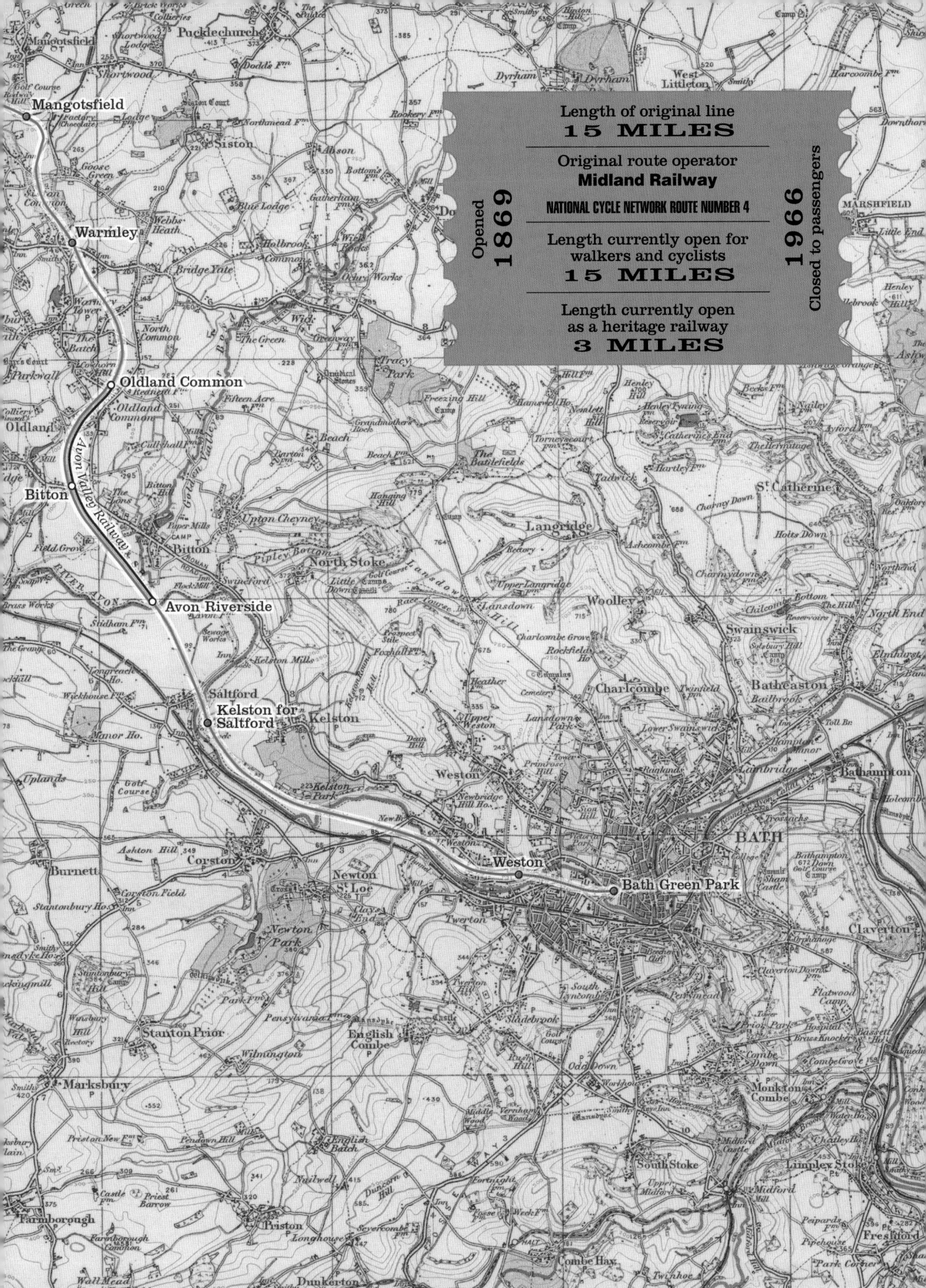

Mangotsfield

Warmley

Oldland Common

Bitton

Avon Riverside

Kelston for
Saltford

Length of original line
15 MILES

Original route operator
Midland Railway

NATIONAL CYCLE NETWORK ROUTE NUMBER 4

Length currently open for
walkers and cyclists
15 MILES

Length currently open
as a heritage railway
3 MILES

Opened **1869**

1966
Closed to passengers

Weston

Bath Green Park

BATH

While the Great Western Railway's (GWR) broad-gauge line from Paddington to Bristol had already reached the city of Bath in 1840, the Midland Railway did not arrive in the city until much later. Meanwhile the Birmingham & Gloucester Railway had opened in 1840 and the Bristol & Gloucester Railway in 1844. Seeking to block a potential GWR takeover of these two railways, George Hudson's newly formed Midland Railway (MR) stepped in and took over both companies in 1845.

The goal of reaching Bath was now possible for the MR but the poor economic climate of the time delayed this until 1864 when a 10-mile double-track branch from Mangotsfield, north of Bristol, to Bath was authorized by Parliament. Crossing the River Avon several times and with intermediate stations at Warmley, Oldland Common, Bitton, Kelston (for Bath Racecourse) and Weston, the line opened to a temporary terminus at Bath in 1869. A permanent two-platform terminus with an overall roof and grand frontage was opened in 1870 and remained as the 'Bath Midland Station' until it was renamed Green Park in 1951. A triangular junction was built at Mangotsfield allowing north-south trains to avoid calling at the draughty station.

The opening of the Somerset & Dorset Railway's Bath Extension across the Mendips in 1874 transformed the MR's branch line, which soon saw the passage of through trains between the North of England and the Midlands and Bournemouth. Of these the most famous was the 'Pines Express' – named in 1927 by the MR's successor, the London Midland & Scottish Railway – which, apart from the war years, continued to run over this route until 1962. Despite Bath Green Park's impressive façade it had only two platforms, on which north-south trains via the Somerset & Dorset line changed engines and reversed direction. Traffic on the line – upgraded to main-line standards in the 1930s – was particularly heavy during the Second World War but the post-war years brought threatening clouds with diminishing traffic. British Railways' regional boundary changes soon threatened the branch and the entire S&D route with closure.

With the northern part of the S&D route now under the control of the Western Region, all through trains ceased in September 1962. This was followed by a recommendation for closure in the 1963 'Beeching Report' although it was another three years before this was enacted: 7 March 1966 was 'Black Monday' for the line when the branch lost its passenger services and the S&D to Bournemouth closed completely. The Bath branch was singled and goods trains continued to serve Bath gas works until July 1971 when the line closed altogether, with the track lifted by June 1972. Meanwhile, trains between Bristol and Gloucester ceased to run over the former MR route between Bristol and Mangotsfield at the end of 1969, being diverted via Yate and Filton.

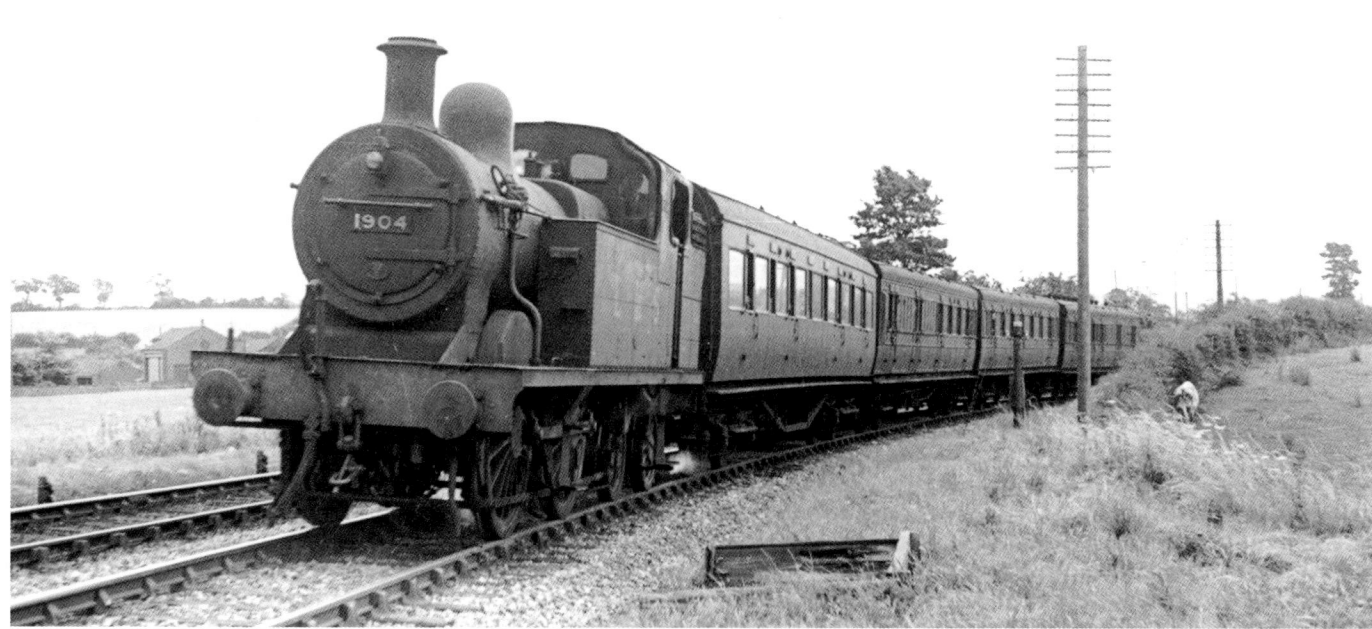

Since closure, the old MR route between Bath and Bristol via Mangotsfield has seen a renaissance. From early beginnings as the Bristol Suburban Railway in 1983, the Avon Valley Railway operates steam trains along three miles of line from its headquarters at the superbly restored Bitton station westwards to Oldland and eastwards to Avon Riverside. Between these points the railway shares the route with the adjacent Bristol and Bath Railway Path.

Almost the entire route of the line from Bristol to Mangotsfield and Bath was reopened by the cycling charity Sustrans between 1979 and 1986 as the first green traffic-free route for cyclists in Britain. Since these early beginnings Sustrans has opened over 10,000 miles of mainly traffic-free routes around the country, many of them following long-closed railway lines. With about 2.5 million trips each year, the popular Bristol and Bath Railway Path forms part of National Cycle Network Route 4 and consists of a wide tarmacked surface along its entire 15-mile route between Lawrence Hill, in central Bristol, and Newbridge, on the western outskirts of Bath. Much of the railway infrastructure remains including Staple Hill Tunnel (lit and open twenty-four hours), several bridges over the River Avon, the old platforms at Staple Hill, Mangotsfield and Warmley stations and of course, the Avon Valley Railway's station at Bitton. Cycle hire shops can be found in Bristol and Bath. A proposal to convert part of the path in the Bristol area into a concrete guided busway has met with much opposition from cycle users.

The *pièce de résistance* of this long-closed railway must surely be the beautifully restored station of Bath Green Park. With its grand frontage and graceful curving overall glass roof, the station now provides cover for car parking for the adjacent Sainsbury's supermarket in addition to stall holders and events. Various shops have taken up residence in the station building.

The Bristol and Bath Railway Path is accompanied by the Avon Valley Railway between Oldland and Avon Riverside. Midway between the two stations, restored Bitton station is the headquarters of this heritage railway.

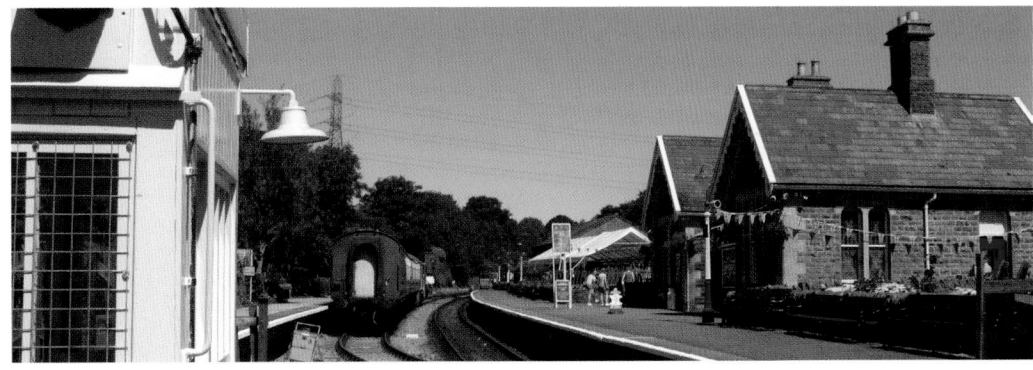

Until closure in 1966 Bath Green Park station saw steam-hauled trains on their way to and from Bournemouth. Since closure it has been beautifully restored and its arched glass roof provides shelter for supermarket car parking, cafés and events.

LEFT: Built at Derby Works in 1932, LMS 0-4-4T No. 1904 heads into Mangotsfield with the 12.20pm train from Bath Green Park to Bristol on 5 July 1947. This locomotive was withdrawn from Lancaster Green Ayre shed in 1959.

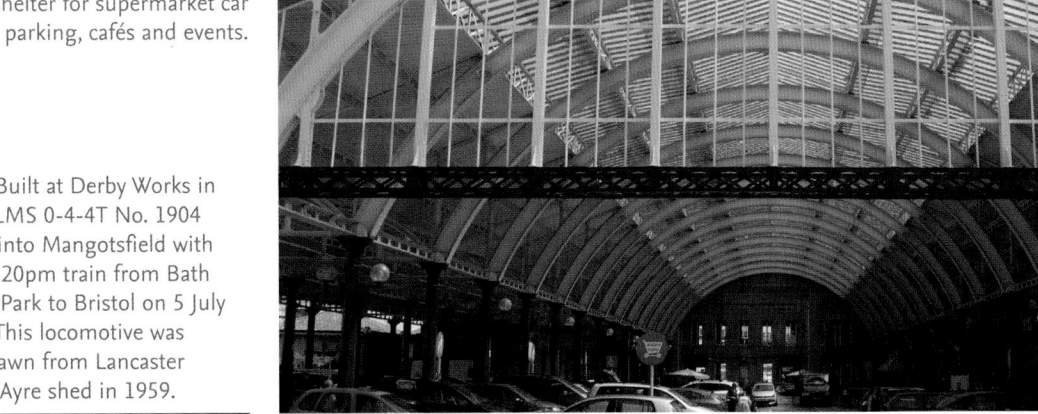

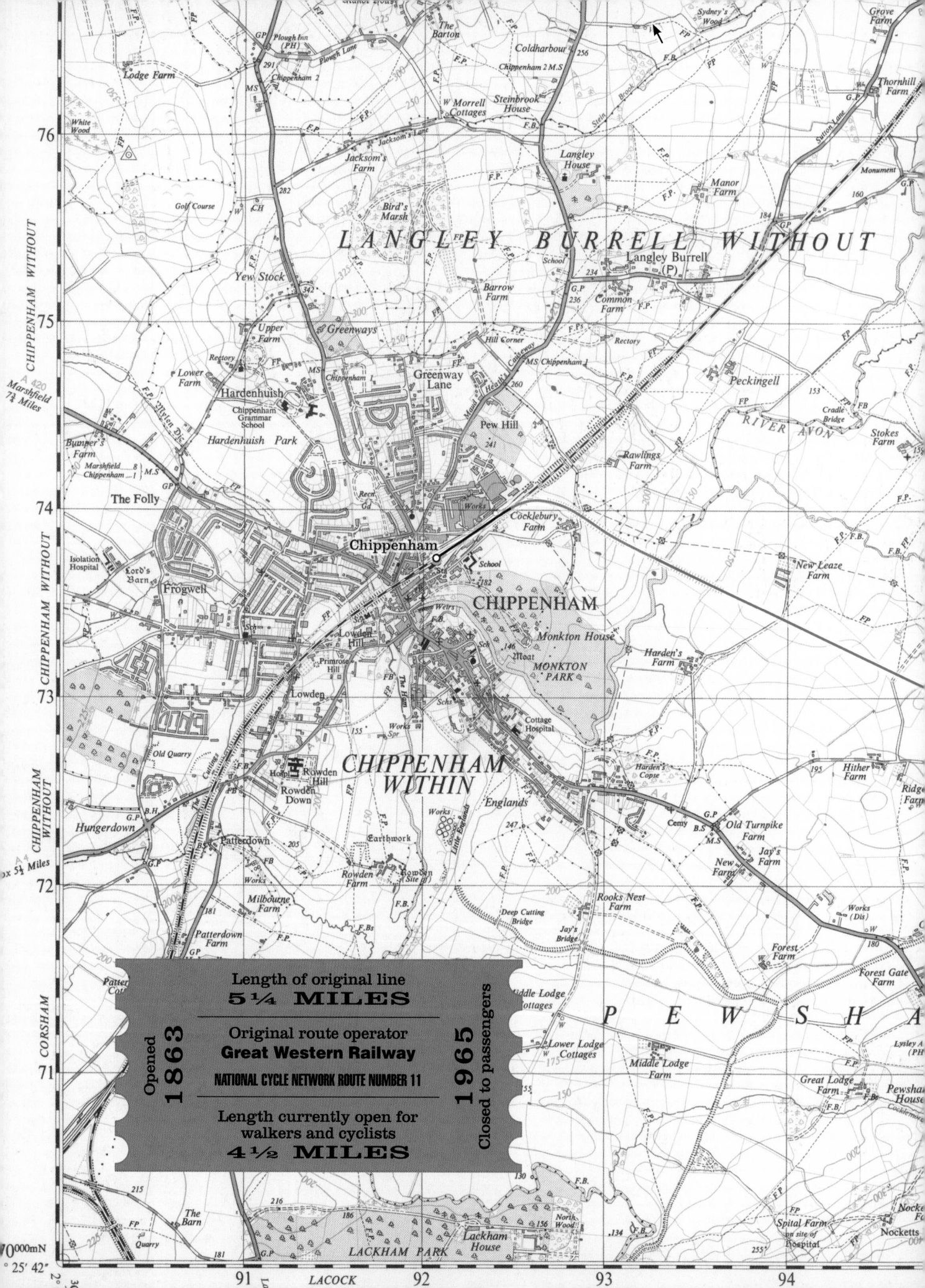

Length of original line
5¼ MILES

Original route operator
Great Western Railway

NATIONAL CYCLE NETWORK ROUTE NUMBER 11

Length currently open for walkers and cyclists
4½ MILES

Opened **1863**

1965 Closed to passengers

CHIPPENHAM
TO
CALNE

CHIPPENHAM TO CALNE RAILWAY PATH

The 5¼-mile branch line from Chippenham to Calne was primarily built to serve the rapidly expanding pork processing family business of Harris's – by the early twentieth century it had become a hugely successful business and was by far the largest employer in the town, with cured bacon, sausages and pork pies sent out by the trainload from the company's two enormous factories. The Second World War brought additional traffic to serve two nearby RAF bases but by the 1950s increased competition from road transport saw the line in terminal decline until closure in 1965. Today, the Harris factories in Calne have long since closed and been demolished, while most of the line has been reopened as a footpath and cycleway.

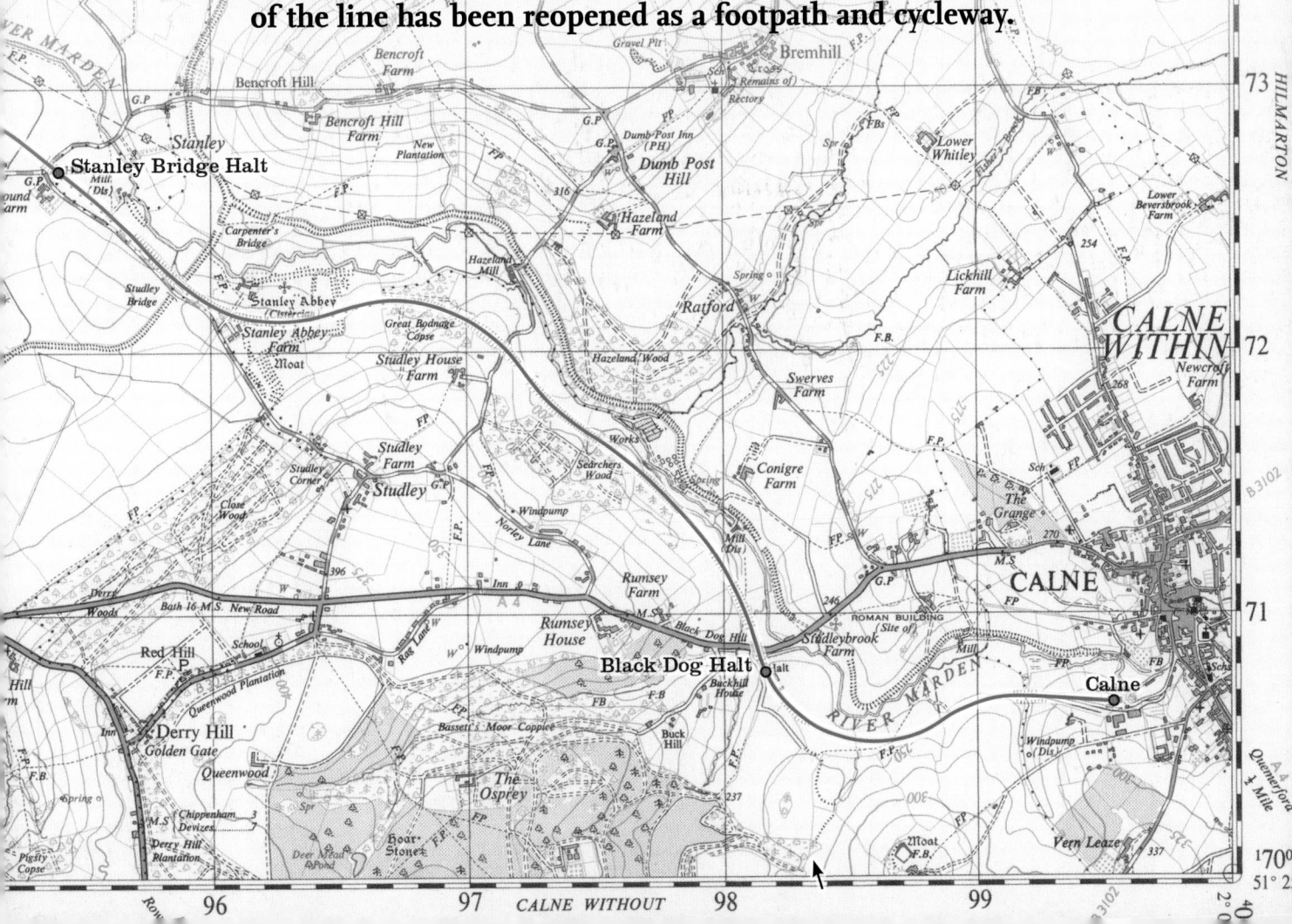

Sitting astride the old London-Bristol stage-coach route south of Chippenham, the town of Calne's one claim to fame was the Harris family's pork processing business that from early beginnings in 1770 had, by the early twentieth century, become an enormously successful business employing around 20 per cent of the town's population. By the mid-nineteenth century the town's only transport link, the Calne branch of the Wilts & Berks Canal, was struggling to keep up with the demand for Harris' products – what was needed was a railway. To this end the Calne Railway Company was authorized to build a 5¼-mile branch line from Chippenham, on the Great Western Railway's (GWR) Paddington-to-Bristol main line, to the town in 1860.

With no major physical obstacles to overcome, construction of the single-track broad-gauge line was fairly straightforward and it opened to great rejoicings in Calne on 3 November 1863. Although the line was worked from the outset by the GWR and converted to standard gauge in 1873, the Calne Railway Company remained independent until it was taken over by the GWR in 1892.

Apart from Lord Lansdowne's private station at Black Dog Siding there were no intermediate stations until Stanley Bridge Halt was opened in 1905. Meanwhile Harris' pork business in Calne was going from strength to strength with enormous quantities of its products – cured bacon, pork pies and sausages – being shipped

out by train each day. To cope with the demand the GWR enlarged the facilities at Calne in 1895. A major expansion of the Harris business followed at the end of the First World War when the company built its own power station, which supplied electricity not only for its factories but also for the town of Calne until 1948. At the same time Harris built two enormous factories and a cattle market next to the station – from its sidings the company's customized refrigerated goods vans started their journey to destinations around Britain.

The opening of two nearby RAF bases brought even more business to the branch line during the Second World War – fuel, coal and servicemen all adding to the daily traffic. The private station at Black Dog Halt first appeared in the public timetable in 1952 but the decade saw a major decline in traffic on the branch with the closure of the RAF bases and the Harris company's increasing use of road transport. Despite the introduction of diesel multiple units on the branch in 1958, traffic continued to fall until it was inevitably listed for closure in the 1963 'Beeching Report'. Goods services were withdrawn in 1964 and passenger services on 18 September 1965, by which time the branch had the dubious honour of making the biggest loss per mile of track of any railway in Britain. The track was lifted in 1967. As for Harris' business, it was taken over by FMC in 1962 but with ever-rising costs brought on by increasing red tape, the factory at Calne was closed in 1981 with the loss of 2,000 jobs.

A 3-car diesel multiple unit awaits departure from a deserted Calne station with a train for Chippenham on 24 June 1965. By this date goods facilities had already been withdrawn and the line was less than three months from complete closure.

Seen here in 1938, Black Dog Halt and its goods siding were originally provided for the personal use of Lord Lansdowne of nearby Bowood House. His Lordship would transport his race horses to meetings in railway horse boxes from this station which only appeared in the public timetable from 1952.

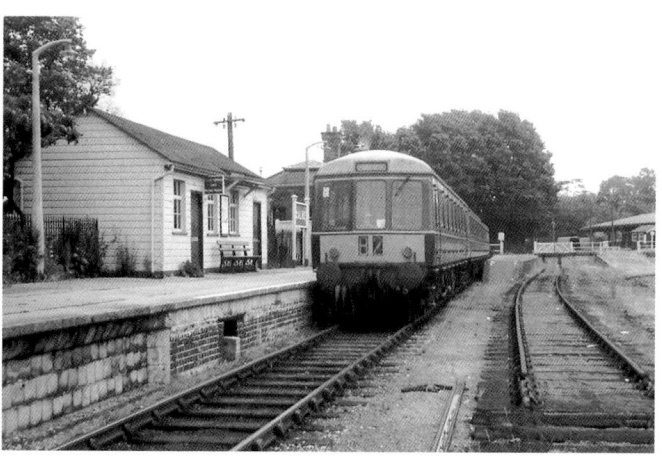

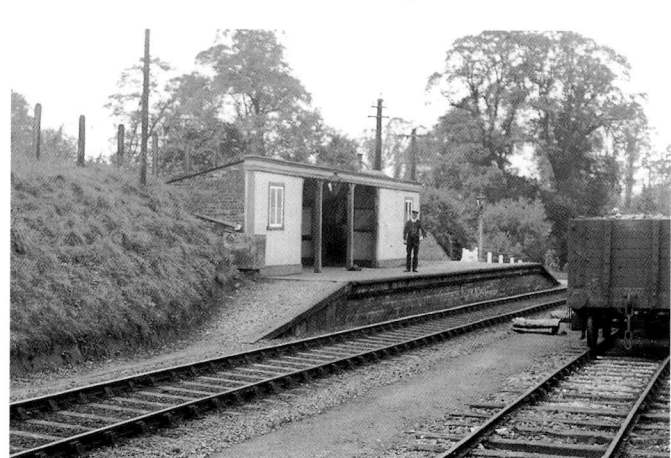

oday, almost the entire route of the Calne branch line is a footpath and cycleway known as the Chippenham to Calne Railway Path. Forming part of National Cycle Network Route 11, the 7-mile traffic-free route starts at Station Road in Calne near the site of the town's long-demolished railway station. A mile west of Calne and immediately to the north of the restored platform and station sign at Black Dog Halt – which was built as Lord Lansdowne's private station in 1863 – the path crosses the A4 on a purpose-built bridge. To the west lie the landscaped grounds of Bowood Estate, once the seat of the Lansdowne family although the majority of Bowood House was sadly demolished in 1955. After crossing the A4 the path heads westwards along the pretty Marden Valley passing under several small road overbridges and the site of Stanley Bridge Halt before ending its journey by crossing the River Avon to the east of Chippenham. Here the path leaves the former railway route to take a detour along the north bank of the river to the town.

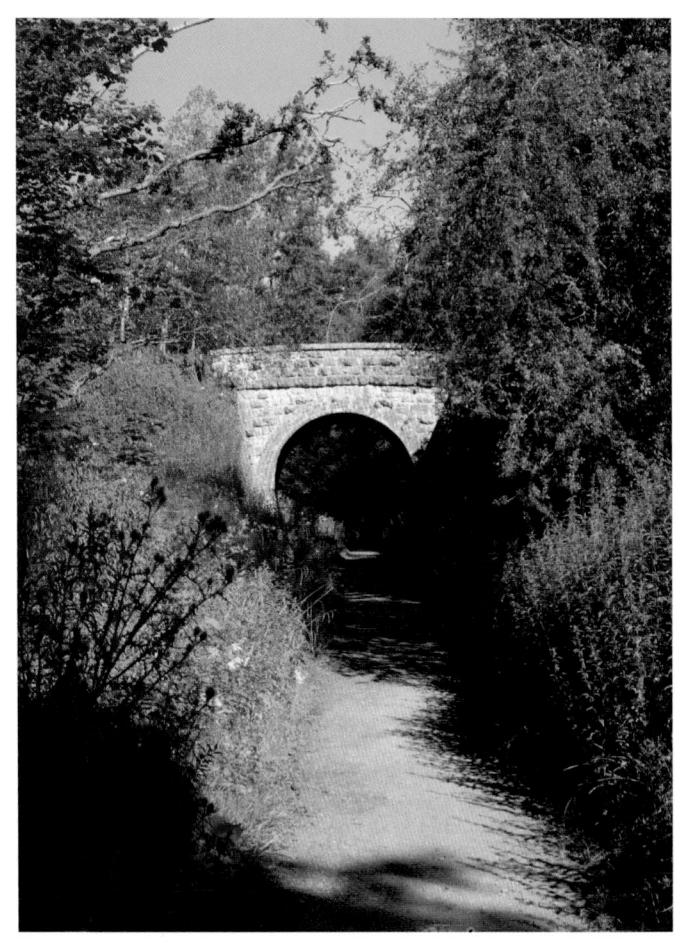

Since closure in 1965 the Chippenham to Calne branch line, seen here north of the village of Studley, has been reopened as a peaceful traffic-free route for walkers and cyclists along the valley of the River Marden.

Opened in 1905 with the introduction of a new steam railmotor service, Stanley Bridge Halt was a typical GWR wayside station complete with pagoda-roofed waiting shelter and gas lights. The halt has long since been demolished but a nearby roadbridge has survived.

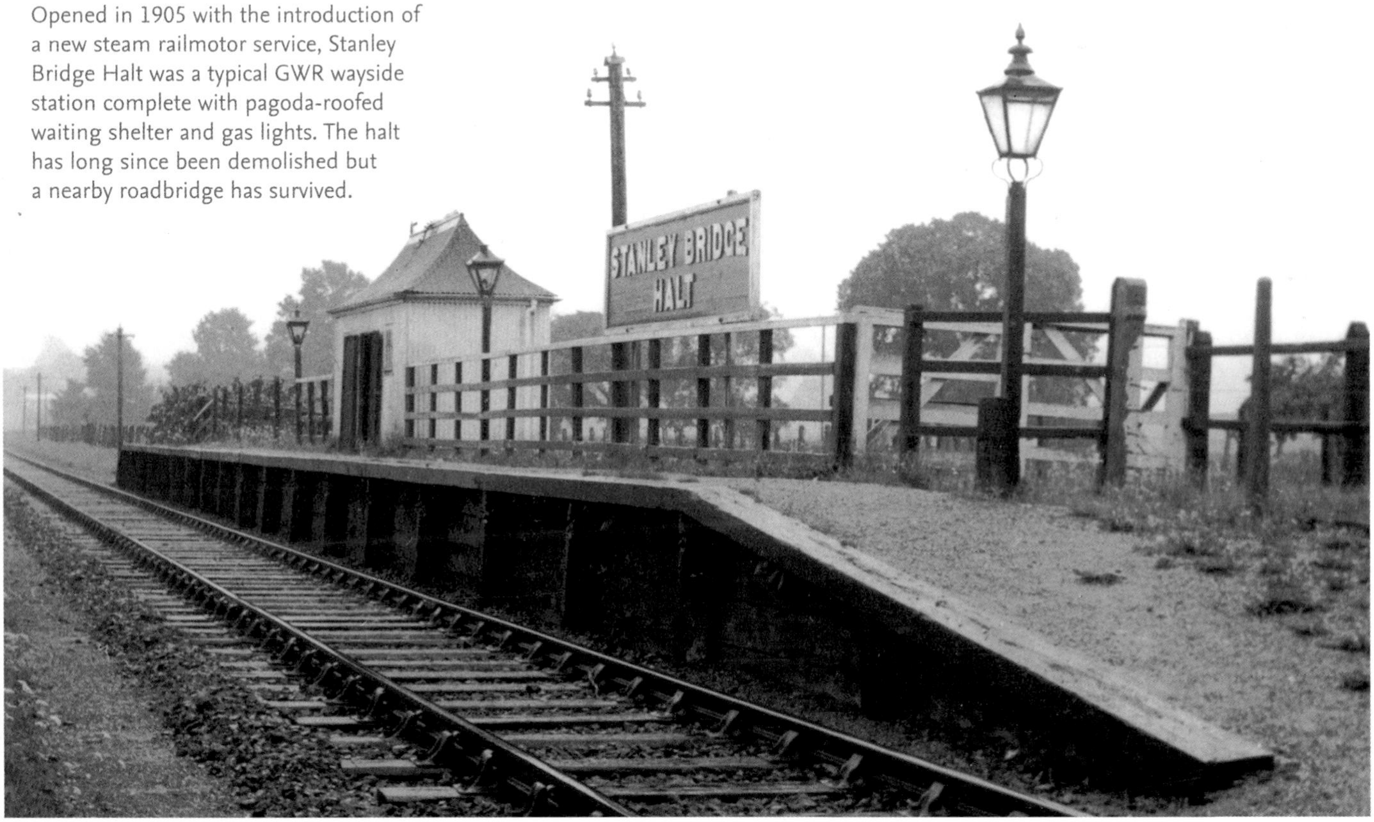

SOUTHERN ENGLAND

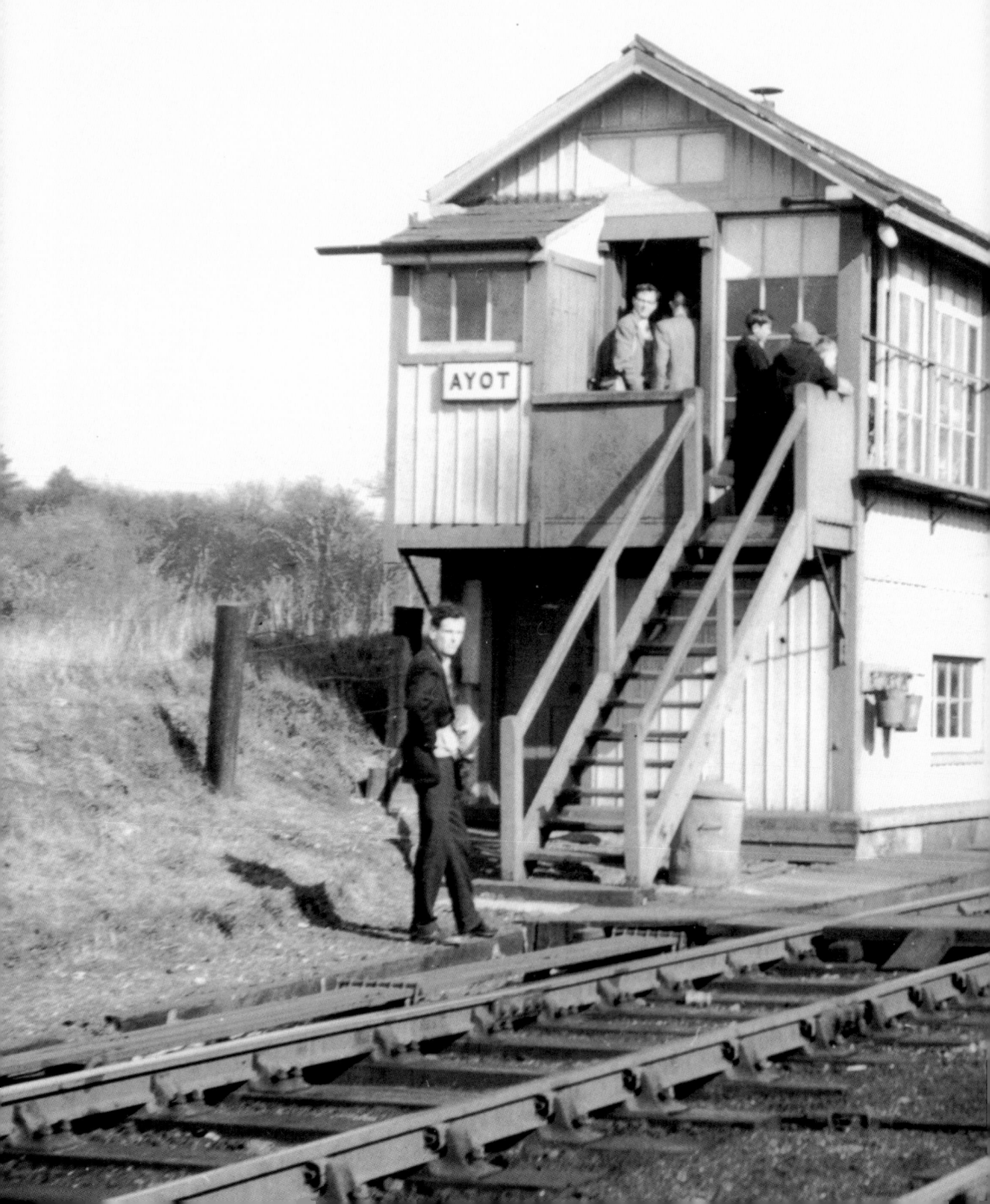

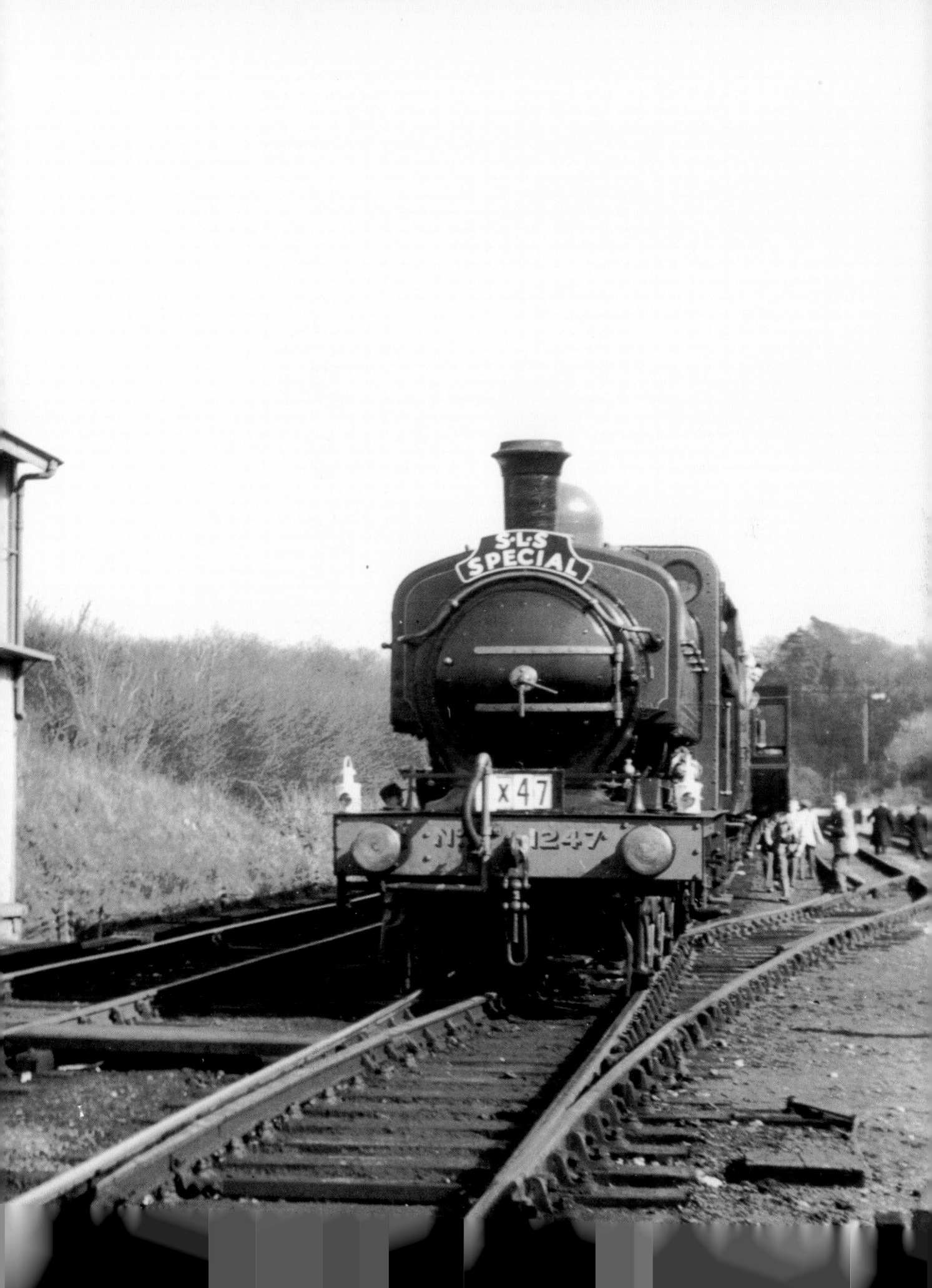

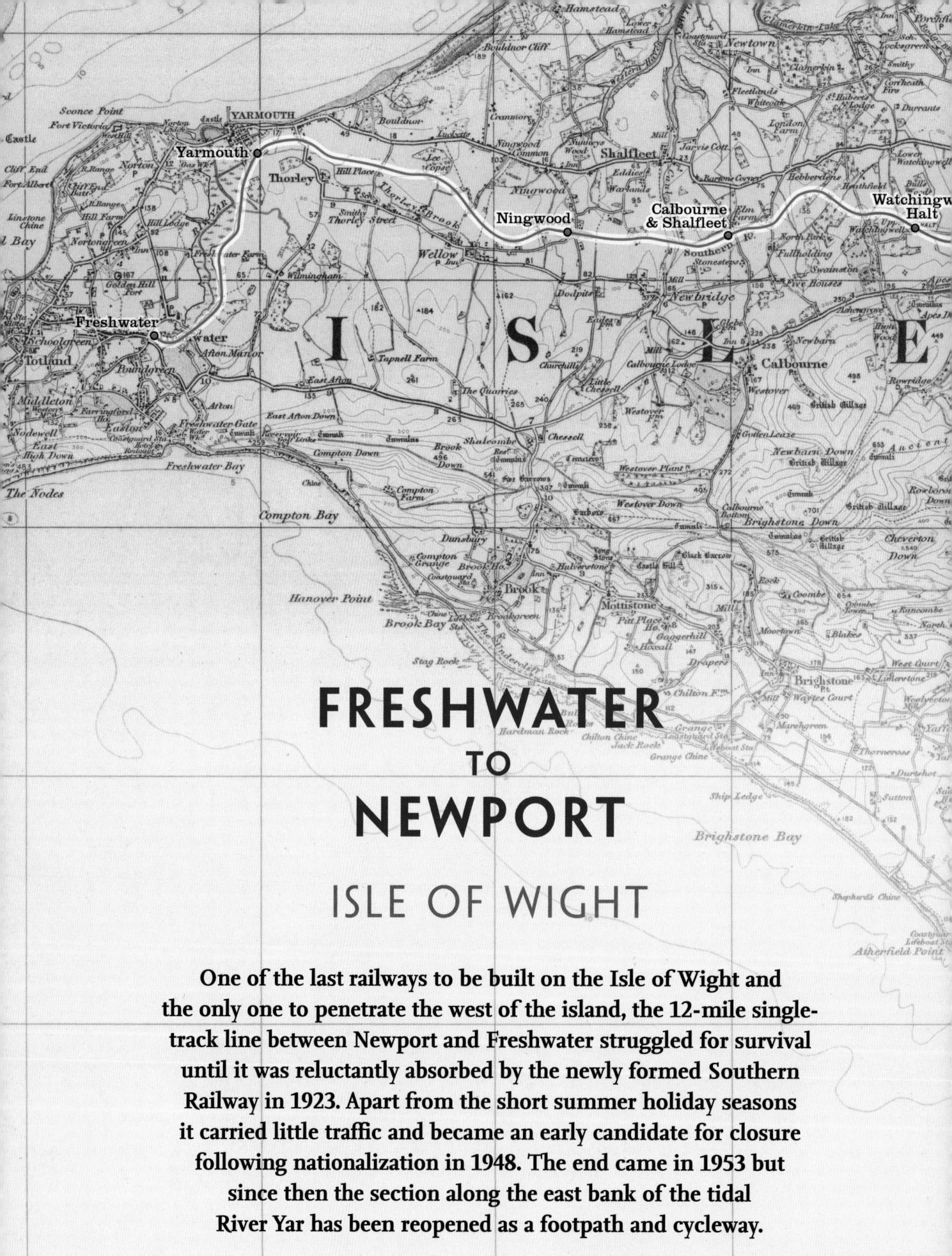

FRESHWATER
TO
NEWPORT
ISLE OF WIGHT

One of the last railways to be built on the Isle of Wight and
the only one to penetrate the west of the island, the 12-mile single-
track line between Newport and Freshwater struggled for survival
until it was reluctantly absorbed by the newly formed Southern
Railway in 1923. Apart from the short summer holiday seasons
it carried little traffic and became an early candidate for closure
following nationalization in 1948. The end came in 1953 but
since then the section along the east bank of the tidal
River Yar has been reopened as a footpath and cycleway.

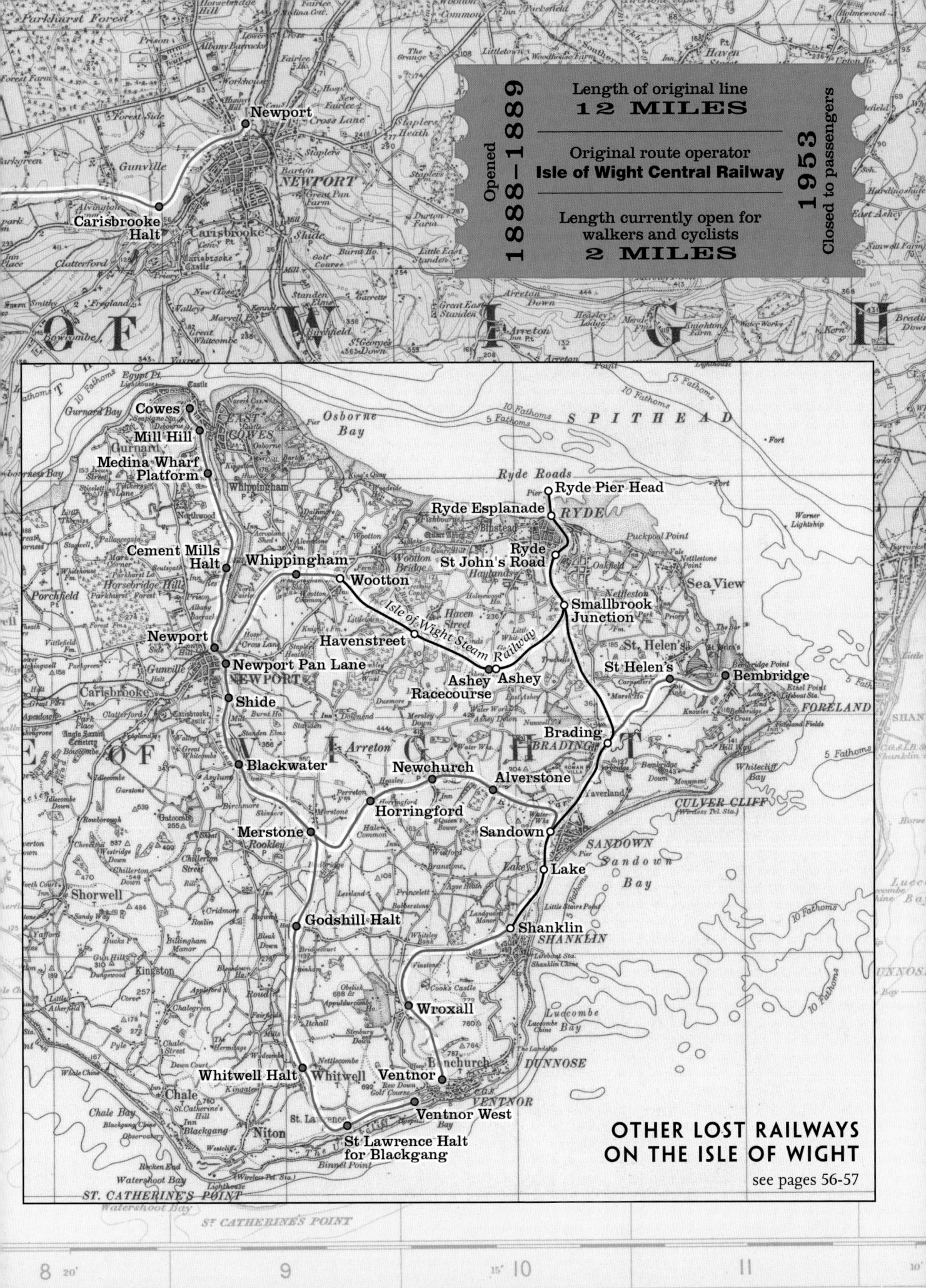

Newport

Carisbrooke
Halt

Opened 1888–1889

Length of original line
12 MILES

Original route operator
Isle of Wight Central Railway

Length currently open for
walkers and cyclists
2 MILES

1953 Closed to passengers

Cowes

Mill Hill

Medina Wharf
Platform

Cement Mills
Halt

Whippingham

Ryde Pier Head

Ryde Esplanade

Ryde
St John's Road

Smallbrook
Junction

Wootton

Havenstreet

Isle of Wight Steam Railway

Newport

Newport Pan Lane

Shide

Ashey
Racecourse

Ashey

St Helen's

Bembridge

Blackwater

Newchurch

Brading

Alverstone

Horringford

Merstone

Sandown

Lake

Godshill Halt

Shanklin

Wroxall

Whitwell Halt

Whitwell

Ventnor

Ventnor West

St Lawrence Halt
for Blackgang

OTHER LOST RAILWAYS
ON THE ISLE OF WIGHT

see pages 56-57

The penultimate railway to be opened on the Isle of Wight, the Freshwater, Yarmouth & Newport Railway (FY&NR) was first authorized to build a 12-mile single-track line between these three locations in 1873. Nothing happened and the company was dissolved in 1877. The second attempt came in 1880 when the company was reincorporated with the blessing of the London & South Western Railway, which was planning on improving its steamer service between Lymington, on the mainland, and Yarmouth.

Initially worked by the Isle of Wight Central Railway (IoWCR), the line opened to goods in 1888 and to passengers the following year. Intermediate stations were initially provided at Carisbrooke, Calbourne & Shalfleet, Ningwood and Yarmouth, while a private station at Watchingwell was opened for the use of Sir John Simeon in 1889. The arrangements at Newport were far from satisfactory as trains to and from Freshwater had to reverse out of or into the IoWCR's station in the town.

The FY&NR was also far from satisfied with the working arrangements provided by the IoWCR and in 1913 took over the running of its own line. Locomotives and rolling stock were purchased but the company was initially barred from using the IoWCR's station at

Newport and so built its own rather minimal terminus. The financial strain of becoming master of its own destiny proved too much for the company however, and it soon went bankrupt – Sam Fay of the Great Central Railway was appointed as Receiver. Despite these setbacks the railway continued to operate independently until it was absorbed, reluctantly, by the newly formed Southern Railway on 1 August 1923.

The new owners of the line breathed fresh life into the railway and in the summer of 1933 introduced the only named train to operate on the Isle of Wight – 'The Tourist' was a through train running between Ventnor and Freshwater via Newport, with an engine change at the latter station. The train was particularly popular with holidaymakers but was withdrawn before the Second World War. Apart from this both passenger and goods traffic on the line was always light.

The early post-war austerity years brought the nationalization of Britain's railways. Eager to dispose of loss-making rural routes the new British Railways' management soon drew up a long list of doomed branch lines. Included were several on the Isle of Wight including the Newport to Freshwater line, which closed completely on 21 September 1953.

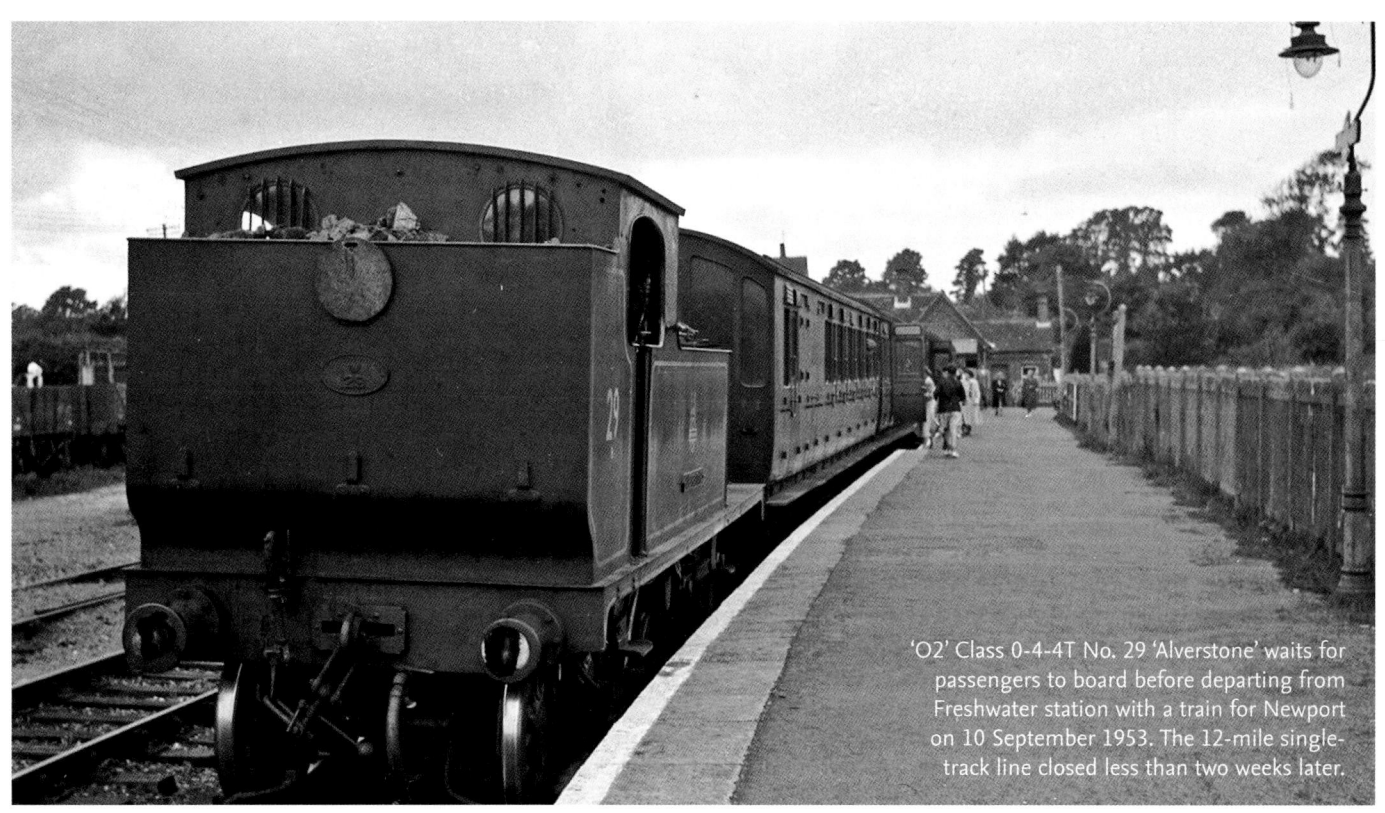

'O2' Class 0-4-4T No. 29 'Alverstone' waits for passengers to board before departing from Freshwater station with a train for Newport on 10 September 1953. The 12-mile single-track line closed less than two weeks later.

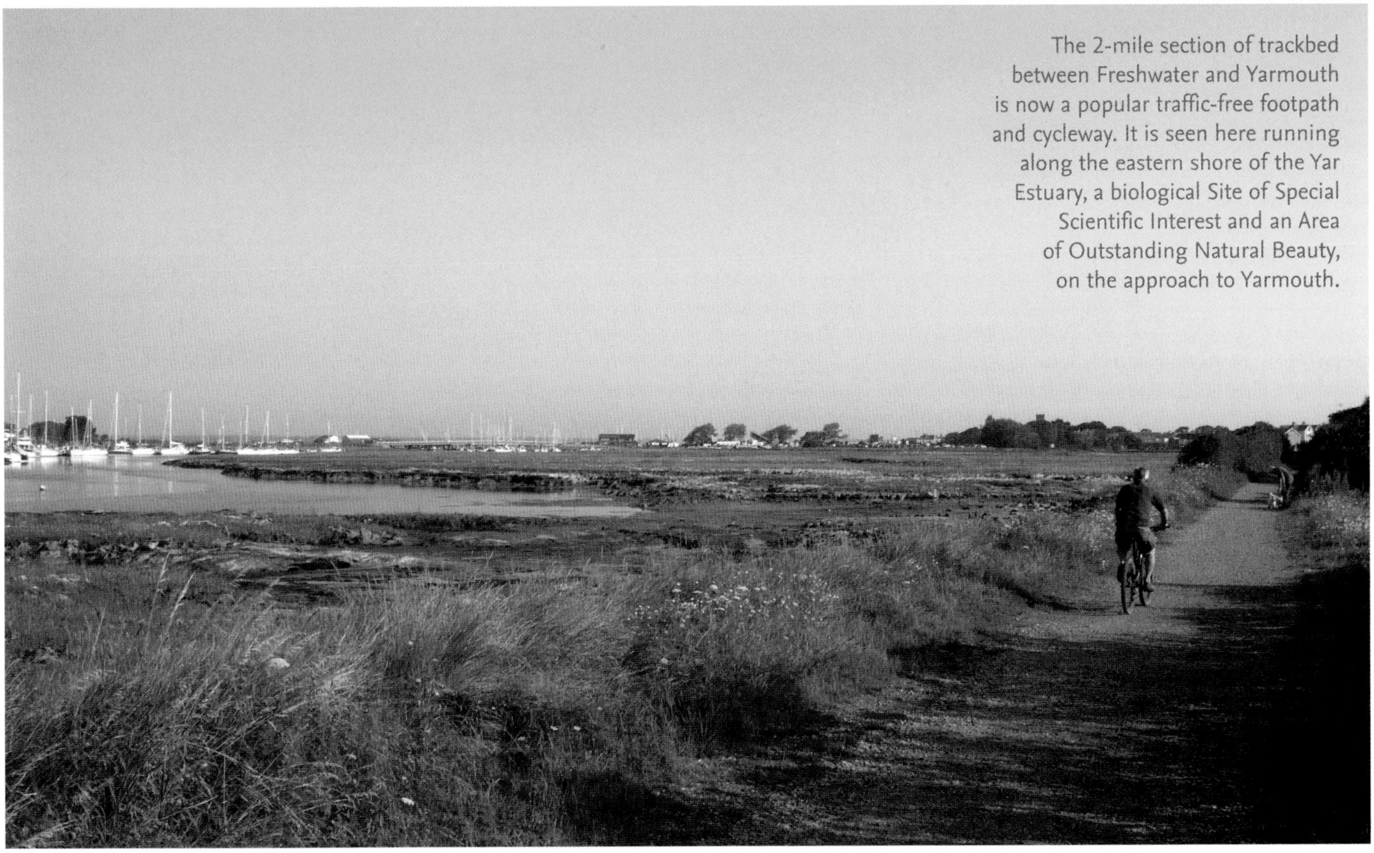

The 2-mile section of trackbed between Freshwater and Yarmouth is now a popular traffic-free footpath and cycleway. It is seen here running along the eastern shore of the Yar Estuary, a biological Site of Special Scientific Interest and an Area of Outstanding Natural Beauty, on the approach to Yarmouth.

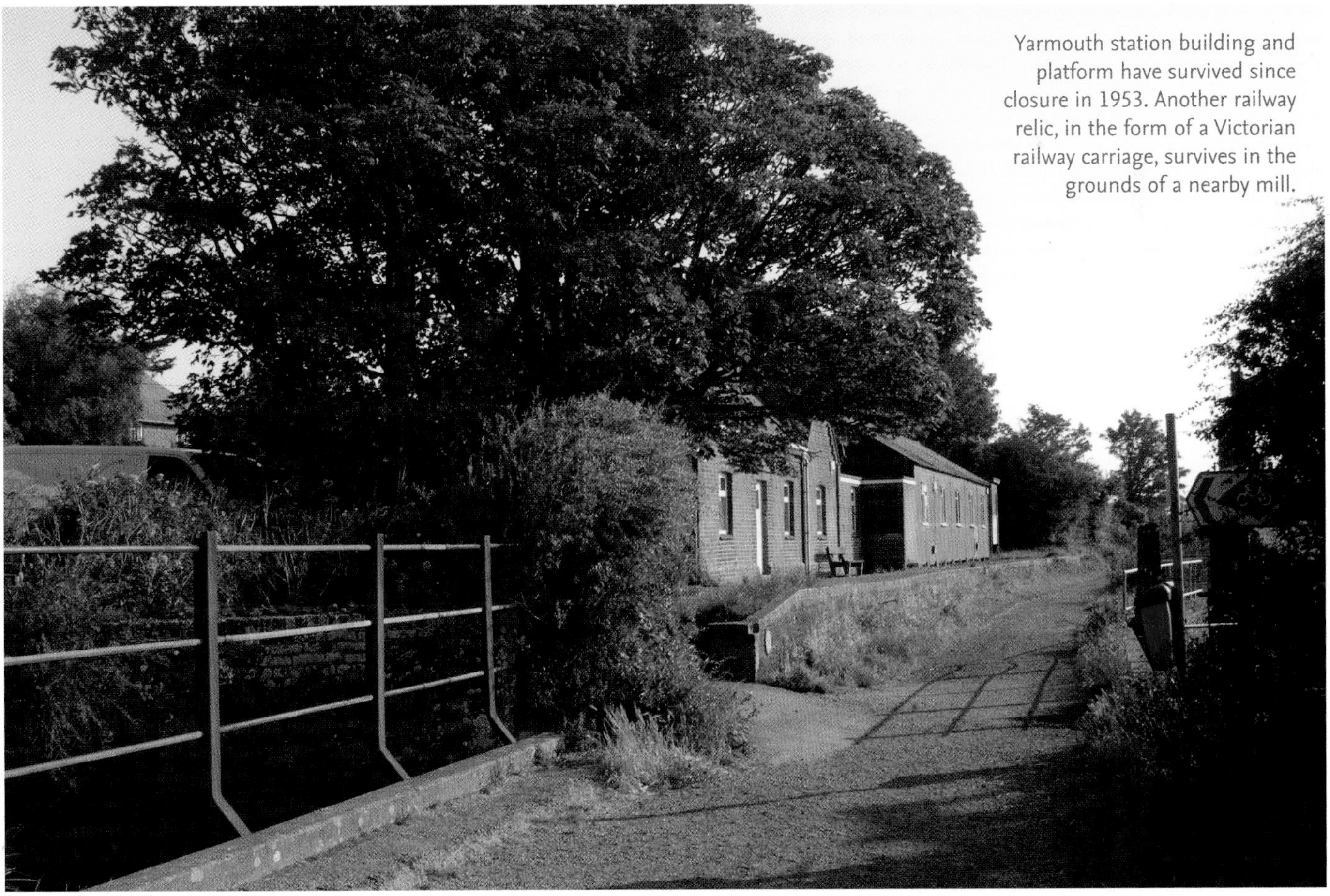

Yarmouth station building and platform have survived since closure in 1953. Another railway relic, in the form of a Victorian railway carriage, survives in the grounds of a nearby mill.

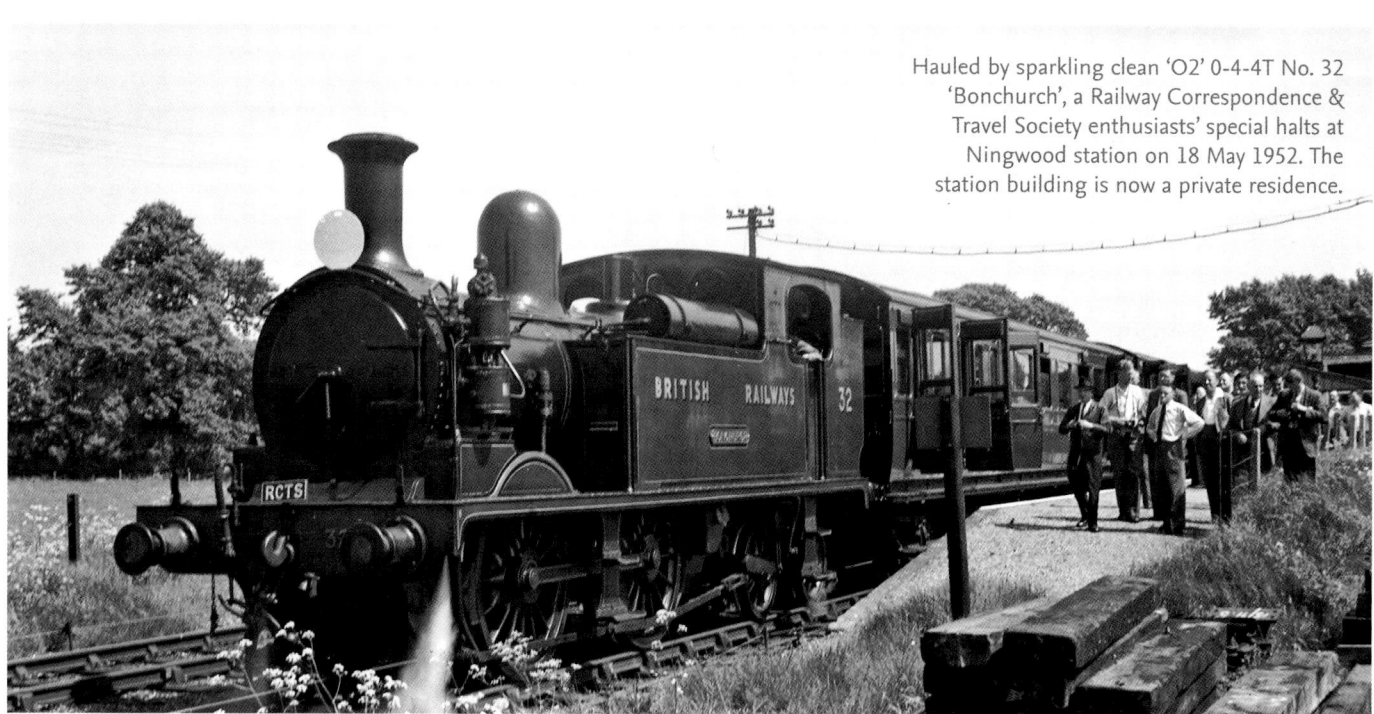

Hauled by sparkling clean 'O2' 0-4-4T No. 32 'Bonchurch', a Railway Correspondence & Travel Society enthusiasts' special halts at Ningwood station on 18 May 1952. The station building is now a private residence.

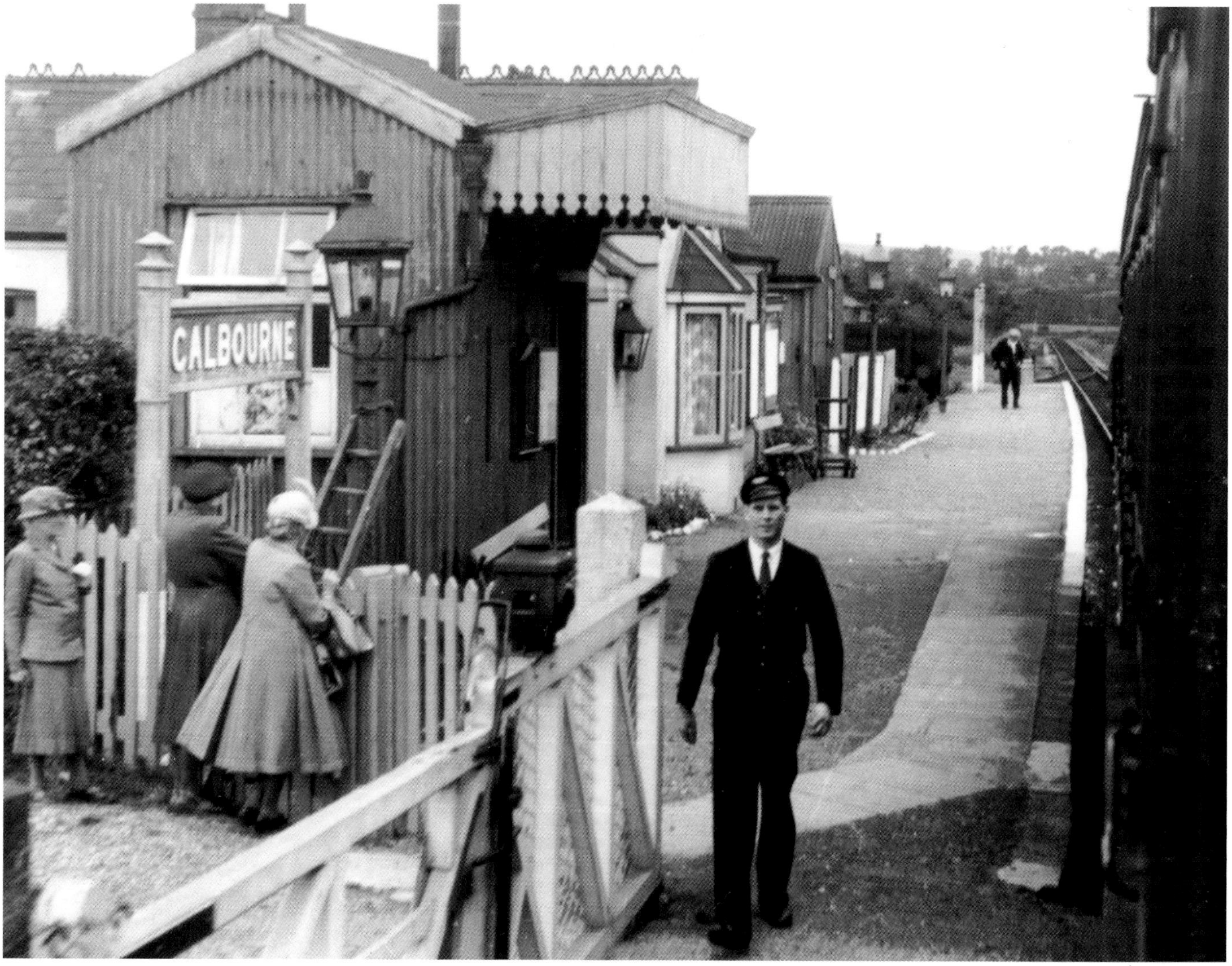

Since closure a 2-mile section of the railway route between Freshwater and Yarmouth has been reopened as a footpath and cycleway. At Freshwater the station site is now occupied by a supermarket and garden centre while the appropriately named End of the Line café, with its mock station canopy, is a convenient place to take refreshments before heading off up the railway path.

From Freshwater the railway path heads north, passing an old crossing keeper's cottage that is now a private residence. From here it closely follows the unspoilt eastern banks of the tidal Western Yar river through stretches of woodland for 1½ miles to Yarmouth. It is located in an Area of Outstanding Natural Beauty and the estuary is also a biological Site of Special Scientific Interest because of its diverse habitats – the saltmarsh, mud flats and sand dunes are home to a rich abundance of wildlife including over-wintering wildfowl and waders.

At Yarmouth the station building and platform have both survived (at the time of writing they were for sale), while in the grounds of a nearby mill the body of a Victorian railway coach has been converted into living accommodation. Refreshments can be taken in the nearby town where there is also a large car park. The railway path continues eastwards from Yarmouth station for half a mile through Rofford Marsh before ending on the B3401 just outside of the town.

Further east, much of the route of the railway has disappeared although a few road overbridges still survive and a 1-mile section at Watchingwell is now a farm track. The station buildings and platforms at Ningwood and Watchingwell are now private residences while the platform at Calbourne & Shalfleet finds itself in the garden of a bungalow. There is no sign of the two stations at Newport – the site of the FY&NR's minimal station is covered by a school playing field while the IoWCR's station has been demolished to make way for a bypass.

LEFT: Watched by the level crossing keeper and three smartly dressed ladies, a Freshwater to Newport train departs from the delightful Calbourne & Shalfleet station on 3 September 1952. The platform survives today in the garden of a modern bungalow.

Plenty of fascinating railway artefacts graced the small platform at Watchingwell station in 1952. The station was originally opened for the use of Sir John Simeon in 1889 and is now a private residence.

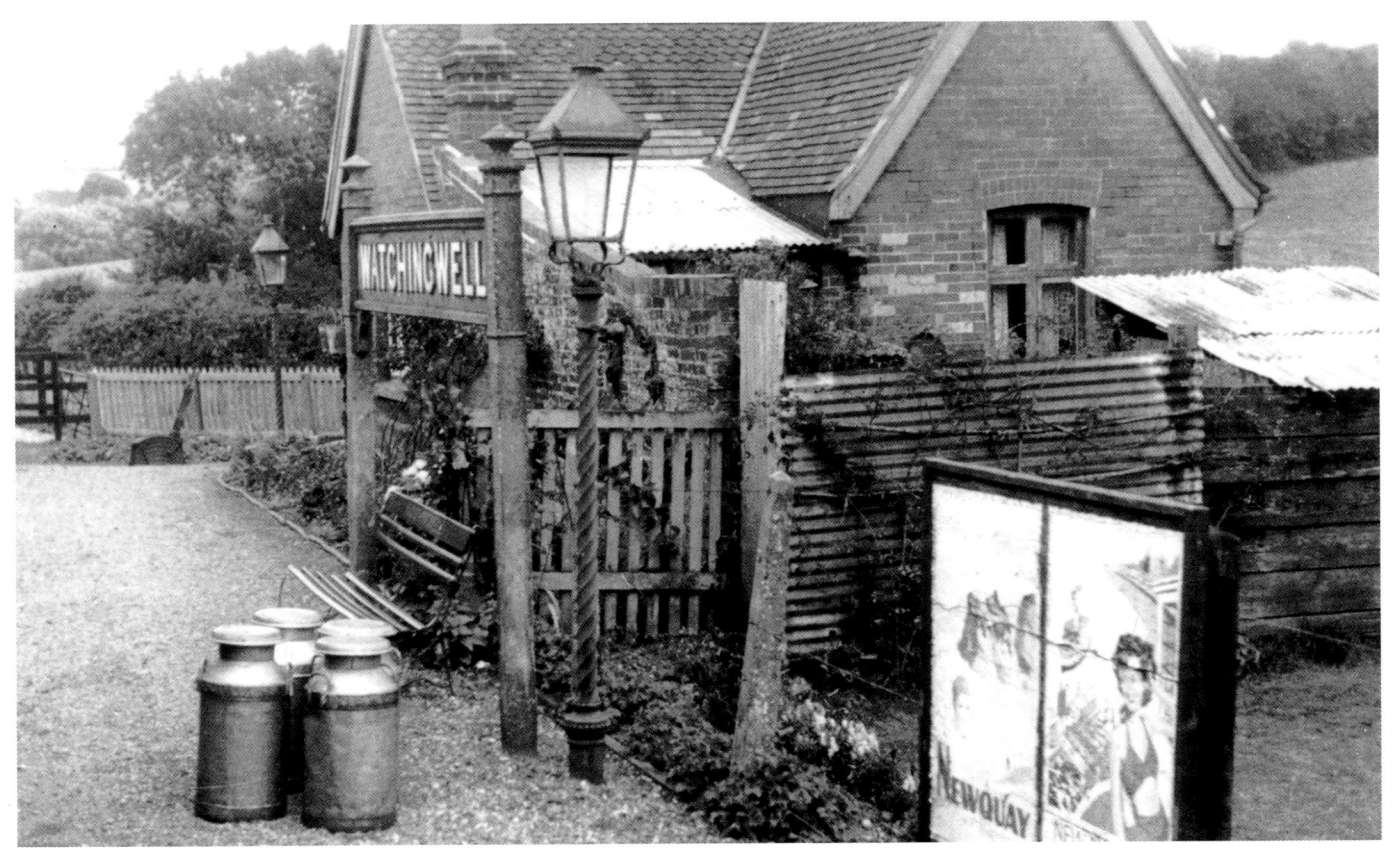

OTHER LOST RAILWAYS ON THE ISLE OF WIGHT

In its heyday the railway system on the Isle of Wight extended to 45¼ route miles. All that remains today of this once-extensive system is the 8½-mile section from Ryde Pier Head to Shanklin, which was converted to third-rail electrification in 1967, and the Isle of Wight Steam Railway that now operates a heritage railway for five miles between Wootton and Smallbrook Junction.

NEWPORT TO COWES

The first railway on the island was the 4¼-mile Cowes & Newport Railway which opened between those two towns in 1862. It remained isolated until the Ryde & Newport Railway (R&NR) opened in 1875. In 1887 it amalgamated with the R&NR and the Isle of Wight (Newport Junction) Railway to form the Isle of Wight Central Railway, eventually becoming part of the newly formed Southern Railway in 1923. British Railways closed the Ryde to Cowes line on 21 February 1966.

Since closure almost the entire route of this line along the west bank of the River Medina has been reopened as a footpath and cycleway.

NEWPORT TO SMALLBROOK JUNCTION

The 7¼-mile Ryde & Newport Railway opened between Newport and Smallbrook Junction (1½ miles south of Ryde St John's Road) in 1875 and was worked jointly with the Cowes & Newport Railway until amalgamating with the Isle of Wight (Newport Junction) Railway to form the Isle of Wight Central Railway in 1887. It became part of the newly formed Southern Railway in 1923 and was closed by British Railways on 21 February 1966.

Since closure five miles of the line between Wootton and Smallbrook Junction have been reopened as a heritage railway by the Isle of Wight Steam Railway, with its headquarters at Havenstreet station.

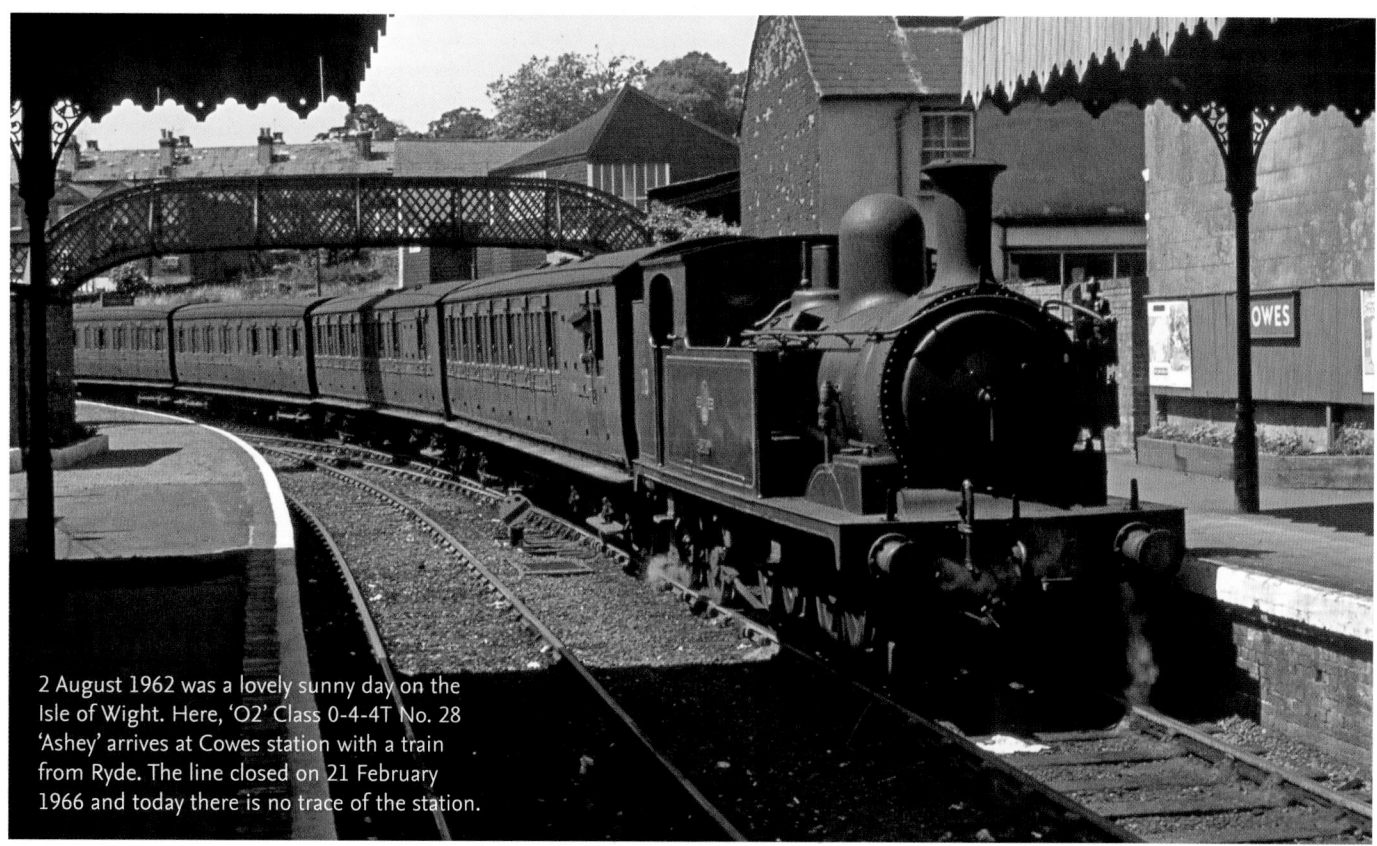

2 August 1962 was a lovely sunny day on the Isle of Wight. Here, 'O2' Class 0-4-4T No. 28 'Ashey' arrives at Cowes station with a train from Ryde. The line closed on 21 February 1966 and today there is no trace of the station.

NEWPORT TO SANDOWN

The 9½-mile Isle of Wight (Newport Junction) Railway opened between Newport and Sandown via Merstone in 1875. It was connected to the Ryde & Newport Railway (R&NR) at Newport via a viaduct in 1879. This bankrupted the company, which was then run by an Official Receiver until amalgamation with the R&NR and Cowes & Newport Railway to form the Isle of Wight Central Railway in 1887. The line became part of the Southern Railway in 1923 and was closed by British Railways on 6 February 1956.

Since closure almost the entire route of the Newport to Sandown line has been reopened as a footpath and cycleway known as the Perowne Way. The island platform at Merstone Junction remains, complete with a piece of art in the shape of a concrete suitcase.

BRADING TO BEMBRIDGE

The Brading Harbour Improvement & Railway opened the 2¾-mile branch line from Brading to Bembridge in 1882. It was absorbed by the Isle of Wight Railway in 1898 and became part of the Southern Railway in 1923. British Railways closed the branch on 21 September 1953.

Since closure Bembridge station has been demolished but the intermediate station at St Lawrence has become a private residence. Brading station is still served by trains on the Ryde to Shanklin electrified line while the station building, with its restored signalbox, is now a visitor centre and café.

SHANKLIN TO VENTNOR

The second railway to be built on the island was the Isle of Wight Eastern Section Railway, which opened between Ryde and Shanklin in 1864 and extended through the three-quarter-mile Boniface Tunnel to Ventnor in 1866. Meanwhile it had changed its name to the Isle of Wight Railway in 1863. The company took over the Brading Harbour Improvement & Railway in 1898. The line between Shanklin and Ventnor became part of the newly formed Southern Railway in 1923 and was later closed by British Railways on 18 April 1966. The section from Ryde to Shanklin continued with steam haulage until the end of that year and was then electrified using third rail, reopening in March 1967.

Since closure 2½ miles of the railway route between Shanklin and Wroxall have been reopened as a footpath and cycleway.

MERSTONE TO VENTNOR WEST

The last railway to be built on the island was the 6¾-mile Newport, Godshill & St Lawrence Railway, which opened from Merstone to Ventnor West in 1900. It was worked by the Isle of Wight Central Railway, with which it was amalgamated in 1913. The line formed part of the new Southern Railway in 1923 and became the island's first casualty upon its closure by British Railways on 15 September 1952. The station buildings at Godshill, Whitwell, St Lawrence and Ventnor West have all survived as private residences.

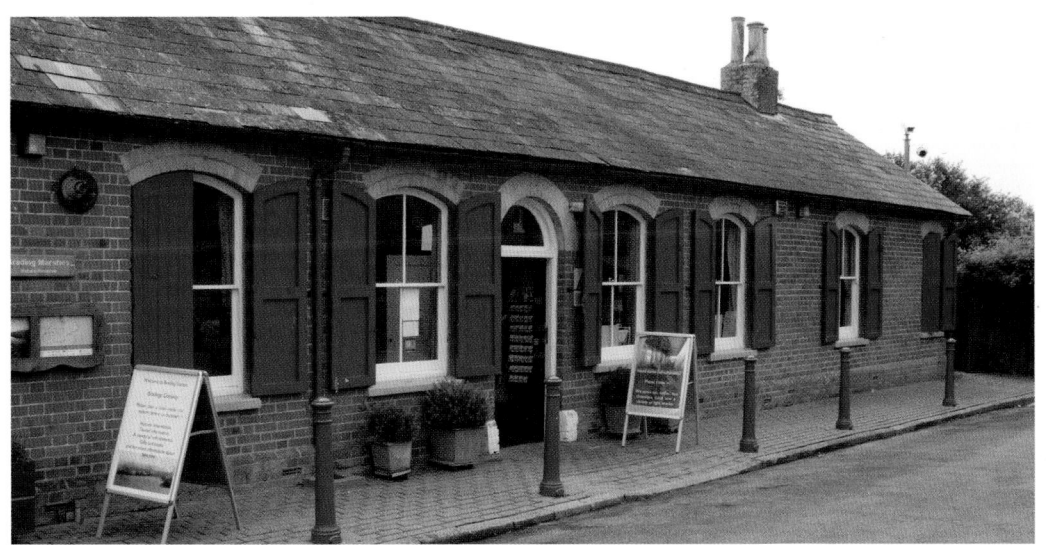

Brading station is still served by Island Line trains on the electrified Ryde Pier Head to Shanklin line. The station building is now a visitor centre and café while the restored signalbox on the island platform is also open to visitors on selected days. It is planned to restore the passing loop here in order to increase the frequency of trains.

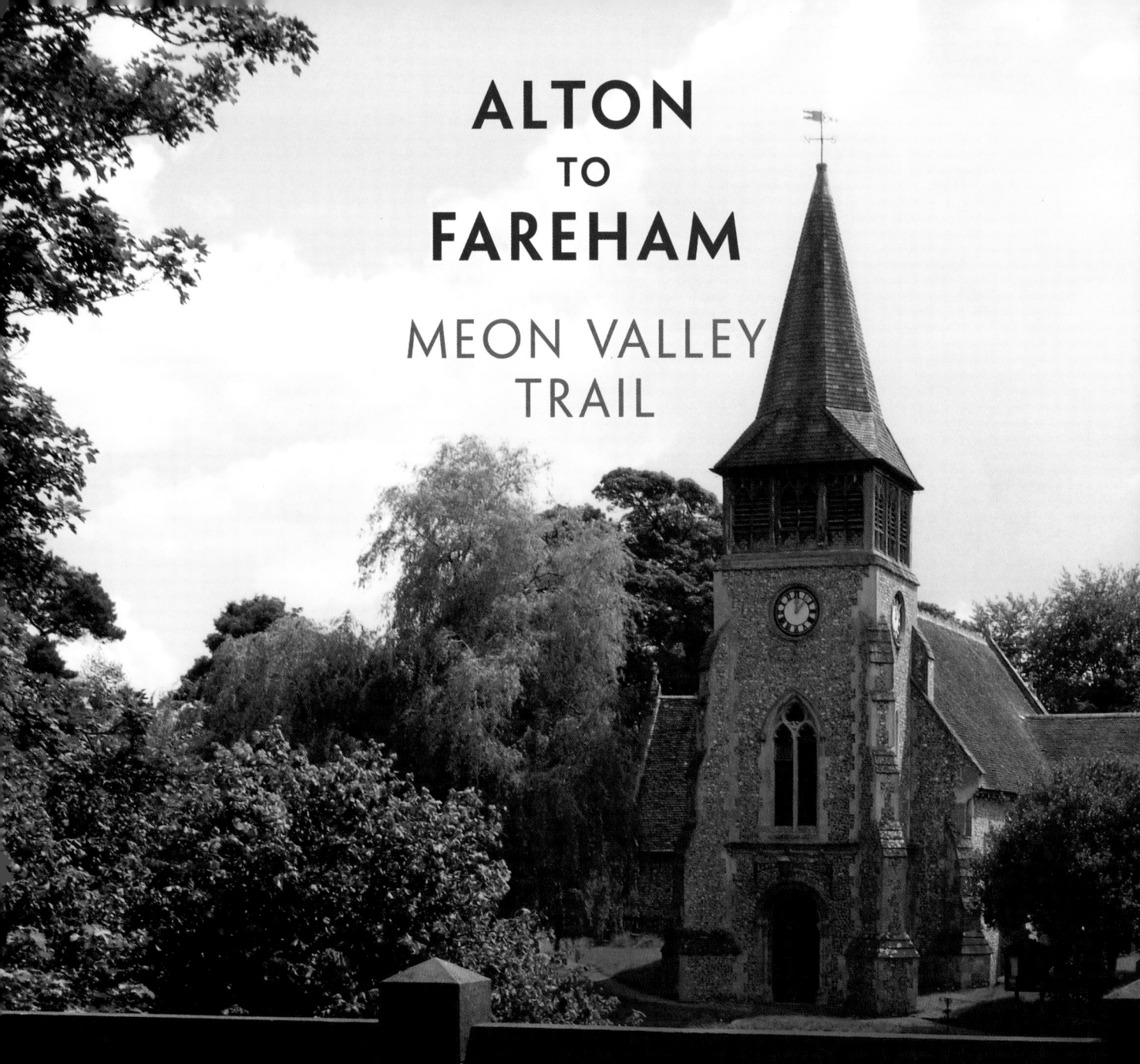

ALTON
TO
FAREHAM

MEON VALLEY
TRAIL

Originally planned as a double-track main line linking London
Waterloo with Gosport and Stokes Bay, the Meon Valley Railway failed
miserably to live up to its promoters' expectations and soon faded into
obscurity as a bucolic branch line serving only small villages along its
22¼-mile route. Its only brief claim to fame came in 1944 when
Winston Churchill and the Allied leaders met secretly at Droxford
station in the run-up to the D-Day landings. Closure to passengers
came in 1955 but sections of the line lived on until the 1960s for goods
traffic. A scheme to reopen part of it in the 1970s as a preserved railway
came to nothing but the southern section from West Meon to Knowle
Junction has since been reopened as a footpath and cycleway.

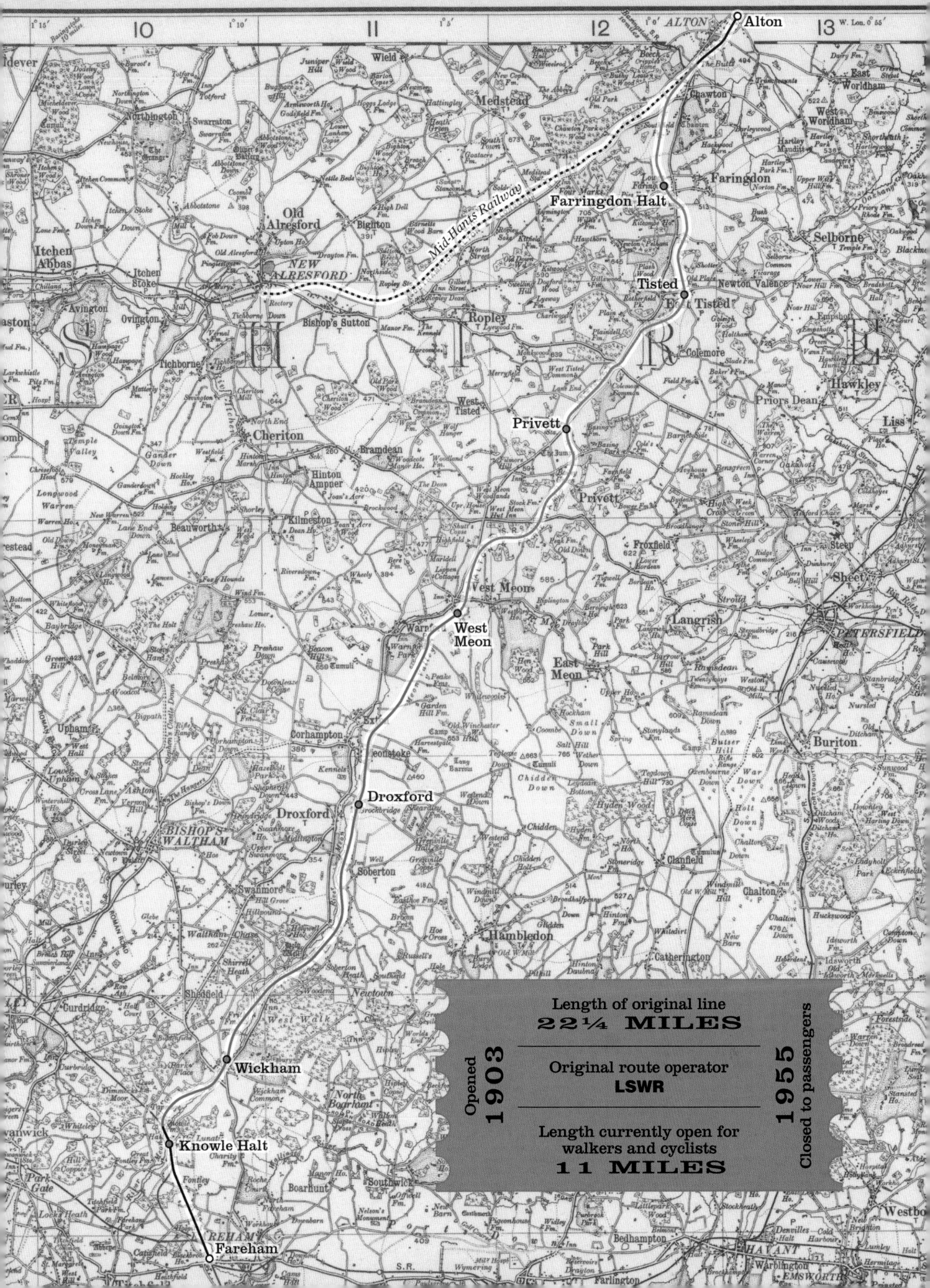

Length of original line
22¼ MILES

Original route operator
LSWR

Length currently open for
walkers and cyclists
11 MILES

Opened
1903

1955
Closed to passengers

Ex-LSWR 'T9' Class 4-4-0 No. 30732 runs round its train at Tisted station on 6 February 1955. This, the last train to run over the entire Meon Valley route before closure the next day, was double headed with sister engine No. 30301.

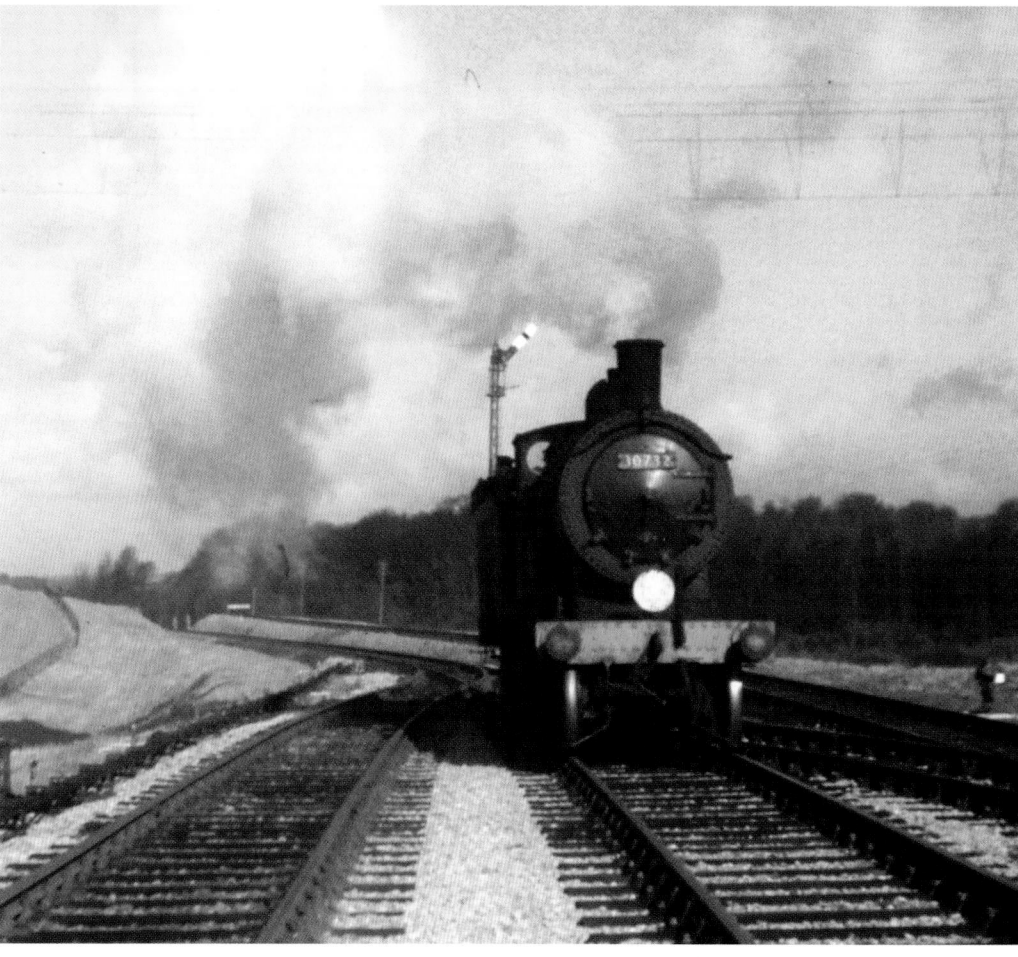

PREVIOUS SPREAD:
The railway along the Meon Valley once served a string of sleepy Hampshire villages. Today a cast-iron bridge provides walkers along the Meon Valley Trail with a grandstand view of Wickham's fine twelfth-century St Nicholas church.

Closely following the meandering course of the River Meon along much of its route, the 22¼-mile Meon Valley Railway was opened between Alton and Fareham by the London & South Western Railway as late as 1903 – becoming one of the last 'main lines' to be opened in Britain during the twentieth century. The railway's construction involved numerous embankments and cuttings, two tunnels and a viaduct to accommodate a double-track main line to carry express trains between London Waterloo, Gosport and Stokes Bay, where the LSWR operated a ferry service to the Isle of Wight. The stations along the route were built in a grand mock-Tudor style with 600-ft platforms capable of accommodating lengthy trains. Despite all this grandeur the Meon Valley Railway was opened as a single-track line with passing places and failed miserably to live up to its parent company's expectations. The hoped-for development of Gosport and Stokes Bay as resorts and ferry terminals along with a flow of military traffic between Aldershot and Portsmouth never materialized and by the First World War the through train service to and from Waterloo had ceased completely.

With virtually no through traffic and only a local service operating between Alton and Fareham, the route had been downgraded to branch-line status by the early 1920s. Its days as a through route ended completely with the removal of the access from the Waterloo to Alton line at Butts Junction in 1931. All that remained was a daily pick-up goods service and a two-coach push-pull service for the dwindling passenger traffic that remained. Although the line saw little military traffic during the Second World War, its one claim to fame came in June 1944 when a special train carrying Winston Churchill, General Eisenhower and other Allied leaders to a meeting to finalize the D-Day landings was parked for several days in a siding at Droxford station.

This delightful rural railway was plainly uneconomical and under British Railways' management its closure was a foregone conclusion. The Meon Valley Railway closed to passengers on 7 February 1955, years before Dr Beeching and his 'Axe' appeared on the scene. The last train ran on 6 February and was double headed by 'T9' Class 4-4-0s Nos. 30301 and 30732, following which the section

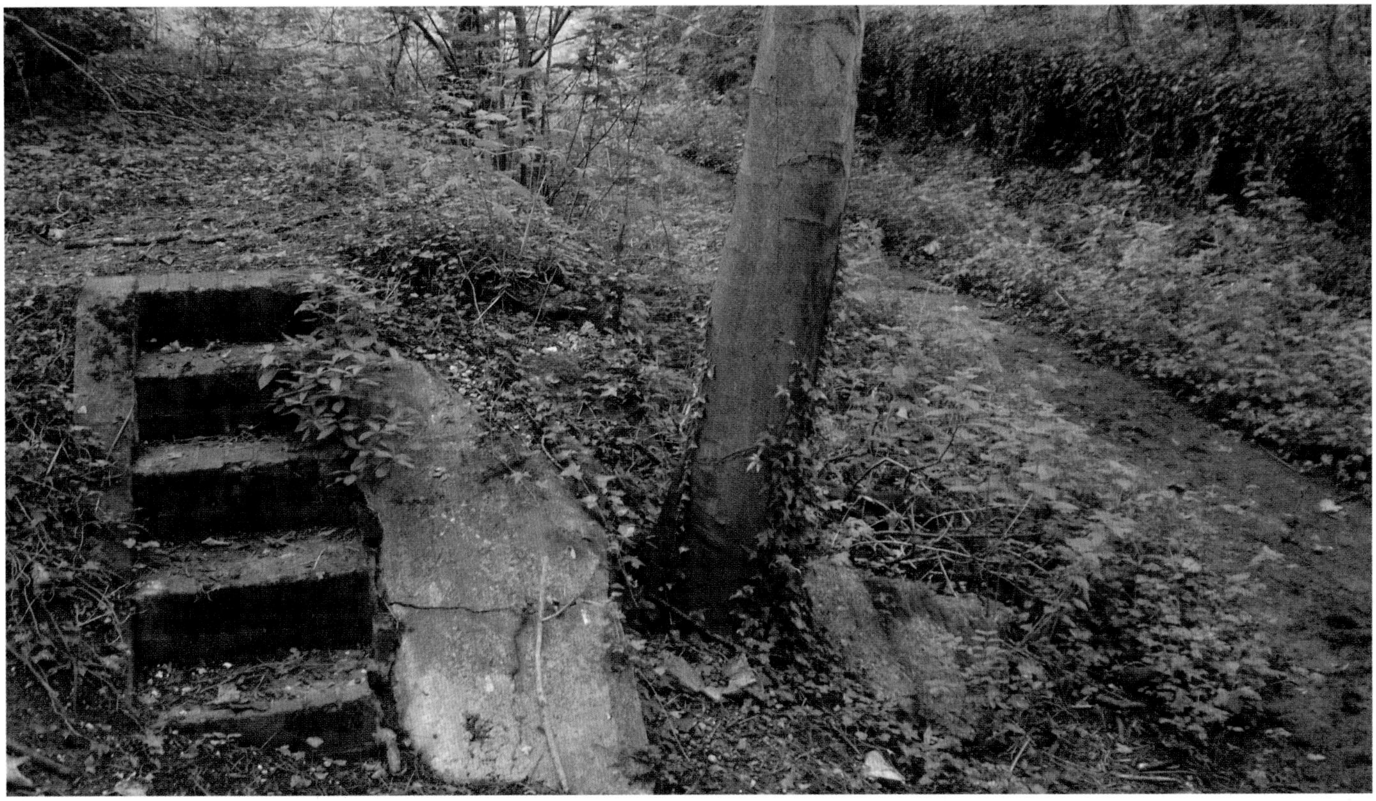

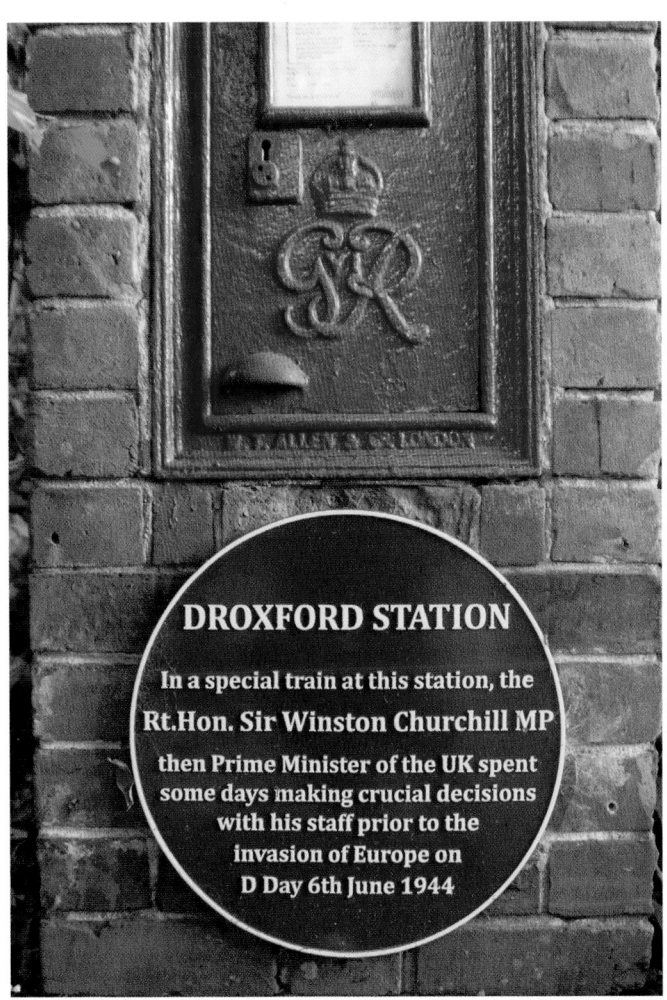

Some 60 years since closure of this rural railway backwater and nature has taken over but keen-eyed lost railway sleuths can usually find something to excite them. Here, hidden away in the undergrowth at the start of the Meon Valley Trail, are the remains of the platform of West Meon station.

DROXFORD STATION

In a special train at this station, the Rt.Hon. Sir Winston Churchill MP then Prime Minister of the UK spent some days making crucial decisions with his staff prior to the invasion of Europe on D Day 6th June 1944

between Farringdon and Droxford was closed completely. Goods trains continued to use the southern section from Fareham to Droxford until June 1962 and ran along the northern section from Alton to Farringdon until August 1968.

An inventor, Charles Ashby, subsequently hired out the southern section of the line, basing himself at Droxford station, to test a new lightweight railbus. The curious Sadler Rail Coach had a bus body mounted on pneumatic tyres with flanged wheels that kept it on the track. Despite using the line as a test bed for his new creation the inventor failed to find any customers for it. Several redundant steam locomotives were also based at Droxford by a preservation society but the hopes of reopening the line as a heritage railway were dashed when BR severed the connection at Knowle Junction, near Fareham, in the early 1970s. Ashby continued to use the isolated line for his creations until 1975 when the track was lifted.

The 11-mile section of the railway between West Meon and Knowle Junction is now a footpath and cycleway known as the Meon Valley Trail.

North of West Meon there are still glimpses of this long-lost railway. The Mock-Tudor 'Arts & Crafts' style stations have been beautifully restored at East Tisted and Privett, the latter marking the summit of the line at 519 ft above sea level. Both the S-shaped 1,056-yd Privett Tunnel and the 560-yd West Meon Tunnel survive and are now used for storage and inhabited by colonies of protected bats. At West Meon little remains of the enormous steel-girder viaduct that once carried the railway across the valley – costing £10,000 and using 725 tons of steel this 62-ft-high structure was sadly demolished for scrap in the 'enlightened' 1960s.

The Meon Valley Trail starts at a car park on the site of West Meon station where railway sleuths will find the overgrown platforms hidden in nearby woodland. Nearly all the bridges and embankments have survived along this section to Knowle Junction, making it a very level route for both walkers and cyclists, although the surface can get very muddy during the winter months. South of West Meon, the tree-lined Trail leads through rich farmland, offering fine views of the Hampshire countryside and Old Winchester Hill on the approaches to Meonstoke. At Droxford a green plaque fixed to the post box next to the station commemorates the meeting of the Allied leaders here in June 1944. The station has been beautifully restored as a private residence although views of the platform, canopy, station building and other railway artefacts are rather hidden from view by a high fence. Opposite the station is the conveniently located Hurdles country pub. Still heading south down the delightful Meon Valley, the wooded Trail criss-crosses the river to arrive at the village of Wickham where, to the east, the fine twelfth-century flint and Bath stone church of St Nicholas overlooks the Trail from its mound. Roadside parking is available in the village and at the famed eighteenth-century King's Head coaching inn. The Trail continues on to the site of Knowle Junction but here cyclists and walkers will need to retrace their journey back to Wickham.

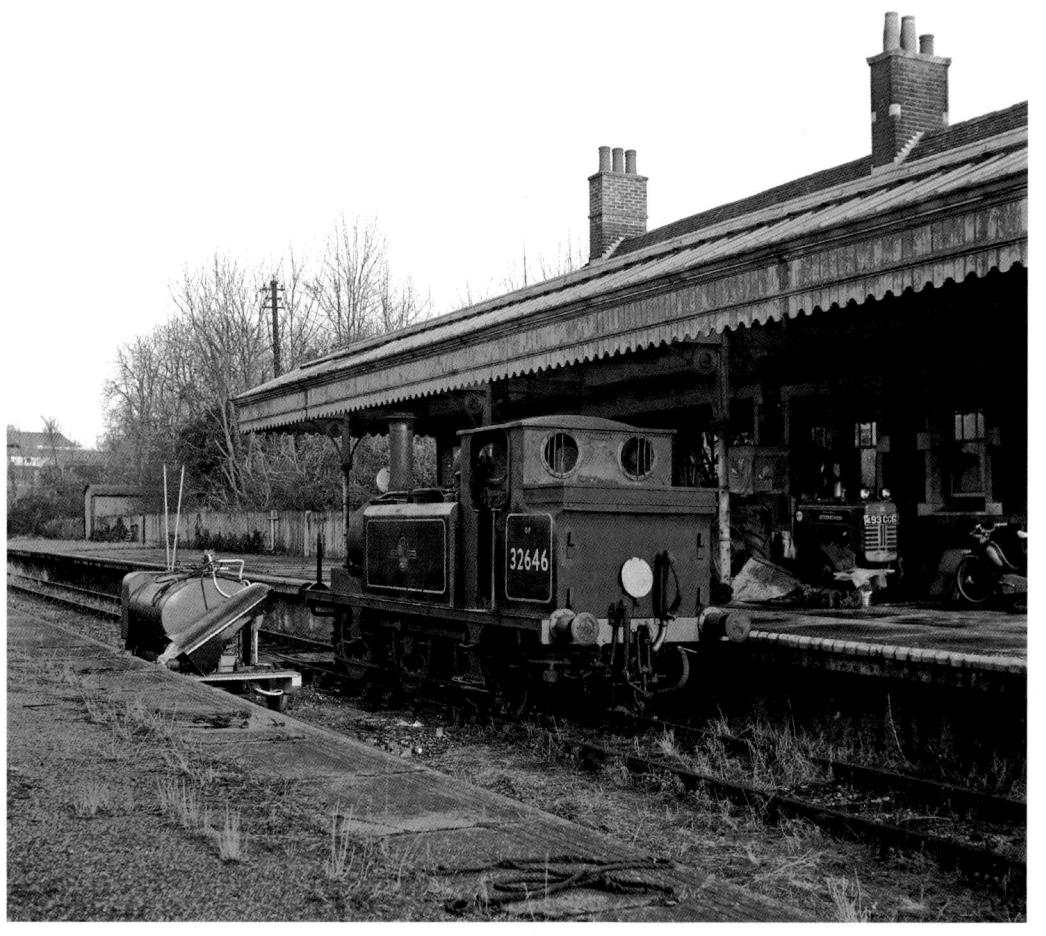

Ex-LB&SCR Class 'A1X' 0-6-0T No. 32646 stands at the long-closed Droxford station on 19 December 1965, two years after withdrawal from service on British Railways. The strange contraption on the left looks like a weed killing trolley but I could be wrong! The Sadler Railcar Company's preservation scheme at Droxford fell apart when BR severed the connection with the main rail network at Knowle Junction in the early 1970s. The diminutive locomotive went on to stand on a plinth outside a pub in Hayling Island until being purchased and restored by the Isle of Wight Steam Railway.

RIGHT:
North of the village of Meonstoke, the Meon Valley Trail skirts rolling farmland to the west of Old Winchester Hill. The hill, 646 ft above sea level, is surmounted by an Iron Age hill fort and a Bronze Age cemetery and is a Site of Special Scientific Interest and a National Nature Reserve.

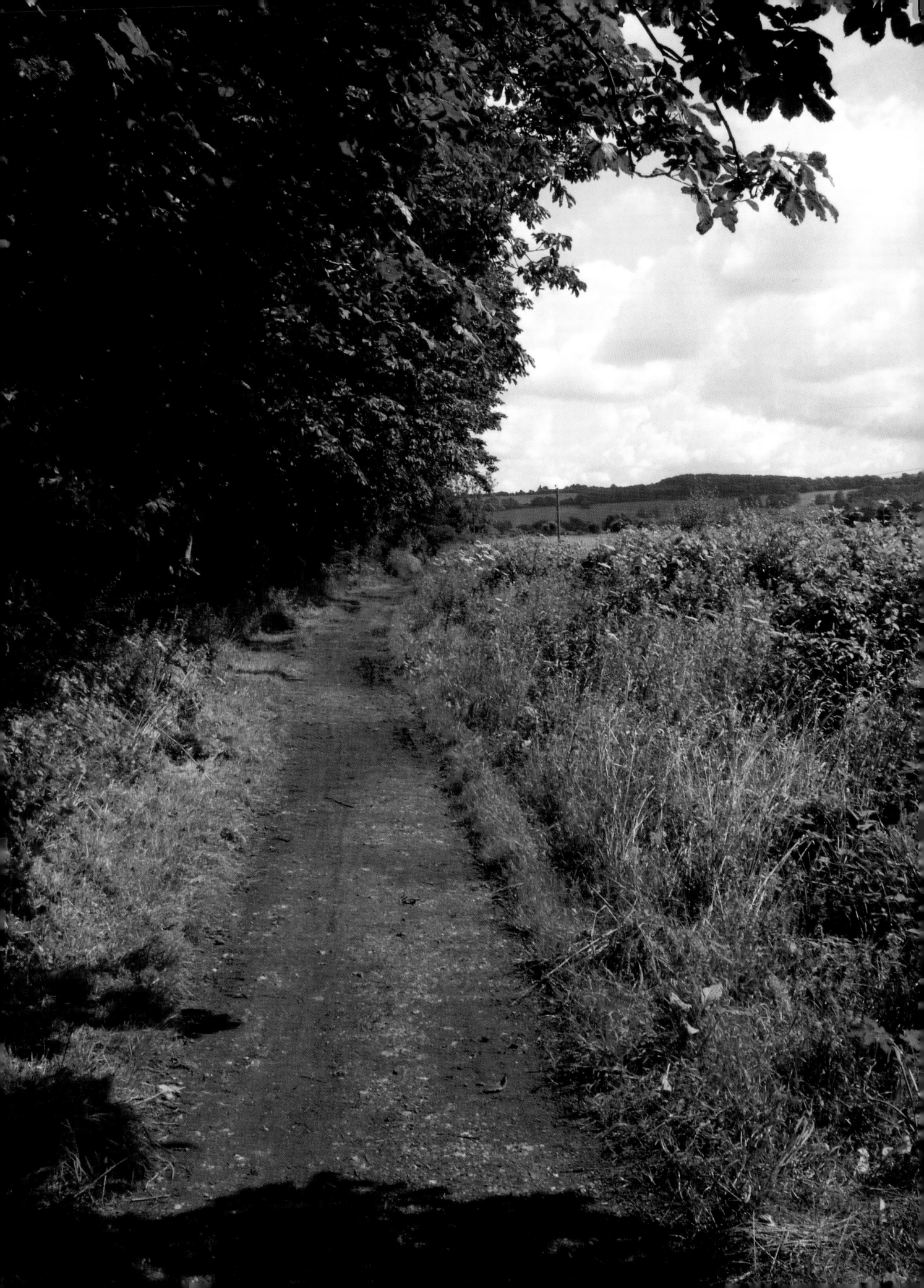

ANDOVER JUNCTION
TO
ROMSEY
TEST WAY

Known as the 'Sprat & Winkle Line', the railway between Andover
Junction and Romsey had many false starts before finally opening along
the winding route of a disused canal in 1865. Leading a fairly quiet life
serving communities along the Test Valley, the railway was also used
by the trains operating between Cheltenham and Southampton via
the Midland & South Western Junction Railway's route from 1894
until 1961. Since closure in 1964 Hampshire County Council
has reopened an 8½-mile section to walkers and cyclists as
part of the Test Way Long Distance Footpath.

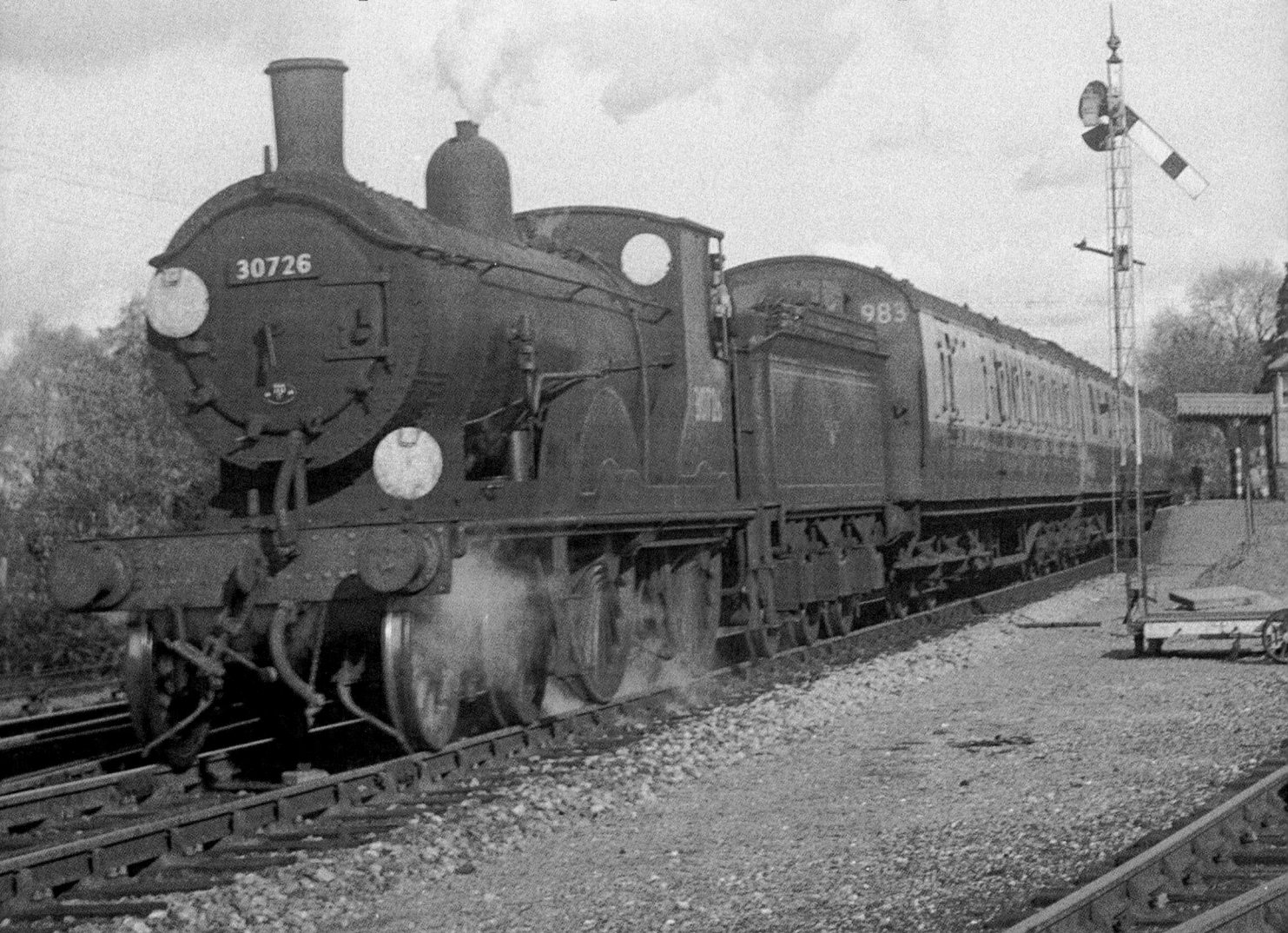

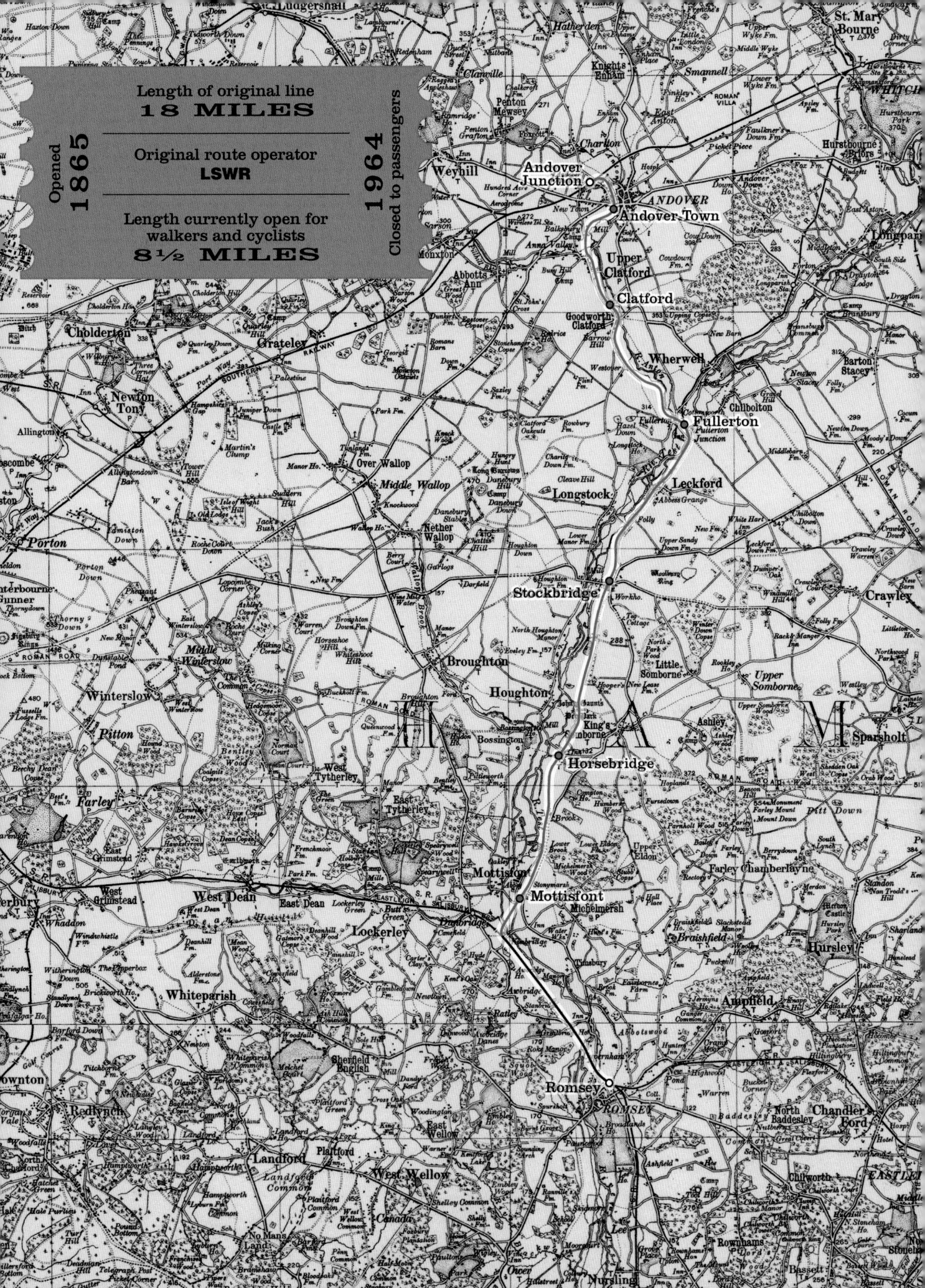

Length of original line
18 MILES

Opened **1865**

Original route operator
LSWR

Closed to passengers **1964**

Length currently open for
walkers and cyclists
8½ MILES

What became known as the Sprat & Winkle Line started life in 1794 as the Andover Canal. Carrying agricultural produce, coal and manure between Southampton and Andover, the canal was never a financial success and various proposals were put forward to rebuild it as a railway. The first of these was the grandly named Manchester & Southampton Railway (M&SR) which, at the height of Railway Mania in 1845, agreed to buy the canal. Unfortunately the M&SR had also agreed to share the new railway with the London & South Western Railway (LSWR), causing its bitter rival, the Great Western Railway (GWR) to object to the 'marriage'. The Parliamentary Bills for the new line were thrown out in 1846 and again in 1848.

PREVIOUS SPREAD:
Ex-LSWR 'T9' 4-4-0 No. 30726 restarts an Andover Junction to Eastleigh train formed of one of the earlier design Bulleid coaches painted in carmine and cream from Horsebridge station in 1957. Since closure the station has been beautifully restored as a wedding reception venue. The 'T9', or 'Greyhounds' as the class was called, was built by Dübs of Glasgow in 1900 and was withdrawn in August 1959.

More twists and turns in the story of this railway followed. After the two defeats in Parliament the LSWR was more successful, obtaining authorization to buy the canal and build the railway. Although construction began it had stopped by 1849 and the canal had still not been paid for! Enter the Andover & Redbridge Railway (A&RR), which was incorporated in 1858 and with GWR support planned to build a broad-gauge railway over the canal. Work started on building the line again but the A&RR soon went bust. After yet another tussle with the GWR the LSWR finally took over in 1863 and opened the line in 1865. Built along the course of the canal, the railway negotiated many twists and curves which inevitably led to operating problems.

The LSWR opened a new double-track line from Hurstbourne, on their Basingstoke to Salisbury main line, to Fullerton on the Sprat & Winkle Line in 1885. At the same time the twists and curves of the latter were straightened out and the line doubled. A new station at Fullerton Junction was also opened, replacing the original (Fullerton Bridge) slightly to the north. The line to Hurstbourne was singled

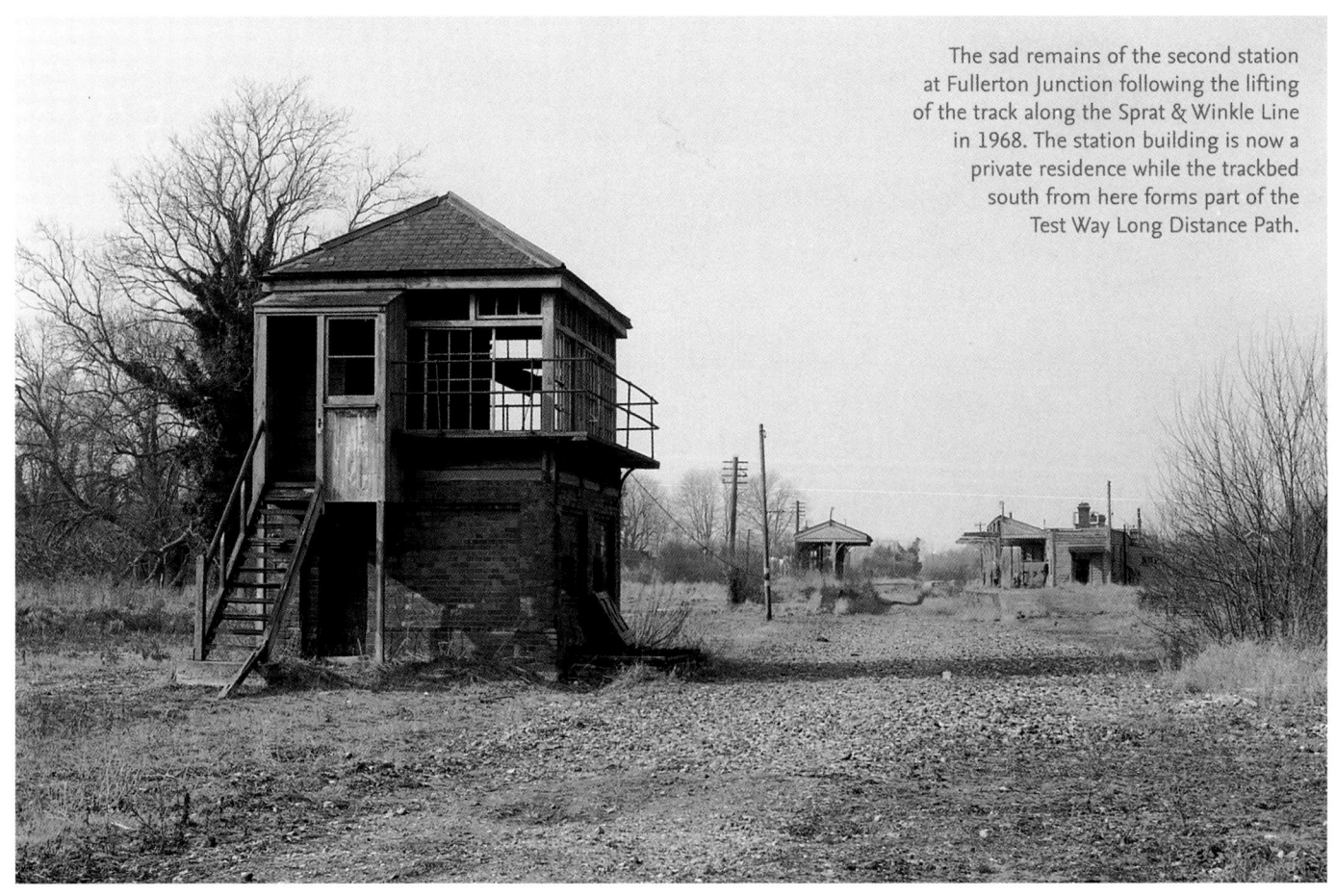

The sad remains of the second station at Fullerton Junction following the lifting of the track along the Sprat & Winkle Line in 1968. The station building is now a private residence while the trackbed south from here forms part of the Test Way Long Distance Path.

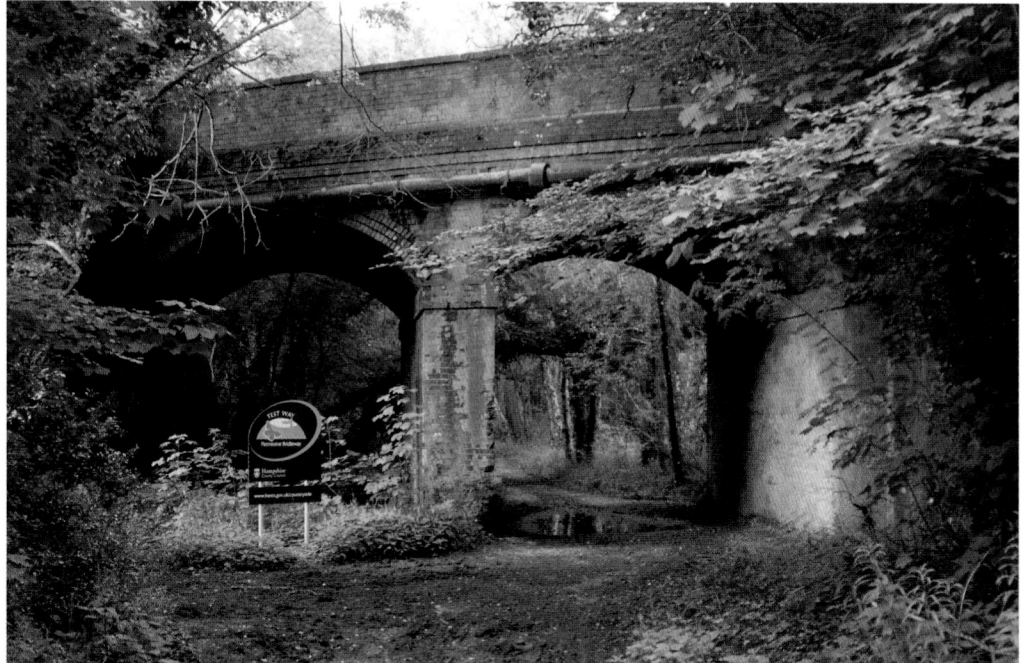

The muddy Test Way at Leckford passes beneath this twin-arched road overbridge. The second arch was added when the single-track railway along the Test Valley was doubled in 1885.

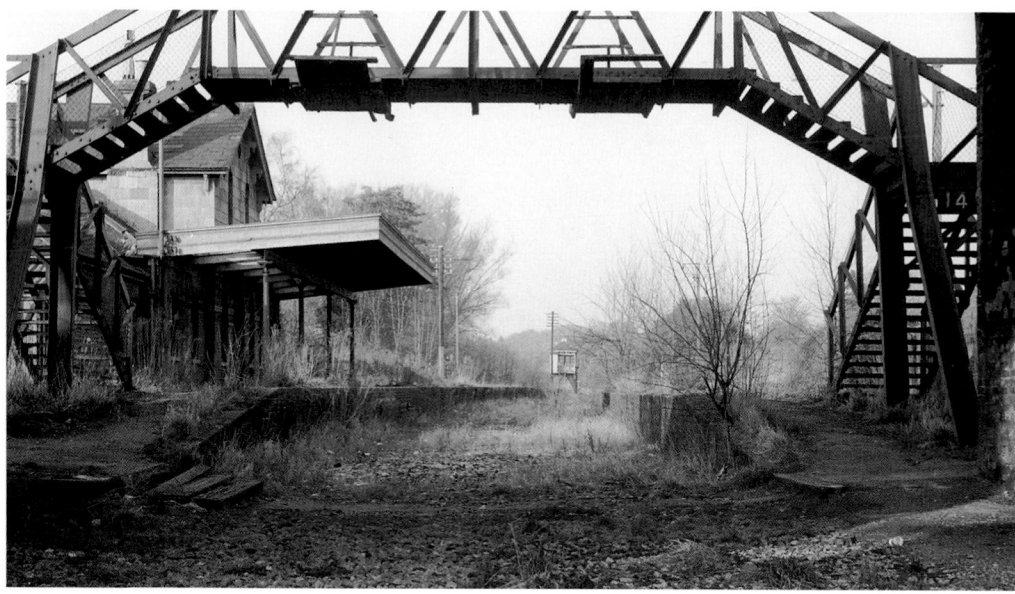

A poignant view of Stockbridge station following track lifting in 1968. The route of the railway through the town has since been obliterated by 'improvements' to the A3057 but the Test Way Long Distance Path resumes its course along the trackbed a mile to the south.

in 1913 and closed to passengers in 1931 although goods traffic continued to run between Fullerton and Longparish until 1956.

The opening of the Midland & South Western Junction Railway's north-south route between Cheltenham and Andover Junction in 1894 injected additional traffic onto the Sprat & Winkle, with a daily service between the Cotswold spa town and Southampton running over the line until it closed north of Andover Junction in 1961. Running for much of its length down the meandering Test Valley, the railway spent its last years serving a regular-interval passenger service between Andover Junction and Southampton. No longer useful as a through route, the line from Andover Junction to Kimbridge Junction, north of Romsey, was listed for closure in the 1963 'Beeching Report'. The end was quick and the line closed completely on 7 September 1964 with the exception of a short section from Andover Junction to Andover Town, which was kept open for freight until 18 September 1967. After twenty years of birth pains and ninety-nine years of faithful service to the communities along the Test Valley, the Sprat & Winkle had finally bitten the dust.

Following closure the rusting track of the Sprat & Winkle Line slowly disappeared into the encroaching undergrowth for four years until it was finally lifted. Since then Hampshire County Council has reopened 8½ miles of the trackbed between West Down, close to the site of Fullerton Junction, and Mottisfont as part of the Test Way Long Distance Path. A public car park and the popular riverside Mayfly pub at West Down make a good start point from which to explore this lost railway. Immediately to the north of here lies Fullerton Junction station, now restored as a private residence, with the remains of the concrete platforms and iron bridge over the Test still visible in the undergrowth. The twin-arched road bridge over the railway at the start of this walk is a reminder of the doubling of the railway back in 1885. Closely following the River Test and its meandering tributaries, the path southwards can be very muddy at times as it passes through the village of Leckford and skirts nearby Longstock before reaching the small town of Stockbridge. 'Improvements' to the A3057 have long obliterated the railway's route through the town but it can soon be rejoined in the water meadows to the south – here the quiet world of reed beds is a popular haunt of waterfowl.

Continuing southwards the Test Way reaches the village of Horsebridge, an ancient crossing point of the river with its John of Gaunt pub and beautifully restored Victorian railway station. An important staging post for soldiers, munitions, horses and equipment on their way to France during the First World War, the station building, platforms, canopy, signalbox and a 1922 Southern Railway carriage at Horsebridge are open to the public for afternoon teas on certain weekends during the year – for opening days visit www.horsebridgestation.co.uk

The final stretch of the old railway route is sandwiched between the Test and the A3057 before reaching the eastern outskirts of Mottisfont. Here the old station is now a private residence but it is only a brief walk into the village, which is famed for its National Trust-owned Abbey. A short distance to the southwest lies the sparsely patronised Mottisfont & Dunbridge station, which is still served by trains running between Salisbury and Southampton. The Mill Arms country pub is situated opposite the station. The original Sprat & Winkle signalbox at Romsey, dating from 1865, has been restored to working order and is open to the public on the first Sunday of each month, excluding January. For details visit: www.romseysignalbox.org.uk

RIGHT: Mottisfont station, seen here from a northbound train on 22 May 1957. The railway section of the Test Valley Way ends here although the station building has survived as a private residence.

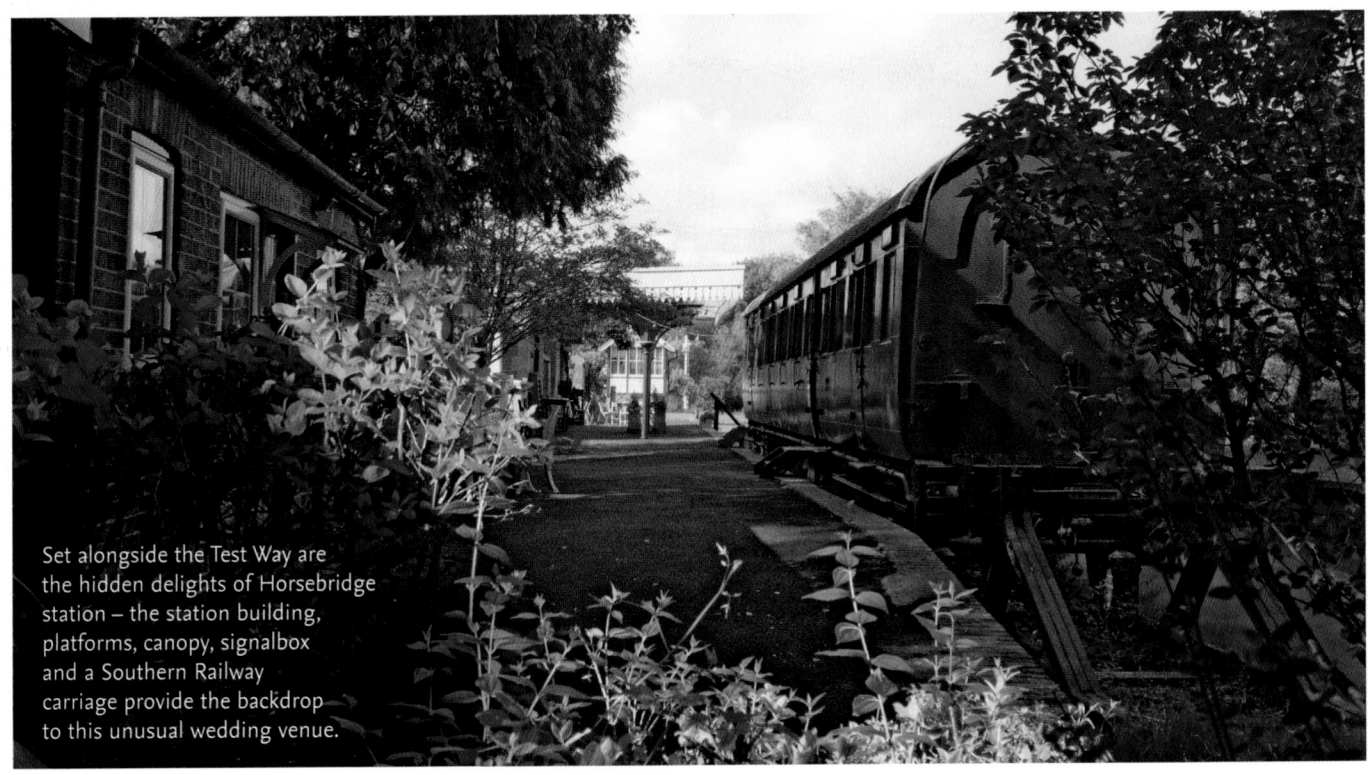

Set alongside the Test Way are the hidden delights of Horsebridge station – the station building, platforms, canopy, signalbox and a Southern Railway carriage provide the backdrop to this unusual wedding venue.

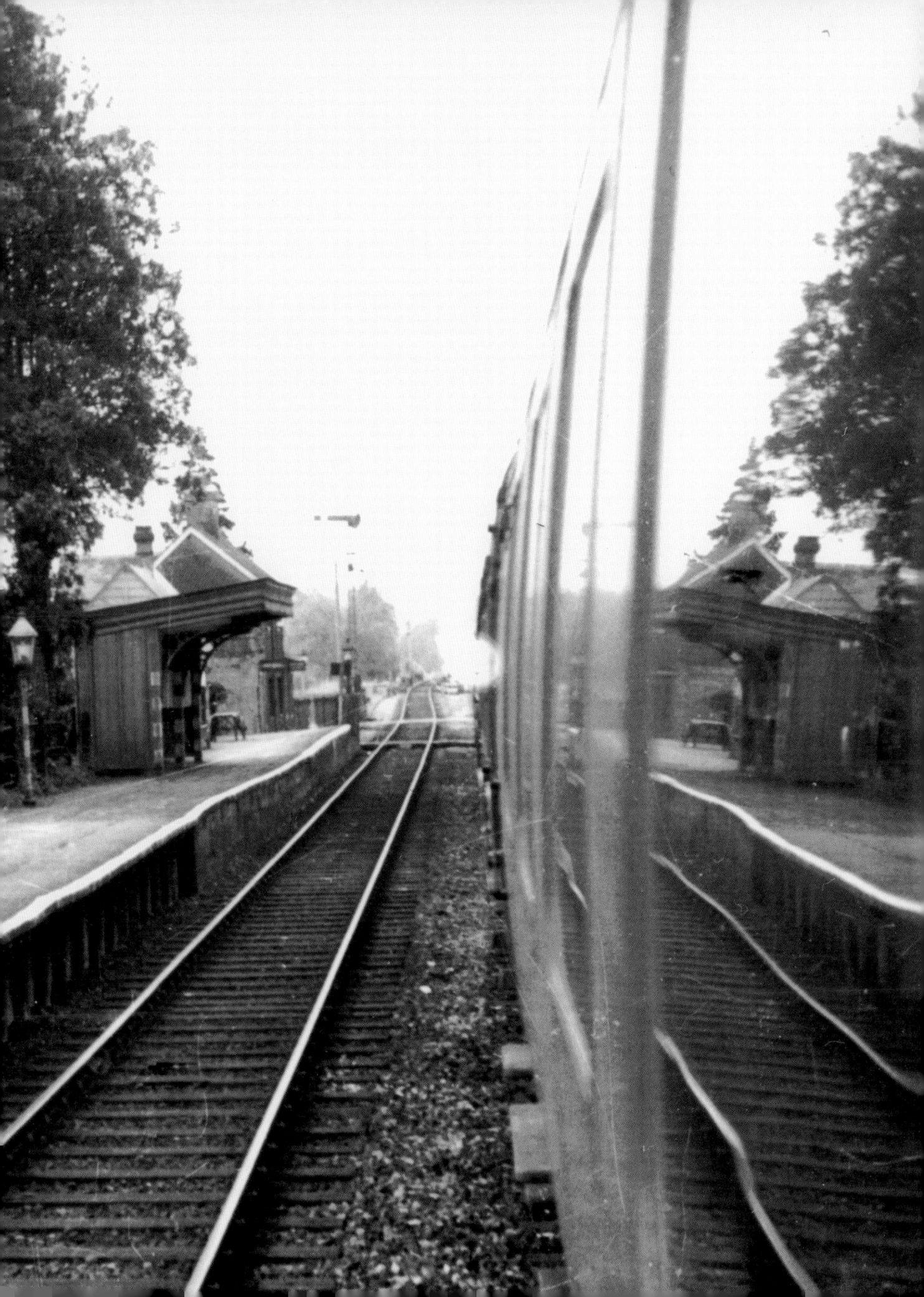

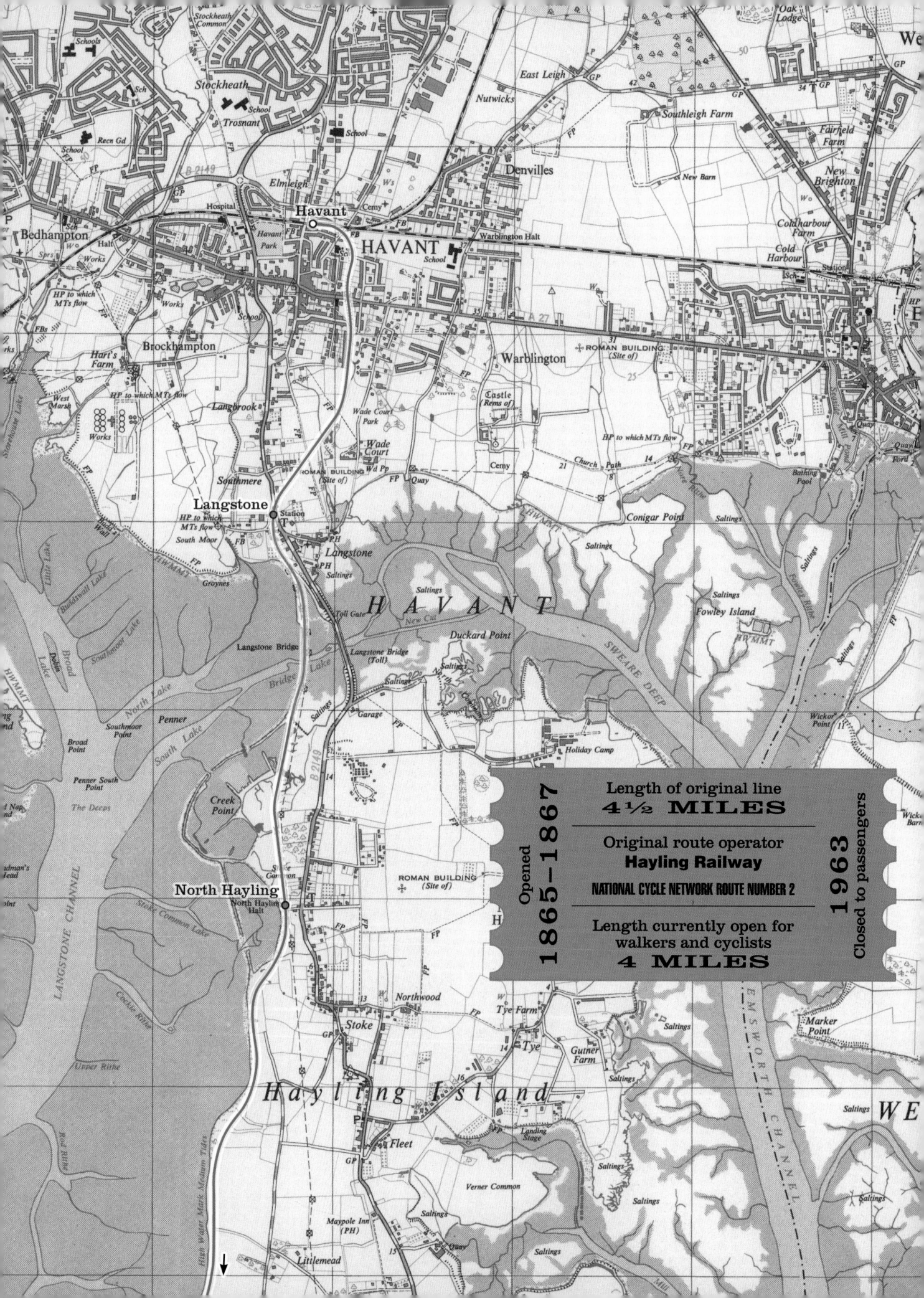

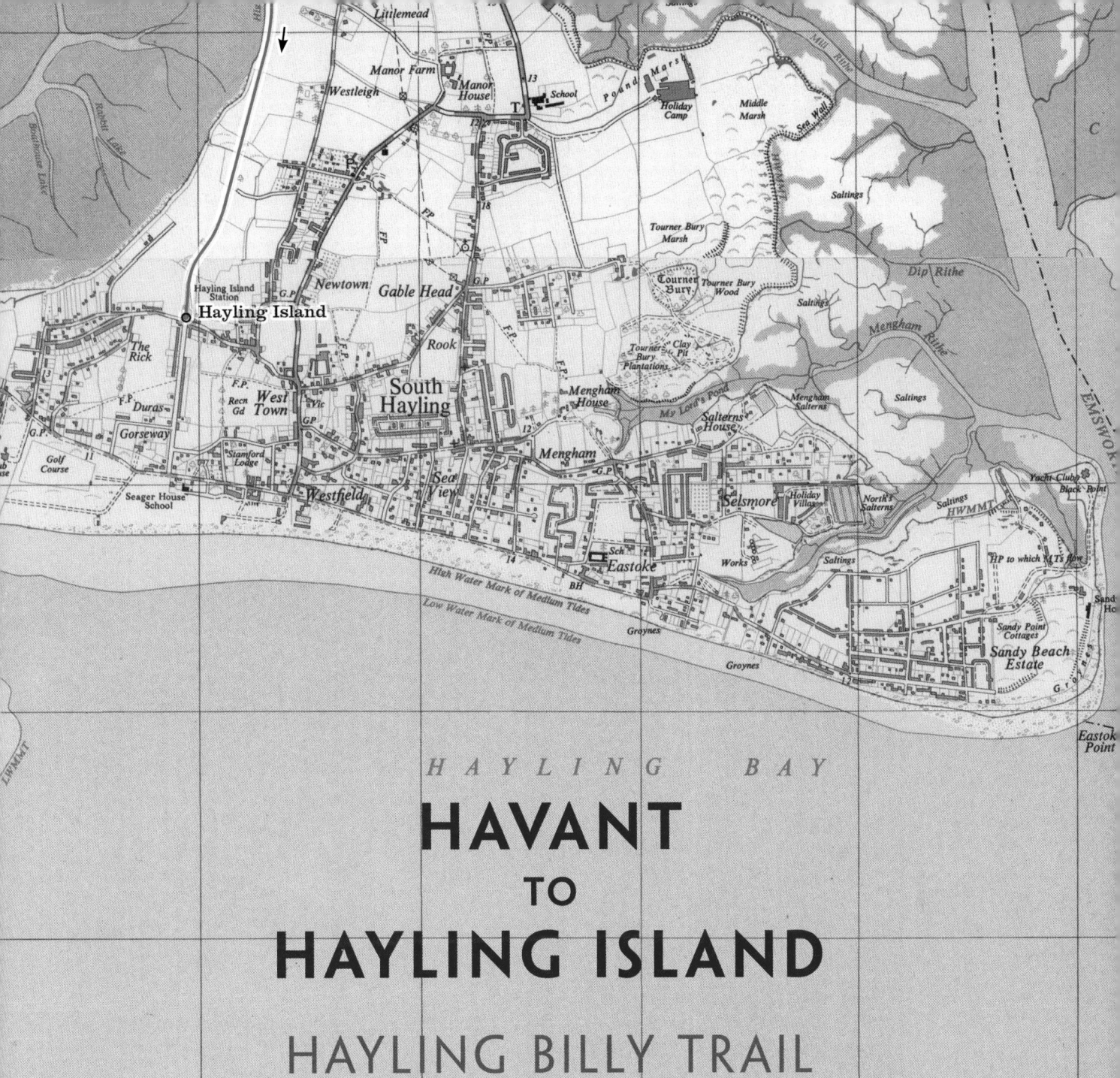

HAYLING BAY

HAVANT
TO
HAYLING ISLAND

HAYLING BILLY TRAIL

Featuring a long, timber swing bridge across Langstone Harbour, the Hayling Railway brought holidaymakers in their thousands during the summer months to the popular resort of Hayling Island. Due to weight restrictions on the bridge, diminutive Stroudley 'Terrier' locomotives dating from the 1870s provided the motive power until closure of the line in 1963. Since then the only road on to the island has become gridlocked during the summer months while almost the entire route of the railway has been reopened as a footpath and cycleway known as the Hayling Billy Trail.

Promoted by local businessmen eager to transform Hayling Island into a holiday resort, the Hayling Railway was authorized in 1860 to build a 4½-mile single-track line from Havant, on the London, Brighton & South Coast Railway's (LB&SCR) coastal route from Brighton to Portsmouth, to Hayling Island. Construction of the line was slow owing to the building of a 1,100-ft timber bridge with a central swing section across Langstone Harbour and an embankment on the mud flats along the west coast of the island. Costs escalated and were made worse when the Board of Trade inspector delayed the line's opening after he discovered damaged rails and rotten wooden sleepers. Goods trains started to run in 1865 but passenger services were delayed until 17 July 1867 – by coincidence the second day of the inaugural meeting of Hayling Races, which took place on the foreshore opposite the Royal Hotel in South Hayling.

For the first four years of its existence the line's contractor operated the Hayling Railway using ancient four-wheeled carriages hired from the London & South Western Railway. The LB&SCR took over operations in 1872 and leased the line from 1874. Despite this, the Hayling Railway Company remained independent until it was absorbed by the newly created Southern Railway in 1923.

With intermediate stations at Langstone and North Hayling – both diminutive wooden structures, although the latter was used to transport oysters from nearby oyster beds – the line proved very popular with holidaymakers and day trippers during the summer months. In the winter it was a different story however, with few passengers and virtually empty trains. Owing to weight restrictions imposed on the timber bridge at Langstone, the only locomotives allowed to use the branch line were the Stroudley 'Terrier' Class 'A1X' 0-6-0Ts, which remained in service until closure – these diminutive locos were affectionately known by locals as Hayling Billies.

Although the Hayling Island branch made a modest profit it was listed for closure in the 1963 'Beeching Report' – the reason given was the estimated £400,000 cost of replacing the ageing timber bridge at Langstone. That last summer still saw a very intensive service on the line with fifteen weekday services, twenty-four on Saturdays and twenty-one on Sundays – at weekends the trains were often filled to overflowing with daytrippers. The end came on 4 November 1963 when it closed for good – the last train to travel over the line had been an enthusiasts' special, double headed by two 'Terrier' locos on Sunday, 3 November.

Following closure, attempts were made to reopen the line as an electric tramway but this came to nothing, and the track was lifted and Langstone Bridge demolished in 1966.

Ex-LBSCR 'A1X' Class 'Terrier' 0-6-0T No. 32662, adorned with wreath, climbs away from Langstone with the 2.35pm Havant to Hayling Island train on the last day of service, 2 November 1963. The veteran 'Terrier' was built at Brighton in 1875, withdrawn from Eastleigh shed on 30 November 1963 and is now preserved at the Bressingham Steam Museum in Norfolk.

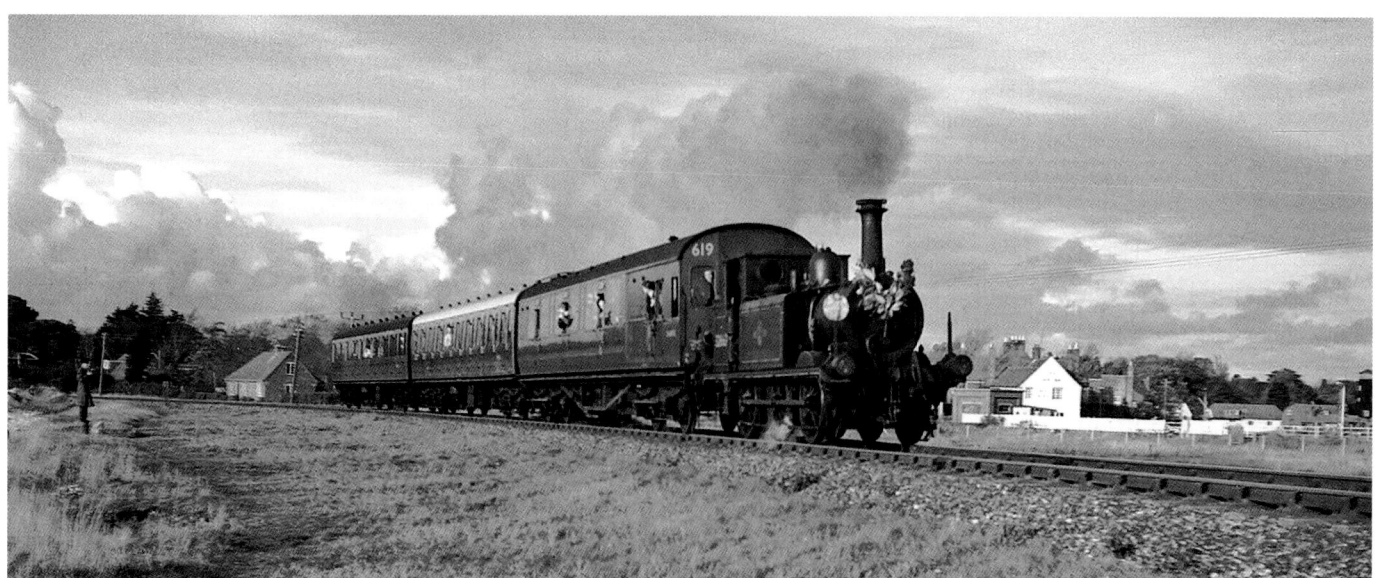

Since the railway's closure the only road to the island has become gridlocked on summer weekends. By comparison the peaceful railway trackbed from Langstone to South Hayling has been reopened as a footpath and cycleway known as the Hayling Billy Trail, which now also forms part of National Cycle Network Route 2. Havant station is still served by trains on the Portsmouth Direct Line from Waterloo and also by trains on the West Coastway Line between Southampton and Brighton.

The route of the railway from Havant station to the north of Langstone Harbour is also a footpath, and a short detour via the road bridge over the harbour leads to the start of the Hayling Billy Trail. With car parking available nearby, the piers of the old swing bridge can be seen clearly at low tide, while a lonely signal post still stands as a forlorn reminder of this once busy railway. Heading south and with fine views across Langstone Harbour to Portsmouth, the path reaches the site of North Hayling station. The station itself is long gone but this coastal stretch is now internationally recognized for its wildlife. The nature reserve through which the path passes is home to a wide variety of protected species of wildfowl, wading birds, butterflies and plantlife.

The Hayling Billy Trail ends at the site of Hayling Island station where there is car parking. The station itself has long been demolished but the 1900-built goods shed has been tastefully converted into a theatre for the Hayling Island Amateur Dramatic Society. A short walk away from the station is the Hayling foreshore with its amusement arcades, beaches and narrow-gauge Hayling Seaside Railway. All in all a great day out!

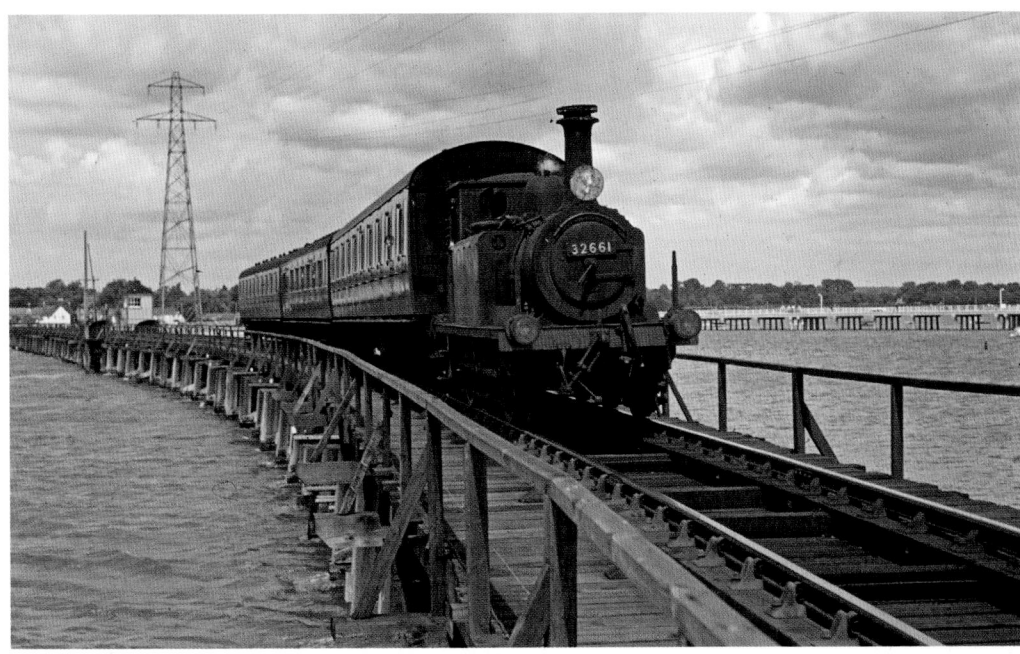

'Terrier' 0-6-0T No. 32661 rumbles off Langstone Bridge with a Havant to Hayling Island train on 4 August 1962. The wooden bridge was subsequently demolished but the trackbed to the south and north of here is now a footpath and cycleway.

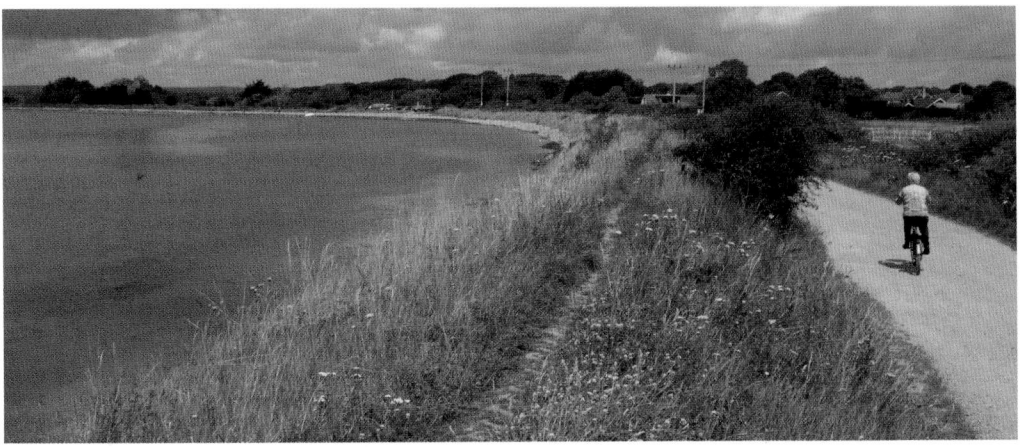

The Hayling Billy Trail skirts the eastern shore of Langstone Harbour from where there are far-reaching views across to Portsmouth. This popular traffic-free footpath and cycleway offers visitors to Hayling Island an alternative route to the single, congested road onto the island.

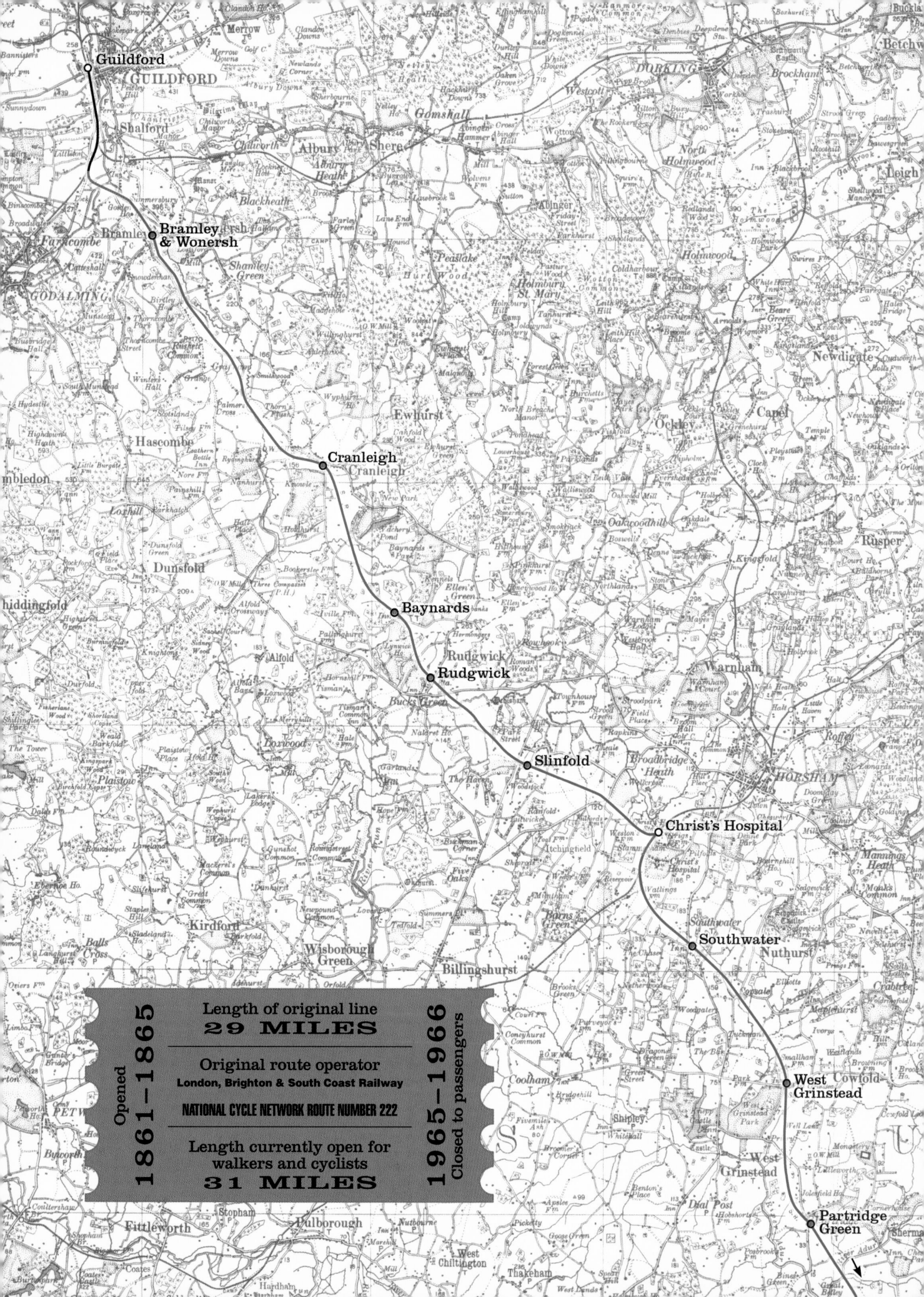

Guildford

Bramley & Wonersh

Cranleigh

Baynards

Rudgwick

Slinfold

Christ's Hospital

Southwater

West Grinstead

Partridge Green

Opened
1861–1865

Length of original line
29 MILES

Original route operator
London, Brighton & South Coast Railway

NATIONAL CYCLE NETWORK ROUTE NUMBER 222

Length currently open for
walkers and cyclists
31 MILES

1965–1966
Closed to passengers

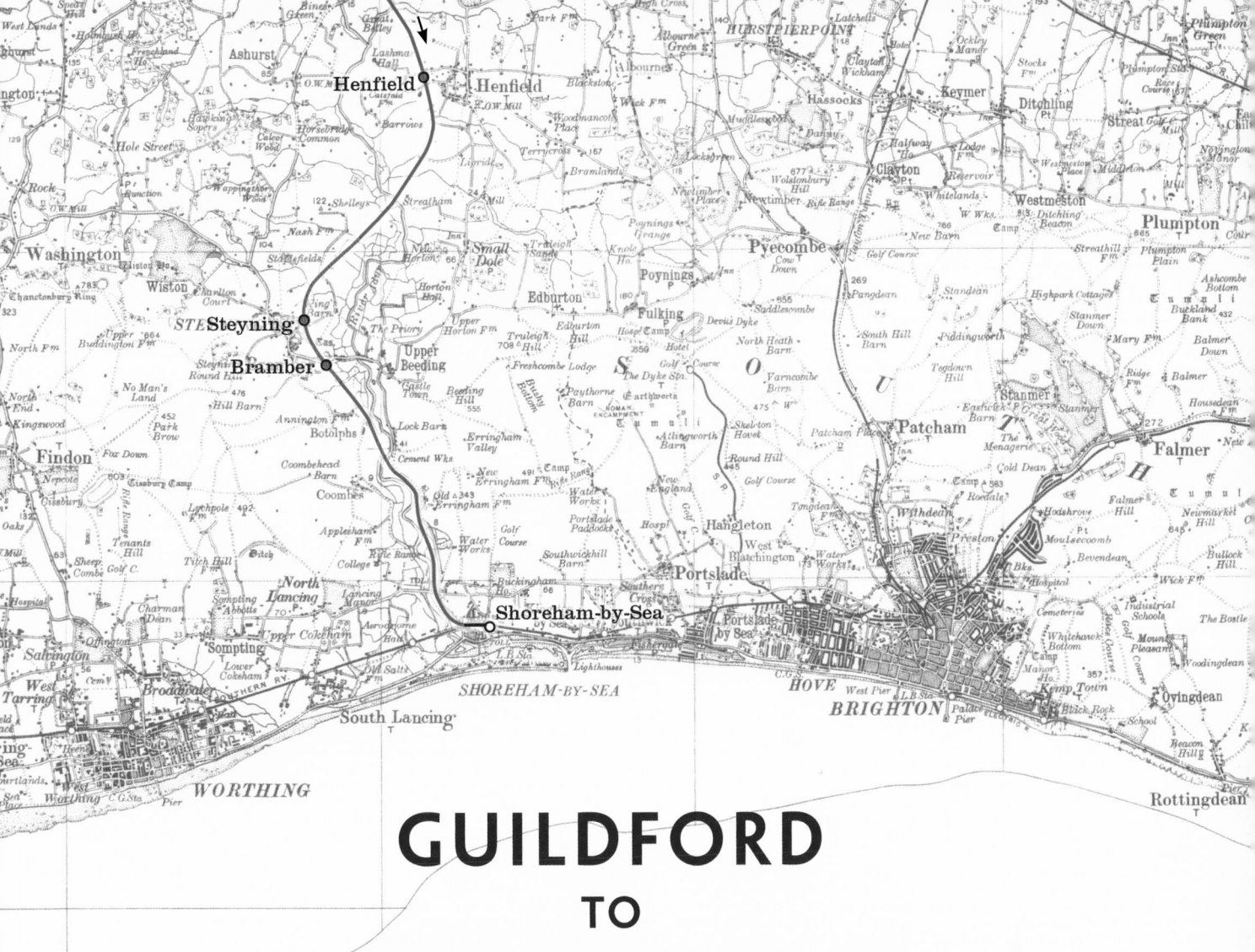

GUILDFORD
TO
SHOREHAM-BY-SEA

DOWNS LINK

Although seen as a through route from Guildford to the south coast, this long cross-country railway across Surrey and Sussex was effectively operated as two separate entities. Suffering attacks from German planes during the Second World War, both lines missed out on third-rail electrification although they were well used by excursion traffic during the summer months. The less patronized Guildford to Christ's Hospital section remained steam-worked until closure in 1965, while the Steyning line continued with buoyant passenger numbers, aided by a regular interval service of diesel-electric multiple units, until it, too, was closed a year later. Almost the entire route has since been reopened as the Downs Link footpath, bridleway and cycleway.

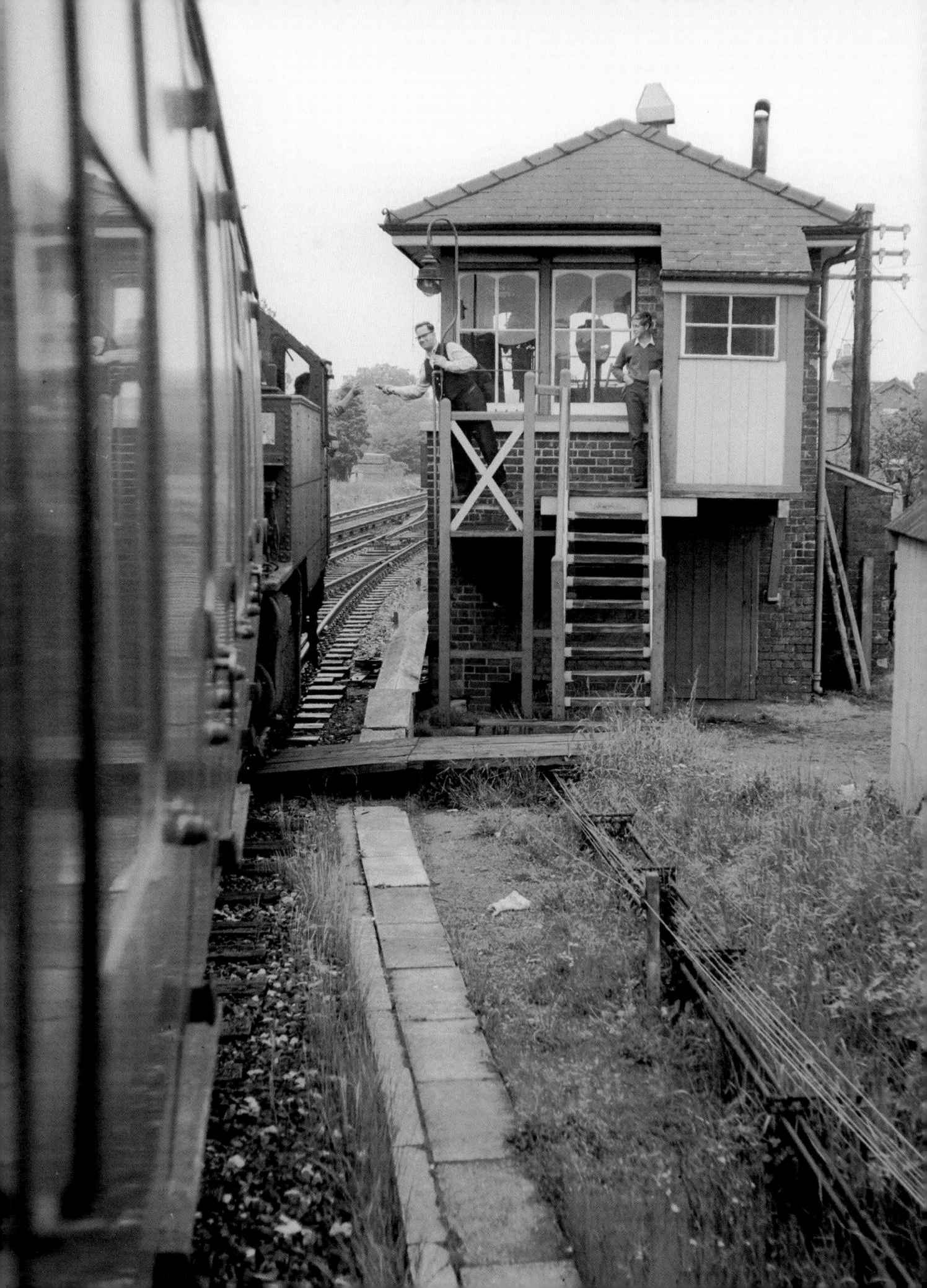

With its goal of reaching Portsmouth from London, the London & South Western Railway (LSWR) had already reached Guildford from Woking in 1845. The company not only had Portsmouth in its sights but was also looking at ways of reaching the port of Shoreham in Sussex by building a cross-country line from Guildford via Horsham. However, this would have encroached on the territory of the rival London & Brighton Railway (L&BR), which put forward its own scheme, the London & Brighton (Steyning Branch) Railway, gaining authorization in 1846. The L&BR soon amalgamated with the London & Croydon Railway to become the London, Brighton & South Coast Railway (LB&SCR).

The Steyning line from Horsham to Shoreham-by-Sea was effectively a 20-mile branch from the LB&SCR's main line that it planned to build from Dorking to Arundel and Chichester. However, the severe financial depression that followed the period known as Railway Mania soon put an end not only to the LSWR's aspirations but also to the LB&SCR's line to Chichester and the Steyning branch. By 1848 the LB&SCR had only reached Horsham and this was via a branch line from its London to Brighton main line at Three Bridges – it was to take another fifteen years before the LB&SCR's main line from Horsham to Chichester was completed.

Several proposals had been put forward to resurrect the Steyning line before a Parliamentary Inquiry was held and approval finally given for the LB&SCR scheme to go ahead. With intermediate stations at Bramber, Steyning, Henfield, Partridge Green, West Grinstead and Southwater the line opened throughout in 1861, joining the uncompleted Horsham to Chichester line at Itchingfield, south of Horsham.

Meanwhile, the Horsham & Guildford Direct Railway had been incorporated in 1860 to build a 15½-mile single-track line between Peasmarsh Junction, on the LSWR's Portsmouth line south of Guildford, and Stammerham Junction, on the LB&SCR's line south of Horsham. Construction was slow and costly and the company was taken over before completion by the LB&SCR in 1864. Running powers over LSWR metals into Guildford station were obtained and a triangular junction was built at Itchingfield to allow through running between Guildford and Shoreham. With intermediate stations at Bramley, Cranleigh, Baynards, Rudgwick and Slinfold the line opened in 1865 – its arrival sounding the death knell for the nearby Wey & Arun Canal which had been abandoned by 1871.

The anticipated through traffic between Guildford and the South Coast failed to materialize owing to the obstruction

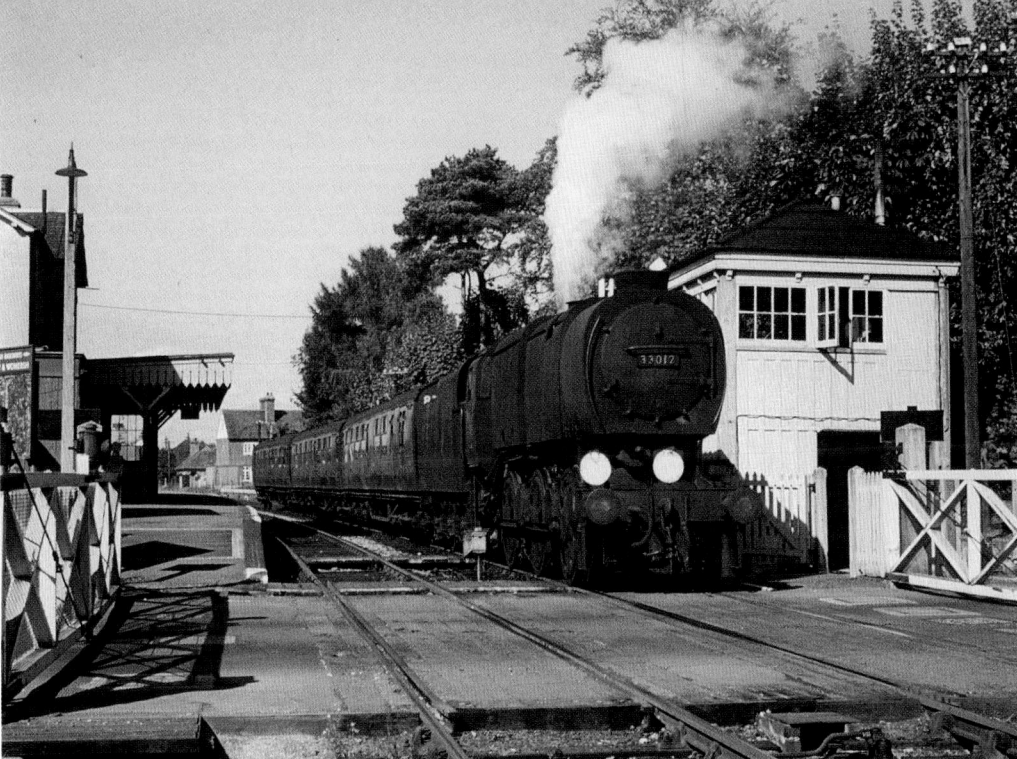

Oliver Bulleid's wartime 'Q1' Class 0-6-0 No. 33012 calls at Bramley & Wonersh station with a Guildford to Horsham train on 26 September 1964. Bombed by German planes in 1942, the station site, complete with platforms and level crossing gates, is now a stopping place on the Downs Link Long Distance Path.

LEFT:
The signalman and driver exchange single-line tokens at Peasmarsh Junction south of Guildford on the last day of regular services, 12 June 1965. The train, the 6pm from Horsham, was hauled by Ivatt Class '2' 2-6-2T No. 41287.

of the LSWR at Guildford, so the spur at Itchingfield Junction was closed as early as 1867. Thereafter the Steyning Line and the Cranleigh Line led completely separate existences apart from meeting up at Stammerham Junction for the final 2½ miles into Horsham. The grand station of Christ's Hospital (West Horsham) was built at the junction to serve the relocated public school nearby in 1902.

Of the two railways, the Guildford to Horsham line was by far the quieter, with passenger and goods traffic falling far short of expectations because of the LSWR's machinations at Guildford. The First World War saw the line busier than normal but when the Southern Railway's third-rail electrification reached Guildford and Horsham in 1937 the Cranleigh line missed out. However, the 1930s did see increased usage of the route by excursion trains to the south coast during the summer months from as far afield as the Great Western Railway. During the Second World War the line sustained serious damage from German bombers and a passenger train was strafed near Bramley in 1942, killing the driver, guard and six passengers, and injuring thirty-six. In the post-war years the line suffered from a reduced service and poor connections at Guildford and Horsham – it was as if British Railways (BR) was hell-bent on closing the line and the 1955 rail strike further contributed to the line's

downfall. Judged by BR to be uneconomical, with losses at around £45,000 per year, the Cranleigh line was listed for closure in the 1963 'Beeching Report'. With goods services already having been withdrawn in 1962, it was announced that the line would close in November 1963. There were many objections to the closure but, despite a public enquiry, at which BR conceded that passenger numbers were actually rising, the line, steam-worked to the end, closed on 14 June 1965. The track was hastily lifted and the so-called replacement bus services also soon bit the dust.

Meanwhile, back on the Steyning line, the 1926 General Strike had already brought about the permanent loss of important milk traffic to road transport. However, the line still carried large amounts of incoming gypsum and coal to a cement factory at Beeding with outgoing cement being transported to Southampton. On the passenger side the line was popular with ramblers and heavily used during the summer months by excursion trains. Military traffic was also heavy during both World Wars. The Southern Railway proposed third-rail electrification in 1946, but the newly nationalized British Railways cancelled this golden opportunity in 1948. Despite this short-sighted decision, passenger numbers, no doubt helped by a frequent regular interval service, saw a steady increase well into the

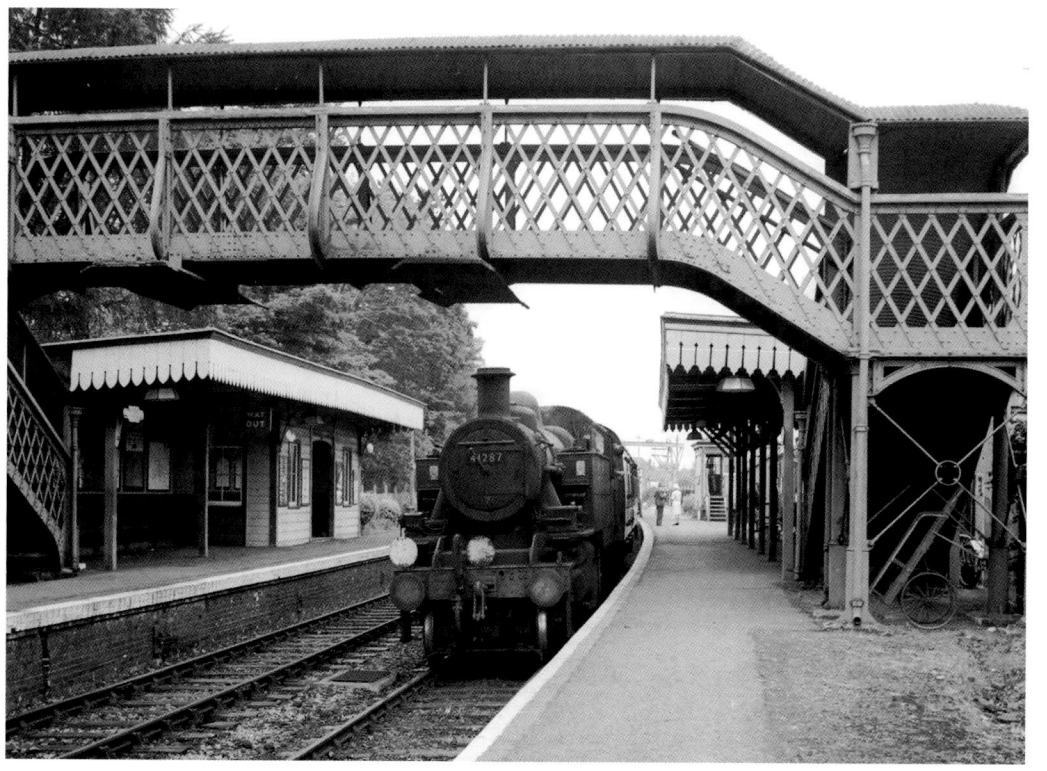

Ivatt Class '2' 2-6-2T No. 41287 pauses at Cranleigh station with the 9.08am Guildford to Baynards train on the last day of regular services on the line, 12 June 1965. Cranleigh station has since been demolished to make way for modern shops and housing.

RIGHT:
The unique double bridge between Rudgwick and Slinfold. The line's opening was delayed while an iron bridge was built on top of the brick arch bridge to lessen the gradient up to Rudgwick station. The double bridge symbol is depicted on signposts along the Downs Link.

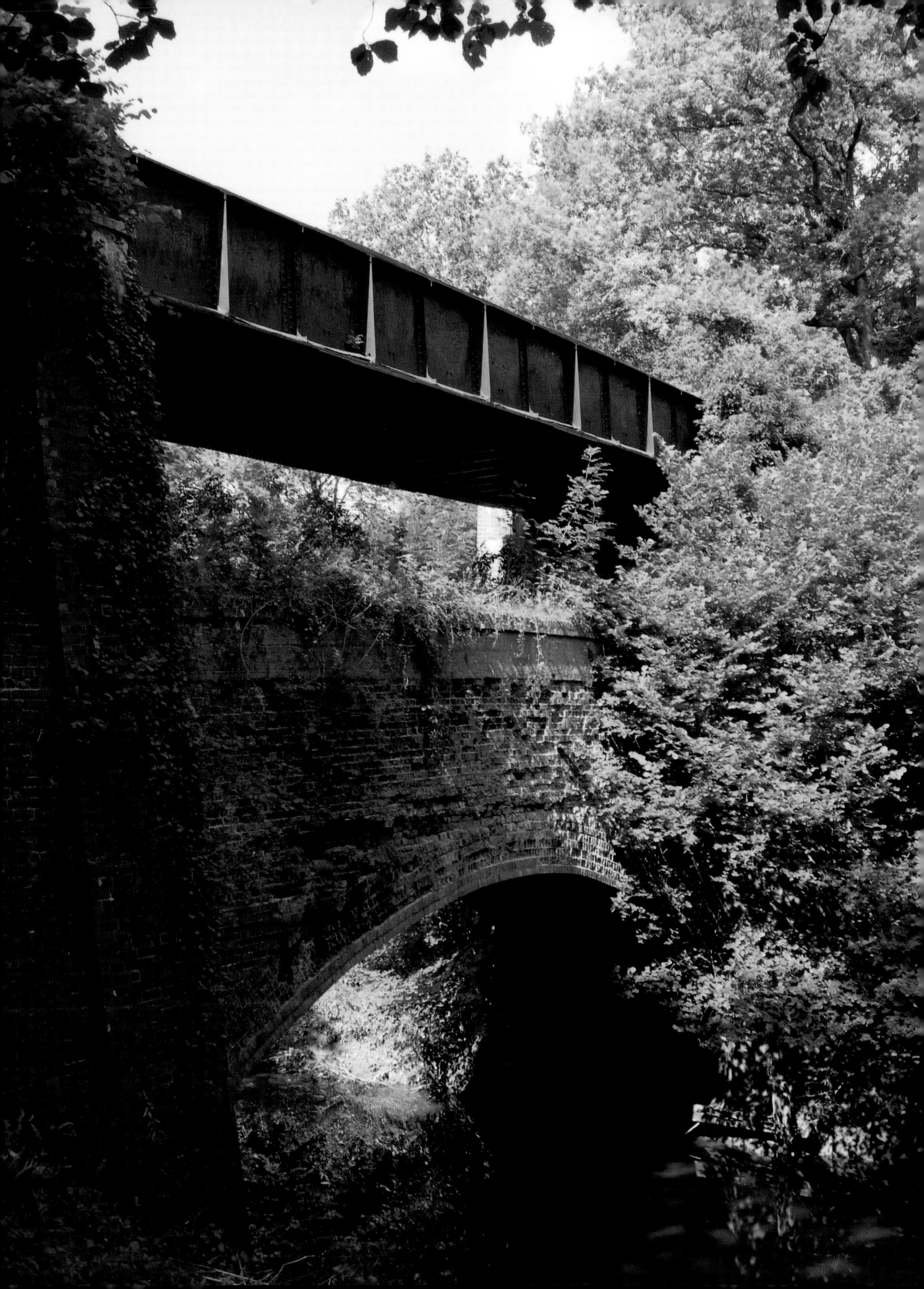

1960s, with steam giving way to diesel-electric multiple units in 1964.

By this time the Steyning line had already been listed for closure in the 'Beeching Report' and, despite a public inquiry and several passenger traffic surveys, the end came on 7 March 1966 when passenger services were withdrawn. The replacement bus service fared no better! Although goods traffic continued to serve the cement works at Beeding until 1991 the rest of the track was soon lifted following complete closure.

⊦⊦⊦⊦⊦⊦⊦⊦⊦⊦⊦⊦⊦⊦⊦

BR sold the overgrown trackbeds of the Cranleigh and Steyning lines to Surrey County Council and what was to become Waverley Borough Council in 1970. The two local authorities managed the land and cleared the embankments and cuttings to allow public access. Since 1984 the trackbed has been incorporated to form most of the 37-mile Downs Link footpath and bridleway that links the North Downs Way at St Martha's Hill, southeast of Guildford, to the South Downs Way near Steyning and on to the coast at Shoreham-by-Sea. In more recent years it has also become part of National Cycle Network Route 222 (Sussex Downs Link).

An excellent starting point for walkers or cyclists is Bramley & Wonersh station, south of Guildford, where a car park, restored platforms, concrete station signs, a waiting shelter and level crossing gates can be found. A plaque on the shelter wall remembers the eight deaths and 36 injuries resulting from the attack on a passenger train by a German plane in 1942.

From Bramley & Wonersh the path heads off for five miles in a southeasterly direction, closely following the disused Wey & Arun Canal for a while before reaching the site of Cranleigh station, once spelt as 'Cranley'. The station has long been demolished to make way for modern shops and housing. Now heading south, the path passes through peaceful Surrey countryside for three miles to reach the beautifully restored station at Baynards – apart from the missing track very little has changed at this delightful rural spot. Next comes Rudgwick, where a medical centre now occupies the station site, before the path heads through

woodland – great care must be taken when crossing the treacherously fast A281 – to reach the unique double bridge across the River Arun. Here the line's opening was delayed while an iron girder bridge was built on top of a brick arch bridge to lessen the gradient up to Rudgwick station – the double arch symbol is depicted on signposts along the Downs Link.

Continuing southeastwards the path passes Slinfold station, now a private residence, before taking a short diversion away from the Cranleigh line at Christ's Hospital. Albeit a shadow of its former self, the station here is still served by trains between Horsham and the South Coast.

The Downs Link regains the trackbed of the Steyning line close to Christ's Hospital School, following it through Southwater, where shops, a police station and a library now occupy the station site – the only reminder of the railway here is the old roadbridge and a replica station sign. The path heads under the A24 dual carriageway, passing a convenient car park at Copsale (with its popular Bridge House pub) before reaching the idyllic site of West Grinstead station. Here the two platforms, station nameboard and a latticework signal have survived, while a marooned BR Mk 1 coach adds railway atmosphere to a picnic site and the nearby small car park. Immediately to the west of the station site is a large restaurant and pub.

Heading south from West Grinstead the path makes use of old railway bridges to dive under the A272 and over the B2135, passing through Partridge Green and crossing the River Adur north of Henfield – both villages' station buildings have long since been demolished. A refreshment stop at one of Henfield's several pubs is highly recommended before embarking on the next 3¾-mile isolated section, which crosses the Adur again before reaching Steyning. Here the station site has long disappeared beneath housing development but the attractive town is at least more peaceful following the building of a bypass along the railway trackbed to the east. Following a diversion through the town, the Downs Link regains the trackbed close to the site of the cement works at Beeding before ending its journey along the east bank of the River Adur and diving under the A27 dual carriageway to enter Shoreham-by-Sea.

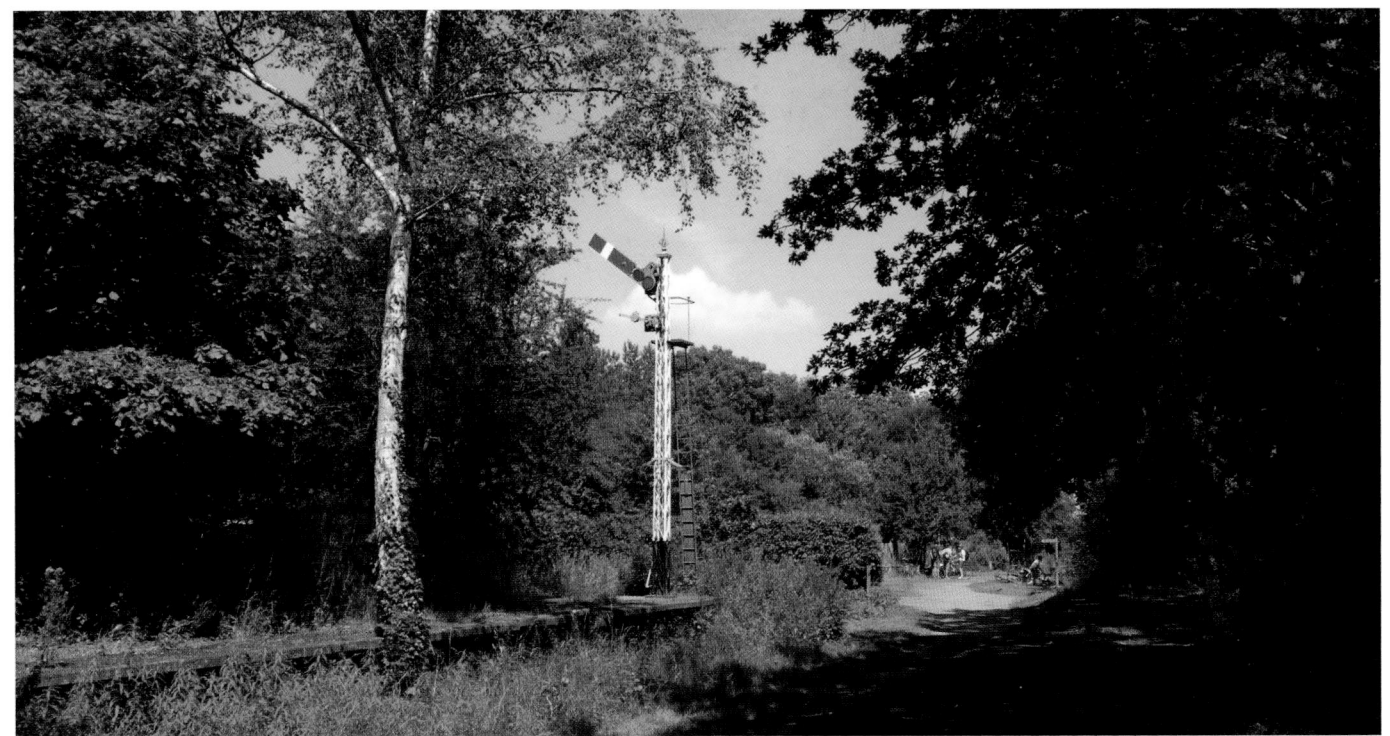

A train is due to arrive and all that is missing at West Grinstead station is the track. This idyllic spot features a picnic site, both platforms, a road overbridge, home signal and a BR Mk 1 coach standing on an isolated piece of track.

Watched by a few stalwarts from the coal yard and allotment, a Locomotive Club of Great Britain railtour prepares to leave from Partridge Green station behind 'N' Class 2-6-0 No. 31866 on a wet and windy 5 December 1965. The locomotive was withdrawn a month later while the line from Christ's Hospital to Shoreham closed two months after that.

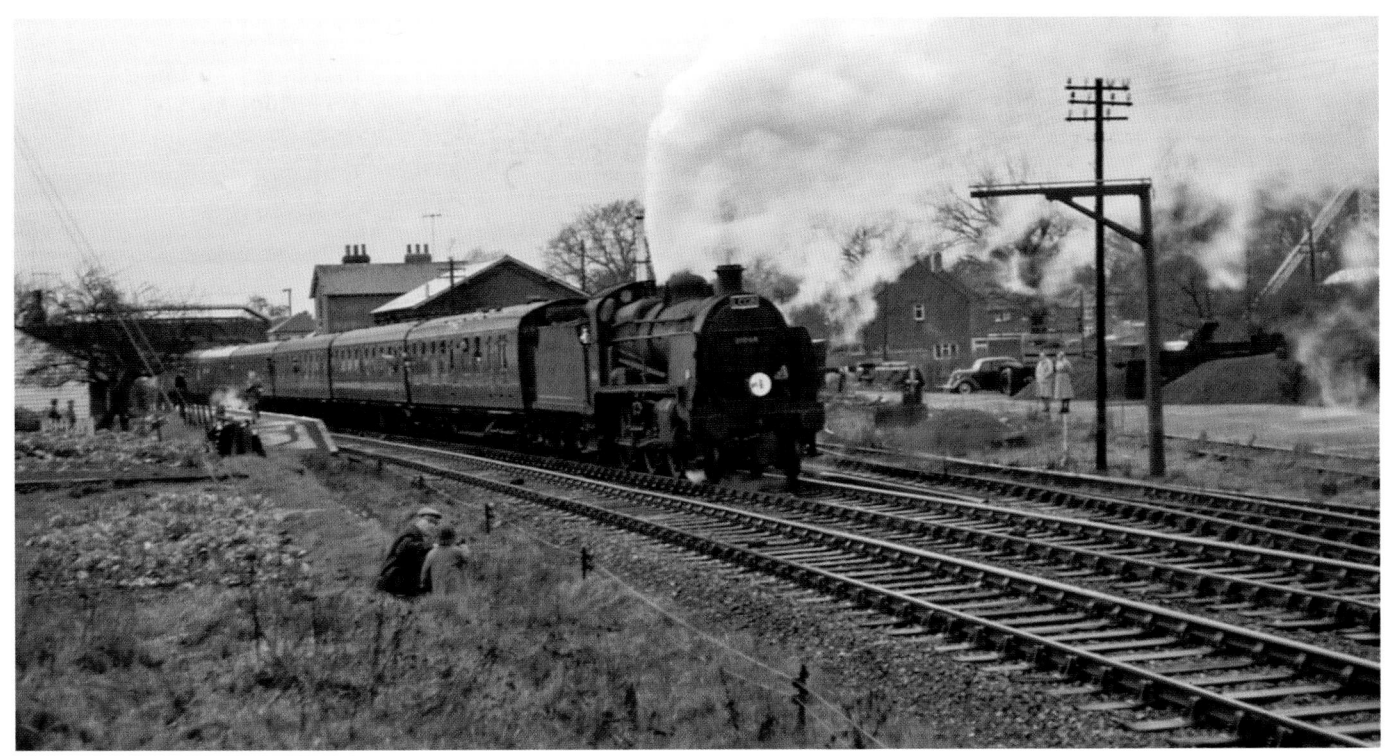

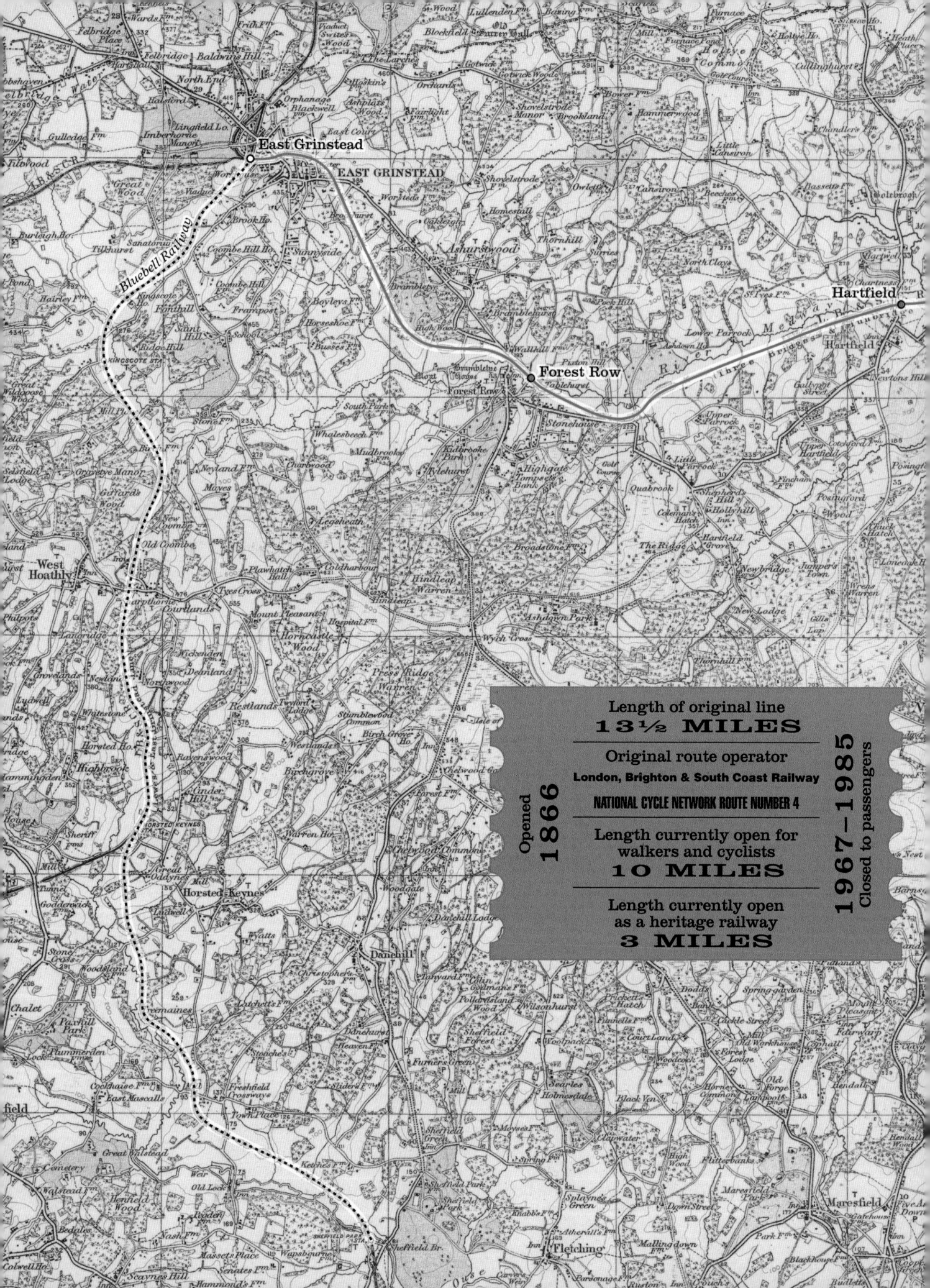

East Grinstead

EAST GRINSTEAD

Bluebell Railway

LB&SCR

Forest Row

Hartfield

Hartfield

West Hoathly

Horsted Keynes

Danehill

Opened
1866

1967–1985
Closed to passengers

Length of original line
13½ MILES

Original route operator
London, Brighton & South Coast Railway

NATIONAL CYCLE NETWORK ROUTE NUMBER 4

Length currently open for
walkers and cyclists
10 MILES

Length currently open
as a heritage railway
3 MILES

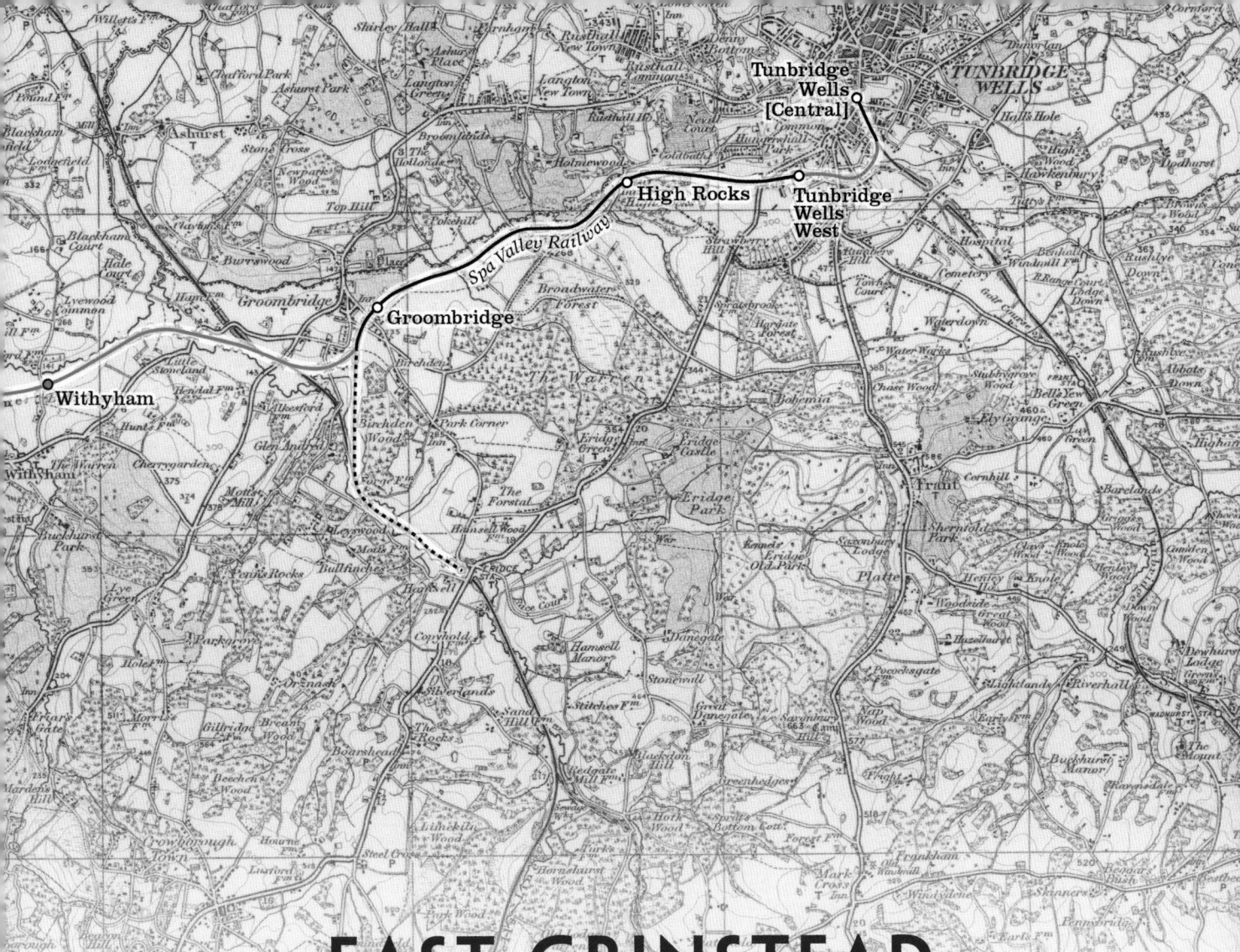

EAST GRINSTEAD
TO
TUNBRIDGE WELLS

FOREST WAY

Linking two wealthy towns through the tranquil Wealden countryside, this quintessentially English rural railway led a very quiet existence for just over 100 years. Despite its proximity to the home of Dr Beeching, the line closed between East Grinstead and Groombridge in 1967, while the remainder stayed open for trains to and from Eridge until 1985. Since closure the East Grinstead to Groombridge section has been reopened as a footpath and cycleway known as the Forest Way, while the Spa Valley Railway has reopened the rest.

With the Greenwich Meridian running through its centre, the wealthy market town of East Grinstead witnessed the arrival of its first railway in 1855, when the East Grinstead Railway opened a 6¾-mile single-track branch line from Three Bridges, on the London to Brighton main line. The London, Brighton & South Coast Railway (LB&SCR) worked it from the outset and took it over in 1865.

Meanwhile the East Grinstead, Groombridge & Tunbridge Wells Railway (EGG&TWR) had been authorized in 1862 to build a 13½-mile line through the peaceful Wealden countryside, linking the three towns. Running powers were obtained over the Brighton, Uckfield & Tunbridge Wells Railway (BU&TWR) between Groombridge and Tunbridge Wells, which was in the course of construction. With intermediate stations at Forest Row, Hartfield, Withyham and Groombridge, the EGG&TWR was the first to open in 1866, with the BU&TWR joining it from the south at Groombridge two years later. Meanwhile both companies had been absorbed by the LB&SCR in 1865.

To facilitate through working between Three Bridges and Tunbridge Wells a new station had also been opened at East Grinstead in 1866, but this had to be resited once again when the railways from Oxted in the north and Lewes in the south were opened to East Grinstead in 1883. The two lines were at a lower level so the new station on the Three Bridges to Tunbridge Wells line was renamed High Level. The LB&SCR station at Tunbridge Wells, later named Tunbridge Wells West, was linked to the town's South Eastern Railway's station via a short tunnel in 1876.

Apart from commuter traffic running between London and Forest Row (in later years the home of Dr Beeching), passenger traffic on the East Grinstead to Tunbridge Wells line was light and only warranted a steam-hauled push-pull service. By the 1950s traffic had declined to such an extent that British Railways was seriously considering closure of the line. This threat passed temporarily but East Grinstead still lost its railway link from Lewes in 1958 (it has since reopened northwards from Sheffield Park as the Bluebell Railway). Despite the introduction of diesel-electric multiple units along the route, the 1963 'Beeching Report' was the final nail in the coffin for the Three Bridges to Tunbridge Wells line, which was listed for closure along with the connection from Eridge, on the Uckfield line, to Groombridge. Despite strong local objections following this announcement, the line between Three Bridges, East Grinstead (High Level) and Groombridge closed on 2 January 1967.

The link to Tunbridge Wells West from Eridge via Groombridge remained open for many more years until it, too, closed on 8 July 1985. It was reopened in 2011 as a heritage railway known as the Spa Valley Railway (for details visit www.spavalleyrailway.co.uk).

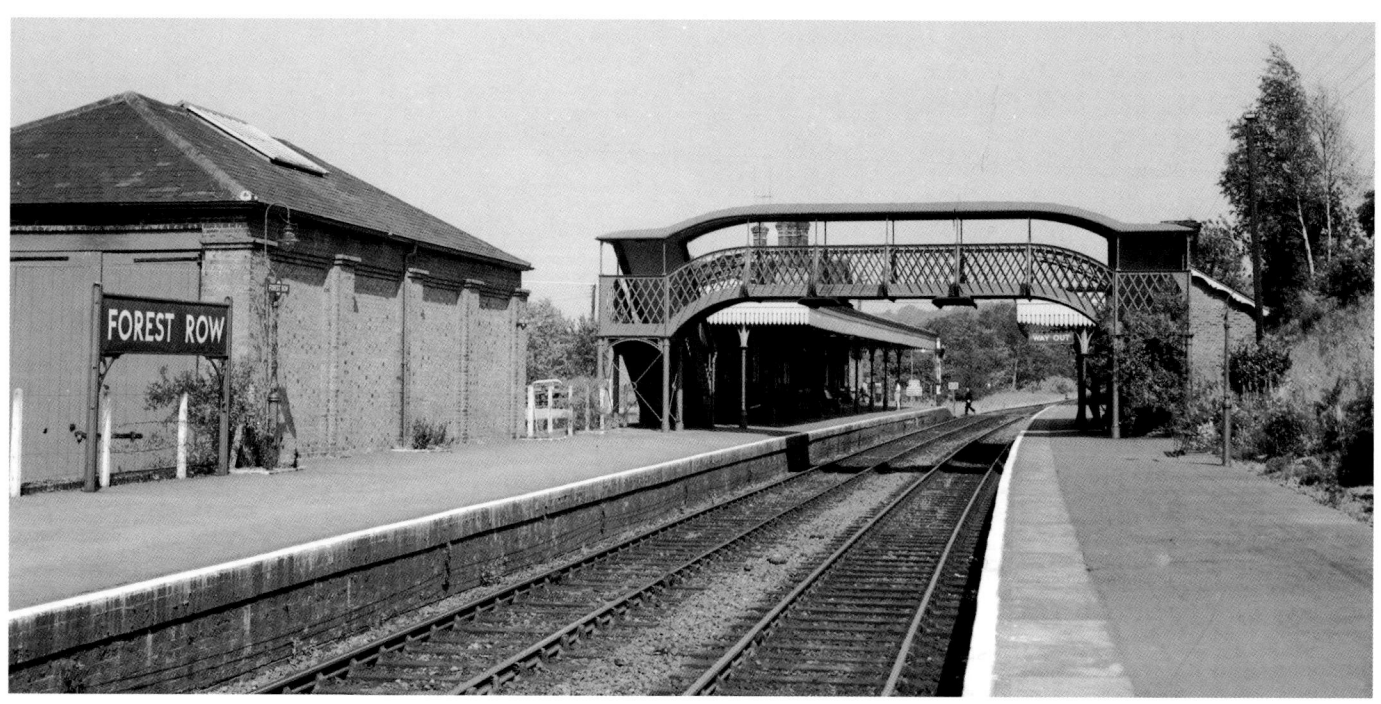

By 1970 all the track between Three Bridges and Groombridge had been lifted. The section to the west of East Grinstead was reopened in 1979 as a footpath and cycleway known as the Worth Way, while to the east much of it has since been reopened by East Sussex County Council as a 10-mile footpath and cycleway to Groombridge, known as the Forest Way. Set in the High Weald Area of Outstanding Natural Beauty, the route skirts Ashdown Forest, providing an important habitat for wildlife along its green corridor, and has formed part of National Cycle Network Route 21 since 2002.

The Forest Way starts at Herontye Drive in East Grinstead, just off the busy A22 in the southeastern corner of the town, and heads off through open countryside towards Forest Row. Here an old railway platform and goods shed are now part of an unsightly industrial estate and waste-recycling centre. There is also a large car park and refreshments can be taken at the Riverview Café, which was once the local coal merchant's office served by the railway.

Heading eastwards from Forest Row along the valley of the River Medway, the tree-lined route enters Hartfield station under an attractive stone overbridge. Now used as a playschool, the front of the station (complete with SR green nameboard) has changed little since closure but the rear of the building is screened off alongside a short diversion of the path. Beyond the station the former goods shed is barely recognizable in its new guise as a private residence. Refreshments can be taken at the attractive Anchor Inn in the nearby village, which was once home to A. A. Milne, the creator of Winnie the Pooh. His house was later acquired by the one of the Rolling Stones' founders, Brian Jones, who was found dead in his swimming pool in 1969.

Following the lush Medway Valley eastwards from Hartfield, the Forest Way soon arrives at Withyham station – now a private residence well-screened from walkers and cyclists – before continuing eastwards to meet the Oxted to Uckfield railway, which it parallels for a short distance before ending in Groombridge. Refreshments can be taken at the appropriately named Junction Inn or at the nearby station café. The rest of the journey from this picturesque village to Tunbridge Wells can now be taken on the Spa Valley Railway, which operates heritage trains to and from Eridge on weekends, bank holidays and selected days between April and October.

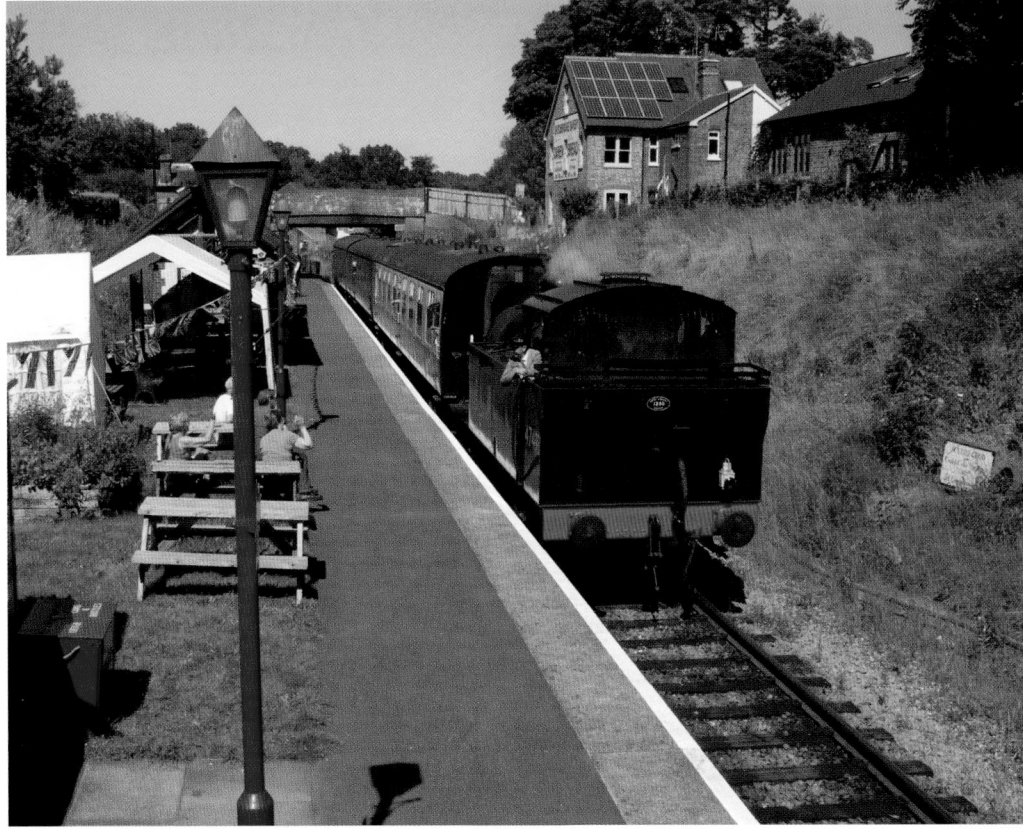

Saved from the scrapyard, visiting ex-LMS 'Jinty' 0-6-0T No. 47493 calls at Groombridge station with a Tunbridge Wells West to Eridge train. This stretch of line remained in use until closure in 1985 and has since been reopened as the Spa Valley Railway.

LEFT: The near-deserted station of Forest Row is seen here on 15 June 1959. Little now remains of this station although the trackbed forms the Forest Way footpath and cycleway.

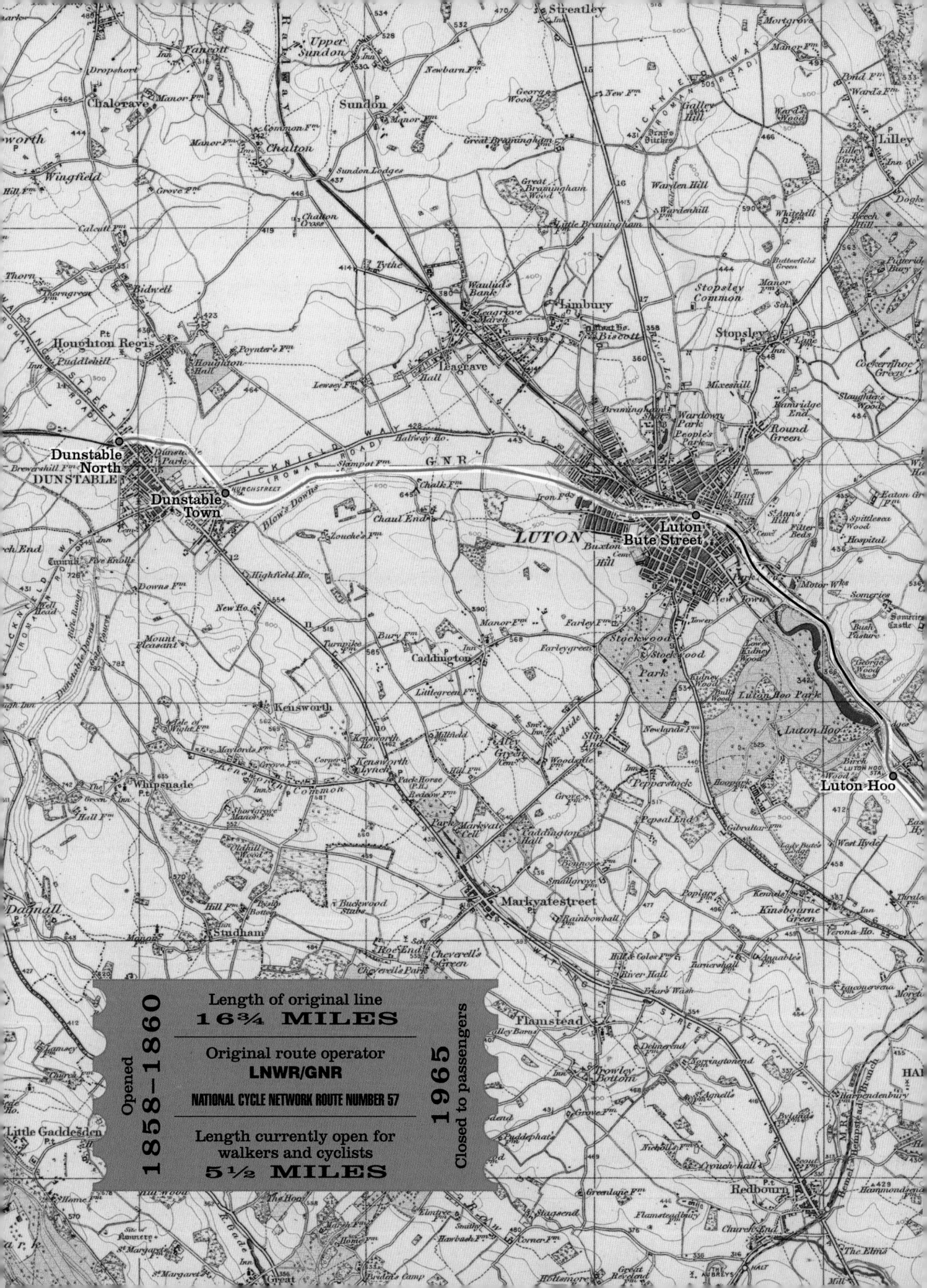

Length of original line
16¾ MILES

Original route operator
LNWR/GNR

NATIONAL CYCLE NETWORK ROUTE NUMBER 57

Length currently open for
walkers and cyclists
5½ MILES

Opened **1858–1860**

1965 Closed to passengers

WELWYN
TO
DUNSTABLE

For its first eight years, this rural railway provided the growing town of Luton with its only link to the outside world. Its importance declined following the opening of the Midland Railway's main line through the town but it was kept alive by trainloads of gravel destined for London and rubbish for landfill in the opposite direction – even elephant dung from London Zoo was carried! Once frequented by the writer George Bernard Shaw who lived at Ayot St Lawrence, the line became a victim of the 'Beeching Report', losing its passenger service in 1965, although sections of it remained open for freight traffic until 1989. Two separate sections have since been reopened as footpaths and cycleways.

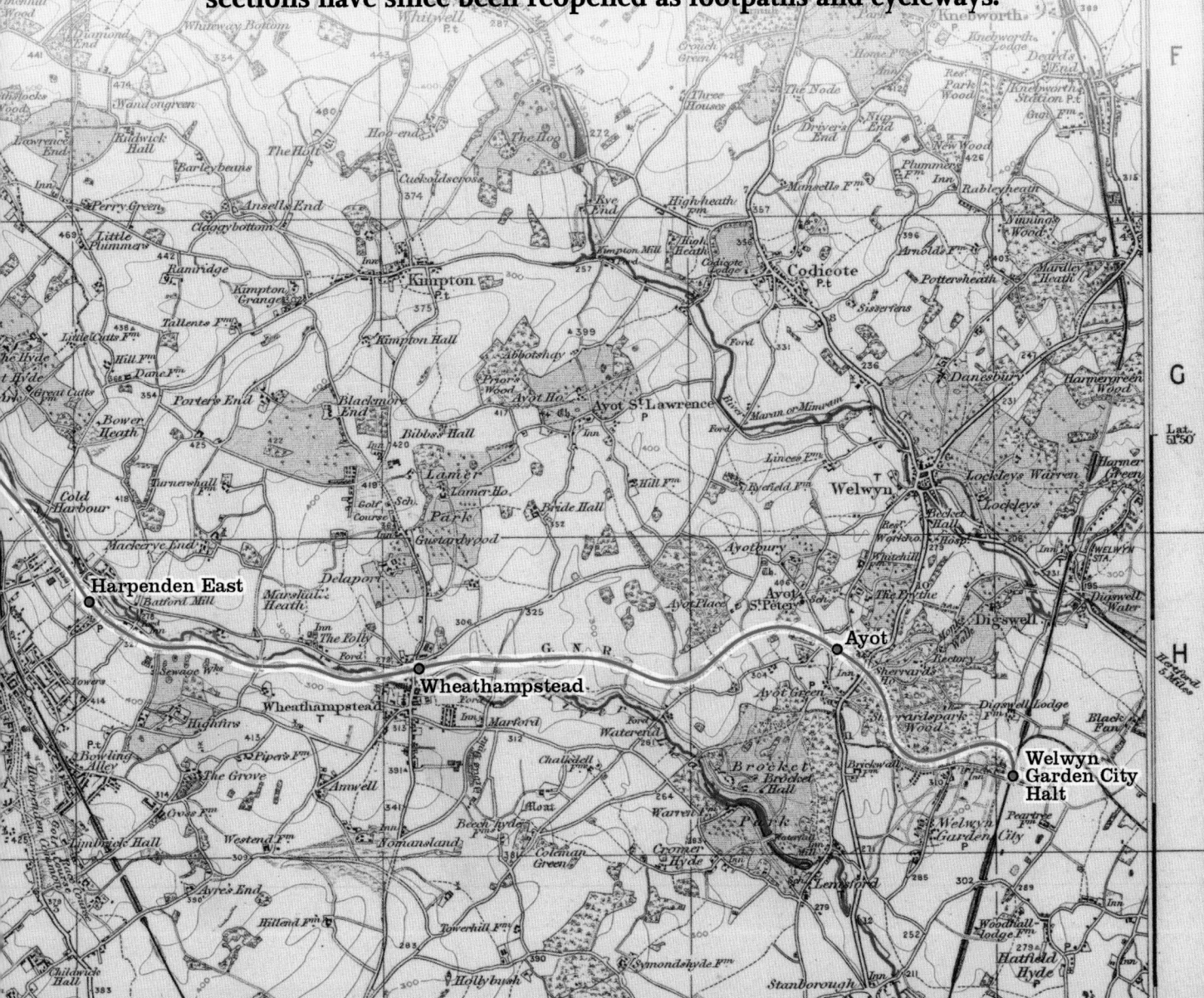

By the mid-nineteenth century the townsfolk and businessmen of Luton were clamouring for their own railway. With a population of over 11,000 and important industries such as hat making, the town was by far the largest in Bedfordshire with no railway connection. To make matters worse the neighbouring town of Dunstable, five miles to the west, had got its own branch line from Leighton Buzzard as early as 1848. To the east, the Great Northern Railway had opened from King's Cross to Doncaster in 1852 and it was from Welwyn Junction, north of Hatfield, that the Luton, Dunstable & Welwyn Junction Railway (LD&WJR) was authorized in 1855 to build its 16¾-mile railway. Strangely, construction began in Dunstable, where the new railway's station in Church Street was linked to the London & North Western Railway's (LNWR) station at the end of the branch from Leighton Buzzard. The 5-mile double-track section from Dunstable to Luton opened in 1858 but was worked by the LNWR until 1860 when the rest of the single-track line opened eastwards through Wheathampstead to Welwyn. From the opening day on 1 September the whole branch line was worked by the GNR.

Meanwhile the LD&WJR had amalgamated with the Hertford & Welwyn Junction Railway in 1858 to form the Hertford, Luton & Dunstable Railway – the latter was absorbed by the GNR in 1861 and the branch lines from Dunstable and Hertford were extended to run parallel to the main line between Welwyn and Hatfield.

Competition for traffic between Luton and London heated up in 1868 when the Midland Railway opened its main line between St Pancras and Bedford. Luton soon became a boom town, with major engineering companies such as

Vauxhall setting up new factories and replacing the hat-making industry as the town's main employers. The GNR branch to Welwyn and Hatfield, with its massive goods warehouse at Luton Bute Street, was kept busy with coal, and agricultural and livestock traffic. This was supplemented in 1900 by trainloads of gravel that were transported from pits at Blackbridge, just north of Wheathampstead, to London and by the 1920s these trains were bringing back landfill waste from the capital. Even elephant dung from London Zoo was carried by rail to Wheathampstead station to help grow lettuces! During the inter-war years the village of Wheathampstead became a popular destination for Londoners wishing to spend a weekend playing golf or fishing. The station's most famous customer was George Bernard Shaw, who would cycle from his home in nearby Ayot St Lawrence to travel by train to London – a poor timekeeper, Shaw often made the train late as it was held back for him. Ayot station was destroyed in a fire in 1948 and never rebuilt.

Increasing road competition in the 1950s saw a decline in traffic on the railway and it was listed for closure in the 1963 'Beeching Report'. To cut running costs diesel multiple units had already been introduced in 1962 and, while the Leighton Buzzard to Dunstable branch was closed to passengers in the same year, the Dunstable to Hatfield line soldiered on until 1965, with 6 January scheduled as the closure date. This was postponed following objections but the inevitable came on 26 April when passenger services were finally withdrawn. Landfill waste trains continued to serve the section from Hatfield to Blackbridge Sidings until 1971 while oil traffic continued between Luton and Dunstable until 1989, when that section of the line was mothballed.

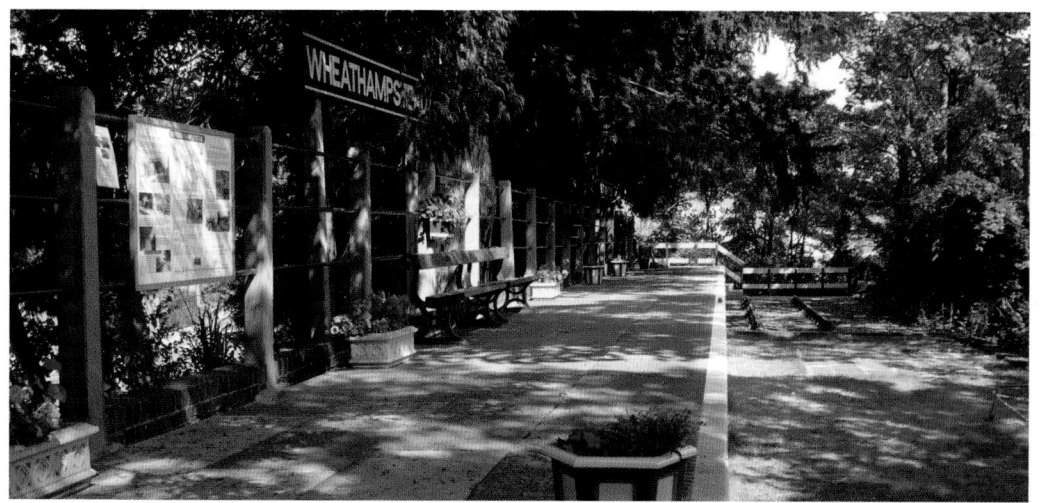

The hidden station site at Wheathampstead has recently been restored by local volunteers. Once frequented by George Bernard Shaw on his trips to London, this delightful spot features the restored platform complete with nameboard, seats and birdfeeders.

Since complete closure, much of the trackbed of the Welwyn to Dunstable line has had a new lease of life. While the formerly mothballed section between Dunstable and Luton is reopening as a concrete guided busway, two other sections have been reopened as footpaths and cycleways. To the east the three-mile Ayot Greenway (part of National Cycle Network Route 57) follows the pleasant tree-lined route of the railway from Ayot St Peter, west of Welwyn Garden City, to Wheathampstead. Here, the tranquil wooded station site has miraculously been restored by local volunteers with the platform, station name board, seats and bird feeders making it a pleasant spot from which to contemplate one of Britain's lost railways. Immediately to the west of the station the bridge over the road and the station master's house have long since been demolished to make way for road improvements – however, 'Station Road' still exists in name!

The shorter section from Harpenden East to Luton Hoo now forms part of the 50-mile Lea Valley Walk, which runs from the source of the River Lea near Luton to the Thames at Limehouse. A new bridge has replaced the old railway bridge to carry the Walk over the busy B653, while Luton Hoo station and platform still survive as a private residence.

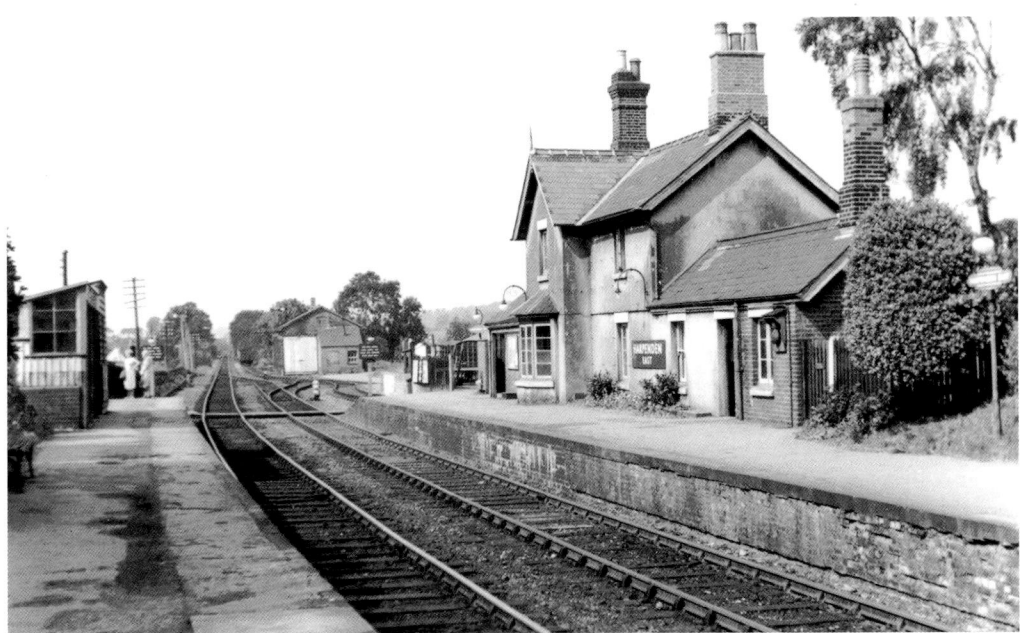

A couple of ladies chat at Harpenden East station while they wait for the next train to Luton and Dunstable on 5 September 1959. The station has been demolished to make way for housing but in its heyday was kept busy handling livestock, agricultural produce, coal, coke and even elephant manure from London Zoo.

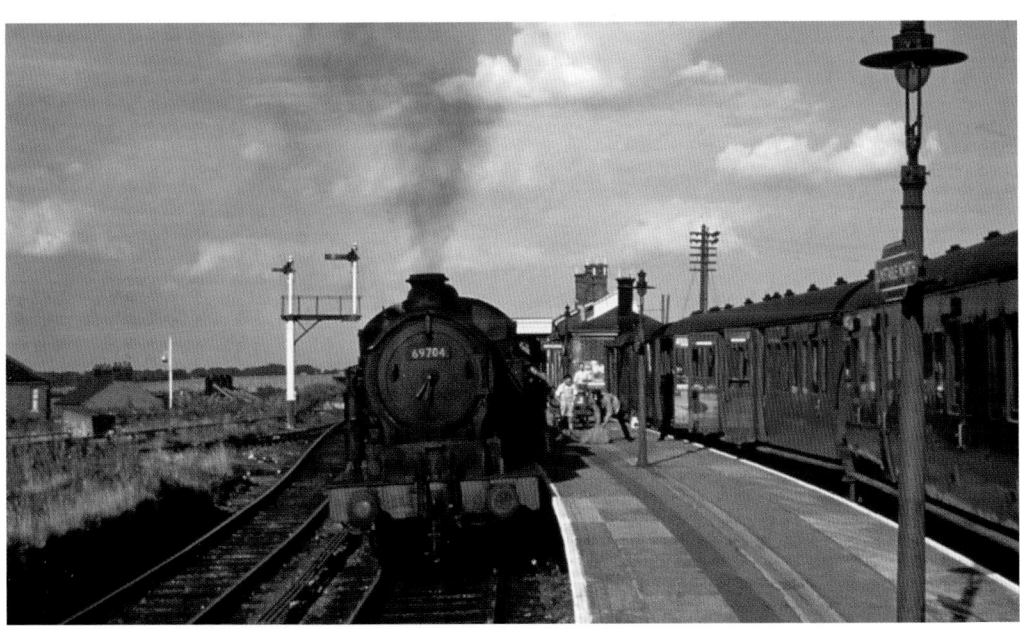

Ex-LNER Class 'N7/3' 0-6-2T No. 69704 has just arrived at Dunstable North station with a train from Hatfield in July 1959. The passengers and mail bags are transferring across the platform for the branch train to Leighton Buzzard.

HARPENDEN
TO
HEMEL HEMPSTEAD

NICKY LINE

Suffering from a lack of through traffic due to a few 'local difficulties' at Hemel Hempstead, this single-track branch line was never a financial success and lost its passenger service during a period of coal shortage in 1947. Despite this, the line continued to be used by a manufacturer of building blocks until complete closure in 1979. The route was purchased by two local councils in the 1980s and has since reopened as a footpath and cycleway known as the 'Nicky Line'.

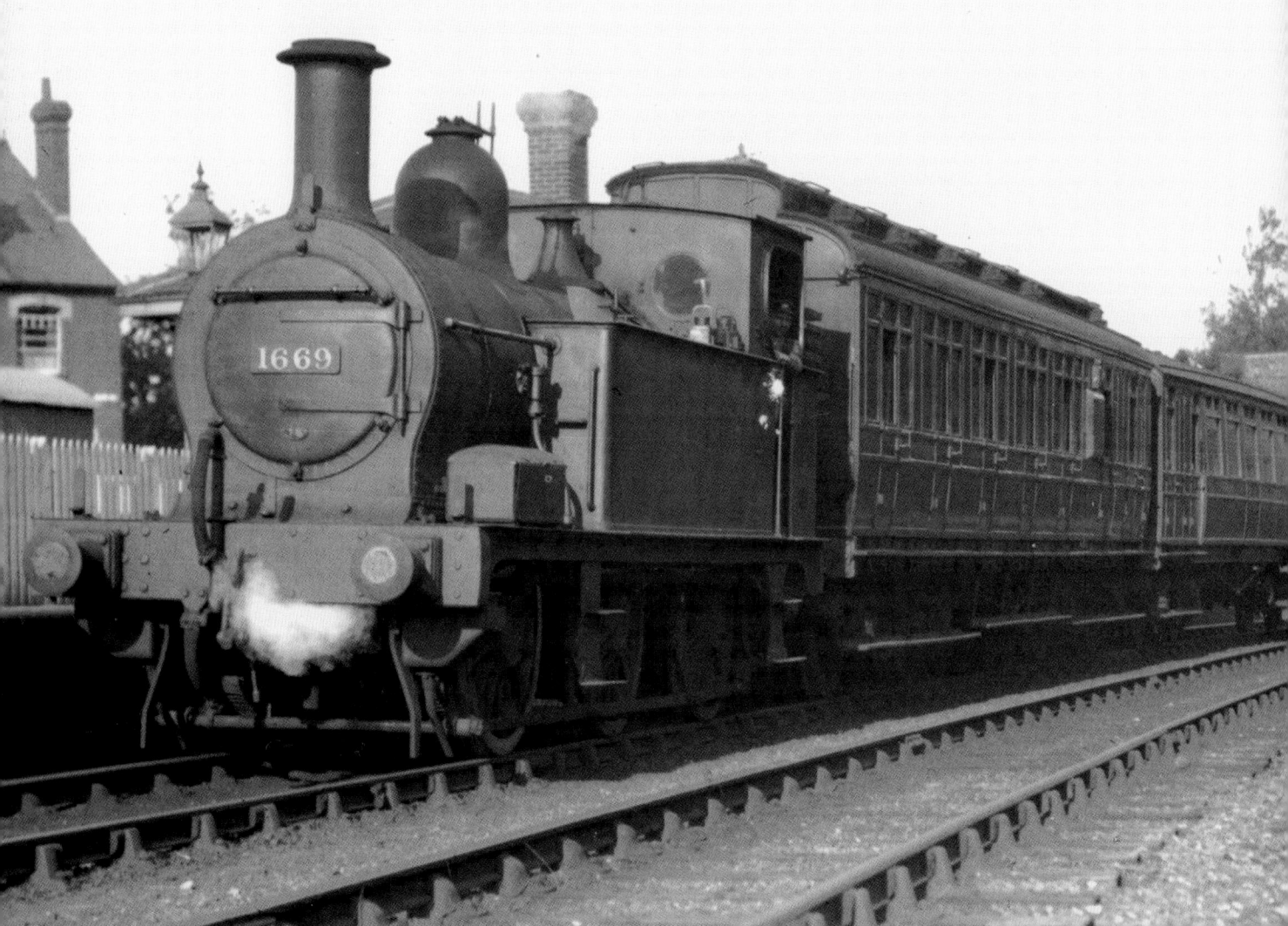

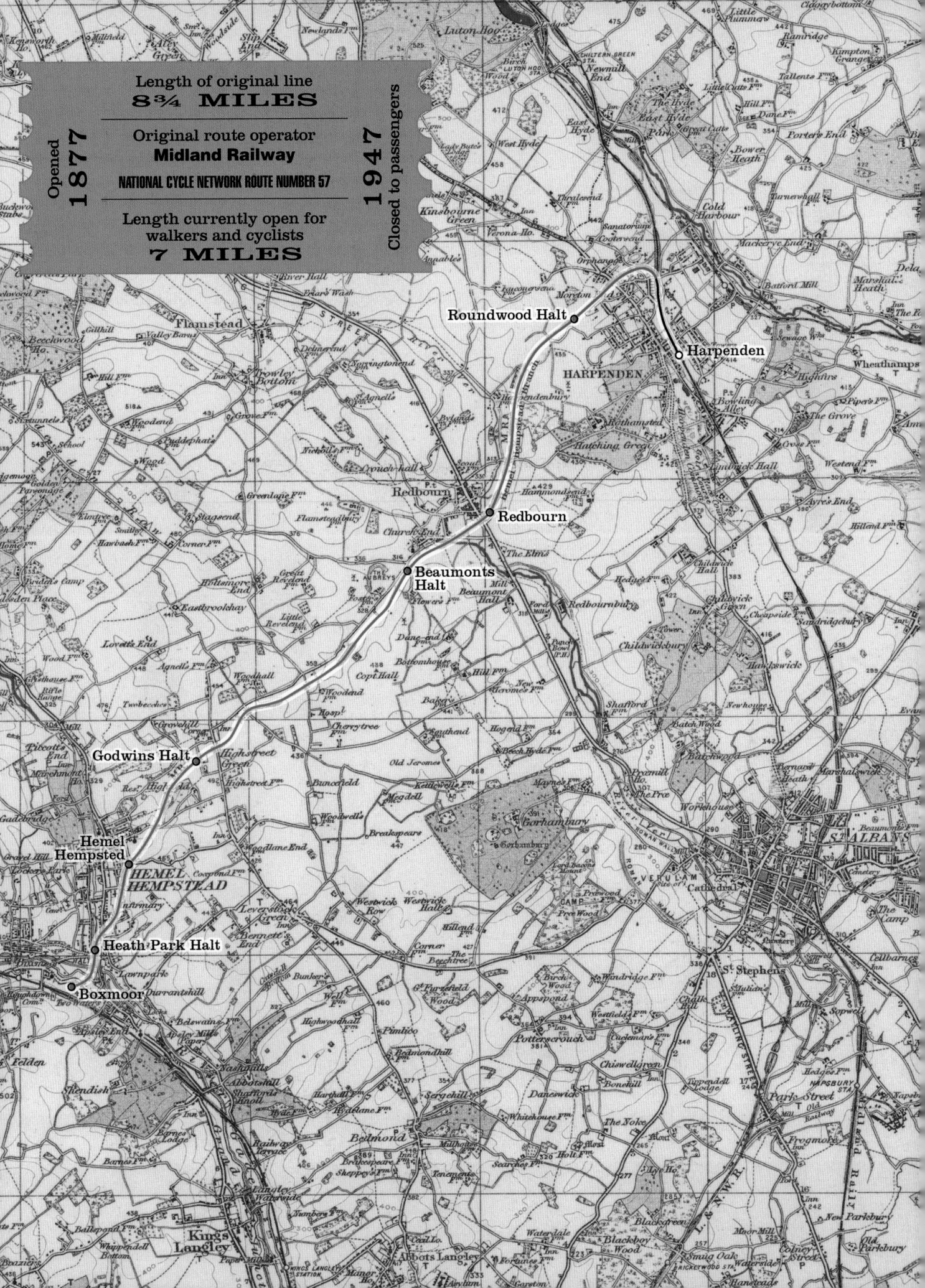

Length of original line
8¾ MILES

Original route operator
Midland Railway

NATIONAL CYCLE NETWORK ROUTE NUMBER 57

Length currently open for
walkers and cyclists
7 MILES

Opened **1877**

Closed to passengers **1947**

Roundwood Halt

Harpenden

Redbourn

Beaumonts Halt

Godwins Halt

Hemel Hempsted

Heath Park Halt

Boxmoor

When the London & Birmingham Railway opened in 1837 its route took it some distance from the town of Hemel Hempstead on the opposite side of the Grand Union Canal and the River Gade. A station was provided at Boxmoor and named 'Boxmoor & Hemel Hempstead'.

Pressure grew from Hemel's residents and businessmen for a rail link into their town and in 1863 the Hemel Hempstead Railway Company was formed to build a short branch line from Boxmoor to the town. The scheme foundered due to obstruction from local landowners and financial problems but in 1866 a proposal to extend the line eastwards from Hemel through Redbourn to Harpenden finally saw the light of day and construction of the line began. Progress was very slow with the first section from Boxmoor to Hemel taking five years to build, by which time the company had again run into financial difficulties.

Enter the Midland Railway (MR), which had already opened its main line through Harpenden and Luton in 1868 and was keen to see the connection from Hemel Hempstead completed. The MR financed the completion of the line and agreed to work it from its opening on 16 July 1877, absorbing it in 1886. However passenger trains ran only between the new MR station in Hemel and Chiltern Green north of Harpenden – the physical link between Boxmoor and Hemel was a white elephant due to restrictions placed on the connection by the rival London & North Western

Railway (LNWR). In effect the MR route was just a branch line and suffered from the lack of through traffic. To compete with the LNWR's new bus service from Boxmoor station to Hemel the MR opened a new western terminus at Heath Park Halt in 1906 – this remained the furthest extent of passenger services in Hemel until closure.

During its early years the railway benefitted from its direct link with the town of Luton via Chiltern Green station on the MR main line – straw plait made in Hemel was quickly transported to the hatters in Luton. By 1886 this trade had dwindled and the west-north connection to the MR main line was replaced by a west-south connection allowing trains to run into Harpenden.

Traffic was never heavy on the 8¾-mile single-track line and in order to reduce operating costs the London Midland & Scottish Railway (successor to the MR) experimented in 1932 with a road-rail vehicle known as a Ro-Railer. Built by Karrier, this was a single-deck bus that also had raisable flanged wheels allowing it to run on both railway tracks and roads. After test runs on the Hemel branch it went on to be used for a short while between Blisworth and Stratford-upon-Avon but it was not successful and was soon withdrawn.

The Hemel branch struggled on through the Second World War only to see its passenger service temporarily suspended on 16 June 1947 due to the national coal

PREVIOUS SPREAD: Ex-MR 0-6-0T No. 1669 has just arrived at Hemel Hempstead station with the 1.58pm train from Harpenden on 19 October 1929. Passenger services along the 'Nicky Line' ceased in 1947 following a supposedly temporary suspension because of national coal shortages.

BELOW: Seen here just before closure to passengers in 1947, tiny Roundwood Halt was located on the western outskirts of Harpenden. The concrete platform and distant signal still survive today alongside the 'Nicky Line' footpath and cycleway, which heads off through a long tunnel of trees that have grown up since the line's complete closure in 1979.

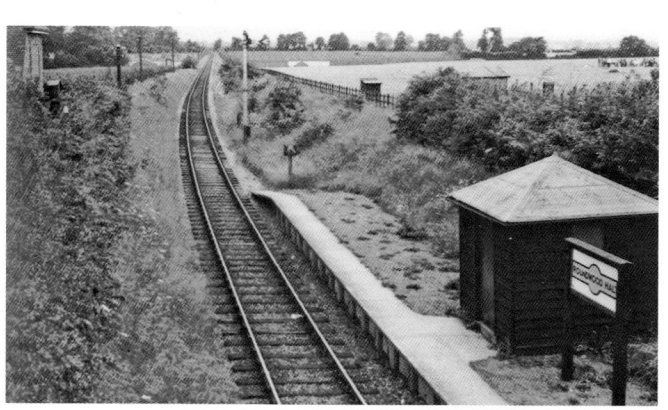

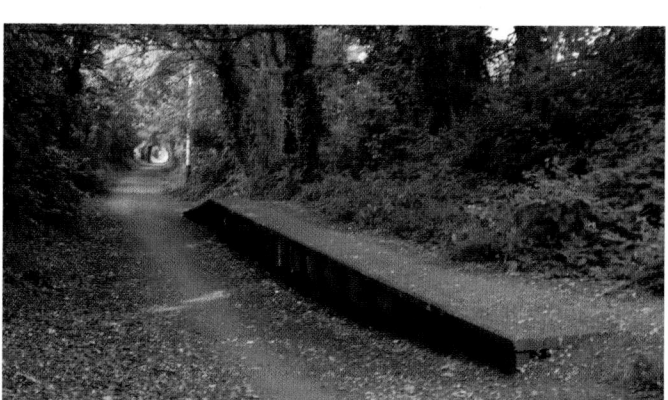

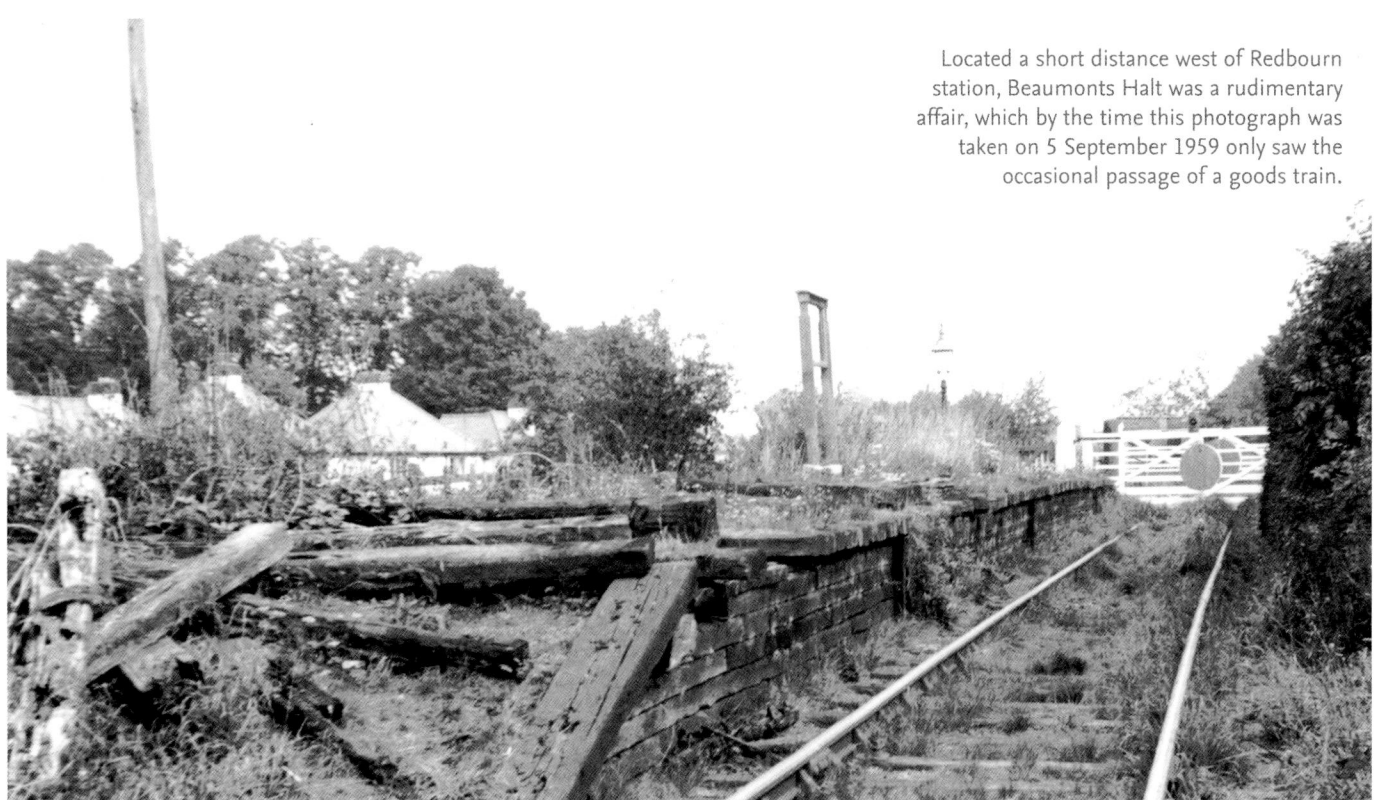

Located a short distance west of Redbourn station, Beaumonts Halt was a rudimentary affair, which by the time this photograph was taken on 5 September 1959 only saw the occasional passage of a goods train.

shortage. As it turned out this became a permanent closure although coal trains continued to supply the local gasworks at Hemel until 1959. The dormant line was sold to the Hemelite Company in 1968 and was used to transport residual ash and clinker from power stations to their yard at Cupid Green for use in the manufacture of building blocks. This traffic ceased in 1979 when the connection with the main line at Harpenden was severed and the line closed completely.

††††††††††††††††††

With some foresight, St Albans District Council and Dacorum Borough Council purchased much of the railway's route in the 1980s. The once little-used section west of Hemel to Boxmoor has long-since disappeared beneath road improvements and housing and industrial development – the viaduct carrying the railway over the Gade Valley was demolished in 1960. The remaining seven miles of the trackbed was reopened as the Nicky Line footpath and cycleway in 1985. The railway had been nicknamed the Nicky Line for years but its origins have since been lost in the mists of time.

The route can be joined alongside the St Pancras to Nottingham main line north of Harpenden station.

Heading in a southwesterly direction it soon crosses the busy A1081 on an impressive brick viaduct before reaching the site of Roundwood Halt where part of the concrete platform and a distant signal have miraculously survived. Here there is level access to the route from local roads.

Leaving the suburbs of Harpenden behind, the Nicky Line heads towards the village of Redbourn through what is now a verdant tunnel (as is common with many old railway routes, the lineside vegetation along here has grown considerably since closure). Although Redbourn station and platforms have long been demolished the site is now a picnic area. Immediately west of the Redbourn station site the route passes over Watling Street on the original 1870s wrought-iron bridge. It soon burrows under the ugly concrete structure of the M1 motorway before reaching the northwest suburbs of Hemel Hempstead at Cupid Green, once the site of the railway-connected building-block factory. The Nicky Line continues its journey through the built-up suburbs of Hemel before ending close to the Midland Hotel. Opposite the hotel once stood the MR station, which was demolished in the late 1960s to make way for a block of flats. Curiously, both the MR and its successor the LMS insisted on spelling the station's name on signs, tickets and timetables as 'Hemel Hempsted'.

BOURNE END
TO
HIGH WYCOMBE

Originally opened as a part of a broad-gauge through route between Maidenhead and Oxford, the Bourne End to High Wycombe line lost this traffic when the more direct GWR/GCR Joint Railway opened in 1906. Despite this loss it was well patronized by local residents and carried considerable amounts of freight traffic to and from local paper mills until after the Second World War. Despite not being listed for closure in the 'Beeching Report', the line fell on hard times in the late 1960s and closed in 1970. While the Maidenhead-Bourne End-Marlow lines remain open, a short section of the closed High Wycombe line from Bourne End is now a footpath and cycleway.

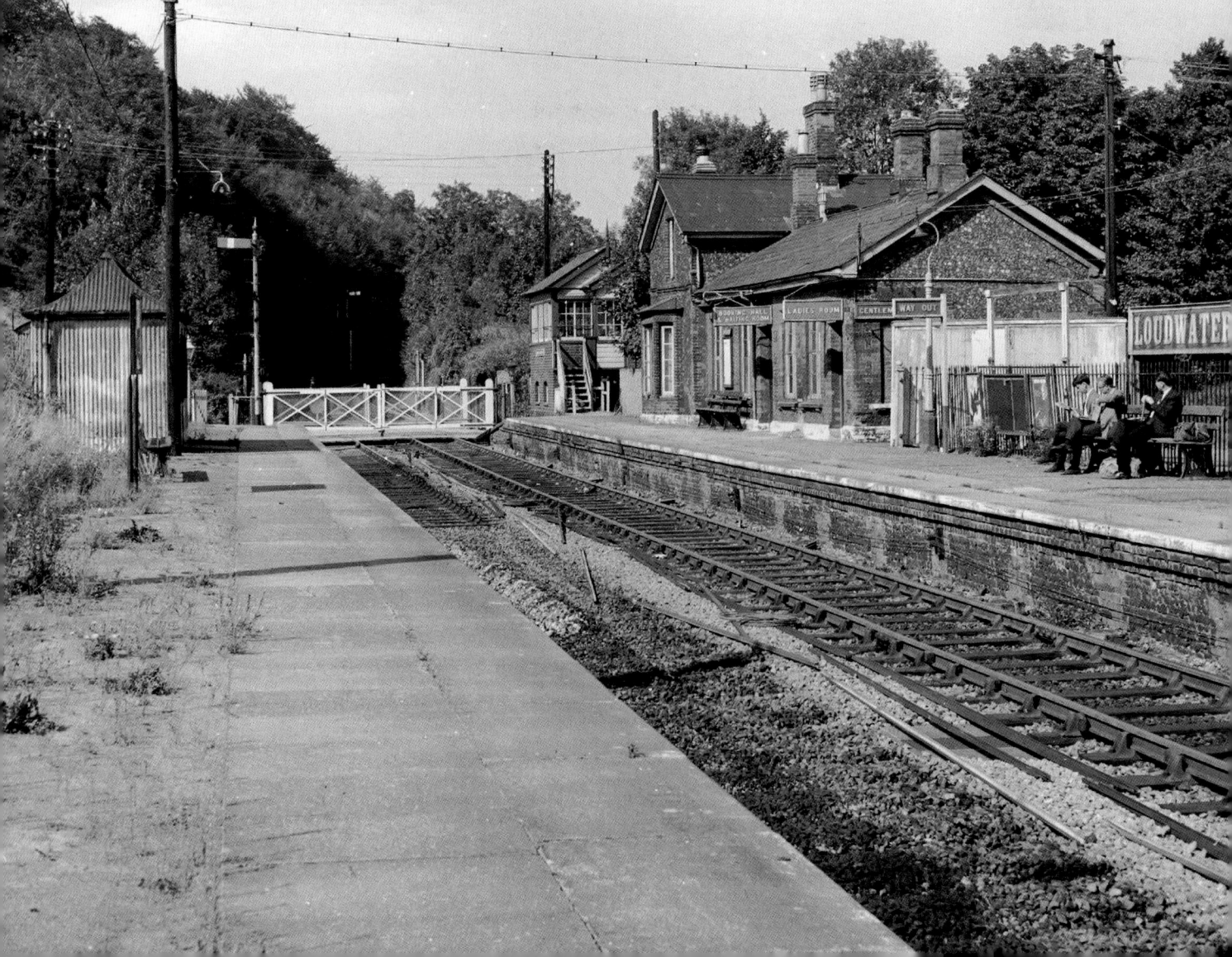

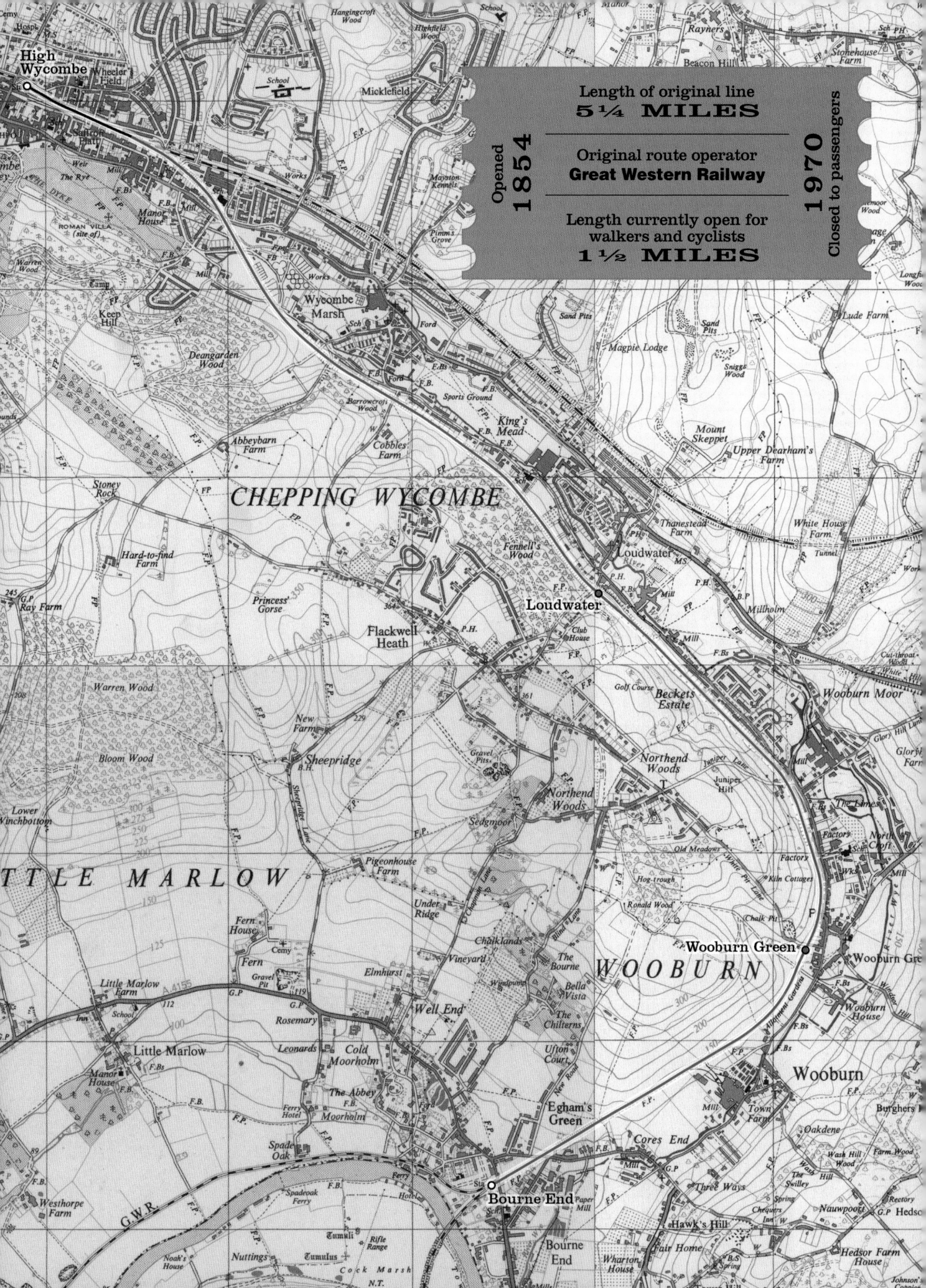

High Wycombe

Length of original line
5 ¼ MILES

Opened
1854

Original route operator
Great Western Railway

1970
Closed to passengers

Length currently open for
walkers and cyclists
1 ½ MILES

CHEPPING WYCOMBE

Loudwater

LITTLE MARLOW

WOOBURN

Wooburn Green

Bourne End

As we shall see on page 100, the Wycombe Railway began operating when it opened a single-line broad-gauge railway from Maidenhead, on the Great Western Railway's (GWR) Paddington to Bristol main line, to High Wycombe in 1854. The company went on to extend its railway to Princes Risborough and Thame in 1862 and to Oxford in 1864. The GWR worked this line from the outset, allowing its trains an alternative route between Paddington and Oxford. The Wycombe Railway lost its independence in 1867 when it was taken over by the GWR and the entire route was converted to standard gauge in 1870.

Through traffic ended when the more direct Great Western & Great Central Joint Railway opened between Northolt Junction and High Wycombe in 1906. A 2¾-mile branch line was opened by the Great Marlow Railway from Bourne End – originally named Marlow Road (Bourne End) – on the Maidenhead to High Wycombe line, in 1873. The company was taken over by the GWR in 1897.

Despite losing its through traffic, the Maidenhead to High Wycombe line was well used by local people and much freight traffic was generated to and from the giant Soho corn and paper mill near Wooburn Green and other mills along the valley. The 1963 'Beeching Report' brought good news for rail users on the Maidenhead to High Wycombe and Bourne End to Marlow lines as they were not listed for closure, and even the building of the M40 motorway over the railway at Loudwater in the late 1960s failed to disrupt services. However this optimism soon disappeared when the through service between Maidenhead and Aylesbury was withdrawn on 5 May 1969 and the service on the Bourne End to High Wycombe section was considerably reduced. This came under scrutiny again in 1970 when British Railways requested £60,000 from High Wycombe Council to keep the line open. This was all to no avail and despite strong local objections the line closed on 4 May. A determined Passengers' Association fought off a closure threat to the Maidenhead-Bourne End-Marlow line in 1972 – the line is still open today providing a useful service for commuters to and from London.

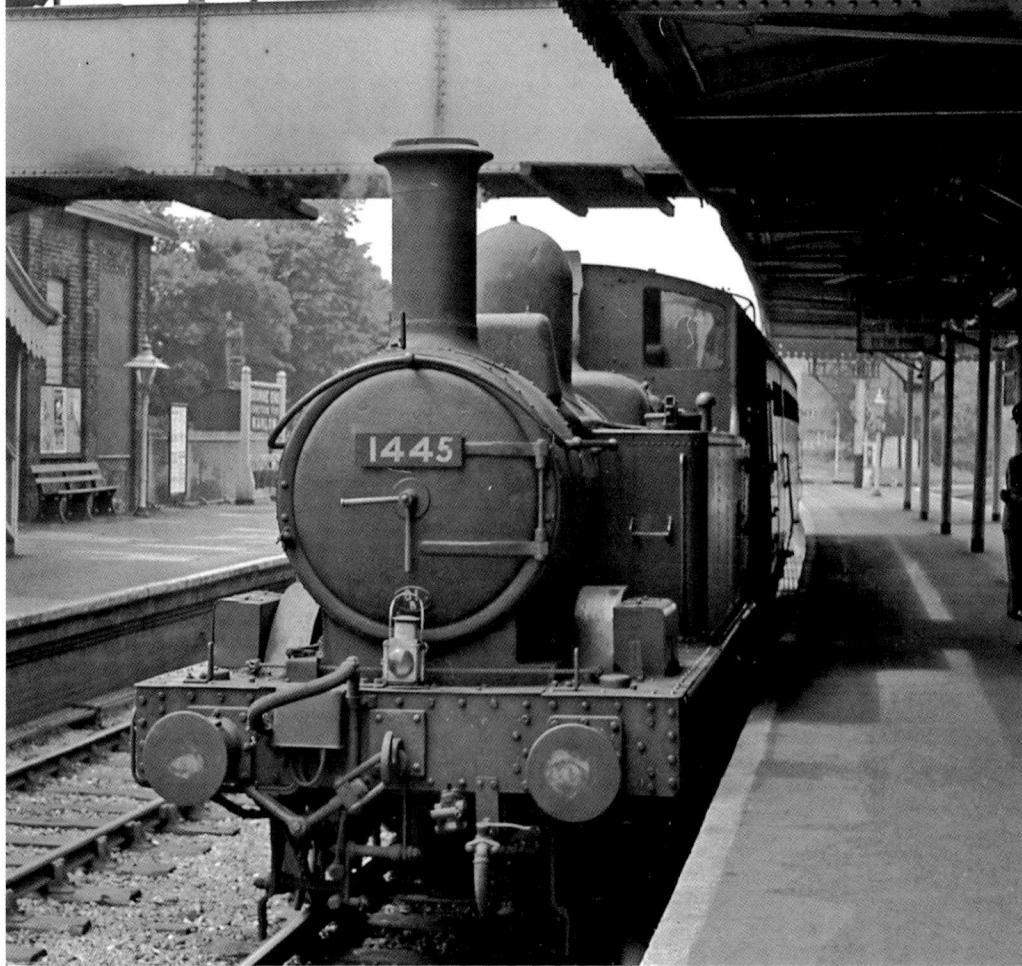

Slough shed's ex-GWR '1400' Class 0-4-2T No. 1445 halts at Bourne End with an auto train for High Wycombe in July 1962. Built at Swindon in 1935, this locomotive was withdrawn from Gloucester Horton Road shed in September 1964.

PREVIOUS SPREAD:
Three intrepid explorers of lost railways sit in the sunshine at Loudwater station as they await the next train to Bourne End and Maidenhead on 17 September 1966. Sadly this wondrous scene was soon to disappear, with the station being demolished shortly after the line's closure in 1970. The site is now an industrial estate.

Arriving by train at the pretty station of Bourne End, the intrepid railway detective can follow the long-closed line to High Wycombe up the valley of the River Wye on foot for a distance of 1½ miles (try a bacon sandwich at the adjacent station café before setting off!). The station at Bourne End was originally named Marlow Road and it is here that trains from Maidenhead reverse direction to reach Marlow.

Often muddy, the tree-lined path starts behind a modern industrial estate across the road from Bourne End station and skirts a housing estate and open countryside for a short distance before ending at Wooburn Green. The station here, as at Loudwater, was demolished soon after closure. Beyond, little remains of the railway route although it can be traced sandwiched between the A4094 and Flackwell Heath Golf Club, where the concrete gate post of a foot crossing survives in the undergrowth. Beyond the M40 several brick-arch bridges survive between Loudwater and High Wycombe, where stretches of the trackbed can be walked. Brunel's original station at High Wycombe is virtually unrecognizable as it is now a tyre and exhaust centre, despite the fact that it is a listed building.

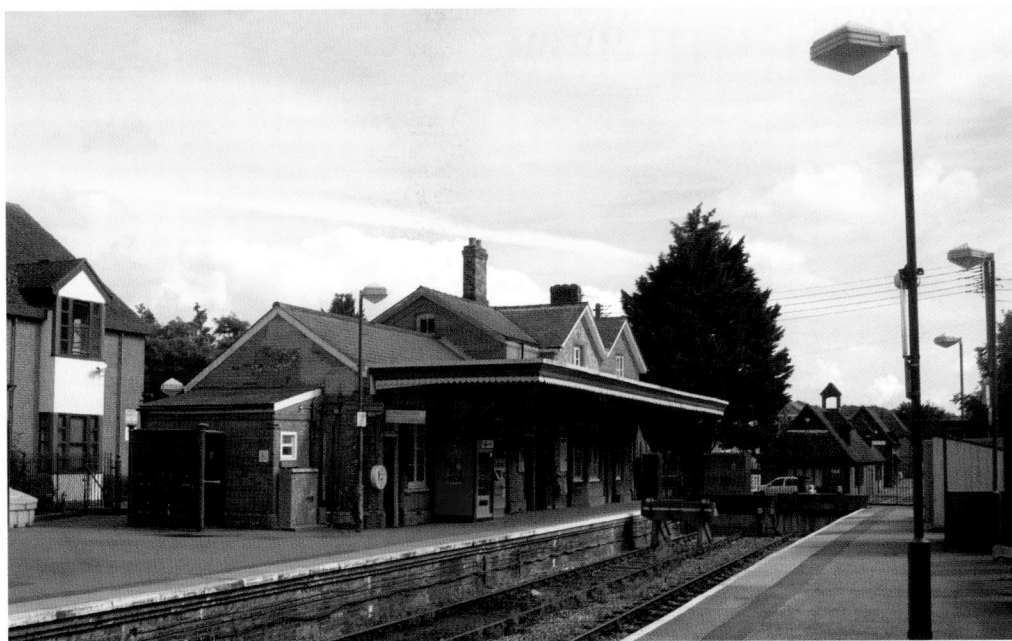

End of the line at Bourne End. Trains from Maidenhead to Marlow still reverse direction here, while trains for High Wycombe once continued over a level crossing beyond the bufferstops until that line closed in 1970.

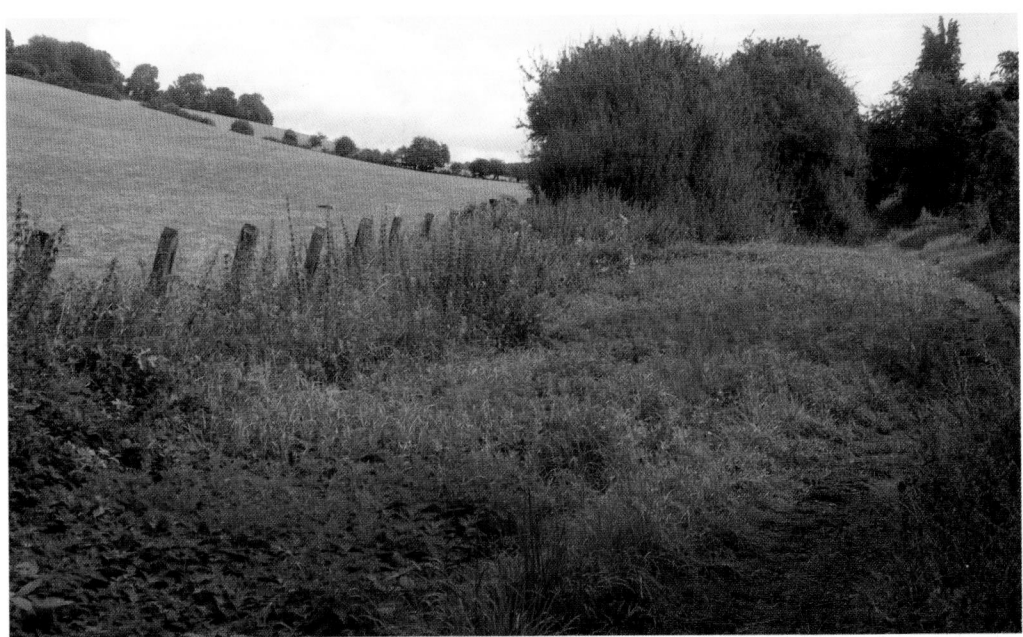

Beyond Bourne End the route of the line to High Wycombe along the valley of the River Wye is now a footpath as far as Wooburn Green. Lost railway sleuths will note the original fencing still in place along this section.

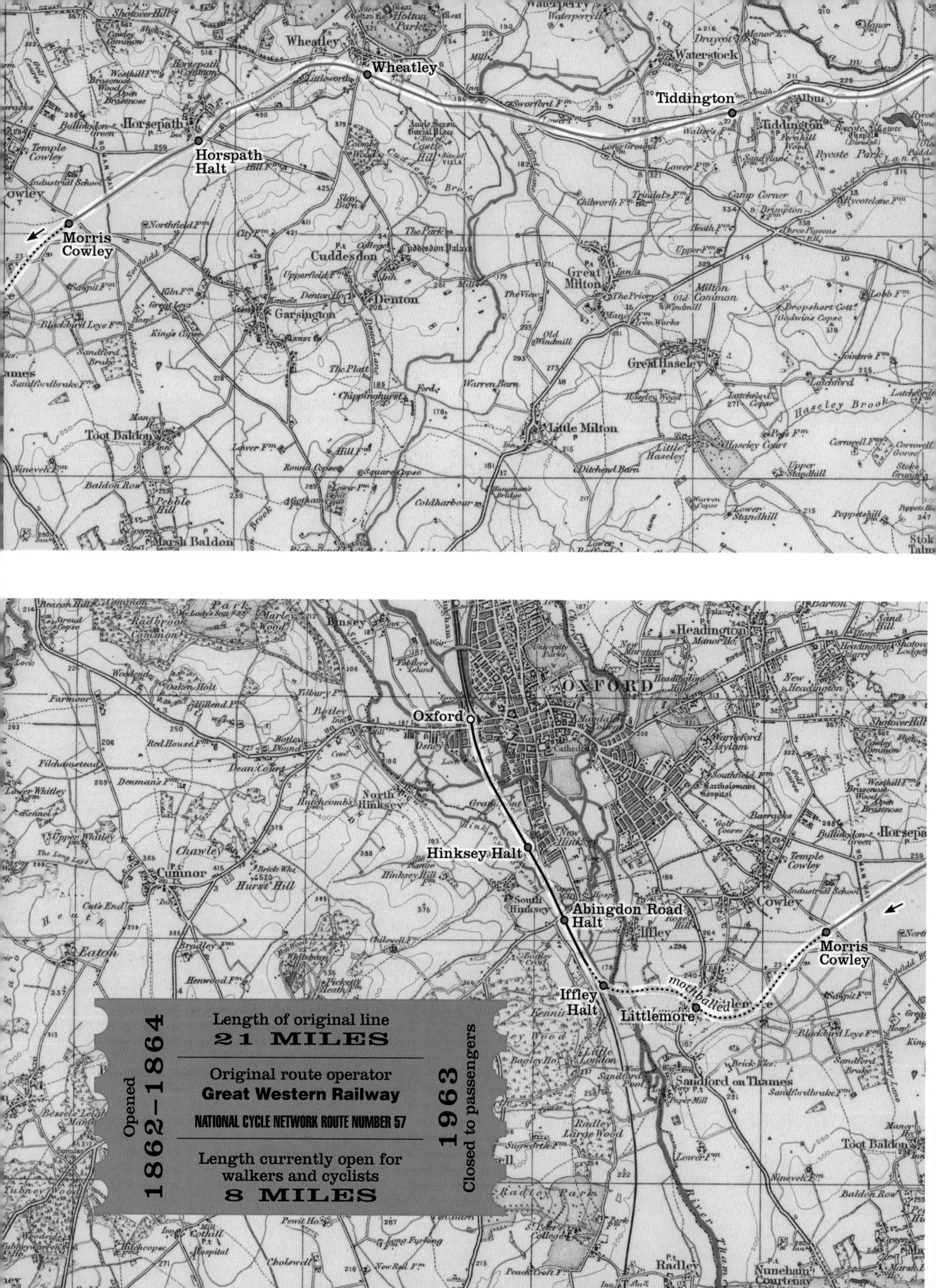

Shotover Hill
Wheatley
Wheatley
Littleworth
Tiddington
Tiddington
Horsepath
Horspath
Halt
Morris
Cowley
Cuddesdon
Denton
Garsington
Great
Milton
Great Haseley
Little Milton
Toot Baldon
Marsh Baldon

Binsey
Headington
OXFORD
Oxford
Hinksey Halt
Abingdon Road
Halt
Iffley
Cowley
Temple
Cowley
Morris
Cowley
Iffley
Halt
Littlemore
mothballed
Sandford on Thames
Radley
Toot Baldon
Radley
Nuneham
Courtenay

Opened
1862–1864

Length of original line
21 MILES

Original route operator
Great Western Railway

NATIONAL CYCLE NETWORK ROUTE NUMBER 57

Length currently open for
walkers and cyclists
8 MILES

1963
Closed to passengers

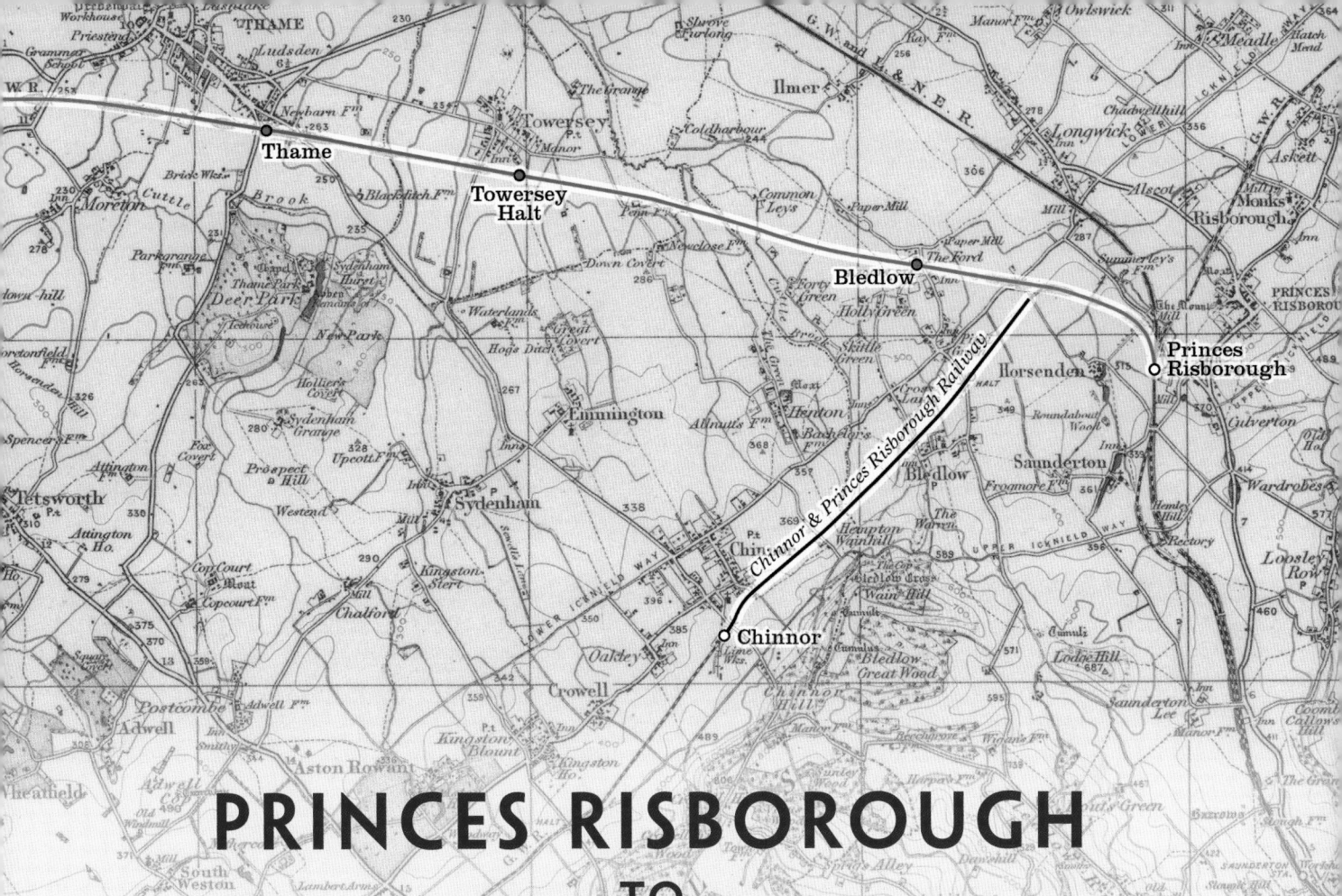

PRINCES RISBOROUGH
TO
OXFORD

PHOENIX TRAIL

This western extension of the broad-gauge through route between
Maidenhead and Oxford via High Wycombe and Princes Risborough
lost its importance in 1910 with the opening of the new Aynho Cut-off
Line to Banbury. Despite the opening of new halts and the
introduction of an early steam railmotor service, this cross-country
line went on to lead a fairly quiet existence apart from on Sundays,
when London to Birmingham expresses used it as a diversionary
route during engineering work on the main line. Following closure
to passengers in 1963, the eastern section to Thame remained open
for oil traffic until 1991. The western section remains open to serve
the Morris Cowley factory near Oxford. Since complete closure the
eastern section from Princes Risborough to Thame has reopened
as a footpath and cycleway known as the Phoenix Trail.

The Princes Risborough to Oxford line was built by the Wycombe Railway but the Great Western Railway (GWR) operated it from the start. Incorporated by an Act of Parliament in 1846 and engineered by Isambard Kingdom Brunel, the Wycombe Railway began operating when it opened a single-line broad-gauge railway from Maidenhead, on the GWR's Paddington to Bristol main line, to High Wycombe in 1854 (see page 94). An extension to the railway was opened from High Wycombe to Princes Risborough and Thame in 1862, with a branch line from Princes Risborough to Aylesbury following in 1863. The company's final thrust westwards came in 1864 when it extended the Thame line to Kennington Junction, just over two miles south of Oxford. The 21-mile railway between Princes Risborough and Oxford was now open and allowed GWR trains to run between Paddington and Oxford via this alternative route. The Wycombe Railway lost its independence in 1867 when it was taken over by the GWR, and the entire route was converted to standard gauge in 1870.

The Maidenhead-High Wycombe-Princes Risborough-Oxford route lost its through traffic when the more-direct Great Western & Great Central Joint Railway opened between High Wycombe and Northolt Junction in 1906. Four years later the High Wycombe to Princes Risborough section was doubled to enable trains from Paddington to reach Birmingham via the new Aynho Cut-off Line to Banbury.

The remaining section from Princes Risborough to Oxford settled down to a fairly quiet existence although the GWR did try to attract more passengers by opening halts at Horspath, Garsington Bridge and Iffley in 1908. Steam railmotors were also introduced to reduce operating costs but these were withdrawn in 1915. Iffley, Garsington Bridge and Horspath halts were closed in 1915 – Garsington Bridge was reopened to serve the Morris Cowley factory in 1928 while Horspath was reopened in 1933 along with a new halt at Towersey.

With ever-increasing competition from road transport, the years following the Second World War saw passenger and goods traffic in rapid decline. By the late 1950s there were just five return trains on weekdays (plus an extra on Saturdays) with only two running on Sundays. However, the railway did come to life occasionally on Sundays when expresses between Paddington and Birmingham were diverted away from the main line to the north due to engineering work. With annual losses estimated by British Railways to be around £35,000 closure was inevitable, with the end coming for passenger services on 7 January 1963 – nearly three months before the publication of the 'Beeching Report'.

The western section from Kennington Junction remained open to serve the Morris Cowley factory (known today as Plant Oxford) while the eastern section from Princes Risborough to Thame was kept open to serve an oil depot until 1991.

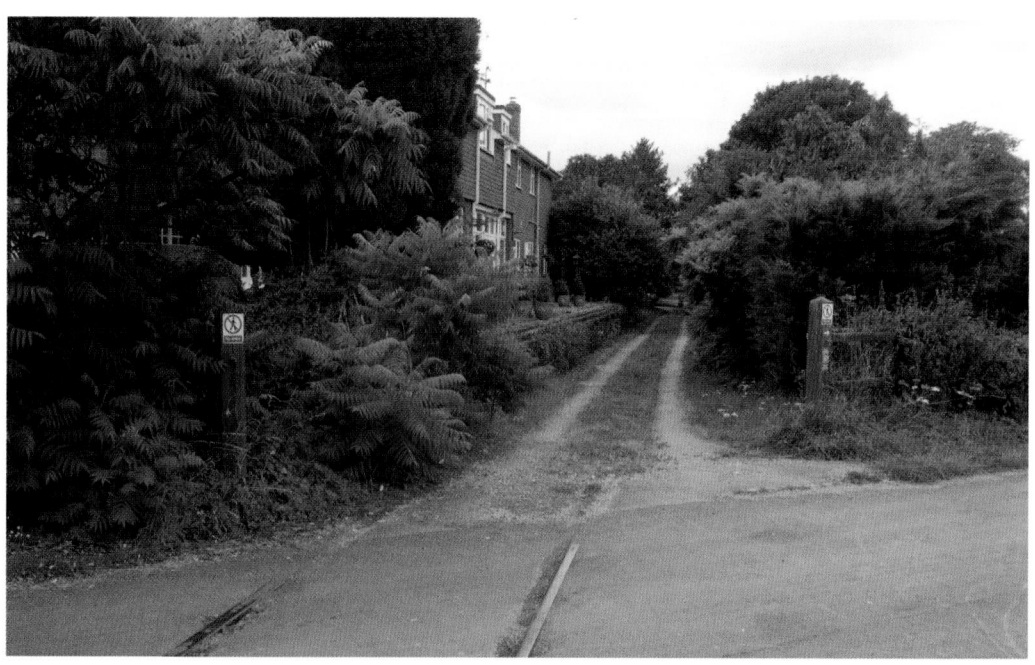

The station building and platform at Bledlow survive as a private residence. Here walkers and cyclists along the Phoenix Trail take a short diversion before rejoining the trackbed of the railway. Surprisingly, the track on this level crossing has also survived despite complete closure of this line in 1991.

Following closure of the Princes Risborough to Thame section in 1991 the trackbed was purchased by the cycling charity Sustrans and resurfaced as an 8-mile footpath and cycleway known as the Phoenix Trail. Forming part of National Cycle Network Route 57, it is also suitable for wheelchairs and pushchairs, with seating provided every 500 metres. Sightings of red kites are common along the Trail, which is further enhanced by 30 sculptures built by Angus Ross and furniture students. The Trail starts near Horsenden Church in Princes Risborough and ends in the attractive town of Thame. Car parking is available in both locations while refreshments can also be taken at the Three Horseshoes pub in Towersey. Princes Risborough station is served by Chiltern Railways' trains running between London Marylebone and Birmingham Moor Street and to and from Aylesbury.

One and a half miles west of Princes Risborough is the former station at Bledlow, where the platform and station building have survived as a bed and breakfast establishment. The level crossing here remained in use until the line closed in 1991 and the rails can still be clearly seen embedded in the roadway. Further west nothing remains of Towersey Halt, while at Thame only the remains of the down platform can still be seen alongside the Phoenix Trail near the Thame Park Road overbridge. Further west, the railway's route through the Oxfordshire countryside as far as Morris Cowley has disappeared, although the local parish council now manages a cutting at Horspath as a nature reserve. The short Horspath Tunnel is owned by Oxfordshire County Council as a safe retreat for colonies of bats. The railway is still in place from Kennington Junction to the old Morris Cowley factory, which has been owned by BMW since 2001 and currently makes models of the Mini.

CHINNOR & PRINCES RISBOROUGH RAILWAY

With a short detour, visitors to the Phoenix Trail can also visit the nearby Chinnor & Princes Risborough Railway, which runs along part of the GWR's Watlington branch between the village of Chinnor and Thame Junction at Princes Risborough. Although closed to passengers in 1957, the line remained open to a cement works at Chinnor until 1989. Today, steam-hauled heritage trains operate from the delightfully restored station at Chinnor; however there is currently no access to the railway at Princes Risborough until the line is extended a short distance into the station. For operating days visit: www.chinnorrailway.co.uk

A busy moment at Thame station in March 1961 as ex-GWR '6101' Class 2-6-2T No. 6111 takes on water before departing with an eastbound train to Princes Risborough and sister locomotive No. 6156 arrives with a Princes Risborough to Oxford service. Opened in 1862, Thame station, with its Brunel-style overall timber roof, was demolished following withdrawal of passenger services in 1963. The Phoenix Trail cycleway and footpath now pass through the site.

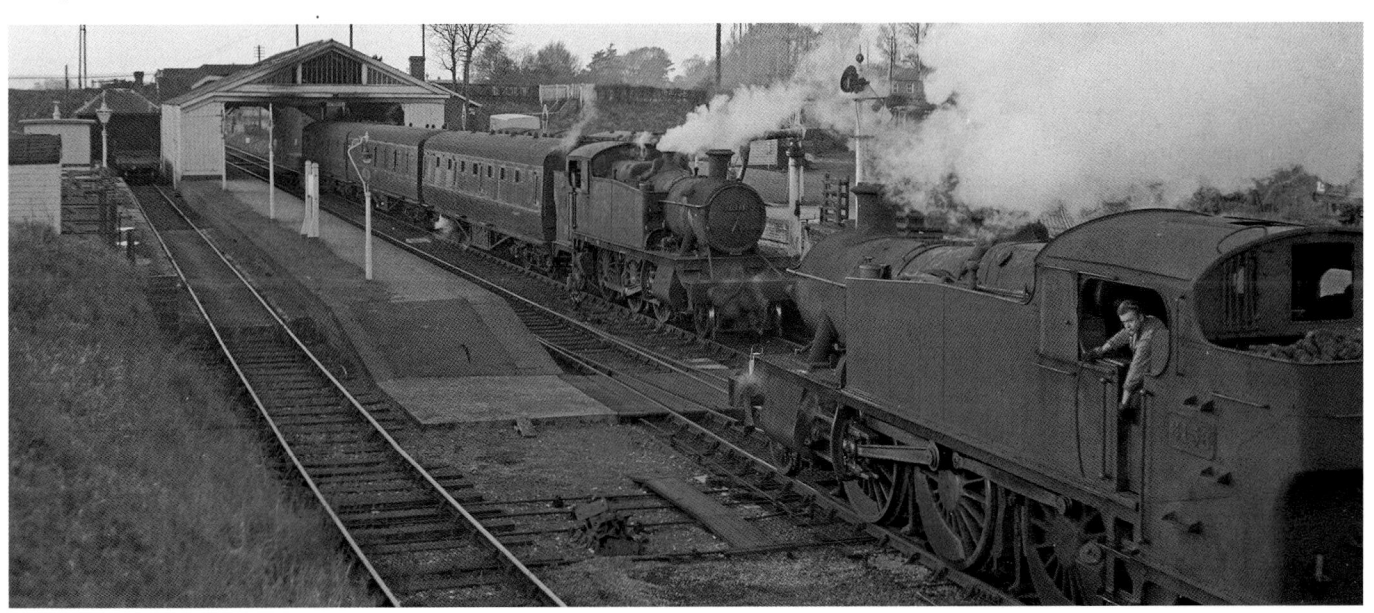

EASTERN ENGLAND

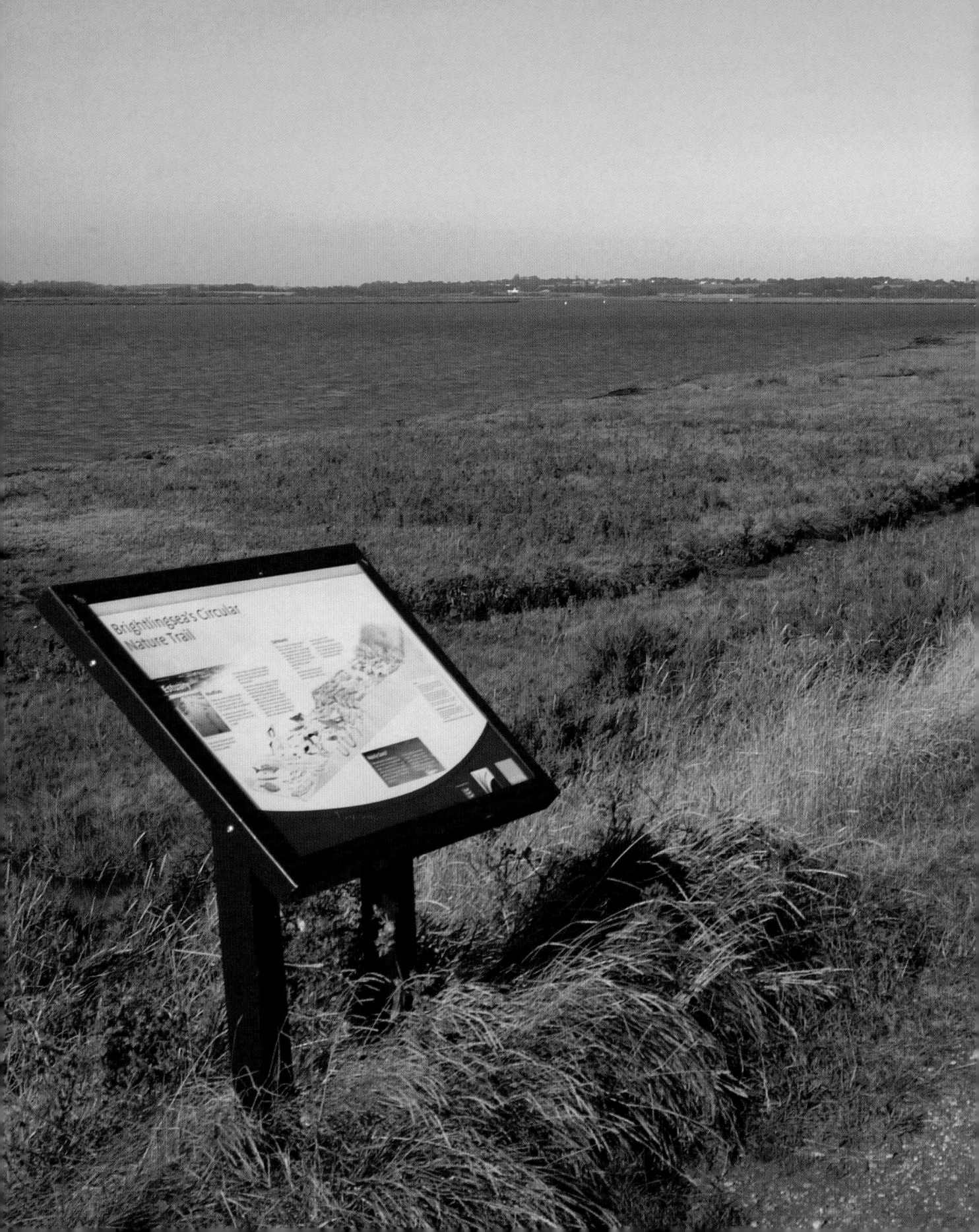

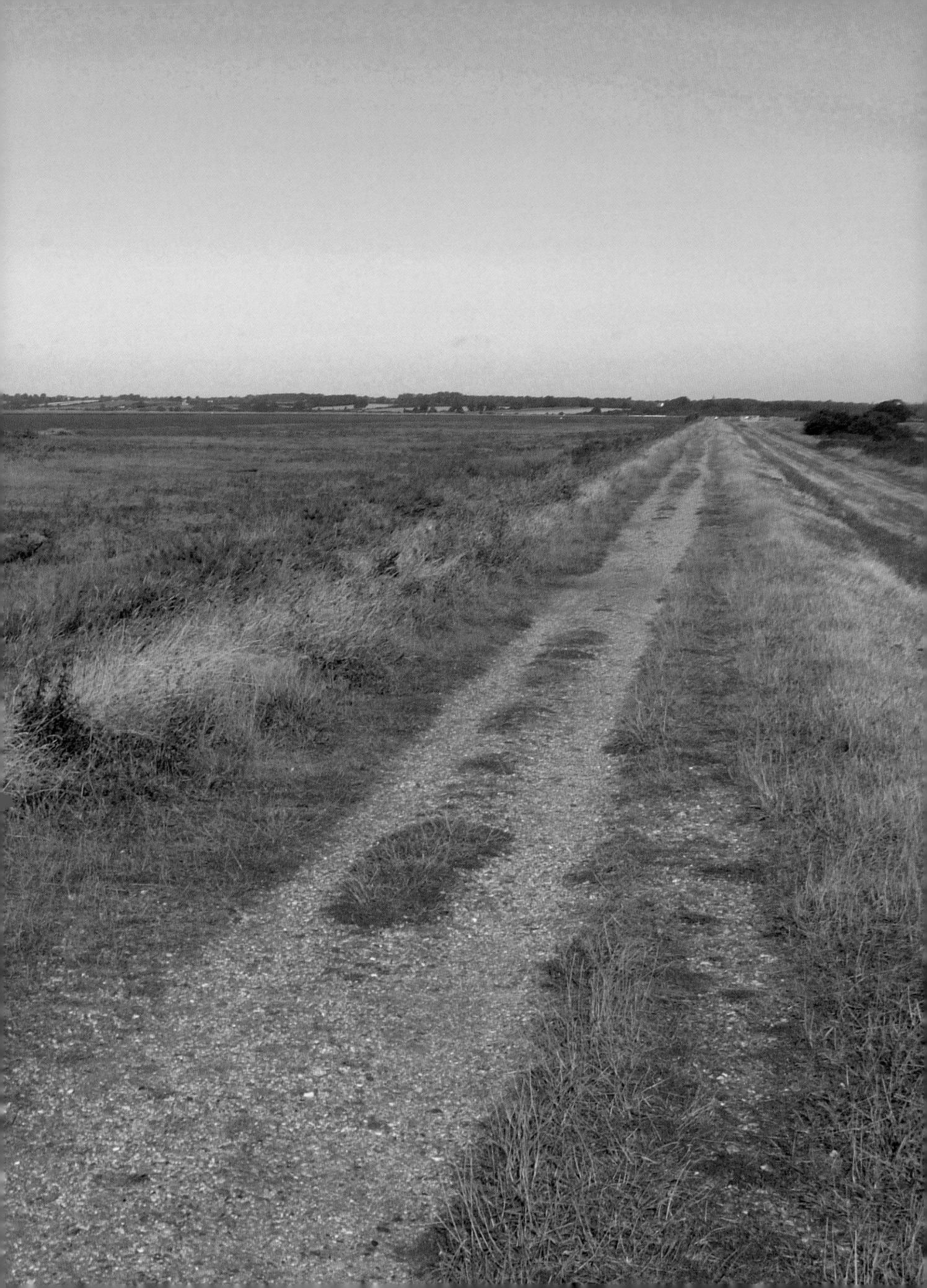

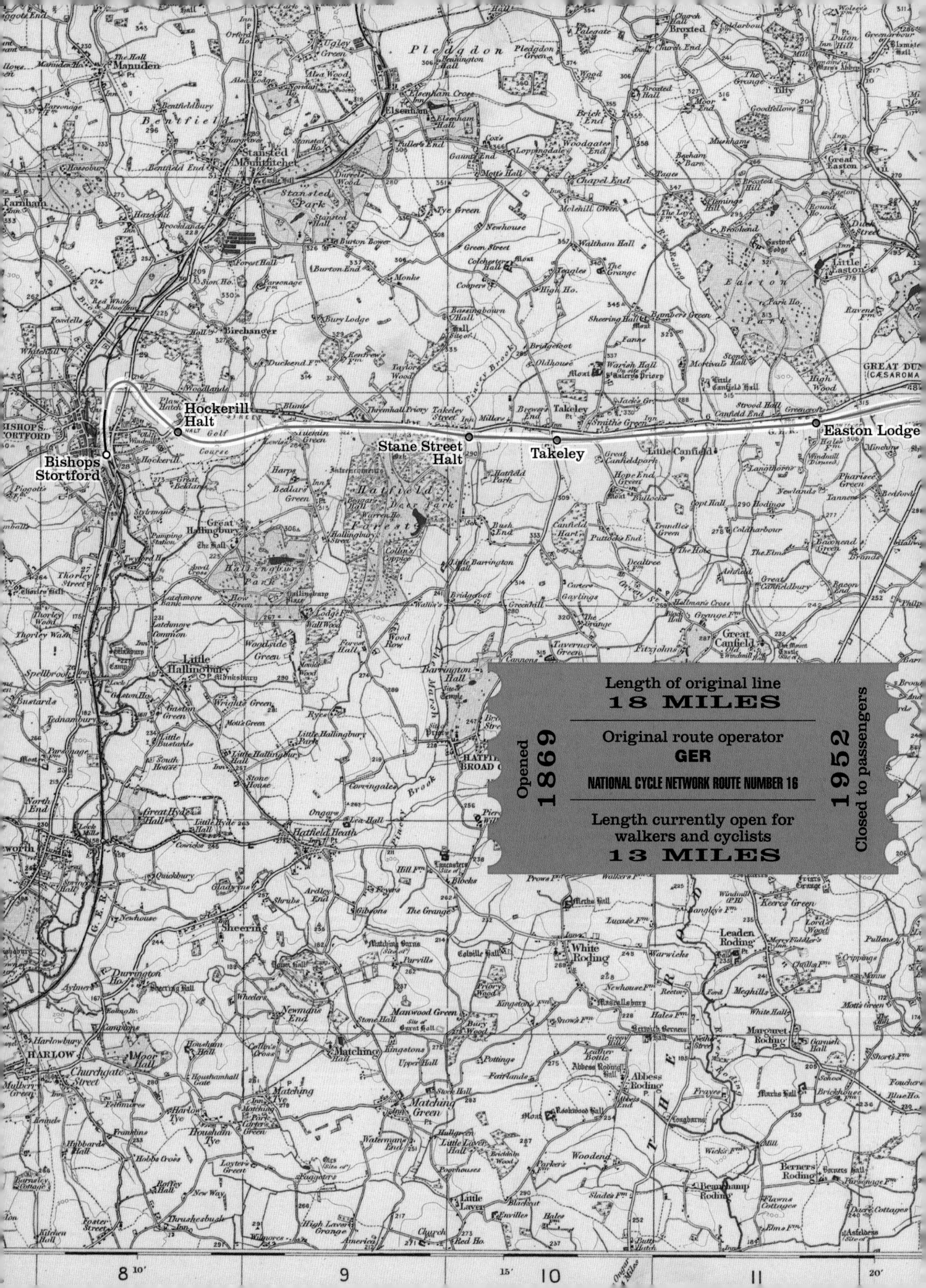

Bishops Stortford

Hockerill Halt

Stane Street Halt

Takeley

Easton Lodge

Opened **1869**

Length of original line
18 MILES

Original route operator
GER

NATIONAL CYCLE NETWORK ROUTE NUMBER 16

Length currently open for
walkers and cyclists
13 MILES

Closed to passengers **1952**

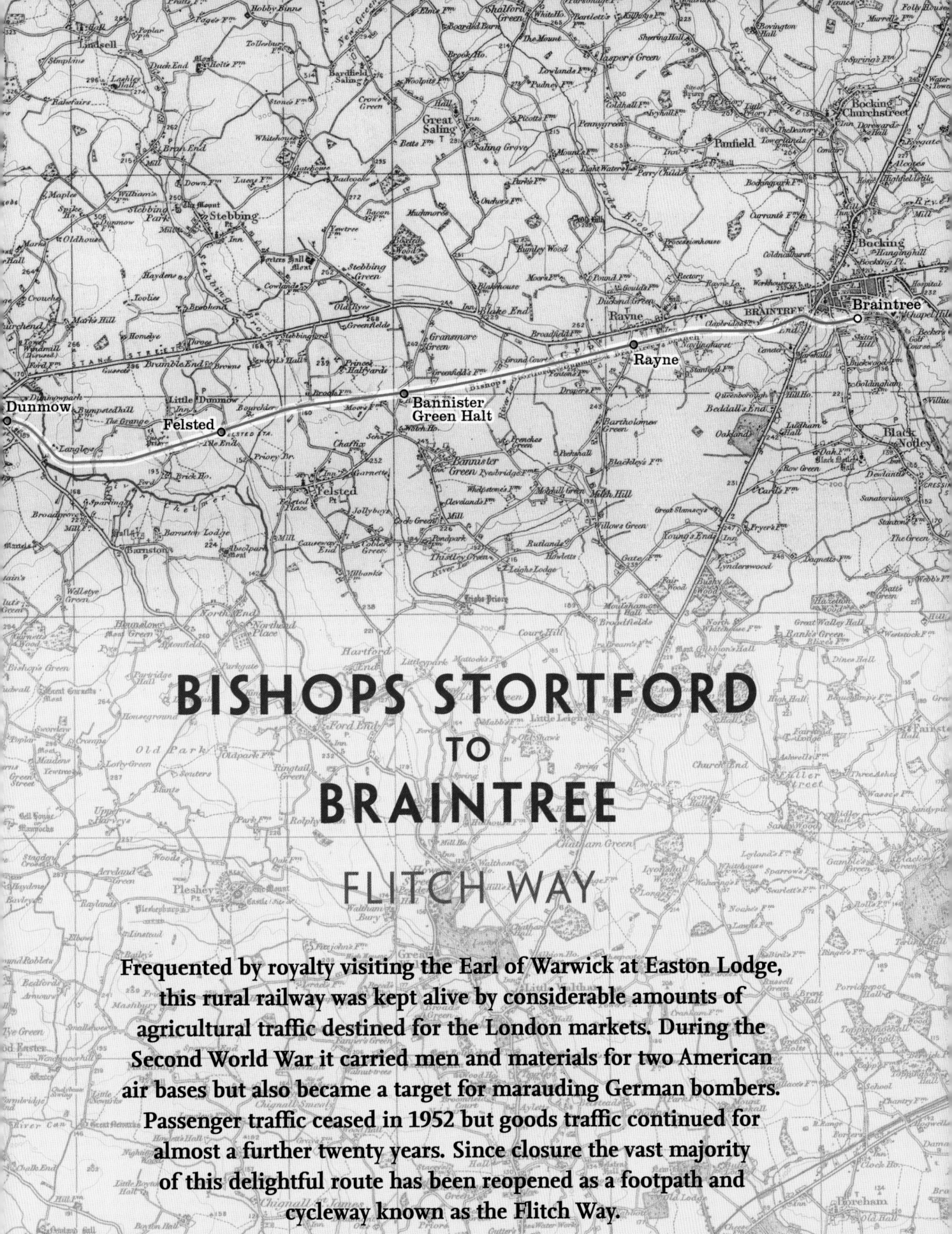

BISHOPS STORTFORD
TO
BRAINTREE

FLITCH WAY

Frequented by royalty visiting the Earl of Warwick at Easton Lodge, this rural railway was kept alive by considerable amounts of agricultural traffic destined for the London markets. During the Second World War it carried men and materials for two American air bases but also became a target for marauding German bombers. Passenger traffic ceased in 1952 but goods traffic continued for almost a further twenty years. Since closure the vast majority of this delightful route has been reopened as a footpath and cycleway known as the Flitch Way.

Originally seen as part of a grand trunk route linking London and York, the Northern & Eastern Railway (N&ER) opened its line from London to Bishops Stortford in 1842. Unusually the railway was built to a gauge of five feet but this incompatibility with other railways soon led to its conversion to the standard 4-ft-8½-in gauge in 1844. By then the railway had been leased to the Eastern Counties Railway (ECR), which went on to become one of the major constituent companies that formed the Great Eastern Railway (GER) in 1862. Nevertheless, N&ER remained an independent company until its eventual absorption by the GER in 1902.

Meanwhile the Bury St Edmunds Railway had proposed a line linking that town with London via the ancient market town of Dunmow. This met with much opposition from the ECR, which supported an extension of the Epping Railway from Ongar to Dunmow. This received Parliamentary approval in 1859 but the line was never built. Instead, a group of local businessmen, eager to transport their produce such as malt and barley from West Essex, formed the Bishops Stortford, Dunmow & Braintree Railway. Supported financially by the ECR,

the company received Parliamentary approval to build the 18-mile single-track railway in 1861.

A long drawn out process of land purchases delayed construction of the line until 1864 and by that time the newly formed GER had taken over, completing it in 1869. The railway opened on 22 February with intermediate stations at Takeley, Easton Lodge, Dunmow, Felsted and Rayne – the small halt at Easton Lodge was opened for the use of the Earl and Countess of Warwick who lived nearby. Passenger traffic was always light, although the line was frequented by many distinguished visitors including the Prince of Wales (later Edward VII) when they visited the Warwicks at Easton Lodge. By contrast goods traffic remained buoyant well into the twentieth century – agricultural produce destined for London markets such as wheat, barley, milk, coal and livestock all kept the line busy.

The Second World War saw the line stretched to capacity transporting men, materials and armaments for two nearby American air bases – the line's importance to the war effort also made it a target for German planes –

Despite losing its passenger service in 1952 the Bishops Stortford to Braintree line continued to be used by goods trains until 1971. Seen here on 9 September 1962, Takeley station has recently reopened as a café on the Flitch Way.

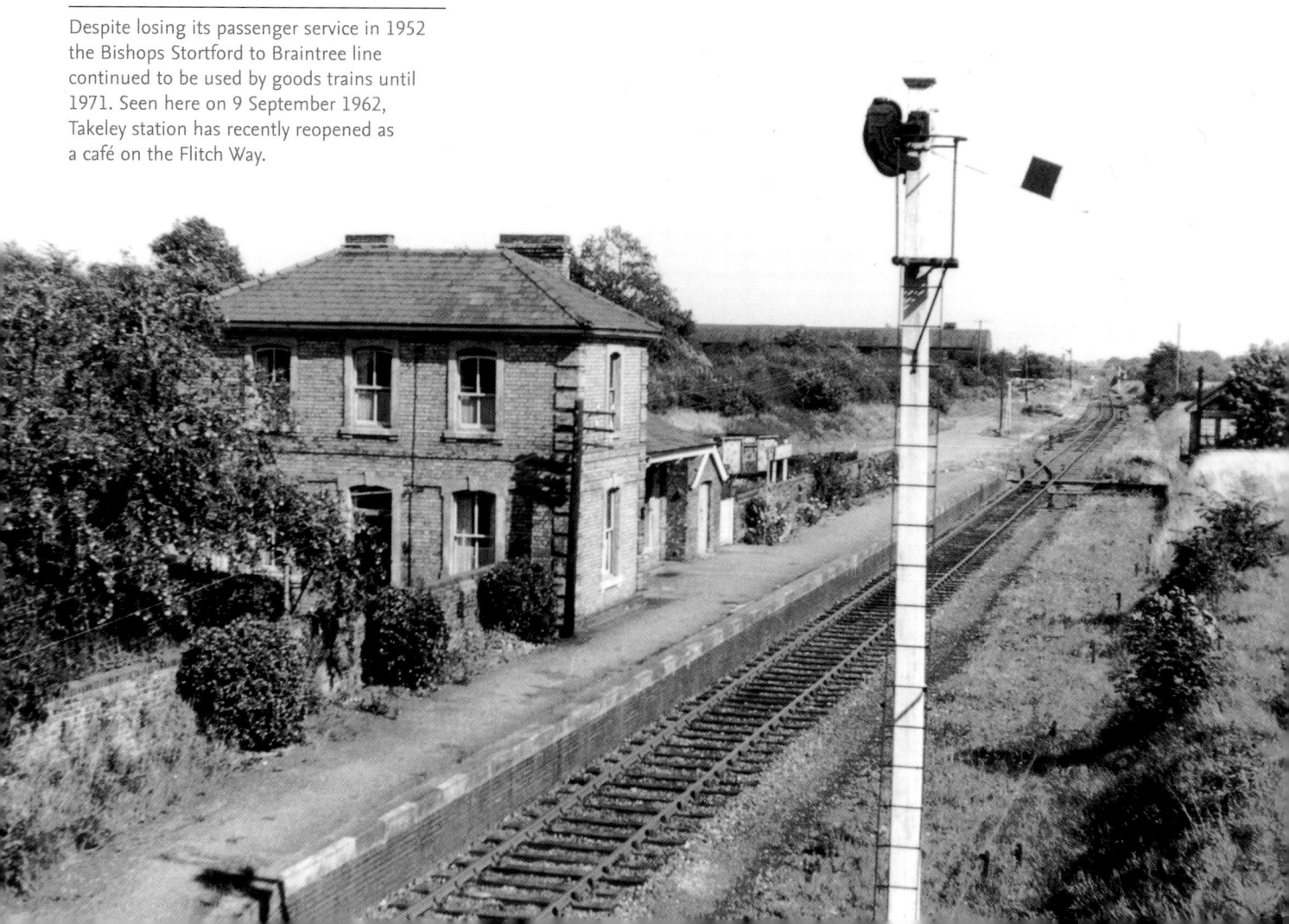

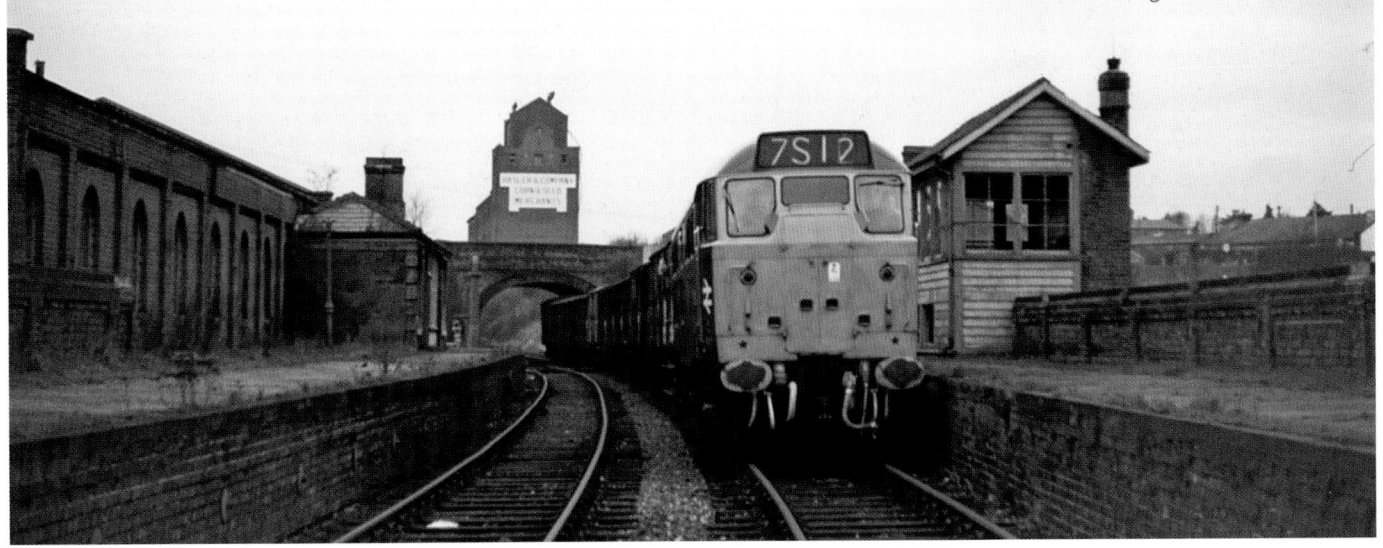

Sparkling clean Class 31 diesel No. 5639 trundles through the ghostly closed station at Dunmow with a freight train on 15 April 1969. The station site has since disappeared beneath a realignment of the A120.

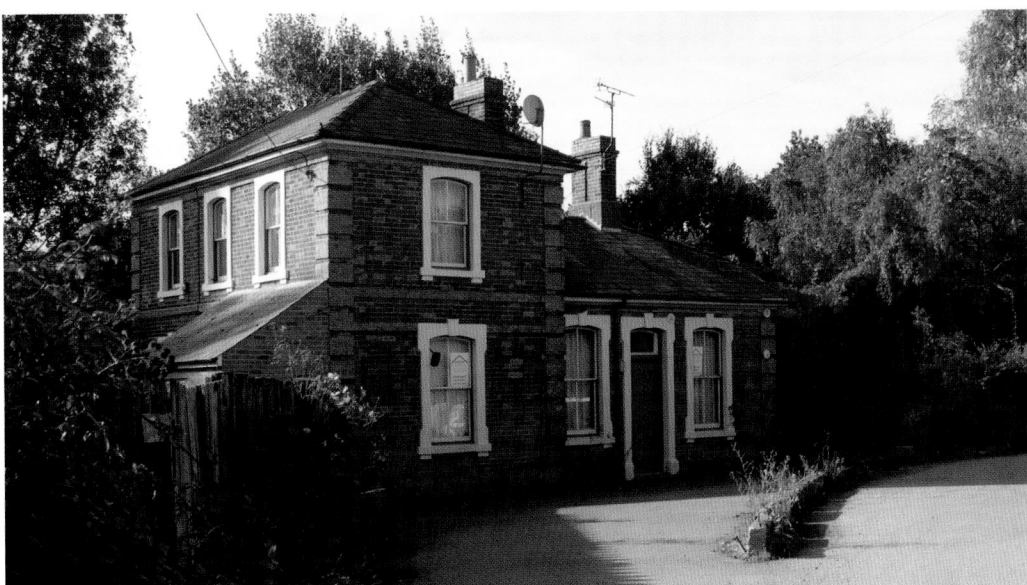

Like many country stations the one at Felsted was some distance from the village it served. The Flitch Way makes a detour around the station where walkers and cyclists now have to cross the road on the level as the railway bridge to the east has long been demolished.

and, following the D-Day landings, for ambulance trains delivering wounded soldiers to a hospital on the eastern outskirts of Bishops Stortford.

The post-war austerity years of the newly nationalized railways saw many little-used branch lines around Britain lose their passenger services. The Bishops Stortford to Braintree line was no exception, closing to passengers on 3 March 1952, although it was used to test British Railways' prototype 'Road-Railer' vehicle in 1960. Despite the loss of passenger services the line continued to flourish, carrying large amounts of freight, supplemented by deliveries of unripe bananas to a new Geest depot opened at Easton Lodge in 1962. Sadly, by the late 1960s much of this business had been lost to road transport and all freight traffic ceased on 17 February 1972. A final enthusiasts' special was run from Bishops Stortford to Easton Lodge in July and by the end of that year the majority of the track had been lifted. Braintree is still served by trains on the electrified branch line from Witham that was opened by the ECR in 1848.

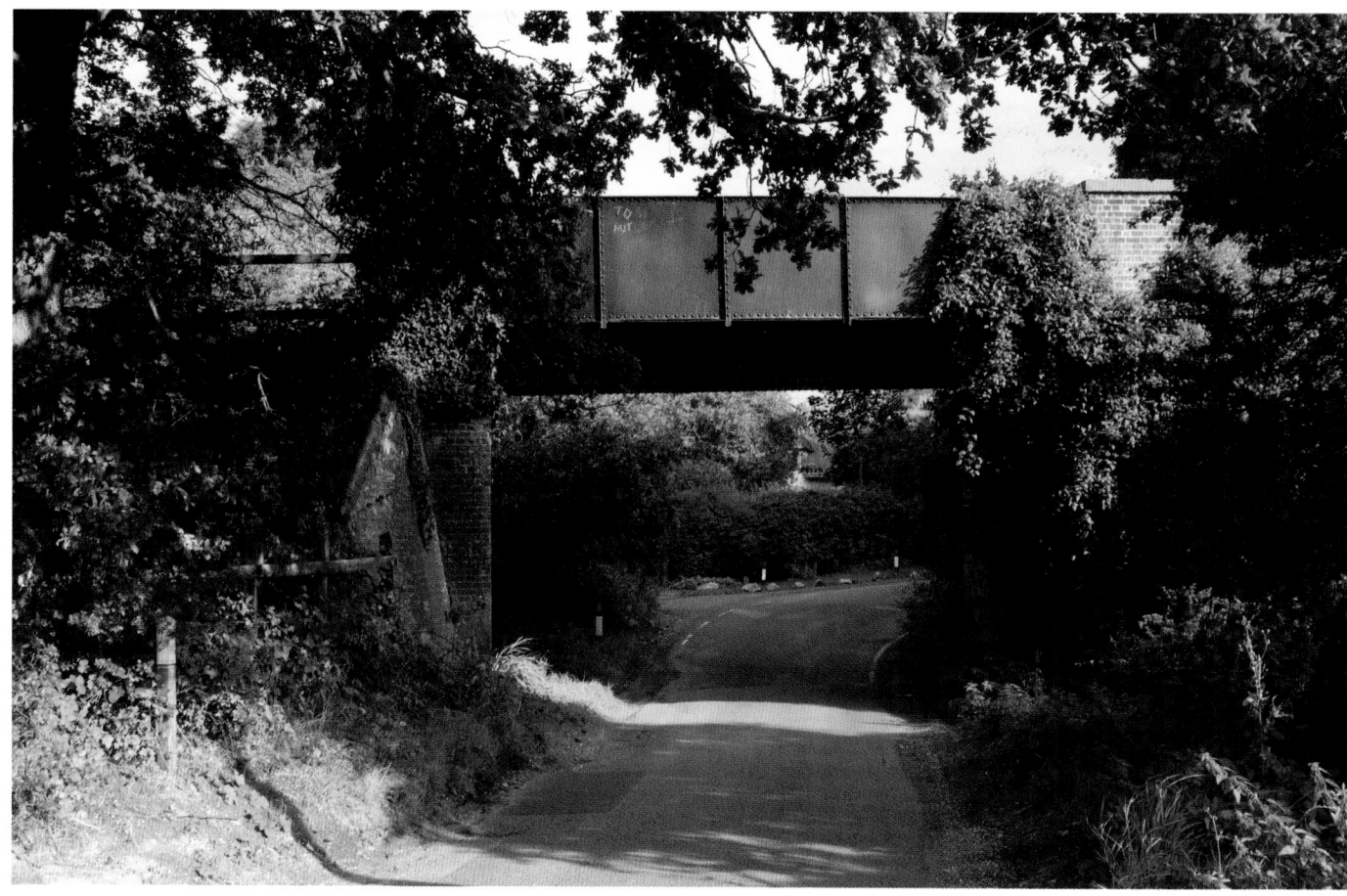

Since closure in 1972 Essex County Council has reopened much of the route as a footpath and cycleway. Known as the Flitch Way it also forms part of National Cycle Network Route 16 – its name comes from a medieval ceremony which takes place in Dunmow every four years when married couples try to prove they haven't argued for a year and a day; if successful they are presented with a Flitch (or side) of bacon. Although the Flitch Way starts in the centre of Bishops Stortford it only joins the old railway route at Tilekiln Green, to the east of the M11 and south of Stanstead Airport, following it for fifteen miles to the centre of Braintree.

Passing through cuttings rich with wildlife, under Victorian arched brick overbridges and across embankments with views over farmland and villages, there is much to discover on this fairly level well-surfaced route. Heading east the former station and its platform at Takeley have remarkably survived over sixty years since closure and the building has recently reopened as a café. At Easton Lodge, where the Prince of Wales once alighted to visit the Earl of Warwick,

the crossing keeper's cottage and wooden signal hut also survive – even the nearby banana depot is still in business!

The Way diverts around the busy A120 dual carriageway before ending the first part of its journey through a long cutting on the western outskirts of Great Dunmow. The railway route and station in this historic town have long disappeared beneath the A120 Dunmow bypass but the signposted Flitch Way resumes again on the banks of the River Chelmer near Little Dunmow. Still heading east the Way detours around the privately owned former station at Felsted before heading out once more into open countryside. Crossing the A120 on a new bridge the route soon enters Rayne where the level crossing gates, platform and station building have been superbly restored – the building is now home to a café and visitor centre, and is the ranger base for the Flitch Way.

Leaving Rayne the Flitch Way wends its way into Braintree, crossing streets on old railway bridges before ending its journey near the single-platform Braintree station. Here there are hourly rail connections to Witham and Liverpool Street.

LEFT: The Flitch Way crosses a quiet country lane to the north of Felsted on this single-span steel girder bridge. A popular traffic-free route across rolling Essex farmland, this well-surfaced footpath and cycleway now forms part of National Cycle Network Route 16.

A welcome sight for walkers and cyclists, the sympathetically restored Rayne station is now home to a café and visitor centre, and is also the ranger base for the Flitch Way. Even the level crossing gates to the west of the station have been restored.

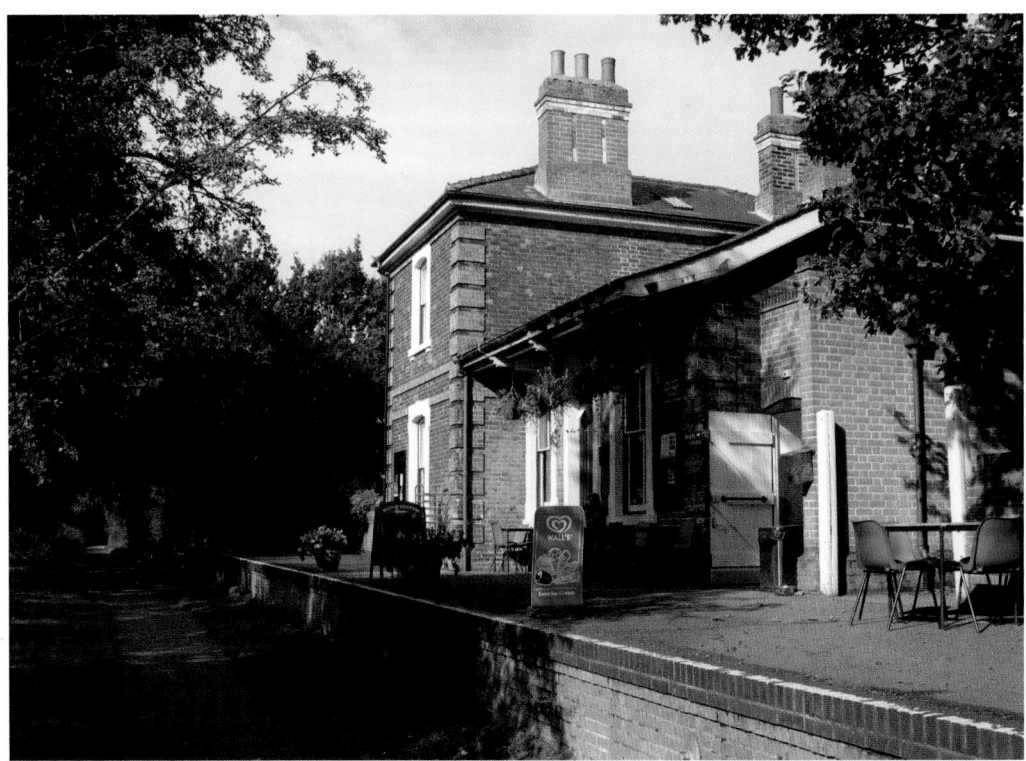

A passenger train waits to depart from Braintree station for Witham on 26 May 1956. While passenger trains from Bishops Stortford were withdrawn in 1952, the station remains open for trains to and from Liverpool Street via Witham today.

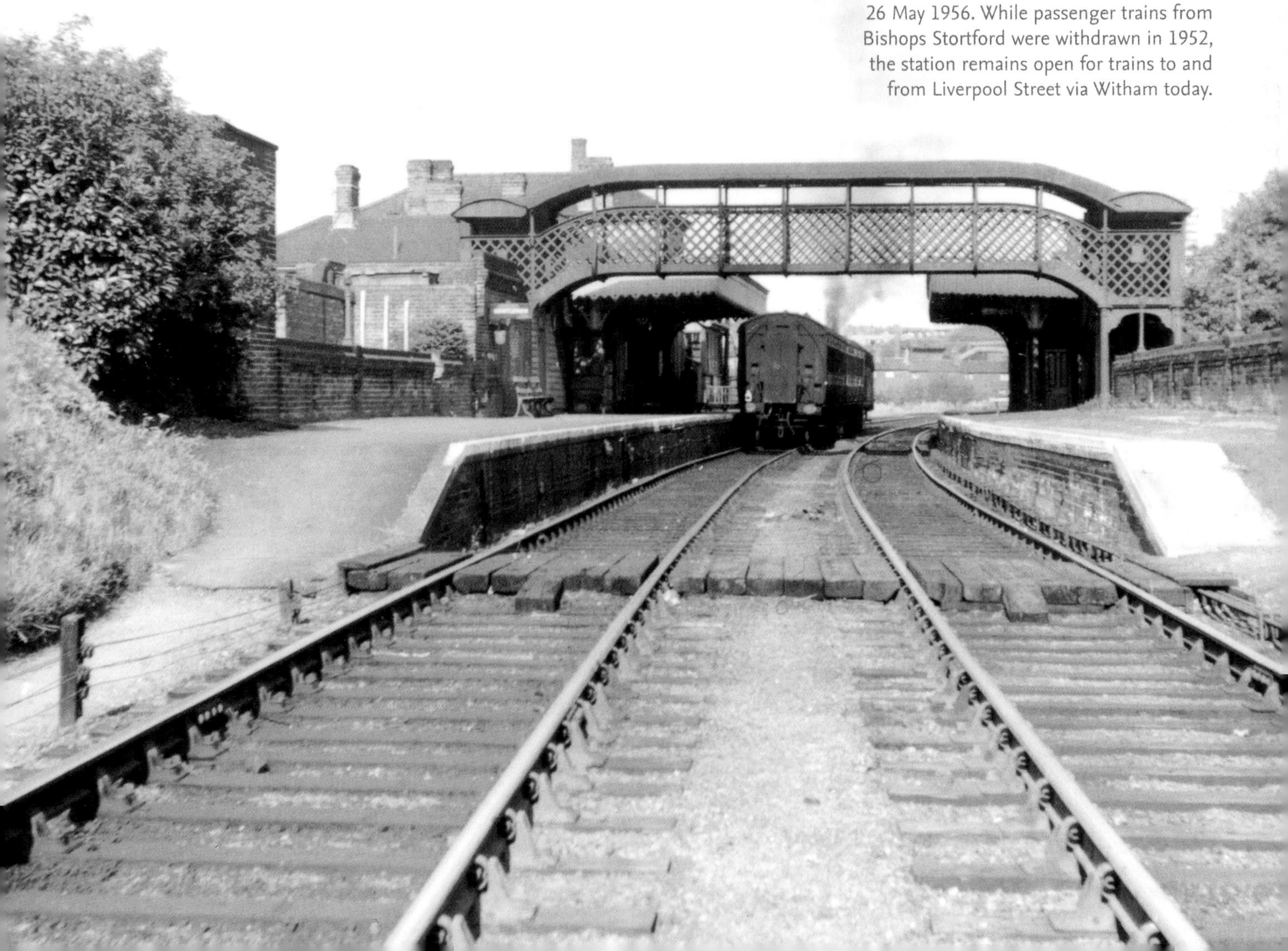

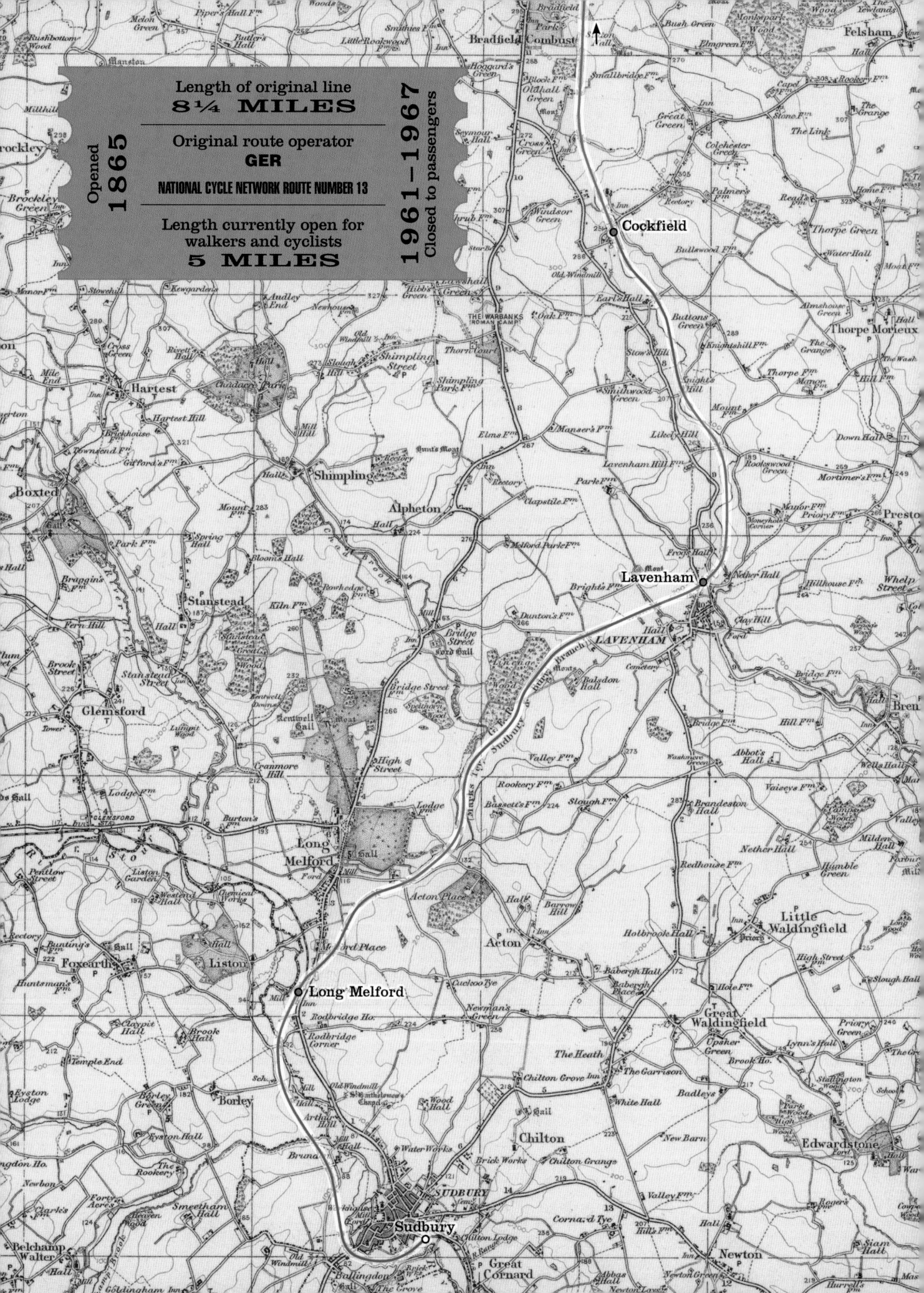

Length of original line
8¼ MILES

Opened **1865**

Original route operator
GER

NATIONAL CYCLE NETWORK ROUTE NUMBER 13

Length currently open for
walkers and cyclists
5 MILES

1961–1967
Closed to passengers

Cockfield

Lavenham

Long Melford

Sudbury

SUDBURY
TO
BURY ST EDMUNDS

This route consists of two separate railways. The 'main line' from Sudbury to Haverhill formed part of a through route served by trains running between Cambridge and Colchester, while the branch line from Long Melford to Bury St Edmunds led a fairly quiet existence. Both lines came alive during the Second World War carrying men and materials for several American air bases, but the post-war years saw declining traffic and a consequent reduction in services. Since closure in the 1960s the section between Sudbury and Long Melford, alongside the River Stour, has been reopened as a footpath and cycleway, while a two-mile stretch southwest of Lavenham has been reopened as a footpath.

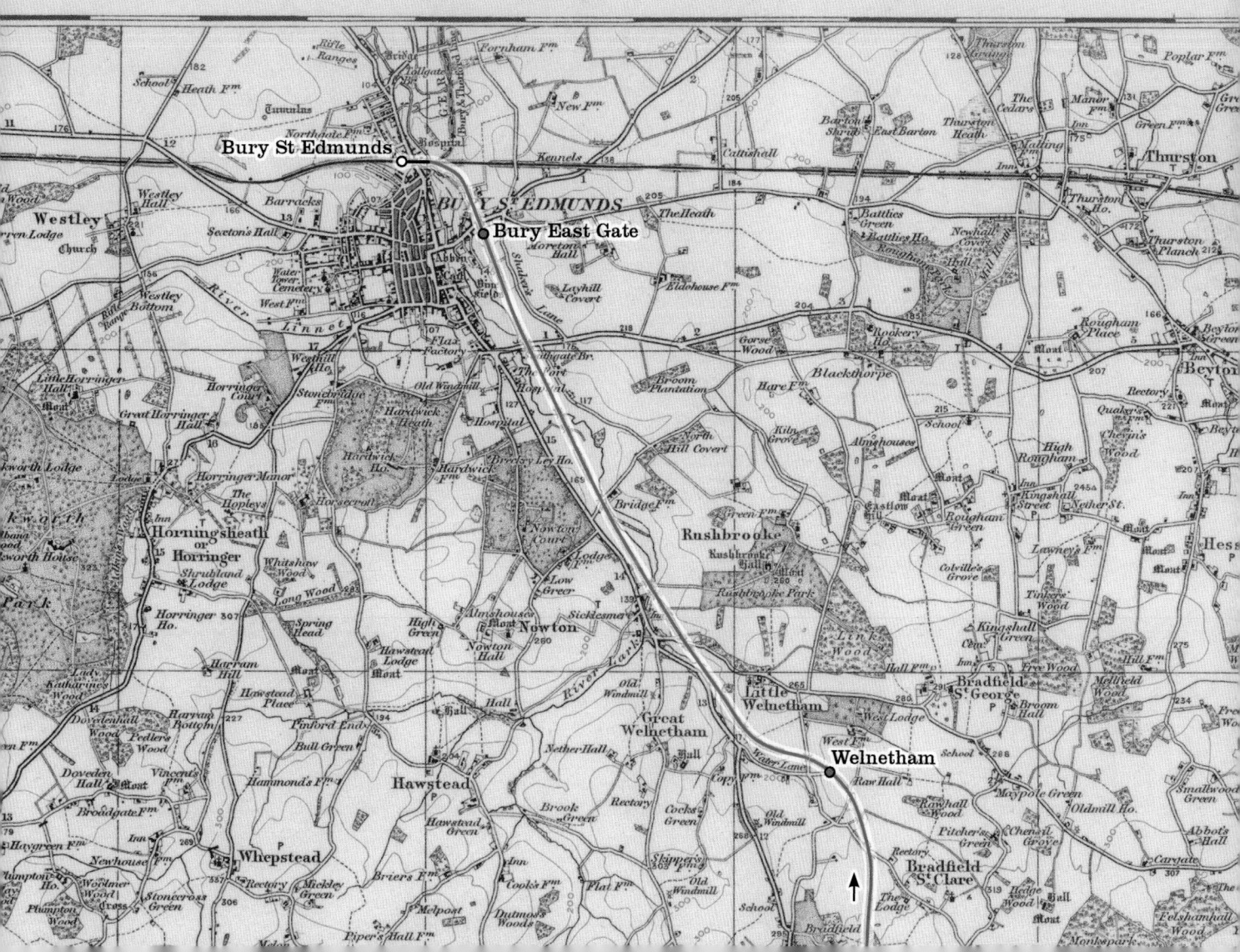

The Colchester, Stour Valley, Sudbury & Halstead Railway (CSVS&HR) opened from Marks Tey, on the Eastern Counties Railway main line from London to Colchester, to the market and silk-weaving town of Sudbury in 1849. Although the heavily engineered 11¾-mile railway was in direct competition with the then recently modernized Stour Navigation, both forms of transport lived in harmony until the 1890s, by which time most freight traffic had been transferred to rail. Originally leased to the Eastern Union Railway, the CSVS&HR was taken over by the Great Eastern Railway in 1898.

The railway was extended northwards to Long Melford and west to Clare and Haverhill (for Cambridge) in 1865. Passenger services consisted mainly of through trains running between Haverhill or Cambridge and Colchester while the backbone of the goods traffic was the carrying of cattle, grain and farm produce. The railway was particularly busy during the Second World War delivering fuel and bombs to RAF bases in the area. Steam traction was replaced by diesel multiple units in 1959 but steadily declining passenger and freight traffic saw the line listed for closure in the 'Beeching Report' – the Marks Tey to Sudbury section was reprieved owing to future growth prospects for the town but the line to Long Melford and Haverhill closed on 6 March 1967.

Meanwhile, back in 1865, the Great Eastern Railway had also opened a 16½-mile single-track line from Long Melford, on the Sudbury to Haverhill line, to the market town of Bury St Edmunds. The original station at Bury St Edmunds was known as Eastgate Street but this closed in 1909, leaving the Long Melford trains to use the main-line station in the town. Serving intermediate stations at Lavenham, Cockfield and Welnetham, this delightful rural railway led a very quiet life. Prior to the coming of the railway the medieval village of Lavenham had been an important centre for weaving but by the mid-nineteenth century this was in terminal decline. During the Second World War a nearby USAAF base brought increased traffic to the line, which was protected by numerous concrete pillboxes. The post-war years saw increased competition from road transport and a subsequent reduction in passenger trains. As a cost-saving measure diesel multiple units were introduced in 1959 but this failed to stem the drift away from the railway. The final winter 1960/61 timetable shows only four return services over the line on weekdays – most of these trains originated at or continued to Sudbury, Marks Tey or Colchester.

Closure of this loss-making rural railway was inevitable, with passenger services between Bury St Edmunds and Long Melford ceasing on 10 April 1961. Goods traffic lingered on between Bury St Edmunds and Lavenham until complete closure on 19 April 1965. The Sudbury to Haverhill line was closed completely on 6 March 1967.

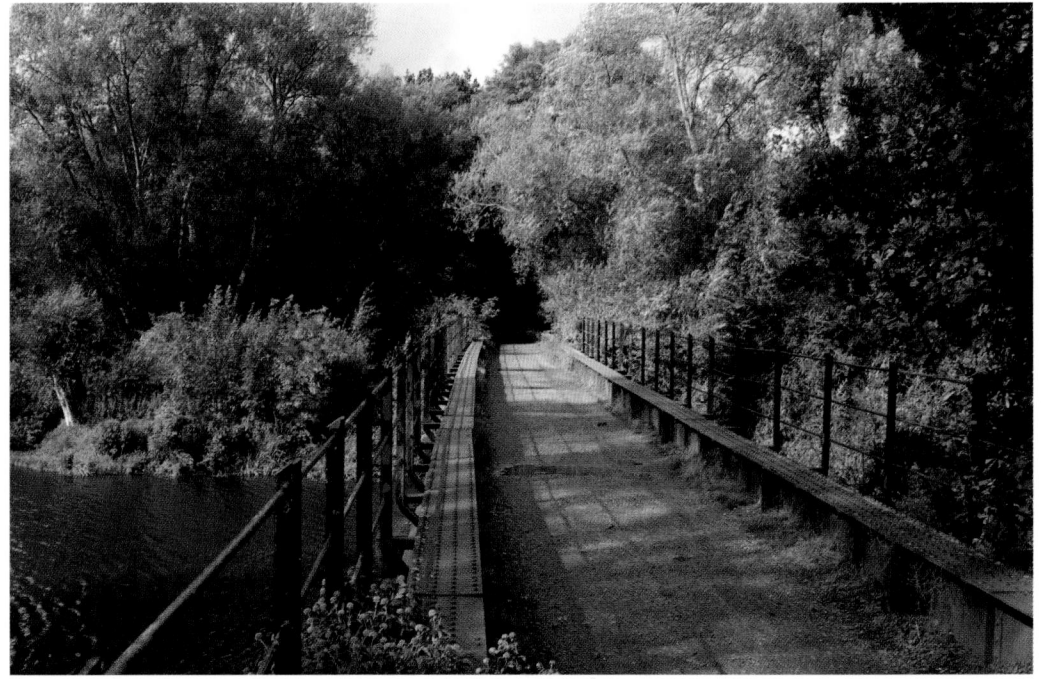

At Sudbury the picturesque and tree-lined footpath and cycleway to Long Melford loops westwards around the town, crossing the River Stour on this sturdy old railway girder bridge. There are fine views of watermeadows and restored riverside warehouses along this section of old railway trackbed.

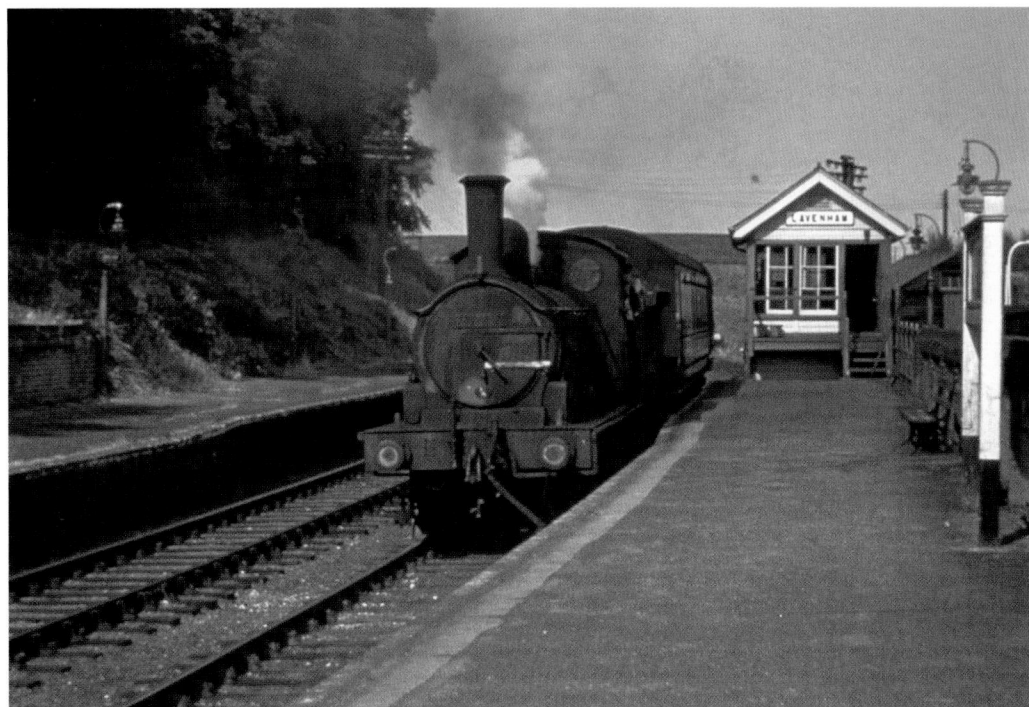

The Long Melford to Bury St Edmunds line had long been the stamping ground of veteran GER locomotives. Here, Class 'J15' 0-6-0 No. 65475 rolls into delightful Lavenham station with a local for Sudbury in July 1959. The introduction of diesel multiple units failed to save this bucolic railway which closed in 1961.

Since closure, the section of the railway from Sudbury to the outskirts of Long Melford has been reopened as a 3-mile footpath and cycleway, forming part of National Cycle Network Route 13. Sudbury is still served by trains from Marks Tey, on the Liverpool Street to Colchester main line. While the original 1865 station at Sudbury has been demolished to make way for the Kingfisher Leisure Centre and car park, the new, single-platform station has only the minimum of passenger facilities. On leaving the station walkers and cyclists will need to head westwards through the leisure centre car park before rejoining the former trackbed. Popular with local residents, the picturesque tree-lined route closely follows the meandering River Stour, which it crosses on an iron-girder bridge followed by a similar structure over the A131 on the western outskirts of the town – glimpses of restored riverside warehouses and water meadows make this a delightful stretch before open country is reached.

Passing under several brick-arched overbridges, the path heads north past the riverside mill at Borley before reaching a car park and picnic site at Rodbridge Corner. From here the railway path crosses the meandering River Stour on another iron-girder bridge before ending on the southern outskirts of Long Melford. Here walkers and cyclists must use the B1064 into the village before regaining the railway path on the opposite side of the road just north of the former railway station.

Sandwiched amongst new housing, this fine building has been restored as a private residence, while the former railway goods yard to the south now awaits redevelopment.

The railway path continues around the eastern perimeter of Long Melford before petering out near the A134 bypass. However, for walkers, the old railway route to Lavenham can be reached by following the Stour Valley Path and St Edmund Way (both long-distance footpaths) from the car park at Rodbridge Corner to the north of the National Trust's Melford Hall. Here, St Edmund Way heads east to rejoin the old railway trackbed for the last two miles to the western outskirts of Lavenham.

The station at Lavenham has long been demolished and the site is currently under redevelopment – here, in pride of place, is the magnificent sweeping red-brick arched overbridge that carries the A1141 over the western approach to the site. Beyond Lavenham much of the railway route has long since disappeared beneath farmland although the occasional bridge survives as a reminder. A section south of Cockfield is now a public footpath, while the station and platform here have survived in near original condition. Further north a section of the trackbed at Welnetham is now part of the St Edmund Way LDP, while the station at Welnetham is now a private residence.

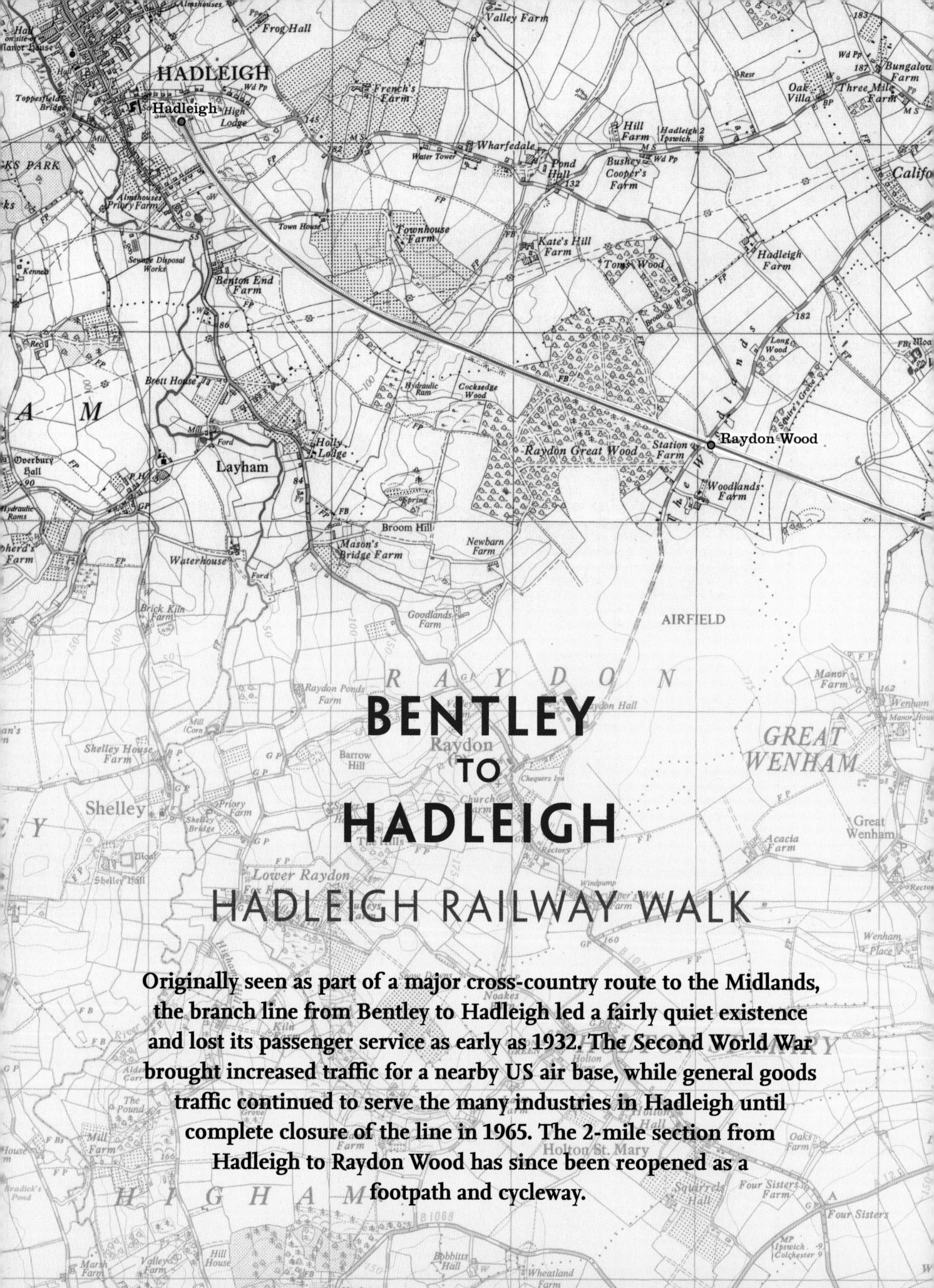

BENTLEY
TO
HADLEIGH

HADLEIGH RAILWAY WALK

Originally seen as part of a major cross-country route to the Midlands, the branch line from Bentley to Hadleigh led a fairly quiet existence and lost its passenger service as early as 1932. The Second World War brought increased traffic for a nearby US air base, while general goods traffic continued to serve the many industries in Hadleigh until complete closure of the line in 1965. The 2-mile section from Hadleigh to Raydon Wood has since been reopened as a footpath and cycleway.

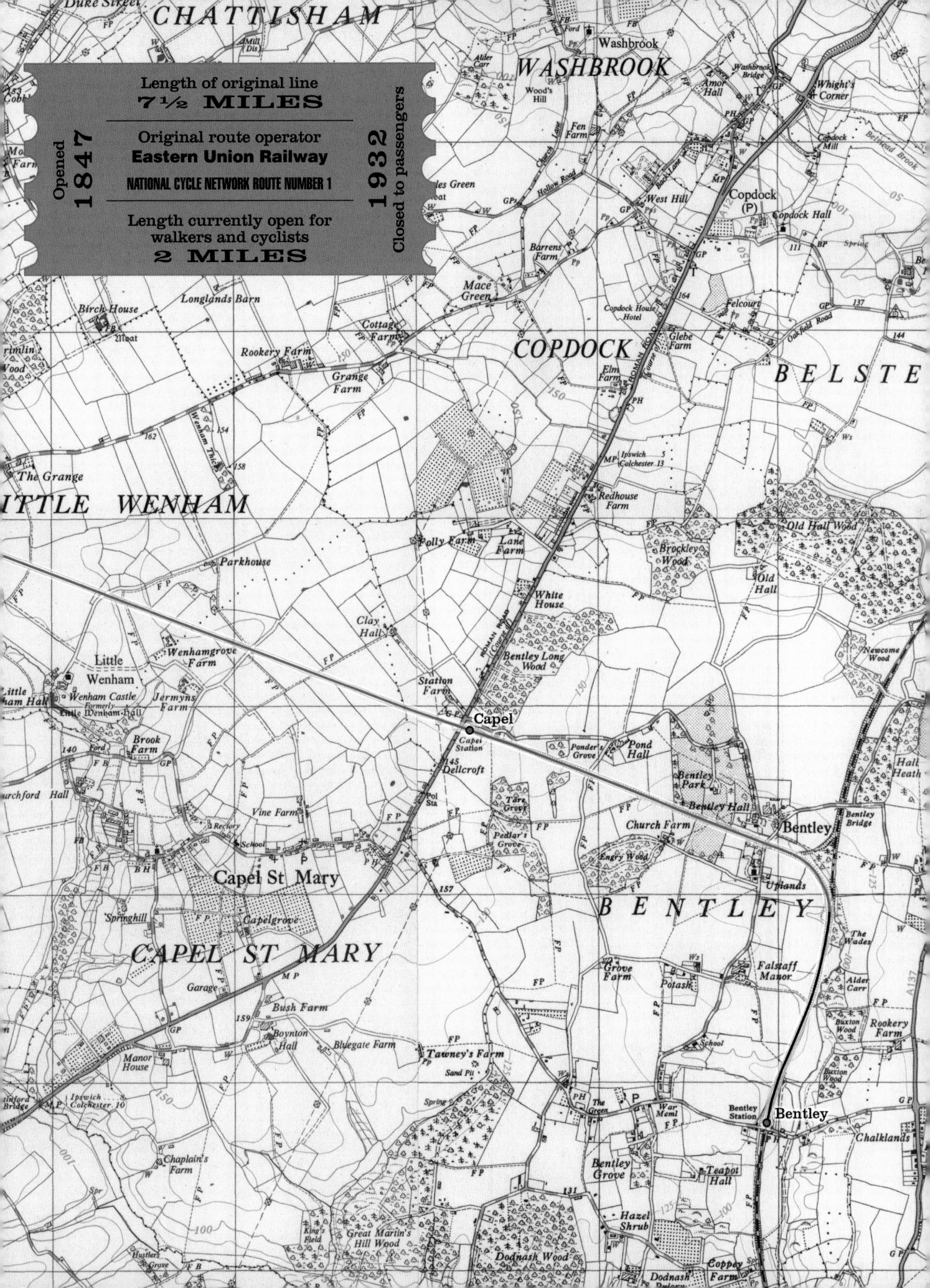

CHATTISHAM

WASHBROOK

Length of original line
7½ MILES

Opened **1847**

Original route operator
Eastern Union Railway

NATIONAL CYCLE NETWORK ROUTE NUMBER 1

Closed to passengers **1932**

Length currently open for
walkers and cyclists
2 MILES

COPDOCK

BELSTE

LITTLE WENHAM

Capel

CAPEL ST MARY

CAPEL ST MARY

BENTLEY

Bentley

Bentley

riginally seen as part of a cross-country route between Ipswich and the Midlands, the 7½-mile single-track branch line from a triangular junction at Bentley, on the mainline between London and Ipswich, to the town of Hadleigh was incorporated in 1846. Although the Eastern Union & Hadleigh Junction Railway started the construction work, it was soon purchased by the Eastern Union Railway, which opened the line in 1847. The only major engineering feature on this level-and-straight line was a 50-ft embankment and bridge over a tributary of the River Brett near Hadleigh. A proposal to extend the line in a northwesterly direction up the Brett Valley to Lavenham was quietly forgotten.

With intermediate stations at Capel and Raydon Wood, the line was initially served by local trains that continued south from Bentley to Manningtree and north from Bentley to Ipswich. However, the northern part of the triangular junction at Bentley was closed as early as 1875. For a short time Hadleigh was also served by a through coach to and from Liverpool Street – the up coach was attached to an express at Bentley while the down one was slipped here.

Passenger traffic on the line was always light and the introduction of a direct bus service to Ipswich in the early 1930s soon brought about the railway's demise and it closed to passengers on 29 February 1932. Despite this the flourishing local businesses of milling, malting, clothing and coconut matting in Hadleigh kept the line open for goods traffic for over 30 years more. Both Raydon Wood and Capel were kept busy during the Second World War handling fuel and armaments for a nearby American air base (now the home of Netley Enterprise Park). The post-war years saw increasing competition from road haulage, and with dwindling freight traffic the line closed completely on 19 April 1965.

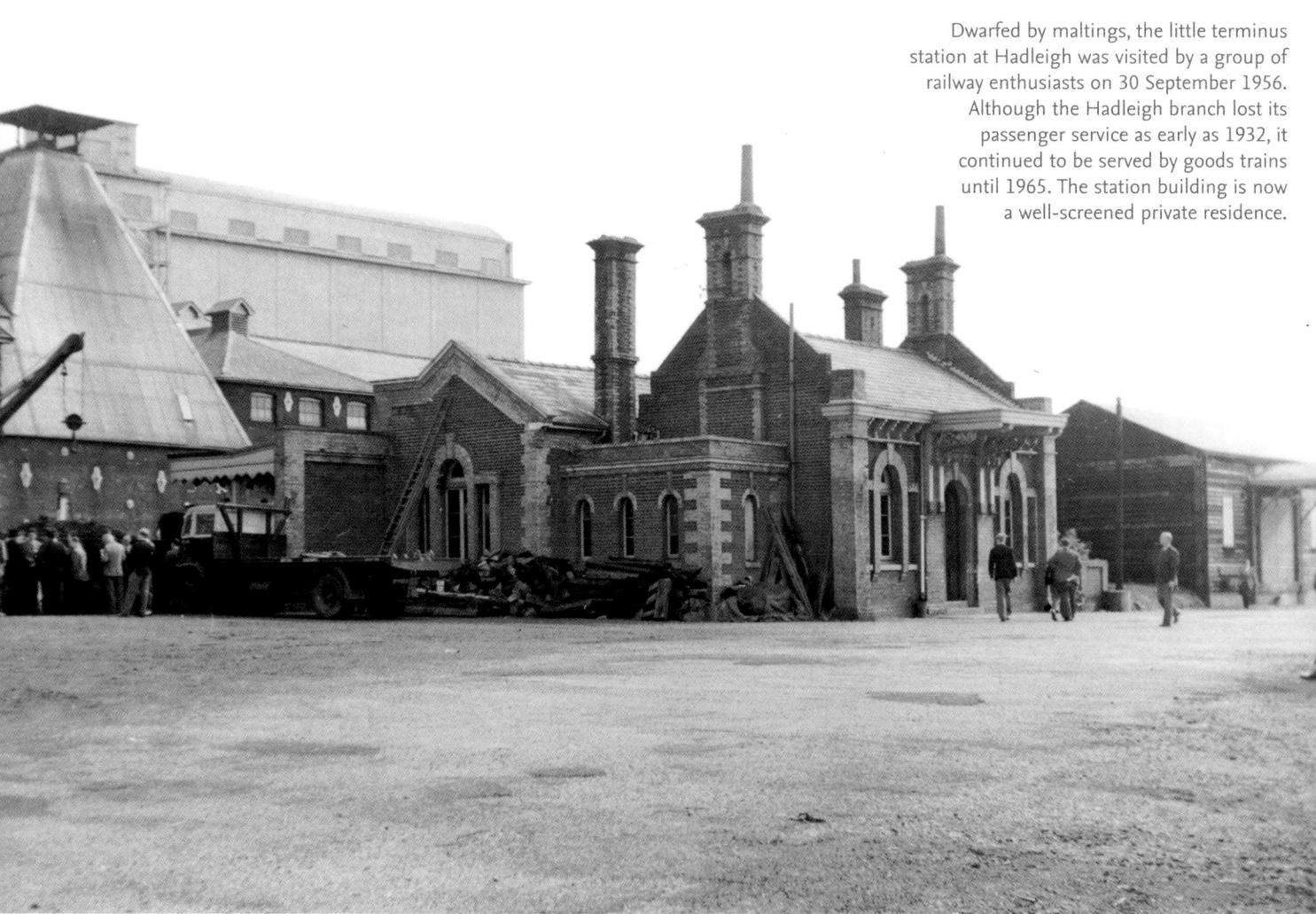

Dwarfed by maltings, the little terminus station at Hadleigh was visited by a group of railway enthusiasts on 30 September 1956. Although the Hadleigh branch lost its passenger service as early as 1932, it continued to be served by goods trains until 1965. The station building is now a well-screened private residence.

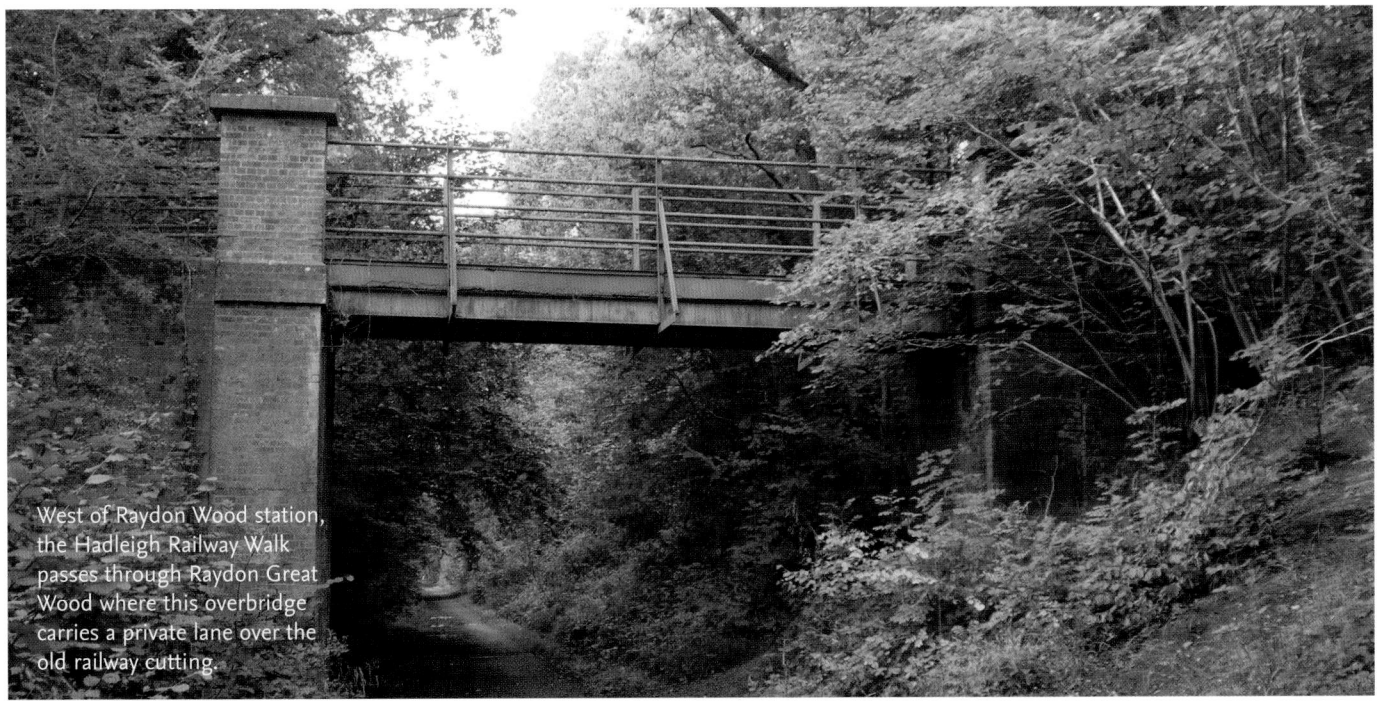

West of Raydon Wood station, the Hadleigh Railway Walk passes through Raydon Great Wood where this overbridge carries a private lane over the old railway cutting.

Since closure of the line, the 2-mile section from Hadleigh to Raydon Wood has been reopened as the Hadleigh Railway Walk. It is also suitable for cyclists and forms part of National Cycle Network Route 1. The walk starts at a car park close to the former railway station at Hadleigh, its building with tall ornate double chimneys and arched windows now a well-screened private residence amidst new housing development in the old maltings. Passing a Sustrans National Cycle Network sculpture, the tree-lined route soon enters a cutting and passes through a nature reserve before crossing the 50-ft-high embankment built in 1846. Another cutting is encountered as the Walk enters Raydon Great Wood and passes under Hunters Bridge before ending at a car park opposite Raydon Wood station. Here the derelict station building and platform, fenced off because of their dangerous state, share the old goods yard with a coal depot. Beyond Raydon Wood much of the former railway is utilized as farm tracks, although it is severed by the 'new and improved' A12 dual carriageway to the west of Bentley Park Hall. Bentley station, now a private residence, was closed to passengers on 7 November 1966 but still sees the passage of electric trains between Liverpool Street and Norwich.

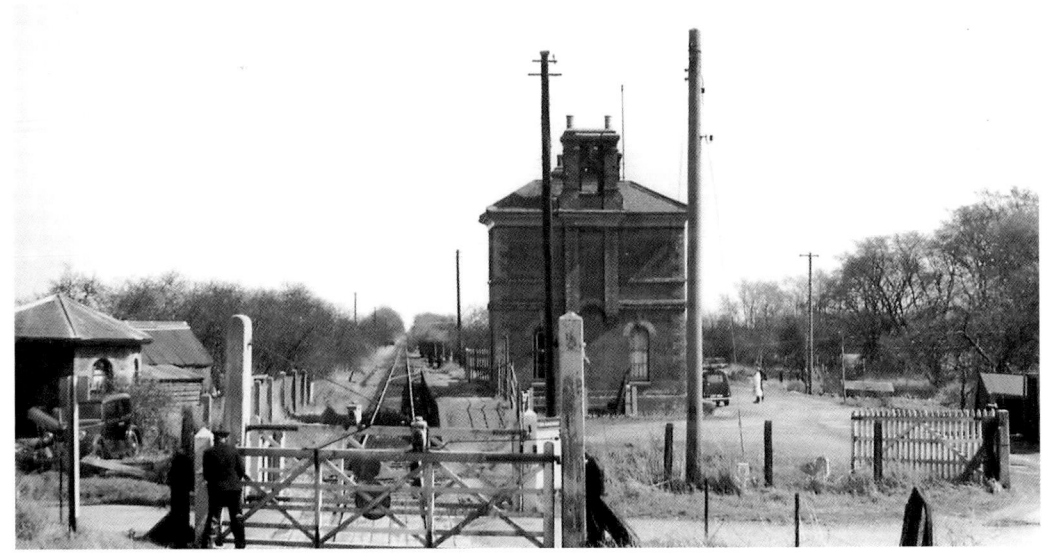

The crossing keeper gets ready to open the level-crossing gates at Raydon Wood station in the 1950s. Despite closure to passengers over 80 years ago, the derelict station building still survives adjacent to a coal depot.

WIVENHOE
TO
BRIGHTLINGSEA

Hugging the eastern shore of the Colne Estuary, the single-track railway from Wivenhoe to the harbour town of Brightlingsea had no intermediate stations and featured a swing bridge over Alresford Creek. The line was kept busy with trainloads of fish throughout the year and throngs of day trippers during the summer months. Three miles of track was washed away in the Great Storm of 1953 but the railway reopened, only to become a victim of Dr Beeching's 'Axe' in 1964. Today much of the railway's embankment alongside the estuary provides enjoyment for walkers and cyclists taking in the bracing sea air.

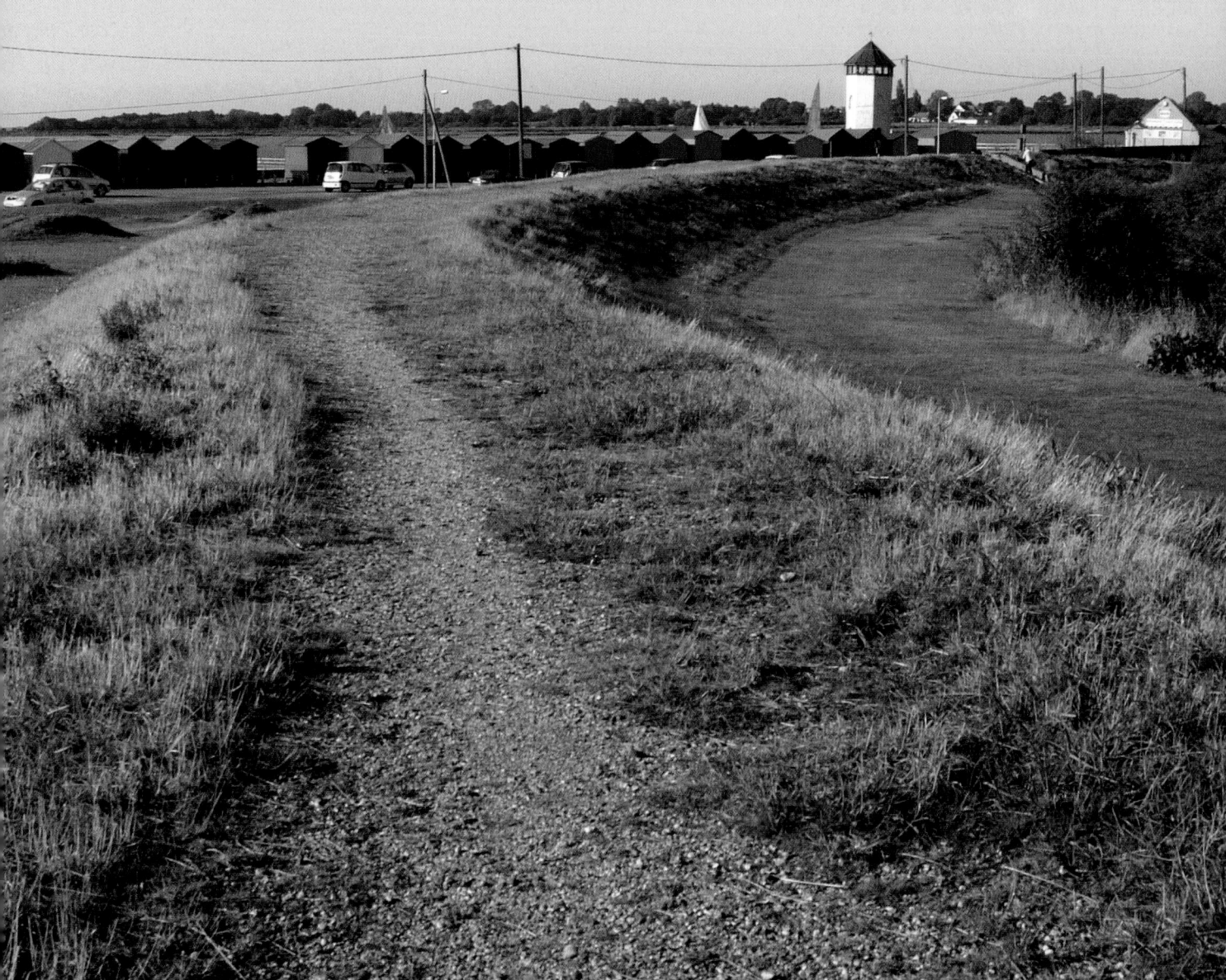

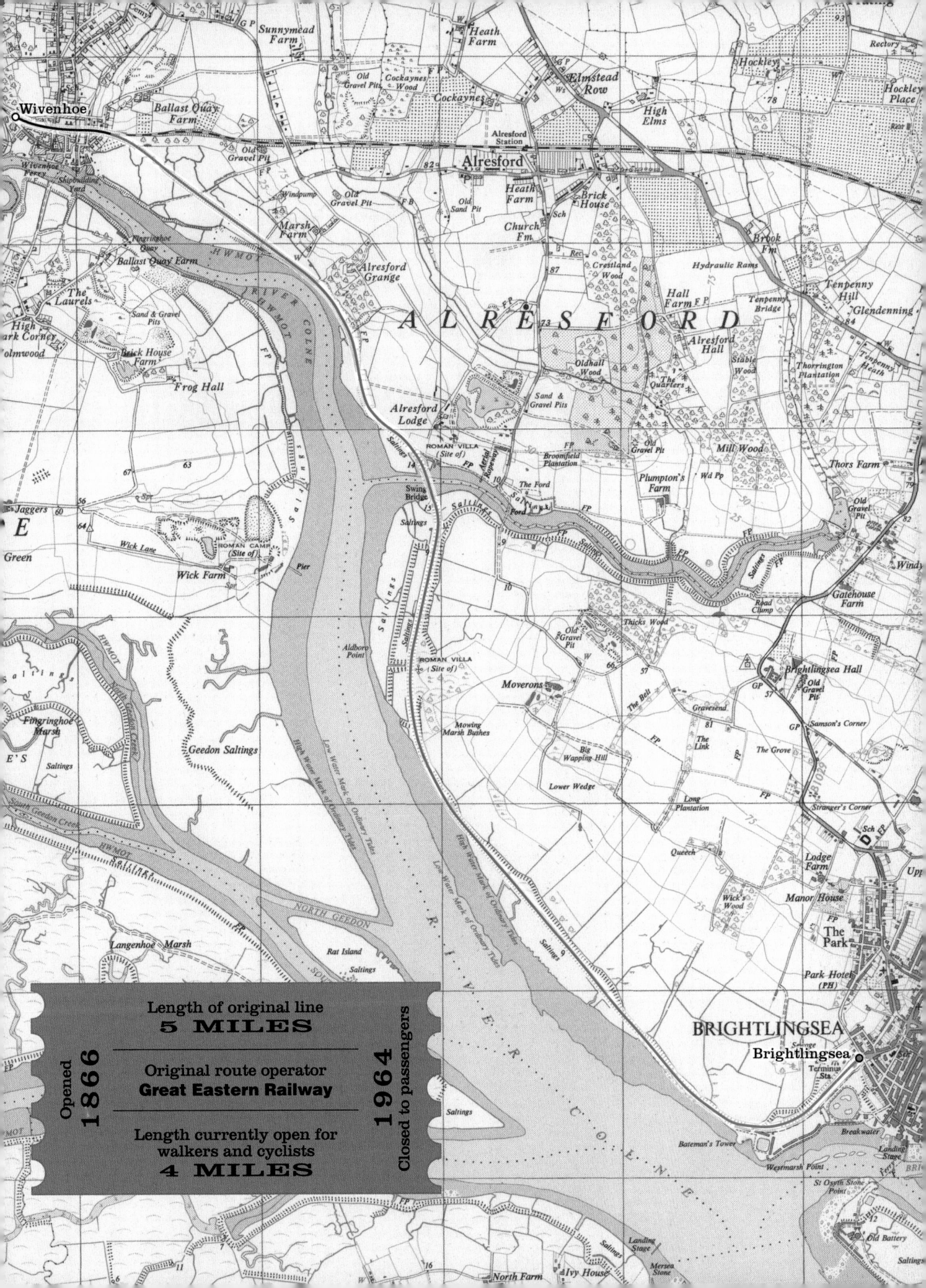

Length of original line
5 MILES

Original route operator
Great Eastern Railway

Length currently open for
walkers and cyclists
4 MILES

Opened **1866**

1964 Closed to passengers

Railways first reached the port of Wivenhoe in the upper reaches of the Colne Estuary when the 2½-mile Tendring Hundred Railway (THR) opened in 1863. Connecting with the Great Eastern Railway's (GER) Hythe branch from Colchester, the line was worked by GER for 70% of its receipts. A terminus station at St Botolph's in Colchester (now known as Colchester Town station) was opened in 1866. The THR was extended to the coast at Walton-on-the-Naze in 1867 and the company was absorbed by the GER in 1883.

Meanwhile, with an eye on gaining lucrative fish trade, the Wivenhoe & Brightlingsea Railway had been authorized in 1861 to build a railway connecting the two towns. With no intermediate stations the single-track line hugged the east shore of the Colne Estuary for its entire five miles, with a swing bridge over Alresford Creek being the only engineering feature of importance. The line opened with financial support from the GER, who worked it for 40% of receipts until buying it lock, stock and barrel in 1893 for £31,000.

Despite plans for a new harbour which never materialized, the coming of the railway saw Brightlingsea flourish both as a seaside resort for day trippers and as a yachting centre. Its heyday was in the early twentieth century when trainloads of fish, including sprats destined for the continent during the winter and local Pyfleet oysters, were despatched to distant markets. Like many other branch lines around Britain the Brightlingsea branch went into decline after the Second World War due to ever-increasing competition from road transport. Its coastal route was also at the mercy of storms and in the Great Storm of January 1953 almost three miles of track were washed away. Although immediate closure was threatened, the line had been reopened by the end of that year and in 1957 diesel multiple units were introduced as a cost-saving measure. This was all to no avail as with passenger numbers continuing to decline, the branch was listed for closure in the 1963 'Beeching Report'. Despite strong local objections the end came on 15 June 1964 when the line closed completely.

Following closure, Brightlingsea station building survived until 1968 when it was badly damaged in a fire and then demolished – the original station building had also been destroyed by fire, in 1901.

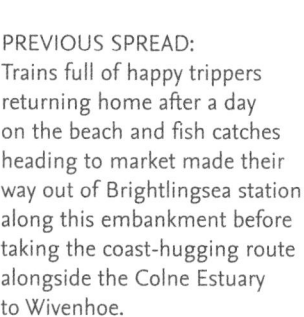

The route of the railway from Brightlingsea ran along this embankment following the eastern shore of the Colne Estuary. Today it provides walkers with far-reaching views across to Mersea Island while taking in the bracing sea air. Inland from the embankment is the Brightlingsea Marsh National Nature Reserve.

PREVIOUS SPREAD:
Trains full of happy trippers returning home after a day on the beach and fish catches heading to market made their way out of Brightlingsea station along this embankment before taking the coast-hugging route alongside the Colne Estuary to Wivenhoe.

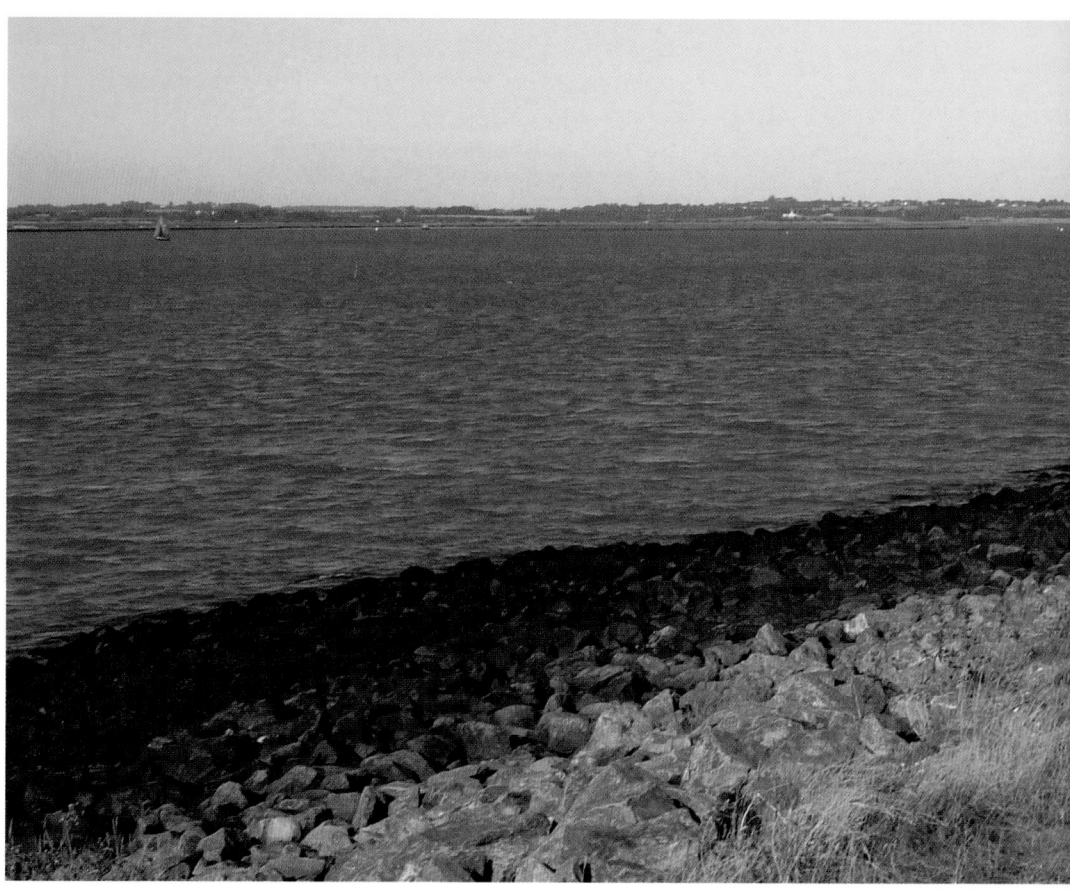

While the site of Brightlingsea station is now a community centre, the Railway Tavern across the road is still open for business. A well-surfaced footpath now follows the top of the railway embankment from the station site for 2¾ miles alongside the Colne Estuary as far as Alresford Creek – there is a large car park and charming seaside café near the beginning of the path at Brighlingsea. The embankment has been raised to aid flood defences since closure of the railway and gives wind-blown walkers panoramic views across the estuary to Mersea Island and the creeks and marshes along the opposite bank. On a fine day myriad yachts, along with an occasional sailing smack, can be seen tacking through the water on their way out to Brightlingsea Reach and the sea.

Inland from the embankment are the 50 hectares of Brightlingsea Marsh, now a National Nature Reserve and home to a wide variety of specialist plants, insects and birdlife. Although the swing bridge at Alresford Creek has long been demolished, it is possible to rejoin the tracked on the opposite bank – via a detour around the creek – from where a path continues along the river bank to Wivenhoe. Here, Greater Anglia trains serve the town, running between Liverpool Street, Colchester, Walton-on-the-Naze and Clacton-on-Sea.

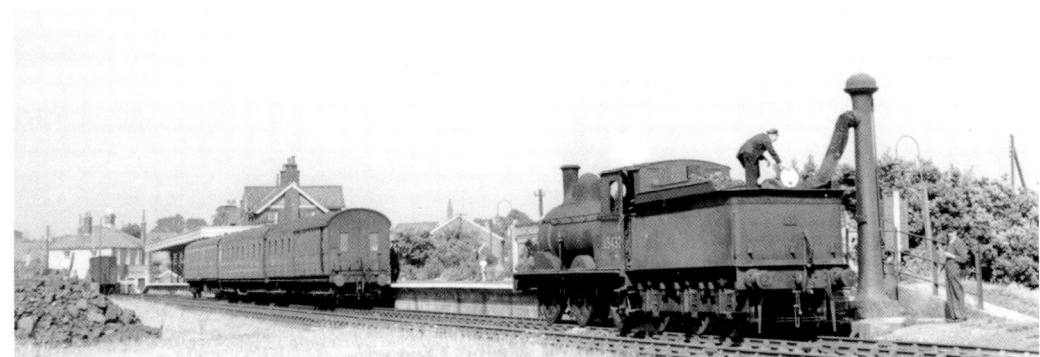

Ex-GER Class 'J15' 0-6-0 No. 65432 takes on water at Brightlingsea on 7 July 1956 before departing with the 4.48pm train to Colchester. This long-running locomotive was built in 1900 and withdrawn in March 1958. Despite the introduction of new diesel multiple units on the Brightlingsea branch in 1957, the line closed in 1964.

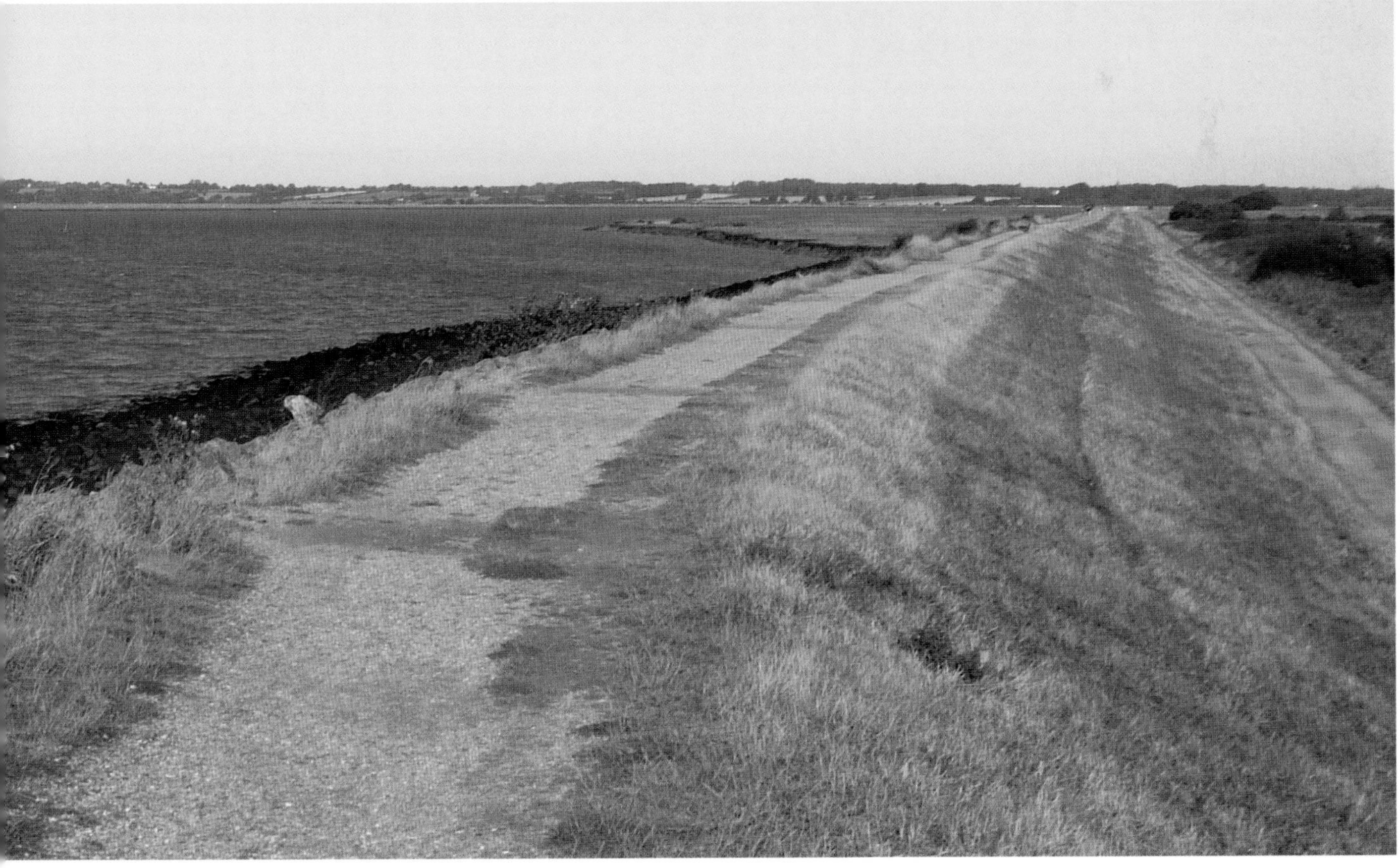

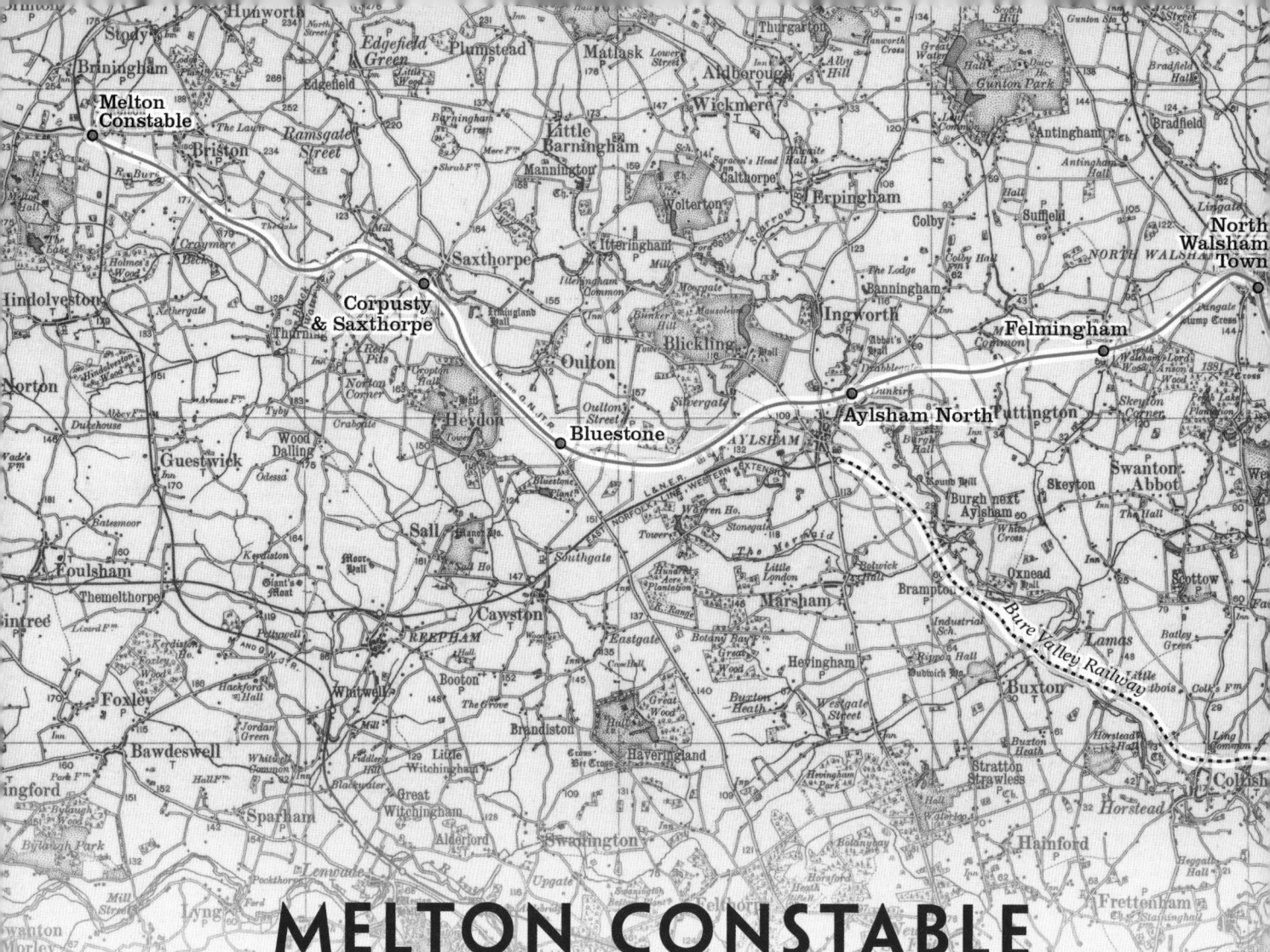

MELTON CONSTABLE
TO
YARMOUTH

Built by a motley collection of local railway companies, what was
to become the Midland & Great Northern Joint Railway had its
workshops in the Norfolk 'railway village' of Melton Constable.
Saved from bankruptcy by the Great Northern and Midland railways
in 1893, this joint railway eventually possessed a sprawling, mainly
single-track, 180-mile network with tentacles reaching out to King's
Lynn, Spalding, Little Bytham, Peterborough, Norwich, Cromer and
Great Yarmouth. Despite healthy through traffic from the Midlands
during the summer holiday season, the antiquated system struggled to
survive in the years following the Second World War. Closure for most
of the railway came in 1959, since when several sections in northeast
Norfolk have been incorporated into a long-distance path.

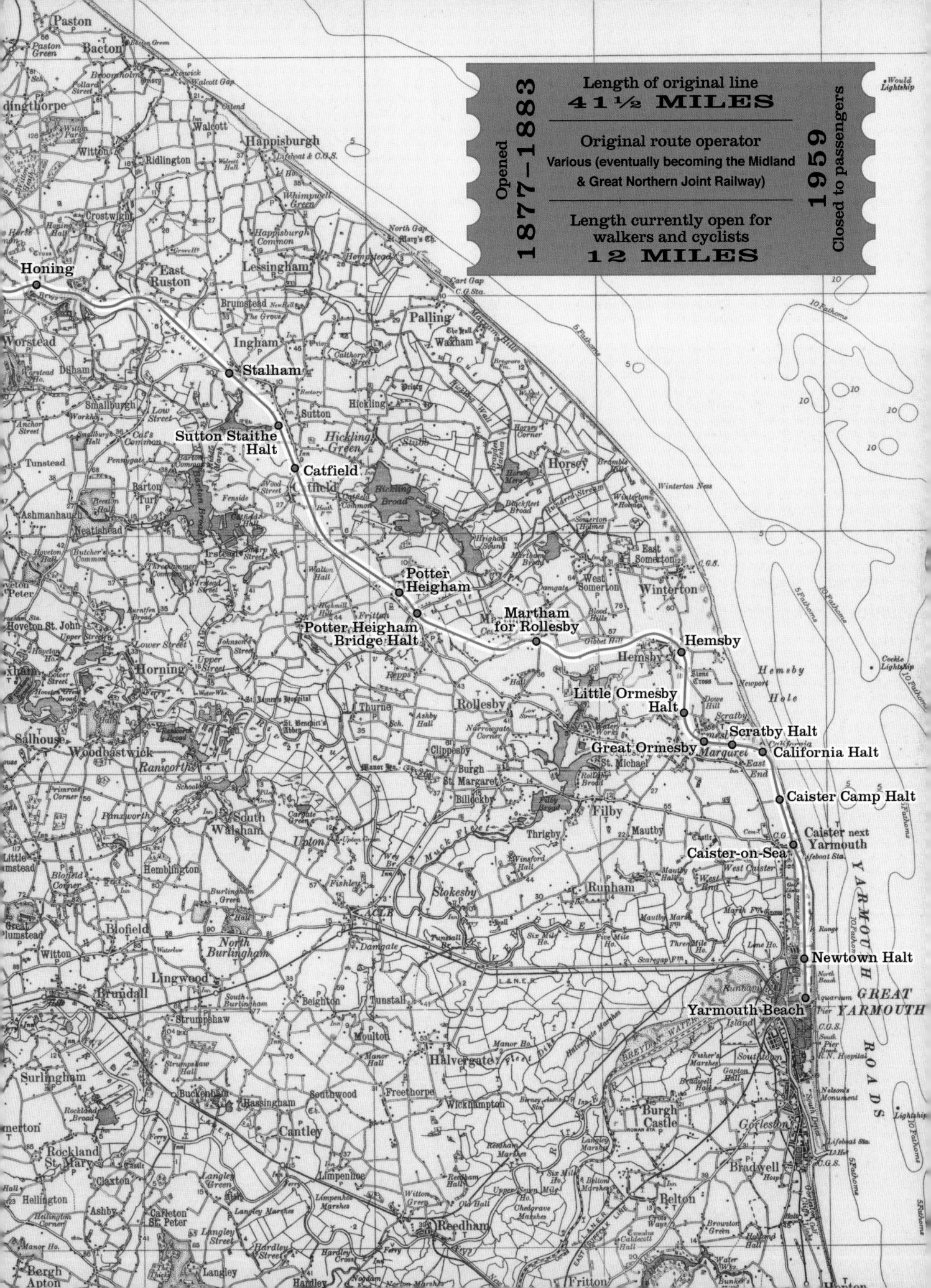

Paston
Paston Green
Bacton
Bacton Green
dingthorpe
Broomholm
Keswick
Walcott Gap
Walcott
Happisburgh
Ridlington
Lessingham
Ingham

Honing
Worstead
Stalham
Sutton Staithe Halt
Catfield
Potter Heigham
Potter Heigham Bridge Halt
Martham for Rollesby
Hemsby
Little Ormesby Halt
Scratby Halt
Great Ormesby
California Halt
Caister Camp Halt
Caister-on-Sea
Caister next Yarmouth
Newtown Halt
Yarmouth Beach
GREAT YARMOUTH

Opened 1877-1883

Length of original line
41½ MILES

Original route operator
Various (eventually becoming the Midland & Great Northern Joint Railway)

Length currently open for walkers and cyclists
12 MILES

1959 Closed to passengers

Railways were late coming to northeast Norfolk, with the network that eventually became the Midland & Great Northern Joint Railway starting life as a motley collection of local companies.

First on the scene was the Great Yarmouth & Stalham Light Railway, which was authorized in 1876 to build a single-track line between the two towns. It opened from Yarmouth to Ormesby in 1877 and to Hemsby in 1878. The company was renamed the Yarmouth & North Norfolk Light Railway and by 1880 it had extended its line to Stalham. An extension to join the Lynn & Fakenham Railway (L&FR – see below) near Fakenham was authorized in 1881 when the company changed its name again, becoming the Yarmouth & North Norfolk Railway. This new company extended its line from Stalham to North Walsham in the same year and then amalgamated with the L&FR and three other railway companies – the Yarmouth Union Railway, the Midland & Eastern Railway and the Peterborough, Wisbech & Sutton Bridge Railway – to form the Eastern & Midlands Railway (E&MR) in 1883.

Meanwhile, in 1880 the L&FR had completed its single-track line between King's Lynn and Fakenham. An extension to the village of Melton Constable opened in 1882 and it was here that the company established its railway works on land donated by Lord Hastings of nearby Melton Constable Hall. The missing link between Melton Constable and North Walsham was completed by the E&MR in 1883. By 1889 the E&MR was seriously overstretched and possessed a sprawling 180-mile network of lines, the majority of which were single track, stretching from Little Bytham Junction

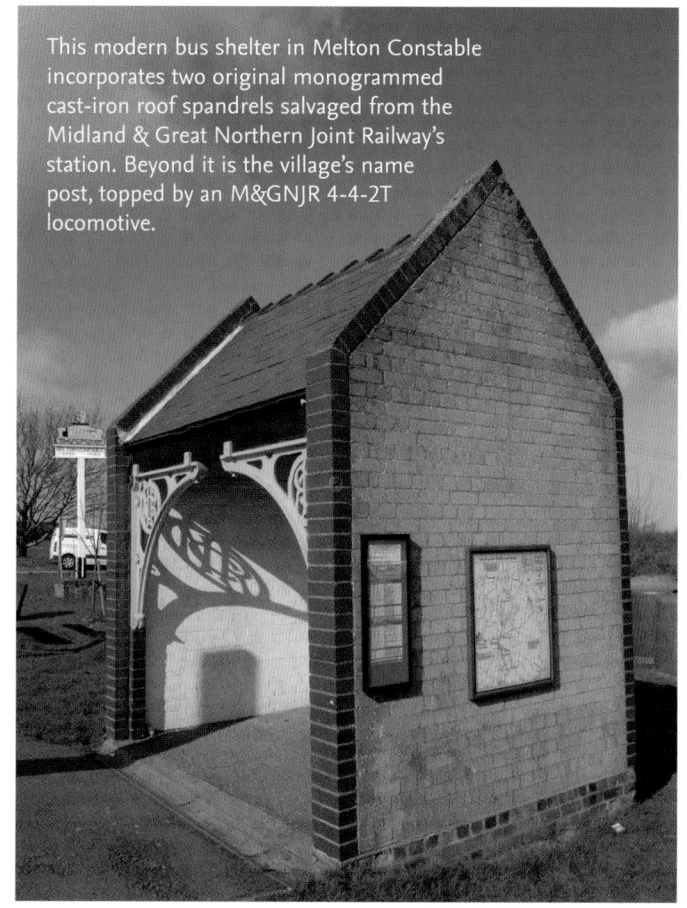

This modern bus shelter in Melton Constable incorporates two original monogrammed cast-iron roof spandrels salvaged from the Midland & Great Northern Joint Railway's station. Beyond it is the village's name post, topped by an M&GNJR 4-4-2T locomotive.

BELOW: A luggage porter whiles away his time in the sunshine at Melton Constable station on 16 April 1947. This railway village depended on the M&GNJR works for much of its employment until they were closed by the LNER in 1936. It was also the hub of the network, with lines radiating out to King's Lynn and beyond, as well as to Norwich, Great Yarmouth and Cromer.

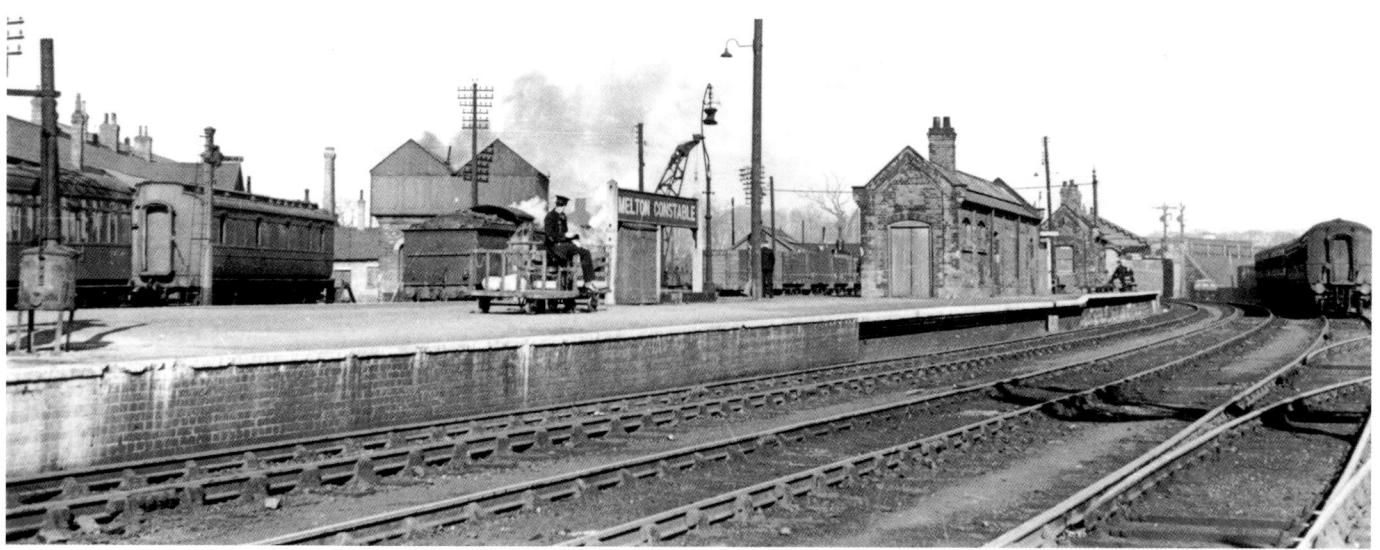

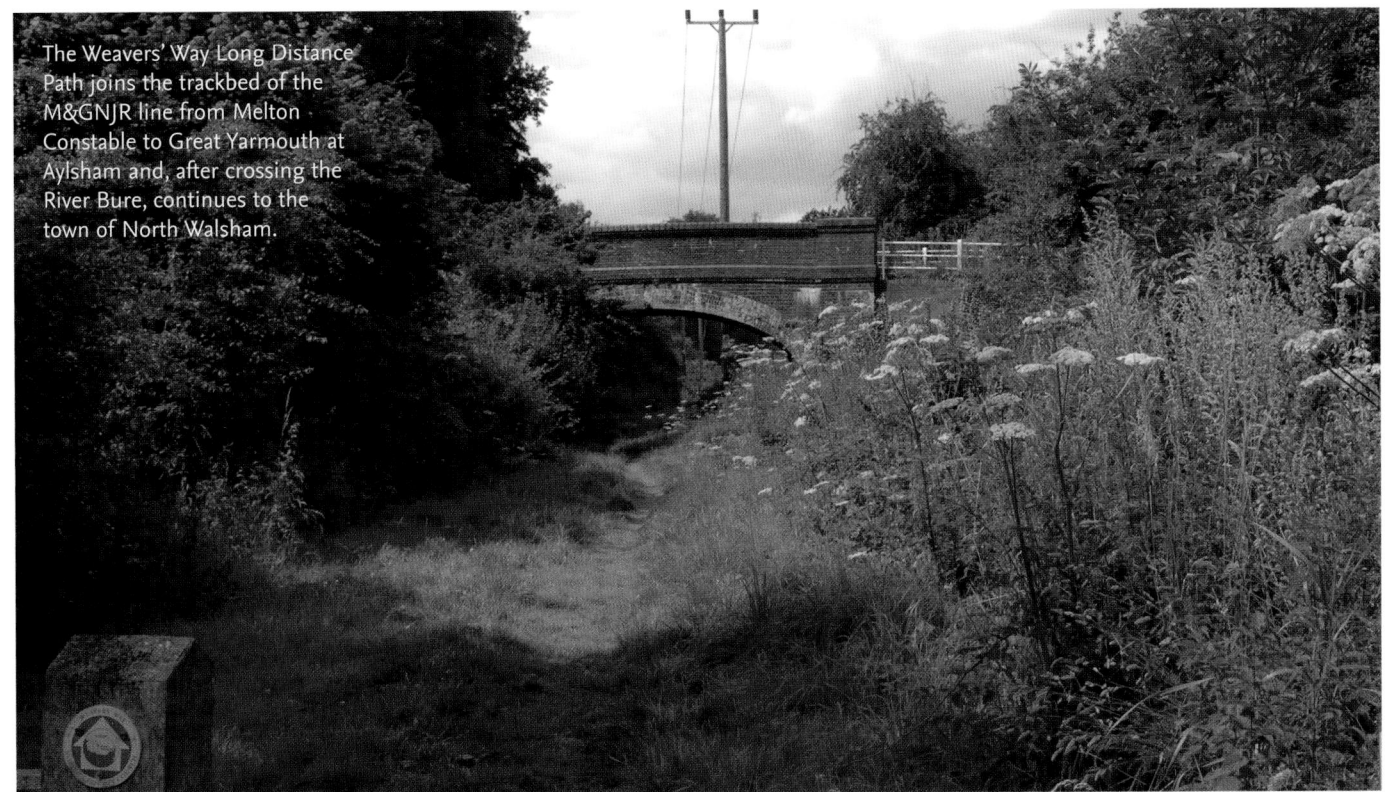

The Weavers' Way Long Distance Path joins the trackbed of the M&GNJR line from Melton Constable to Great Yarmouth at Aylsham and, after crossing the River Bure, continues to the town of North Walsham.

in Lincolnshire (where there was a connection with the Midland Railway) to Yarmouth. It also owned branch lines from Sutton Bridge to Peterborough, Melton Constable to Cromer and Melton Constable to Norwich.

With a financial crisis on its hands the E&MR turned to the Midland Railway (MR) and the Great Northern Railway (GNR), on which it was largely dependent on through traffic, for help. Thus the Midland & Great Northern Joint Railway (M&GNJR) was born in 1893, jointly owned by the MR and GNR with headquarters at King's Lynn and railway works at Melton Constable. Striking right into the heart of Great Eastern Railway territory, the M&GNJR offered its two parent companies the opportunity of siphoning off lucrative trade to and from the region. However, this duplication of efforts was to be the railway's eventual downfall.

The Big Four Grouping of 1923 saw the newly formed London Midland & Scottish Railway (LMS) and London & North Eastern Railway (LNER) jointly take over the running of the M&GNJR. This arrangement lasted until 1936 when the LNER took complete responsibility for working the line – at the same time the King's Lynn HQ and most of the railway works at Melton Constable were

closed. Through running was the lifeblood of the railway, with passenger trains from King's Cross, the Midlands and the North to Cromer, Norwich and Yarmouth keeping it very busy during the summer months. Seasonal agricultural goods traffic was also heavy but the mainly single-track railway struggled to cope with demand during the peak holiday weekends. This all came to an end with the outbreak of the Second World War.

The austerity post-war years saw the M&GNJR nationalized and struggling for survival. With long journey times and serving only small communities along most of its length, it could not compete with road transport. Many of its routes were also duplicated by former GER lines and in those straitened times closure of the entire network soon became a reality. Apart from a few isolated sections retained for freight, and the Cromer to Melton Constable section, the M&GNJR closed completely on 2 March 1959. The last vestige of passenger train services ended on 6 April 1964 when the section from Sheringham to Melton Constable closed completely – this has since been reopened as a heritage railway as far as Holt by the North Norfolk Railway. Today the section from Sheringham to Cromer is the only part of the former M&GNJR system that is still served by trains on the national rail network.

Despite closure over 50 years ago there is still much of the M&GNJR to explore. Our journey starts at Melton Constable, once the hub of the system and home to the company's railway works. Here, although the station and Lord Hasting's private waiting room have long been demolished, much of the former railway works has been incorporated into an industrial estate. The large water tower also survives, complete with damage sustained during an air attack in the Second World War. Two ornamental roof supports from the station have been incorporated into a bus shelter, while an attractive village name board features a painting of an M&GNJR 4-4-2T in the company's distinctive yellow-ochre livery.

To the east, the station and platform at Corpusty & Saxthorpe have survived on the edge of a sports field, while the station at Bluestone (closed to passengers in 1916) is now a private residence. From here to the outskirts of Aylsham the railway's route is now

utilized as farm tracks. At Aylsham the viaduct over the River Bure has survived and is now incorporated into the Weavers' Way long-distance path. The attractive town of Aylsham is also the western terminus of the 15-in-gauge Bure Valley Railway to Wroxham. Aylsham North station has been demolished and its site is now a car park for the Weavers' Way, which utilizes the trackbed for the next five miles to North Walsham. En route there is a car park at Felmingham where the platform and station building (now restored as a private residence) survive alongside the path. The latter continues to follow the railway route before ending at a car park in North Walsham – the town is still served by trains on the Bittern Line between Norwich and Sheringham but the M&GNJR station of Aylsham North has long since been demolished.

South of Aylsham the M&GNJR route has been swallowed up by 'improvements' to the A149 as

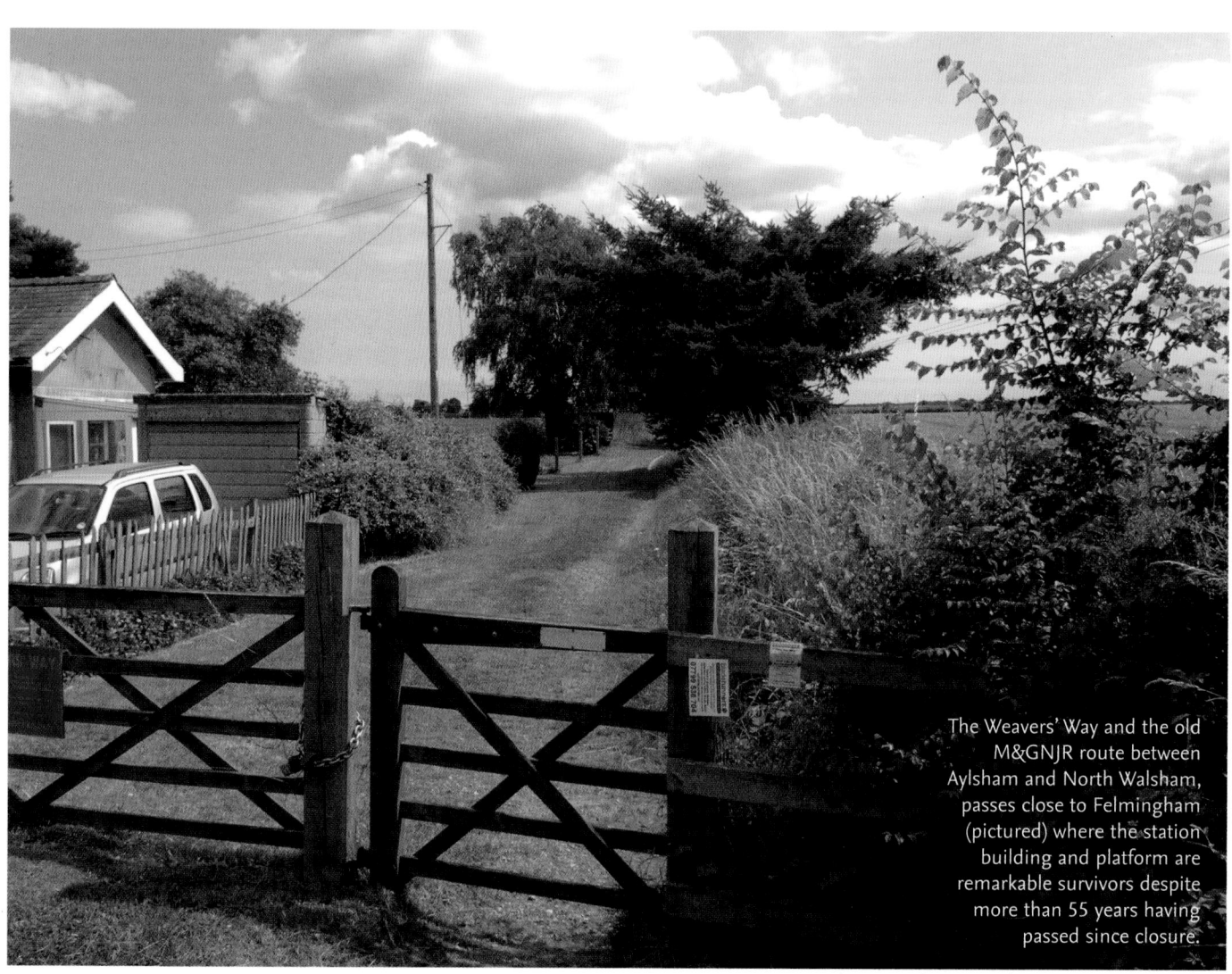

The Weavers' Way and the old M&GNJR route between Aylsham and North Walsham, passes close to Felmingham (pictured) where the station building and platform are remarkable survivors despite more than 55 years having passed since closure.

far as Benngate, where there is a car park for users of the Weavers' Way, which has been rerouted via quiet lanes from North Walsham. For the next five miles the Way utilizes the railway route as far as Stalham. Heading east from Benngate, the Way soon crosses over the privately owned but disused North Walsham & Dilham Canal before reaching another car park near Briggate. Soon the derelict remains of Honing station are reached – here the two platforms, along with the remains of the waiting room, signal box foundations and M&GN-style lattice fencing, wait to be explored in the undergrowth.

Heading away from Honing alongside the disused canal, the Weavers' Way reaches yet another car park at East Ruston. From here it follows the dead-straight course of the railway for two miles to the village of Stalham where refreshments can be taken at the Swan Inn. The former station building at Stalham was dismantled and rebuilt at Holt on the North Norfolk Railway.

South of Stalham the route of the railway is now used by the realigned A149 for five miles to Potter Heigham, where remains of the platform and station buildings have survived. Here, the Weaver's Way parts company and heads east while the railway route becomes much more difficult to follow south of the River Thurne. The route through Martham, Hemsby and Scratby has long since disappeared beneath farmland but, as it reaches the coast at California, once the site of a small halt, it can once again be followed on foot along the coastline to Caister-on-Sea. The end of the line was at Yarmouth Beach station, where thousands of happy holidaymakers once arrived after their long journey from the Midlands. The station remained intact until 1986 when it was demolished to make way for a new bus station. All that remains as a memorial is a brick plinth with a short length of track and a couple of cast-iron roof spandrels decorated with the M&GNJR and E&MR logos.

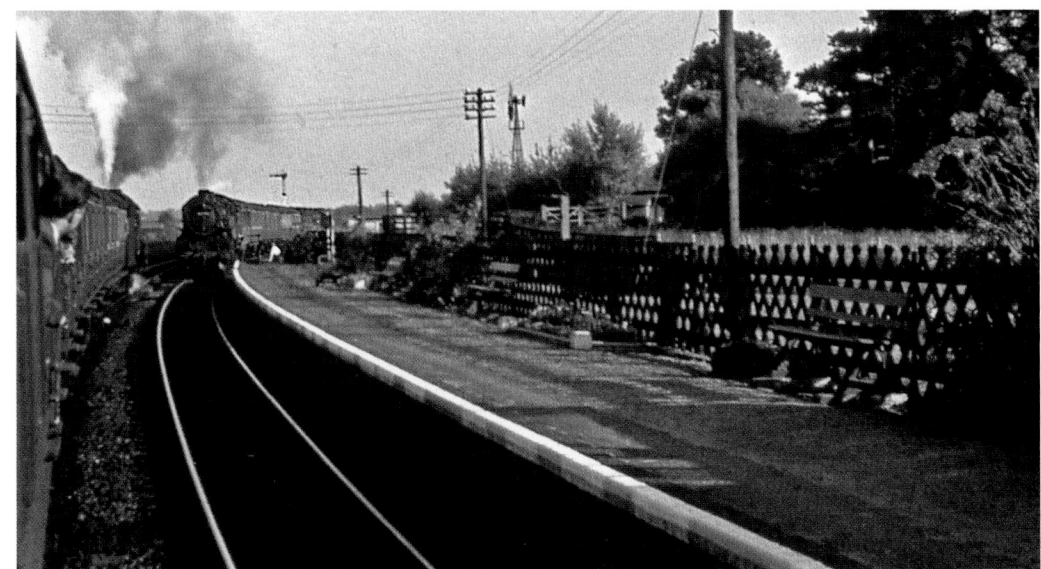

Two trains full of holidaymakers, hauled by Ivatt Class '4MT' 2-6-0s pass at Potter Heigham station on 13 September 1958, the final summer of service on the old M&GNJR network which closed less than six months later. Although parts of this station have survived, the former railway route is now used by the realigned A149.

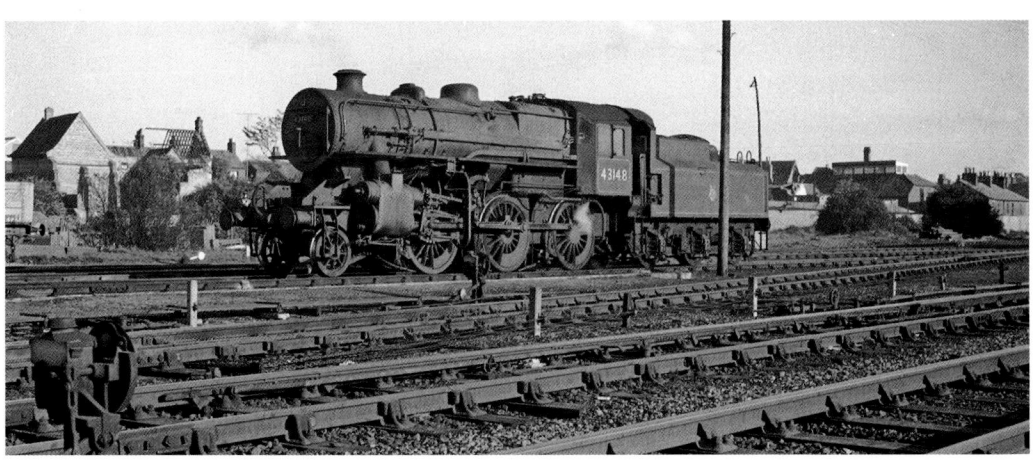

Affectionately known as 'Doodlebugs', 'Flying Pigs' or 'Mucky Ducks', Ivatt Class '4MT' 2-6-0 No. 43148 is seen here between turns at Yarmouth Beach, c.1958. Built by BR at Doncaster in 1951 this powerful but ungainly locomotive had a short life and was withdrawn from Staveley Barrow Hill shed in April 1965.

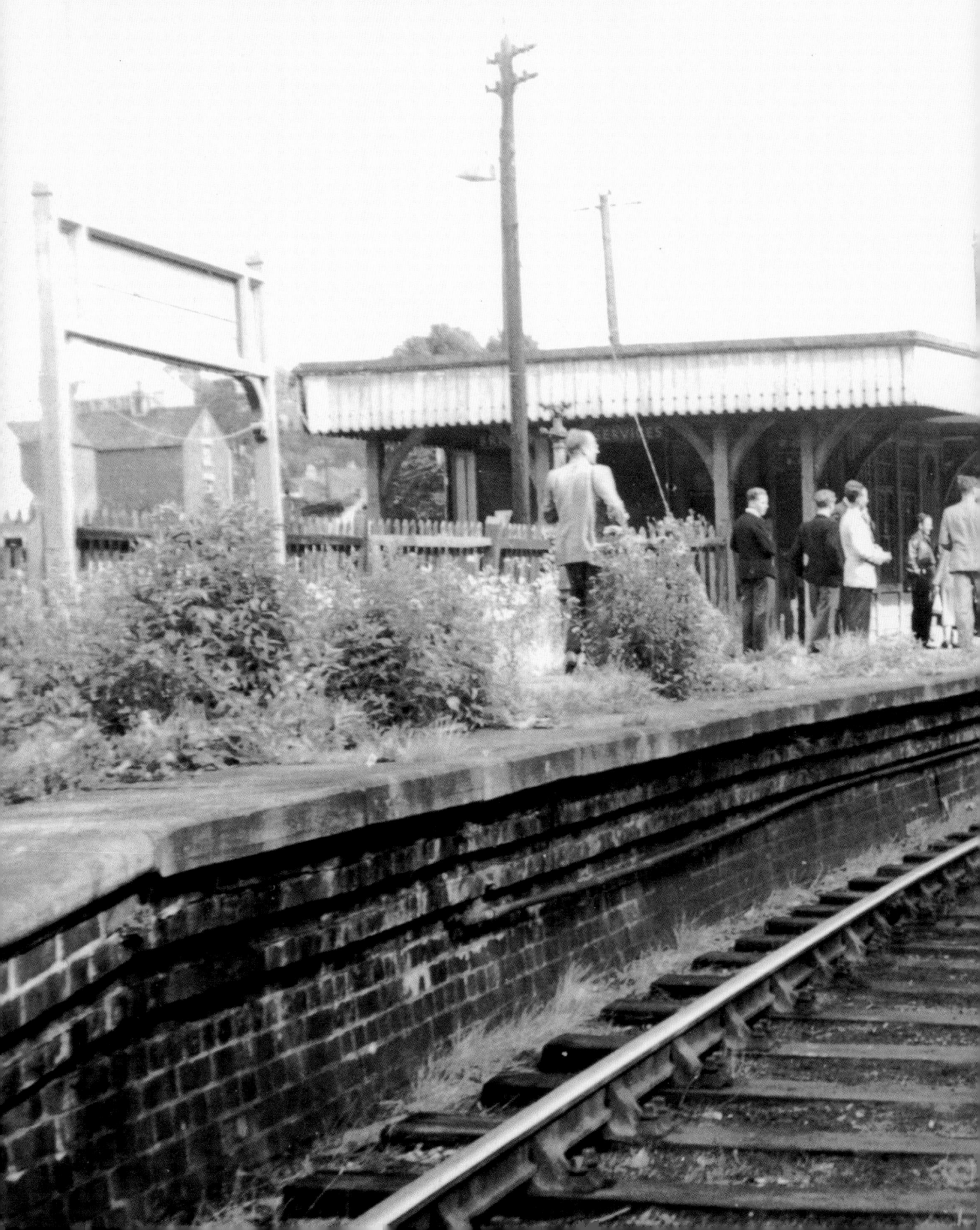

CENTRAL ENGLAND

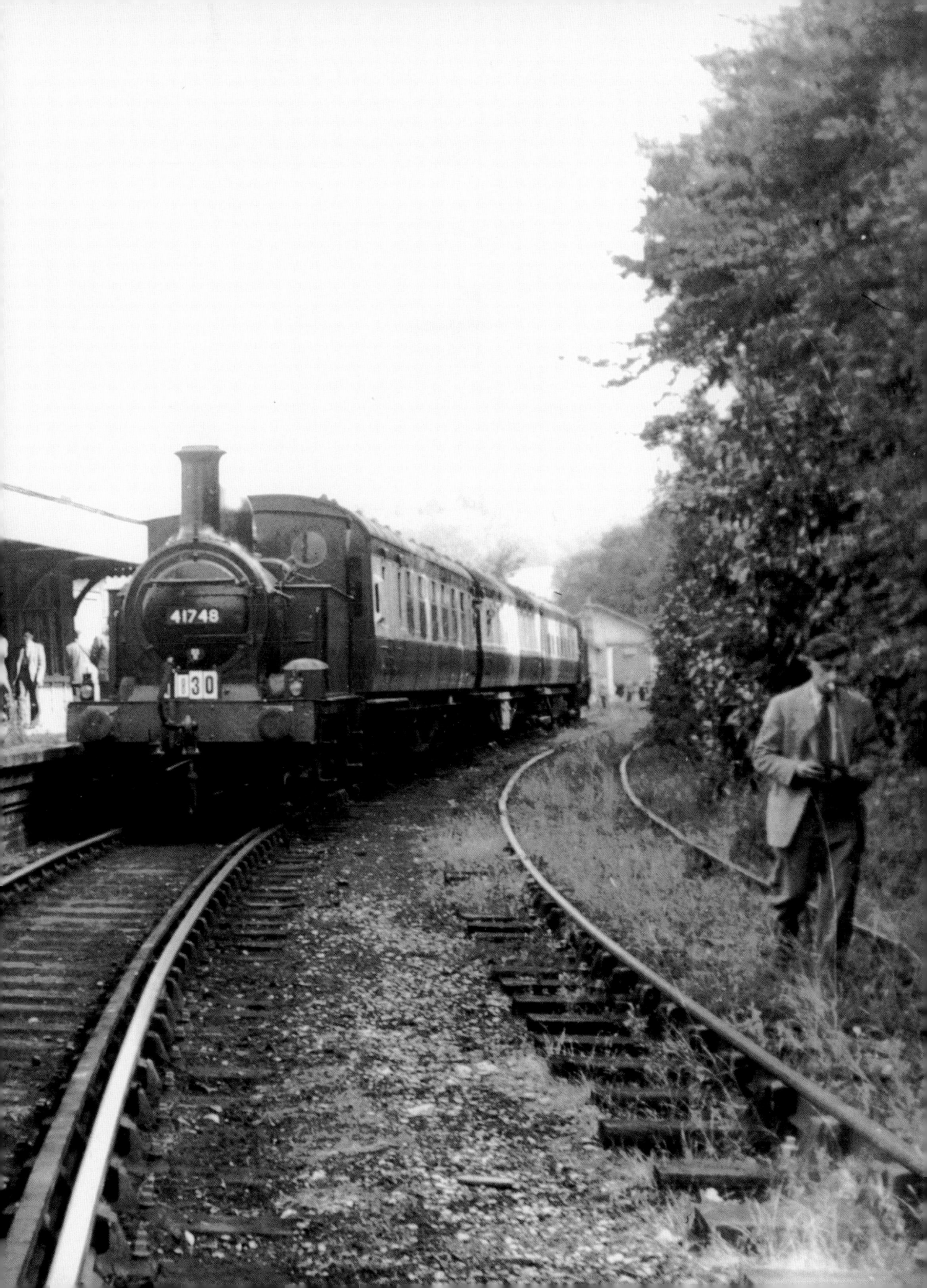

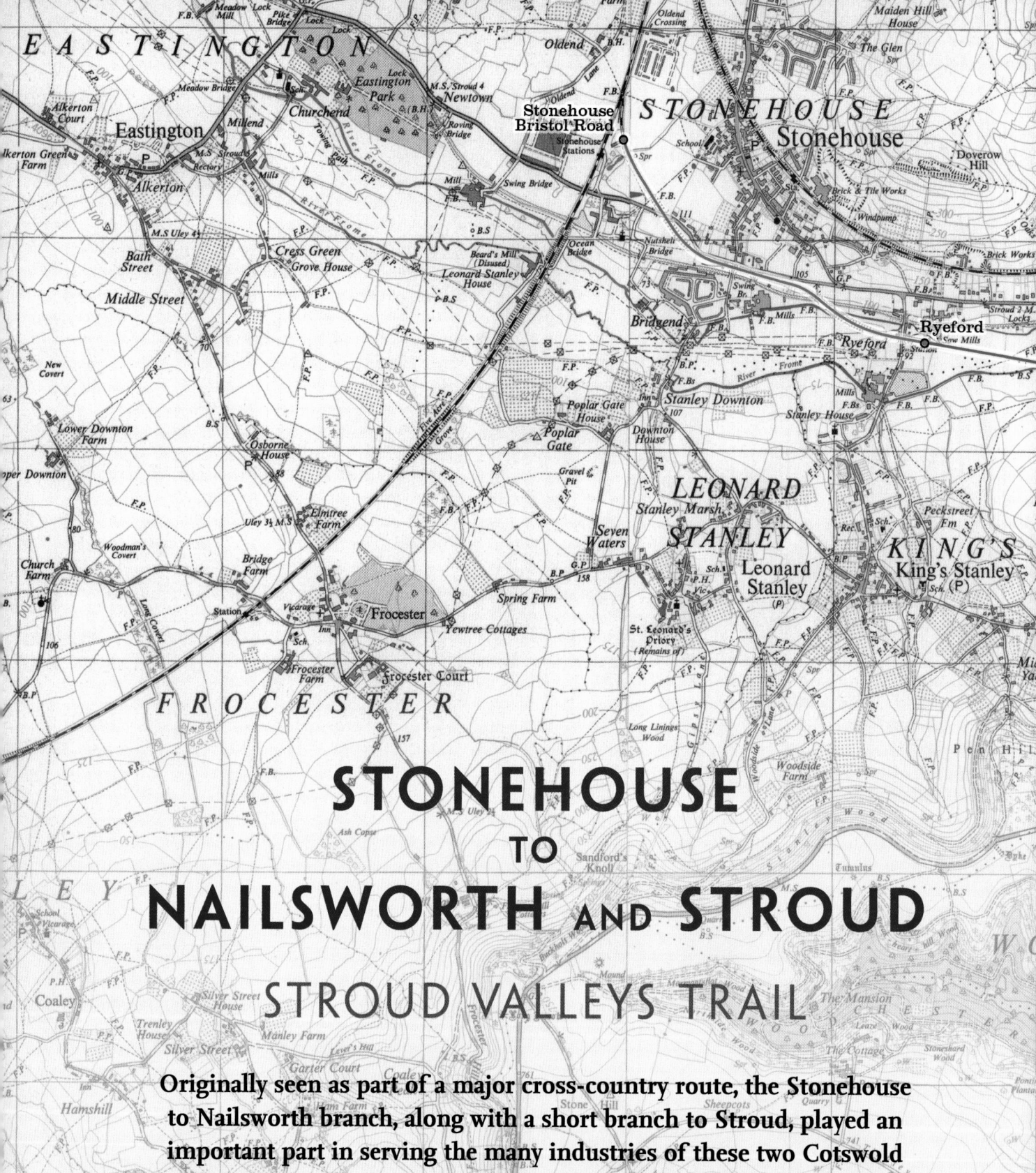

STONEHOUSE
TO
NAILSWORTH AND STROUD

STROUD VALLEYS TRAIL

Originally seen as part of a major cross-country route, the Stonehouse to Nailsworth branch, along with a short branch to Stroud, played an important part in serving the many industries of these two Cotswold valleys until 1966. Passenger traffic, on the other hand, was relatively light with the service first being suspended in 1947 following a national coal shortage and then officially withdrawn in 1949. Since closure the section from Ryeford to Nailsworth has been reopened as a footpath and cycleway.

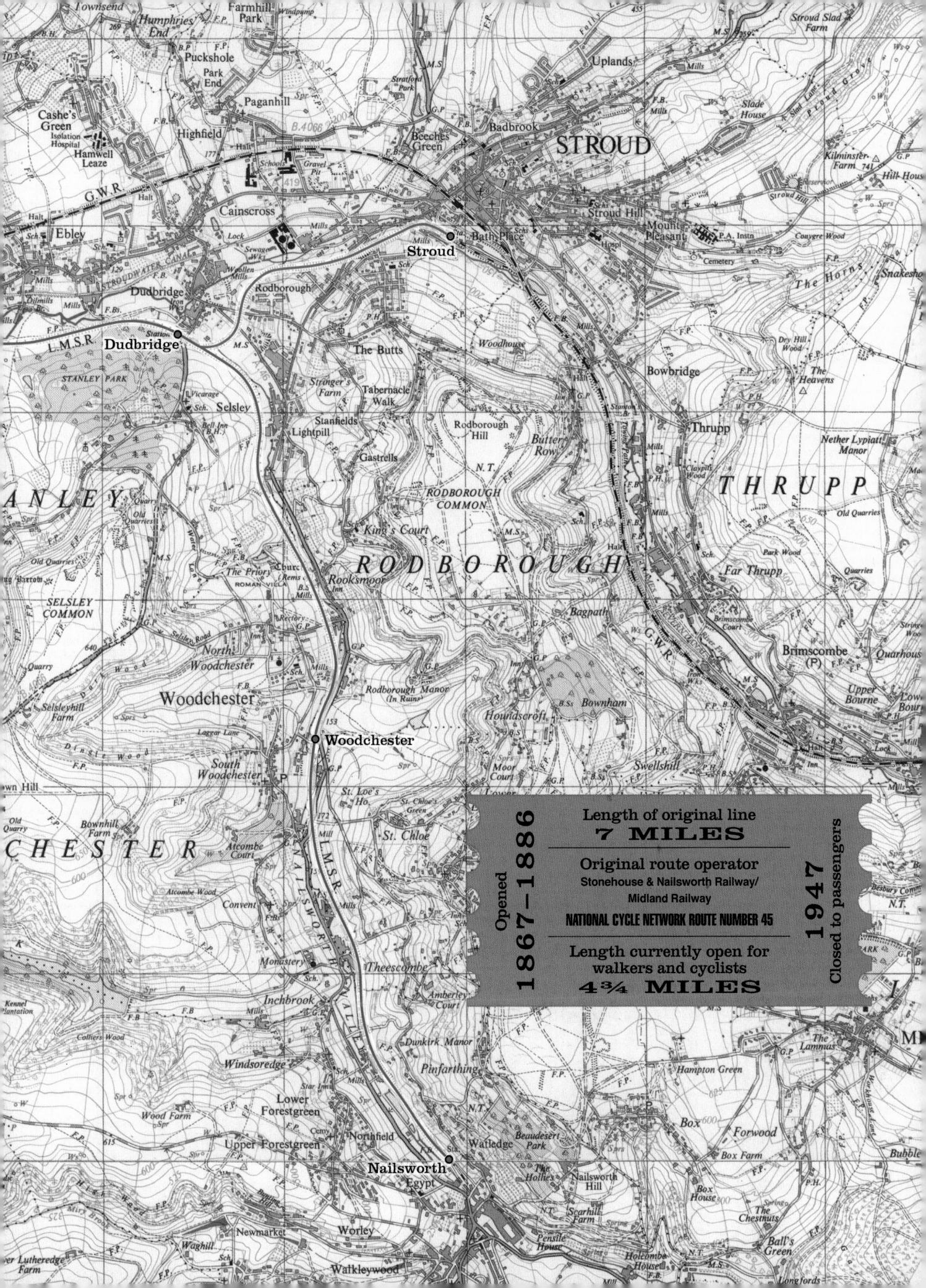

STROUD

THRUPP

RODBOROUGH

Stroud

Dudbridge

Woodchester

Nailsworth

Opened 1867–1886

1947 Closed to passengers

Length of original line
7 MILES

Original route operator
Stonehouse & Nailsworth Railway/
Midland Railway

NATIONAL CYCLE NETWORK ROUTE NUMBER 45

Length currently open for
walkers and cyclists
4¾ MILES

An important centre for weaving and brewing since the seventeenth century, the Cotswold town of Stroud received its first modern link with the outside world in 1779, when the Stroudwater Canal opened from the River Severn. The opening of the Thames & Severn Canal between Stroud and Lechlade via the long and dank Sapperton Tunnel in 1789 further improved communications. The first railway to reach the Stroud Valley was the broad-gauge Great Western Railway (GWR), which opened from Kemble to Standish Junction in 1845.

Three miles south of Stroud, the small town of Nailsworth was also once a centre for woollen mills and brewing. Ambitious proposals to build a railway through the area from the Midland Railway's (MR) Bristol to Gloucester main line at Stonehouse to link up with the GWR's Malmesbury branch came to naught and in the end the Stonehouse & Nailsworth Railway was authorized to build a 5¾-mile branch line from Stonehouse by paralleling the Stroudwater Canal as far as Dudbridge and then heading south up the valley to Nailsworth. The railway opened in February 1867 but the company was soon in dire financial straits and an official receiver was appointed at the end of that year. While the railway continued to operate, negotiations for a takeover by the MR were extremely protracted. Agreement was not reached until 1874 and it was a further four years before this was authorized by a new Act of Parliament.

With the MR in control the company was soon looking at ways to make an incursion into GWR territory at Stroud. The outcome of their deliberations was a 1¼-mile branch line, built at great cost, from Dudbridge, on the Nailsworth branch, which opened for goods in 1885 and for passengers a year later. To avoid confusion with the nearby GWR station, the MR's station was named Stroud Wallgate. Goods traffic was especially heavy on this short route, which featured a 9-arch viaduct on the approach to the terminus, and by the end of the century the MR had installed improved goods handling facilities at stations and industrial sidings along the whole route.

By 1922 passenger traffic was catered for by six return trains each weekday along the Nailsworth branch while the connecting service from Dudbridge met both up and down trains – the journey to Stroud Wallgate in a push-pull carriage propelled or hauled by ancient MR 0-4-4 tank locos took only three minutes! Becoming part of the newly formed London Midland & Scottish Railway (LMS) in 1923, the passenger services on the Nailsworth and Stroud branches clung to life until 16 June 1947 when they were suspended, never to return, during a period of national coal shortage. Following nationalization of the railways in 1948, the new bosses at British Railways were quick to rid themselves of loss-making branch lines and the suspended passenger services on the two branches were officially withdrawn on 8 June 1949.

Despite the loss of passenger services, the Nailsworth and Stroud branches remained open for goods traffic, with steam traction lasting until the end of 1965. The end came on 1 June 1966 – ninety-nine years after opening – when they were completely closed.

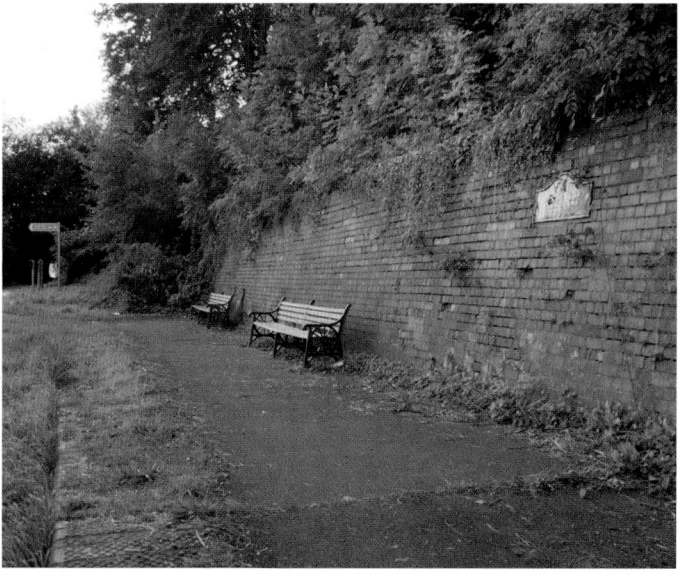

All that remains today of Dudbridge station, once the junction for the short branch line to Stroud. A plaque on the retaining wall records the station's demolition in 1969 while, beyond, a modern claustrophobic tunnel leads to the footpath and cycleway along the trackbed to Nailsworth.

RIGHT: 6 July 1963: Gloucester Barnwood's ex-LMS Class '3F' 'Jinty' 0-6-0T No. 47308 is watched by a few locals and a bored looking young lad from the weed-infested platform of Woodchester station on the occasion of an enthusiasts' special to Nailsworth. Judging by the sea of faces looking out from the carriages the trip must have been a sell-out!

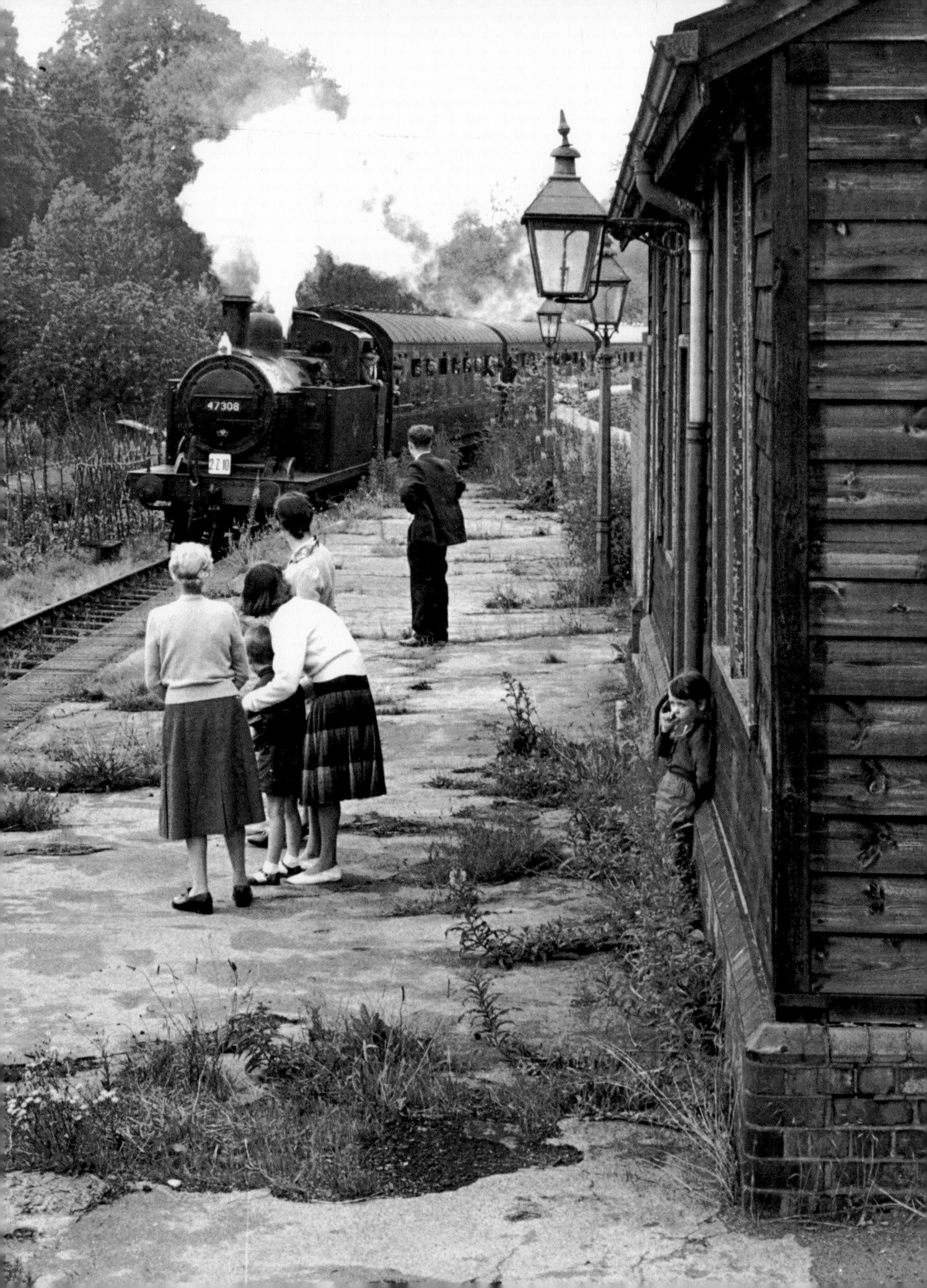

Seen here on 18 February 1976, the derelict state of Nailsworth station contrasts greatly with the superbly restored building that is now a private residence.

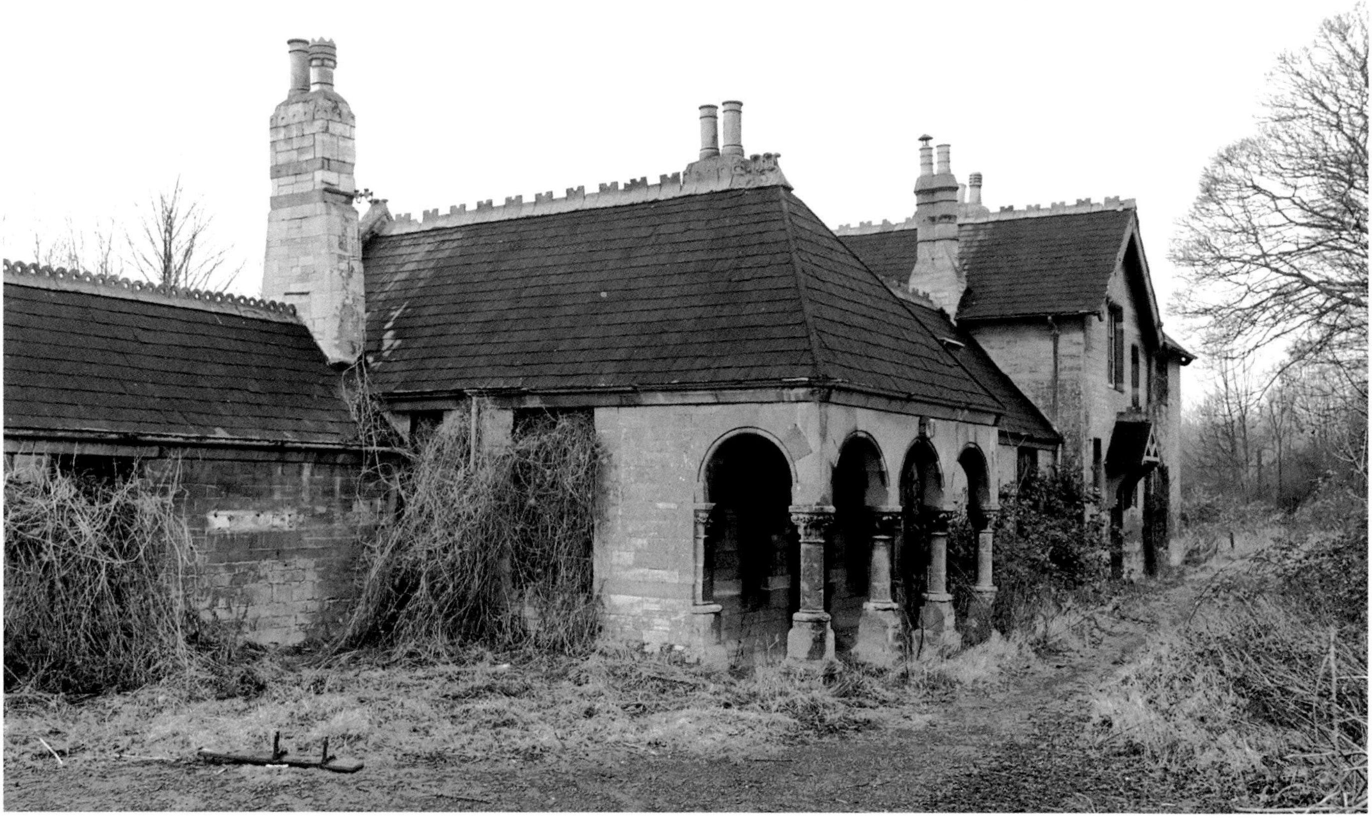

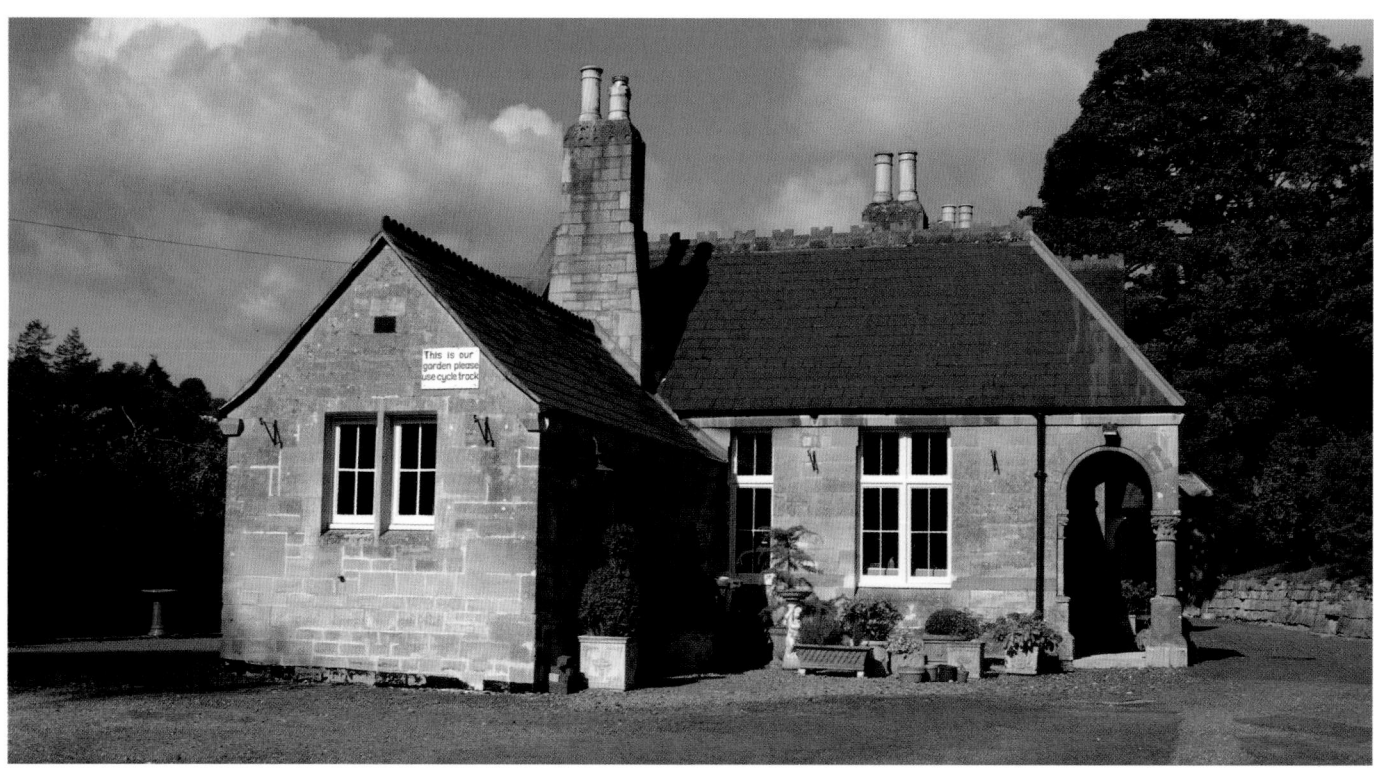

Since closure much of the trackbed of the Stonehouse to Nailsworth branch line has been reopened as a 4¾-mile footpath and cycleway known as the Stroud Valleys Trail. It also forms part of National Cycle Network Route 45. The path starts at a car park off the A419 near King's Stanley and, after a short distance, joins the trackbed near the site of Ryeford station, now an industrial estate, and Stroud Cricket Club's grounds. Heading east the path closely follows the meandering River Frome and the restored section of the Stroudwater Canal. Featuring a MR brick-arched bridge over a farm track, the route along this stretch has recently been planted with a variety of apple and pear trees.

At Dudbridge the site of the station has long disappeared beneath a roundabout but the high retaining wall and one of the platforms have survived – a plaque on the wall reminds us that the station was demolished in 1969. From Dudbridge the path enters a narrow tunnel under the B4066 before heading south up the Nailsworth Valley to the site of Woodchester station, passing through a tree-lined cutting where an iron road bridge has more recently been reinforced to take the weight of modern vehicles. Approaching Woodchester the path crosses the Nailsworth Stream on a small girder bridge; the fast-running waters below once provided power for the many mills along the valley.

At Woodchester, where the wooden station building has long been demolished, the path crosses Station Road where trains once passed over a level crossing – only the former crossing keeper's cottage and a concrete post still survive – then dives under the A46 to enter a heavily wooded section on a ledge above the valley. Below are the now-silent five-storey-high Dunkirk Mills, which have been tastefully restored into flats. The Stroud Textile Trust has restored part of the mill as a visitor centre where pride of place goes to an enormous cast iron overshot wheel, made in Stroud in 1855, which is operated on open days.

The final tree-lined approach into Nailsworth passes the former railway station (built in a grand style with Ionic pillars) and goods shed which have been tastefully restored as a private residence. The path ends in the old railway goods yard near Egypt Mill. Located on the edge of the River Frome this sixteenth-century corn mill has been beautifully converted into a hotel. The former warehouse also survives in the yard while, across the road, the old Railway Hotel (the name still proudly emblazoned across its frontage) is now a private residence. It is but a short distance from here to the town centre and car parking.

The end of the line at Nailsworth on 7 May 1962, with ex-LMS Class '4F' 0-6-0 No. 44045 shunting some wagons into the goods shed. Despite the passage of time since complete closure in 1966, much of this scene remains today – the goods shed, warehouse and Railway Hotel have all survived, albeit with different uses.

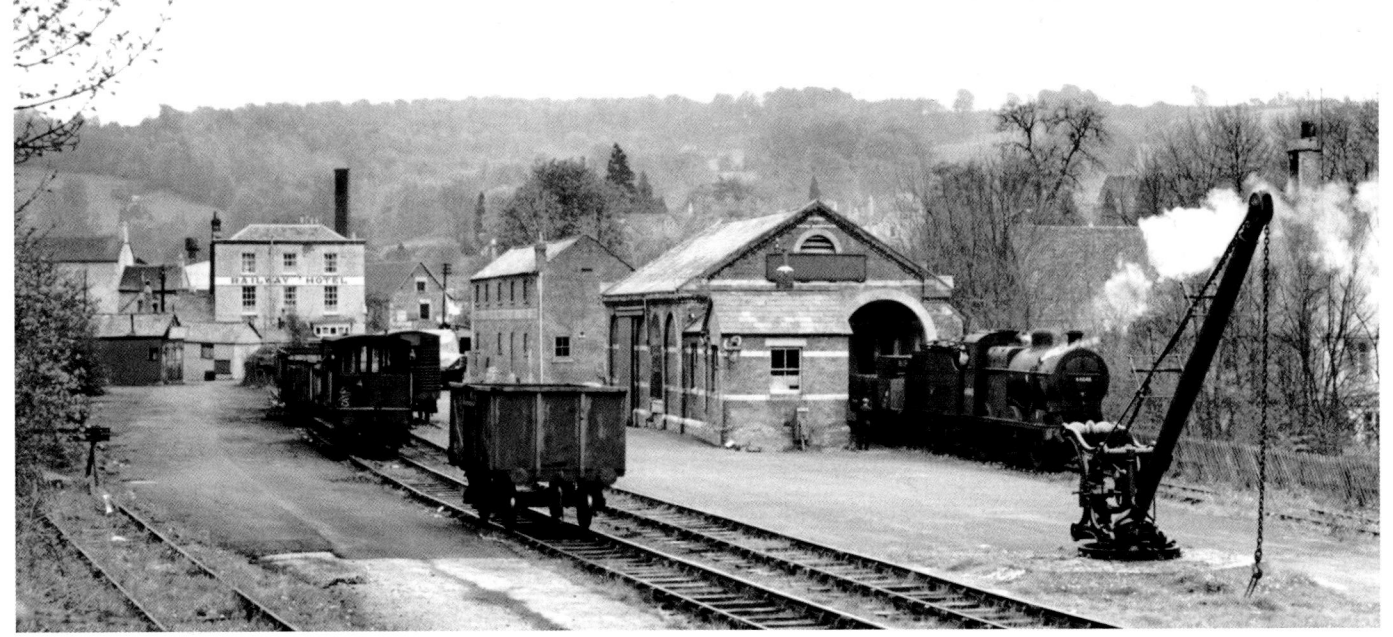

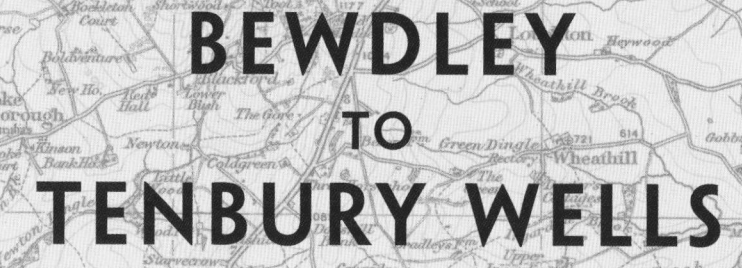

BEWDLEY
TO
TENBURY WELLS

WYRE FOREST

Crossing the River Severn on a substantial bridge north of Bewdley, this delightful rural line headed off west through the Wyre Forest, serving small communities along its length. From 1908 the eastern section also carried munitions for the Admiralty depot at Ditton Priors and stone from a quarry at Clee Hill via a branch line from Cleobury Mortimer. At Tenbury Wells the line met a 5½-mile branch from Woofferton but this little-used through route ended with the branch's closure in July 1961.

The rest of the line soldiered on until its closure in 1962 west of Cleobury Mortimer. Remaining Admiralty traffic for Ditton Priors continued until complete closure in 1965. Two miles of the trackbed in the Wyre Forest have recently been reopened as a footpath and cycleway.

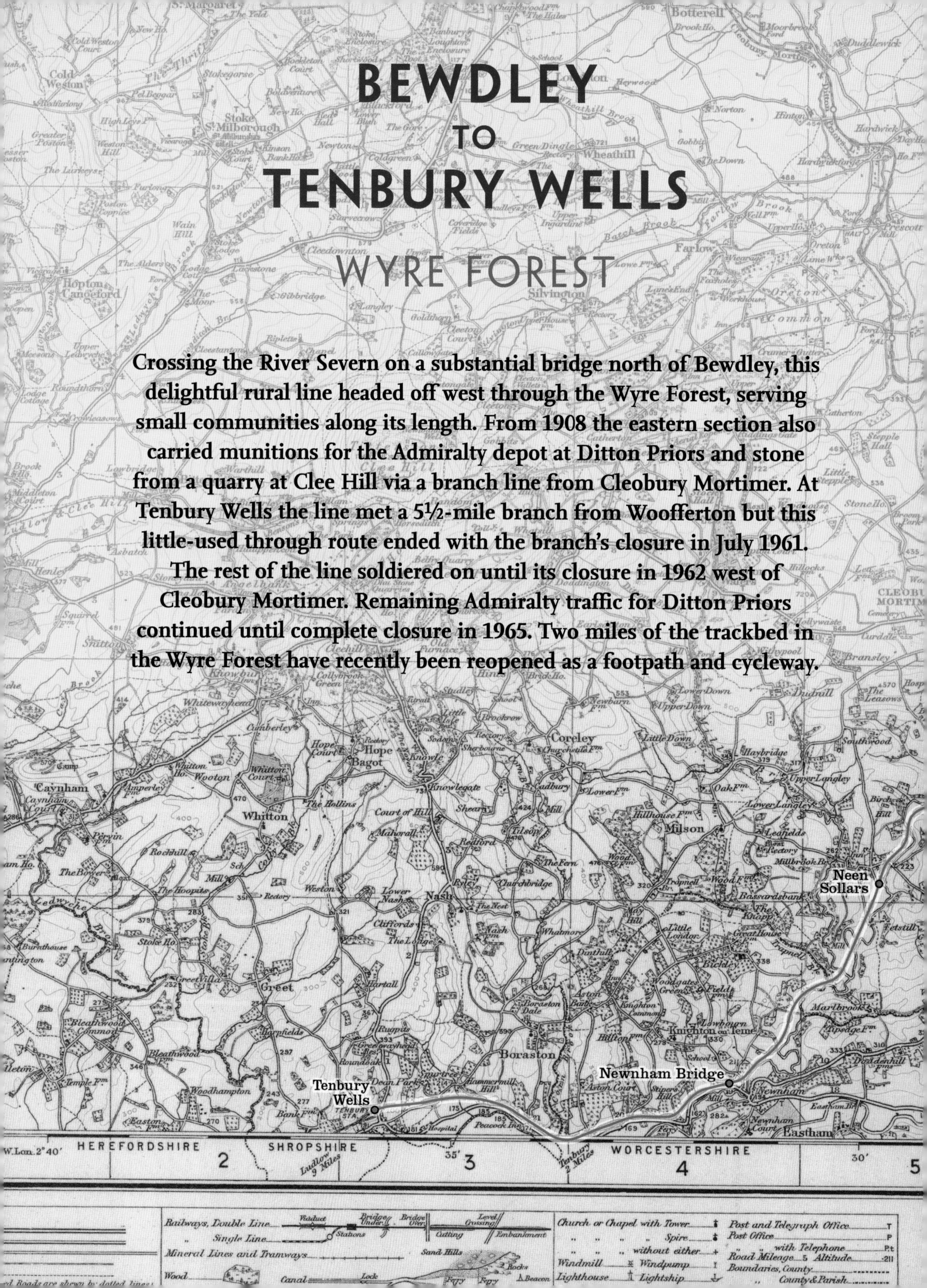

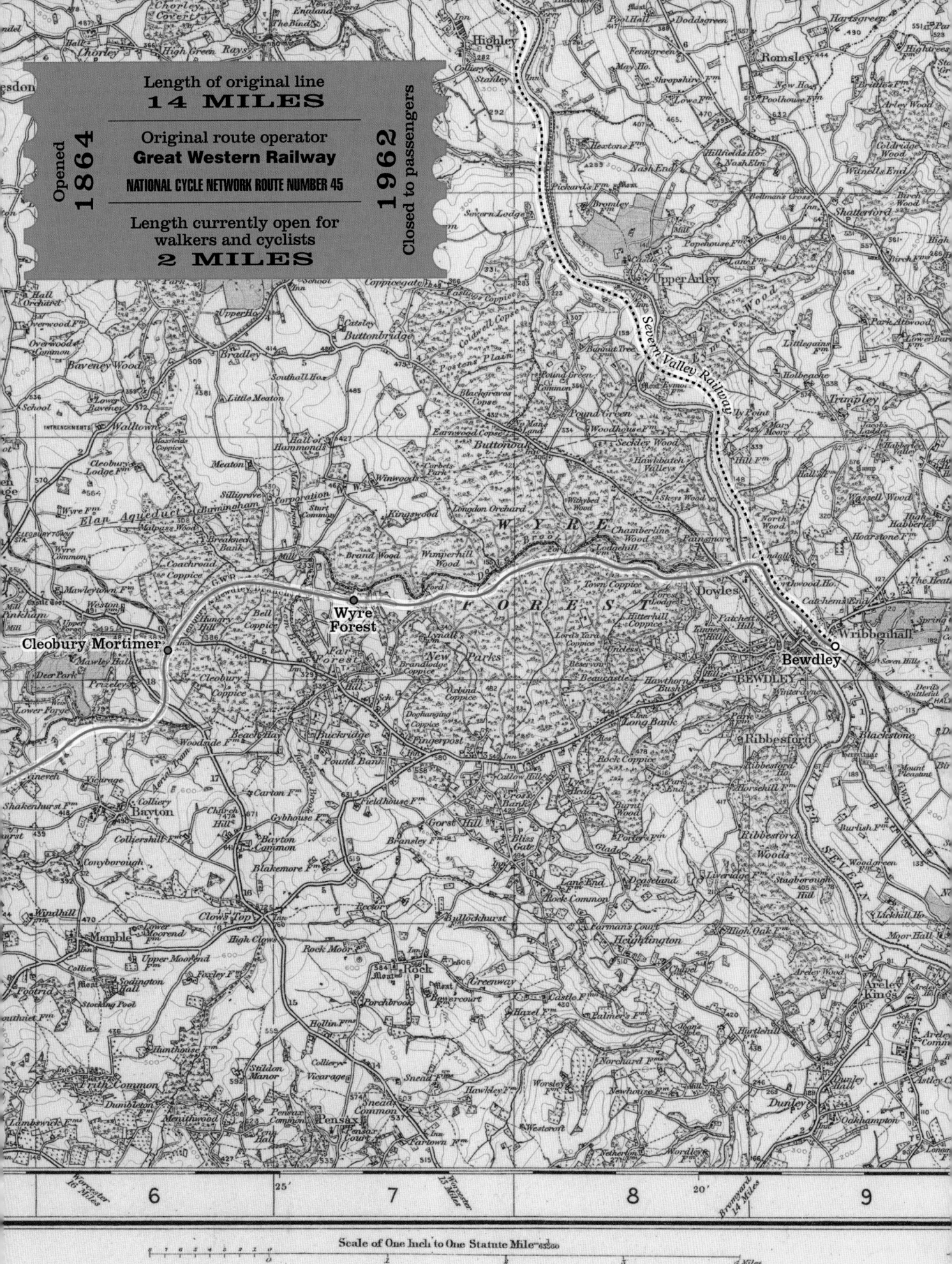

Length of original line
14 MILES

Opened **1864**

Original route operator
Great Western Railway

NATIONAL CYCLE NETWORK ROUTE NUMBER 45

Closed to passengers **1962**

Length currently open for
walkers and cyclists
2 MILES

The Severn Valley Railway (SVR) had opened its 40¾-mile single-track line between Hartlebury, north of Worcester, and Shrewsbury in 1862. Originally leased by the West Midland Railway (WMR), the SVR was absorbed by the Great Western Railway (GWR) in 1872. It closed between Shrewsbury and Bewdley in 1963, and between Bewdley and Hartlebury, and Bewdley and Kidderminster, in 1970, later reopening as a heritage railway between Kidderminster, Bewdley and Bridgnorth.

Meanwhile the Tenbury & Bewdley Railway (T&BR) had been incorporated in 1860 to build a 14-mile single-track branch line from Bewdley, on the SVR line, to Tenbury Wells. Here, the railway was to meet the 5½-mile branch line from Woofferton, on the Hereford to Shrewsbury main line, which had opened along part of the route of the defunct Leominster Canal in 1861.

The T&BR opened in 1864 and, together with the line from Woofferton, was worked by the GWR from the start, eventually becoming absorbed by the company in 1869. From Bewdley it paralleled the SVR line for one mile before heading west across the River Severn on Dowles Bridge and then through the Wyre Forest. Serving intermediate stations at Wyre Forest, Cleobury Mortimer,

Neen Sollars and Newnham Bridge – all built in a distinctive red-brick style – this delightful rural railway led a fairly leisurely existence, although the eastern section became busier when the 12¾-mile Cleobury Mortimer & Ditton Priors Light Railway opened in 1908. This branch line initially served quarries at Clee Hill and, later, an Admiralty munitions depot at Ditton Priors. Absorbed by the GWR in 1922, it lost its meagre passenger service in 1938 and was taken over by the Admiralty in 1957 before being closed in 1965.

In 1961 the Woofferton-Tenbury Wells-Bewdley passenger service was threatened with closure – like many other rural railways it had lost most of its traffic to road transport and by this time the few remaining passengers were easily accommodated in streamlined ex-GWR railcars. At the eleventh hour the Tenbury Wells to Bewdley service was reprieved but the line to Woofferton closed completely on 31 July 1961. A sparse weekday service continued to operate on the rest of the line for another year but the end came on 1 August 1962 when all passenger services ceased and the line west of Cleobury Mortimer closed completely. East of here the line remained open for trains from the Admiralty depot at Ditton Priors until 16 April 1965.

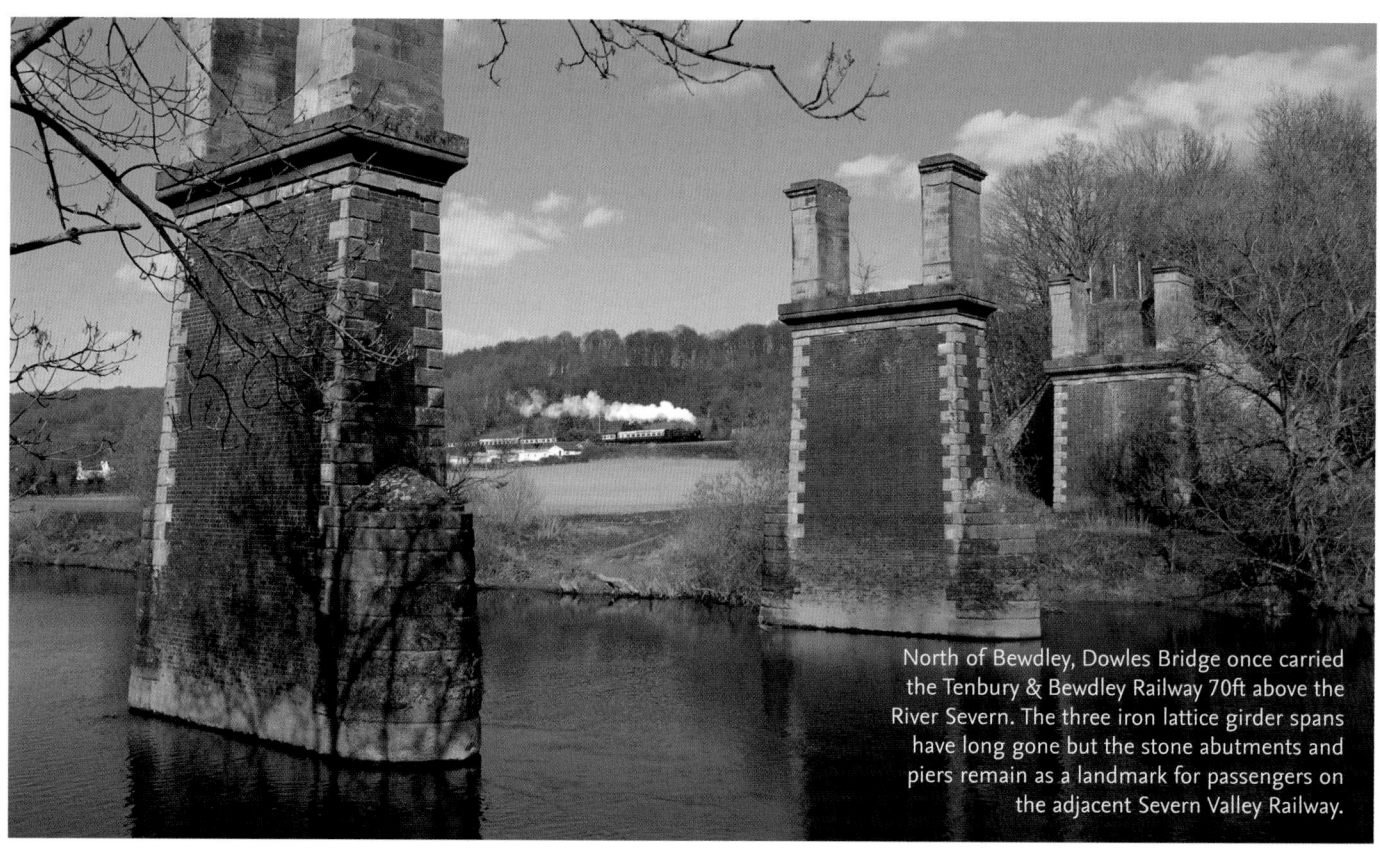

North of Bewdley, Dowles Bridge once carried the Tenbury & Bewdley Railway 70ft above the River Severn. The three iron lattice girder spans have long gone but the stone abutments and piers remain as a landmark for passengers on the adjacent Severn Valley Railway.

Since the closure of the railway, most of the attractive station buildings along the line have been converted into private residences and steam trains now serve Bewdley station on the reopened Severn Valley Railway. West of Wyre Forest station the railway's route along the Rea and Teme Valleys to Tenbury Wells is still recognisable in the form of embankments, cuttings and bridges but none of this route has so far been reopened as a footpath. The exception is the 2-mile heavily wooded section through the Wyre Forest from north of Bewdley, on the west bank of the Severn, which has recently been reopened as a footpath and cycleway. It also forms part of National Cycle Network Route 45. Owned by the Forestry Commission, the 6,500 acres of forest is a designated National Nature Reserve and is rich in wildlife. Many of the trails and paths that criss-cross the forest can be accessed from a Forestry Commission visitor centre on the A417 three miles west of Bewdley. The railway path starts at a car park at Dry Mill Lane, one mile northeast of Bewdley – to reach it follow the NCN Route 45 signs from the town centre. In addition to the railway path, three other waymarked trails also start here, allowing circular walks to be completed.

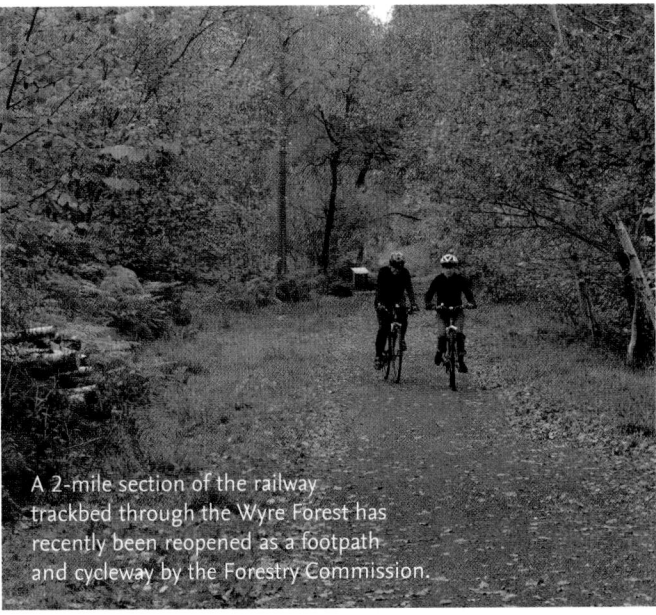

A 2-mile section of the railway trackbed through the Wyre Forest has recently been reopened as a footpath and cycleway by the Forestry Commission.

To the east lies the River Severn, where the gaunt stone piers of Dowles Bridge can be clearly seen by passengers on the Severn Valley Railway. The remains of the bridge can also be reached on foot along either bank of the river from Bewdley.

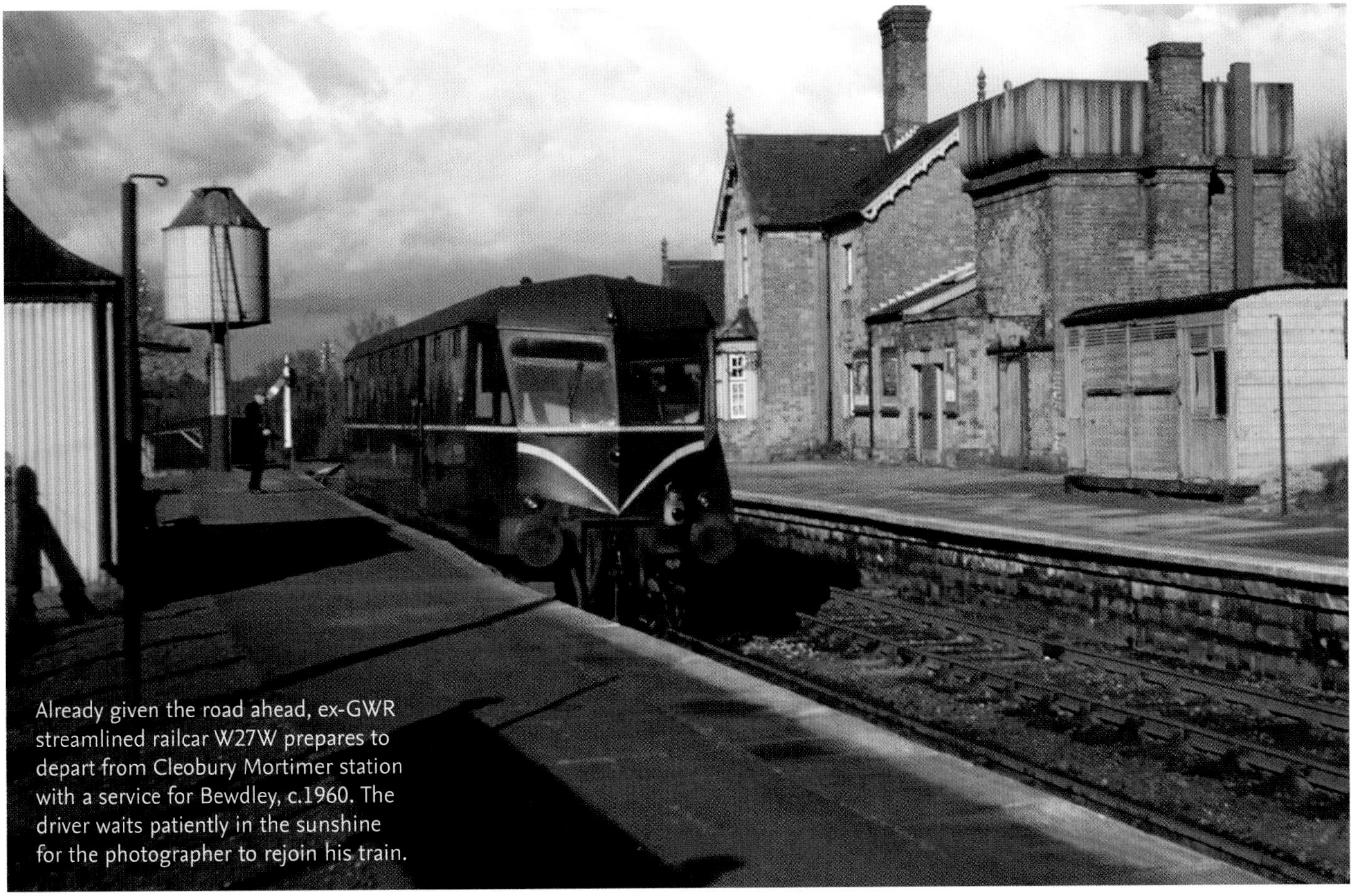

Already given the road ahead, ex-GWR streamlined railcar W27W prepares to depart from Cleobury Mortimer station with a service for Bewdley, c.1960. The driver waits patiently in the sunshine for the photographer to rejoin his train.

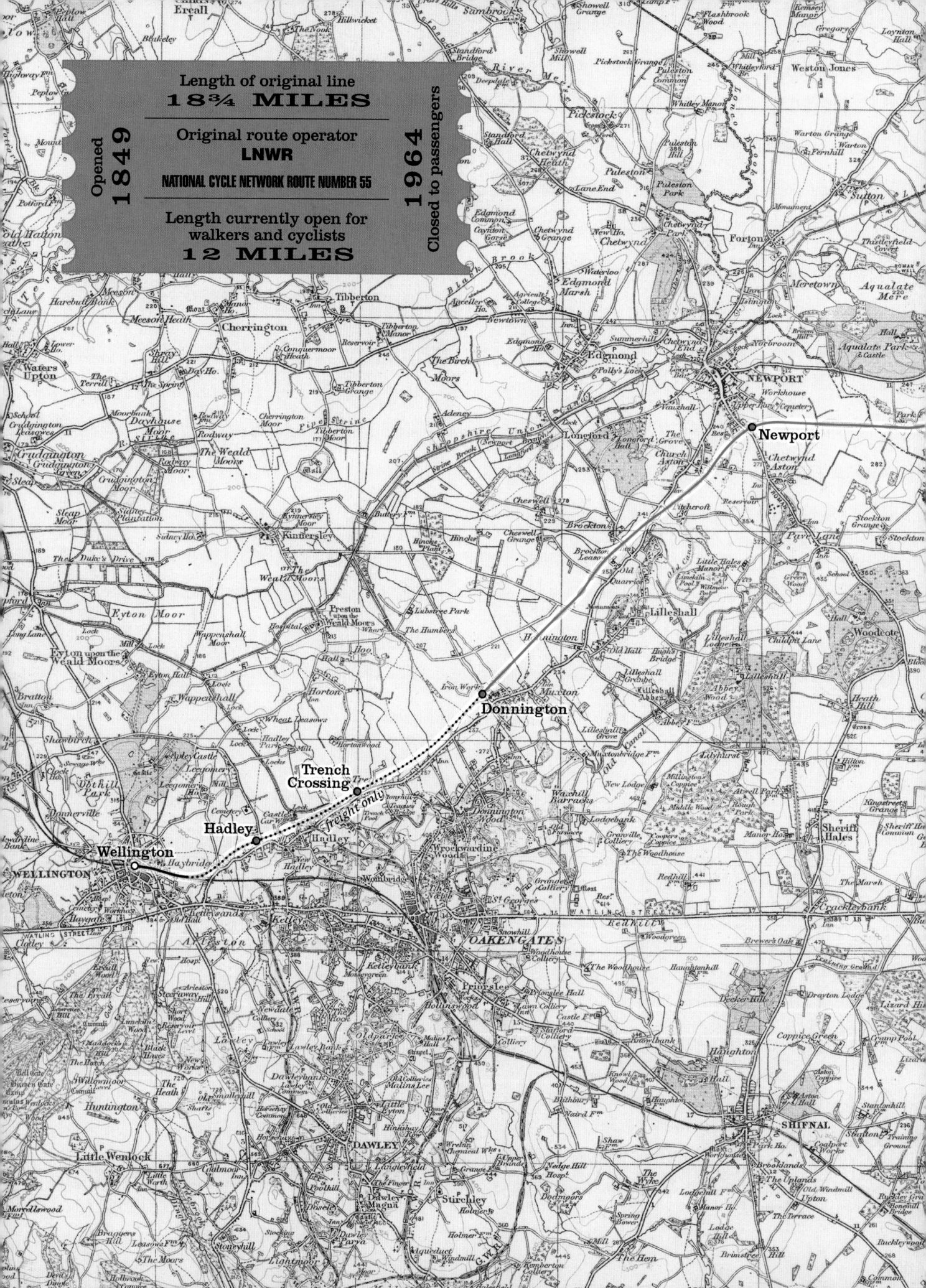

Opened **1849**

Length of original line
18¾ MILES

Original route operator
LNWR

NATIONAL CYCLE NETWORK ROUTE NUMBER 55

Length currently open for
walkers and cyclists
12 MILES

1964 Closed to passengers

Newport

Donnington

Trench
Crossing

freight only

Hadley

Wellington

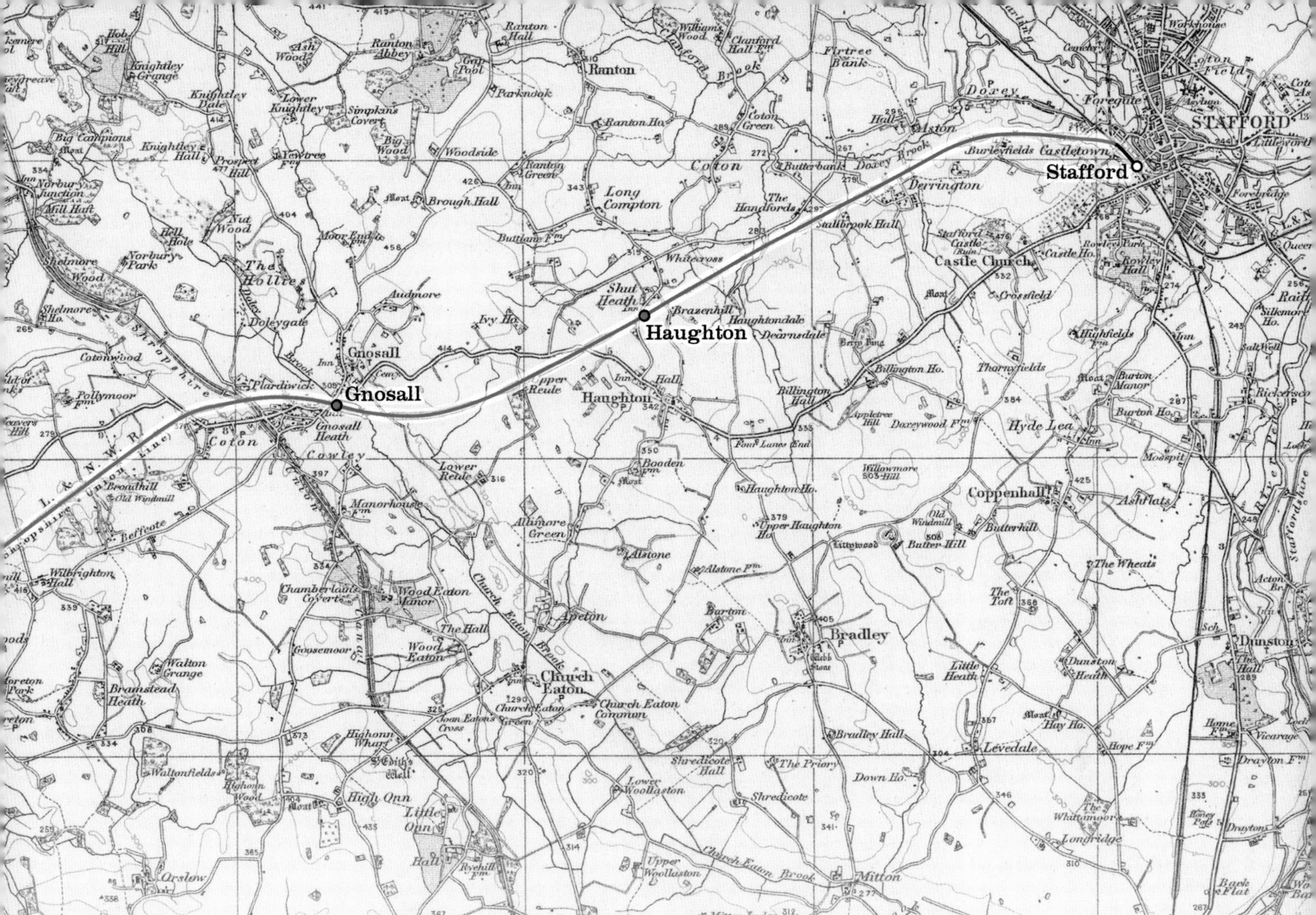

STAFFORD
TO
WELLINGTON

WAY FOR THE MILLENNIUM

Even before it opened, Britain's only railway to be built solely by
a canal company was quickly seen by the London & North Western
Railway as a way of expanding its influence into Shropshire and North
Wales. Intermediate local traffic was light but the double-track line
served an important role as a through route between Staffordshire
and Shrewsbury. Passenger services ceased in 1964 and the line
closed completely east of Donnington in 1966. Since closure,
the twelve-mile section between Stafford and Newport has
been reopened as a footpath and cycleway.

The advent of the railway age in the first half of the nineteenth century saw Britain's canal network swiftly lose its monopoly on transporting goods around the country. Railways were quicker and could tackle gradients with ease whereas canals were slow and relied on lock systems to overcome natural obstacles.

With great foresight several canal companies in the West Midlands joined forces and, under an Act of Parliament in 1846, formed the Shropshire Union Railways & Canal Company (SUR&CC). The aim of this new company was to build railways along their existing canal routes and to take over other canals for the same purpose. In reality it built only one railway line and had a joint share in another. The former was the 18¾-mile double-track railway from Stafford to Wellington while the latter was the 10¼-mile double-track main line between Wellington and Shrewsbury, which it shared with the Shrewsbury & Birmingham Railway (S&BR).

Meanwhile the London & North Western Railway (LNWR) was taking a keen interest in the SUR&CC, seeing it as a way of expanding its influence into Shropshire and mid-Wales. In 1847, one year after the SUR&CC was formed, the LNWR took on a lease of the company – this not only included its planned railways but also its canal business. The Stafford to Wellington line opened in 1849 and was worked from the outset by the LNWR. The completion of the jointly owned Wellington to Shrewsbury line in the same year therefore gave the LNWR direct access into the heart of Shropshire.

The S&BR was merged with the Great Western Railway (GWR) in 1854 and the Wellington to Shrewsbury section continued to be run as a joint railway. The LNWR bought out the SUR&CC in 1922 before becoming part of the newly formed London Midland & Scottish Railway in the 1923 Big Four Grouping.

With intermediate stations at Haughton, Gnosall, Newport, Donnington, Trench Crossing and Hadley, the Stafford to Wellington line was mainly served by through trains running between Stafford and Shrewsbury. The winter 1948/49 timetable shows six of these trains in each direction plus two running only between Stafford and Wellington on weekdays. There was also an overnight through train in each direction that ran between Euston and Shrewsbury via this route. On Sundays just two trains ran between Stafford and Wellington. Although local freight traffic was light, consisting mainly of coal and munitions from Donnington, the line was heavily used by through freight trains.

Listed for closure in the 1963 'Beeching Report', the Stafford to Wellington line lost its passenger service on 7 September 1964. Through freight traffic continued until 1966 until complete closure east of Donnington in July 1967. The 3¾-mile stub at the western end remained open to serve a colliery at Donnington until 1979. The track remained in situ and now serves the little-used Telford International Freight Park.

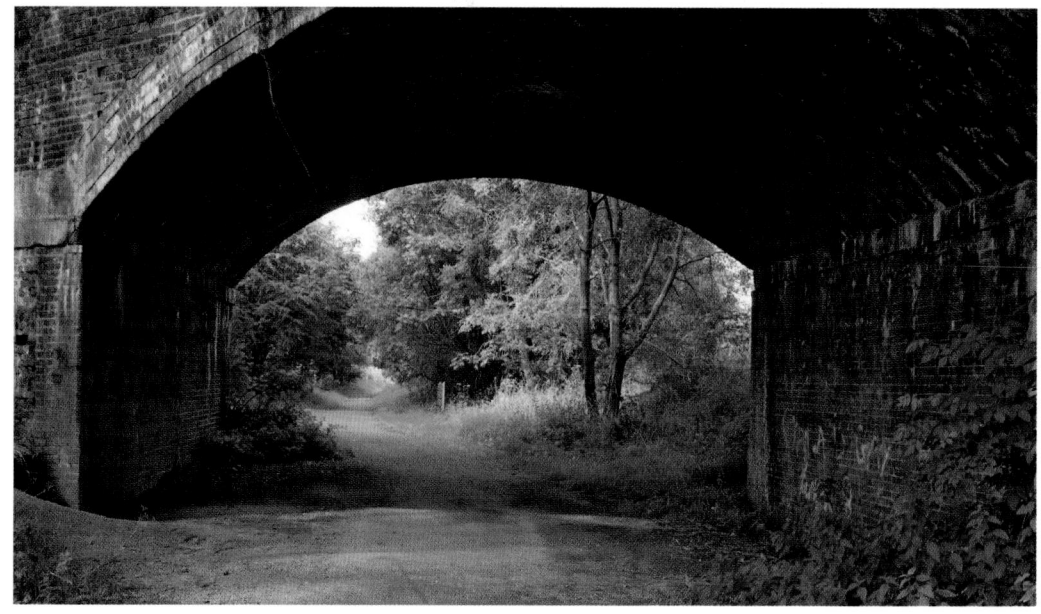

The Newport to Stafford Greenway passes under this impressive road bridge at the site of Haughton station. Although the platforms have long gone, the waiting room and ticket office were unusually located under another arch to the left of this photograph.

Since closure the twelve miles of the Stafford to Newport section of this line has been purchased by Staffordshire County Council and reopened as a footpath and cycleway known as the Newport to Stafford Greenway. It also forms part of National Cycle Network Route 55. The route has expansive views over the surrounding countryside and provides a habitat for plants and wildlife. It is one of the best areas in the county for butterflies thanks to the abundance of plants and wildflowers whose growth is stimulated by the railway limestone ballast that forms the foundations of the route. In 1999 Staffordshire County Council incorporated the Greenway into the 41-mile Way for the Millennium, which mainly follows canal towpaths from Burton-upon-Trent before joining the old railway route at Stafford.

While none of the stations along this route have survived, all the bridges – built to accommodate double track – are intact. Westwards from Stafford the Greenway passes under the M6 motorway, with the motte and baileys of Stafford Castle lying to the south, before arriving at the

village of Derrington and the nearby Red Lion pub. To the west of the village lies the fourteenth-century Smallbrook Hall and a railway crossing-keeper's cottage where remains of the level crossing gates can still be seen. Continuing westward the route passes through the site of Haughton station – here the waiting room and ticket office were located under the impressive road overbridge while the present car park is the site of the old goods yard and station. All that remains are a few stones that were once used in the platform.

The Greenway continues its westward route, first passing through a long cutting before arriving at the village of Gnosall. Here the old railway route passes over the Shropshire Union Canal with its leisure cruisers, locks and the waterside Navigation Inn. Engineered by Thomas Telford, the canal was the last trunk narrow canal to be built in Britain. Linking the Midlands to Ellesmere Port on the River Mersey, it opened in 1835. Purchased by the LNWR in 1922, the Shropshire Union continued to carry commercial traffic until the 1960s and since then has become a popular pleasure-cruising waterway.

Beyond Gnosall, the Greenway heads through open countryside before ending at Outwoods, two miles east of Newport. In 2009 a report by the Association of Train Operating Companies recommended reopening the railway. We shall see!

Ex-LMS 'Jubilee' Class 4-6-0 No. 45578 'United Provinces' leaves Newport (Shropshire) with the 3.59pm Stafford to Shrewsbury train on 5 August 1961. The locomotive was built by the North British Locomotive Company in 1934 and withdrawn from Newton Heath shed in May 1964.

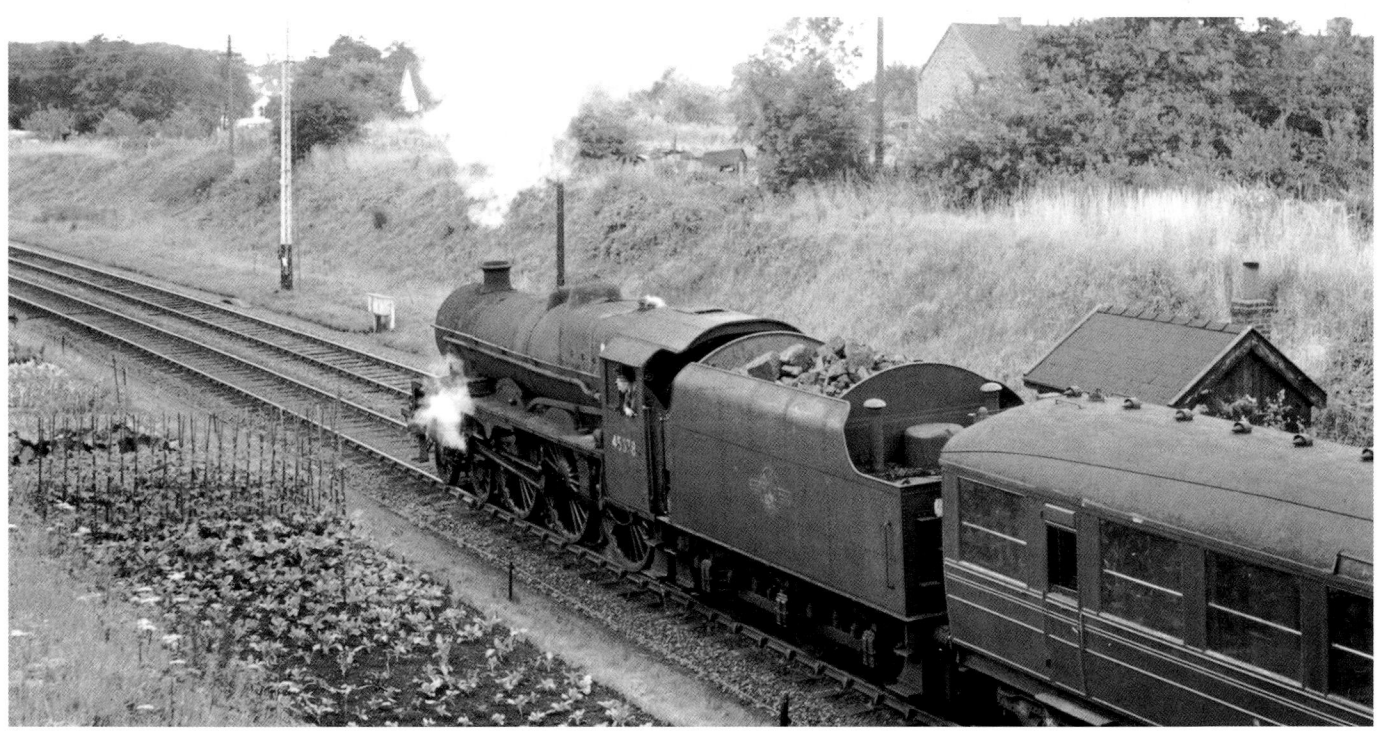

MARKET HARBOROUGH
TO
NORTHAMPTON
MIDSHIRES WAY

Built to transport iron ore from a large opencast quarry, this 18-mile railway was originally built as a single-track line. Increasing traffic soon led to it being doubled, an exercise that included construction of two extra single-bore tunnels alongside the existing ones at Kelmarsh and Oxendon. In its latter years the line was served by trains operating between Northampton and Nottingham but these were withdrawn in 1960 when the remaining intermediate stations were also closed. The line was intermittently reopened for through passenger traffic until 1973 and to through freight traffic until 1981. Since then the majority of the route has been reopened as a linear park, footpath and cycleway known as the Brampton Valley Way.

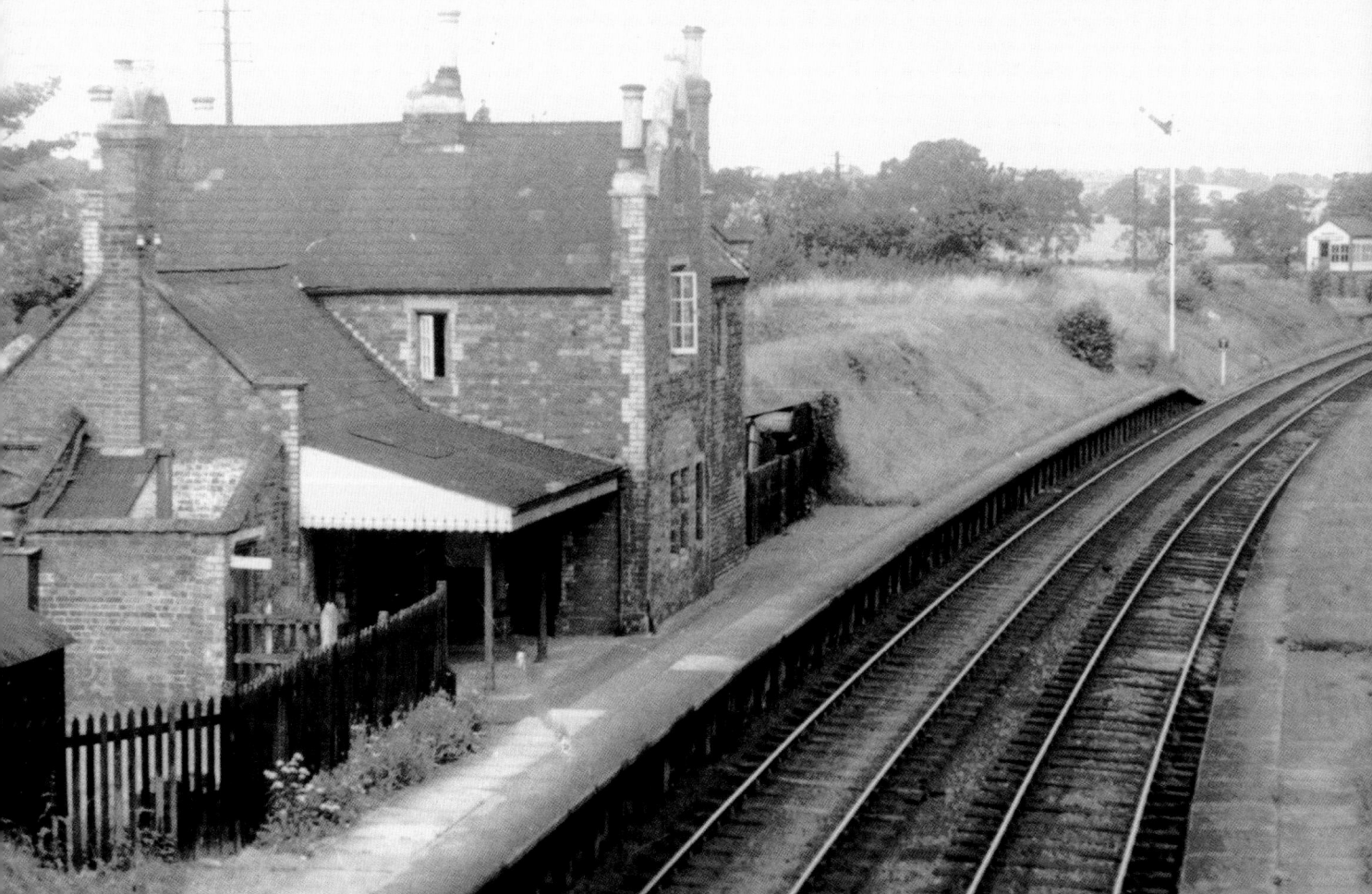

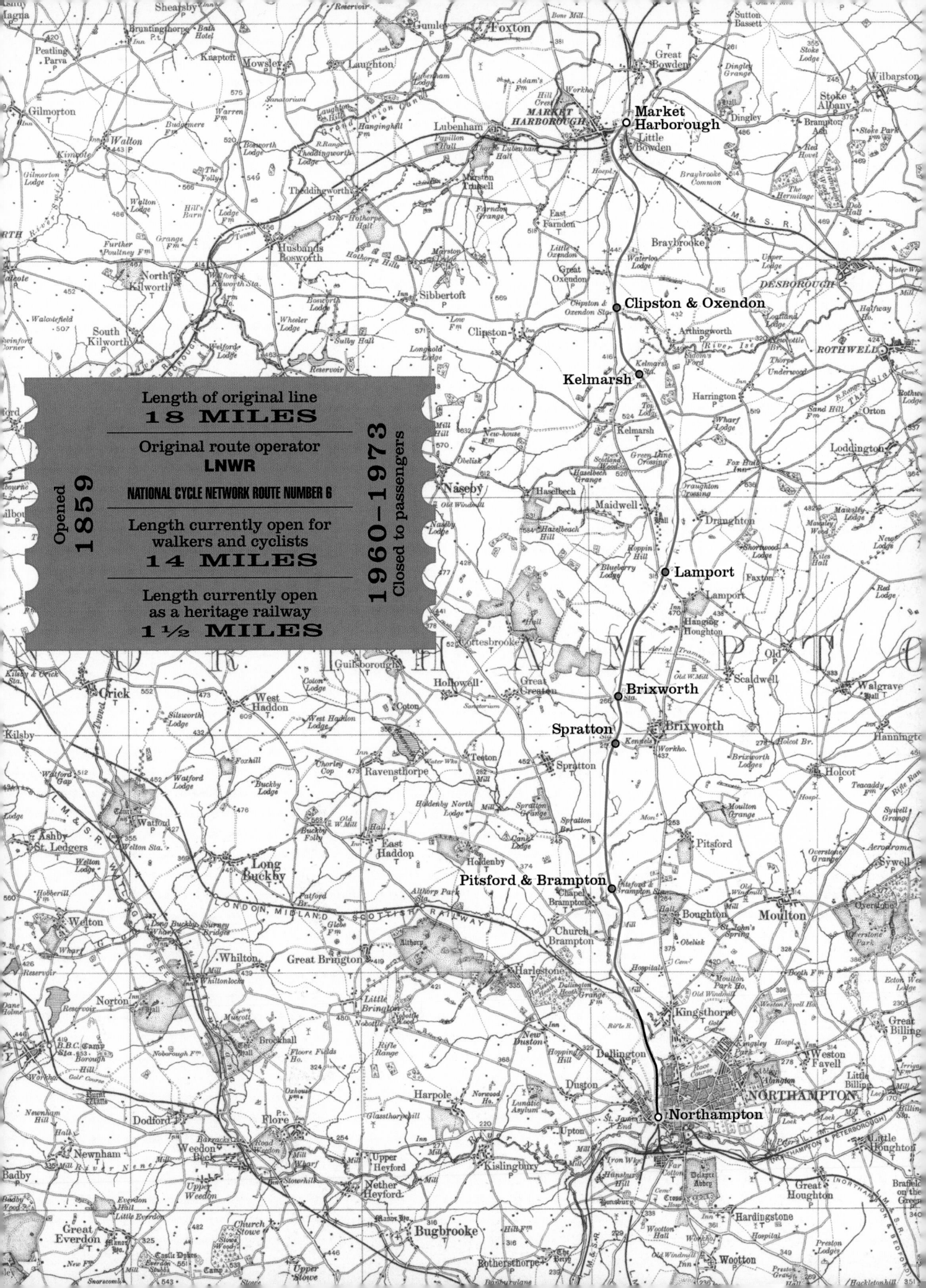

Length of original line
18 MILES

Original route operator
LNWR

NATIONAL CYCLE NETWORK ROUTE NUMBER 6

Length currently open for
walkers and cyclists
14 MILES

Length currently open
as a heritage railway
1 ½ MILES

Opened
1859

1960-1973
Closed to passengers

Market
Harborough

Clipston & Oxendon

Kelmarsh

Lamport

Brixworth

Spratton

Pitsford & Brampton

Northampton

There were no trains in sight as Richard Casserley took this photograph of the closed station at Clipston & Oxendon on 10 May 1965. Walking towards him is his father, the famous railway photographer Henry Casserley. The rickety wooden waiting shelter in the foreground appears to be in an imminent state of collapse.

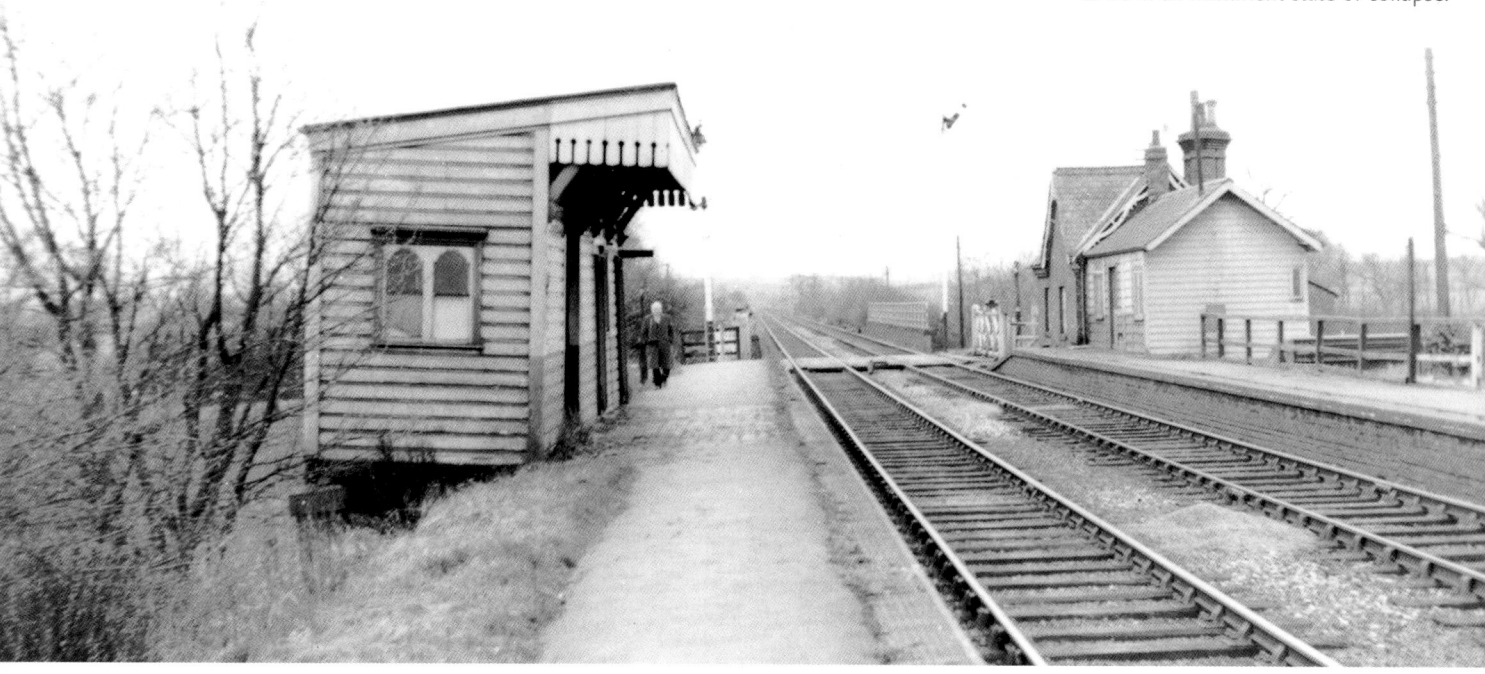

When large deposits of iron ore were discovered in Northamptonshire in 1851, the London & North Western Railway (LNWR) put forward a proposal to build a railway to tap into this lucrative trade. Involving the boring of tunnels at Kelmarsh and Oxendon, the 18-mile single-track railway between Market Harborough and Northampton was opened in 1859. In addition to the tunnels there were four intermediate stations (from north to south: Kelmarsh, Lamport, Brixworth and Pitsford & Brampton) and five level crossings. A station was also planned for Boughton but the 5th Earl Spencer of nearby Althorp had insisted on a more convenient station at Pitsford & Brampton. Two further stations were later opened: Clipston & Oxendon in 1863 and Spratton in 1864. At about this time the entire route was doubled along with additional single-bore tunnels at Kelmarsh and Oxendon.

Although passenger traffic was never heavy on the line it did carry large quantities of locally grown sugar beet from Pitsford & Brampton and also served a large opencast ironstone quarry at Scaldwell near Brixworth. The Ministry of Food built a large cold store as a supply

depot adjacent to Pitsford & Brampton station during the Second World War

By the early 1920s passengers were served by eight southbound trains and seven northbound trains all of which, apart from one service in each direction, stopped at every intermediate station. By 1948 this had dropped to five southbound and six northbound, with three trains in each direction starting or finishing their journeys at Nottingham. The 64¾ miles between Northampton and Nottingham took up to a leisurely three hours!

The railway's final years were marked by a series of closures and reopenings. While Spratton station closed in 1949 and Pitsford & Brampton followed suit in 1950, the line remained open to passenger traffic until 4 January 1960. Freight trains continued to use the route for many more years and it was reopened to through passenger trains on 6 January 1969, closed again on 1 May 1972, reopened for a northbound service on 10 July 1972 and permanently closed to passenger services on 26 August 1973. Freight services continued until 16 August 1981 when the line closed completely.

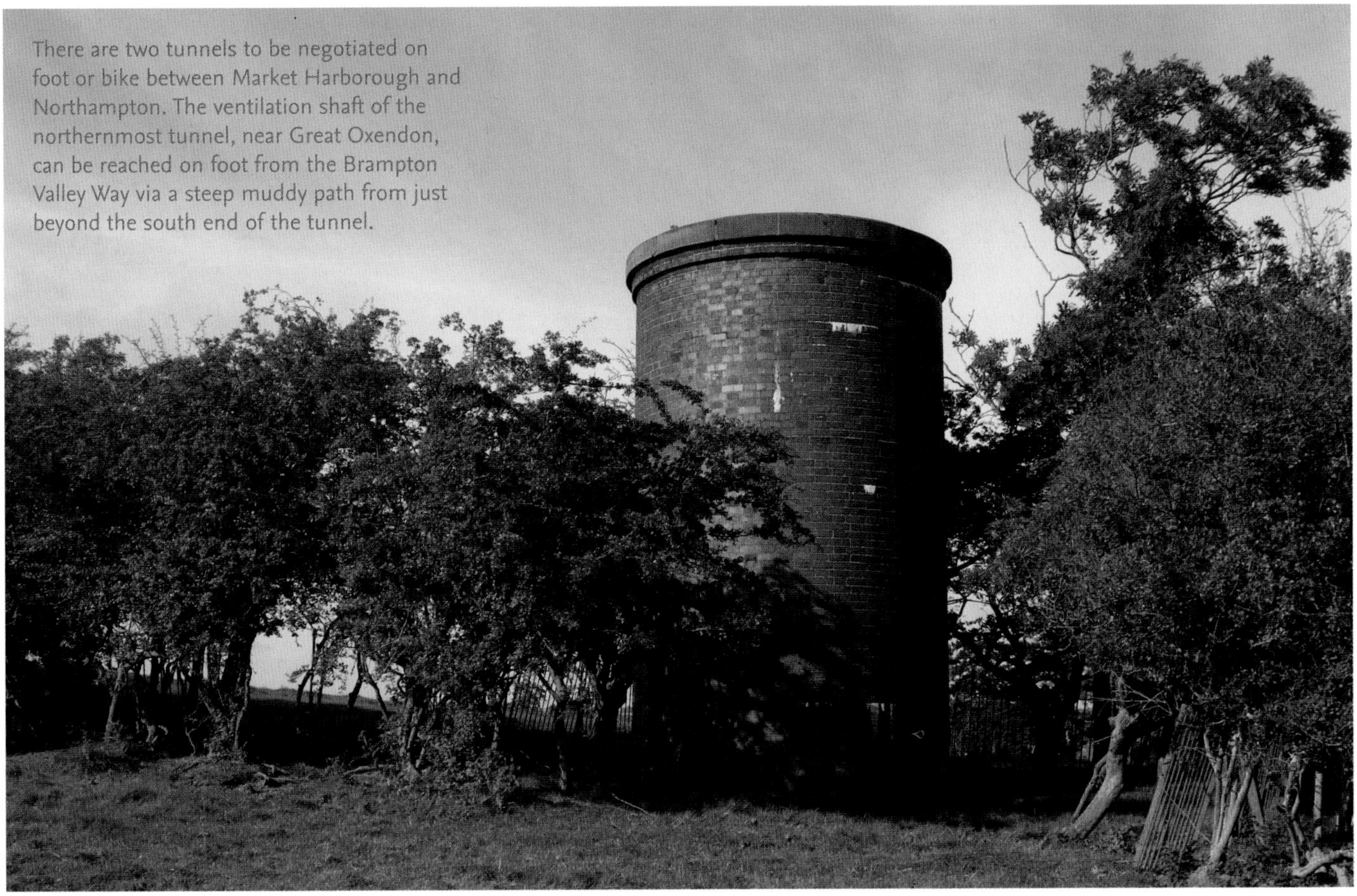

There are two tunnels to be negotiated on foot or bike between Market Harborough and Northampton. The ventilation shaft of the northernmost tunnel, near Great Oxendon, can be reached on foot from the Brampton Valley Way via a steep muddy path from just beyond the south end of the tunnel.

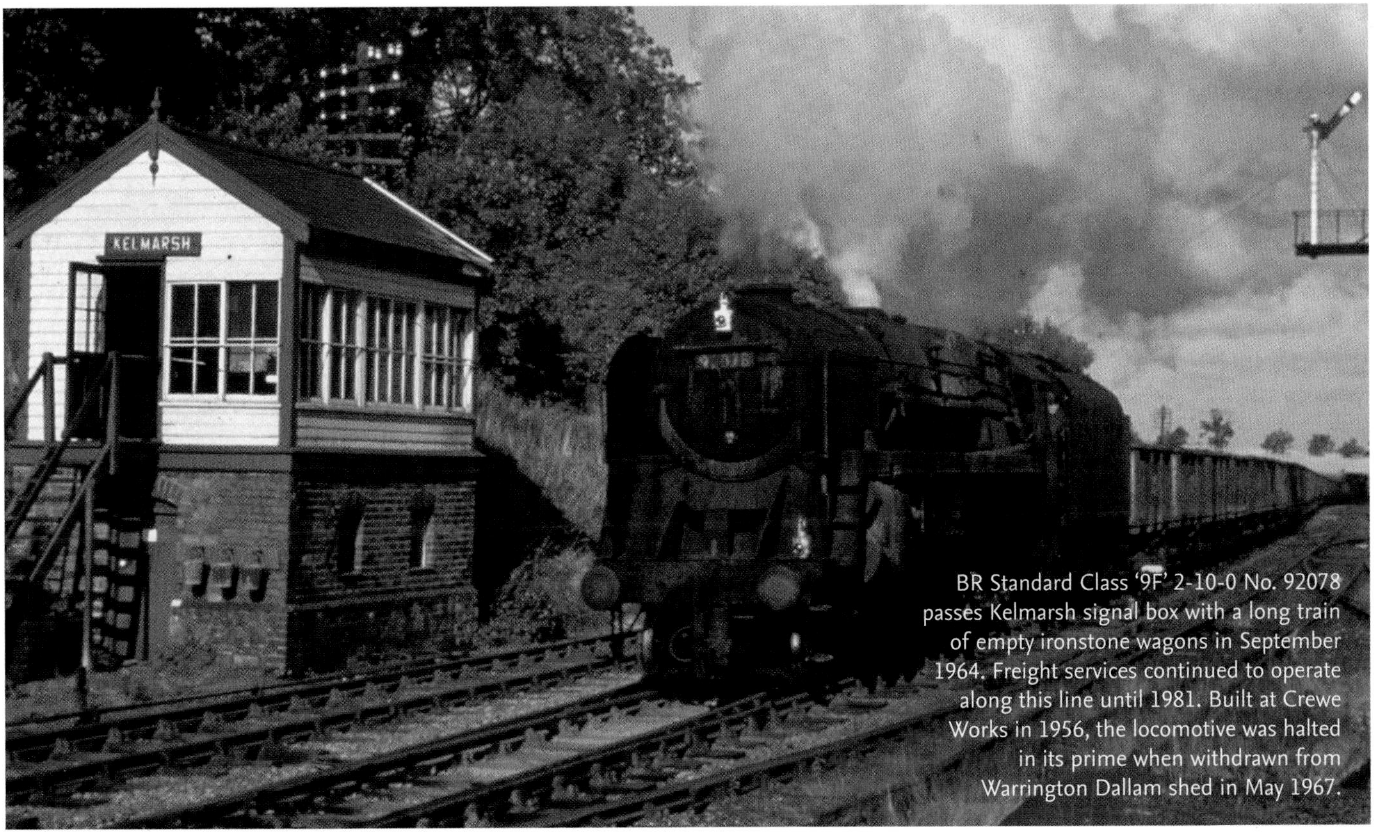

BR Standard Class '9F' 2-10-0 No. 92078 passes Kelmarsh signal box with a long train of empty ironstone wagons in September 1964. Freight services continued to operate along this line until 1981. Built at Crewe Works in 1956, the locomotive was halted in its prime when withdrawn from Warrington Dallam shed in May 1967.

The track was lifted following the line's closure in 1981. Thirteen miles of the trackbed was sold to Northampton County Council and one mile at the northern end to Leicestershire County Council in 1987. It was reopened as a linear park known as the Brampton Valley Way in 1993 and now also forms part of National Cycle Network Route 6 and the Midshires Way Long Distance Path. Never far from the A508 and its regular bus service, the footpath and cycleway starts close to a car park at the Bell Inn on Northampton Road, Market Harborough, and soon enters open country. Near Great Oxendon one of the two single-bore tunnels is now used by the Brampton Valley Way – the 462-yd tunnel is unlit so torches or cycle lights are recommended. Further south, the Way reaches the site of Kelmarsh station where there is a car park and picnic site. Here a retaining wall and steps are the only survivors of the long demolished building. South of here the Way passes over one of the original road overbridges before reaching the single-bore 525-yd Kelmarsh Tunnel – travelling through this unlit tunnel on foot or by bike is an eerie experience.

Beyond the Kelmarsh Tunnel the Way soon dives under the busy A14 dual carriageway before reaching the car park and picnic site at Draughton Crossing. Continuing southwards through open country, the tree-lined Way crosses the A508 at the site of Lamport station, where the station building has survived, before heading on to Brixworth. Refreshments can be taken in the attractive village nearby, which has fortunately been bypassed by the A508 in recent years.

South of Brixworth the Brampton Valley Way soon meets up with the Northampton & Lamport Railway, which now

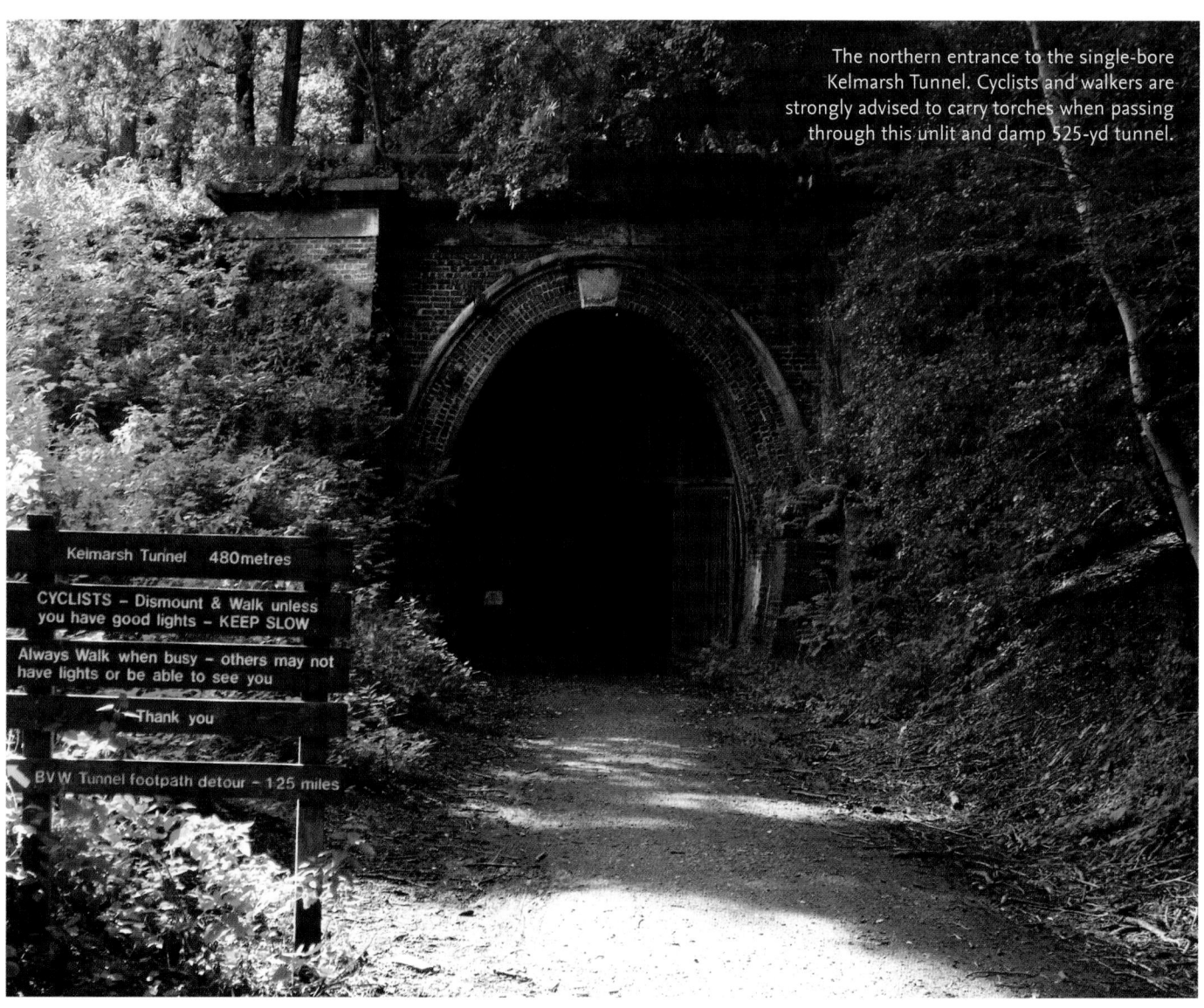

The northern entrance to the single-bore Kelmarsh Tunnel. Cyclists and walkers are strongly advised to carry torches when passing through this unlit and damp 525-yd tunnel.

Kelmarsh Tunnel   480metres

CYCLISTS – Dismount & Walk unless you have good lights – KEEP SLOW

Always Walk when busy – others may not have lights or be able to see you

Thank you

BVW Tunnel footpath detour – 1·25 miles

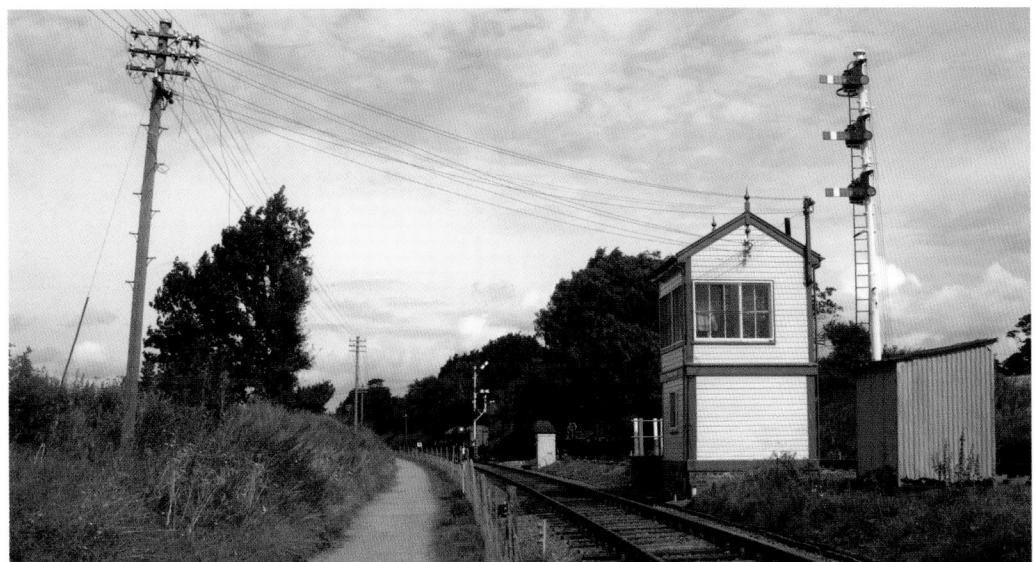

At Pitsford Sidings the Brampton Valley Way parallels the Northampton & Lamport Railway. This scene, with its network of telegraph wires, telegraph posts and semaphore signals, brings back memories of how our railways looked 50 years ago. The restored working LNWR signalbox was originally located at Wolverton Works.

shares the trackbed (separated by heavy-duty fencing) for two miles through its headquarters at Pitsford & Brampton station to a new southern terminus. This heritage railway opened to the public in 1996 and is currently planning to extend northwards over the River Nene to Brixworth.

The headquarters of the railway at Pitsford & Brampton is made up of a single through platform with portable buildings and the LNWR working signalbox, which was moved from Little Bowden Crossing, south of Market Harborough and rebuilt on its present site. The booking office is the top half of the signal box from Lamport station. The railway has an eclectic mix of locomotives, both steam and diesel, although many are currently awaiting restoration. Car parking is available on a railway-owned field on open days (normally Sundays, March to October) and there are two pubs located nearby.

South of the station the Way and the railway keep company past Pitsford Sidings signal box, which was moved from its original location at Wolverton Works on the West Coast Main Line. Still following the Nene Valley the railway reaches its southern terminus at Boughton, under construction at the time of writing, where there is car parking and a pub. South of Boughton the Brampton Valley Way continues along the railway trackbed to the site of the junction with the Northampton Loop Line before joining the streets of Northampton to end its journey at the town's station.

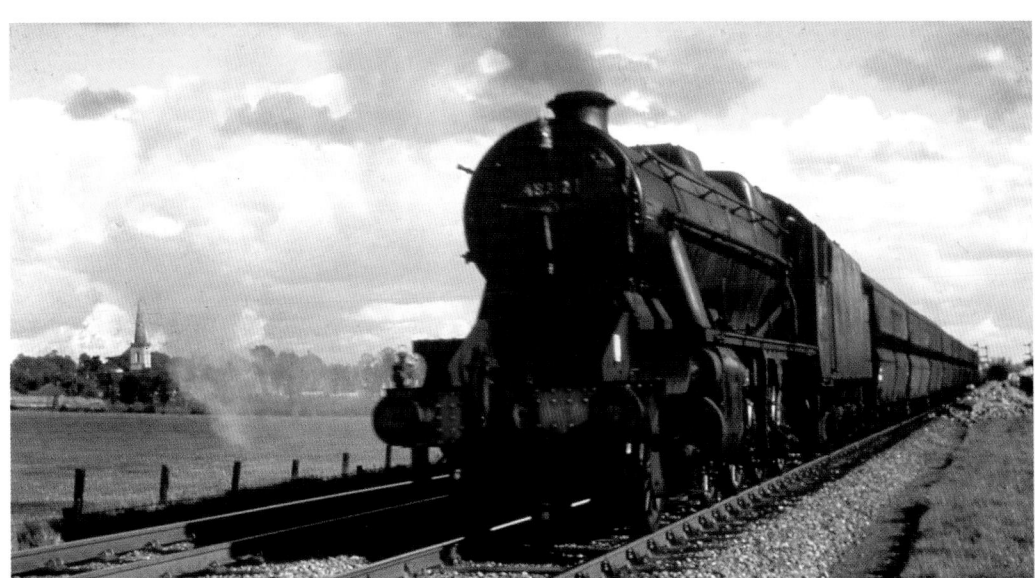

Ex-LMS Stanier Class '8F' 2-8-0 No. 48312 hauls a long train of empty hoppers from Stonebridge Park past Kingsthorpe Church, near Northampton, en route for Market Harborough in May 1962. Walkers and cyclists now take this route on the Brampton Valley Way.

MARPLE
TO
MACCLESFIELD

MIDDLEWOOD TRAIL

Originally planned as a joint railway to avoid the London
& North Western Railway's (LNWR) obstructiveness south
of Manchester, the Macclesfield, Bollington & Marple Railway's
raison d'être disappeared even before it had opened when the
LNWR relented over routing of traffic. While the northerly station
at Marple Rose Hill was kept busy with Manchester commuter
traffic, the rest of the line was never a great success and eventually
succumbed to Dr Beeching's 'Axe' in 1970. Since closure the
entire route south of Marple has been reopened as a
footpath and cycleway known as the Middlewood Trail.

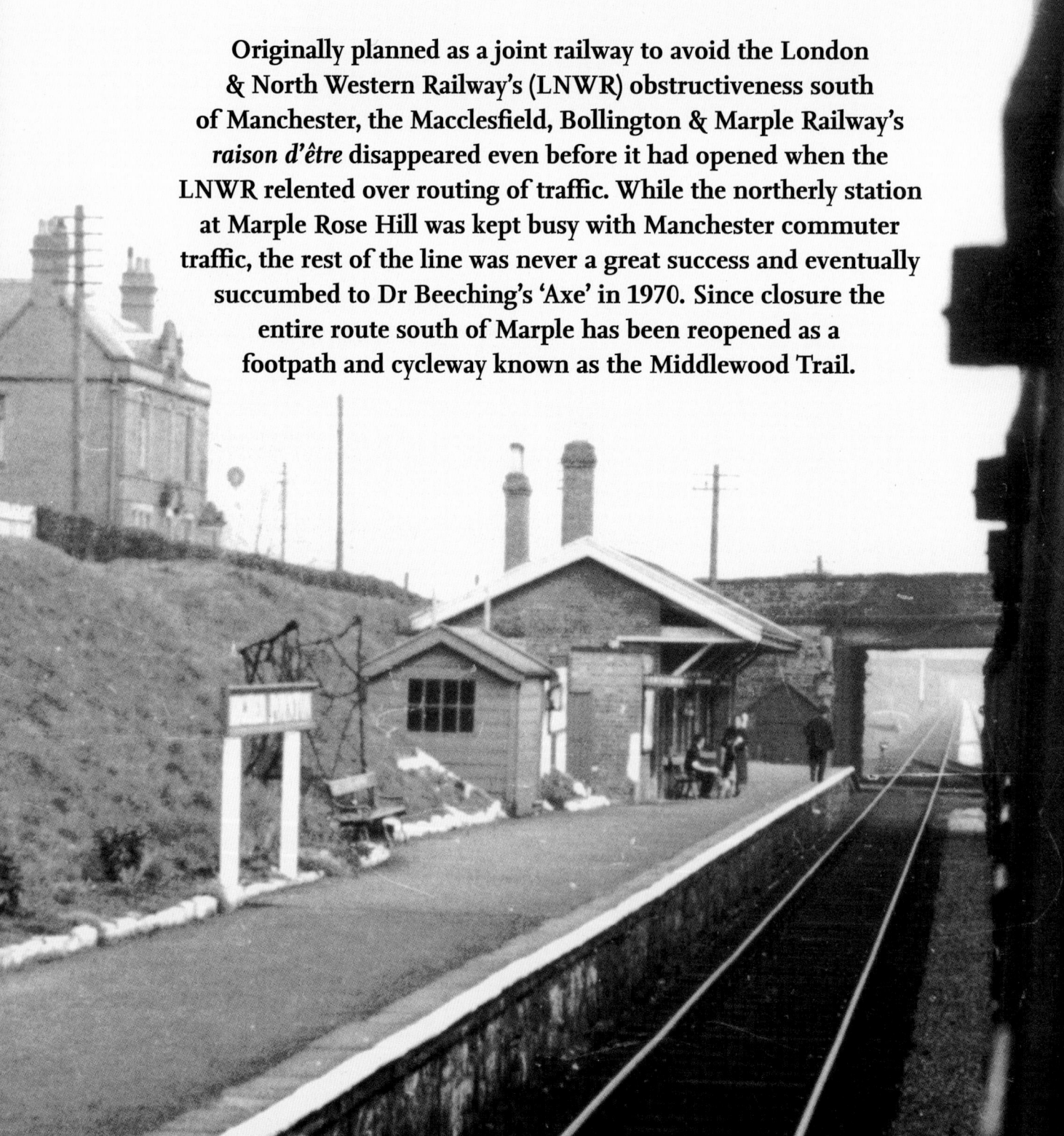

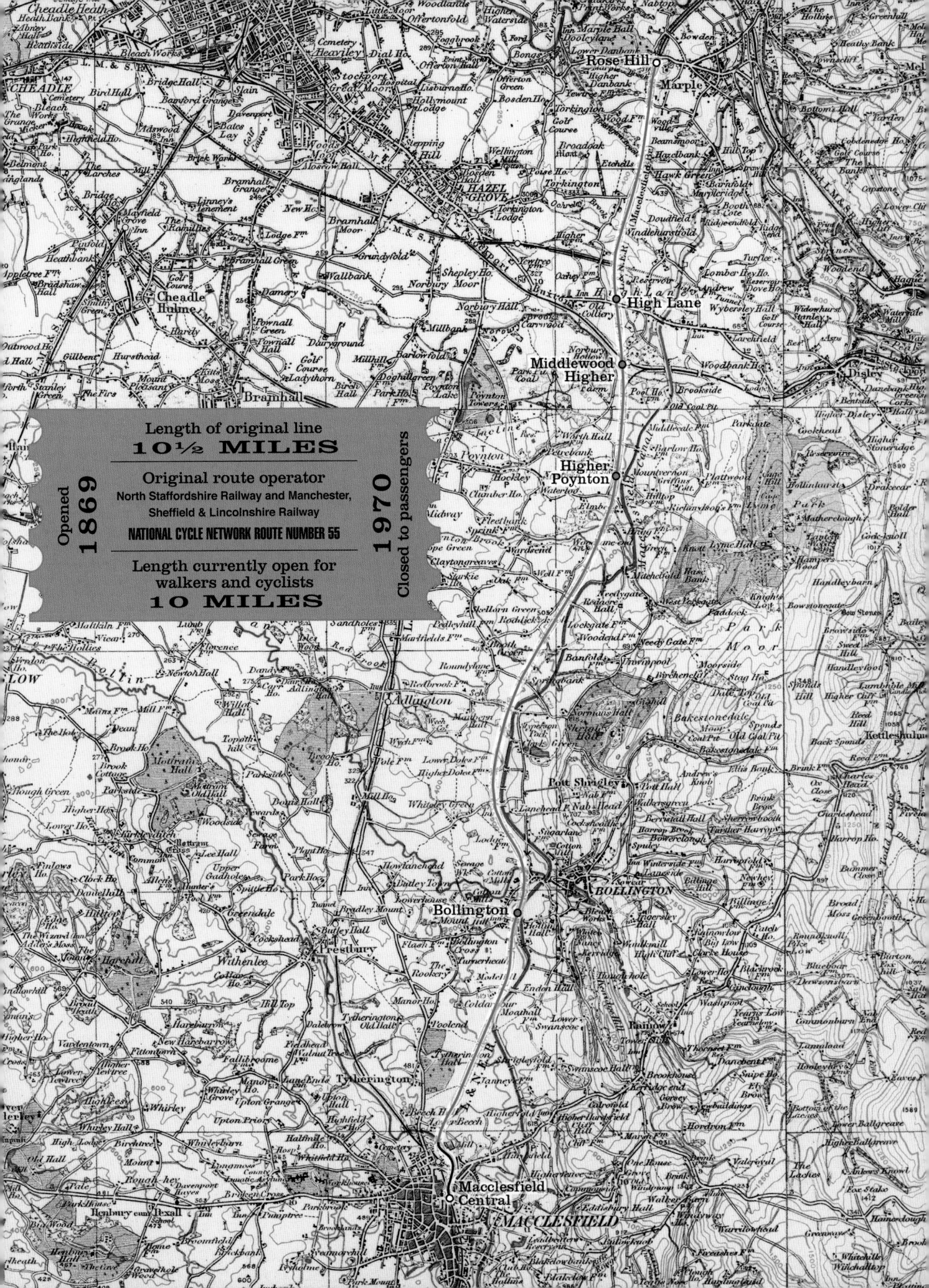

Length of original line
10½ MILES

Original route operator
North Staffordshire Railway and Manchester,
Sheffield & Lincolnshire Railway

NATIONAL CYCLE NETWORK ROUTE NUMBER 55

Length currently open for
walkers and cyclists
10 MILES

Opened **1869**

1970 Closed to passengers

The North Staffordshire Railway (NSR) had reached the town of Macclesfield in 1849, but found its progress northwards towards Manchester effectively blocked by its bigger neighbour, the London & North Western Railway (LNWR). The latter had also opened a branch line from Cheadle Hulme to the town in 1845 but insisted that all traffic between the Potteries and Manchester had to travel along their lines via Crewe. Similarly, the Manchester, Sheffield & Lincolnshire Railway (MS&LR – later to become the Great Central Railway) found its southward progress also blocked by the LNWR.

As the years went by the businessmen of Macclesfield became more and more frustrated by the lack of a direct rail link with Manchester. Once the world's biggest producer of silk, the town had seventy-one silk mills in the 1830s and was also the home of Hovis bread.

Macclesfield had been connected to Manchester by canal in 1831 when the Macclesfield Canal was opened but in the new Railway Age this means of transport was extremely slow. To the north of the town lay Bollington, then an important cotton town, and beyond were quarries and collieries around Poynton. Eventually, in 1863, a Macclesfield businessman, Thomas Oliver, promoted a scheme to link these places by building a railway between Macclesfield and a junction at Marple on the MS&LR's newly opened extension to New Mills (see page 156).

The MS&LR's directors seized on Oliver's proposal, seeing it as a route for the company's traffic to the south, and so the Macclesfield, Bollington & Marple Railway (MB&MR) was formed. It was incorporated in 1864 to be built and operated jointly by the NSR and the MS&LR. The LNWR then relented and came to an amicable agreement with

PREVIOUS SPREAD: Seen here from a southbound train on 18 April 1954, the station at Higher Poynton was just across the road from a magnificent pub that is visible centre left. While the tracks have long gone, the pub (the Boars Head), the station platforms and the road overbridge survive today along the route of the Middlewood Trail.

BELOW: Viewed from a northbound train, ex-GCR Class C13 4-4-2T No. 67426 calls at High Lane station with the 1.28pm (Saturdays only) train from Manchester to Macclesfield on 4 September 1954. This locomotive was built at Gorton Works in 1904 and withdrawn from Gorton shed just over three months after this photograph was taken.

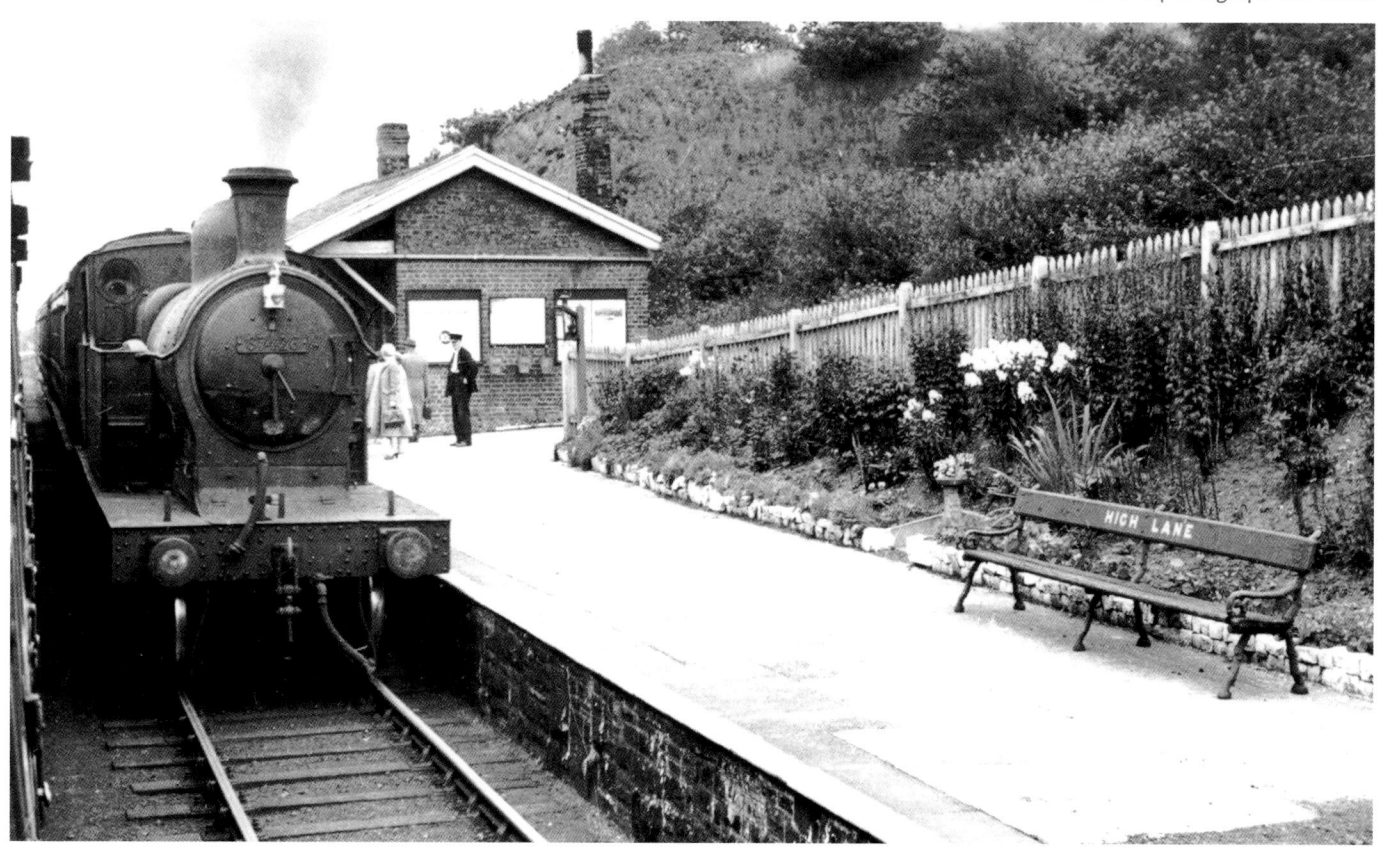

the NSR over the routing of its traffic to Manchester and the whole *raison d'être* of the MB&MR melted away before it had even been built.

Despite this setback, construction of the MB&MR went ahead, albeit very slowly and not helped by the general economic malaise of the 1860s. Although built to accommodate double track, the line was initially single track and later doubled, its only engineering feature of note a 23-arch viaduct at Bollington. With intermediate stations at Marple Rose Hill, High Lane, Higher Poynton and Bollington, the 10½-mile railway opened for passengers in 1869 and for goods the following year. A higher-level interchange station with the LNWR's Stockport to Buxton line at Middlewood was opened in 1879 and a curve was also added here that joined the two lines in 1885 – this allowed a through Stoke-on-Trent

At the site of Middlewood Upper station the Trail passes over the Manchester to Buxton line where the former interchange station of Middlewood Lower is still open for business – it is one of very few stations in Britain to have no road access.

to Buxton service to run in the summer months until it was withdrawn in 1927.

The 1920s and 1930s saw the line kept busy with workmen's trains to and from Manchester and an intensive shuttle service between Macclesfield and Bollington. At the northern end of the line extensive new housing development around Rose Hill brought a massive increase in commuter traffic. Passenger services were handled by ex-GCR 4-4-2T and 4-6-2T locomotives from Gorton shed well into the British Railways' era of the 1950s. The post-war years saw increased competition from cars and buses but the introduction of Derby-built lightweight diesel multiple units in 1957 failed to stop the decline of traffic south of Rose Hill. Even so, by the summer of 1962, those passengers that remained still had the choice of around fifteen trains each way on weekdays and eight on Sundays. With goods traffic also in decline the loss-making Marple to Macclesfield line was listed for closure in the 1963 'Beeching Report', and despite a public enquiry and strong local objections the section from Rose Hill to Macclesfield closed on 5 January 1970. Attempts to reopen it by a local preservation society came to nothing and the track had been lifted by March 1971.

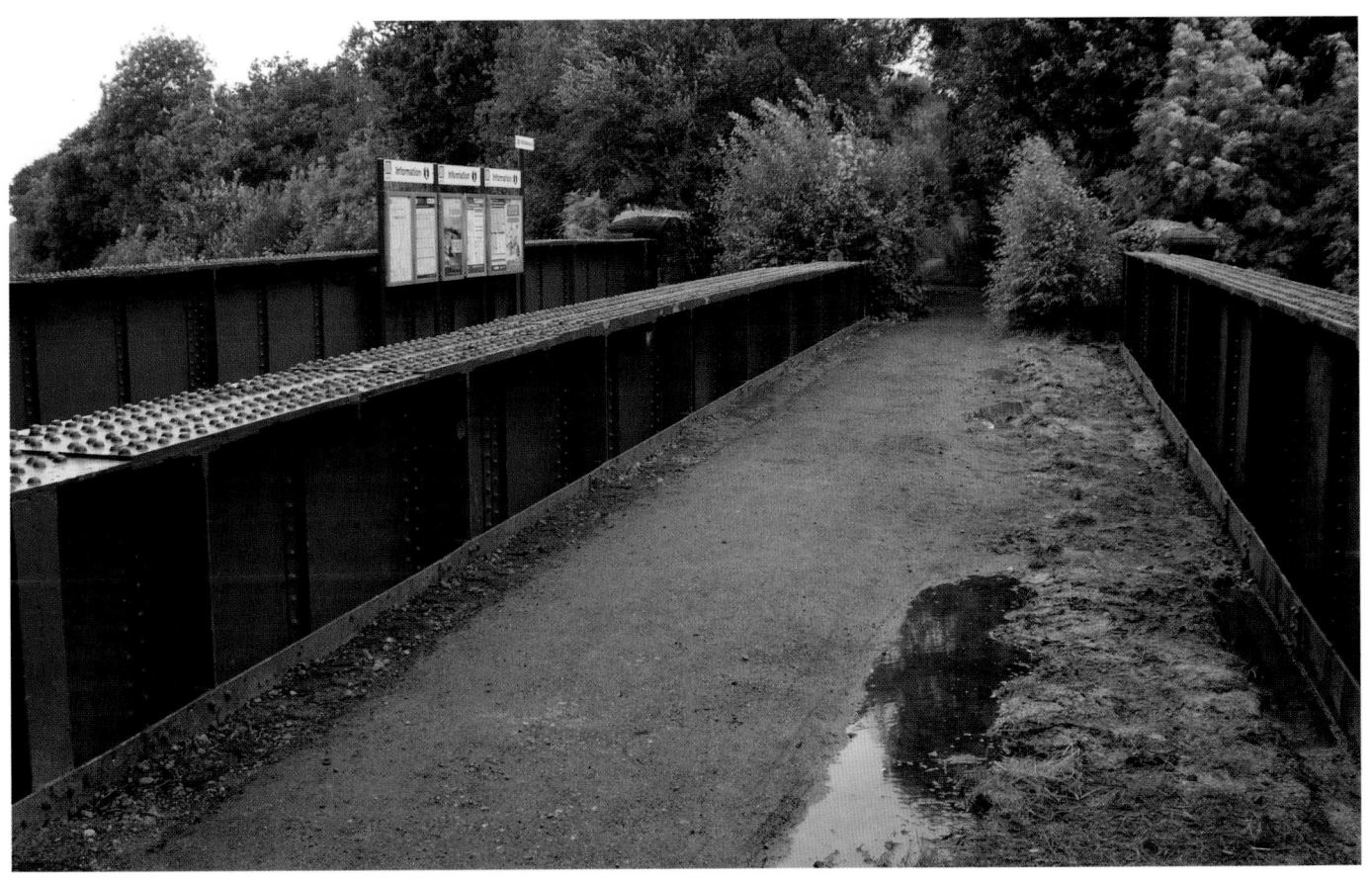

Since closure of the Rose Hill to Macclesfield railway the trackbed reopened in 1985 as a 10-mile footpath and cycleway known as the Middlewood Trail. Closely following the Macclesfield Canal, the Trail also forms part of National Cycle Network Route 55. Stockport Metropolitan Borough Council owns the northern section, from Marple to Middlewood, while Macclesfield Borough Council owns the southern section, from Middlewood to Macclesfield. Other than the section between Bollington and Macclesfield, which is tarmacked, the Trail is suitable only for walkers or mountain bikes.

The Trail starts at Marple Rose Hill station, served by trains from Manchester, where there is a car park and the adjacent Railway Inn. From here the Trail heads south out into open countryside, passing over the western entrance to Disley Tunnel – still open for business on the Manchester to Sheffield main line – to the site of High Lane station. Here the Trail passes through a narrow tunnel under the busy A6 before reaching Middlewood station. Once an interchange station, the lower station at Middlewood is still served by trains running between Manchester and Buxton while the iron railway bridge above it now carries the Middlewood Trail. The low-level station at Middlewood is one of very few in Britain to have no road access and

is reached along woodland paths or from the Middlewood Trail. Despite its remoteness, it was used by over 19,000 passengers in 2010/2011.

South of Middlewood, the Trail heads under several road overbridges and passes the site of Jackson's Brickworks before entering Higher Poynton station. Located close to the Macclesfield Canal, where car parking, the Nelson Pit Visitor Centre and a café are located, the station site at Poynton has been tastefully landscaped with a picnic site set between the two platforms. Just up the station steps and across the road are the Boar's Head pub and a coffee tavern. A mile south of Poynton the canal and railway route rub shoulders at Wood Lanes where there is parking, a picnic site and a café.

Keeping close company with the canal, the Trail continues southward to Bollington. Here it is carried above the town by a low 23-arch viaduct, which can be accessed via a steep flight of steps that lead to a convenient car park. Just across the road are The Vale and Dog & Partridge pubs.

Complete with platforms, the site of Higher Poynton station is now a landscaped picnic site while nearby are a pub, a coffee tavern and the Nelson Pit Visitor Centre alongside the Macclesfield Canal.

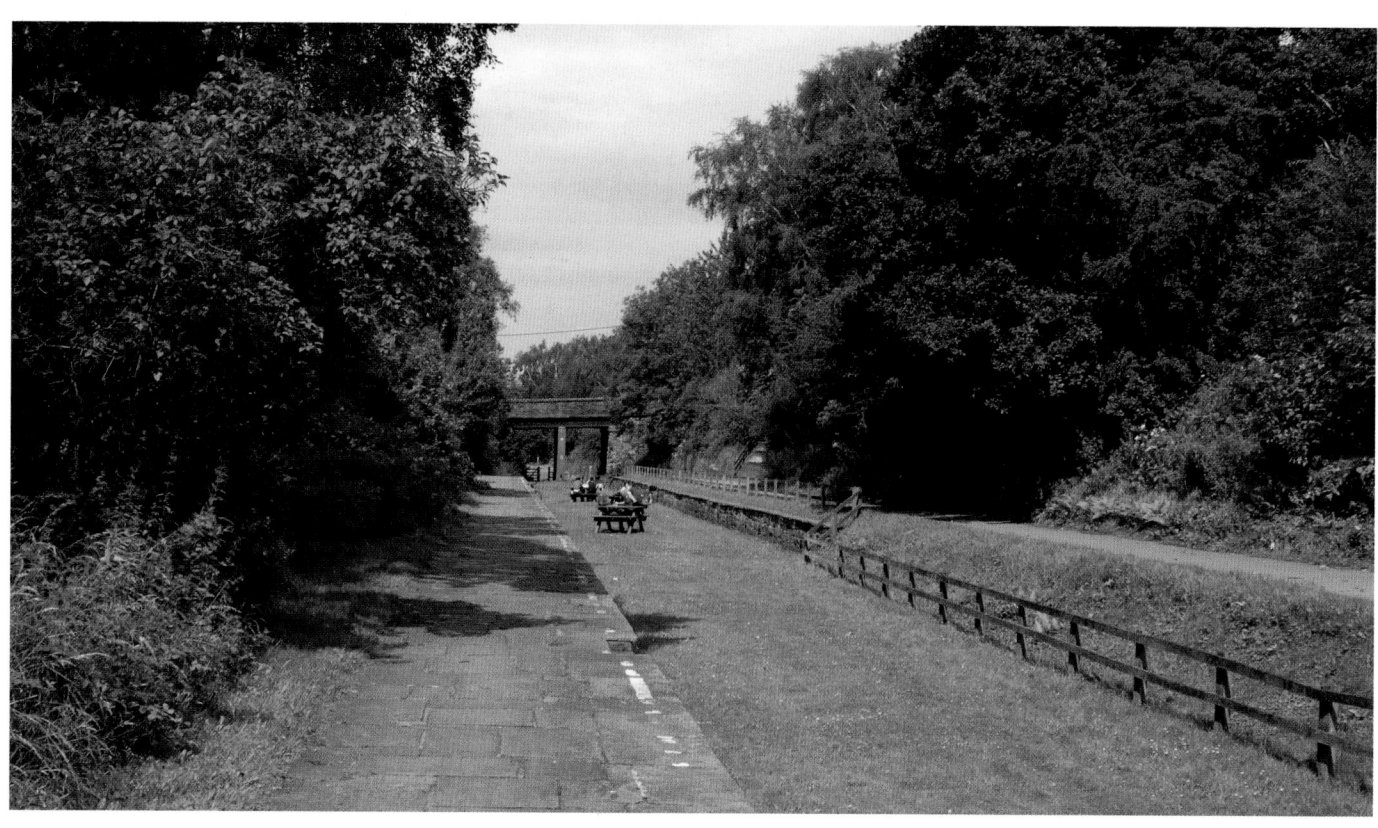

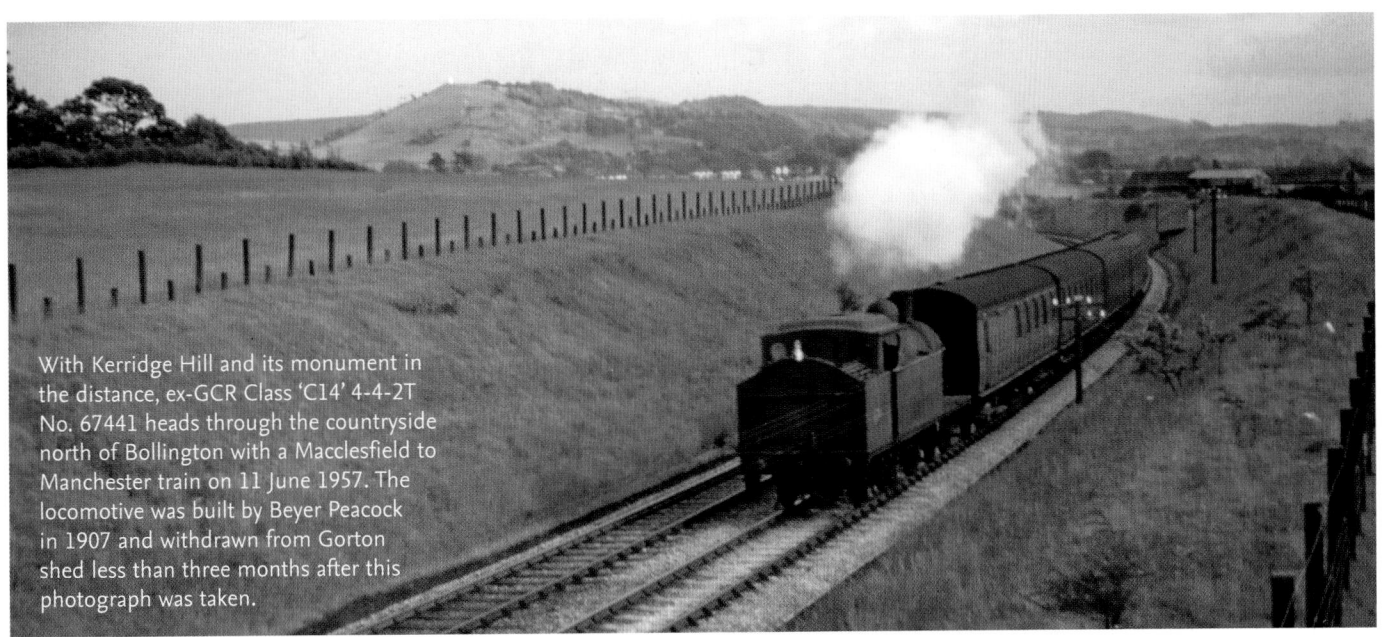

With Kerridge Hill and its monument in the distance, ex-GCR Class 'C14' 4-4-2T No. 67441 heads through the countryside north of Bollington with a Macclesfield to Manchester train on 11 June 1957. The locomotive was built by Beyer Peacock in 1907 and withdrawn from Gorton shed less than three months after this photograph was taken.

Continuing over the viaduct, the Trail soon parts company with the canal and heads alongside the A523 dual carriageway (built for a short distance along the former railway route) into Macclesfield where it ends near the railway station – Macclesfield is served by trains running between Manchester and Stoke-on-Trent via the former LNWR route through Stockport.

Reached via a steep flight of steps from a convenient car park, the Middlewood Trail is carried above the town of Bollington on this 23-arch viaduct.

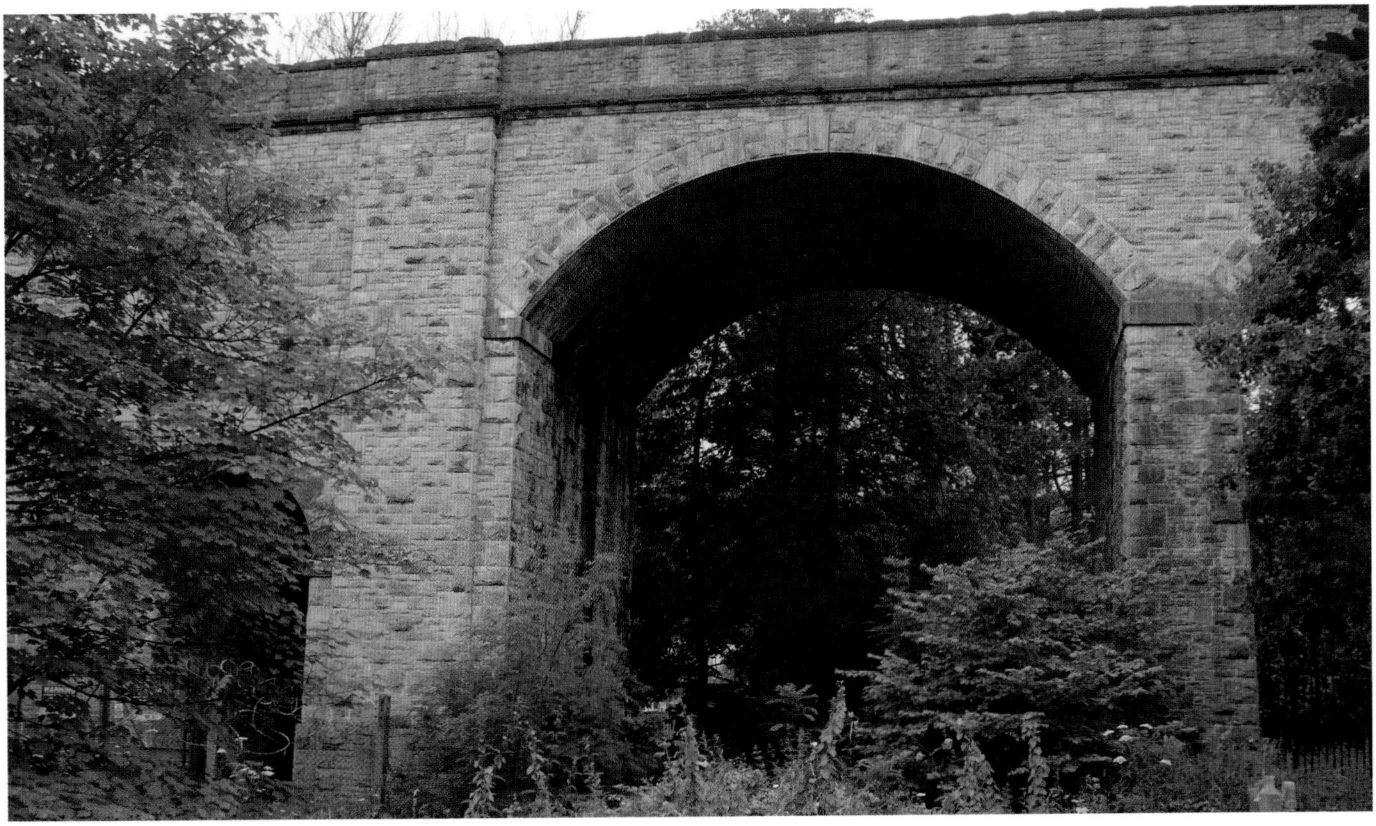

NEW MILLS
TO
HAYFIELD
SETT VALLEY TRAIL

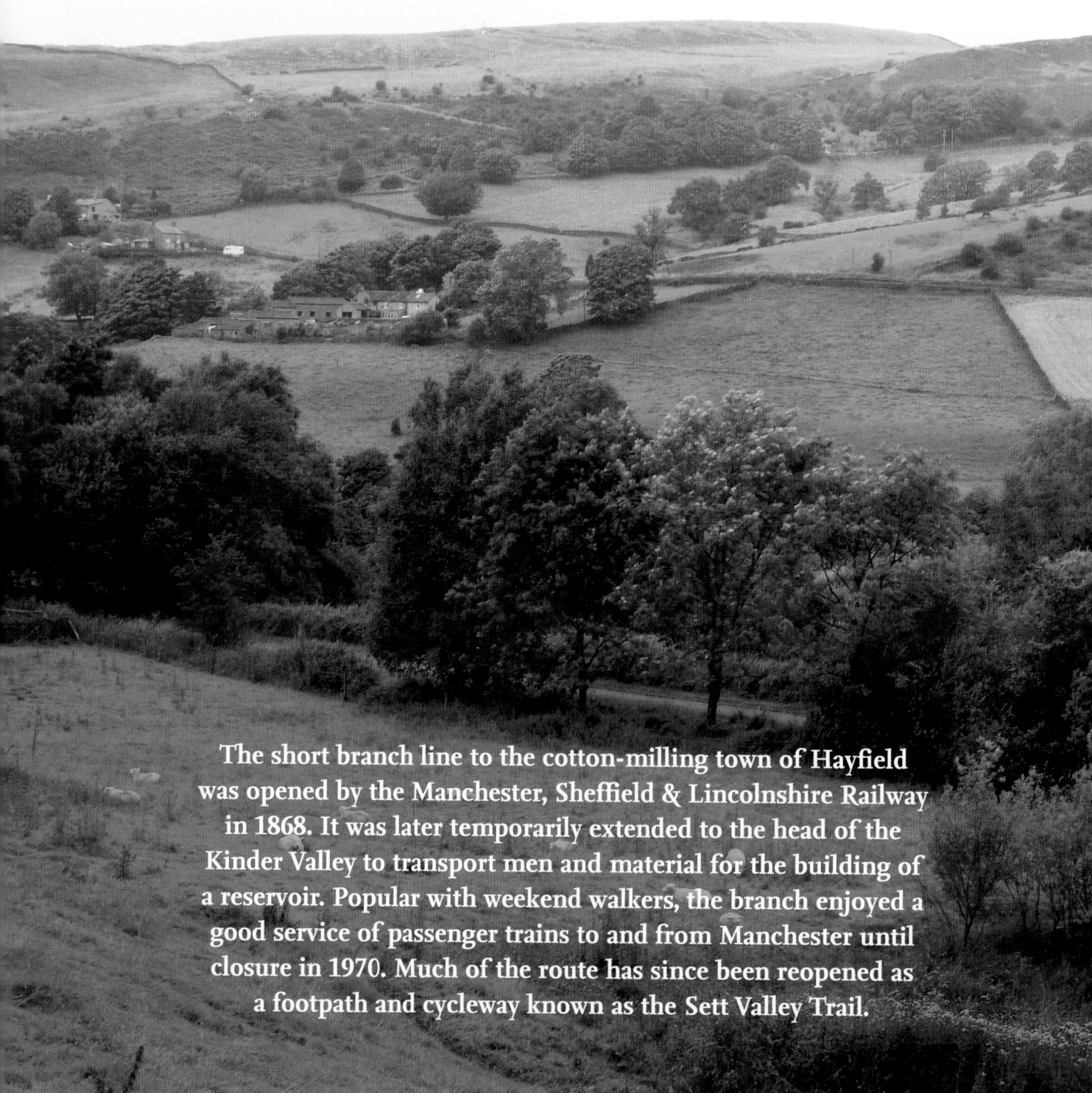

The short branch line to the cotton-milling town of Hayfield was opened by the Manchester, Sheffield & Lincolnshire Railway in 1868. It was later temporarily extended to the head of the Kinder Valley to transport men and material for the building of a reservoir. Popular with weekend walkers, the branch enjoyed a good service of passenger trains to and from Manchester until closure in 1970. Much of the route has since been reopened as a footpath and cycleway known as the Sett Valley Trail.

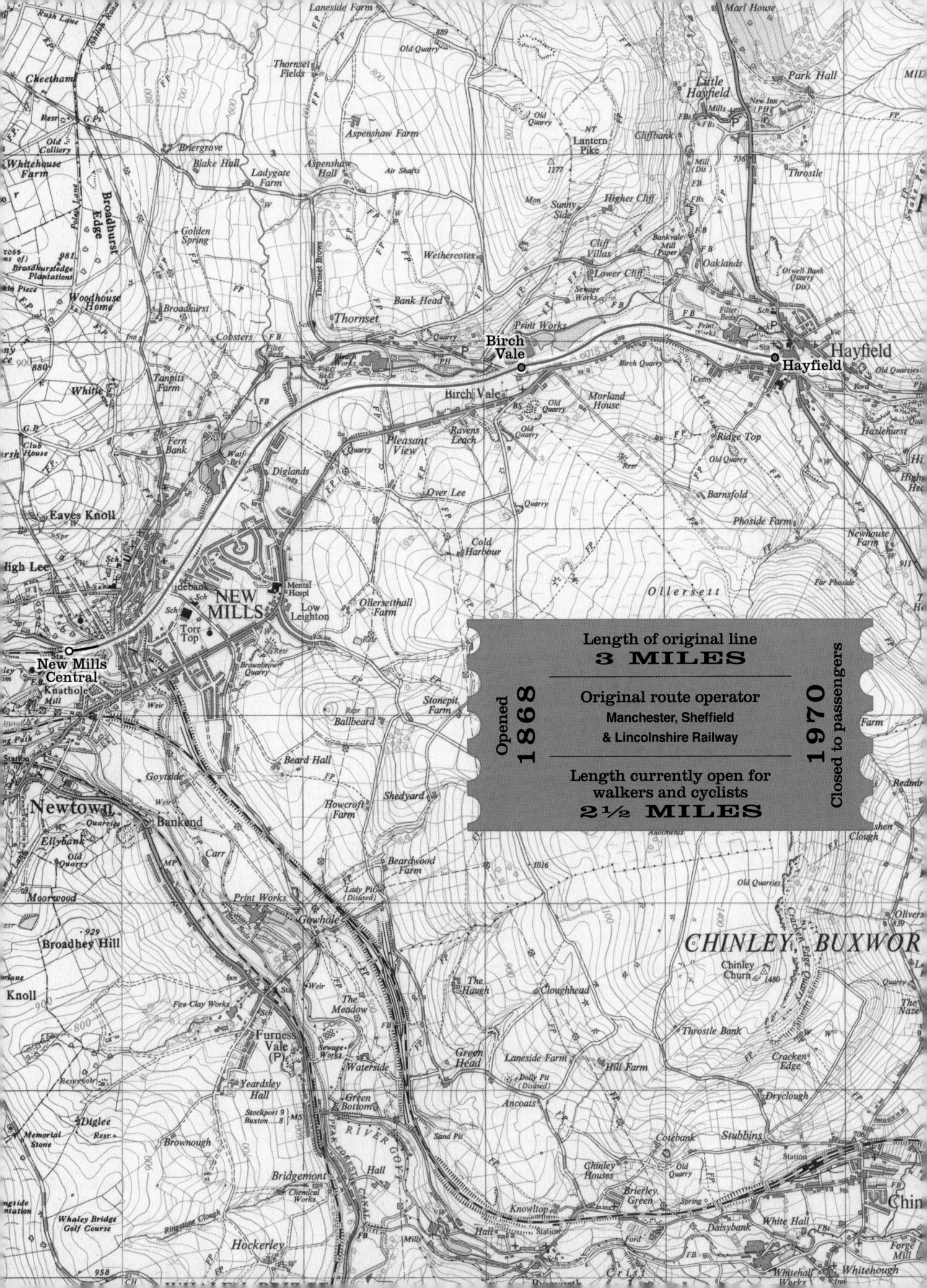

Length of original line
3 MILES

Original route operator
Manchester, Sheffield
& Lincolnshire Railway

Length currently open for
walkers and cyclists
2½ MILES

Opened
1868

1970
Closed to passengers

In the mid-nineteenth century the Manchester, Sheffield & Lincolnshire Railway (MS&LR – predecessor of the Great Central Railway) set its sights on extending its territory southeastwards from the Manchester to Sheffield via Woodhead main line. The first section of this extension was a branch line from Hyde Junction, east of Guide Bridge, to Hyde, which opened in 1858. To the southeast the Midland Railway (MR) reached the spa town of Buxton from Derby in 1863. In its quest to reach Manchester, the MR came to an agreement with the MS&LR allowing the former's trains to reach the city via a new railway to be built from Millers Dale to New Mills, where it would meet an extension of the Hyde branch. The MR opened its line from Millers Dale to New Mills via Dove Holes Tunnel in 1867 and the MS&LW opened the extension of the Hyde branch to New Mills in 1868. The section of line between New Mills and Hyde Junction was vested jointly as the Sheffield & Midland Railway Companies' Committee in 1869.

In addition to extending its line from Hyde to New Mills, the MS&LR continued on up the Sett Valley to the cotton-milling town of Hayfield. With an intermediate station at Birch Vale, this 3-mile single-track branch line also opened in 1868. For the rest of its 102-year life the Hayfield branch was well-served by through trains to and from Manchester – here, both Central and London Road stations were served by trains to and from Hayfield until Central's closure in 1969. The branch line was very popular with walkers during the 1920s and 1930s when up to 5,000 people each weekend would travel from Manchester to trespass on the wild moorlands around Kinder Scout.

At the end of the nineteenth century Stockport Corporation decided to build a new reservoir at the head of the Kinder Valley, two miles east of Hayfield. Hundreds of navvies were housed in the town and the railway was extended up the valley to the construction site. Carrying men and materials, the railway was a familiar scene in the streets of the town until the reservoir was completed in 1912.

Although listed for closure in the 1963 'Beeching Report', the Hayfield branch hung on to life until 5 January 1970 when it closed.

Ex-GCR Class 'A5/1' 4-6-2T No. 69805 heads south away from Hayfield with a train for New Mills and Manchester on a sunny 28 May 1957. Trees now line this route, which is a footpath and cycleway down the Sett Valley. The locomotive was built at Gorton Works in 1911 and withdrawn from Colwick shed in September 1959.

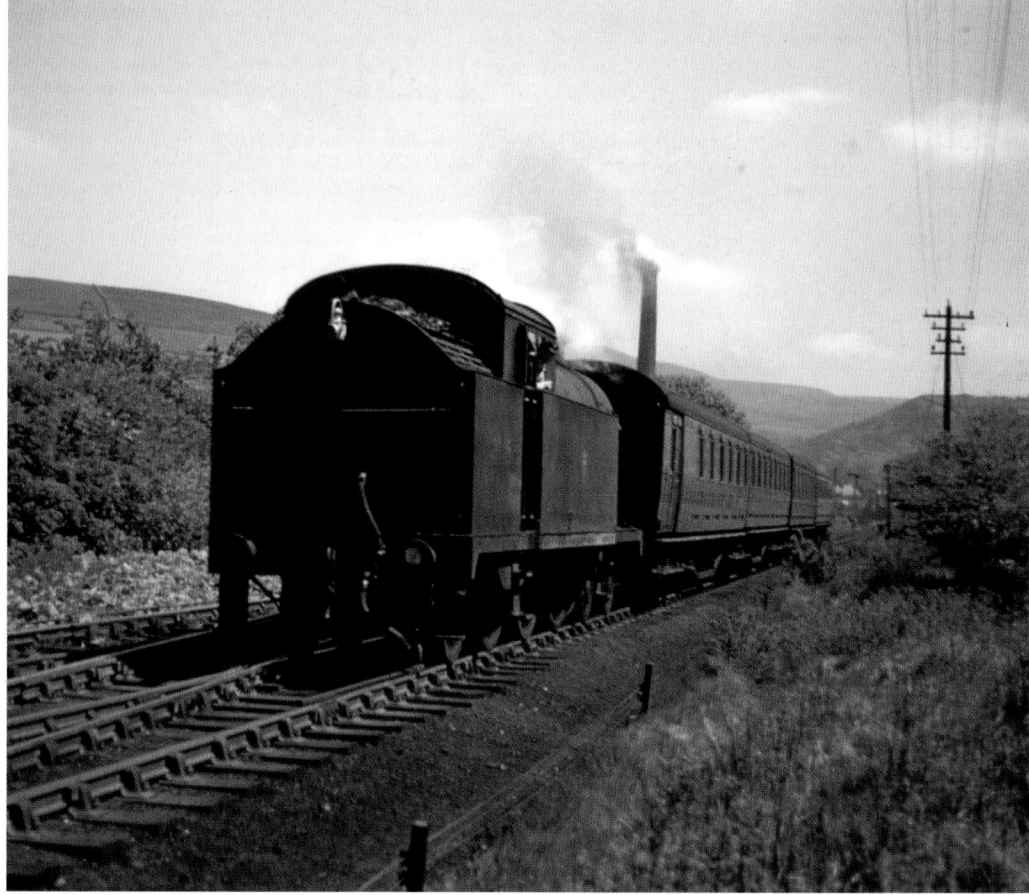

PREVIOUS SPREAD:
The Sett Valley Trail can be seen here passing through an avenue of trees as it heads down from Hayfield to New Mills.

Despite efforts to reopen the Hayfield branch as a heritage railway, the track was soon lifted and the trackbed purchased by Derbyshire County Council in 1973. Although Hayfield station was demolished in 1975, 2½ miles of the railway route from here to New Mills has since been reopened as a footpath and cycleway known as the Sett Valley Trail – the site of Hayfield station is now a car park, information centre and bus station. Much of the route of the reservoir railway from Hayfield can also be walked today.

From Hayfield the tree-lined Trail heads westward down the Sett Valley for a mile to the site of the long demolished Birch Vale station. On the roadside here is a small café that has become popular with users of the Trail. The next 1½ miles threads southwest down the valley before ending at New Mills. The tunnel that was once used by the railway is now blocked up, but a short walk through the town that once boasted nine cotton mills and three weaving mills ends at New Mills Central

station, once the junction for the Hayfield line and still served by trains running between Manchester (via Romiley) and Sheffield via the Hope Valley. Set high on a ledge above the River Goyt and approached down a very narrow lane, Central station has no car parking or turning space but is still worth a visit to see the refurbished MR signal box (semaphore signals were replaced by colour light signals in 2007) and the original station buildings.

Across the valley and close to the Peak Forest Canal is New Mills Newtown station, which is served by trains running between Manchester and Buxton. In between the two stations is a third railway from Manchester via Hazel Grove and Disley Tunnel that bypasses the town but joins the Hope Valley line just to the east of Central station.

Once the junction for the Hayfield branch, New Mills Central station is still served by trains running between Manchester and Sheffield via Romiley and the Hope Valley.

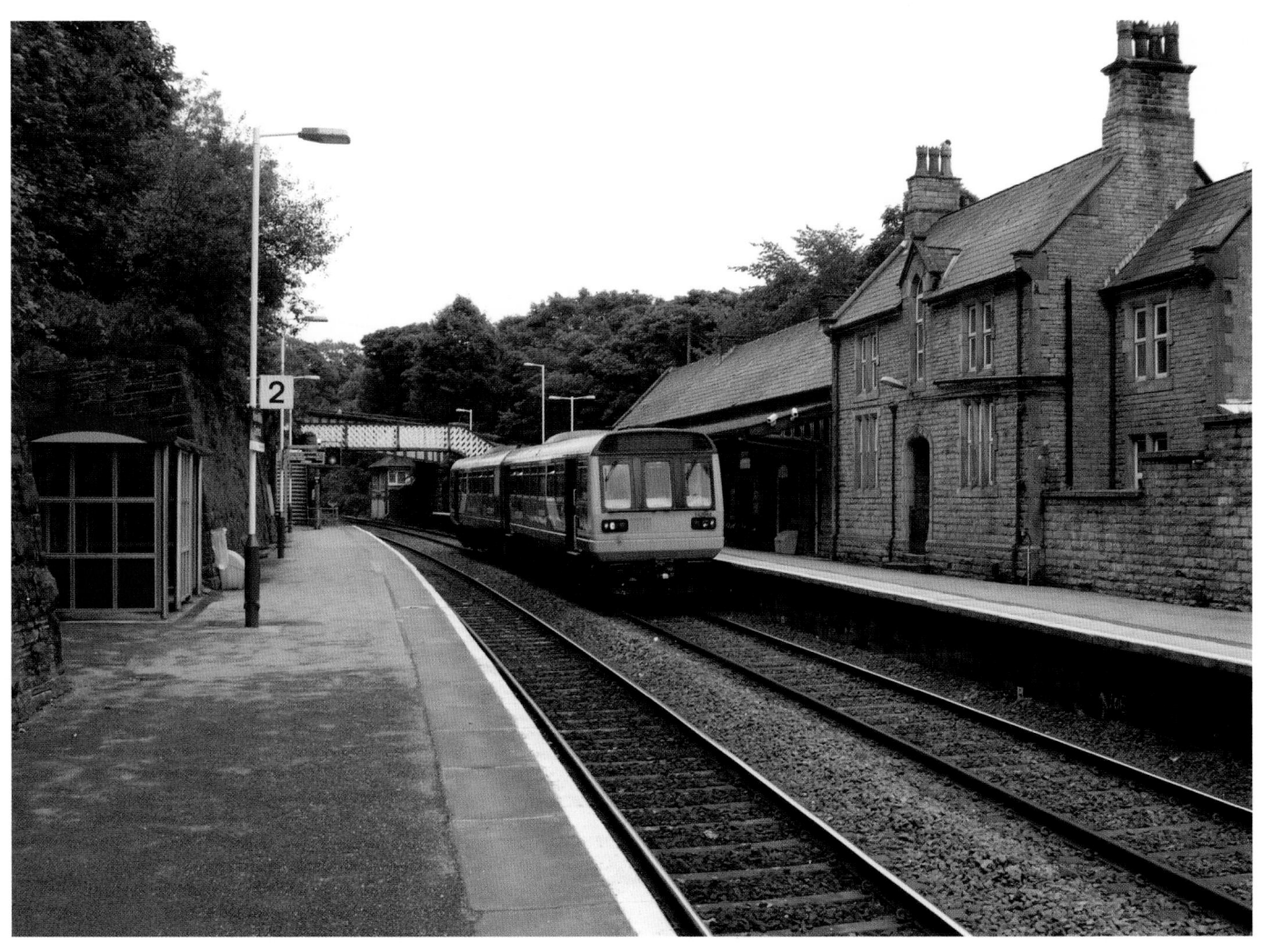

WATERHOUSES
TO
HULME END

MANIFOLD WAY

One of a small handful of narrow-gauge light railways built in England, the Leek & Manifold Valley Light Railway had a short operating life of only thirty years. Its picturesque route threading through the limestone hills of east Staffordshire was fortunately saved in 1937 however, when the parent company, the LMS, gave the redundant trackbed to Staffordshire County Council. Now known as the Manifold Way its well-surfaced, mainly traffic-free route has become extremely popular with walkers and cyclists throughout the year.

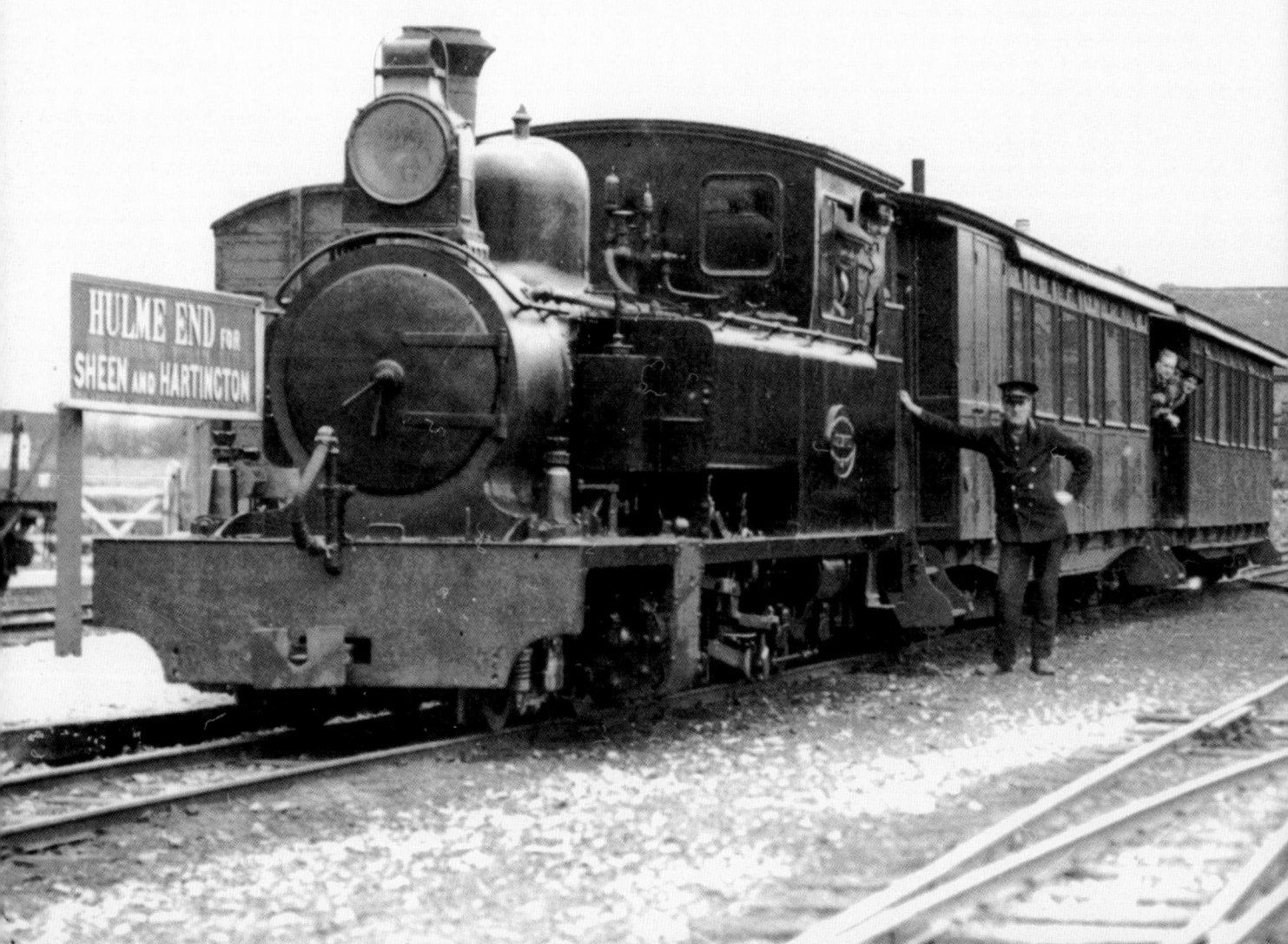

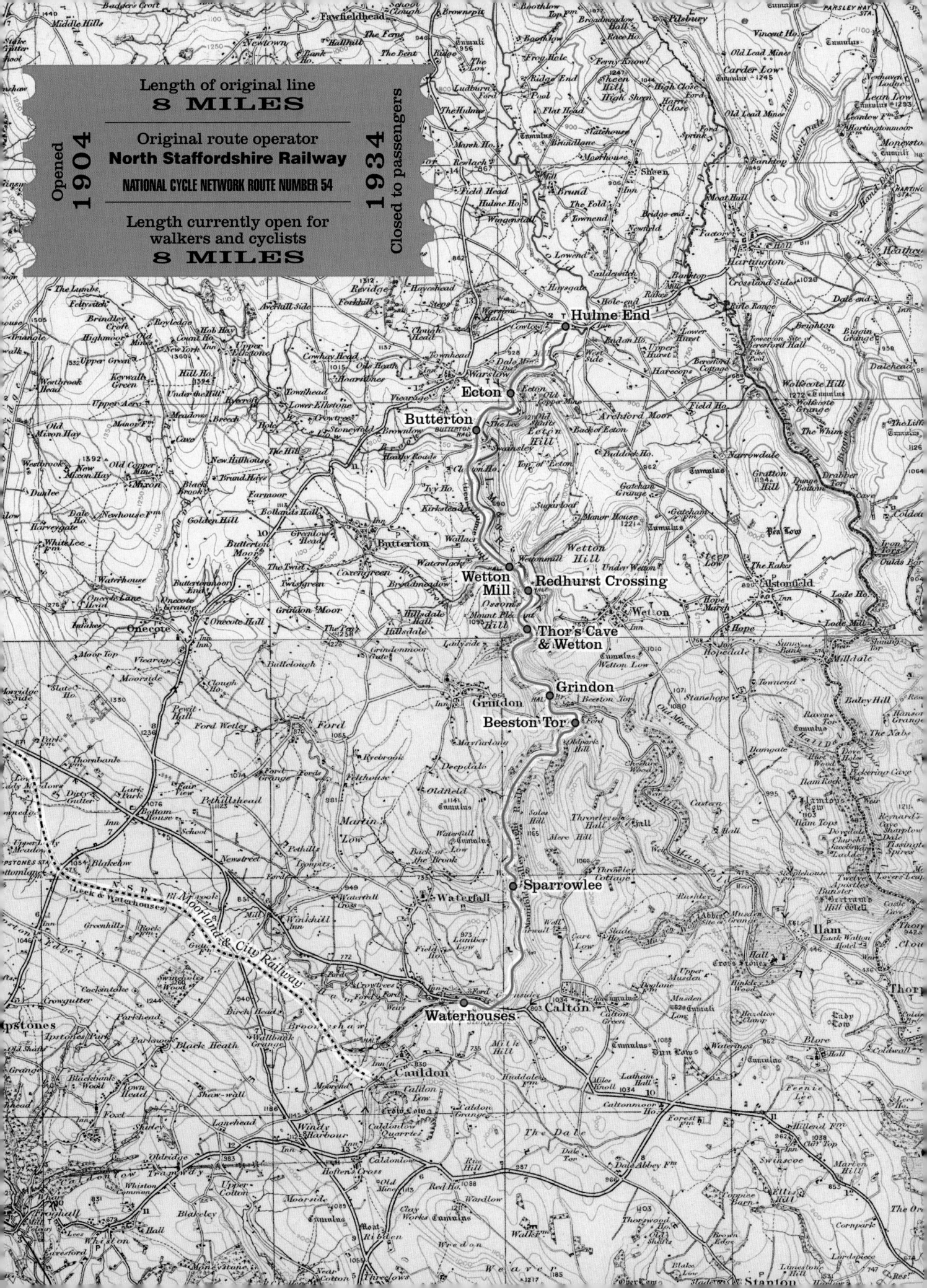

The secluded Manifold Valley, on the border of Derbyshire and Staffordshire, had witnessed the mining of copper and lead ore since the sixteenth century but by the early nineteenth century the workings had become exhausted. Railways first reached the Peak District region of limestone hills in 1849 when the North Staffordshire Railway (NSR) opened its line to Leek. To the southeast the town of Ashbourne was served by the NSR in 1852, while to the north Buxton was reached by the Midland Railway in 1863 and by the London & North Western Railway in 1864. The railway linking Buxton and Ashbourne was opened by the LNWR as late as 1899.

The coming of the railways to the Peak District soon brought Victorians in their droves, eager to explore the region's inspirational scenery, but the Manifold Valley remained virtually untouched by tourism, depending mainly on dairy farming now that mining had ceased. To open up the valley a local MP put forward a proposal for two railways: a 9½-mile standard-gauge line linking Leek with Waterhouses and an 8-mile narrow-gauge line linking Waterhouses with Hulme End along the valley. Parliamentary approval for both railways was obtained in 1899 and Everard Richard Calthrop, formerly an engineer for light railways in India, was appointed consultant engineer for the narrow-gauge line. Both railways were to be owned and operated by the NSR. Known as the Leek & Manifold Valley Light Railway, the 2-ft-6-in-gauge line featured minimal engineering structures and minimal station facilities – the only major feature was the 150-yd Swainsley Tunnel, which was built so that the railway was hidden from the view of the owner of a nearby mansion. To operate services, two steam locomotives were purchased along with four balconied bogie coaches and a variety of goods wagons. Designed by Calthrop, the latter included four transporter wagons that could carry standard-gauge wagons along the line.

While the Leek & Manifold opened for business in 1904, the standard-gauge line from Leek fell behind schedule and was opened a year later. Traffic never lived up to expectations and the little line only came to life on

The former North Staffordshire Railway interchange goods shed at Waterhouses is now home to a cycle hire shop for users of the Manifold Way.

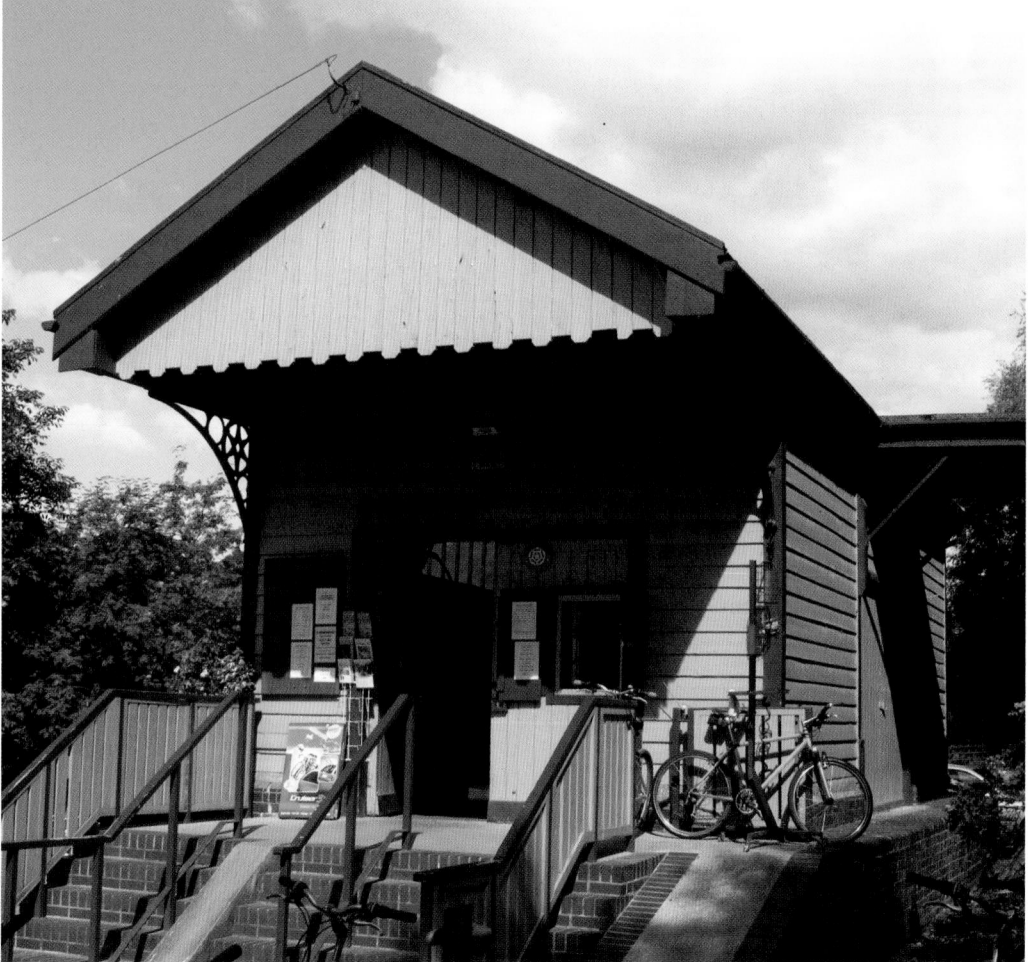

PREVIOUS SPREAD:
No. 2 'J. B. Earle' stands at Hulme End station with a train for Waterhouses in 1933. On the left are standard-gauge wagons, which have been conveyed to the station using the unique transporter wagons designed by the railway's chief engineer, Mr Calthrop. The station building has survived and is now a visitor centre while the engine shed, seen on the right, also remains. Poor old 'J. B. Earle' was cut up at Crewe Works in 1934 but sister engine No. 1 'E. R. Calthrop' survived until 1937 when it was given a temporary reprieve to work the track-lifting train.

summer weekends when hordes of day trippers arrived from the Potteries. The only steady source of income was carrying milk that was collected in churns from the seven wayside halts along the valley. So great was this traffic that an overnight milk train was introduced from Waterhouses to London in 1907. Traffic was further boosted when a creamery was opened at Ecton in 1920, but within a few years the NSR had been swallowed up by the newly formed London Midland & Scottish Railway (LMS) and road transport had begun to encroach. The all-important milk traffic was lost to road haulage in 1932 and the line's days became numbered. Closure of the Leek & Manifold came in 1934 and the track was lifted three years later. The Leek to Waterhouses standard-gauge line closed to passengers in 1935 and to all traffic, apart from the section from Leekbrook Junction to Caldon Low Quarry, in 1943.

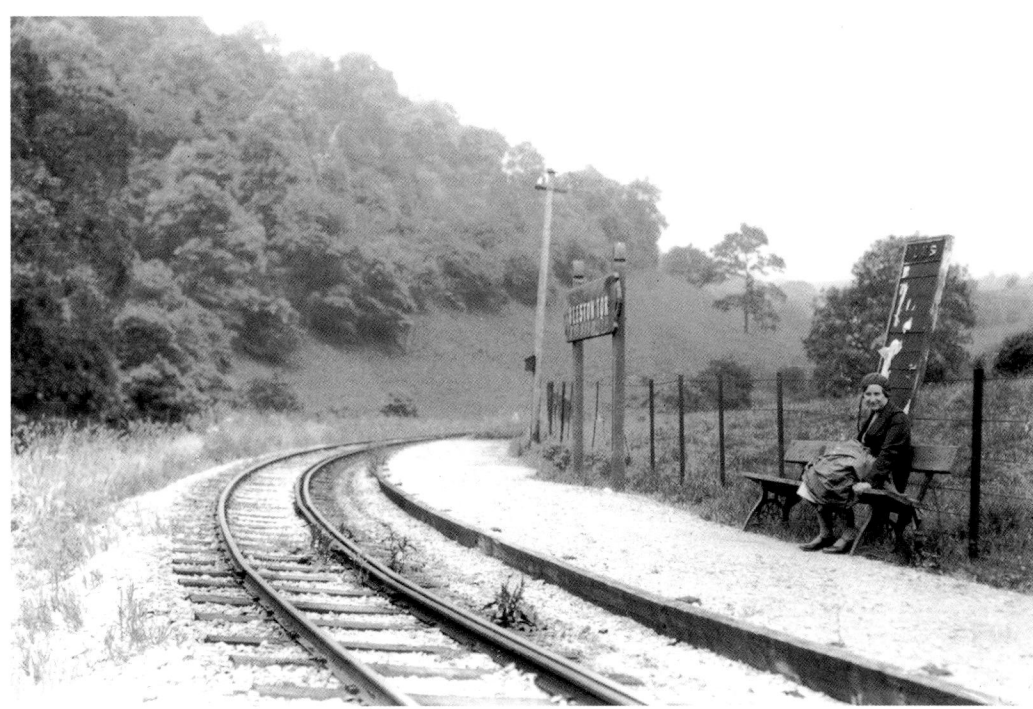

Mrs Kathleen Casserley accompanied her railway photographer husband, Henry, on many of his forays around Britain. Here she looks very relaxed while sitting under an LMS notice board at minimal Beeston Tor station on 28 June 1933. A refreshment room was once located here to quench the thirsts of day trippers who descended on the line on summer weekends and Bank Holidays.

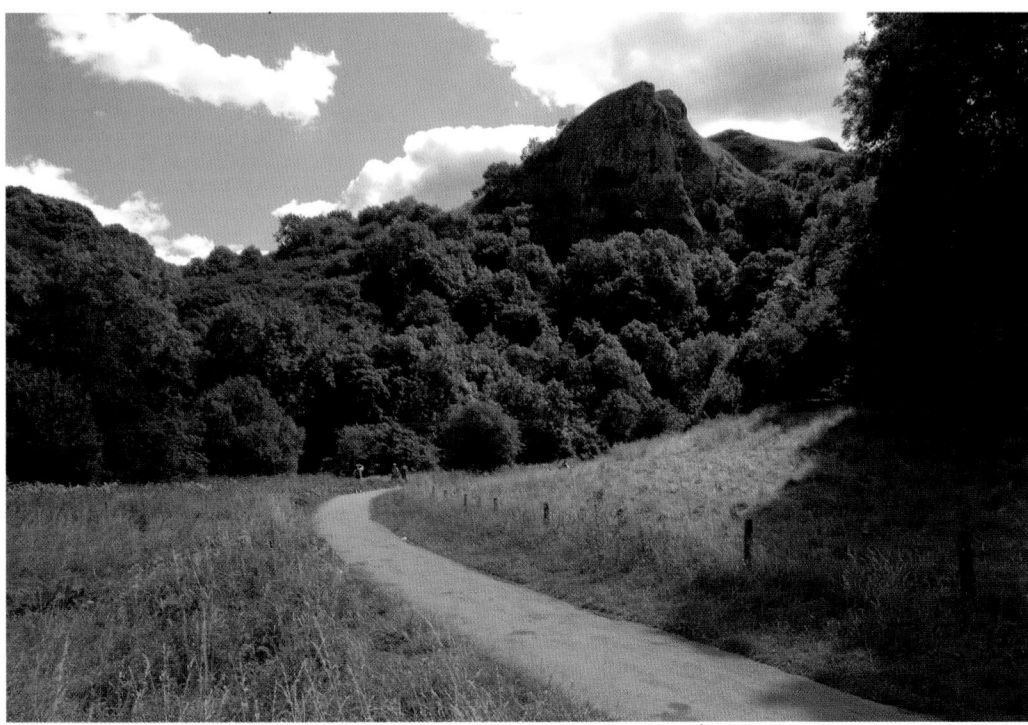

Thor's Cave looms high over the Manifold Way between the sites of Grindon and Wetton Mill stations. Once inhabited by Stone Age man, the cave used to be a popular destination with day trippers travelling by train from The Potteries on summer weekends.

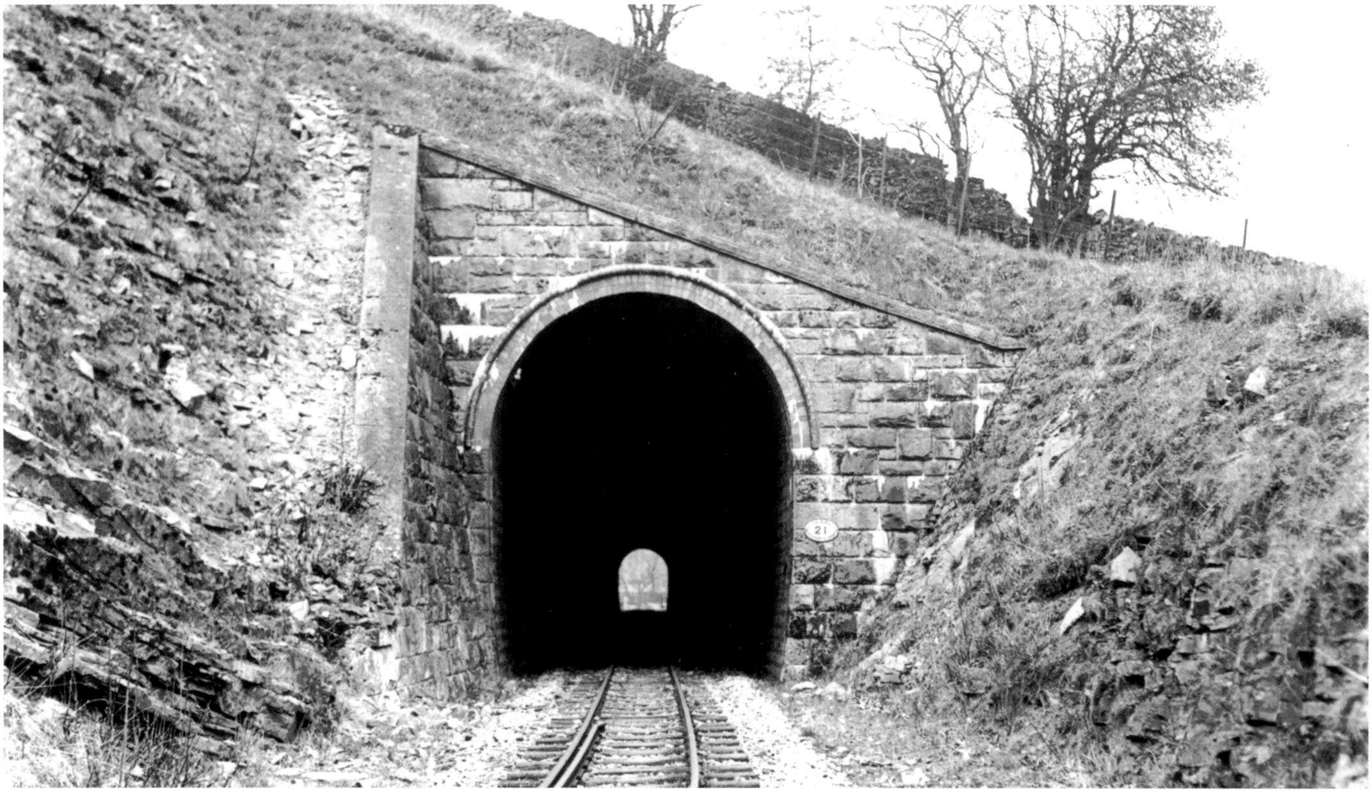

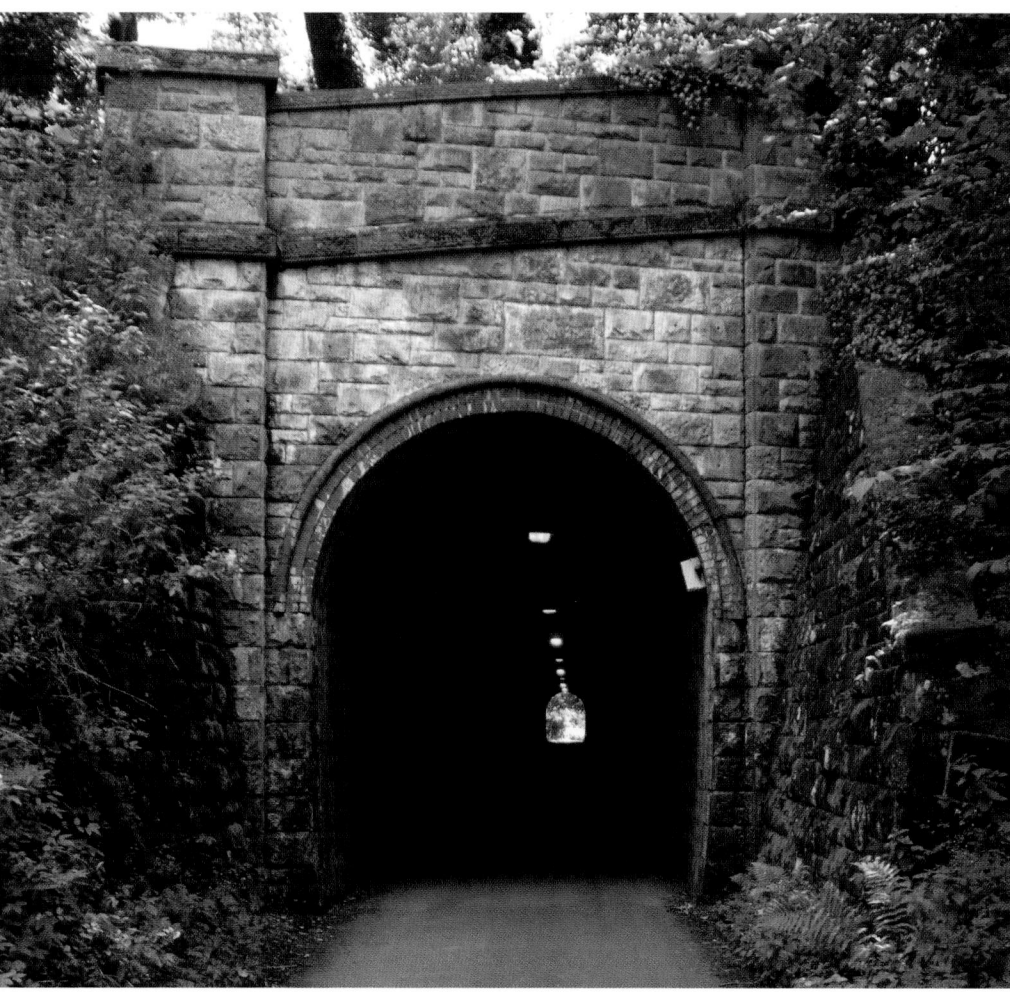

The 150-yd Swainsley Tunnel was built to hide the railway from the sensitive eyes of the owner of a nearby mansion. It is seen here two months after the line's closure on 10 March 1934 although the track was not finally lifted until 1937. That same year the railway's owner, the LMS, gave the trackbed to Staffordshire County Council to use as a footpath. The tunnel is now shared by walkers and cyclists on the Manifold Way as well as vehicles.

Fortunately for us today, the entire route of the short-lived Leek & Manifold Valley Light Railway can be walked or cycled. This came about because the LMS gave the trackbed to Staffordshire County Council who opened it as a footpath in 1937. A 1½-mile section through Swainsley Tunnel to Wetton Mill has been shared with motorists since the 1950s and the entire route has since been resurfaced with tarmac. Today it is known as the Manifold Way and forms part of National Cycle Network Route 54. Extremely popular with walkers and cyclists at weekends, the path starts at the car park on the site of Waterhouses station, where the former NSR goods shed is now a café and cycle hire centre. From here it soon crosses the A52, where there was once a level crossing. Leaving Waterhouses behind, the path crosses the meandering River Hamps on no fewer than fourteen former railway bridges before reaching the site of Beeston Tor station – this was once popular with day trippers visiting the nearby Beeston Tor Cave. Threading through the towering limestone hills, the path soon enters the Manifold Valley to reach a car park at the site of Grindon station. This is the most scenic part of the route and is overlooked by the famous Thor's Cave – once inhabited by Stone Age man – set 250 ft above the valley floor.

North of the site of Thor's Cave station, the path accompanies the road through Wetton Mill where a café provides refreshments for passers by. After making its way through Swainsley Tunnel, the path parts company with the road, passing the site of Ecton station and its creamery before ending at the former terminus station of Hulme End. Here the former station building has been restored and the ticket office is now home to a visitor centre. Nearby is a car park and picnic site and the former engine shed has been completely rebuilt. Refreshments can be taken at the Manifold Inn in the village.

The penultimate station on the Leek & Manifold Valley Light Railway was at Ecton, where a large creamery kept the line in business until milk traffic was lost to road transport in 1932. Today this pleasant spot is enjoyed by walkers and cyclists on the Manifold Way.

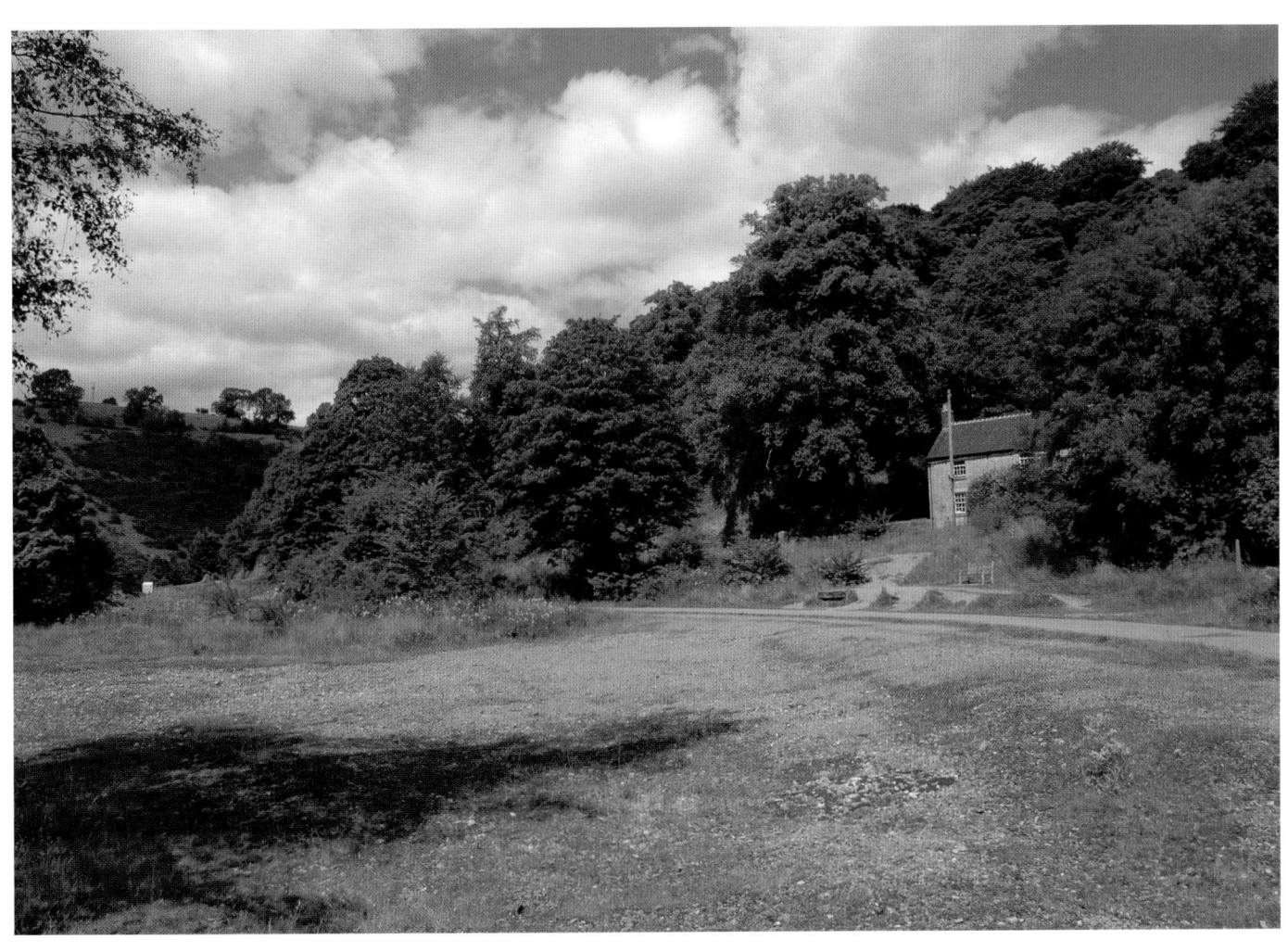

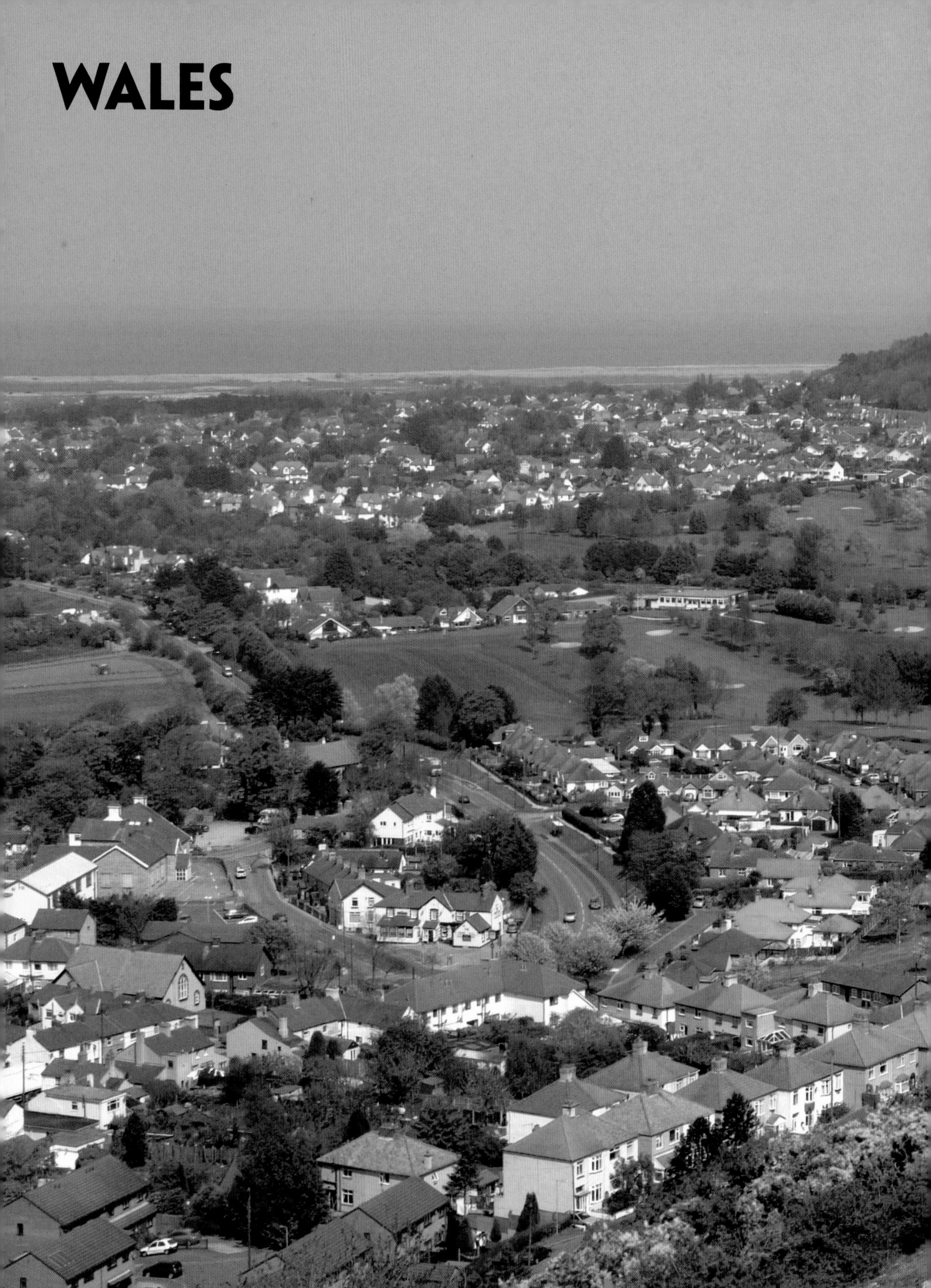

WALES

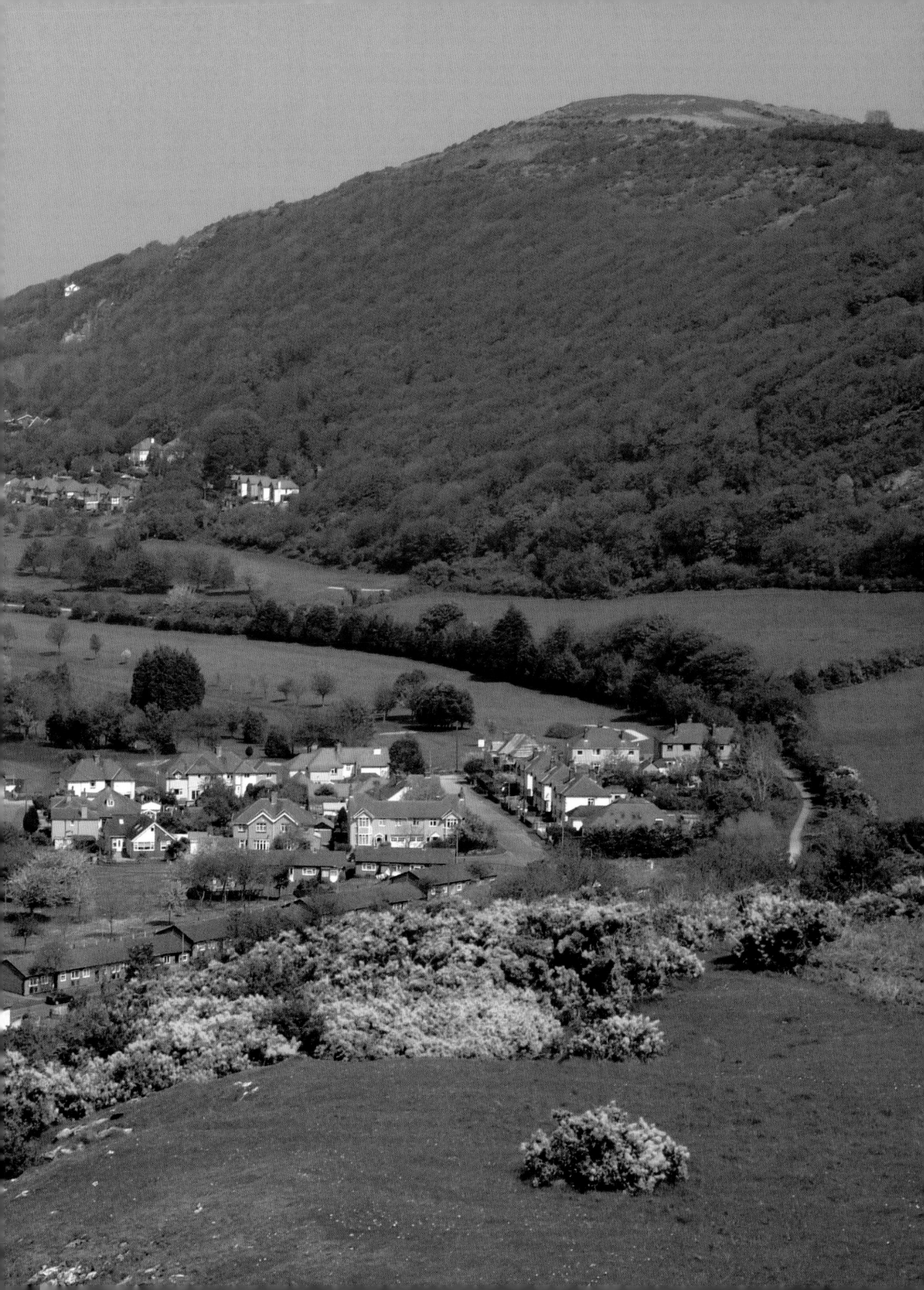

HOLYWELL JUNCTION
TO
HOLYWELL

Starting life as an early horse-drawn tramway serving cotton mills, copper smelters and limestone industries, the 1½-mile branch line to Holywell in Flintshire was also popular with pilgrims visiting a nearby holy well. The railway had mixed fortunes and was an early victim of competition from road transport, closing to passengers in 1954. Today, much of its short route up the Greenfield Valley can be explored on foot.

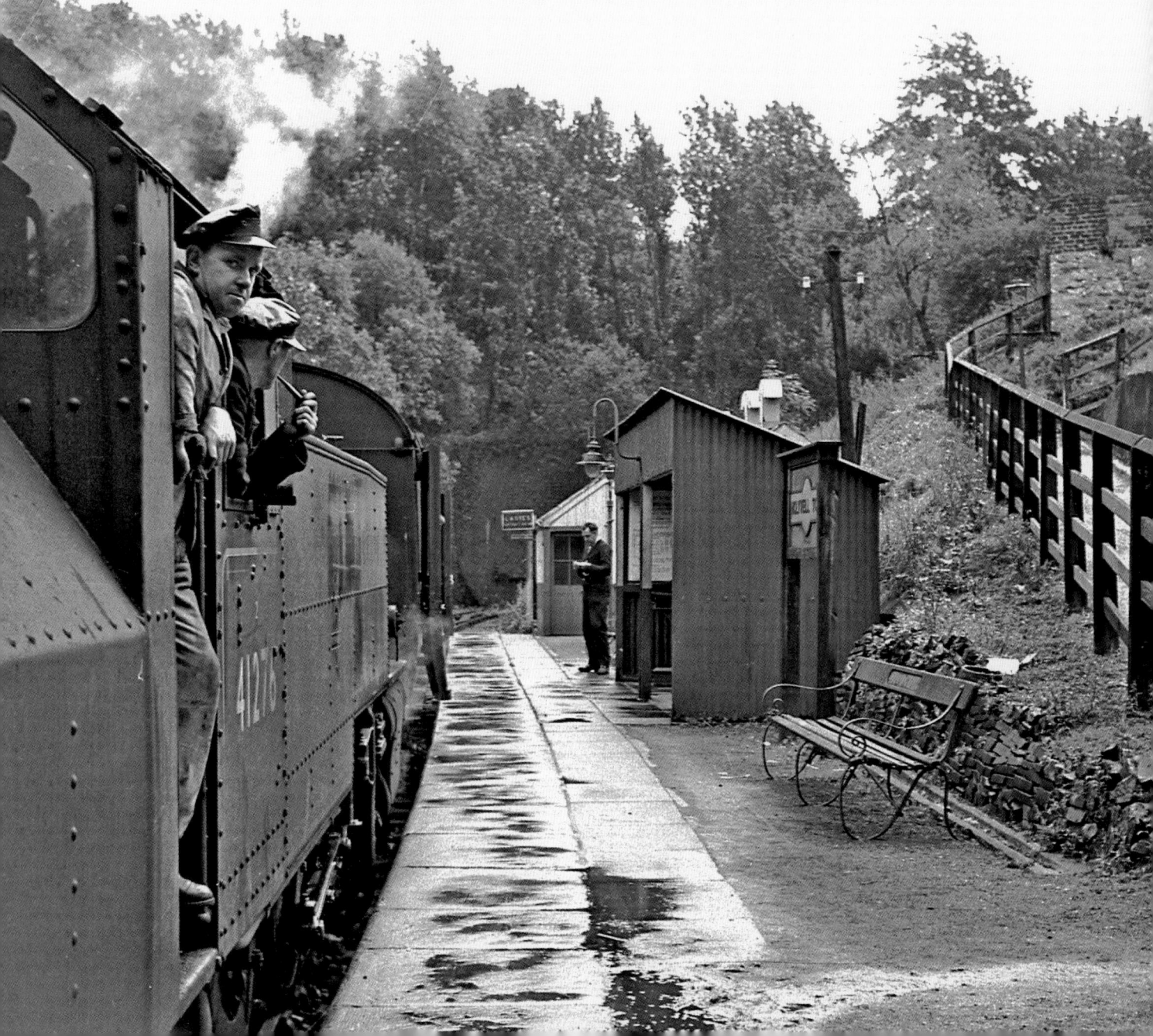

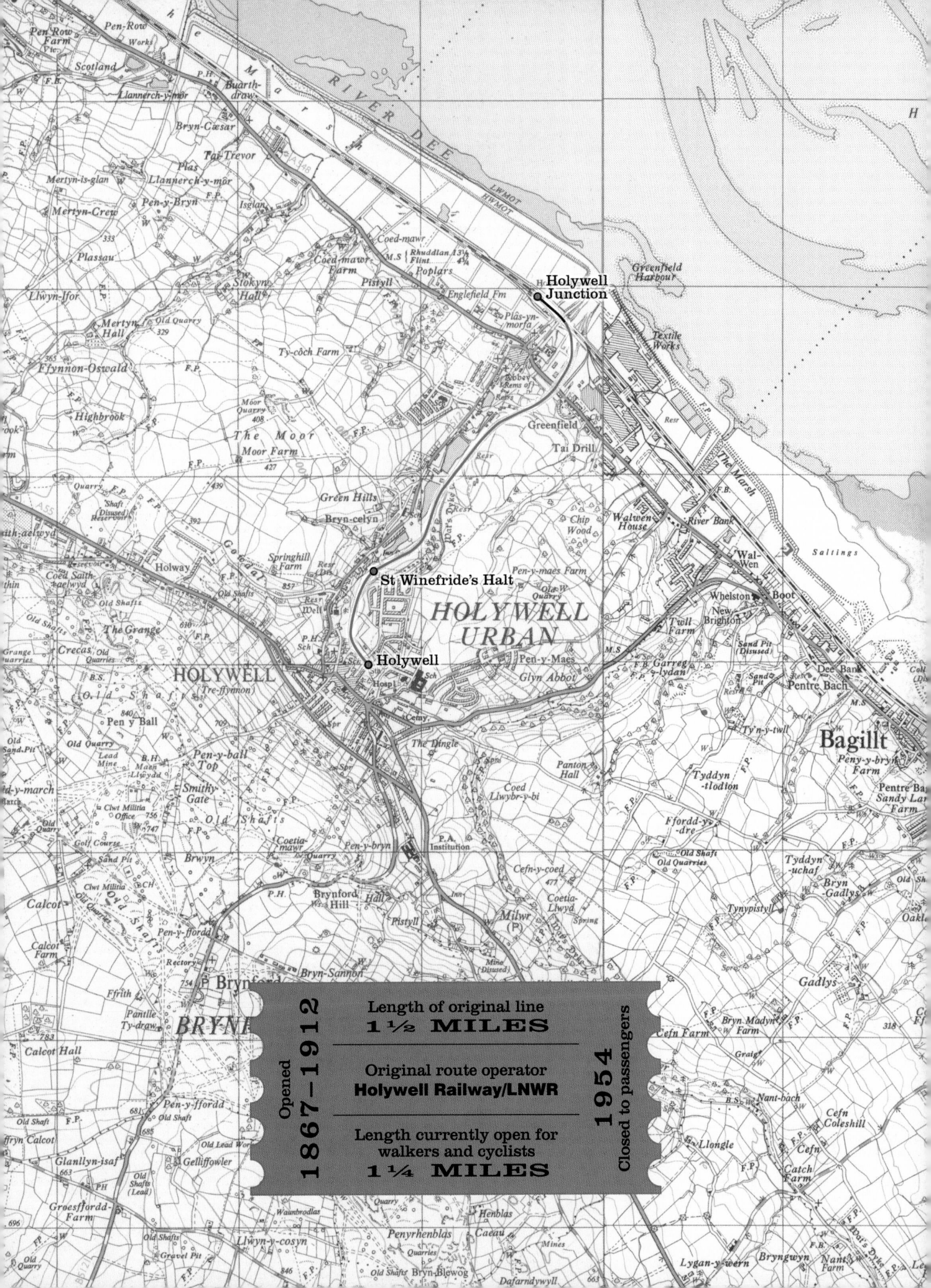

Holywell Junction

St Winefride's Halt

HOLYWELL URBAN

Holywell

HOLYWELL (Tre-ffynnon)

Bagillt

Taking its name from the holy well of St Winefride – a place of pilgrimage since the saint's martyrdom in the seventh century – the market town of Holywell in Flintshire had, by the early nineteenth century, become an important centre for lead mining, limestone quarrying, copper smelting and cotton milling, with mountain streams powering the numerous mills and factories in the Greenfield Valley. By this time a horse-drawn tramway was also operating down the valley, carrying limestone to a small harbour at Greenfield. In the opposite direction copper ore from the giant Parys Mountain mine on Anglesey was taken up the valley to smelters. In 1848 a station (later named Holywell Junction) serving the town was opened 1½ miles to the north on Robert Stephenson's new Chester & Holyhead Railway. The tramway was rebuilt by the Holywell Railway and reopened using steam haulage in 1867 but the decline in the cotton milling, copper smelting and limestone industries led to its abandonment in the 1870s.

The overgrown line lay dormant until 1891 when it was bought by the London & North Western Railway (LNWR), which initially planned to reopen it as an electric tramway – this never transpired but the LNWR started operating a motor bus service from the main line station to the town in 1905. So successful was this that the company eventually reopened the branch line with an intermediate station at St Winefride's (for pilgrims to the holy well) in 1912. Connecting with main line trains at Holywell Junction, the steeply graded branch line – the 1-in-27 gradient was one of the steepest adhesion-worked lines operated by steam in Britain – was well served by a regular passenger service until it closed in 1954, an early victim of increasing competition from road transport. Part of the line remained open to serve textile mills until 1957.

Apart from a short section near the site of Holywell Junction, the entire route of the Holywell Railway up the Greenfield Valley can be explored on foot today. Although closed to passengers in 1966 the grand station at Holywell Junction, now a private residence, still sees the passage of trains along the North Wales Coast Line – the vintage upper quadrant semaphore signalling here is due be replaced by modern colour light signals in the near future.

Set in the 70-acre Greenfield Valley Heritage Park, the route of the Holywell Railway can be accessed from a car park adjacent to the ruined twelfth-century Basingwerk Abbey, which is located north of the A548 at Greenfield/Maes-Glas. Various eighteenth- and nineteenth-century industrial archaeological sites can also be visited along the route including the Battery Factory, which once made pots and pans from sheet brass; Meadow Mill, which produced rolled copper sheets; Lower Cotton Mill; and the ruins of the Abbey Wire Mill. A reconstructed farm and visitor centre is located near Basingwerk Abbey. The 1½-mile railway trail ends under the attractive stone-arched bridge in Holywell Town, where the former station site has now been landscaped. Car parking is available nearby.

PREVIOUS SPREAD: The crew of Rhyl shed's Ivatt Class '2' 2-6-2T No. 41276 look in a pensive mood before departing from Holywell station on the last day of passenger services on the branch, 4 September 1954.

BELOW: The overgrown remains of Holywell Town station as seen on 15 July 1963 contrast greatly with the landscaped site that visitors see today.

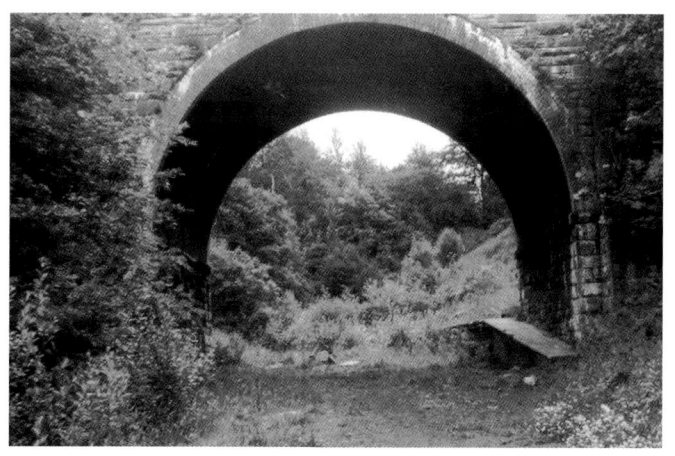

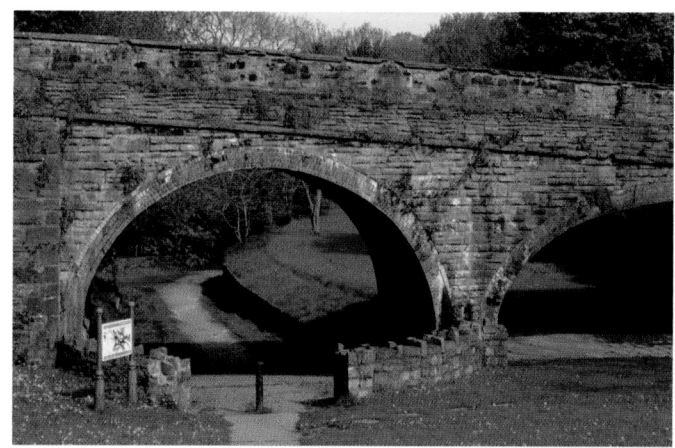

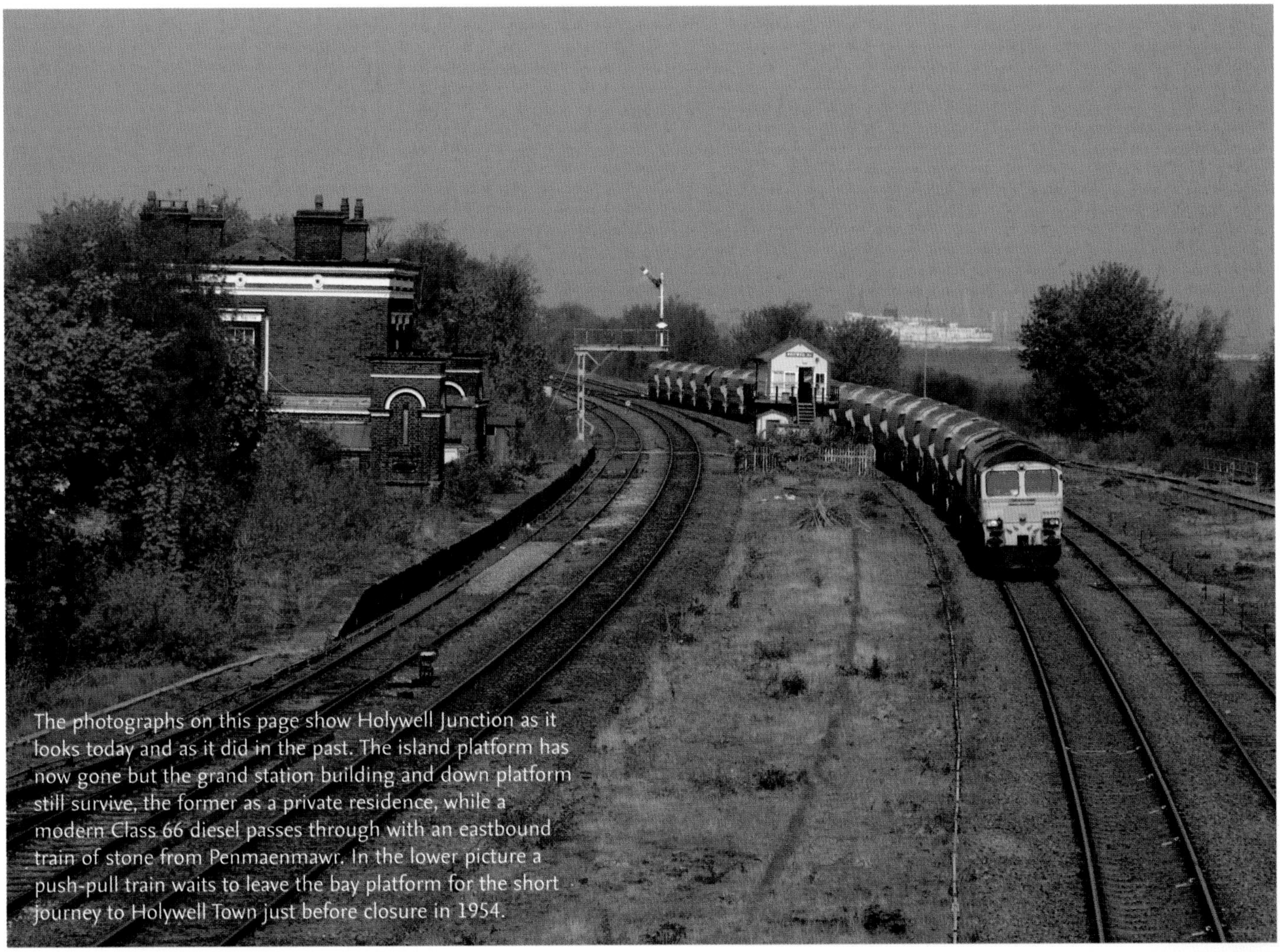

The photographs on this page show Holywell Junction as it looks today and as it did in the past. The island platform has now gone but the grand station building and down platform still survive, the former as a private residence, while a modern Class 66 diesel passes through with an eastbound train of stone from Penmaenmawr. In the lower picture a push-pull train waits to leave the bay platform for the short journey to Holywell Town just before closure in 1954.

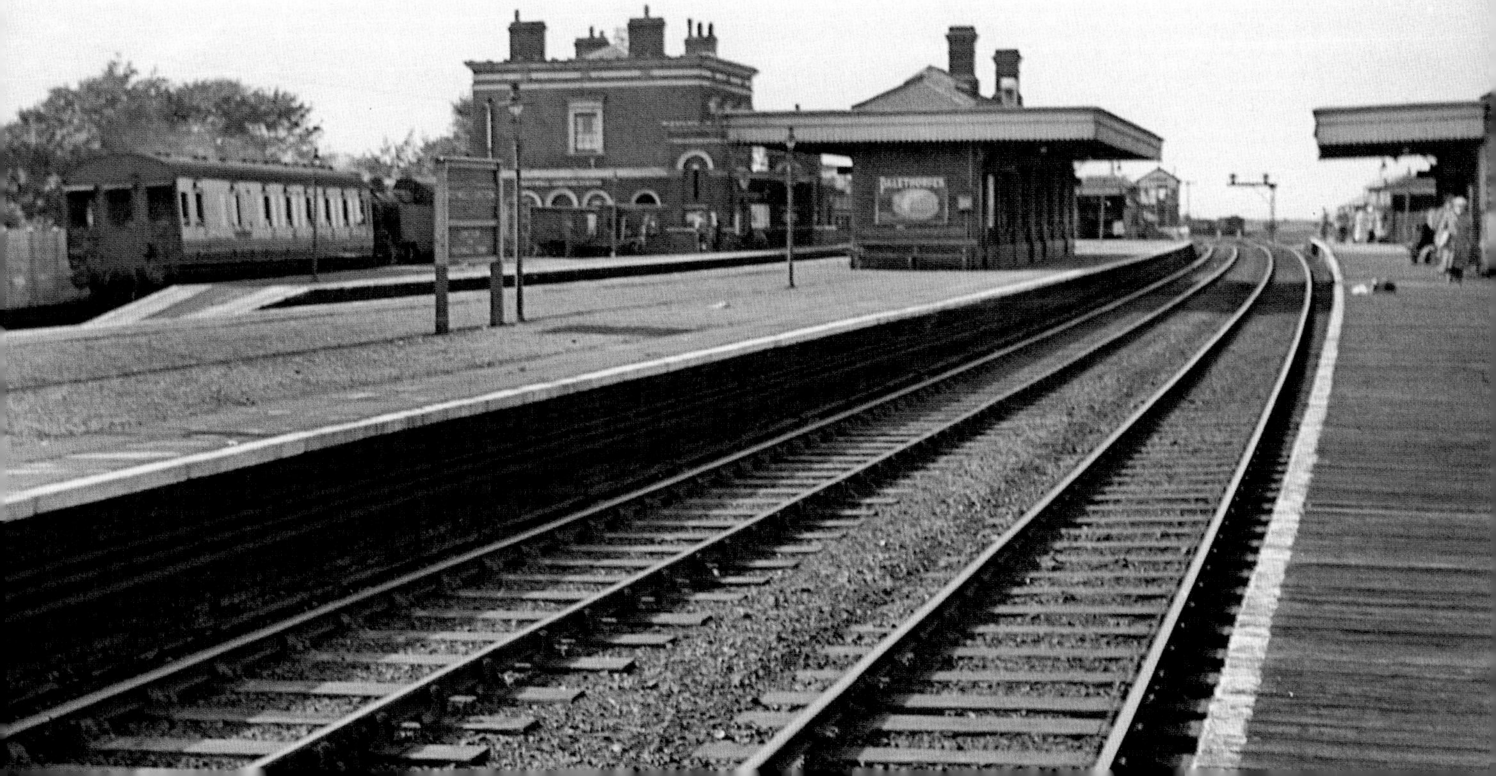

PRESTATYN
TO
DYSERTH

PRESTATYN-DYSERTH WAY

Opened in 1869 to serve mines and quarries in the Dyserth Valley, it took a further thirty-six years before a passenger service was introduced on the three-mile branch line from Prestatyn to Dyserth. Although extremely popular with day trippers, this service became an early victim of competition from omnibuses and ceased in 1930. The line continued to serve limestone quarries at Dyserth until 1973 when it closed completely. Today the entire route is now a well-surfaced footpath and cycleway.

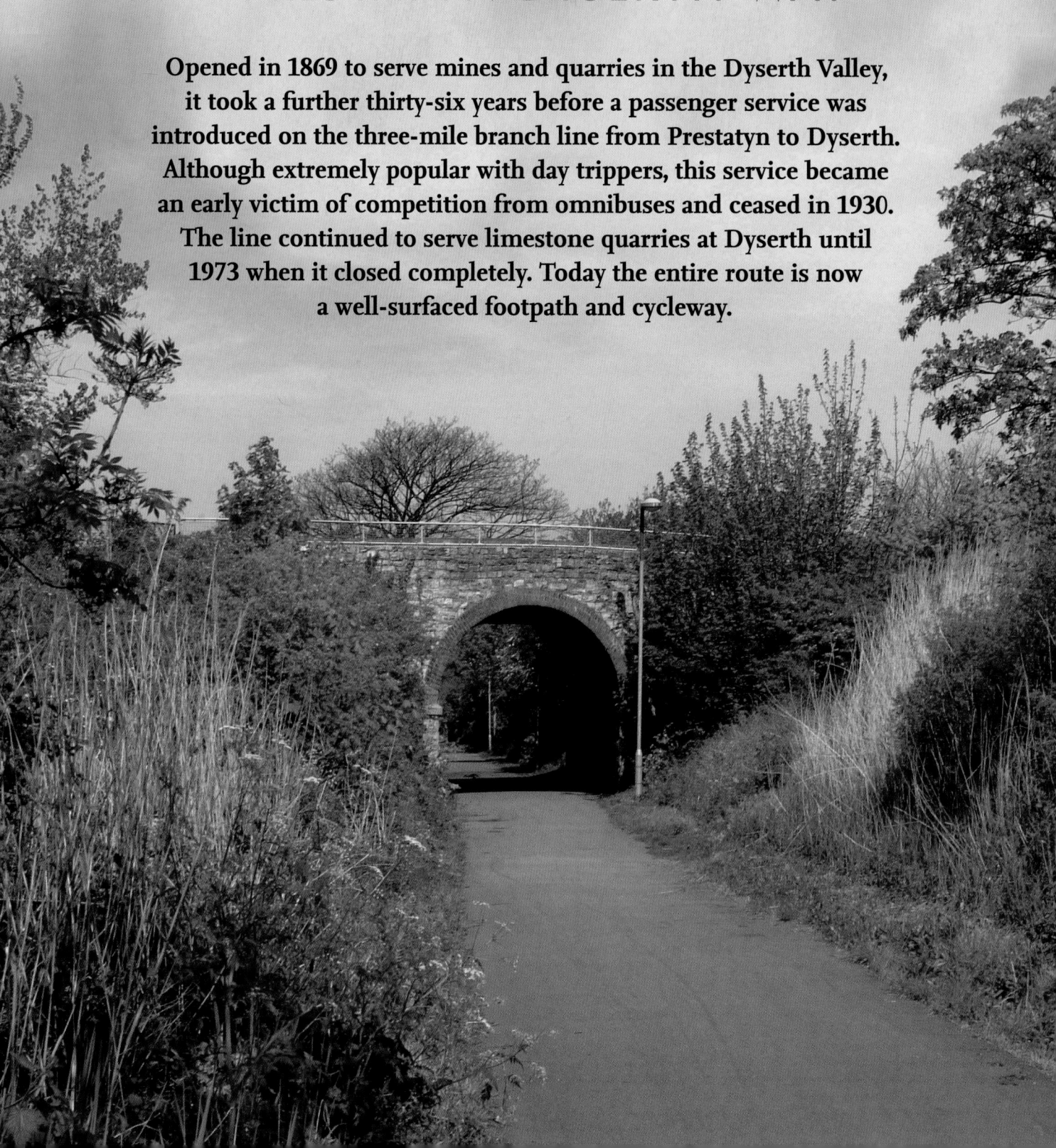

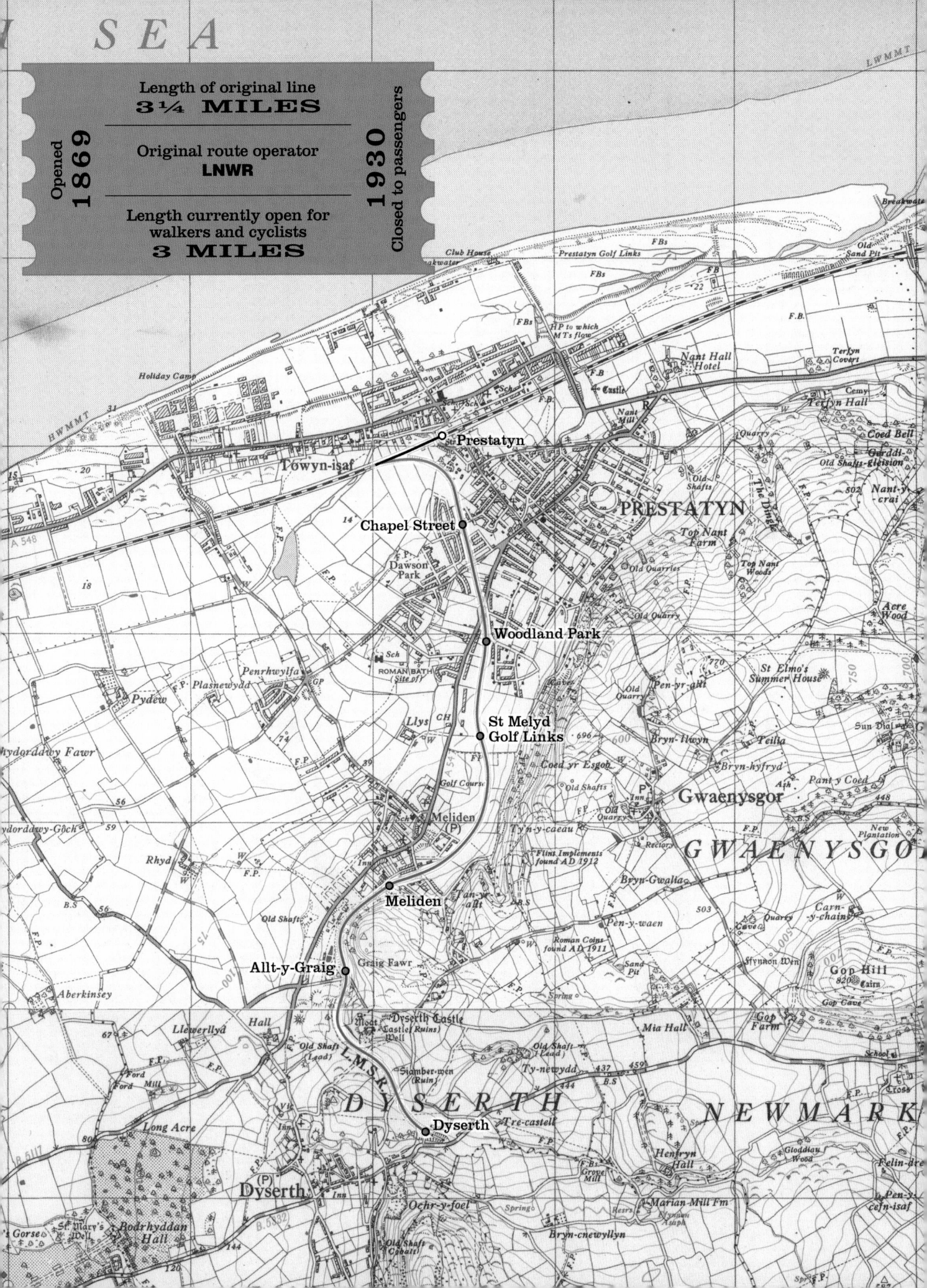

SEA

Length of original line
3¼ MILES

Original route operator
LNWR

Length currently open for
walkers and cyclists
3 MILES

Opened **1869**

1930 Closed to passengers

Prestatyn

Towyn-isaf

Chapel Street

Woodland Park

St Melyd
Golf Links

Meliden

Allt-y-Graig

Dyserth

Lead and copper ore and haematite had been mined at the top end of the Dyserth Valley in Denbighshire since Roman times but transporting it by packhorse overland to Rhuddlan, the nearest port on the River Clwyd, was a costly and time-consuming business. The opening of the Chester & Holyhead Railway along the North Wales coast in 1848 and the Vale of Clwyd Railway in 1858 soon led to proposals for a 4½-mile tramway to be built from Prestatyn, on the coastal railway, to serve the mines and quarries around Dyserth. A proposal put forward in 1864 was seen as too ambitious and would have been abandoned if the London & North Western Railway (LNWR) hadn't stepped in with its own plans. The LNWR's scheme was for a 3¼-mile single-track branch line from Prestatyn to Dyserth, terminating at quarries north of the village. Authorization was received in 1866 and the steeply graded line opened for freight traffic only in 1869.

The scenic charms of the Dyserth Valley and its tourist potential were somewhat lost on the LNWR's directors at Euston until a petition with about 3,500 signatures was received in 1896, requesting a passenger service. After some delay Euston eventually took heed and introduced a steam railmotor service in 1905. Short platforms for this service were opened at Prestatyn main station, Rhuddlan Road, Meliden and Dyserth. The passenger service was an immediate success and further halts were opened at Chapel Street (Prestatyn) in 1906, St Melyd Golf Links in 1923 and Allt-y-Graig in 1928. Apart from Prestatyn, Dyserth was the only station with a ticket office – passengers joining at the halts were issued tickets by an early version of the modern conductor/guard.

The line became so busy with day trippers that a push-pull train was introduced in 1920 – on summer weekends the train ran virtually non-stop up and down the line, carrying thousands of visitors eager to see the ruins of Dyserth Castle and the waterfalls up the valley at Cwm. Sadly the economic depression of the late 1920s, along with competition from buses, saw passenger numbers in decline and the service was withdrawn on 22 September 1930. However, limestone for the steel works at Shotton and other stone traffic from the quarries continued unabated, although the number of trains each weekday had dropped to one by 1953 – again, road transport was to blame for this decline. Meliden goods depot closed in 1957 but stone traffic continued until 8 September 1973 when the line closed completely. Plans to reopen the line as a heritage railway fizzled out as the group of preservationists moved their sights to Llangollen further south. The quarries closed in 1981.

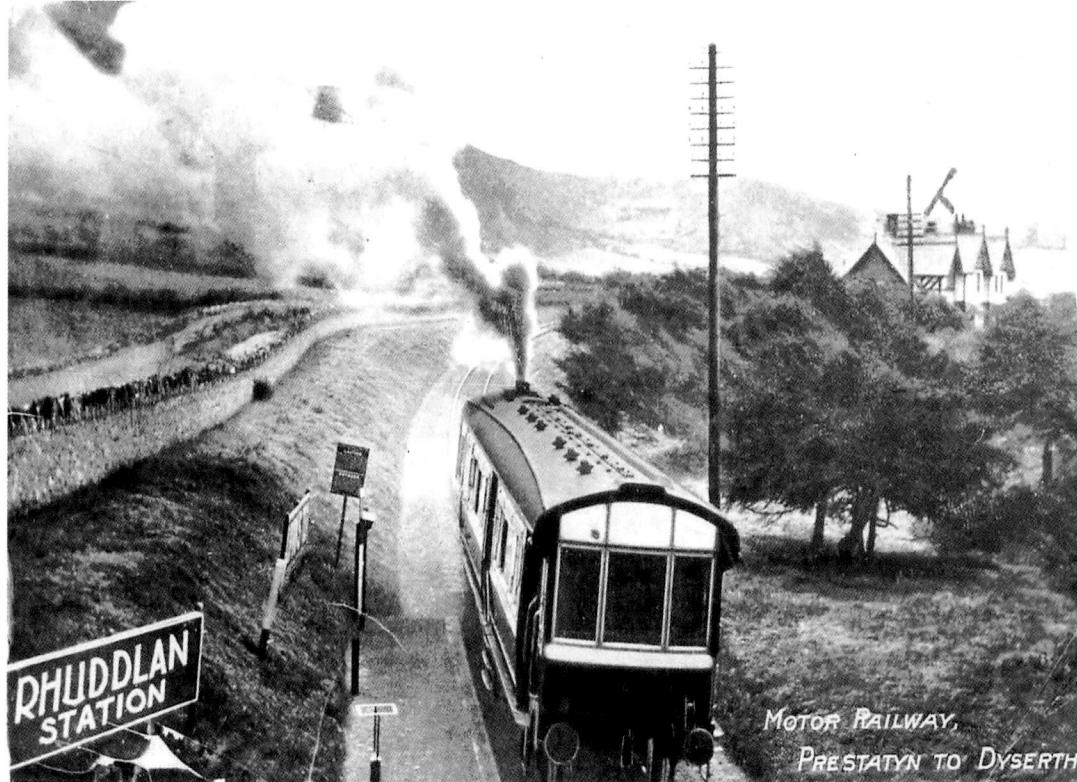

An LNWR steam rail motor departs from Rhuddlan Road Halt on the Dyserth branch, c.1912. During summer weekends and Bank Holidays these rail motors carried thousands of day trippers to Dyserth.

PREVIOUS SPREAD: Seen here on the outskirts of Prestatyn, the trackbed of the 3-mile branch line to Dyserth is now a well-surfaced footpath and cycleway.

Since closure in 1973, almost the entire route of the Dyserth branch from Prestatyn has been reopened as a footpath and cycleway. The well-surfaced 3-mile Prestatyn-Dyserth Way starts close to Prestatyn station, which is served by trains running between Chester and Holyhead. Before long the path passes under several road bridges to the site of Rhuddlan Road station and heads southwards up the Dyserth Valley and into open countryside. After two miles the path enters the site of Meliden station where the goods shed and a loading gauge are remarkable survivors. It was here that trucks of lead ore were once loaded into railway wagons from the nearby Talargoch Mine.

Heading south from Meliden the path skirts the steep slopes of Graig Fawr to the east, its 500-ft summit offering superb views of the tree-lined railway route down the valley to Prestatyn and the Irish Sea beyond. Nearby to the west is the gaunt structure of Clive Engine House, which once pumped water from the Talargoch lead mine. The path continues around the base of Graig Fawr, passing the earthworks of Dyserth Castle before ending its journey under a magnificent 3-arched bridge in a car park at the site of Dyserth goods yard – here an old crane has been restored as a reminder of the

railway's importance to local industries. Nearby is a massive pair of medieval stone walls that once supported a mill's water wheel, driven by water diverted from a nearby waterfall – at one point there were seven flour and fulling mills in Dyserth but most had closed by the end of the nineteenth century. Walkers and cyclists can refresh themselves at the nearby New Inn before returning to Prestatyn along the railway path.

The Vale of Clwyd Farmers' depot and goods yard at Dyserth in 1950. Despite losing its passenger service in 1930, the branch line remained open for stone traffic until 1973.

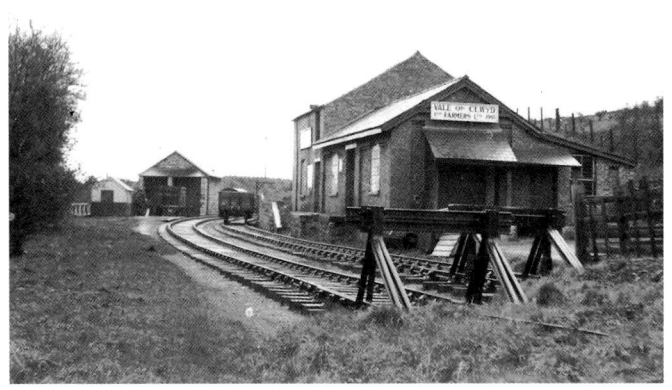

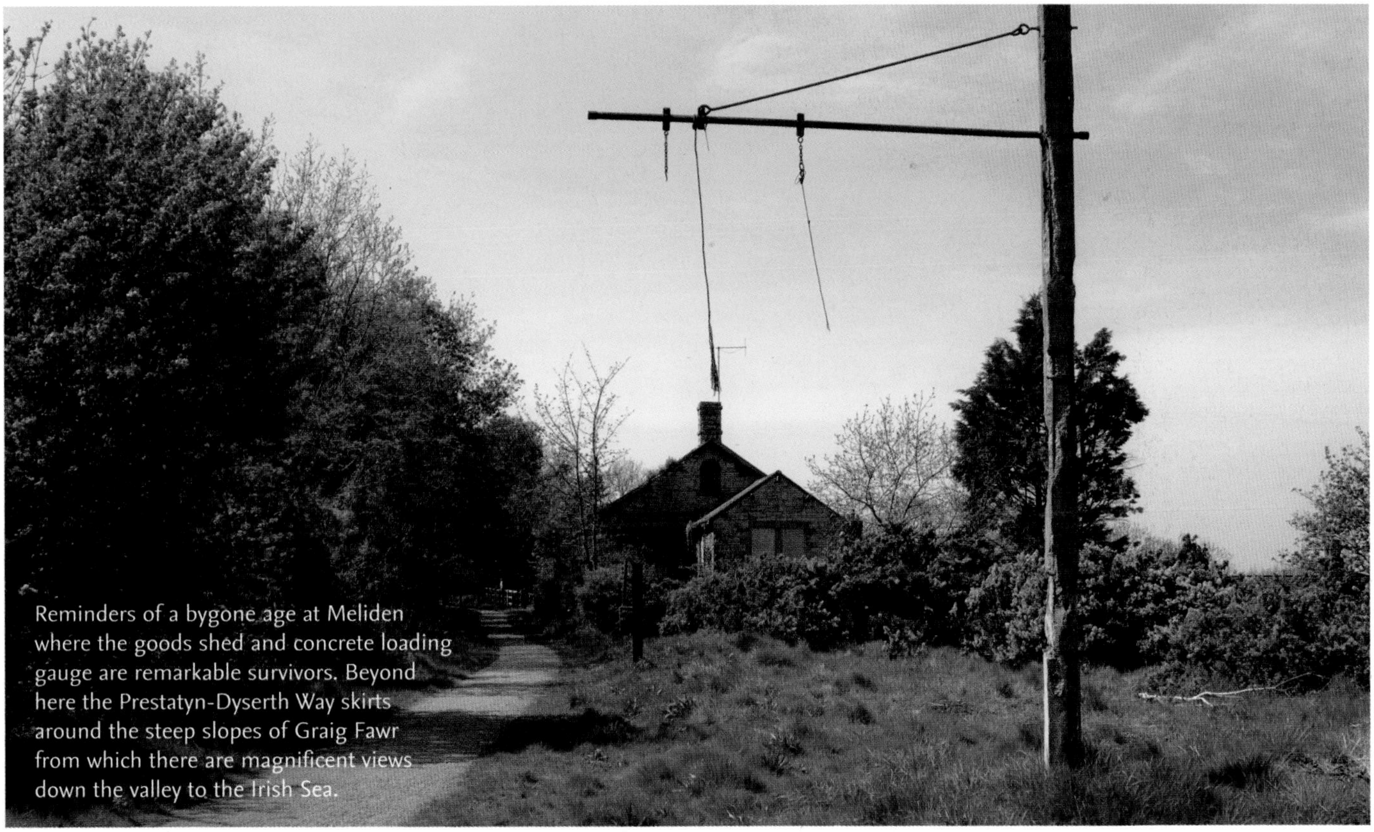

Reminders of a bygone age at Meliden where the goods shed and concrete loading gauge are remarkable survivors. Beyond here the Prestatyn-Dyserth Way skirts around the steep slopes of Graig Fawr from which there are magnificent views down the valley to the Irish Sea.

RHAYADER
TO
CRAIG-GOCH DAM
ELAN VALLEY TRAIL

Built at the end of the nineteenth century to convey men and materials for the construction of the Elan Valley Reservoirs in Central Wales, the Elan Valley Railway served its purpose efficiently and by 1916 had closed. Today, the highly scenic traffic-free route of this long-closed railway, alongside the dams and reservoirs of the remote Elan Valley, is open to walkers and cyclists eager to escape the madding crowd.

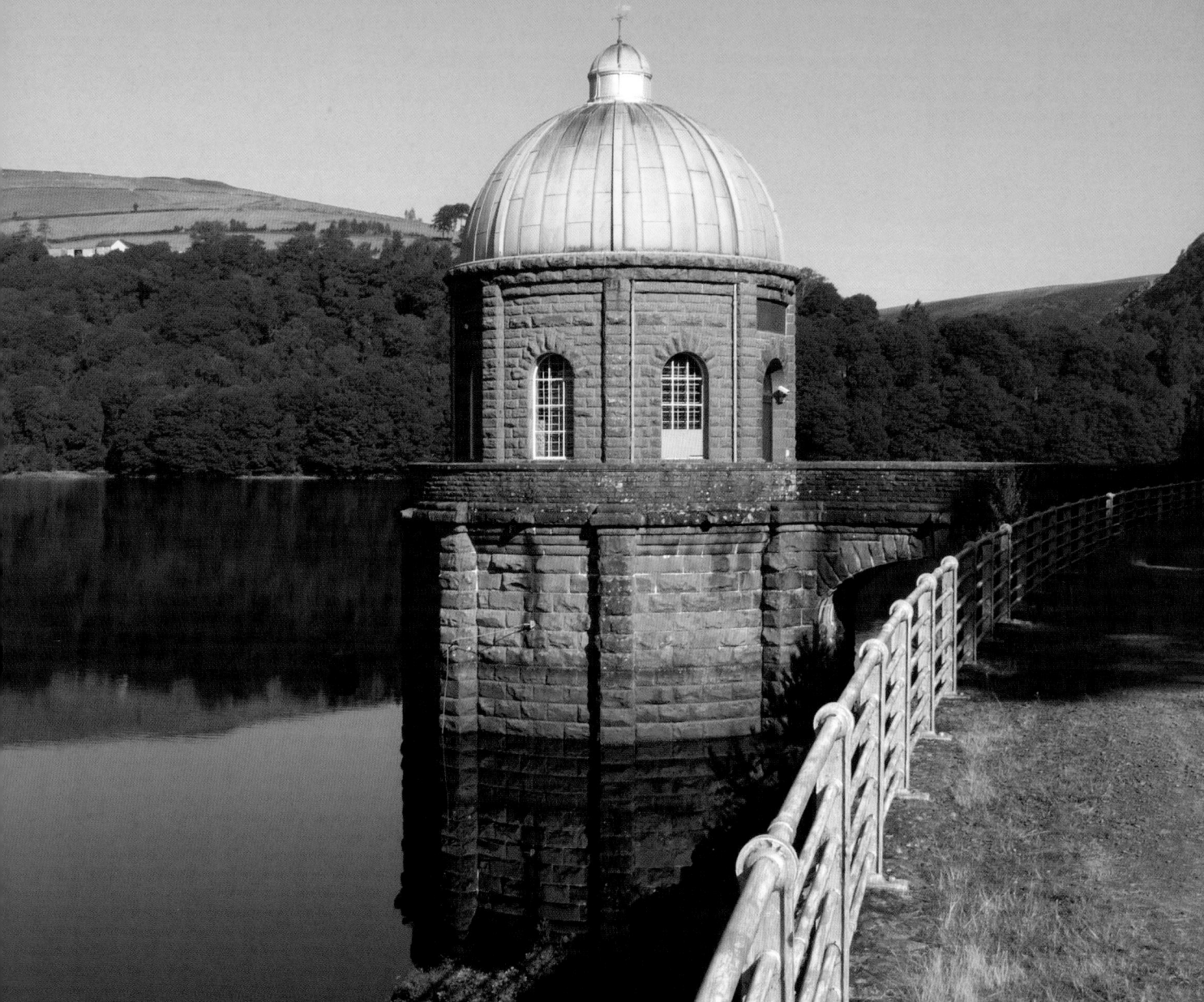

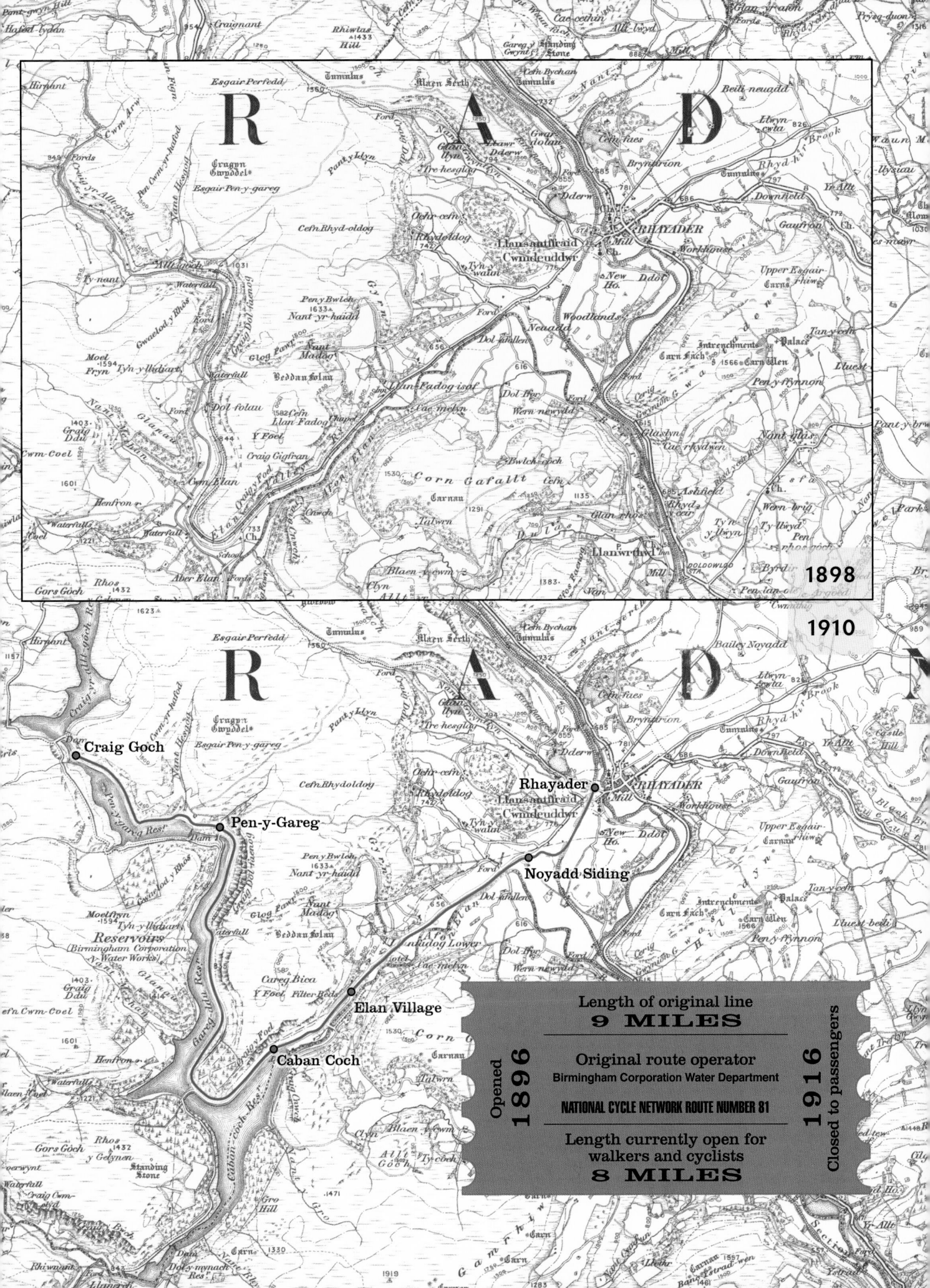

R A D

1898

1910

R A D N

Craig Goch

Pen-y-Gareg

Rhayader

Noyadd Siding

Elan Village

Caban Coch

Length of original line
9 MILES

Original route operator
Birmingham Corporation Water Department

NATIONAL CYCLE NETWORK ROUTE NUMBER 81

Length currently open for
walkers and cyclists
8 MILES

Opened **1896**

Closed to passengers **1916**

Railways first reached the small town of Rhayader in mid-Wales in 1864 when the Mid-Wales Railway opened its single-track line from Llanidloes to Talyllyn Junction, east of Brecon. The railway was worked by Cambrian Railways from 1888 and absorbed by the company in 1904.

Meanwhile the Birmingham Waterworks Committee had been looking for a suitable site on which to build reservoirs to supply drinking water to the burgeoning population of their city – by 1891 its 750,000 inhabitants were consuming over 16 million gallons of water every day. With an average rainfall of around seventy inches per year the sparsely populated Elan Valley, set amidst rugged mountains a few miles west of Rhayader, was a perfect location for such a scheme and the Committee set about planning their enormous building project with typical Victorian zeal.

Authorized by Parliament in 1892, the project involved the purchase of many square miles of land, the construction of six reservoirs and their dams, the building of a model village with all conveniences for construction workers and a 73-mile aqueduct to carry the water to Birmingham. When the aqueduct was completed it took thirty-six hours for water to flow down the 1-in-2300 gradient before reaching Frankley Reservoir on the outskirts of the city. To service this massive building project the Birmingham Corporation Water Department built a standard-gauge railway, which opened in 1896 from exchange sidings at

a junction with the Mid-Wales line at Noyadd south of Rhayader Tunnel. The 'main line', with gradients as steep as 1-in-33, extended for nine miles along the Elan Valley to the site of the furthest dam at Craig-Goch. En route it also served construction sites for dams at Caban-Coch, Carreg-Ddu and Pen-y-Gareg and, together with a branch line to Dol-y-Mynach Dam and numerous sidings and head shunts, totalled thirty-three miles of track.

The Elan Valley Railway also served the new model village that had been built (mainly of timber) to house construction workers and families – in true Victorian style it was alcohol-free and featured a sewage system, hospital, school, chapel and shop. To work the goods trains and services for workmen and schoolchildren, the railway also owned a fleet of steam locomotives built by Leeds manufacturers Hunslet and Manning Wardle, named after the fast-flowing streams that fed the reservoirs.

By 1904 the reservoirs were nearing completion and the Elan Valley Railway was preparing for a royal visit. On 21 July the royal train, carrying King Edward VII and Queen Alexandra, which had travelled from Swansea via the Central Wales line and the connecting spur at Builth Road, reached Rhayader station. From here the royal visitors were carried in ancient four-wheeled Cambrian Railways' coaches headed by Manning Wardle 0-6-0T 'Calettwr' for an inspection of what was then still a giant building site. Despite the royal visit, construction

This view of deserted Rhayader station looking north, c.1950, clearly shows the staggered platform arrangement. The former Cambrian Railways' station site survives today as a council depot.

PREVIOUS SPREAD: Seen here on the right, the Elan Valley Trail follows the eastern shore of Carreg-Ddu Reservoir where, at its southern end, the Foel tower pipes water from the reservoir to the filter beds before flowing along an aqueduct on its 73-mile journey to Birmingham.

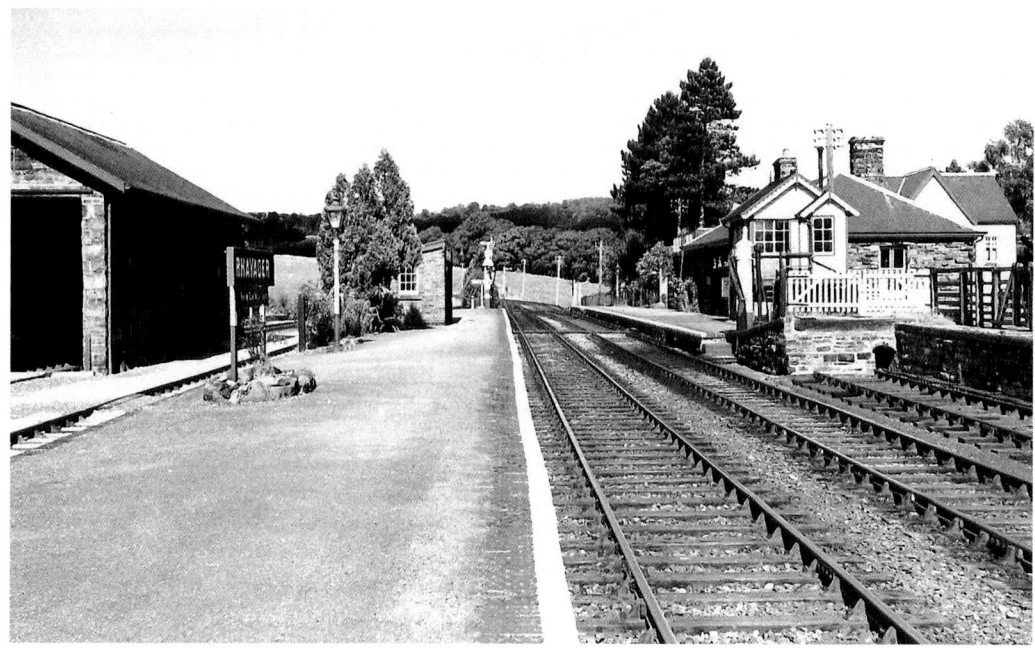

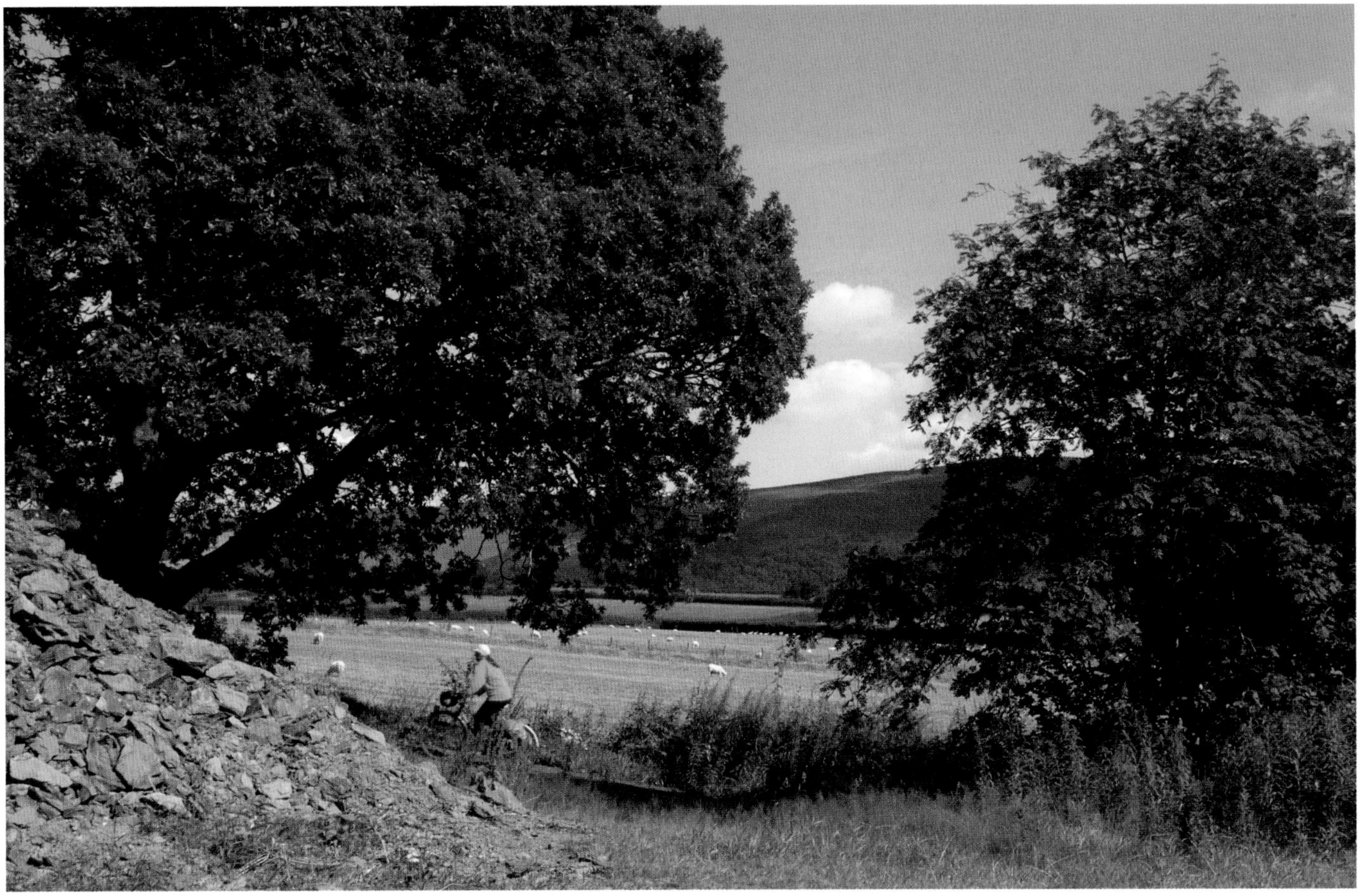

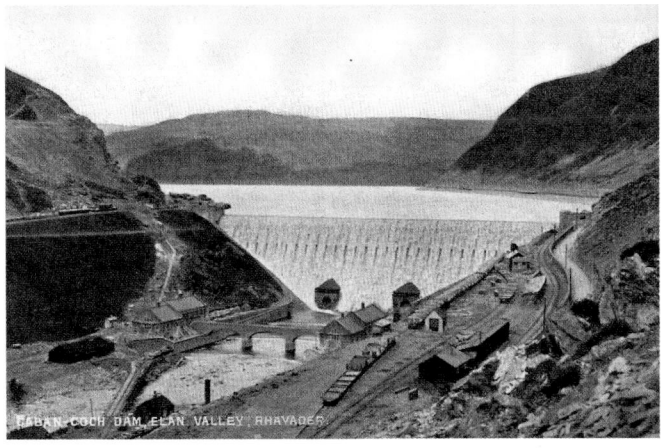

of the dams and reservoirs was not completed until 1906, by which time the Elan Valley Railway had served its purpose. In the meantime the reservoirs had filled up, submerging farms, chapels and the former home of the romantic poet, Percy Shelley.

The branch lines to the various dams had been closed by 1912 and the 'main line' to Craig-Goch was closed in 1916. With their smart green livery and brass nameplates, the company's attractive tank engines went on to find work in the quarries and steelworks of Northamptonshire, with some surviving until the mid-1960s.

Forming part of the Elan Valley Reservoirs system and located in a neighbouring valley, the Claerwen Reservoir and Dam was completed in 1952 – it is by far the largest of the dams at 184 ft high. The Mid-Wales line closed on 31 December 1962, just three months before publication of the 'Beeching Report'. It is now over 100 years since the Elan Valley reservoirs and dams were built, but this herculean feat of Victorian engineering has stood the test of time and still supplies the city of Birmingham with much of its water.

South of Rhayader, the Elan Valley Trail follows the route of the closed Cambrian Railways' Mid-Wales Line for a short distance. On this section the Trail takes a diversion over the top of Rhayader Tunnel, which is now bricked up and home to a colony of bats.

The mighty Caban-Coch dam at the lower end of the Elan Valley soon after completion in 1906. The Birmingham Corporation's standard-gauge railway is seen on the right.

Despite the long passage of time since closure, much of the route of the Elan Valley Railway can be followed today. Known as the Elan Valley Trail, an 8-mile well-surfaced footpath and cycleway from Llansantffraid-Cwmdeuddwr (on the southern outskirts of Rhayader) to Craig-Goch dam, follows the route of the old railway line around four of the Elan Valley reservoirs and their dams. A visitor centre in Elan Village has been converted from the old railway workshops and the adjacent car park was once the site of the locomotive shed and sidings. Bicycles can be hired in Rhayader.

The Trail starts at the dedicated car park near the site of the former Cambrian Railways station in Rhayader – the station buildings have survived and the whole site is now a depot for the local council. Across the road from the car park the Trail is accessed through a set of attractive carved wooden gates and heads uphill to join the trackbed of the Cambrian Railways Mid-Wales line. A detour over the top of the bricked-up Rhayader Tunnel (now home to colonies of bats) is followed by a downhill stretch following the valley of the Afon Elan to the Elan Valley Visitor Centre. En route the Trail passes the former junction with the Mid-Wales Line and the site of the railway's exchange sidings.

At the Visitor Centre, in the shadow of the Caban-Coch Dam, the former railway workshops now house a café and permanent exhibition showing the heritage and natural history of the area. From here it is necessary to retrace our steps from the Centre to regain the Elan Valley Trail proper, which climbs on a ledge above Caban-Coch Dam and around the edge of the reservoir to Carreg-Ddu Dam – this arched structure resembles a viaduct and was built to maintain a constant level in the reservoir during drought conditions. The Trail continues northwards, keeping company with the road along the east shore of Carreg-Ddu Reservoir before it heads uphill away from the road to reach Pen-y-Gareg Dam – in full flow the 123-ft-high dam is an awesome sight during periods of heavy rainfall. The Trail follows the wooded shoreline of Pen-y-Gareg Reservoir before ending at Craig-Goch Dam. Here, a small car park and toilets are reached by a narrow road across the top of the dam. The scenery along the entire Elan Valley Trail is breathtaking!

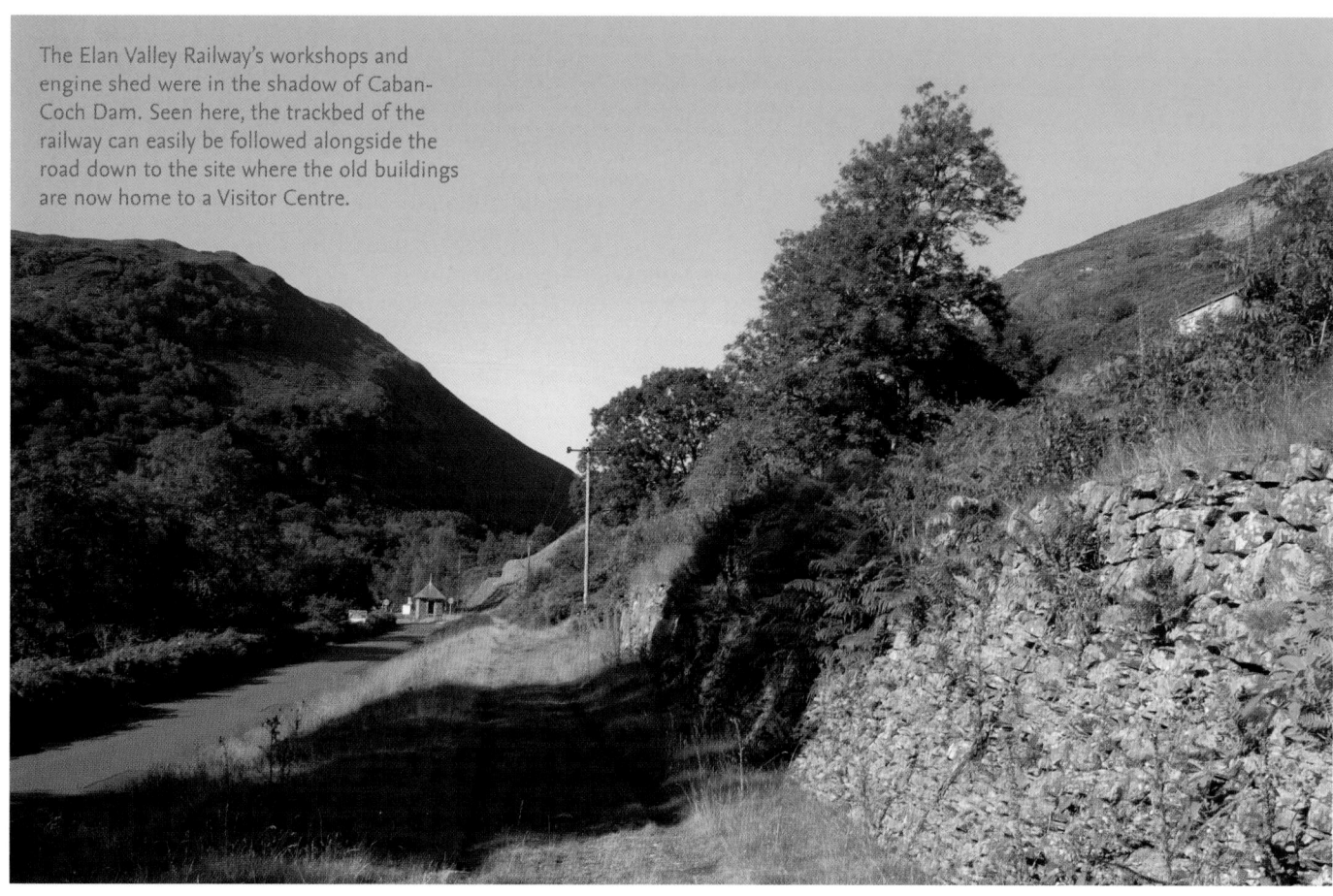

The Elan Valley Railway's workshops and engine shed were in the shadow of Caban-Coch Dam. Seen here, the trackbed of the railway can easily be followed alongside the road down to the site where the old buildings are now home to a Visitor Centre.

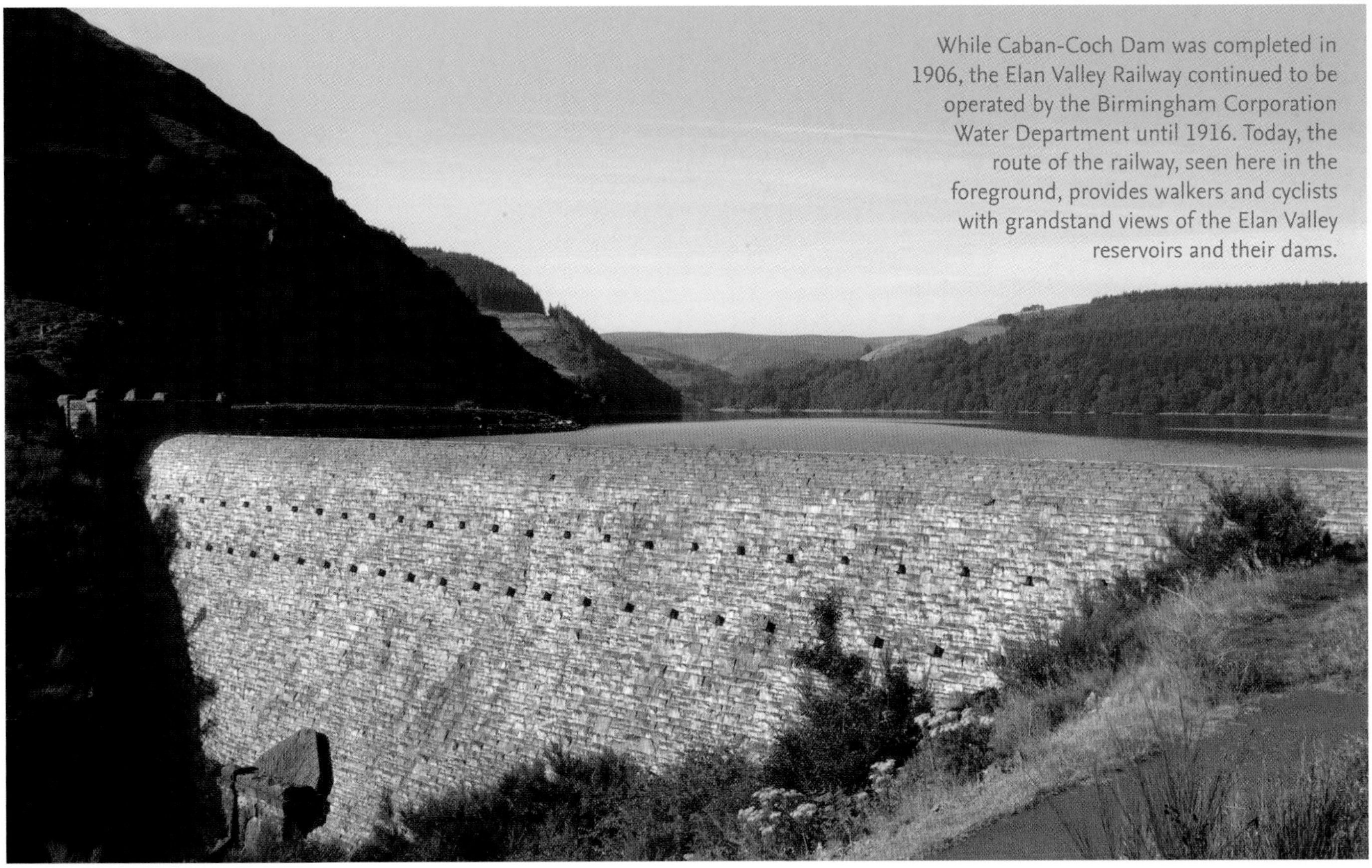

While Caban-Coch Dam was completed in 1906, the Elan Valley Railway continued to be operated by the Birmingham Corporation Water Department until 1916. Today, the route of the railway, seen here in the foreground, provides walkers and cyclists with grandstand views of the Elan Valley reservoirs and their dams.

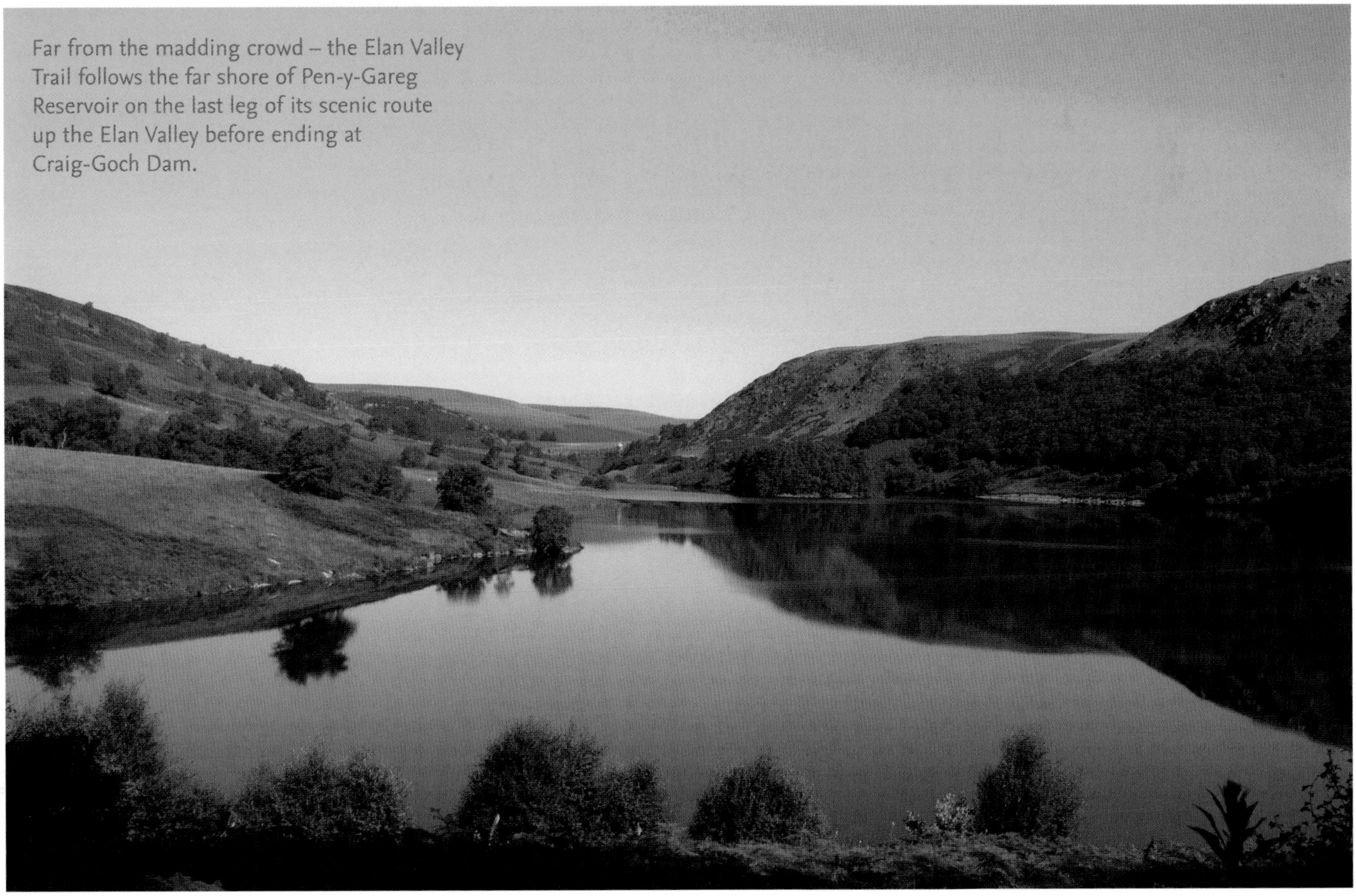

Far from the madding crowd – the Elan Valley Trail follows the far shore of Pen-y-Gareg Reservoir on the last leg of its scenic route up the Elan Valley before ending at Craig-Goch Dam.

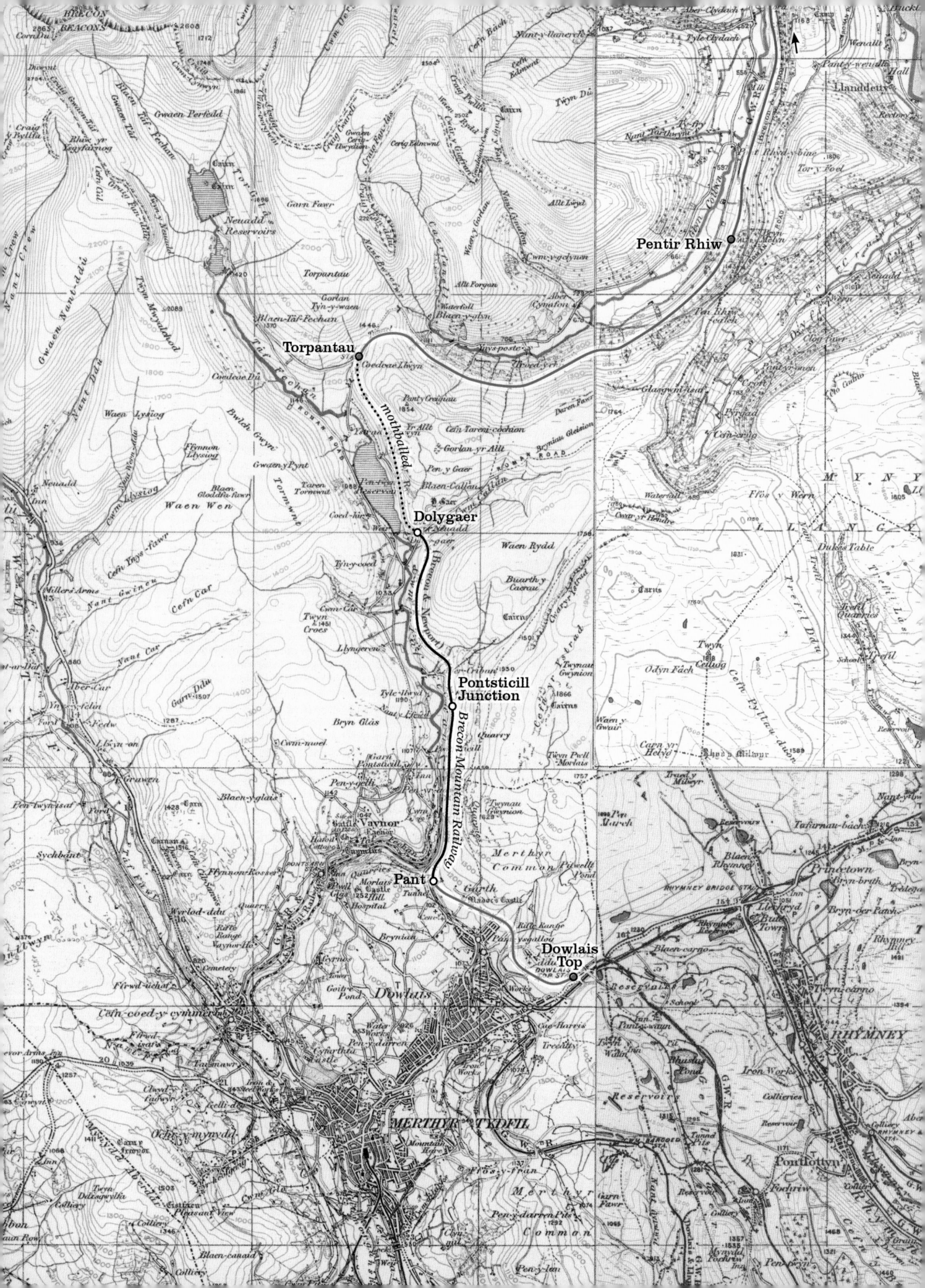

Pentir Rhiw

Torpantau

mothballed

Dolygaer

Pontsticill Junction

Brecon-Mountain Railway

Pant

Dowlais Top

DOWLAIS
TO
BRECON

Featuring Britain's highest railway tunnel at Torpantau, the Brecon & Merthyr Tydfil Junction Railway opened across the remote Brecon Beacons in 1868. Although virtually bankrupt, the company then went on to take over the Rumney Railway to form a railway network stretching from Brecon to Newport. While the section from Pontsticill Junction to Merthyr closed in November 1961, the rest of the route via Dowlais Top succumbed at the end of 1962, three months before the publication of the 'Beeching Report'. Since closure, the section south of Torpantau to Pant has been relaid as a narrow-gauge railway but only 2¼ miles is currently open to the public. North of Beacon Tunnel the trackbed has been reopened as a footpath and cycleway as far as Talybont.

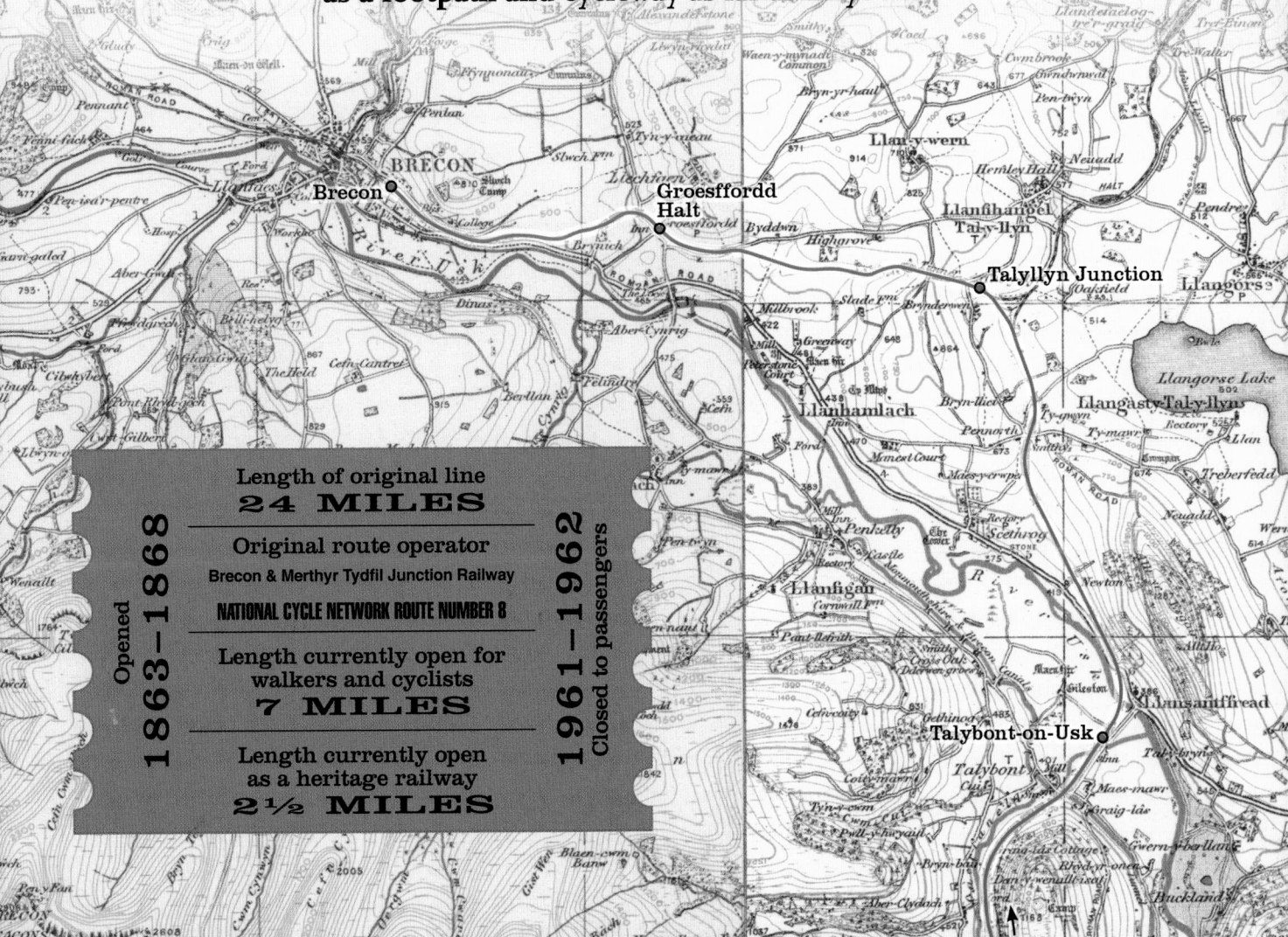

Opened
1863–1868

1961–1962
Closed to passengers

Length of original line
24 MILES

Original route operator
Brecon & Merthyr Tydfil Junction Railway

NATIONAL CYCLE NETWORK ROUTE NUMBER 8

Length currently open for walkers and cyclists
7 MILES

Length currently open as a heritage railway
2½ MILES

Authorized in 1859 and financially supported by the great and good of the county town of Brecon, the Brecon & Merthyr Tydfil Junction Railway (B&MTJR) opened the 6¾ miles of single-track line between Brecon and Talybont-on-Usk in 1863. The first four miles to Talyllyn Junction (for the Mid-Wales line), was built along the route of a narrow-gauge horse-drawn tramway. Meanwhile further authorization had been received in 1860 for a 17¼-mile extension southwards from Talybont-on-Usk to Merthyr Tydfil. This opened across remote countryside in 1868 and involved the building of Beacon Tunnel at Torpantau. The curving 667-yd tunnel – at 1,313 ft above sea level it was the highest railway tunnel in Britain – was approached from the north by a 6½-mile slog up a gradient of 1-in-38 that taxed steam locomotive crews to the limit.

Although virtually bankrupt, the B&MTJR went on to take over the Rumney Railway (RR) in 1863. Originally opened as a 4-ft-2-in horse-drawn tramway in 1826, the RR was an important link between the ironworks and coalfields in the Rhymney Valley and the port of Newport. The missing link between the B&MTJR and the former RR was opened in 1868, allowing through running of trains along the whole of the 47-mile route between Brecon and Newport. The opening up of this through route spelt the end for the Monmouthshire & Brecon Canal which had opened in 1800.

While the lower half of the newly enlarged B&MTJR was intensively worked carrying coal down the valleys and iron ore in the opposite direction, the northern half across the wilds of the remote Brecon Beacons led a fairly quiet existence. Becoming part of the Great Western Railway in 1922 and surviving through to Nationalization in 1948, the entire Brecon to Newport route was facing extinction by the 1950s. By this time much of the coal traffic in the valleys had melted away and competition from cars and buses had made serious inroads into passenger numbers. The end was near!

The 1958 summer timetable for the line shows only three services in each direction on weekdays plus an extra service on Saturdays. Travelling time for the 47-mile journey was around 2½ hours, an average speed of 19 mph! Losing money hand over fist, all the steam-hauled train services to Brecon – from Neath, Moat Lane Junction, Hereford and Newport – had ceased by 31 December 1962. Goods traffic continued to serve Brecon from Newport until 1964 when the line closed completely.

But this wasn't quite the end for the northern section of the railway…

TOP RIGHT: A group of Boy Scouts on their annual summer camp watch ex-GWR '5700' Class 0-6-0PT No. 3661, which has just arrived at remote Torpantau station with a Brecon to Newport train on 9 June 1962. The northbound train for Brecon waits patiently while crew and passengers chat on the platform. An idyllic scene which had disappeared forever by the end of that year.

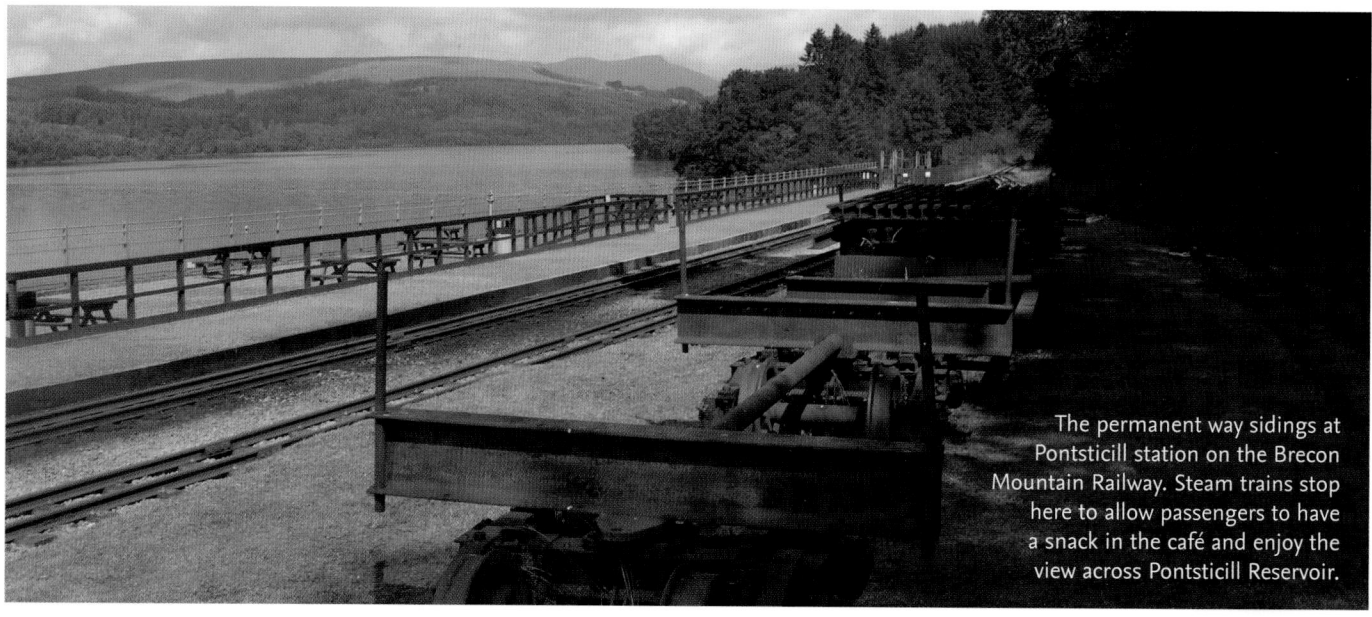

The permanent way sidings at Pontsticill station on the Brecon Mountain Railway. Steam trains stop here to allow passengers to have a snack in the café and enjoy the view across Pontsticill Reservoir.

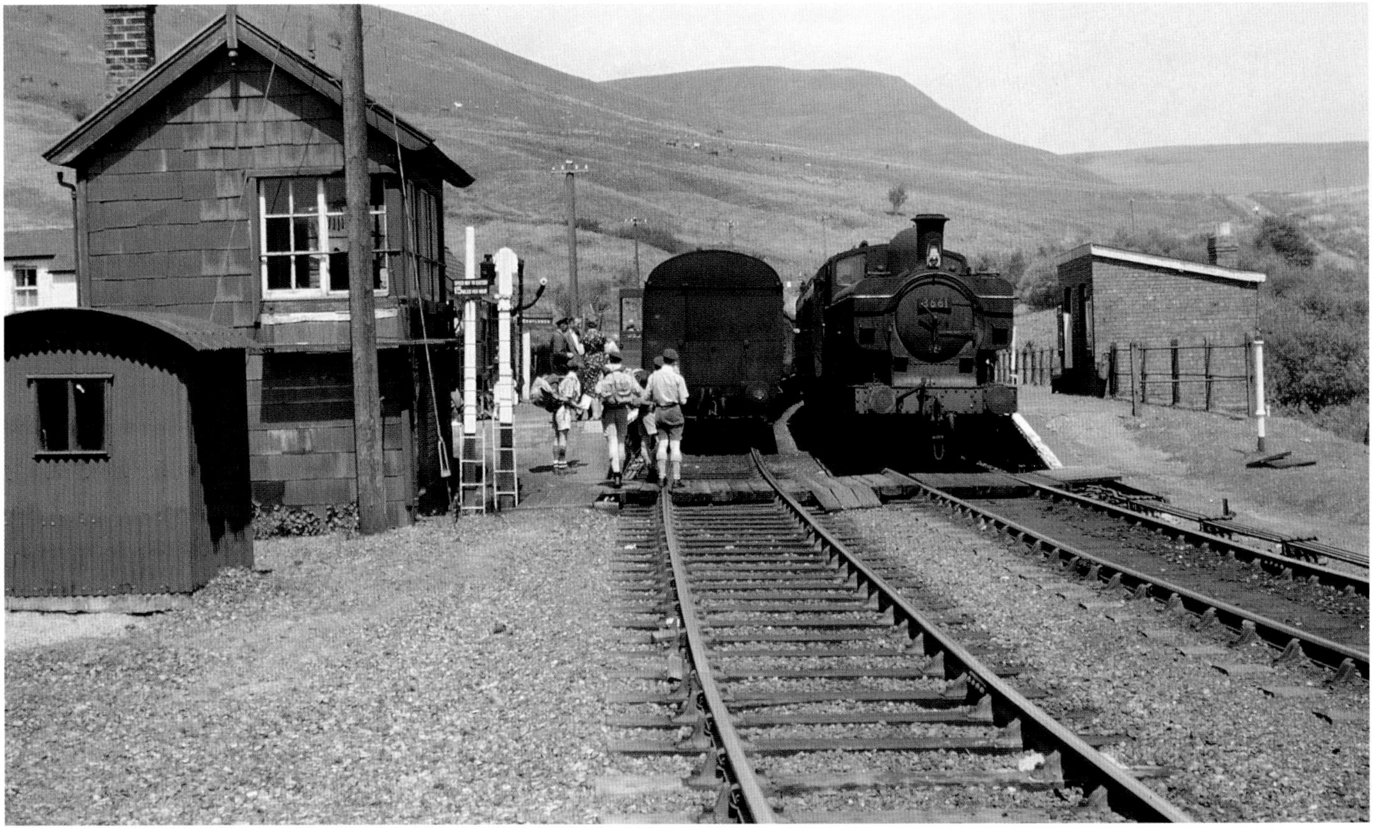

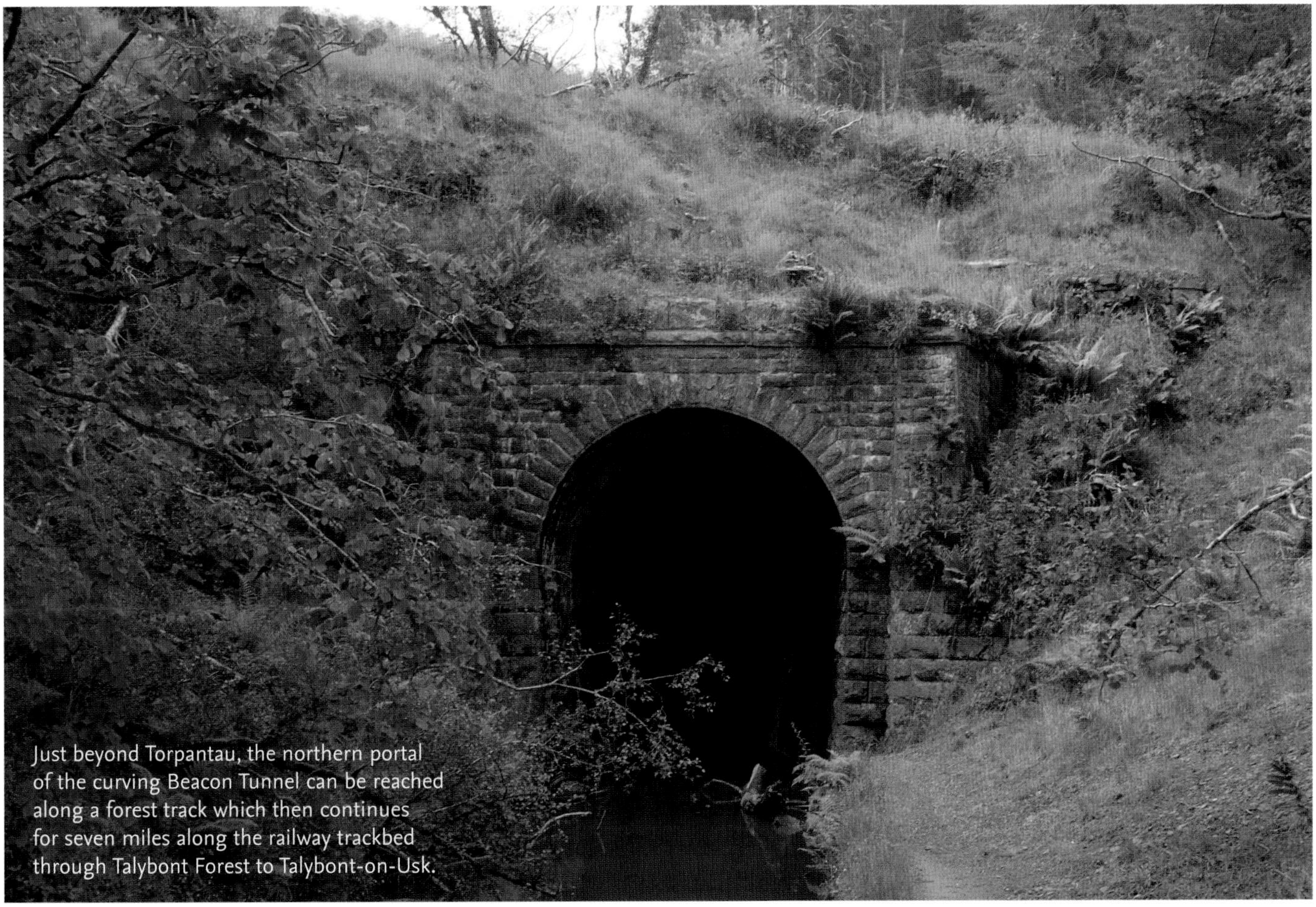

Just beyond Torpantau, the northern portal of the curving Beacon Tunnel can be reached along a forest track which then continues for seven miles along the railway trackbed through Talybont Forest to Talybont-on-Usk.

Opened in stages between 1978 and 1995, the 1-ft-11¾-in-gauge Brecon Mountain Railway (BMR) now operates steam-hauled trains along 2½ miles of the Brecon to Merthyr railway trackbed between its headquarters at Pant, north of Merthyr, and Dolygaer. Pant is home to the company's workshops, where powerful American- and German-built steam locomotives are restored and maintained. The large car park here is built on the site of the former railway branch to Dowlais while 80 ft below lies the former London & North Western Railway's Morlais Tunnel, its course marked by three brick ventilation shafts on the surface.

The first 600 yds of the BMR follows a new alignment before it heads along a ledge high above the picturesque valley of the Taf Fechan. Another mile brings it to Pontsticill station where there are fine views of Pontsticill Dam and Reservoir, and the highest point of the Brecon Beacons – Pen-y-Fan (2,906 ft). The reservoir was completed in 1927 and can hold around 3.5 million gallons of water.

Pontsticill station once possessed three platform faces, a passing loop, sidings and a signal box. Today the station building and signal box survive as a private residence while the goods shed is used by the BMR. BMR trains continue northwards along the eastern shore of the reservoir as far as Dolygaer – here there is a passing loop where the loco runs round its train for the return trip to Pant. There is currently no station here and passengers are not allowed to alight. The nearest car park is a short distance away on the opposite side of the reservoir.

North of Dolygaer the BMR continues for 1½ miles through the forest to Torpantau, where there is a passing loop and low platform. This extension was apparently laid around ten years ago but so far has seen no passenger service. The rusting rails of the narrow-gauge line give this remote spot a certain Marie Celeste quality!

Across the road from the BMR 'terminus' is a car park and the remains of Torpantau station. More than fifty years since closure, little remains of one of the remotest stations in Britain – only the platform edges and brick bases of some of the buildings can still be discerned in this lonely spot. Beyond Torpantau a flooded cutting leads to the southern portal of Beacon Tunnel, although

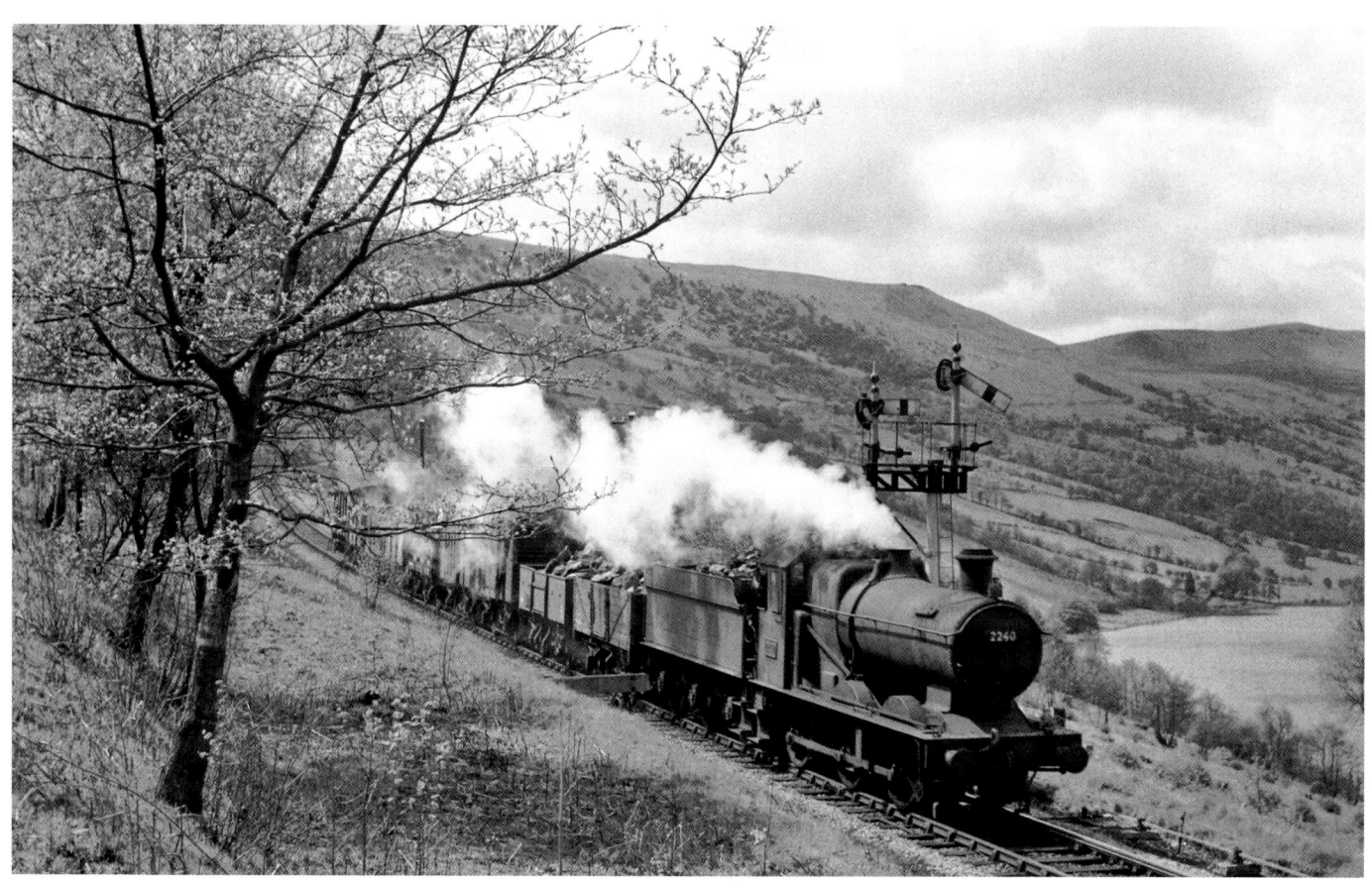

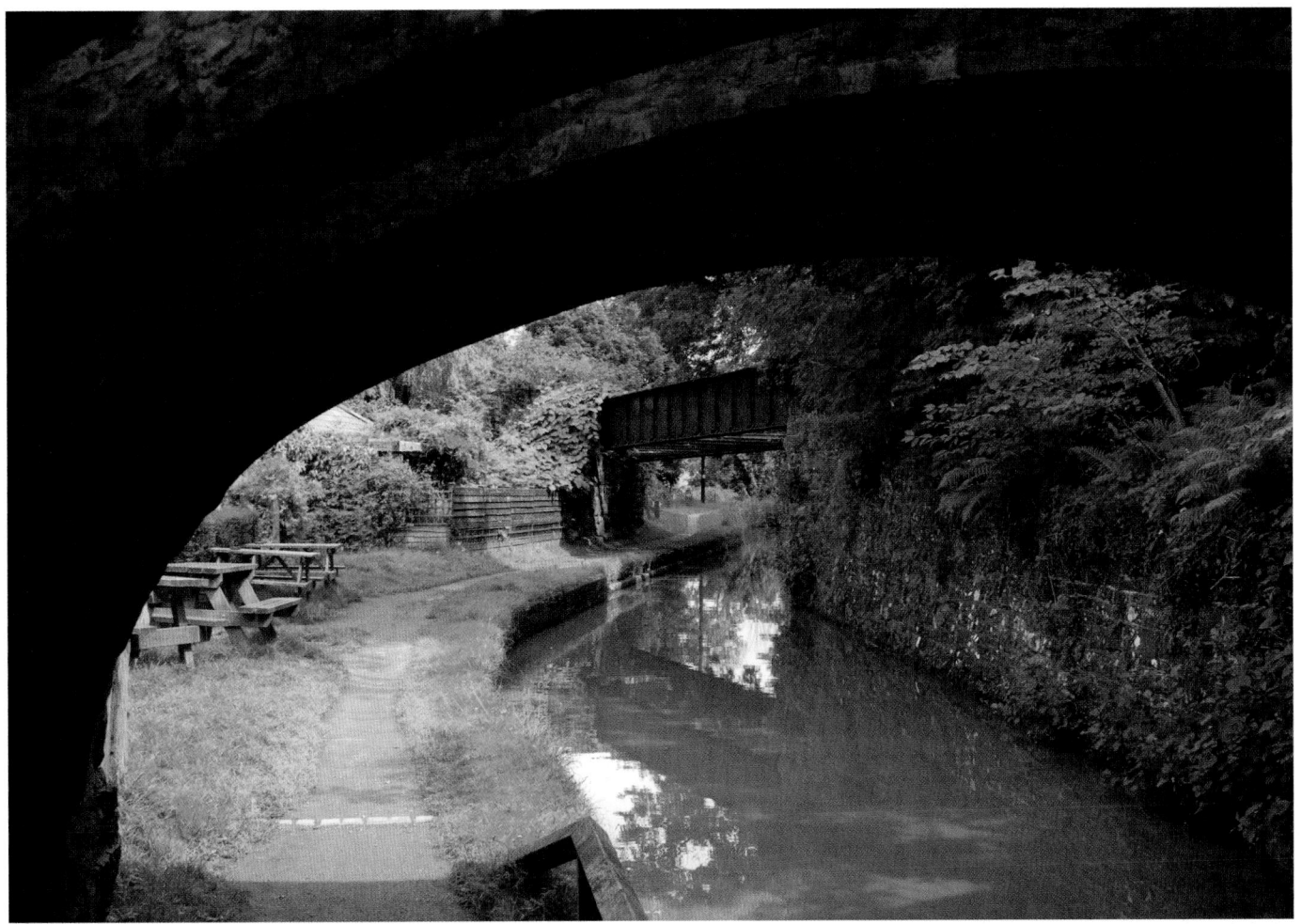

LEFT: Ex-GWR '2251' Class 0-6-0 No. 2240 trundles downhill at Pentir Rhiw with the 7.30am Bassaleg to Brecon goods train on 16 May 1962. While the trackbed here is now a footpath and cycleway, the view of the valley is obscured by extensive forestry plantations.

The railway path from Beacon Tunnel ends at the pretty village of Talybont-on-Usk. Now inaccessible to walkers, the rusting railway girder bridge is seen here crossing the restored Monmouthshire & Brecon Canal close to the canalside White Hart Inn.

access is blocked by vegetation and fencing. The northern (east-facing) portal of the curving tunnel is much easier to reach by walking down a forest track from a small parking area north of Torpantau station. A stream now floods the tunnel entrance but it is still possible to gaze into the stygian depths.

Eastwards from the tunnel, the forest track follows the old railway route down through the Talybont Forest for nearly seven miles to Talybont-on-Usk. This section forms part of the Taff Trail Long Distance Path, The Beacons Way and National Cycle Network Route 8. En route the track passes the site of lonely Pentir Rhiw station before descending alongside Talybont Reservoir where, at the northern end, there is a seasonal tea room and road

access. The railway path ends at the pretty village of Talybont-on-Usk, where the inaccessible railway-bridge girders cross the restored Monmouthshire & Brecon Canal close to the popular White Hart Inn. The canal was once fed by narrow-gauge horse-drawn tramways that carried coal and limestone for onward shipment to South Wales. One of these, the 8-mile Brinore Tramroad (1815-1865), is now a footpath and bridleway from Talybont to Trefil.

While the former station at Talybont-on-Usk survives as a private residence, the railway route beyond here to Talyllyn Junction and Brecon is more difficult to follow. Apart from a few cuttings and the odd road overbridge, it has completely disappeared into the landscape.

NINE MILE POINT
TO
TRELEWIS
CELTIC TRAIL

Starting life in 1805 as a horse-drawn narrow-gauge tramway linking Tredegar Ironworks with the Monmouthshire Canal at Nine Mile Point, the Sirhowy Tramroad was one of the earliest railways to be sanctioned by an Act of Parliament. It was converted to standard gauge with steam haulage in 1863 and effectively taken over by the London & North Western Railway by 1876. Declining coal and passenger traffic after the Second World War led to the line's closure in 1960. Much of the route, along with the closed Great Western Railway line across the impressive Hengoed Viaduct to Trelewis, has since been reopened as a footpath and cycleway.

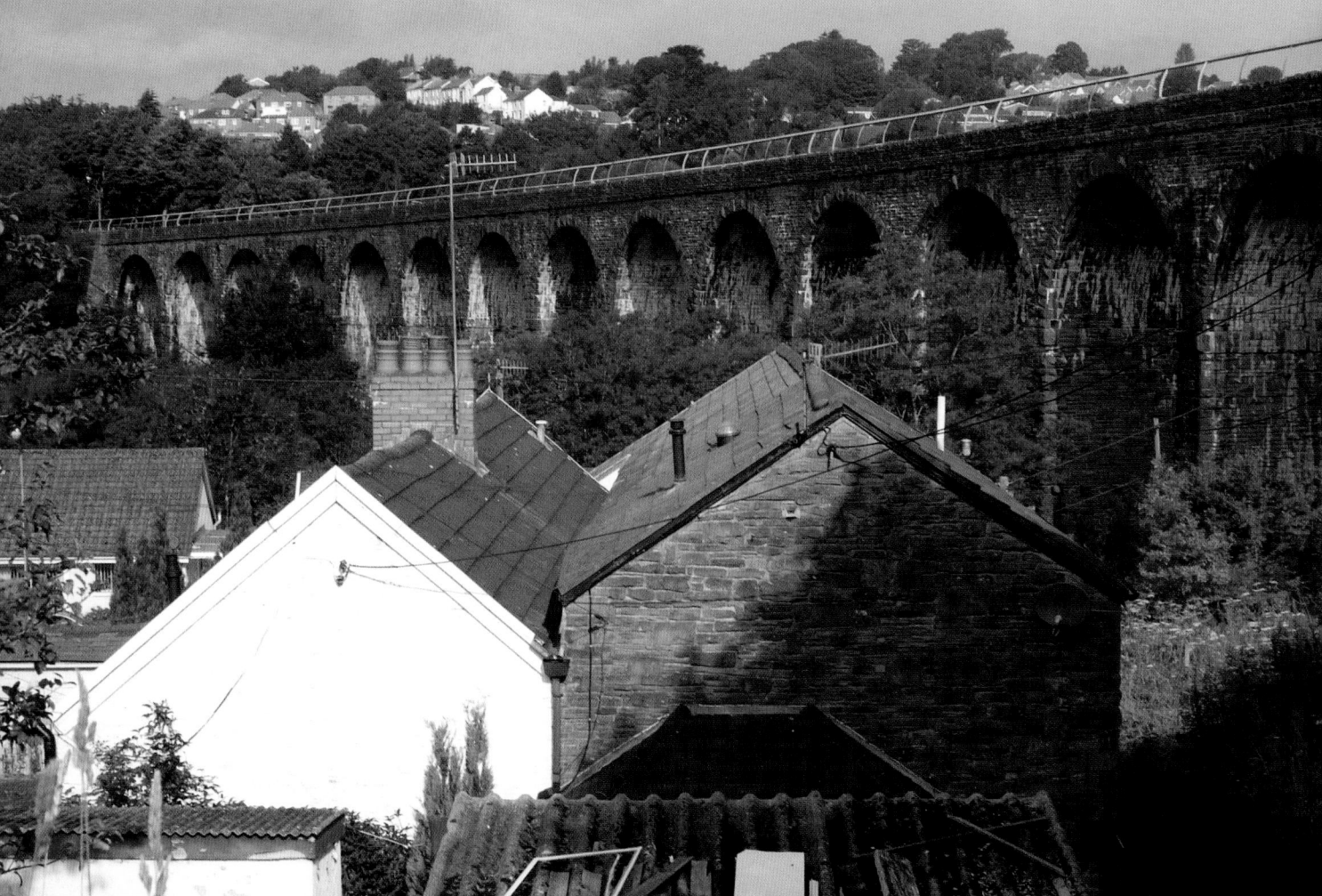

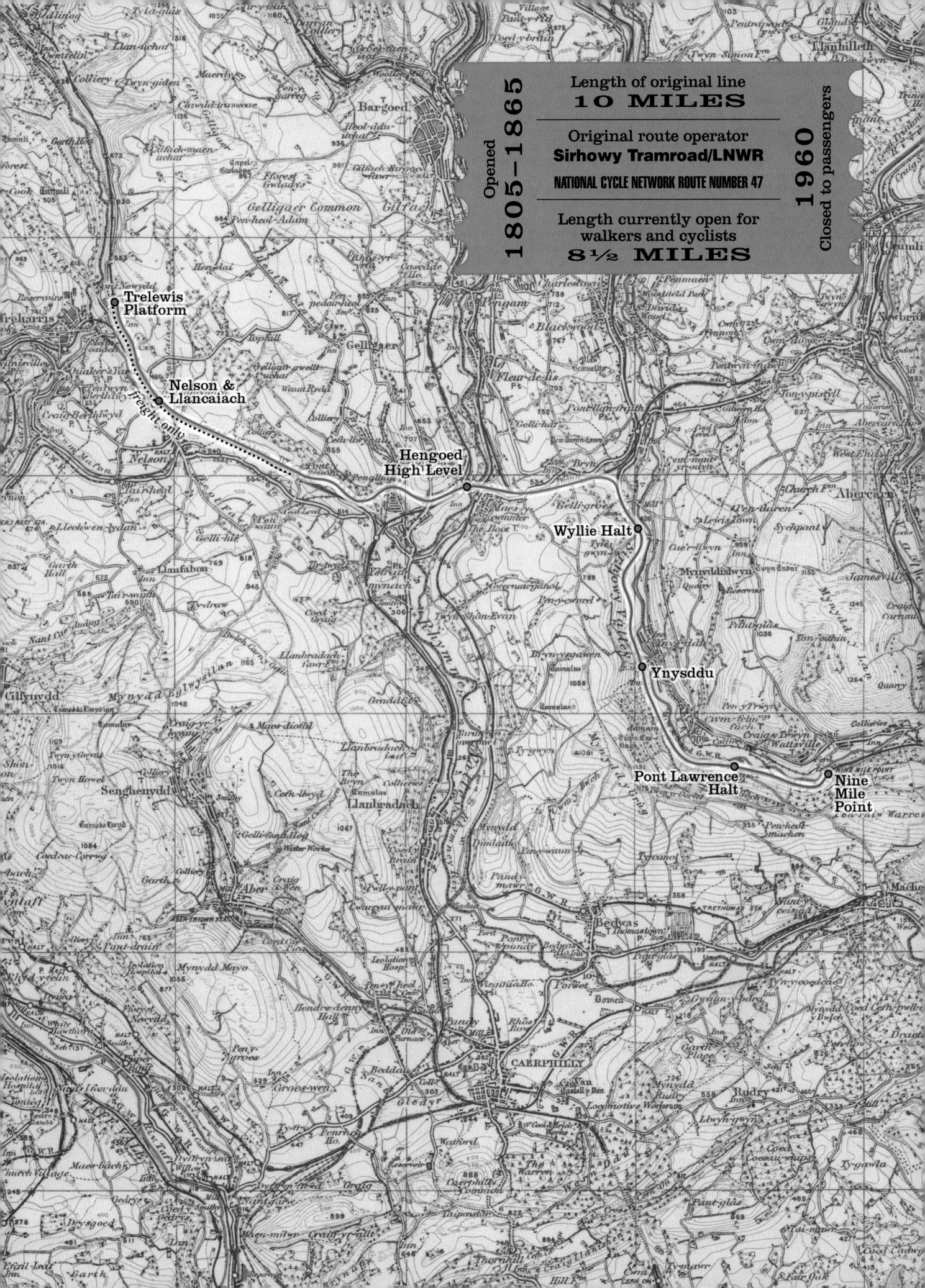

Opened **1805–1865**

Length of original line
10 MILES

Original route operator
Sirhowy Tramroad/LNWR

NATIONAL CYCLE NETWORK ROUTE NUMBER 47

Length currently open for walkers and cyclists
8½ MILES

1960 Closed to passengers

Trelewis Platform

Nelson & Llancaiach

Freight only

Hengoed High Level

Wyllie Halt

Ynysddu

Pont Lawrence Halt

Nine Mile Point

One of earliest railways to be sanctioned by an Act of Parliament, the 4-ft-2-in-gauge Sirhowy Tramroad opened between Tredegar Ironworks and Nine Mile Point in 1805. This early horse-drawn tramway met the Monmouthshire Canal Tramway at Nine Mile Point, from where coal and iron ore were transported to and from Newport Docks. A horse-drawn passenger service was introduced between Newport and Tredegar in 1822 and the first steam locomotive in 1829. In 1860 an Act of Parliament authorized the conversion of the Sirhowy Tramroad into a standard-gauge railway and renamed it the Sirhowy Railway.

In the meantime the Monmouthshire Canal Tramway had already been converted to a standard-gauge railway in 1855 and a new connection was built from its line at Risca to Nine Mile Point, where it met the narrower-gauge Sirhowy Tramroad. The conversion of the latter to standard gauge was completed in 1863 and passenger services were introduced in 1865. The London & North Western Railway (LNWR) took over operations in 1876, having already reached the head of the Sirhowy Valley by leasing the uncompleted Merthyr, Tredegar & Abergavenny Railway (known as the Heads of the Valleys Line) in 1862.

The Sirhowy Railway was eventually taken over by the LNWR in 1876 and Nine Mile Point became the LNWR's most southerly incursion into the South Wales valleys – a sore point not missed by the rival Great Western Railway's (GWR) directors in Paddington. By gaining running powers over the GWR between Nine Mile Point and Newport the LNWR was able to operate passenger services along the 24½ miles from Nantybwch, on the Heads of the Valleys Line north of Tredegar, down the Sirhowy Valley and into GWR territory at Newport. Coal traffic was particularly heavy, especially during the First World War when long coal trains, known as 'Jellicoe Specials', would head northwards via Abergavenny to the far north of Scotland to supply the Royal Navy's fleet at Scapa Flow.

The LNWR routes in South Wales became part of the newly formed LMS in 1923 and subsequently passed to the London Midland Region of British Railways in 1948. The depression of the 1930s had already seen a gradual decline of both freight and passenger services on the line and by the 1950s its outlook was grim. With a journey time of around 1½ hours to cover the 24½ miles between Newport and Nantybwch, the railway could not compete with road transport and closed to passengers on 13 June 1960. Coal traffic continued between Tredegar and Risca until complete closure on 4 May 1970.

An ex-GWR '5700' Class 0-6-0PT waits at Ynysddu station with a Tredegar to Newport train shortly before passenger services were withdrawn in 1960. Despite its small size the basic wooden station building had a booking office and separate waiting rooms for ladies and gentlemen. The trackbed is now a footpath and cycleway and remains of the platform can still be seen here despite closure over 50 years ago.

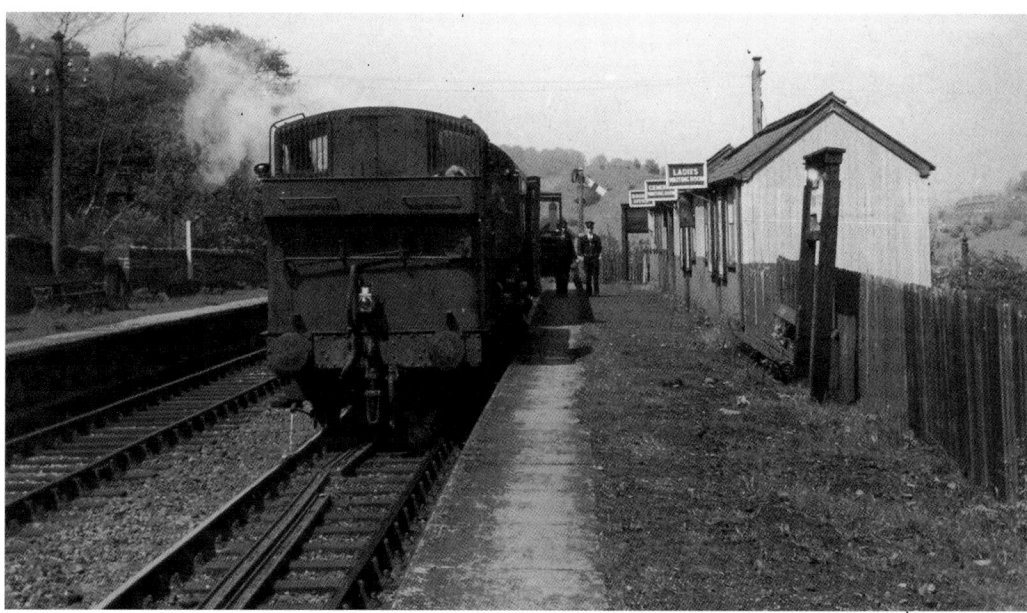

PREVIOUS SPREAD:
The curving 16-arch Hengoed Viaduct, which crosses the Rhymney Valley at Maesycwmmer, was reopened to walkers and cyclists on the Celtic Trail in 2000.

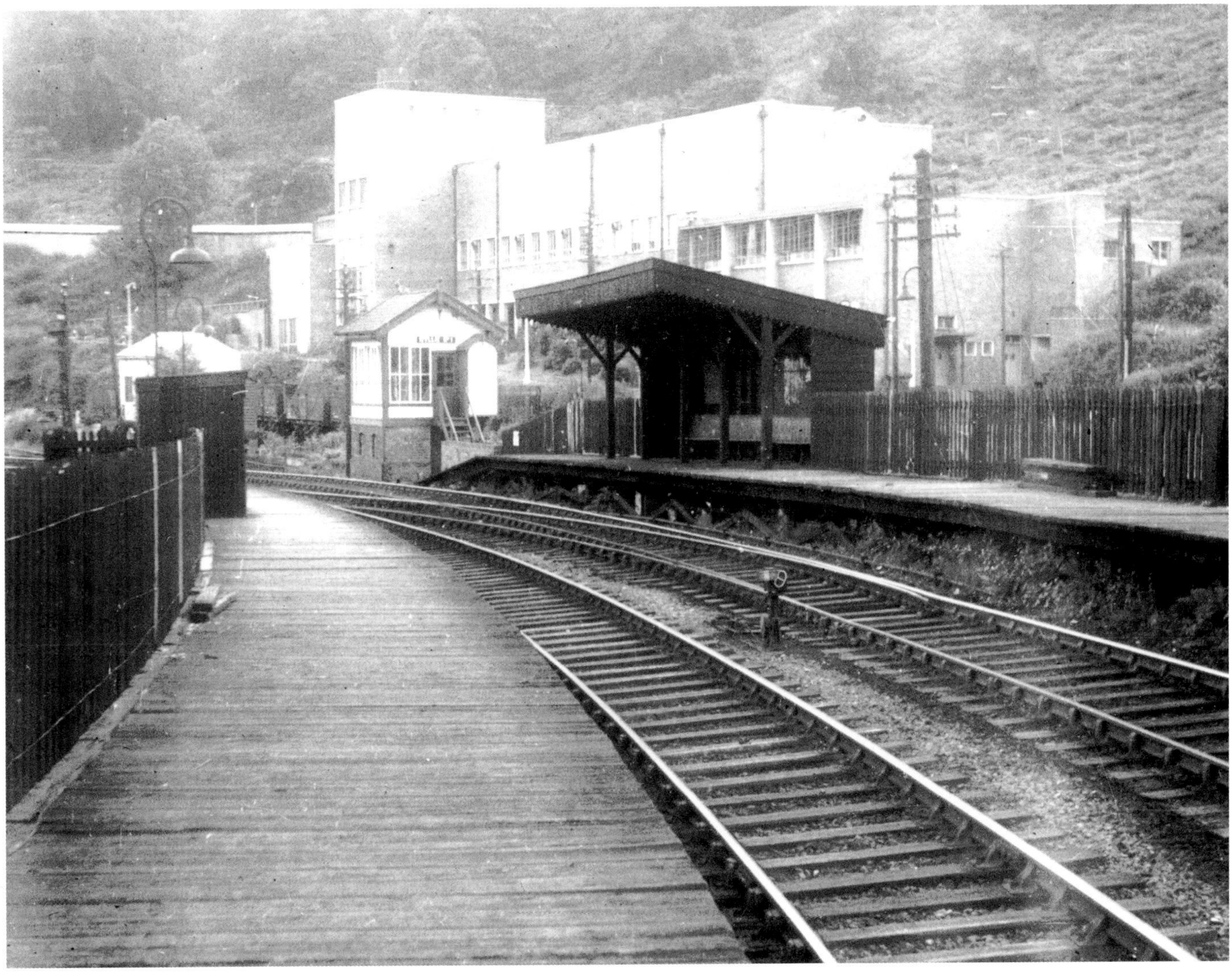

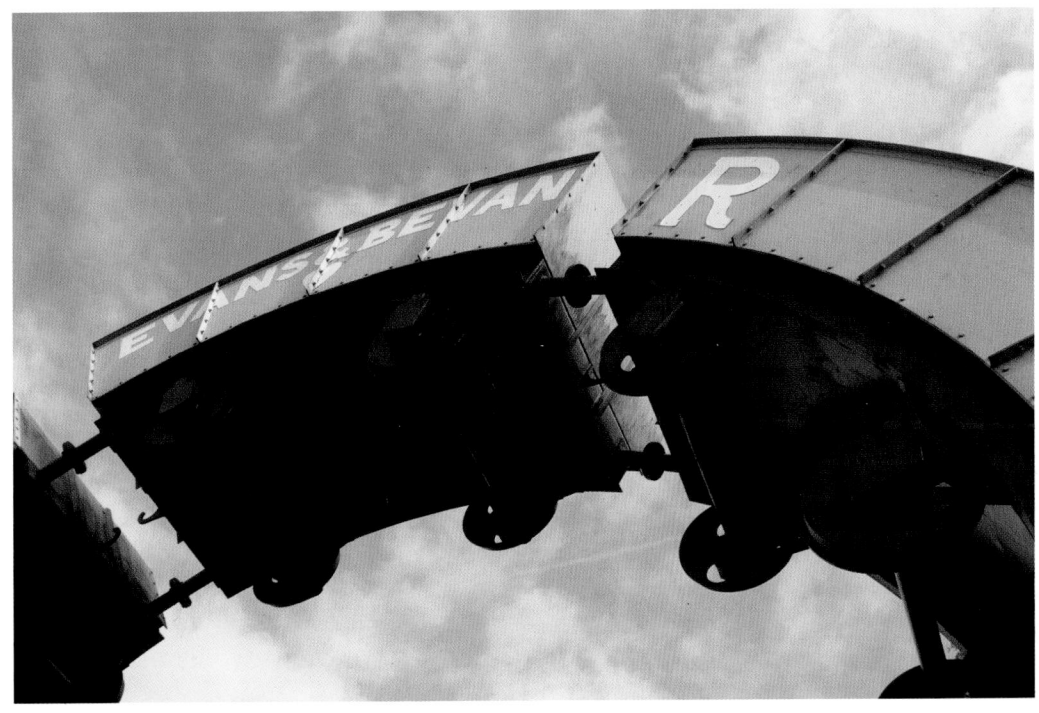

ABOVE: Seen here on 12 July 1958, the deserted Wyllie Halt had only very rudimentary wooden shelter facilities for passengers. The modern colliery building behind was opened by the Tredegar Iron & Coal Company in 1926 and closed in 1968 – it was named after one of the company's directors, Alexander Wyllie. The site is now occupied by modern housing.

In memory of 'King Coal' – featuring a circle of colliery dram wagons, the eye-catching 'Wheel o' Drams' sculpture by Andy Hazell is located at the eastern end of Hengoed Viaduct.

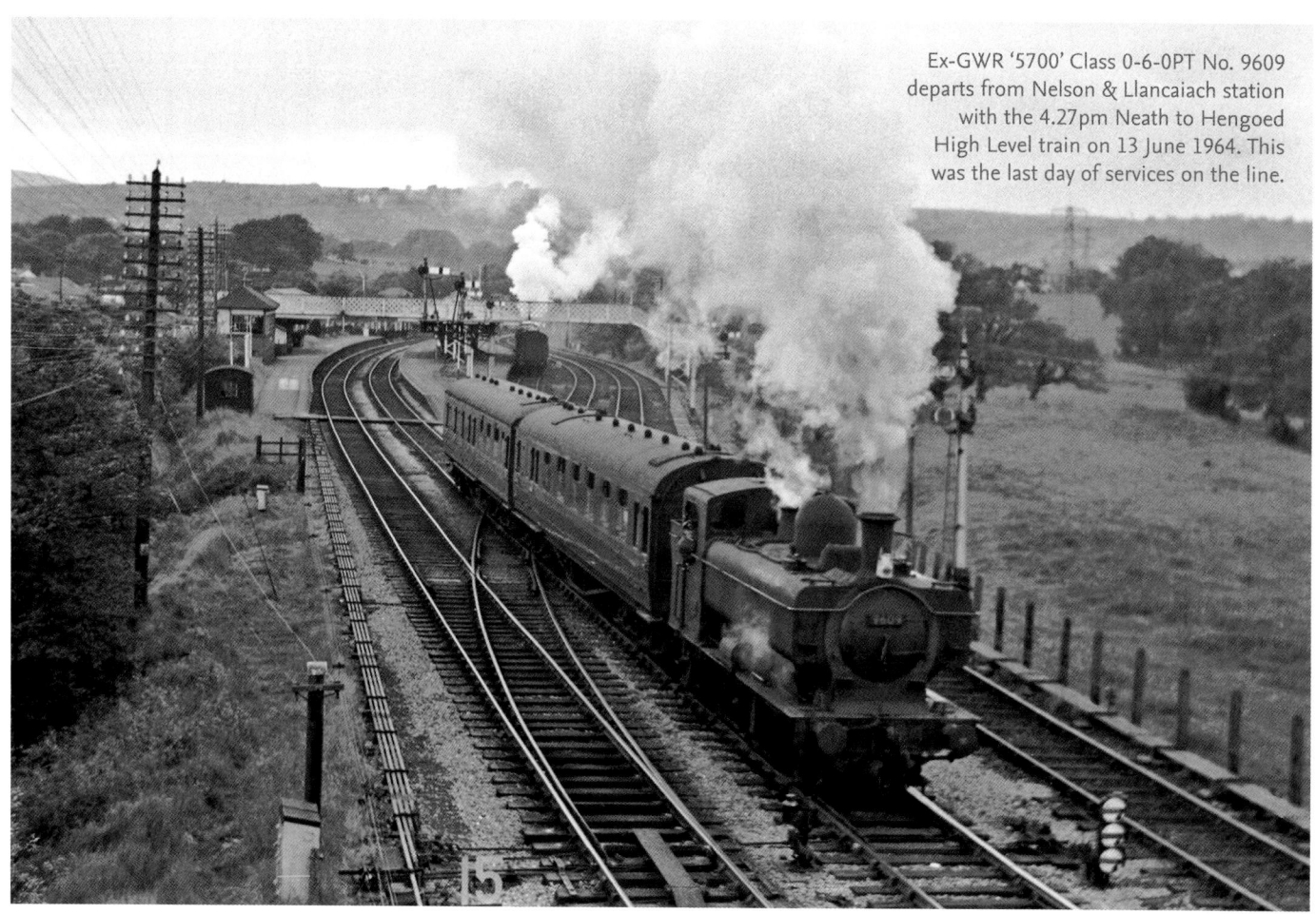

Today, six miles of the Sirhowy Railway between Nine Mile Point and Wyllie forms part of a footpath and cycleway known as the Celtic Trail, which is also used by National Cycle Network Route 47.

Our route starts at the Sirhowy Valley Country Park car park at Half Moon, just off the roundabout at the end of the dual carriageway section of the A4072 from Newport. The nearest railway station is two miles away at Risca, on the reopened Cardiff to Ebbw Vale line. The route of the old railway from Half Moon, where there is a visitor centre in a former railway building, to Nine Mile Point has been resurfaced and is open to visitors' cars during the day. Nine Mile Point is soon reached, where there is a car park and picnic site – a short diversion from here leads to the Penllwyn Tramroad Bridge, which still has original stone sleepers in situ. From Nine Mile Point the route heads up the valley keeping close company with the Sirhowy River, past the site of Pont Lawrence Halt to Ynysddu station. Here there are remains of the old platform from which a steep track leads down to the Black Prince pub.

The tree-lined route continues northwards up the valley to the site of Wyllie Halt and ends ½-mile north of here, close to the A472 dual carriageway.

While the former route of the Sirhowy Railway continues northwards up the Sirhowy Valley, the Celtic Trail cycle route (NCN Route 47) parts company here and heads west alongside the A472 for just over a mile before reaching the magnificent Hengoed Viaduct.

Built of local stone and spanning the Rhymney Valley at Maesycwmmer, the curving 16-arch Hengoed Viaduct was completed in 1854. It is 860 ft long and 130 ft high at its highest point across the valley. Until closure on 15 June 1964, the viaduct was used by trains running on the former GWR line between Pontypool Road and Neath. After being inaccessible to the public for 35 years, the viaduct was reopened as part of the Celtic Trail cycling route (NCN Route 47) in 2000. The structure is now one of only two Grade II* listed railway viaducts in Wales and, in 2004, was the subject of a major restoration funded by the Heritage Lottery

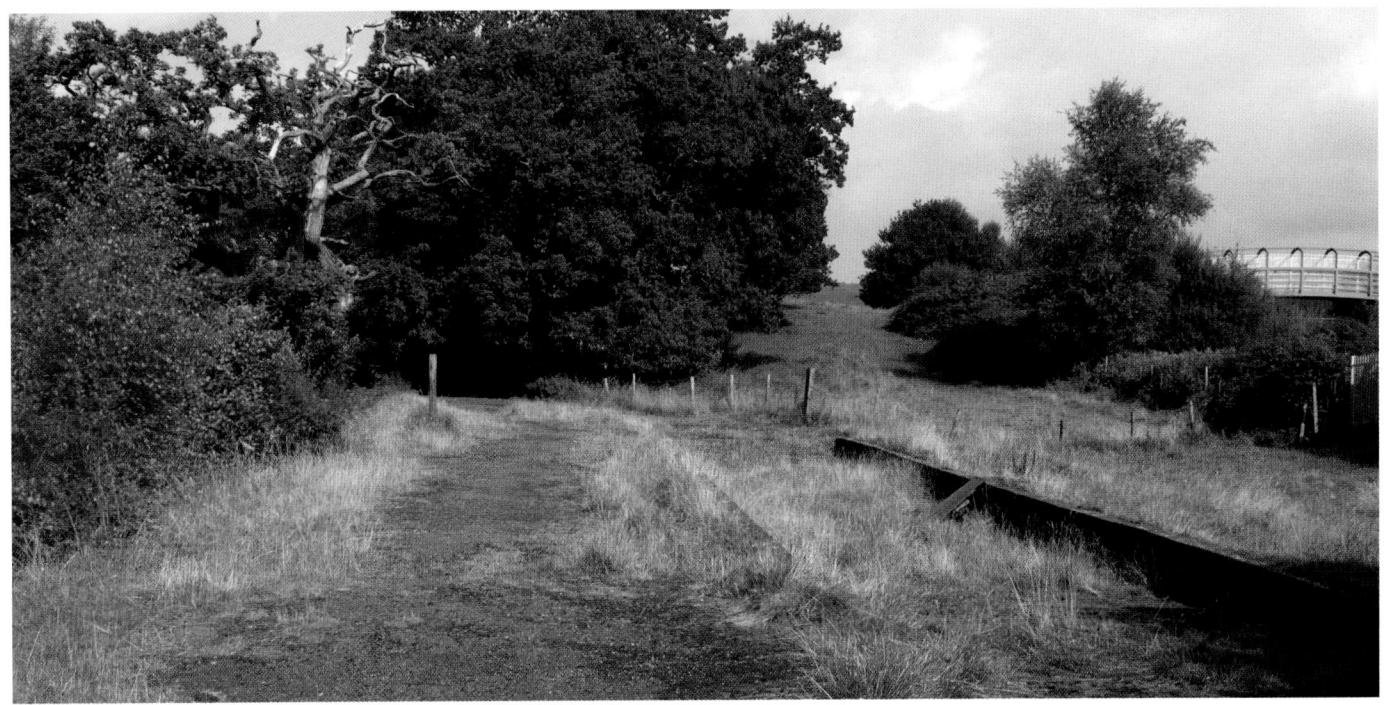

Once a scene of industrial activity, the remains of a colliery branch line at Trelewis are now being gradually overtaken by nature. The Celtic Trail crosses the extant freight-only line to Cwm Bargoed by way of the modern red bridge on the right.

Fund. At the eastern end of the viaduct the eye-catching 'Wheel o' Drams' sculpture by Andy Hazell features a circle of colliery dram wagons.

The Celtic Trail continues westwards from the viaduct through Hengoed before joining the Ystrad Mynach to Cwm Bargoed freight-only line through Nelson & Llancaiach and Trelewis.

The last day! A few local mourners watch as ex-GWR '5600' Class 0-6-2T No. 5662 calls at Trelewis Platform with the 3.17pm train from Ystrad Mynach on 13 June 1964.

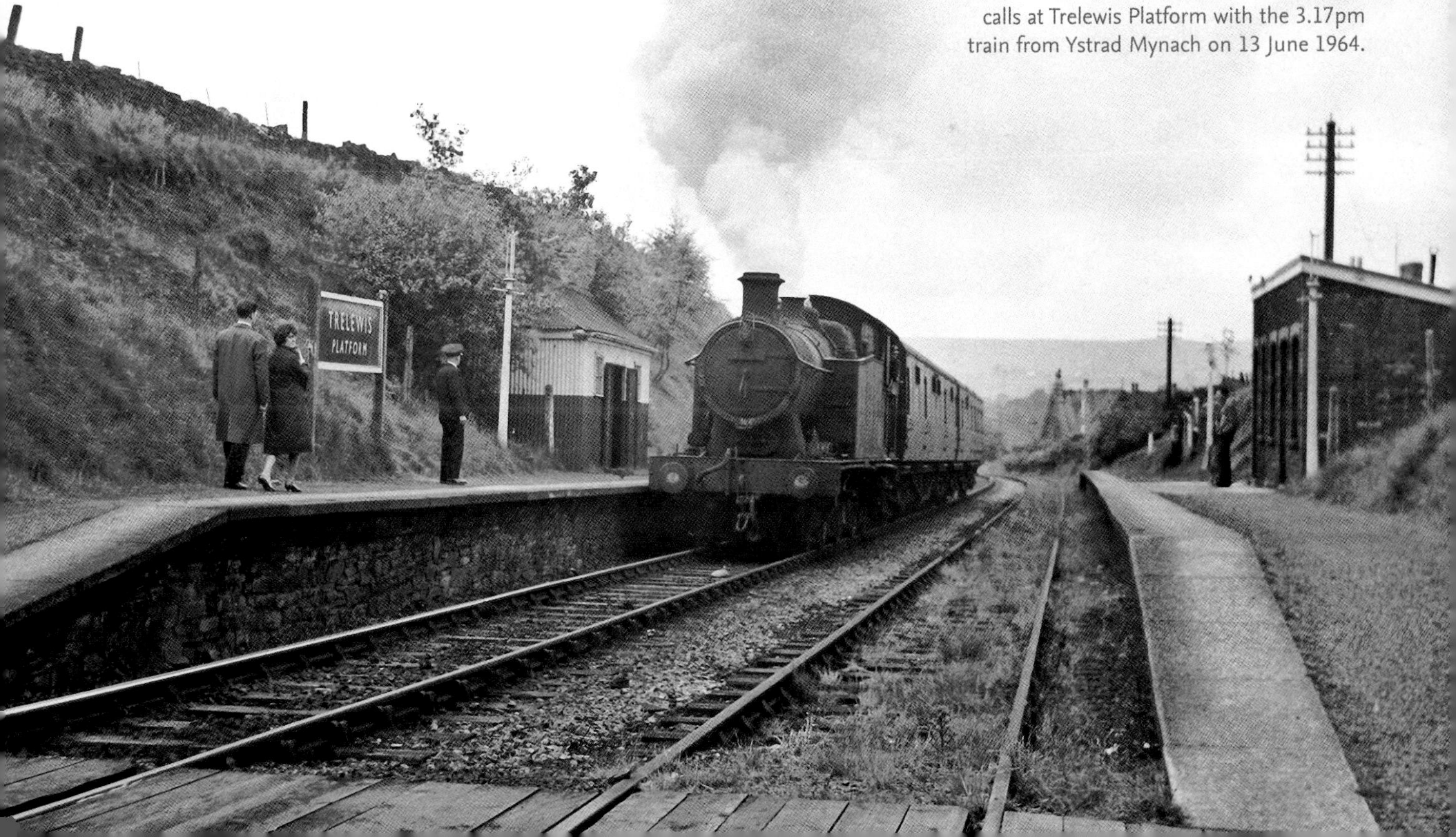

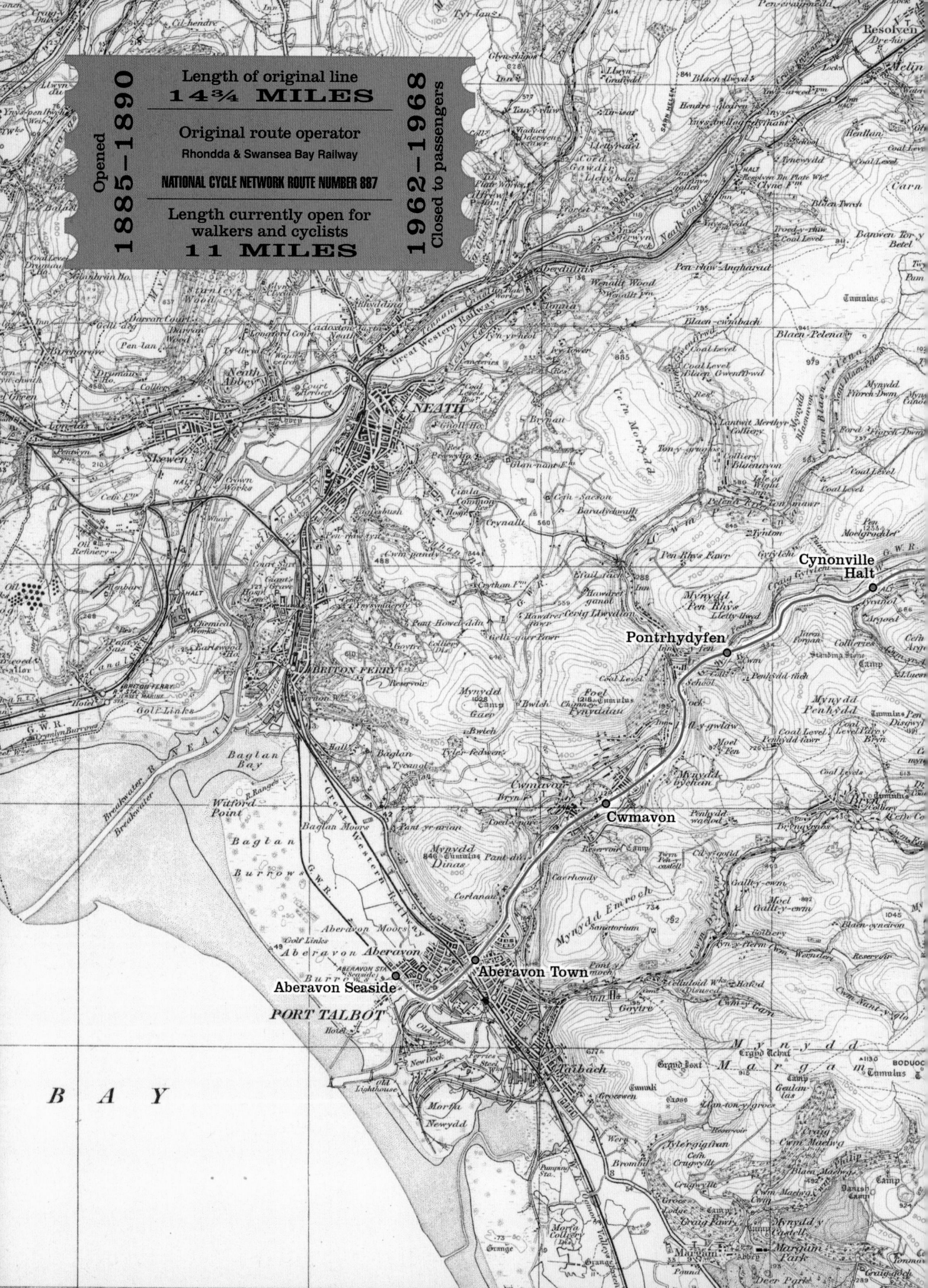

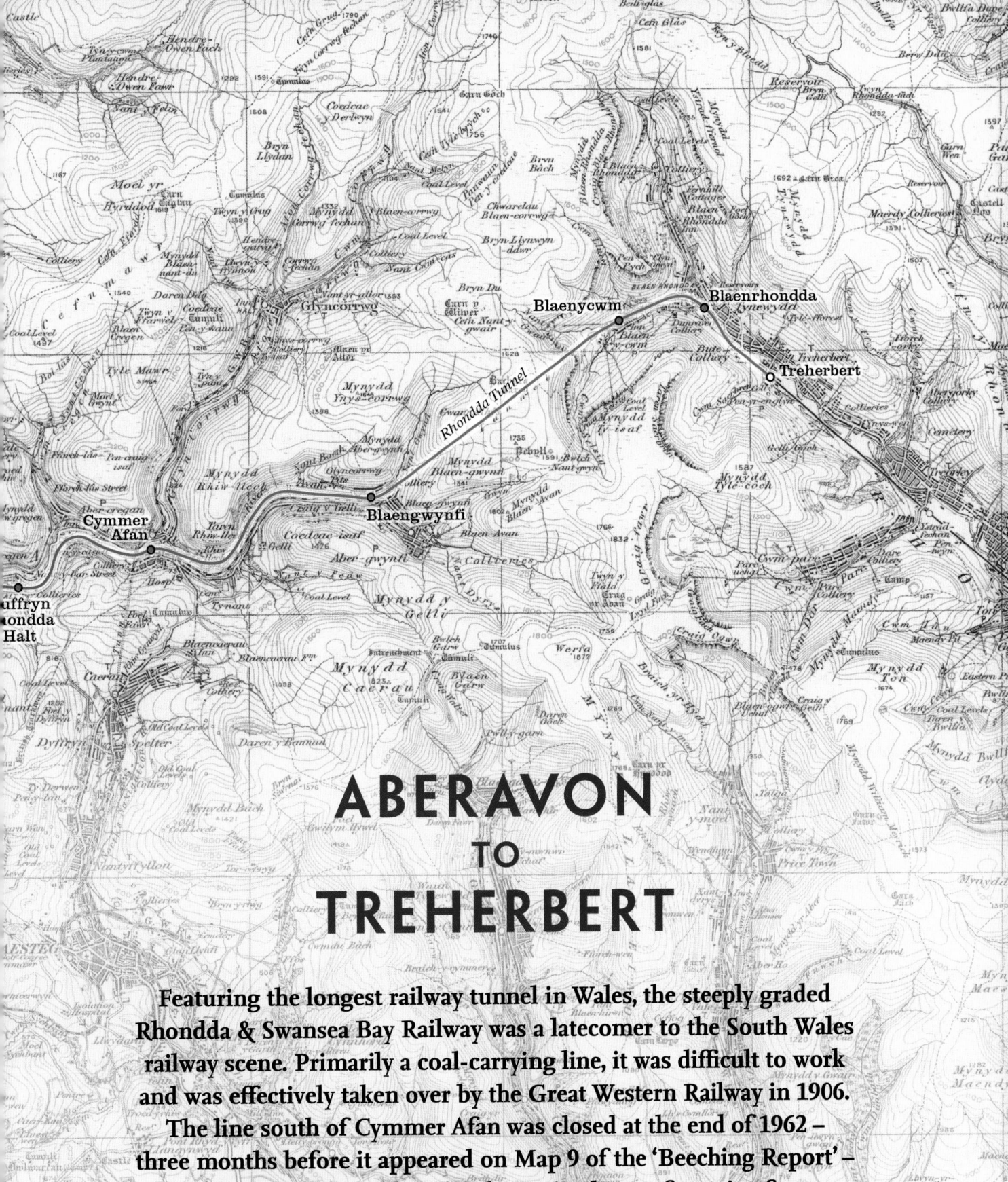

ABERAVON
TO
TREHERBERT

Featuring the longest railway tunnel in Wales, the steeply graded
Rhondda & Swansea Bay Railway was a latecomer to the South Wales
railway scene. Primarily a coal-carrying line, it was difficult to work
and was effectively taken over by the Great Western Railway in 1906.
The line south of Cymmer Afan was closed at the end of 1962 –
three months before it appeared on Map 9 of the 'Beeching Report' –
although the Rhondda Tunnel remained open for trains from
Bridgend via the Llynfi Valley until 1968 when it was closed
because of its poor state of repair. Much of the route from
Aberavon to Blaengwynfi is now a footpath and cycleway.

Despite the coming of the railways to the South Wales' valleys, by the 1880s the industries and port of Swansea were still cut off from the coalfields of the Rhondda Valley, the physical obstacles of the mountains at the head of the valley a seemingly impenetrable barrier. The Victorian railway promoters and builders were not so easily put off however, and thus was the Rhondda & Swansea Bay Railway (R&SBR) formed. The first stage of the railway from Aberavon, up the Afan Valley through Pontrhydyfen, Cymmer and Blaengwynfi and then through the 3,443-yd Rhondda Tunnel to Treherbert, was incorporated in 1882.

With gradients as steep as 1-in-39, the railway opened up the Afan Valley to Cymmer in 1885 but it took another five years before the single-track Rhondda Tunnel was open for business. With a maximum depth of around 1,000 ft below the 1,732-ft peak of Mynydd Blaengwynfi, the tunnel was a feat of Victorian engineering, becoming the longest in Wales and the seventh longest in Britain.

The railway was extended westwards along the coast from Aberavon to Briton Ferry, Neath and Danygraig in 1895, when through passenger services between Swansea Riverside (using the Swansea Harbour Trustees' dock lines to Danygraig) and Treherbert commenced. Working heavy coal trains from Rhondda to Swansea was no mean feat as there was a rising gradient through the Rhondda Tunnel from Treherbert, thus limiting the number of wagons that could be carried. Once through the tunnel, coal trains were faced with descending the Afan Valley to Aberavon – on several occasions trains got out of control, sometimes with fatal consequences. With its long sandy beach, Aberavon became a popular destination on summer weekends for day trippers from Swansea and the Rhondda Valley – today the enormous steelworks at Margam dominates the coastline.

The opening of the R&SBR soon led to congestion at Swansea Docks, so the Prince of Wales Dock, which had opened in 1881, was extended in 1898 to cope with the additional traffic. However, with its steep gradients and the problems of working through the Rhondda Tunnel, the R&SBR struggled to survive and was effectively taken over by the Great Western Railway (GWR) in 1906. It was officially absorbed into the GWR in 1922. Swansea Riverside closed in 1933 and trains were diverted to Swansea East Dock until 1936, when all trains from Aberavon were diverted into the GWR's terminus at High Street.

The station master returns to his office and peace descends once again on Cwmavon station as a northbound train departs on 27 September 1960. Today the trackbed is a footpath and cycleway while a modern art installation here features three past and present local celebrities – Richard Burton, Rob Brydon and Dick Wagstaff.

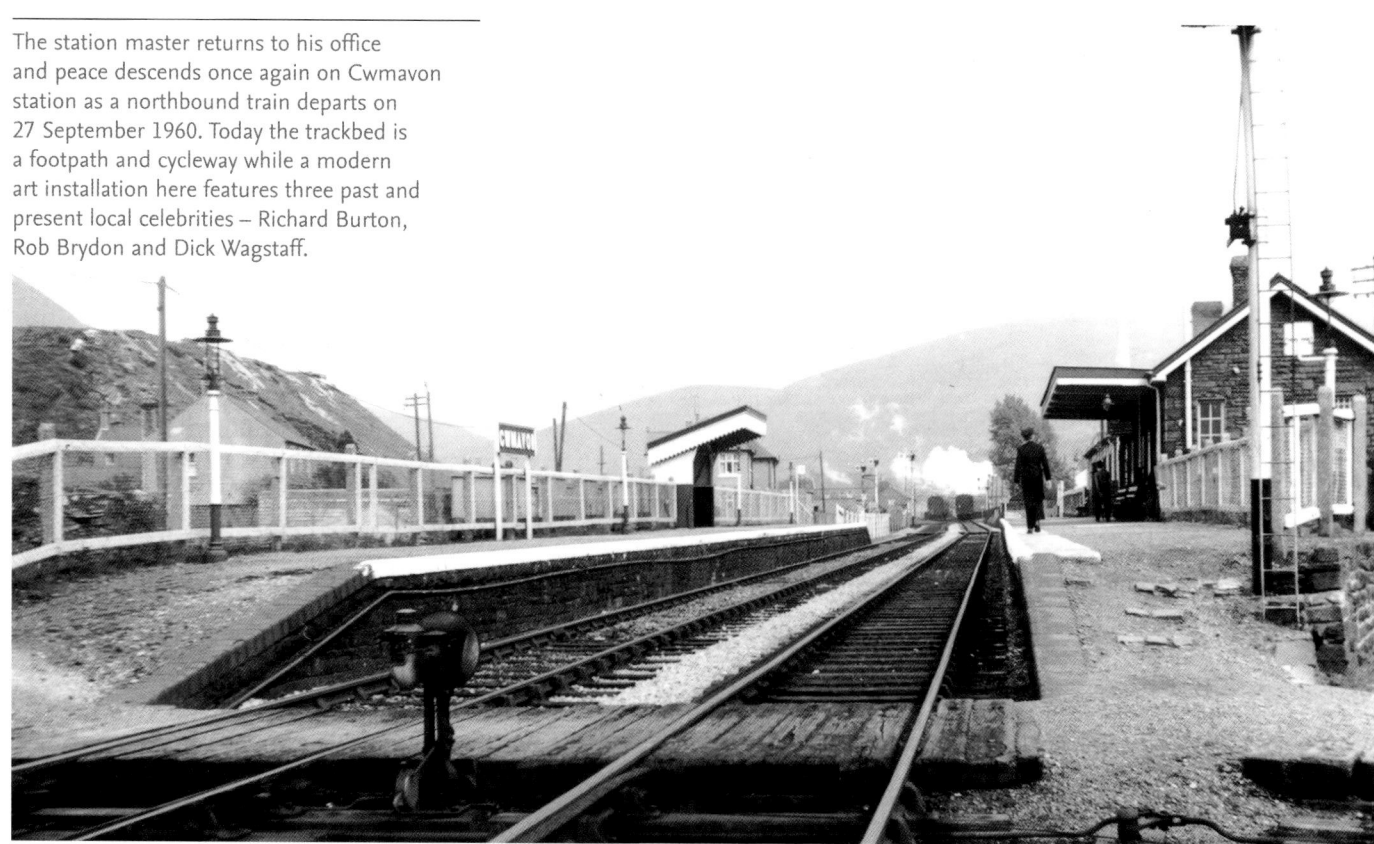

Ex-GWR '5700' Class 0-6-0PT No. 9766 leaves Pontrhydyfen station with the 1.55pm Aberavon to Cymmer Afan train on 27 September 1960. This single-track railway featured severe gradients on its climb up the Afan Valley to the Rhondda Tunnel.

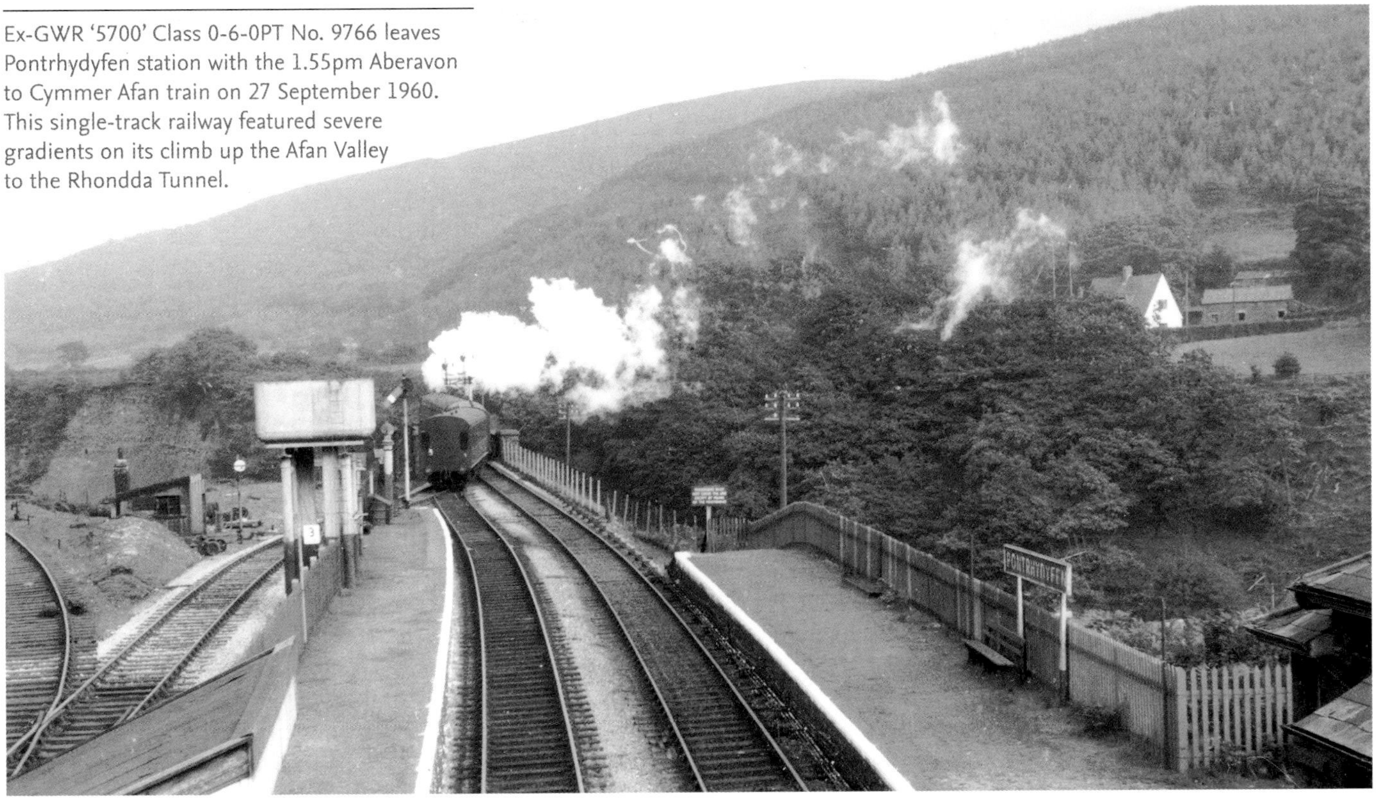

Coal remained the lifeblood of the line until the 1940s but with collieries closing down and a decline in coal exports from Swansea Docks, the line's future looked bleak. With increasing competition from road transport, passenger traffic was also in decline and by 1958 there were only two through trains running between Swansea and Treherbert on weekdays. Other Treherbert trains began or ended their journeys at Neath, with two in each direction on weekdays plus two more on Saturdays.

In 1960, 1½ miles of the R&SB's line between Cymmer and Blaengwynfi was closed to save the cost of repairing a viaduct and the 174-yd Gelli Tunnel – from 13 June all R&SB line trains were diverted onto the parallel former-GWR Llynfi Valley line along this section. Despite this, the line closed to passengers between Briton Ferry and Cymmer Afan on 3 December 1962. The section from Cymmer Afan to Blaengwynfi and Treherbert continued to be served by trains from Bridgend up the Llynfi Valley until 26 February 1968, when the long and dripping Rhondda Tunnel was closed because of its poor state of repair. From that date trains from Bridgend terminated at Cymmer Afan until the Llynfi Valley line from Bridgend and Maesteg closed on 22 June 1970. This line has since reopened to passenger trains between Bridgend and Maesteg with through services to and from Cardiff and beyond.

To the east of Pontrhydyfen the railway path crosses the River Afan on a modern bridge supported on original nineteenth century stone piers. Known as the Afan Forest Country Park, this heavily wooded valley is a popular destination for mountain bikers.

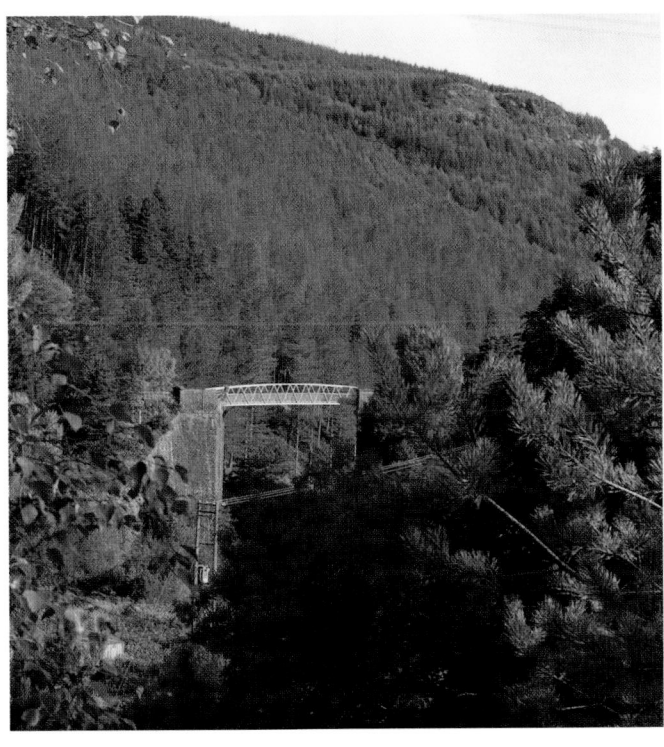

While the railway's coastal route west of Aberavon has long-since disappeared beneath new housing, industrial development and roads, the 9-mile section from Aberavon seafront up the Afan Valley to Cymmer has been reopened as a footpath and cycleway. As Route 887 of the National Cycle Network, it links with Route 4 at Aberavon and Route 885 (for the Llynfi Valley) at Cymmer.

Heading northwards away from Aberavon and Port Talbot – served by trains between Cardiff and Swansea – the railway path closely follows the River Afan through Cwmafan, where there is an art installation featuring local celebrities Richard Burton, Rob Brydon and Dick Wagstaff. It continues up the ever-narrowing wooded valley to Pontrhydyfen where, at the confluence of the Afan and Pelenna Rivers, an aqueduct and a railway viaduct span the valley. The former (now a roadway) was built in 1825 to supply water to blast furnaces at Oakwood Iron Works while the latter was built by the Port Talbot Railway in 1898 to link the Tonmawr collieries to Port Talbot Docks.

To the east of the aqueduct at Pontrhydyfen is a large car park that serves the many footpaths and mountain-bike trails in the Afan Forest Country Park. From here, the route of the railway path continues up the wooded valley and soon crosses the Afan on a modern bridge supported on original nineteenth-century stone piers. With the fast-flowing river far below, the path reaches Cynonville Halt under a stone overbridge. Both platforms are well preserved and a stone shelter is provided for cyclists and walkers.

At Cynonville Halt there are detours to miles of top-class mountain-bike trails across the valley to the north, where the route of the long-closed South Wales Mineral Railway (SWMR) can also be followed along the opposite side of the valley to Cymmer. The Afan Forest Visitor Centre, with its car park, cycle-hire centre, picnic sites, campsite and mining museum, is a short climb from Cynonville Halt to the south via a tunnel under the A4107.

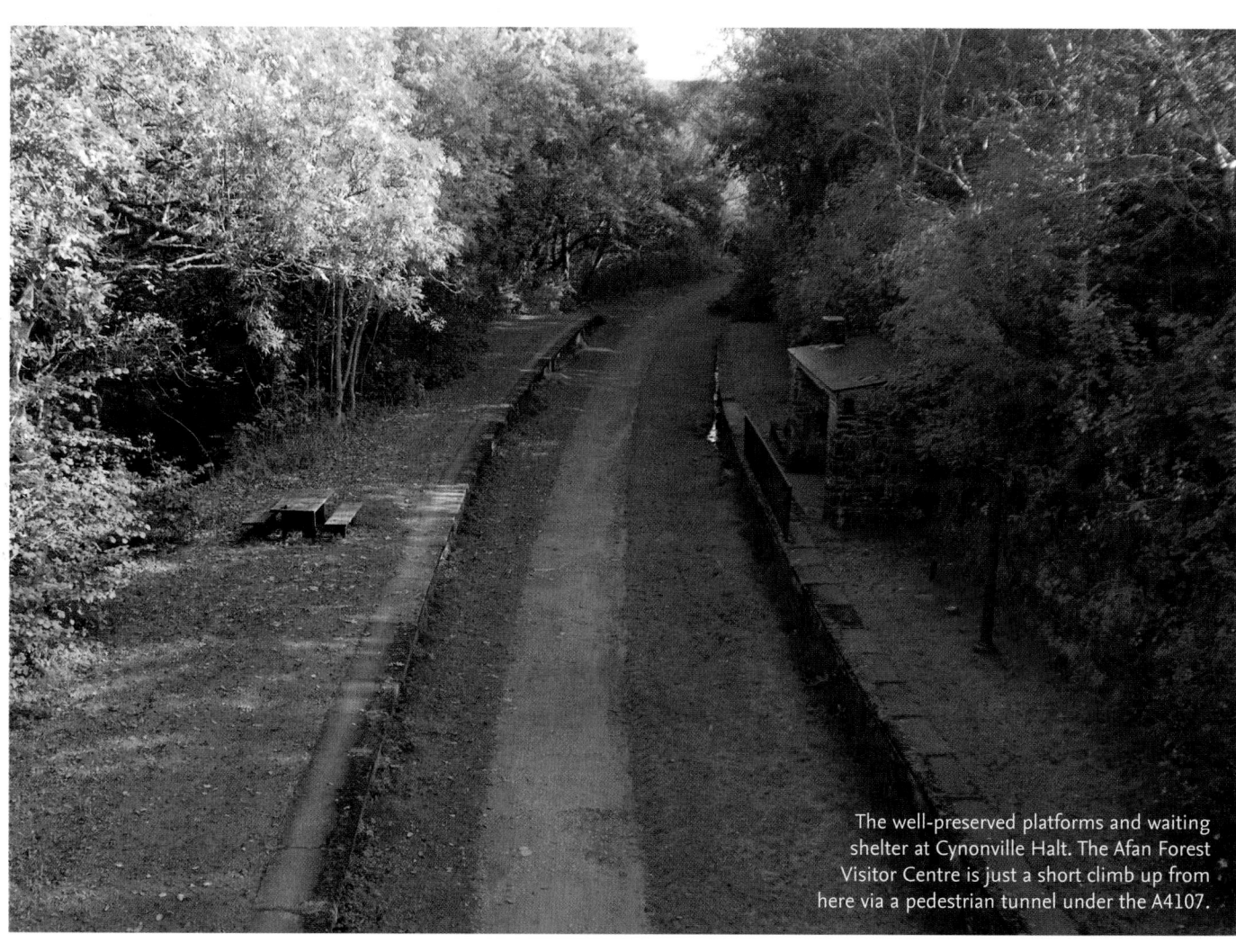

The well-preserved platforms and waiting shelter at Cynonville Halt. The Afan Forest Visitor Centre is just a short climb up from here via a pedestrian tunnel under the A4107.

From Cynonville Halt, the railway path continues eastwards past the site of Duffryn Rhondda Halt and up the wooded valley to Cymmer before ending at Blaengwynfi. At Cymmer, National Cycle Network Route 887 continues across the valley and along the route of the old railway up to Glyncorrwg. The iron viaduct across the valley at Cymmer was built by the Llynfi & Ogmore Railway in 1878 to link the railway with the SWMR and the collieries at Glyncorrwg, but today its rickety structure is inaccessible to walkers and cyclists. On the opposite side of the valley the former SWMR station at Cymmer, from where workmens' trains full of coalminers once slogged up the valley, is now a pub.

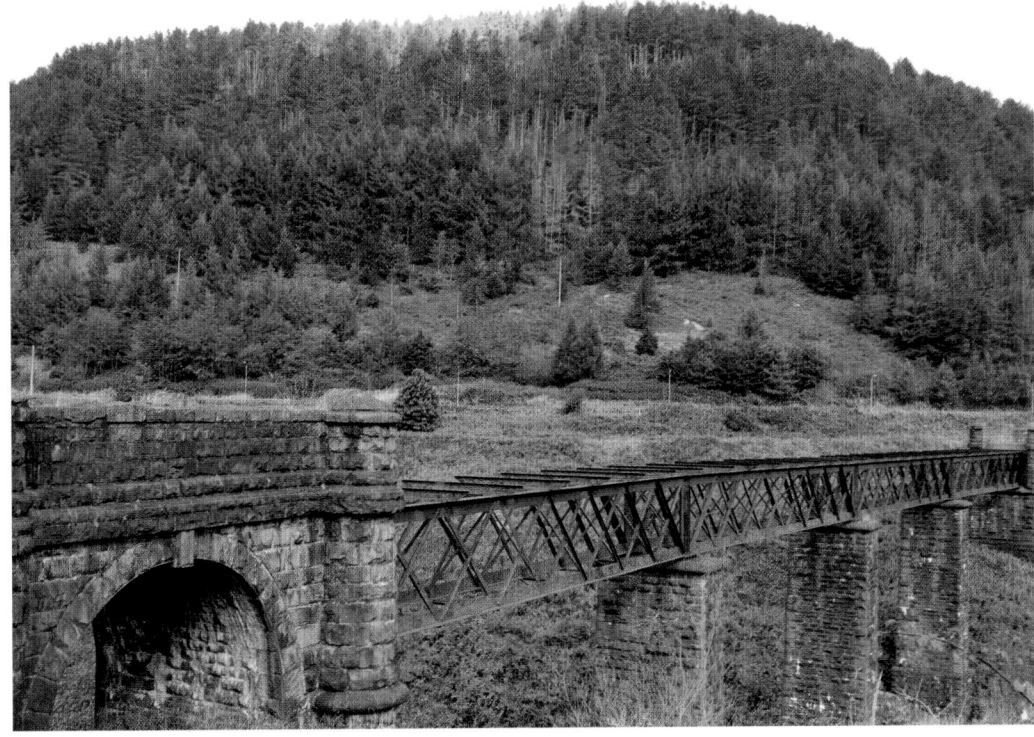

Inaccessible to walkers and cyclists, this viaduct at Cymmer once linked the Llynfi & Ogmore Railway with collieries at Glyncorrwg. On the opposite side of the valley the trackbed of the South Wales Mineral Railway can be followed on foot or bike as far as the bricked up Gyfylchi Tunnel.

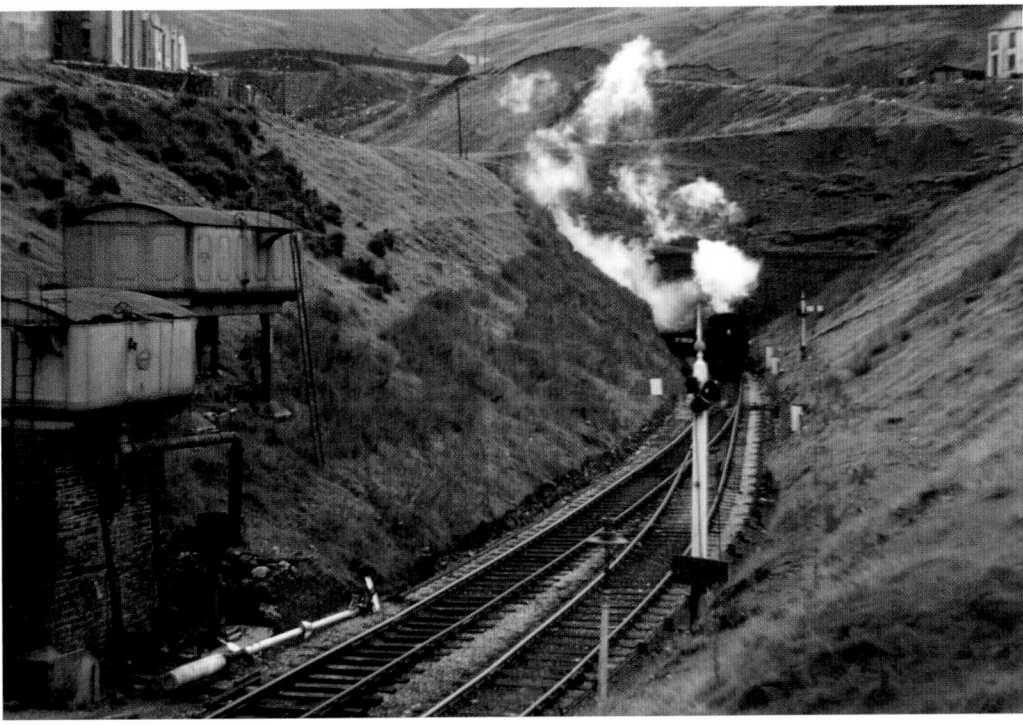

Ex-GWR '5600' Class 0-6-2T No. 6613 emerges from the single-bore hell hole of the 3,443-yd-long Rhondda Tunnel and approaches Blaengwynfi station with a Treherbert to Neath train on 3 August 1959. The tunnel was closed in 1968 owing to its poor state of repair.

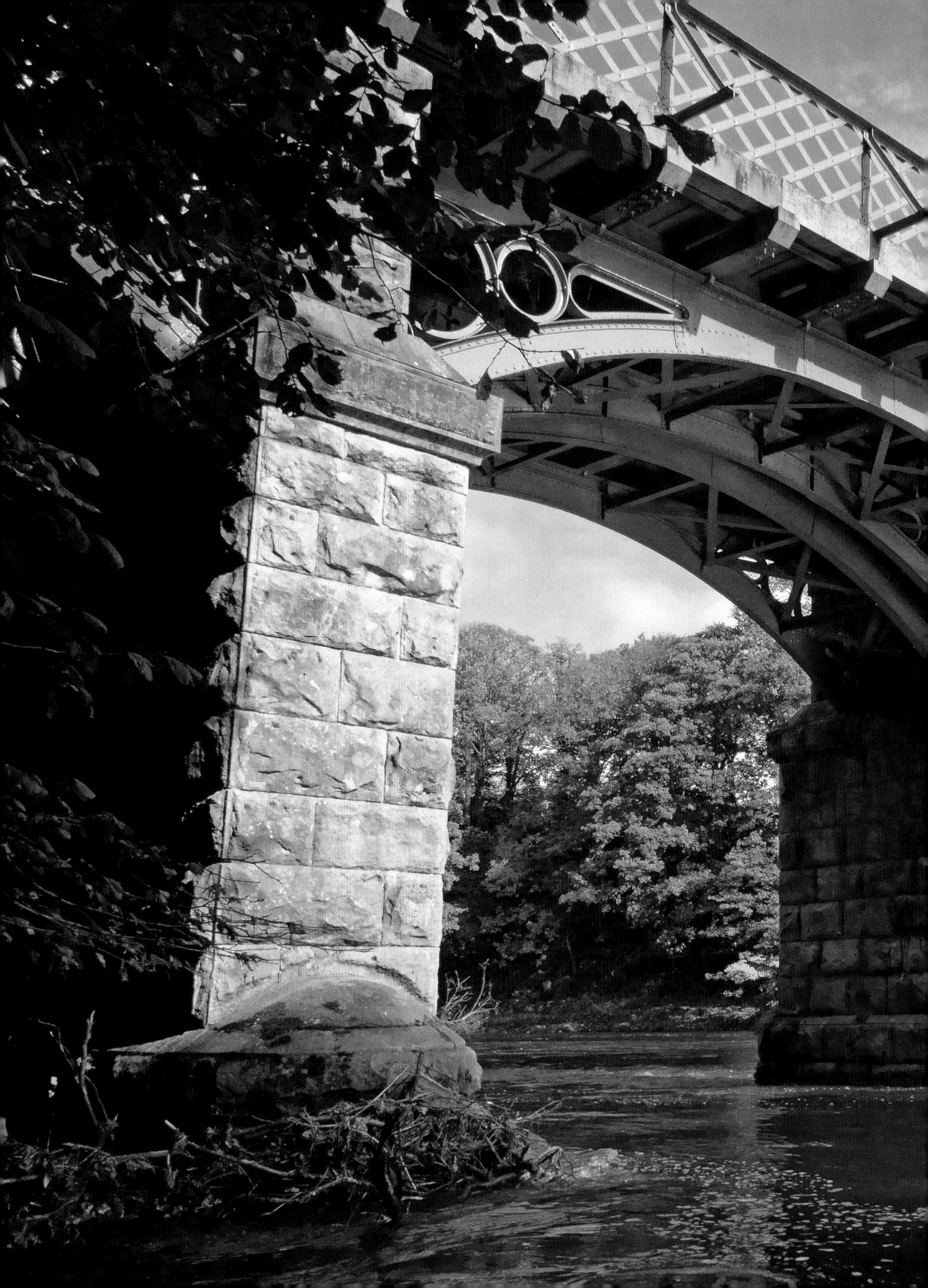

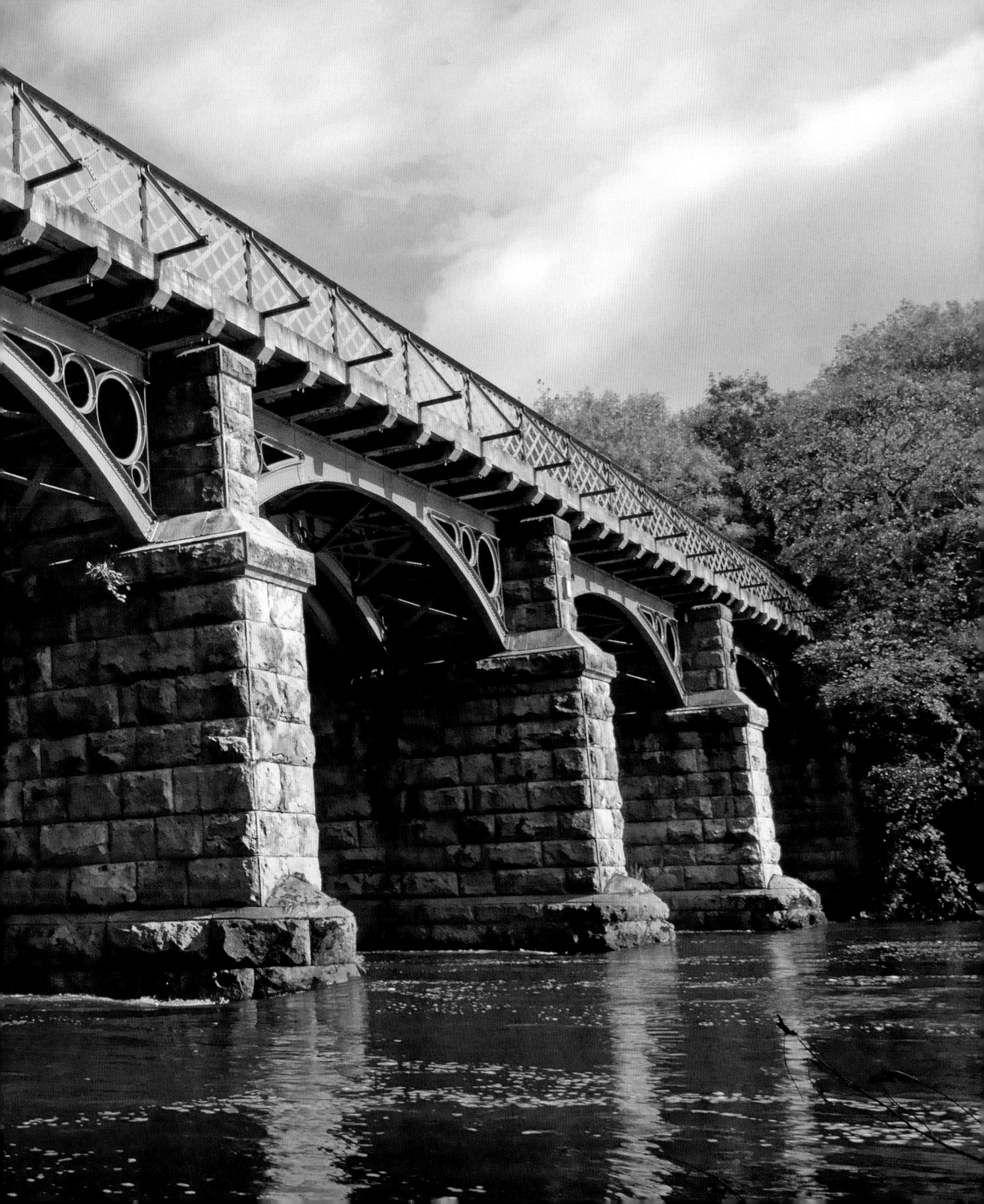

NORTHERN ENGLAND

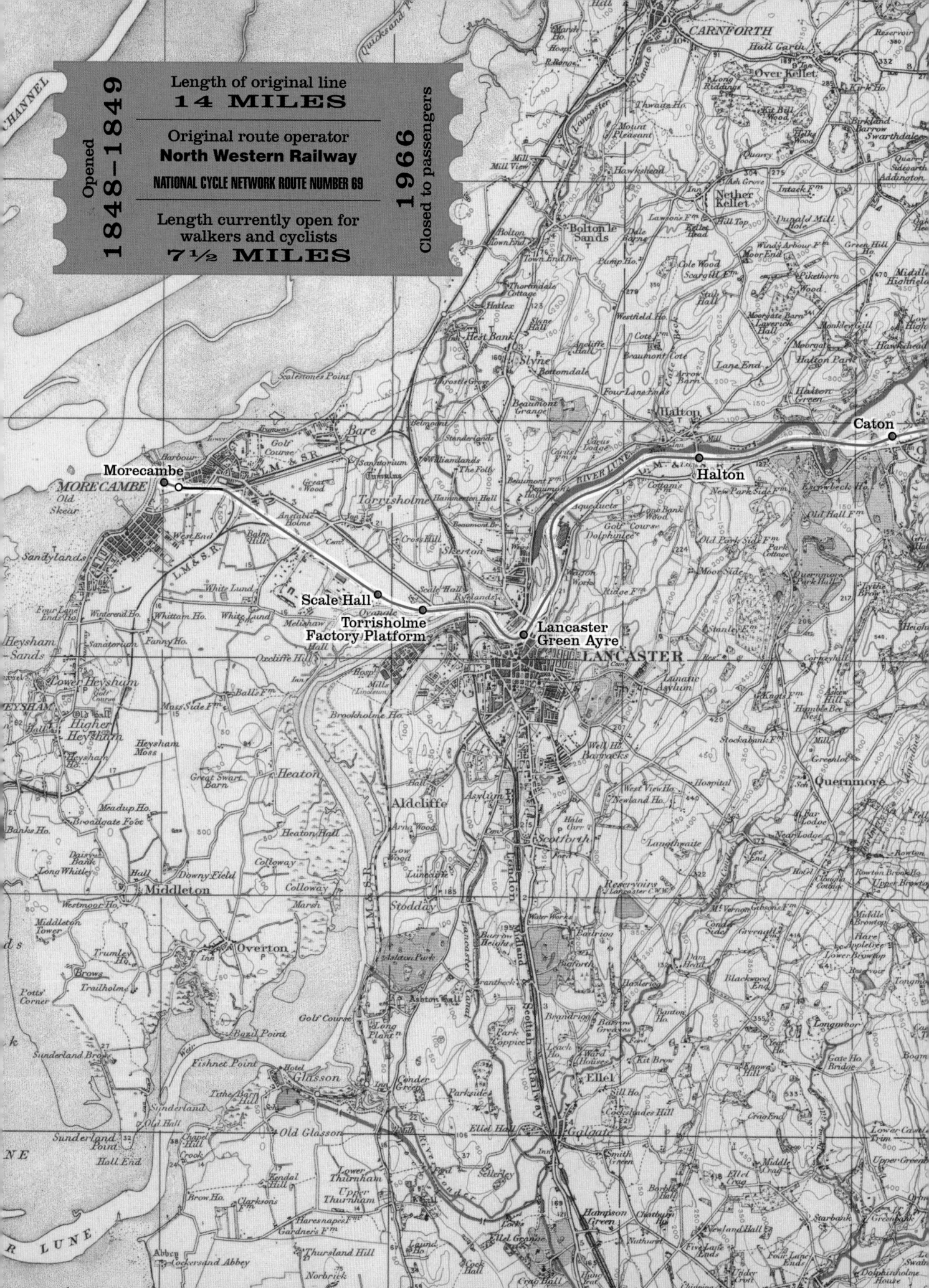

Opened
1848–1849

1966
Closed to passengers

Length of original line
14 MILES

Original route operator
North Western Railway

NATIONAL CYCLE NETWORK ROUTE NUMBER 69

Length currently open for
walkers and cyclists
7½ MILES

Morecambe

MORECAMBE
Old
Skear

Scale Hall

Torrisholme
Factory Platform

Lancaster
Green Ayre

LANCASTER

Halton

Caton

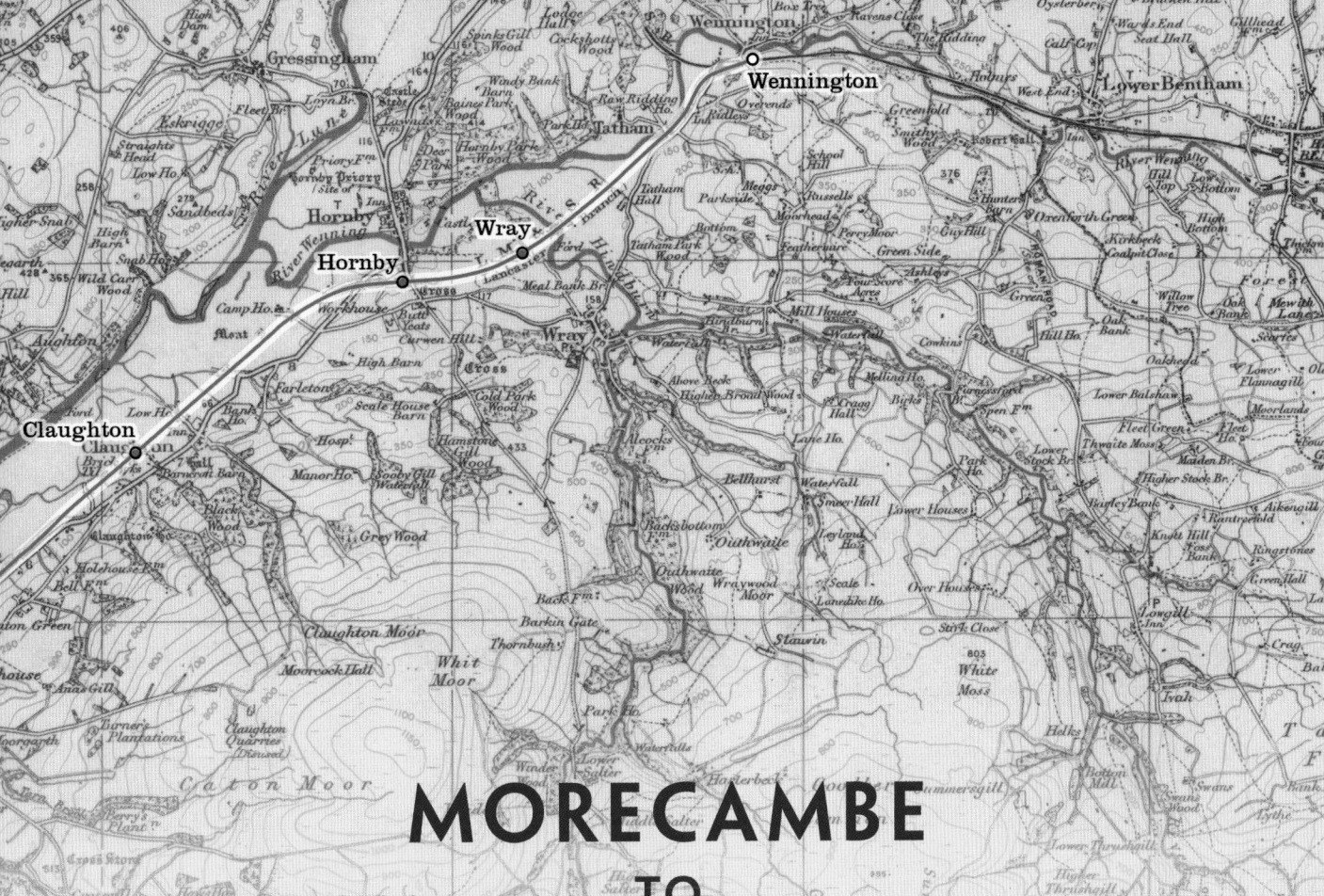

MORECAMBE
TO
WENNINGTON

LANCASTER-MORECAMBE GREENWAY/MILLENNIUM PATH

Before the coming of the railway in 1848, what is now known as the resort town of Morecambe was just a small coastal village by the name of Poulton-le-Sands. The railway changed all that, with its eastern extension to Wennington and Skipton bringing holidaymakers from West Yorkshire by the thousand. Taken over by the Midland Railway in 1871, the section from Lancaster (Green Ayre) to Morecambe became, in 1908, one of the earliest lines in Britain to be electrified using overhead wires. This groundbreaking system remained in use until 1951 when it was converted as a test bed for the high-voltage equipment later used on the West Coast Main Line. Although the section from Morecambe to Wennington closed in 1966 the 7½ miles from Morecambe to Caton is now a footpath and cycleway.

The city of Lancaster received its first railway service when the Lancaster & Preston Junction Railway opened in 1840 – six years later this railway became a link in what would be known as the West Coast Main Line (WCML) when the Lancaster & Carlisle Railway opened.

Just over three miles to the west of Lancaster lies the coast overlooking Morecambe Bay and it was here that the Morecambe Bay Harbour & Railway Company intended to build a harbour linked to Lancaster by a railway. The harbour and railway were authorized by Parliament in 1846. At that time, what was to become the resort town of Morecambe was known as the small resort village of Poulton-le-Sands, but the coming of the railway changed all that! While the construction of the harbour proceeded at a snail's pace the railway opened in 1848, by which time it had amalgamated with the North Western Railway (NWR).

Meanwhile the NWR had been authorized in 1846 to build a railway from Skipton to near Low Gill (where it would connect with the Lancaster & Carlisle Railway's main line) with a branch line from Clapham to Lancaster. The NWR's lines opened in stages: from Skipton to Ingleton via Clapham and from Lancaster Green Area station (from 1870 known as Green Ayre) up the Lune Valley to Wennington in 1849 – the so-called main line never went further north than Ingleton and the company's dreams of running an Anglo-Scottish trunk line came to

nothing. The missing link between Wennington and Clapham opened in 1850 and, with Ingleton now at the end of a useless branch line from Clapham, the entire route from Skipton to Lancaster and thence to Poulton-le-Sands became the NWR's main line.

Through working between Barrow-in-Furness and West Yorkshire became possible in 1867 when the Furness & Midland Joint Railway opened between Carnforth and Wennington – the latter station then became the junction for the Lancaster and Poulton-le-Sands route.

The Midland Railway worked the NWR from 1852, leased it in 1859 and took it over completely in 1871. Now served by through trains from Leeds and further afield, what was once a collection of small coastal villages soon expanded into a popular seaside resort which became officially known as Morecambe in 1889. New hotels and boarding houses were built to cater for the ever-increasing number of holidaymakers that arrived by train from West Yorkshire during the summer months – the famous art deco Midland Hotel, which has been recently restored, was built by the London Midland & Scottish Railway in 1933 to replace an earlier railway-owned hotel that had opened in 1848.

With business booming in Morecambe the MR completed the harbour in 1905 and opened the grand Morecambe station in 1907 – located opposite the old Midland Hotel

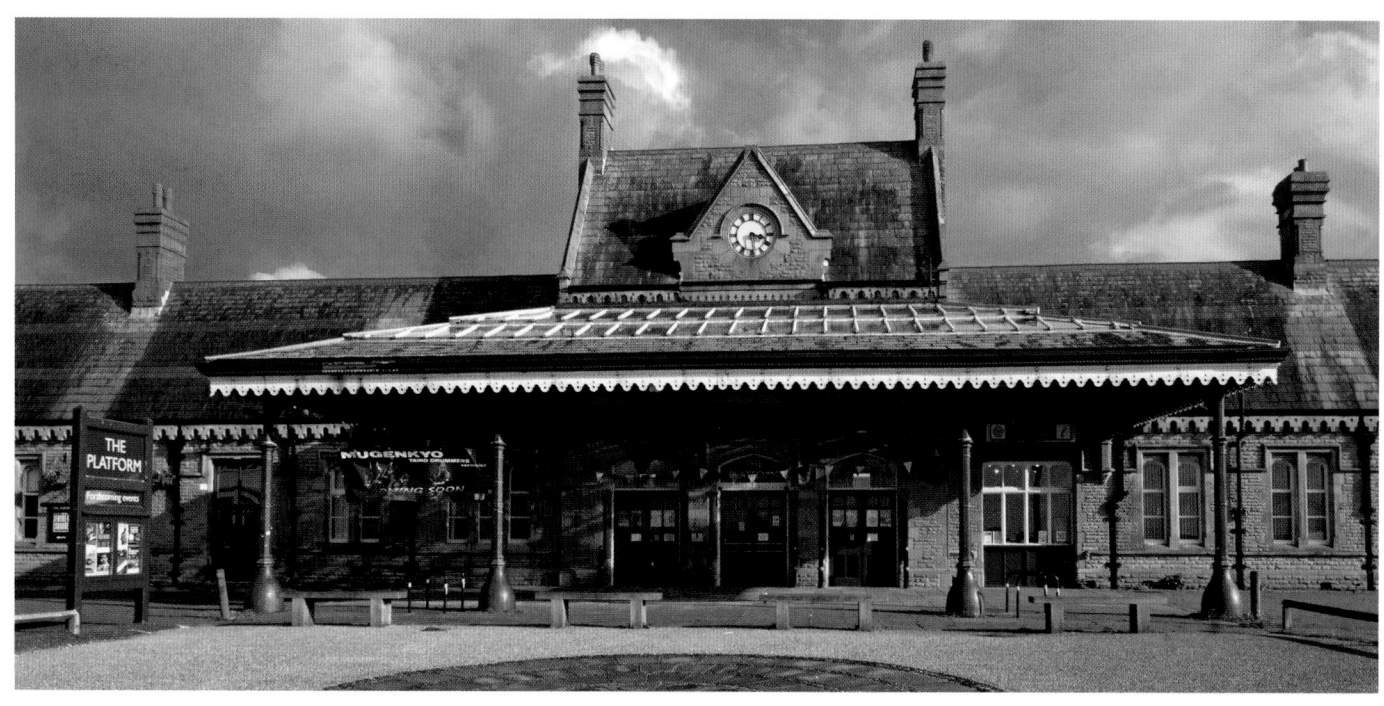

and close to Isle of Man and Belfast steamer jetties, the station had four main platforms built to handle large numbers of passengers and was renamed Morecambe Promenade in 1924. The MR then took a major leap forward in railway technology when it electrified the Lancaster Green Ayre to Morecambe route in 1908 – unusually for this time the electric multiple unit trains collected their power from overhead lines with electricity being supplied from the company's power station at nearby Heysham. This system remained in place until 1951 when steam trains temporarily took over the services. It was reopened in 1953 and became a test bed for the high-voltage equipment that was eventually used on the West Coast Main Line.

Serving intermediate stations at Halton, Caton, Claughton, Hornby and Wray, traffic between Lancaster and Wennington was always light but there was a good service of trains running between Leeds and Morecambe that kept it alive during the summer months. By the 1960s however, Morecambe's image as a holiday resort had become somewhat jaded – cheap foreign holidays and increasing car ownership brought in their wake a rapid decline in passenger numbers and the Wennington-Lancaster (Green Ayre)-Morecambe line was listed for closure in the 1963 'Beeching Report'. The end came on 3 January 1966, although goods traffic continued along the Lancaster to Wennington route for two more years. Passenger trains between Leeds and Morecambe continued to operate but were rerouted via the former Furness & Midland Joint Railway through Carnforth and down the WCML via Hest Bank. Morecambe Promenade station was closed in 1994 and a new terminus station was opened to the east. It is still served by trains running between Lancaster and Heysham via Morecambe South Junction on the WCML – trains to and from Heysham have to reverse direction at Morecambe.

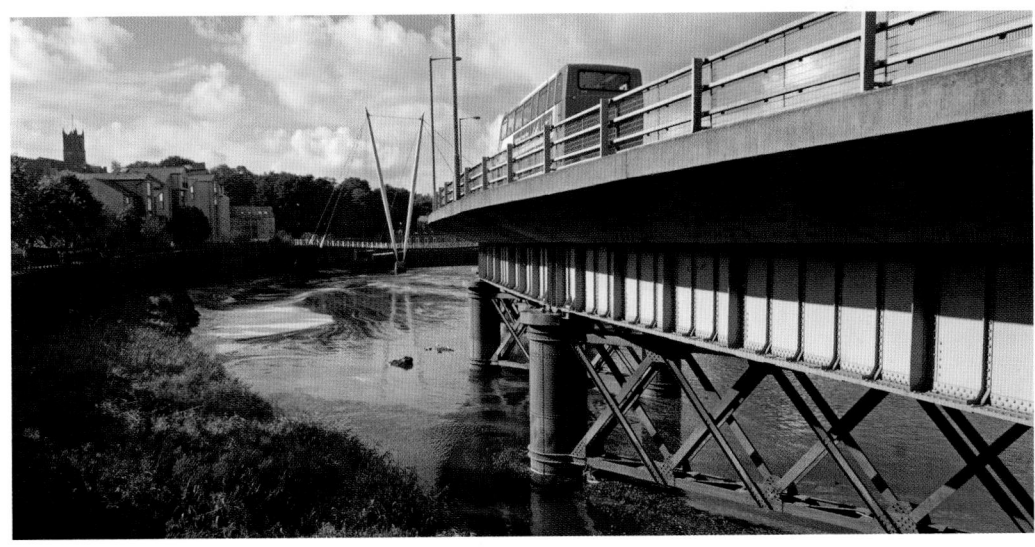

The Greyhound Bridge at Lancaster once carried the Morecambe to Lancaster Green Ayre railway over the River Lune. Since closure of the railway it has been fitted with a concrete deck for road traffic.

LEFT: The Midland Railway's Morecambe Promenade terminus in all its restored glory. While a new basic station has been resited further to the east, the original building now houses a pub, restaurant, arts centre and tourist information office.

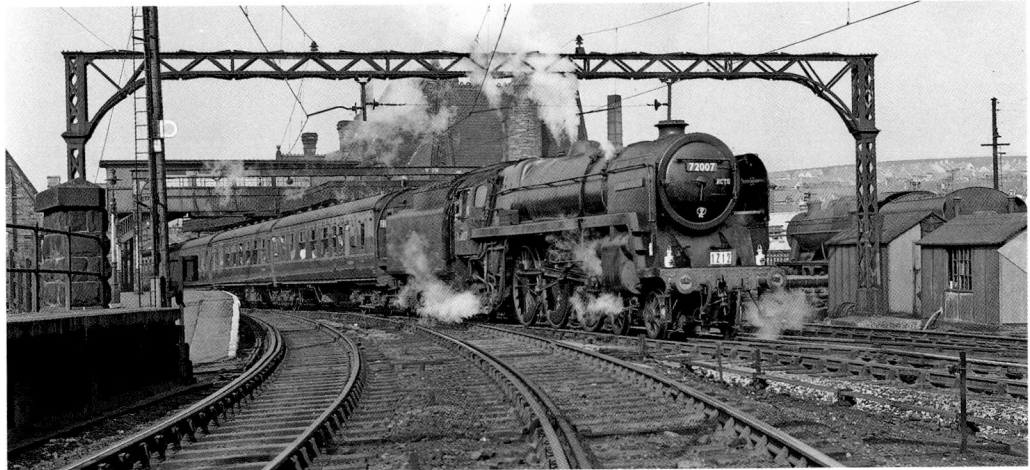

Carlisle Kingmoor shed's spruced up BR Standard 'Clan' Class 4-6-0 No. 72007 'Clan Mackintosh' leaves Lancaster Green Ayre station with the Railway Correspondence & Travel Society's 'Ribble-Lune Railtour' on 23 May 1964. Built at Crewe in 1952, this locomotive had a short working life and was withdrawn in December 1965.

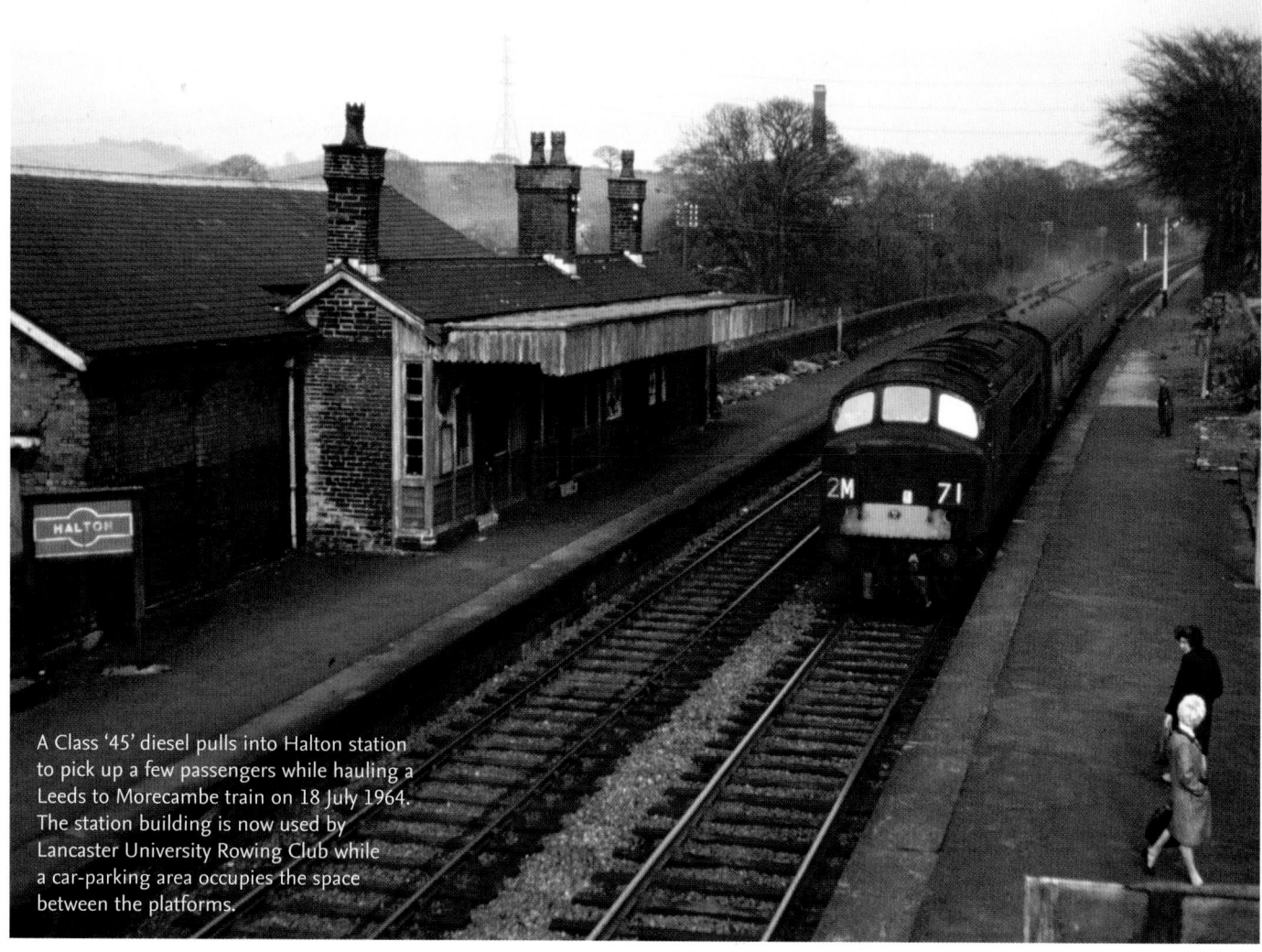

A Class '45' diesel pulls into Halton station to pick up a few passengers while hauling a Leeds to Morecambe train on 18 July 1964. The station building is now used by Lancaster University Rowing Club while a car-parking area occupies the space between the platforms.

Since closure the entire route of the Morecambe to Lancaster section of this railway has been reopened as a 3-mile footpath and cycleway known as the Lancaster – Morecambe Greenway. It also forms part of National Cycle Network Route 69. At Lancaster it connects with the River Lune Millennium Path (North) via the eye-catching Millennium Bridge that was opened across the River Lune in 2001. The Millennium Path makes use of the old railway trackbed for 4½ miles along the Lune Valley from the site of Lancaster (Green Ayre) station to Caton.

The Lancaster – Morecambe Greenway starts at the superbly restored Morecambe Promenade station, which now houses a pub, restaurant, arts centre and tourist information centre. Nearby is the breathtaking art deco Midland Hotel, built by the LMS in 1933, which after years of neglect was completely restored to its former glory in 2008.

Heading southwest, the Greenway follows the straight course of the old electric railway through suburbs before emerging alongside the River Lune in Lancaster. The railway once crossed the river here on the Greyhound Bridge but after closure of the line the bridge was converted in 1972 to carry road traffic. Walkers and cyclists now cross the Lune on the new Millennium Bridge to reach the site of Lancaster (Green Ayre) station.

The site of Green Ayre station is now a car park – the only reminder of the railway here is a goods crane from Hornby station, which has been restored on a plinth – while the site of the locomotive shed is now a supermarket. The railway path closely follows the south bank of the river, passing under the Lancaster Canal aqueduct – designed by John Rennie, this magnificent structure was completed in 1797 – and diving under the M6 to reach Halton station. Destroyed by fire in 1907, the station building was rebuilt in brick and timber. Still sitting on its original platform, the building is now used by Lancaster University Rowing Club while a car-parking area occupies the trackbed. A nice touch here is a sculpture in the shape of an artist's easel with a painting featuring a Midland Railway '3F' 0-6-0 loco entering the station.

Just over one mile east of Halton the railway path crosses a loop of the meandering River Lune twice in quick succession on arched bridges – now Grade II listed structures, designed by Edmund Sharpe. At this beauty spot there is a car park and a picnic site with magnificent views of the Lune Valley. A further mile to the east the railway path ends at the village of Caton where the station is now a private residence and the goods shed has a new life as a Roman Catholic church.

Beyond Caton the railway trackbed awaits reopening as a cycleway to Hornby, where the station site has long-since disappeared beneath housing development. Wennington station, formerly the junction for Lancaster, is still served by Northern Rail trains operating between Leeds and Lancaster.

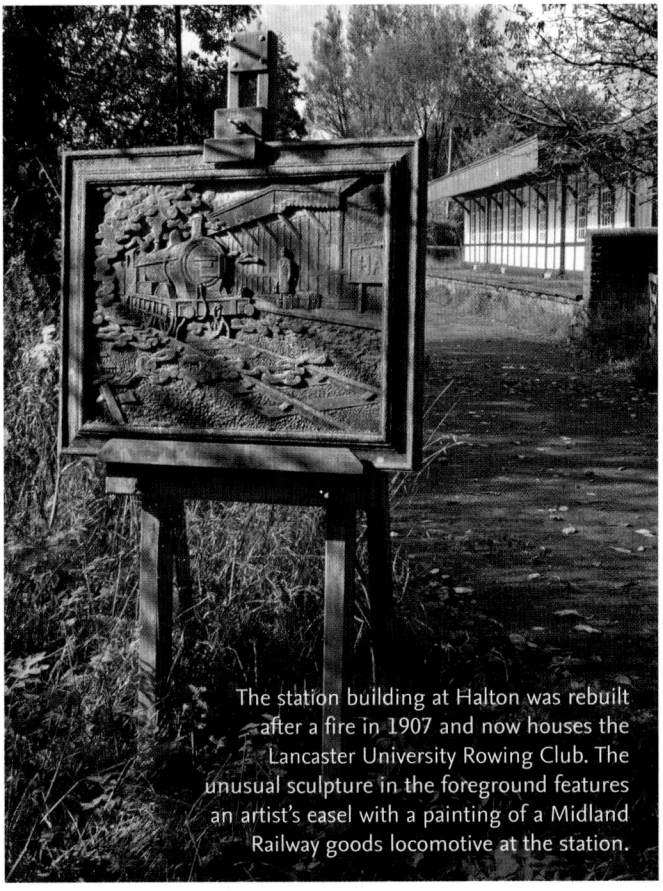

The station building at Halton was rebuilt after a fire in 1907 and now houses the Lancaster University Rowing Club. The unusual sculpture in the foreground features an artist's easel with a painting of a Midland Railway goods locomotive at the station.

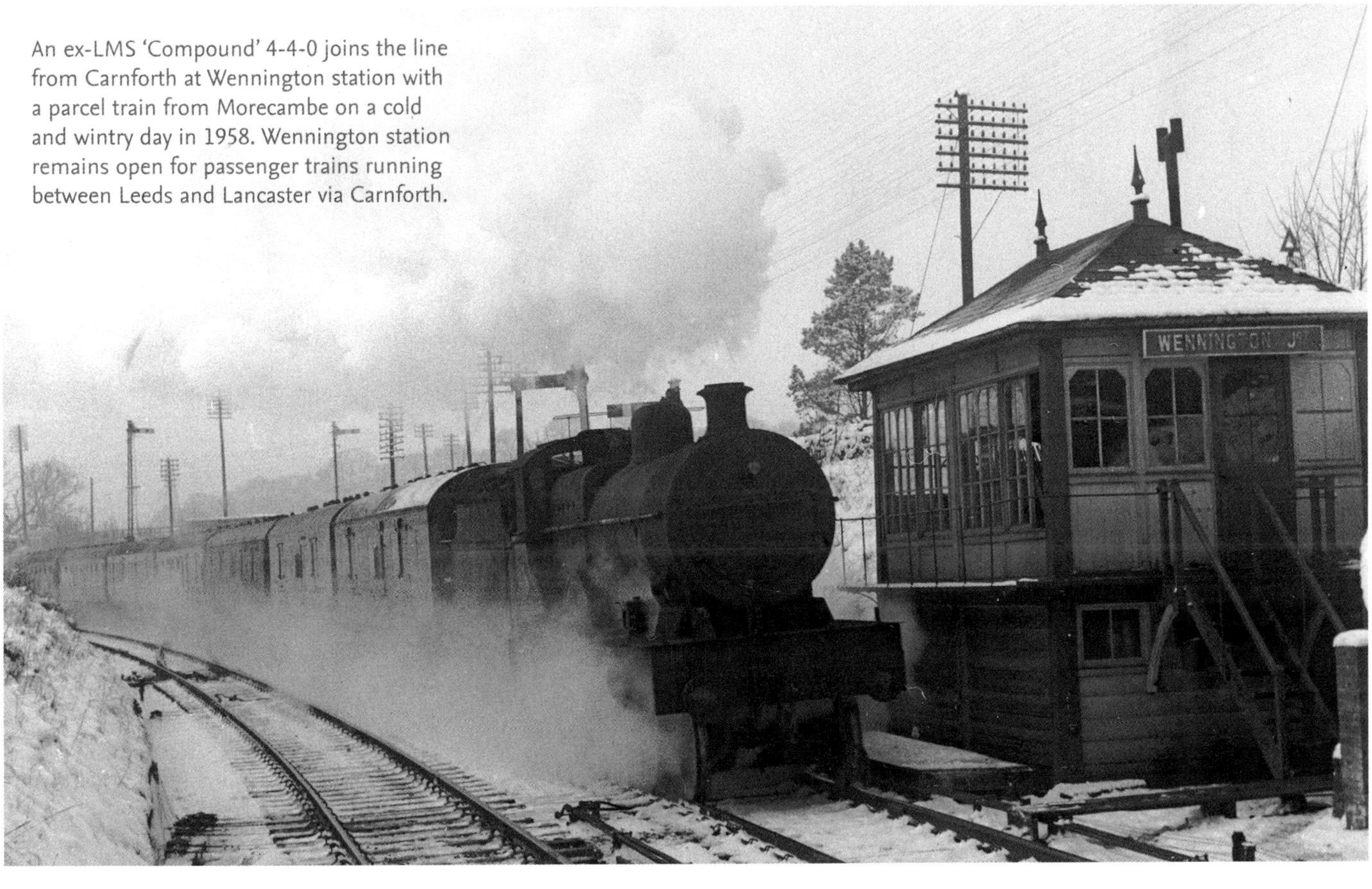

An ex-LMS 'Compound' 4-4-0 joins the line from Carnforth at Wennington station with a parcel train from Morecambe on a cold and wintry day in 1958. Wennington station remains open for passenger trains running between Leeds and Lancaster via Carnforth.

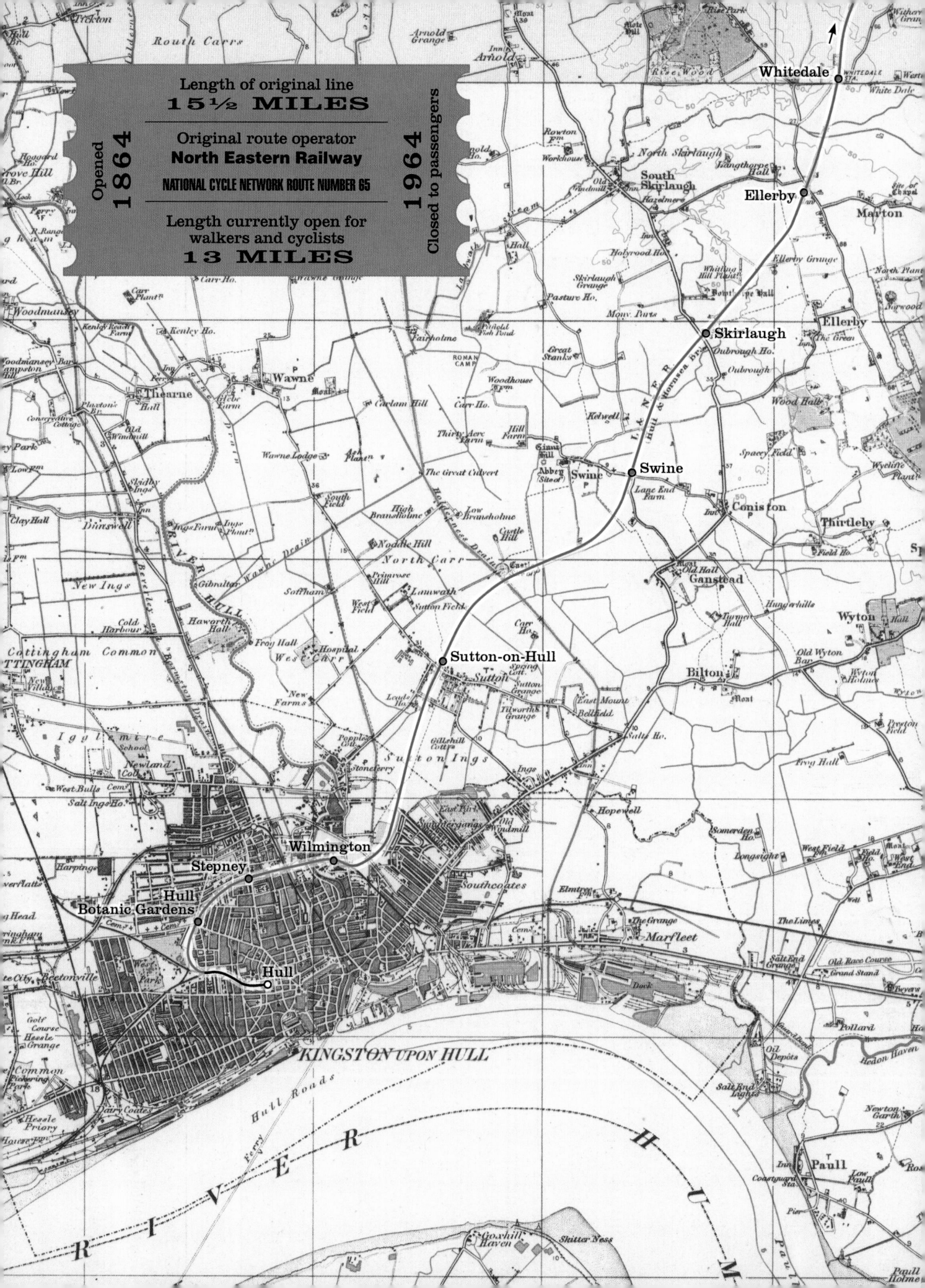

Length of original line
15½ MILES

Original route operator
North Eastern Railway

NATIONAL CYCLE NETWORK ROUTE NUMBER 65

Length currently open for
walkers and cyclists
13 MILES

Opened **1864**

Closed to passengers **1964**

Whitedale

Ellerby

Marton

Skirlaugh

Swine

Coniston

Thirtleby

Ganstead

Wyton

Bilton

Sutton-on-Hull

Wilmington

Stepney

Hull

Botanic Gardens

Hull

KINGSTON UPON HULL

Marfleet

Paull

HULL
TO
HORNSEA

HORNSEA RAIL TRAIL

Opened across the flat Holderness landscape in 1864, the railway's arrival to Hornsea transformed what was then a small coastal village into a thriving resort. The line featured a rare 'market days only' station at Wassand. Despite cost-cutting exercises in the late 1950s, increasing competition from road transport led to the railway's demise after 100 years of service. Since closure, the terminus building at Hornsea has been beautifully restored while almost the entire trackbed has been reopened as a footpath and cycleway known as the Hornsea Rail Trail.

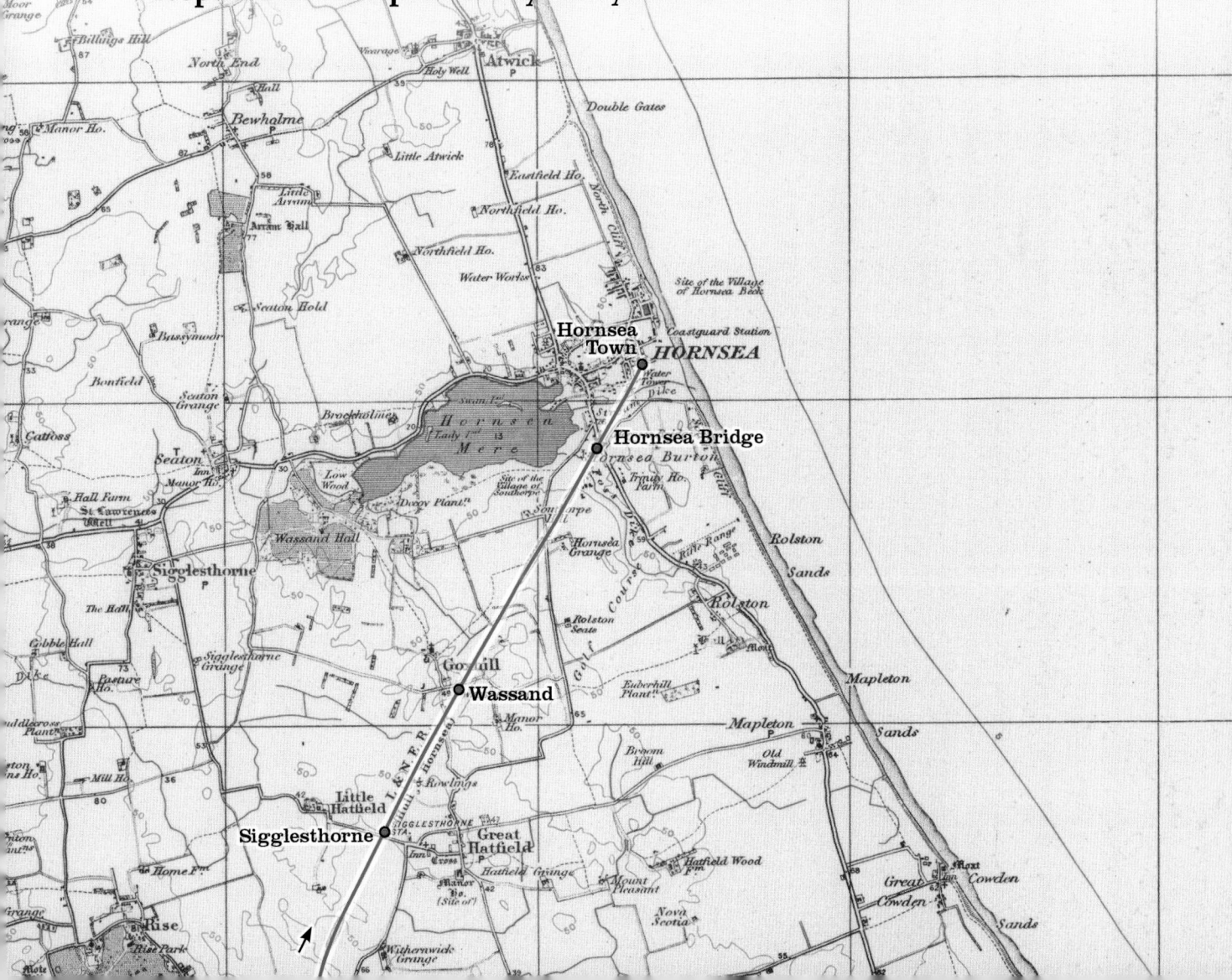

Promoted by local businessman Joseph Wade, who had a vision of turning Hornsea into a thriving seaside resort, the Hull & Hornsea Railway Company received Parliamentary authorization in 1862 to build a 13-mile railway from Wilmington, on the Hull to Withernsea branch line (see pages 214-217), to the small coastal town of Hornsea. The original cost of construction was nearly doubled due to an extension from Hornsea Bridge to the new terminus station close to the seafront – this ½-mile stretch was built on piles due to the boggy nature of the ground. The rest of the single-track line was built across level Holderness countryside – its highest point was only 66 ft above sea level – and opened for traffic in 1864. The North Eastern Railway (NER) worked it from the outset. Intermediate stations were provided at Sutton-on-Hull, Swine, Skirlaugh, Ellerby, Burton Constable, Whitedale, Hatfield (later renamed Sigglesthorne), Goxhill and Hornsea Bridge, although most of these were some distance from the villages they purported to serve.

Goxhill station, renamed Wassand in 1904, was unusual as it was open just for one morning train to Hull and an afternoon service back on market days only.

Services were soon extended into Hull Paragon station and the railway was absorbed by the NER in 1866 before the track was doubled in the early twentieth century. The railway brought vast numbers of day trippers to Hornsea from Hull on summer weekends and within ten years the population of the town had doubled in size. By the twentieth century Hornsea had become a popular seaside resort and a camping coach parked in the station siding was always fully booked during the summer months. Locally generated traffic for commuters working in Hull provided useful all-year-round revenue, with intermediate stations also sending out agricultural produce from local farms. By the summer of 1950 there were eleven trains on weekdays (plus two on Saturdays) between Hull and Hornsea, with twelve (plus two on Saturdays) in the opposite direction. The 'market days

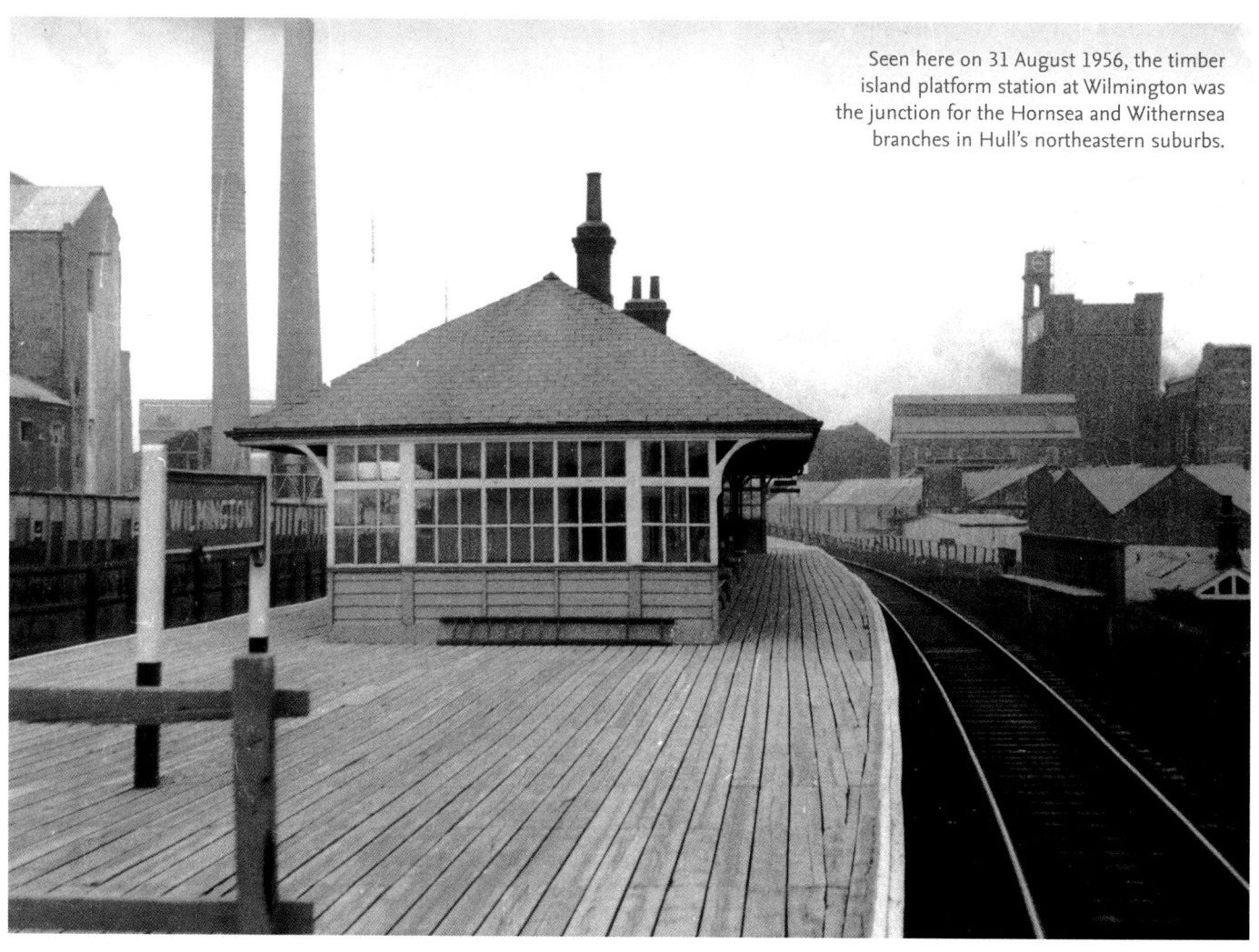

Seen here on 31 August 1956, the timber island platform station at Wilmington was the junction for the Hornsea and Withernsea branches in Hull's northeastern suburbs.

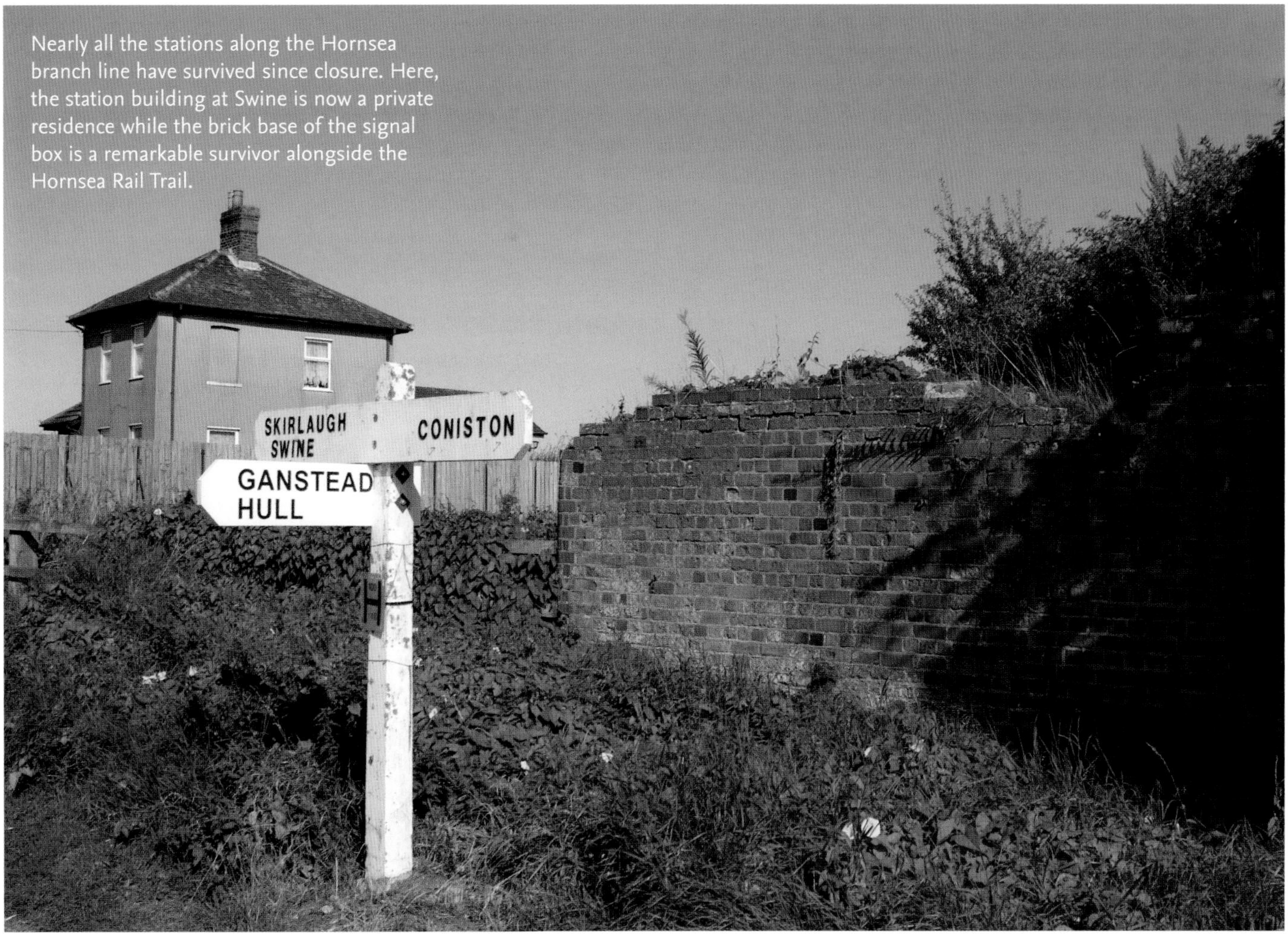

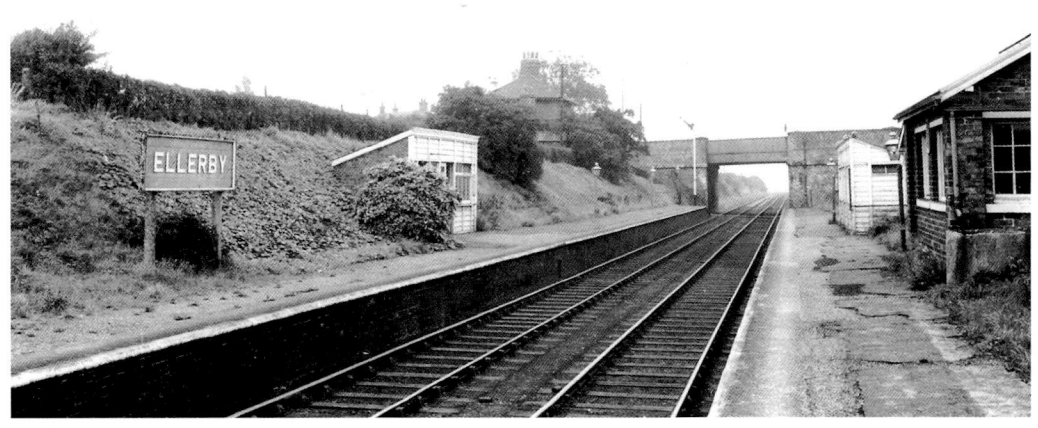

Nearly all the stations along the Hornsea branch line have survived since closure. Here, the station building at Swine is now a private residence while the brick base of the signal box is a remarkable survivor alongside the Hornsea Rail Trail.

only' station at Wassand saw its one-and-only train call on Mondays until 1953. Summer Sundays saw four return services along the line.

By the 1950s, increasing competition from road transport saw passenger numbers declining and the introduction of new diesel multiple units in 1957 failed to stem the tide.

Further cost cutting came in 1960 with stations becoming unstaffed and tickets being issued on the train. Apparently still making a loss, the Hornsea branch was listed for closure in the 1963 'Beeching Report' and despite strong local protests the line closed to passengers on 19 October 1964. Goods trains continued to serve Hornsea Bridge until 3 May 1965.

The ghostly, deserted second station at Ellerby, looking towards Hornsea in 1962. The road overbridge has been infilled since closure but the nearby Railway Inn remains open for business.

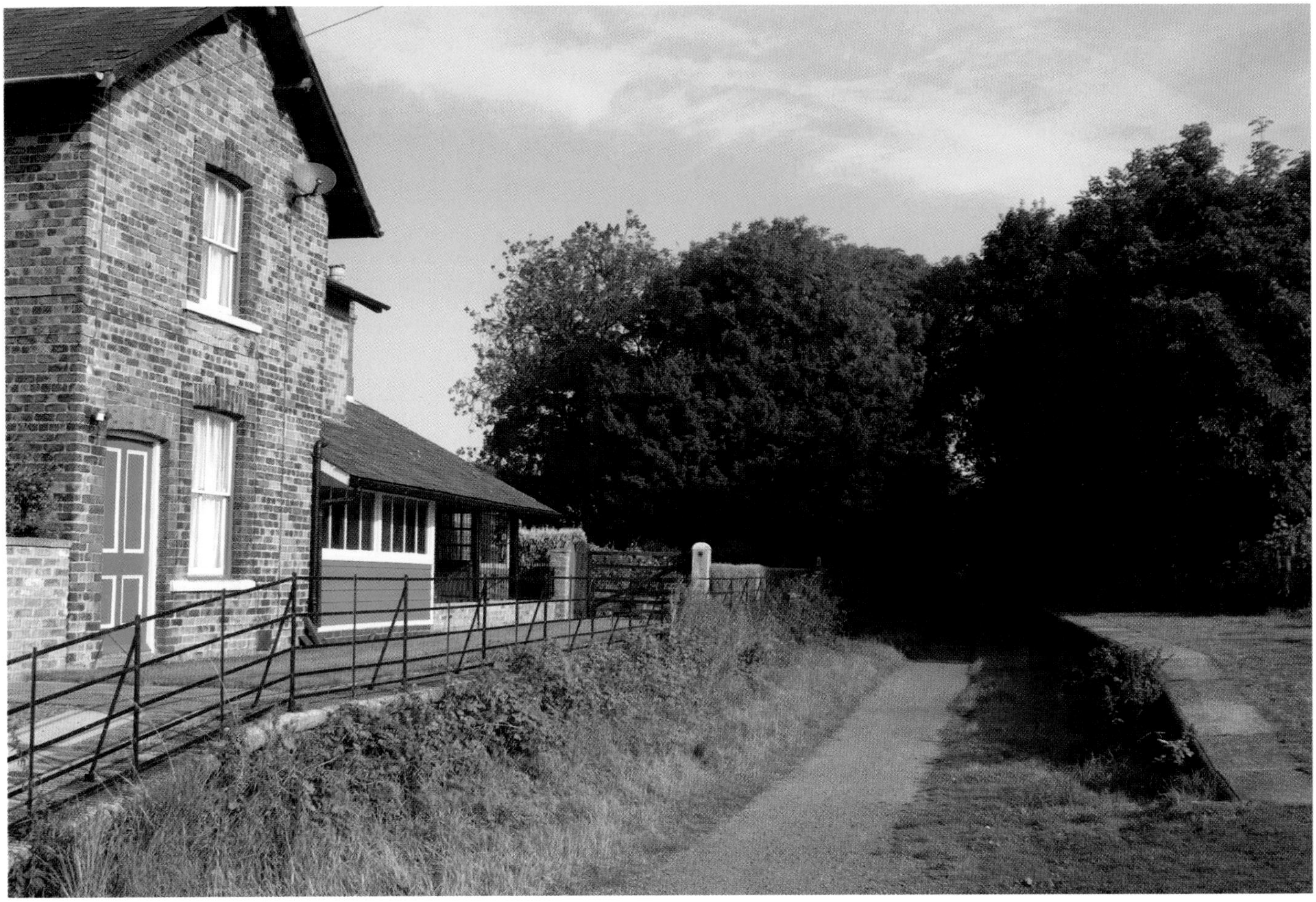

ABOVE: Whitedale station building has been sympathetically restored and is now a private residence as the Hornsea Rail Trail passes between the two platforms.

BELOW: Station staff pass the time of day at Sigglesthorne station in August 1956. The station was originally named Hatfield but was renamed to avoid confusion with other stations of the same name. The staggered platforms either side of the level crossing were common at several of the stations on the Hornsea branch. Today the southbound platform has survived intact alongside the Hornsea Rail Trail, while the station building is now a private residence.

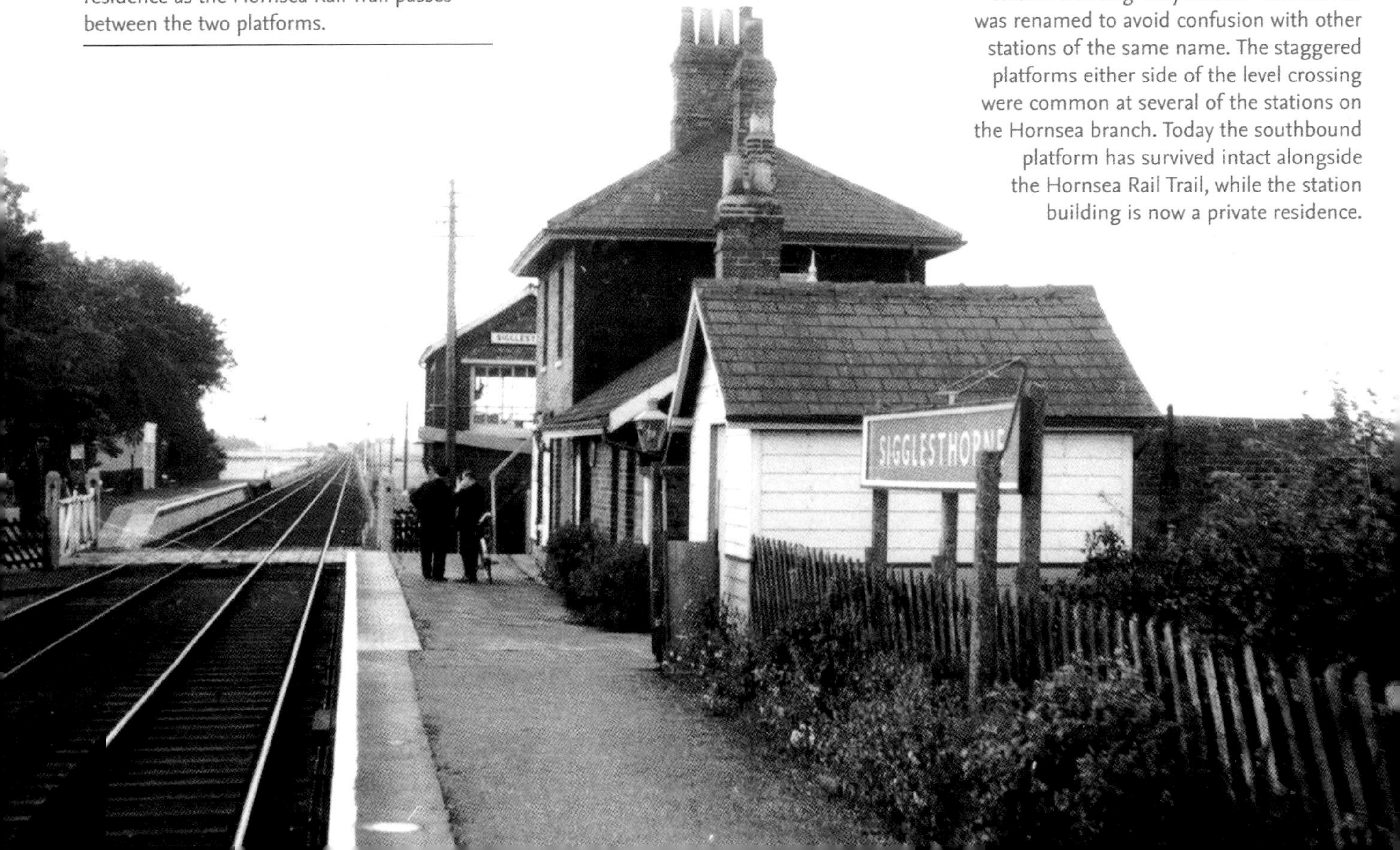

Since closure, almost the entire route of the branch line from Wilmington in Hull to Hornsea has been reopened as a traffic-free footpath and cycleway known as the Hornsea Rail Trail. It also forms part of National Cycle Network Route 65 and the Trans-Pennine Trail.

Although signposted through the streets of Hull as the Trans-Pennine Trail, the off-road section of the Rail Trail starts at Danson Street, about one mile northeast of Hull Paragon station. For the first 2½ miles the Trail heads northwards through the city's suburbs, passing the site of Sutton-on-Hull station en route, which has been landscaped as a children's play area.

The Trail soon reaches open countryside and heads northeast to cross Holderness Drain on a bridge – immediately to the north on the east bank are the earthworks of a prehistoric castle. The Trail then heads across the flat Holderness landscape for 1½ miles to reach the site of Swine station – here the platforms were staggered on either side of a level crossing although only the station building, now a private residence, and the brick base of the signal box have survived. A further 1½ miles from Swine, the Trail crosses the busy A165 to the site of Skirlaugh station, where there is a car park and picnic site in a woodland setting alongside the surviving platforms.

Beyond Skirlaugh, the Trail passes the site of the original Ellerby station which closed in 1902 and is now a private residence, before reaching the village of New Ellerby. Here there is a large car park on the station site – the station was originally named Burton Constable but was renamed Ellerby in 1922. Although there is no sign of the station

building the platform edge can be seen hidden in the undergrowth. The road overbridge here has been blocked up, requiring a short detour up and across the road to rejoin the old railway route. Refreshments can be taken at the adjacent Railway Inn.

The next station along the Trail is at Whitedale, where the beautifully restored station building and its two platforms patiently wait for the next train, which will sadly never arrive. Now following a dead-straight line towards Hornsea through tranquil Holderness farmland, the Trail reaches Sigglesthorne station where the concrete up platform is still in remarkably good condition – the down platform and station building (also a private residence) are on the opposite side of the road which was once guarded by a level crossing. The station was originally named Hatfield but was renamed Sigglesthorne in 1874, despite the fact that its namesake village lies some three miles to the northwest!

From Sigglesthorne the level and straight Trail continues towards Hornsea passing the 'market days only' station of Wassand, now a private residence. It was originally named Goxhill but was renamed in 1904 and closed to passengers in 1953. Continuing northeastwards, the Trail enters a long cutting before passing the site of the demolished Hornsea Bridge station and ending in style at the superbly restored red-brick Hornsea Town station. Although the elegant canopy and platforms have long gone, the station buildings are now used for housing. In front of the station there is a paved area with a modern sculpture celebrating the end (or start) of the Trans-Pennine Trail from Southport. Car parking and the delights of Hornsea seafront are but a short distance away.

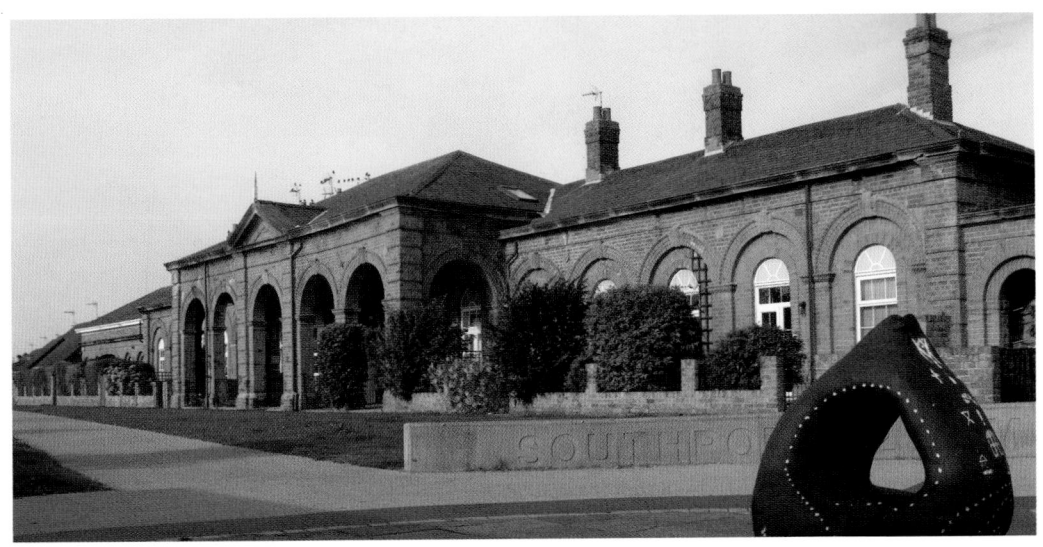

The attractive red-brick station building at Hornsea has been restored as private residences while in the foreground a piece of modern sculpture marks the start of the Trans-Pennine Trail to Southport.

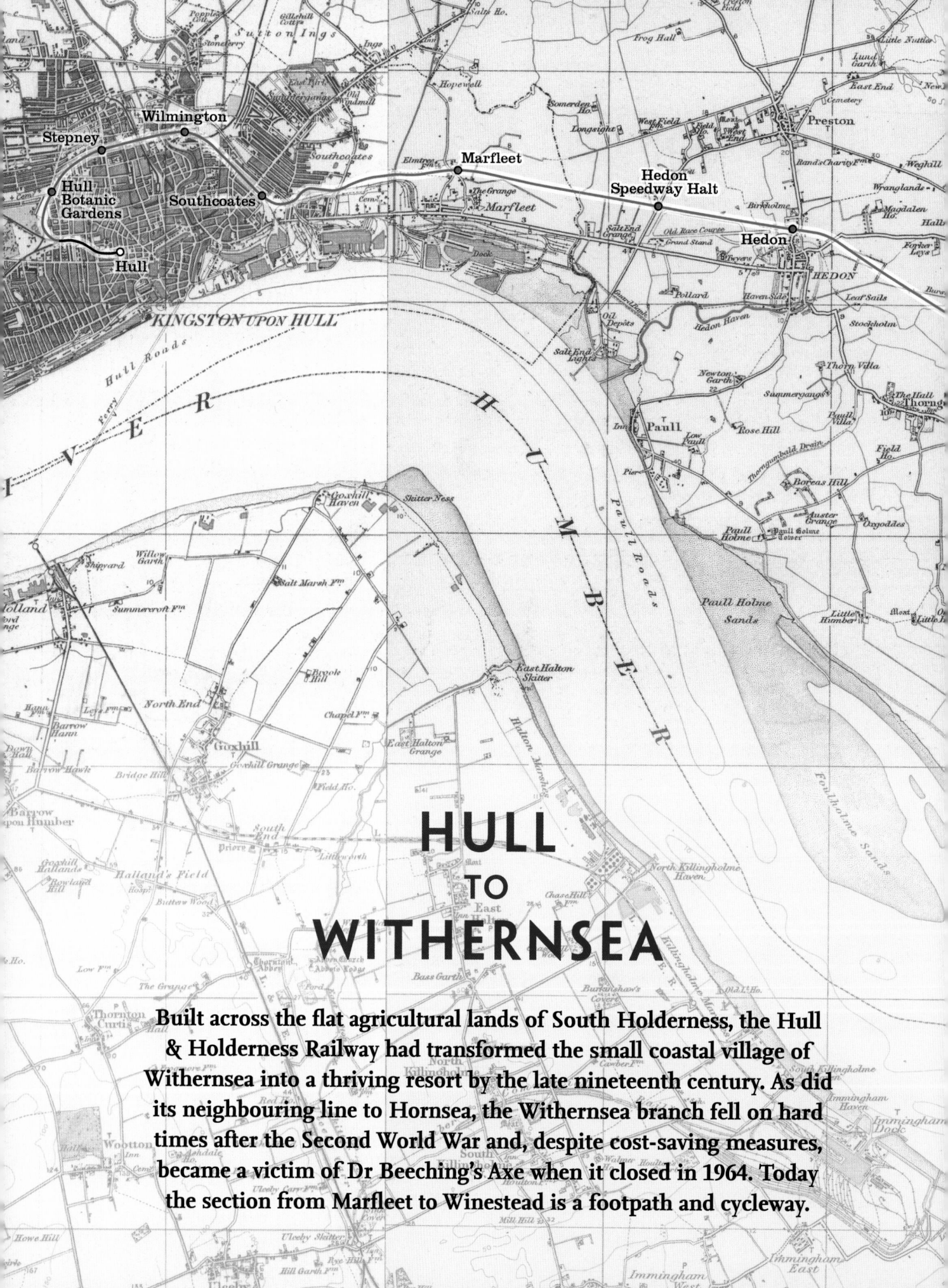

Stepney

Wilmington

Hull
Botanic
Gardens

Southcoates

Hull

Marfleet

Hedon
Speedway Halt

Hedon

KINGSTON UPON HULL

HULL
TO
WITHERNSEA

Built across the flat agricultural lands of South Holderness, the Hull
& Holderness Railway had transformed the small coastal village of
Withernsea into a thriving resort by the late nineteenth century. As did
its neighbouring line to Hornsea, the Withernsea branch fell on hard
times after the Second World War and, despite cost-saving measures,
became a victim of Dr Beeching's Axe when it closed in 1964. Today
the section from Marfleet to Winestead is a footpath and cycleway.

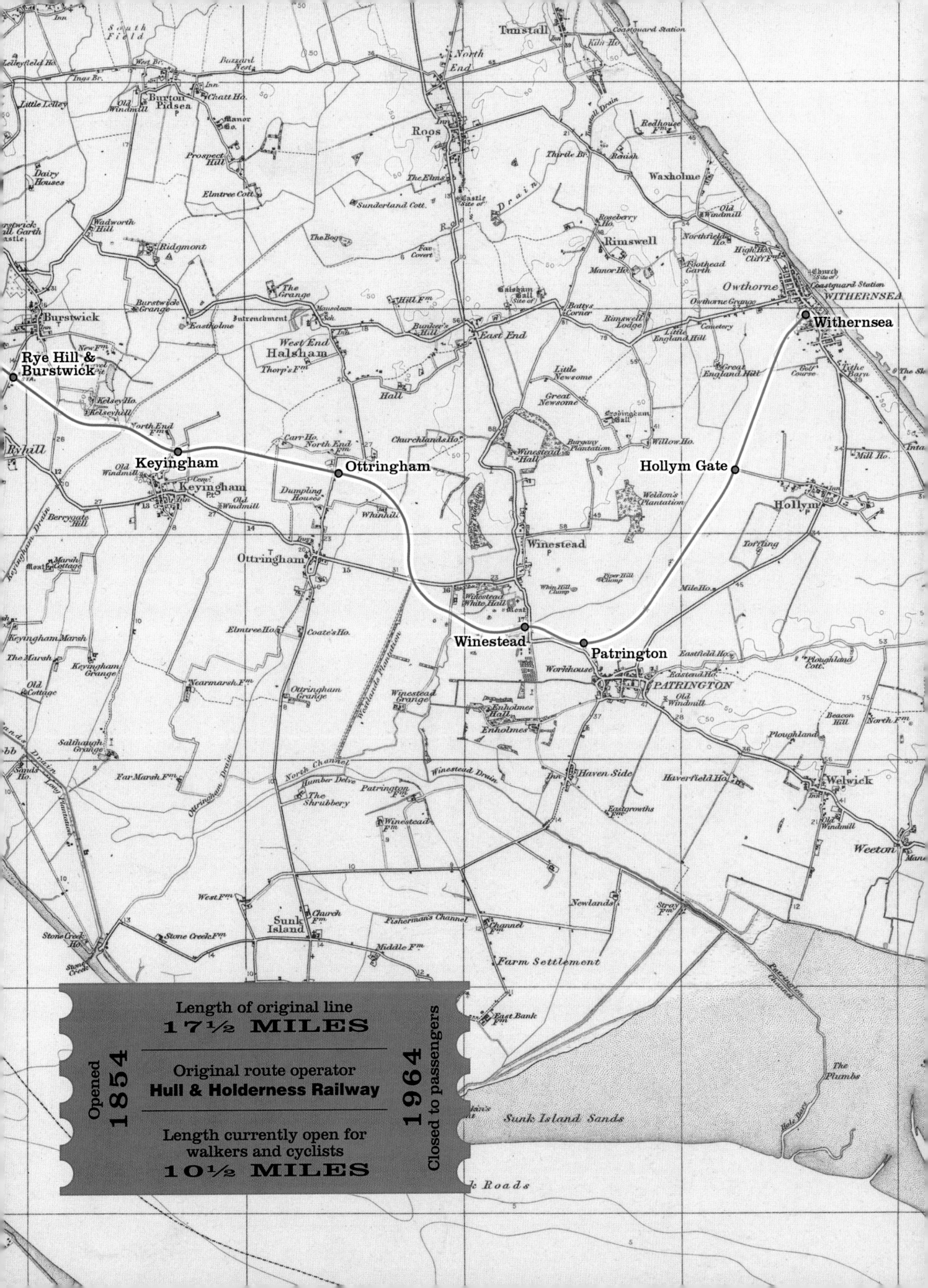

Tunstall

Coastguard Station

North End

Roos

Rimswell

Waxholme

Owthorne

WITHERNSEA

Withernsea

Burstwick

**Rye Hill &
Burstwick**

Keyingham

Ottringham

Halsham

Hollym Gate

Hollym

Winestead

Winestead

Patrington

PATRINGTON

Welwick

Weeton

Sunk Island

Sunk Island Sands

Length of original line
17½ MILES

Original route operator
Hull & Holderness Railway

Length currently open for
walkers and cyclists
10½ MILES

Opened
1854

1964
Closed to passengers

Promoted by a local businessman not only to link the agricultural lands of South Holderness with the port of Hull but also – with a great leap of faith – to develop the tiny village of Withernsea into a seaside holiday resort, the Hull & Holderness Railway received Parliamentary authorization in 1853. Construction across the flat landscape was rapid and the 17½-mile single-track line opened a year later. Intermediate stations were provided at Marfleet, Hedon, Rye Hill & Burstwick, Keyingham, Ottringham, Winestead, Patrington and Hollym Gate. The railway was totally independent, with its own locomotives and rolling stock, but shared Victoria Dock station in Hull with the York & North Midland Railway for a short time until the latter withdrew.

The North Eastern Railway worked the line from 1860 until taking it over two years later. A new curve was opened in 1864 allowing Withernsea branch trains to use the Hull Paragon terminus. Increasing traffic along the line led to three sections being doubled in the early twentieth century – Hull to Hedon, Rye Hill to Ottringham and Winestead to Withernsea. Winestead station closed to passengers in 1904 and there were also short-lived halts provided at Hedon Racecourse and, from 1948, at Hedon Speedway.

Before the coming of the railway, the village of Withernsea had a population of around 100 but within ten years this had dramatically increased (it is now nearly 6,000) and by the end of the nineteenth century hotels, guest houses, a promenade and a pier

had been built to provide all the amenities that Victorian visitors required. The bracing North Sea air and sandy beaches made it a popular destination for visitors from the industrial towns of Yorkshire until the outbreak of the Second World War.

With increasing competition from road transport and the changing habits of holidaymakers, the post-war years saw a decline in passenger numbers. Once carried by rail, the transportation of agricultural produce from the South Holderness farms was also lost to more flexible and cheaper lorry operations – the pattern was being repeated across Britain with branch lines such as this running at an ever-increasing loss.

The 1950 summer timetable shows a healthy frequency of trains running between Hull and Hornsea: on weekdays there were eleven (plus four more on Saturdays) to Withernsea and twelve (plus four on Saturdays) in the opposite direction; on Sundays there were five in each direction. The penultimate station on the line at remote Hollym Gate closed in 1953.

Economies such as introducing diesel multiple units in 1957 and issuing tickets on the trains in 1960 failed to halt the losses and the line was listed for closure in the 1963 'Beeching Report'. The end came on 19 October 1964 when passenger services were withdrawn, although goods traffic continued to Withernsea until 3 May 1965 after which the line was cut back to Hedon – this last section closed in 1968.

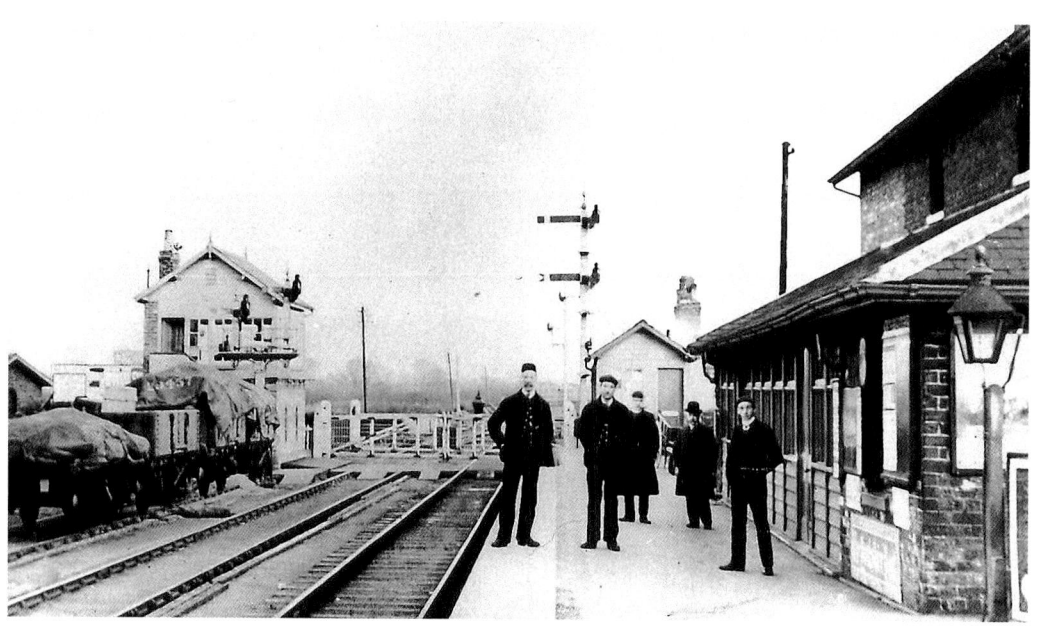

The station staff at Hedon pose for this photograph taken in the early twentieth century. The station buildings, platform and goods shed all survive today while the trackbed is now a footpath.

RIGHT: The railway path from Marfleet to Winestead passes between the platforms at Rye Hill station where the station building is now a private residence.

Today much of the trackbed of the Withernsea branch is a footpath and cycleway. Although the path begins to the east of Marfleet its level course from here – passing depressing industrial complexes en route – to Hedon is not particularly inspiring. Hedon itself makes a good starting point. Here there is a car park and the station building, platform and goods shed have all survived albeit with different uses. From Hedon the path heads southeast for two miles along the northern outskirts of the village and into flat South Holderness countryside to reach Rye Hill & Burstwick station, where the station building and platform have been lovingly restored as a private residence. Half-a-mile along the lane to the north is the Hare & Hounds pub in the village of Burstwick. Resuming its eastward journey, the railway path soon reaches the site of a level crossing over an unclassified road, in the side of which short lengths of double-track rails are still embedded.

A mile further east the path reaches Keyingham station, now a private residence, (from here it is but a short walk into the village for refreshments at the Bluebell Inn) followed by a further mile to Ottringham station. Here there is plenty to interest lovers of lost railways with a short length of rail, concrete level crossing post and the rotting gate hanging on its rusty iron hinge. Across the road lies the station building (now a private residence), platforms, goods shed and small red-brick goods office.

From Ottringham the path heads off south, crossing the busy A1033 on the level before ending near Winestead station, now a private residence. Although the station closed to passengers in 1904 it remained open for goods traffic until 1956 – amazingly one pair of rotting wooden level-crossing gates still hangs precariously from its concrete posts alongside the busy road.

The railway footpath and cycleway currently end near Winestead and the next station site at Patrington is a scrap metal yard. The last three miles of the trackbed to Withernsea is now a farm track but at journey's end there is no trace of the terminus station and its attractive platform canopy, which was demolished to make way for a police station and supermarket in the 'enlightened' 1990s. All that remains of this long-lost railway is the stable block of the also-demolished Station Hotel. Nearby, the delights of Withernsea, in the shape of fish and chip shops, amusement arcades, castellated pier entrance (there is no pier now) and a Cold War nuclear bunker beckon the weary traveller.

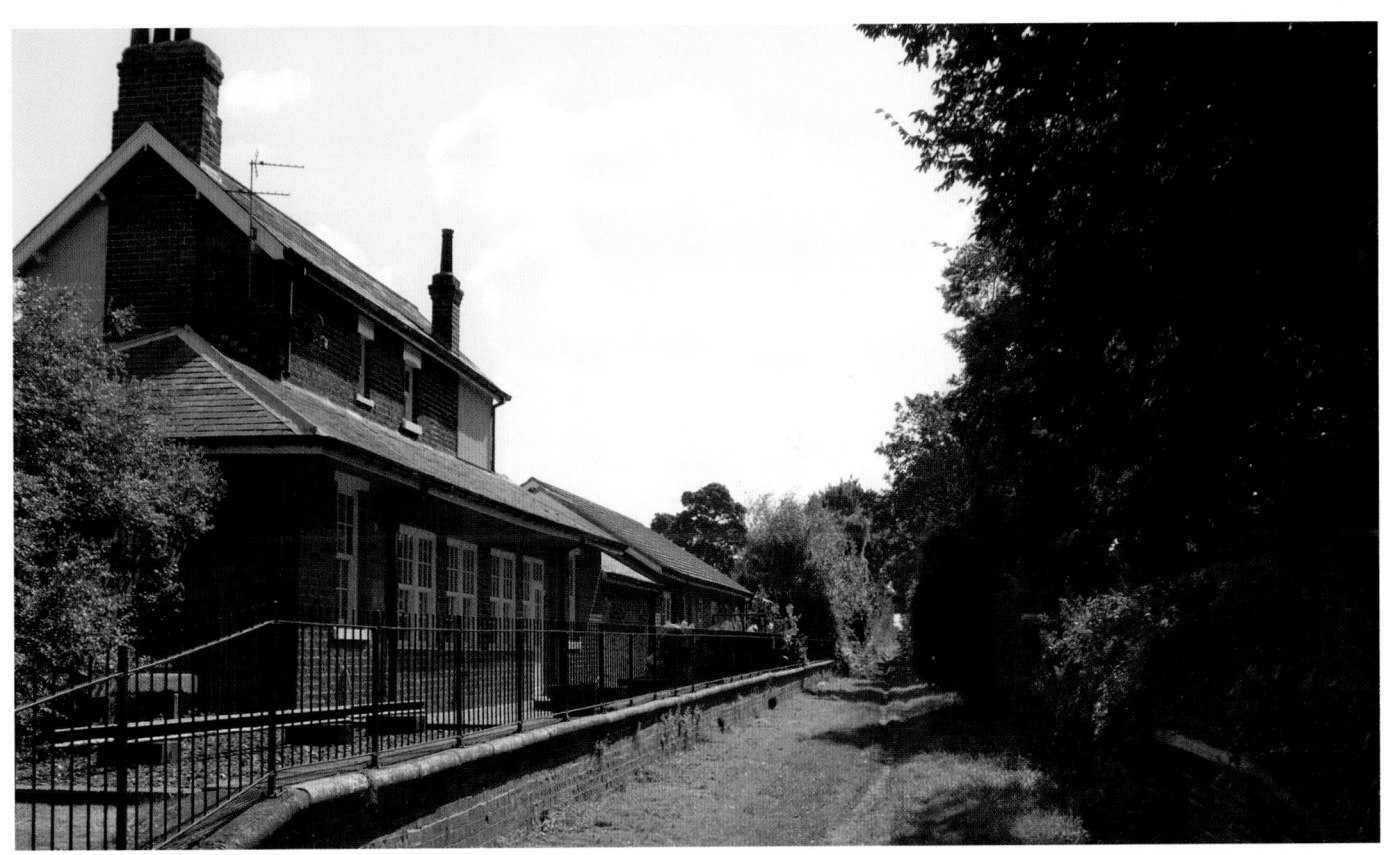

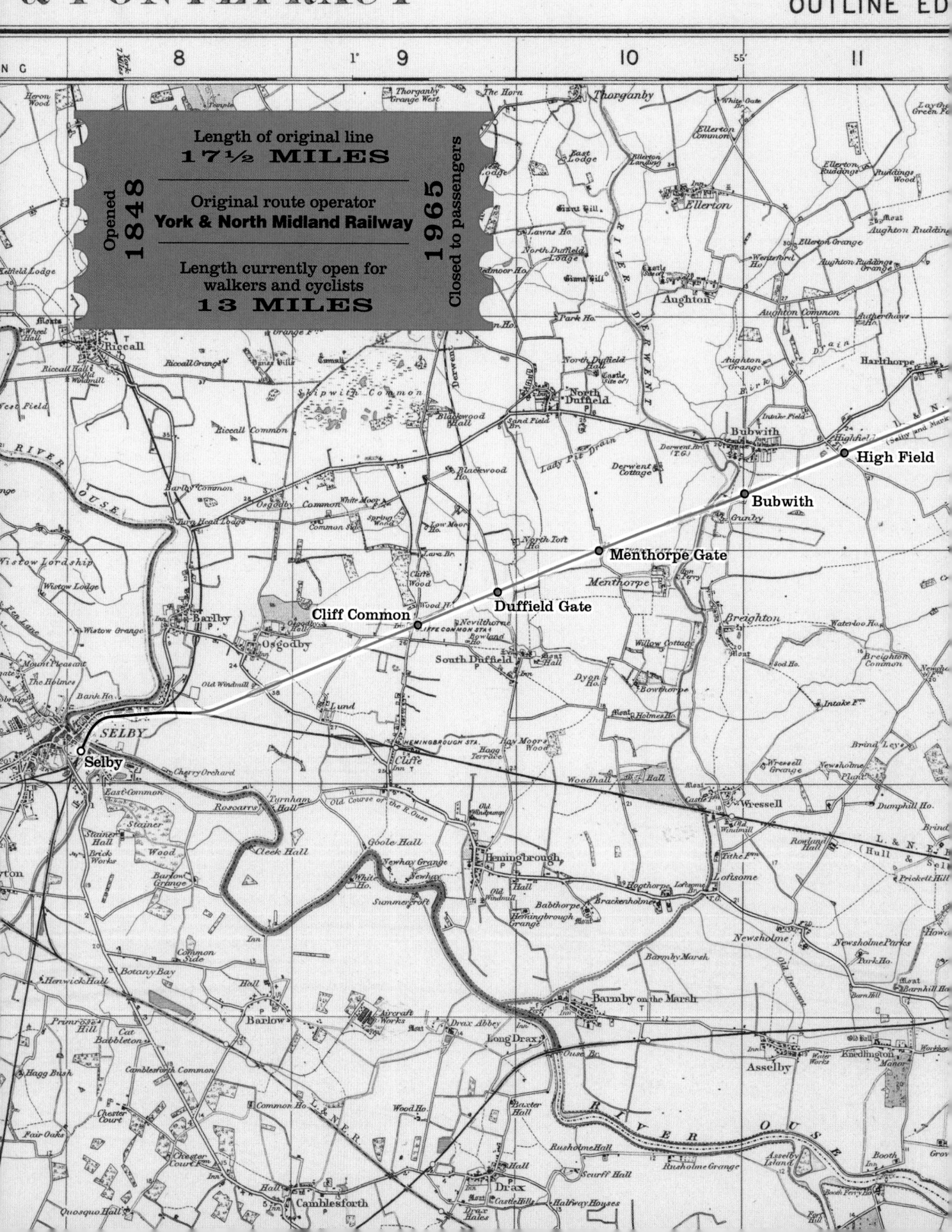

Length of original line
17½ MILES

Original route operator
York & North Midland Railway

Length currently open for
walkers and cyclists
13 MILES

Opened
1848

1965
Closed to passengers

High Field

Bubwith

Menthorpe Gate

Duffield Gate

Cliff Common

Selby

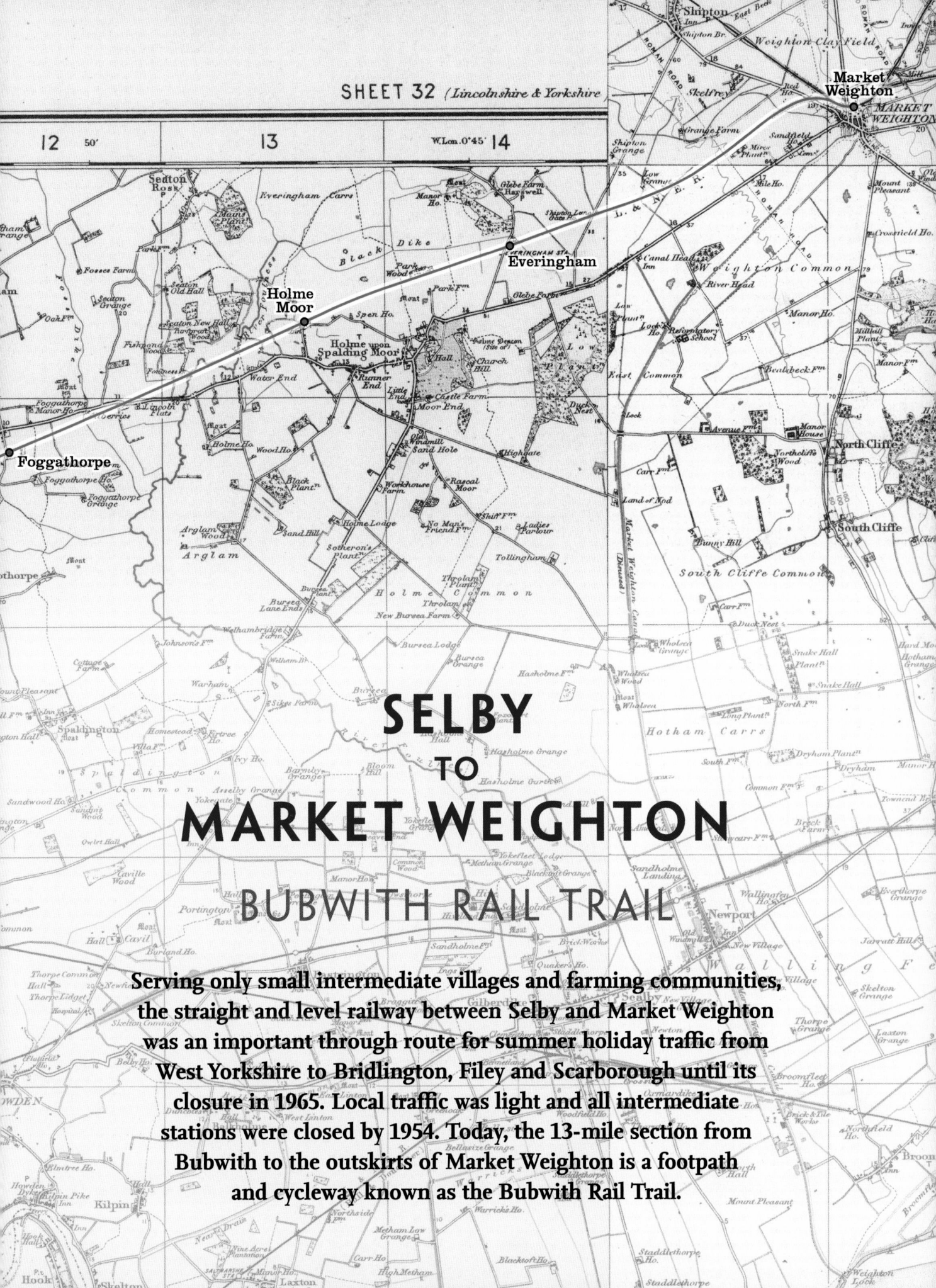

SELBY
TO
MARKET WEIGHTON

BUBWITH RAIL TRAIL

Serving only small intermediate villages and farming communities,
the straight and level railway between Selby and Market Weighton
was an important through route for summer holiday traffic from
West Yorkshire to Bridlington, Filey and Scarborough until its
closure in 1965. Local traffic was light and all intermediate
stations were closed by 1954. Today, the 13-mile section from
Bubwith to the outskirts of Market Weighton is a footpath
and cycleway known as the Bubwith Rail Trail.

To ward off incursions into East Yorkshire by a rival proposal, George Hudson's York & North Midland Railway (Y&NMR) received Parliamentary authorization in 1846 to build a 17½-mile single-track railway between Selby and the town of Market Weighton. With no major engineering features to speak of, the fairly level route was opened in 1848. Intermediate stations were provided at Cliff Common, Menthorpe Gate, Bubwith, High Field, Foggathorpe, Holme Moor and Everingham.

At Market Weighton the railway from Selby met the Y&NMR's line from York, which had opened in 1847. The North Eastern Railway (NER) extended this to Beverley in 1865 (see pages 222-227). Market Weighton became a railway crossroads in 1890 when the Scarborough, Bridlington & West Riding Junction Railway opened its 13¼-mile route between the town and Driffield. The opening of this line allowed through trains to run between the West Yorkshire conurbations, such as Leeds, and the resorts of Bridlington, Filey and Scarborough via Selby and Market Weighton. The Selby to Market Weighton line was doubled in 1890.

In 1913 Cliff Common station became a junction for the newly opened Derwent Valley Light Railway to Layerthorpe in York – this delightful privately owned agricultural line was closed in stages between 1965 and 1981.

Serving only small villages and farming communities, the Selby to Market Weighton route generated little local traffic but was useful as part of a cross-country corridor between West and East Yorkshire – local services were provided by steam railmotors from the 1920s until the Second World War. By the summer of 1950 the line and its intermediate stations were served by only three return services on weekdays. In addition there was one Leeds-Bridlington working via Selby, which only stopped at Market Weighton. The line came to life on summer Saturdays, however, with trains from Sheffield, Leeds, Chesterfield, Bradford, Leicester, Worcester, Manchester and Liverpool all packed with holidaymakers heading for the fleshpots of Bridlington, Butlins Holiday Camp at Filey and Scarborough. Together with an equally heavy flow of return traffic travelling in the opposite direction, the signalmen and crossing keepers (there were twenty-two level crossings!) on the line were kept very busy from early morning to early evening.

While Menthorpe Gate station closed in December 1953, the remaining intermediate stations between Selby

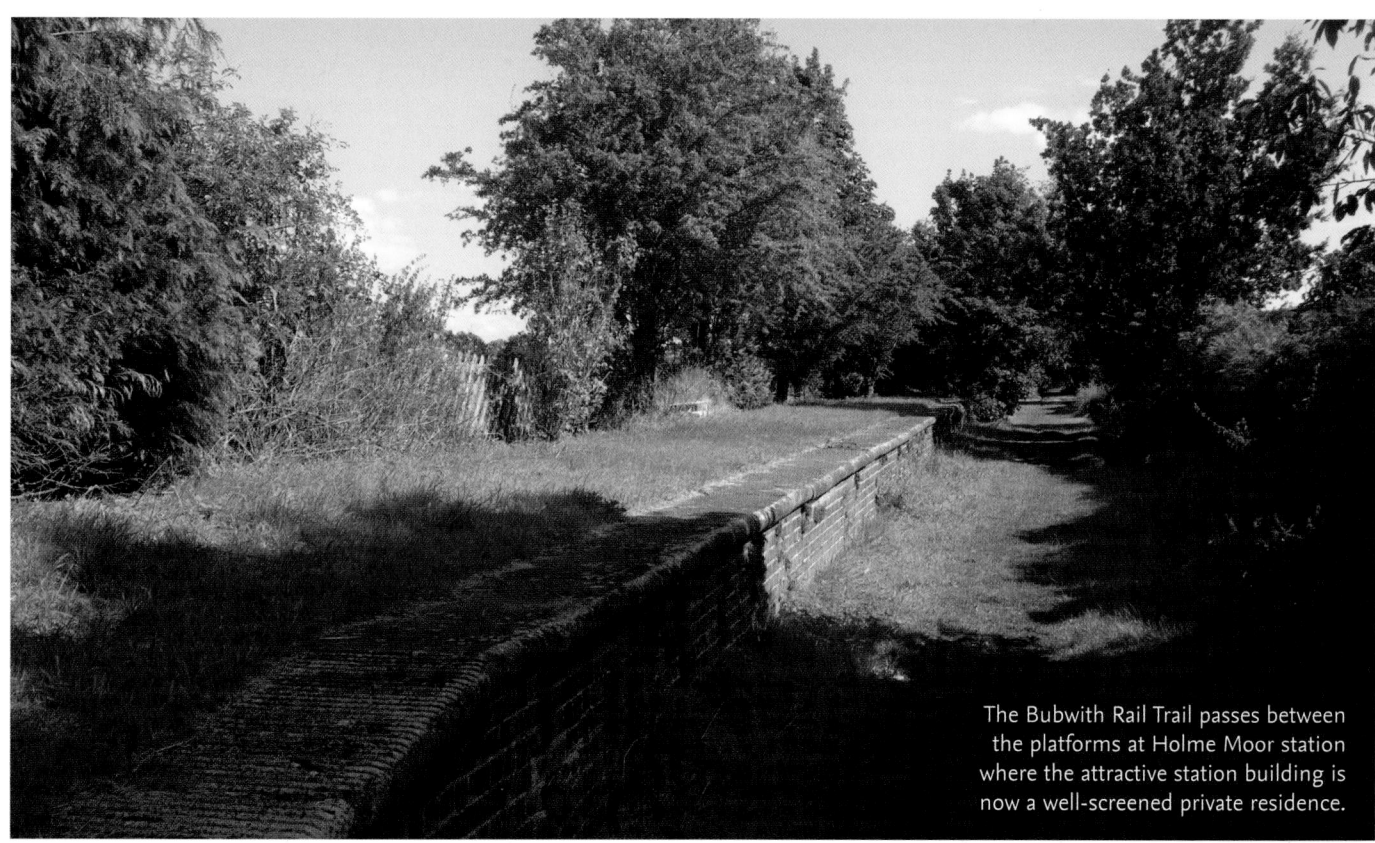

The Bubwith Rail Trail passes between the platforms at Holme Moor station where the attractive station building is now a well-screened private residence.

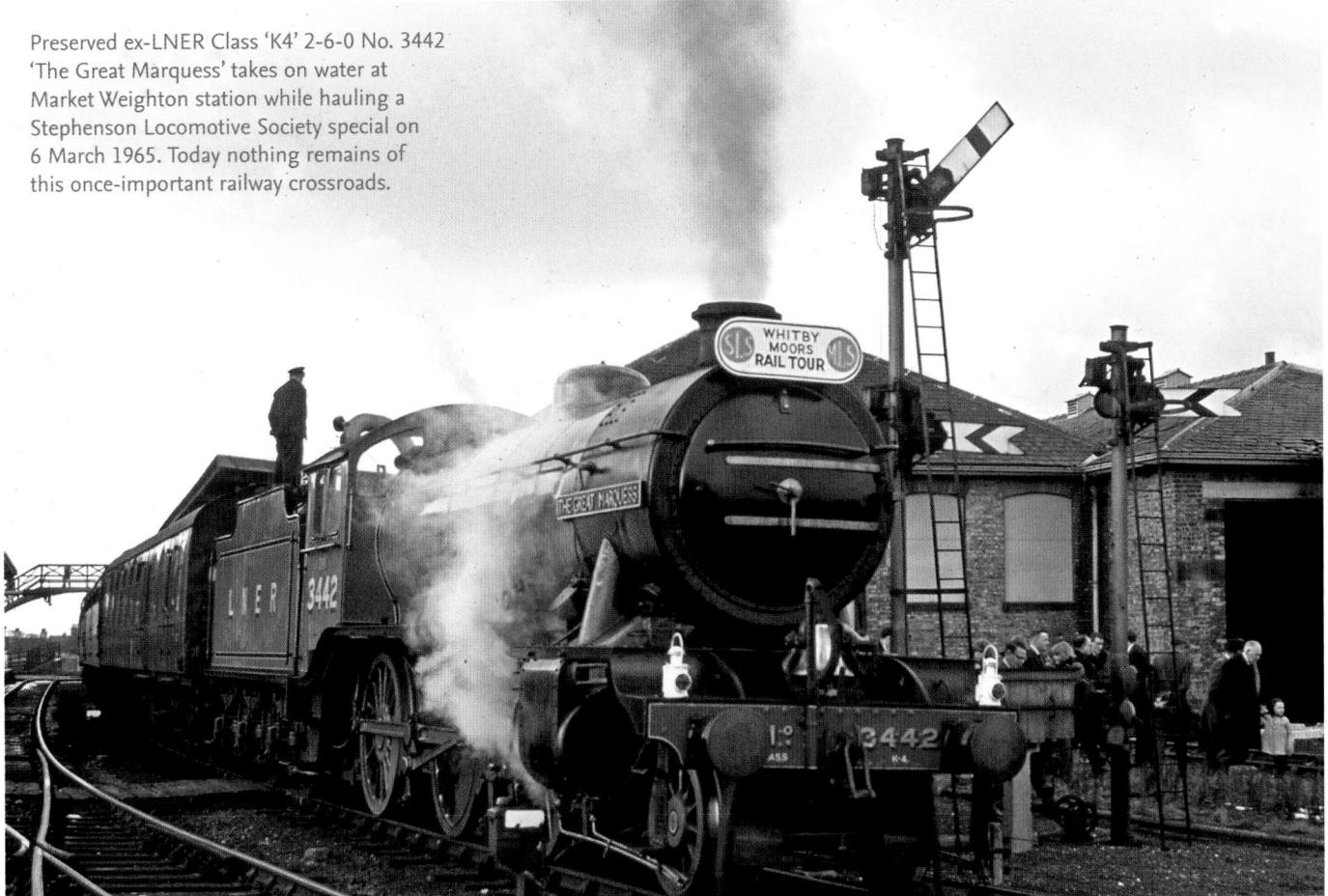

Preserved ex-LNER Class 'K4' 2-6-0 No. 3442 'The Great Marquess' takes on water at Market Weighton station while hauling a Stephenson Locomotive Society special on 6 March 1965. Today nothing remains of this once-important railway crossroads.

and Market Weighton were closed to passengers on 20 September 1954. The line was kept open for through trains during the summer months until 14 June 1965, when the Market Weighton to Driffield line also closed. Goods services to Holme Moor and Everingham continued until complete closure on 2 August 1965.

🚂🚂🚂🚂🚂🚂🚂🚂🚂🚂🚂🚂

Since closure the 13-mile section of the railway from Bubwith to the outskirts of Market Weighton has been reopened as a footpath and cycleway known as the Bubwith Rail Trail. To the west of Bubwith the station buildings at Cliff Common and Duffield Gate are now private residences but the railway bridge over the River Derwent near Bubwith has been demolished.

The Bubwith Rail Trail starts on the east bank of the River Derwent at the village of Bubwith, where there is still much evidence of this lost railway – the stationmaster's house and ticket office are now a private residence while the overgrown platforms

and fencing can be discerned in the undergrowth alongside the Trail. From here the Trail, which can be rather muddy at times, heads eastwards, straight as a die to the outskirts of Market Weighton, passing sleepy villages on its level route through the countryside. Nearly all the stationmasters' attractive houses have survived, with those at High Field (once named Bubwith High Field), Holme Moor and Everingham (Grade II listed) now private residences. Surrounded by high fences, the latter has been beautifully restored and extended. There is a small car park for Trail users at Everingham, where lost railway sleuths will be pleased to find the cast-iron base of a crane that has survived the ravages of time. All the station platforms along the line also survive but are gradually being taken over by encroaching undergrowth and saplings.

The Trail ends two miles short of Market Weighton on the A163. Convenient watering holes along the Trail are the White Swan in Bubwith, the Black Swan at Foggathorpe and Ye Olde Red Lion at Holme.

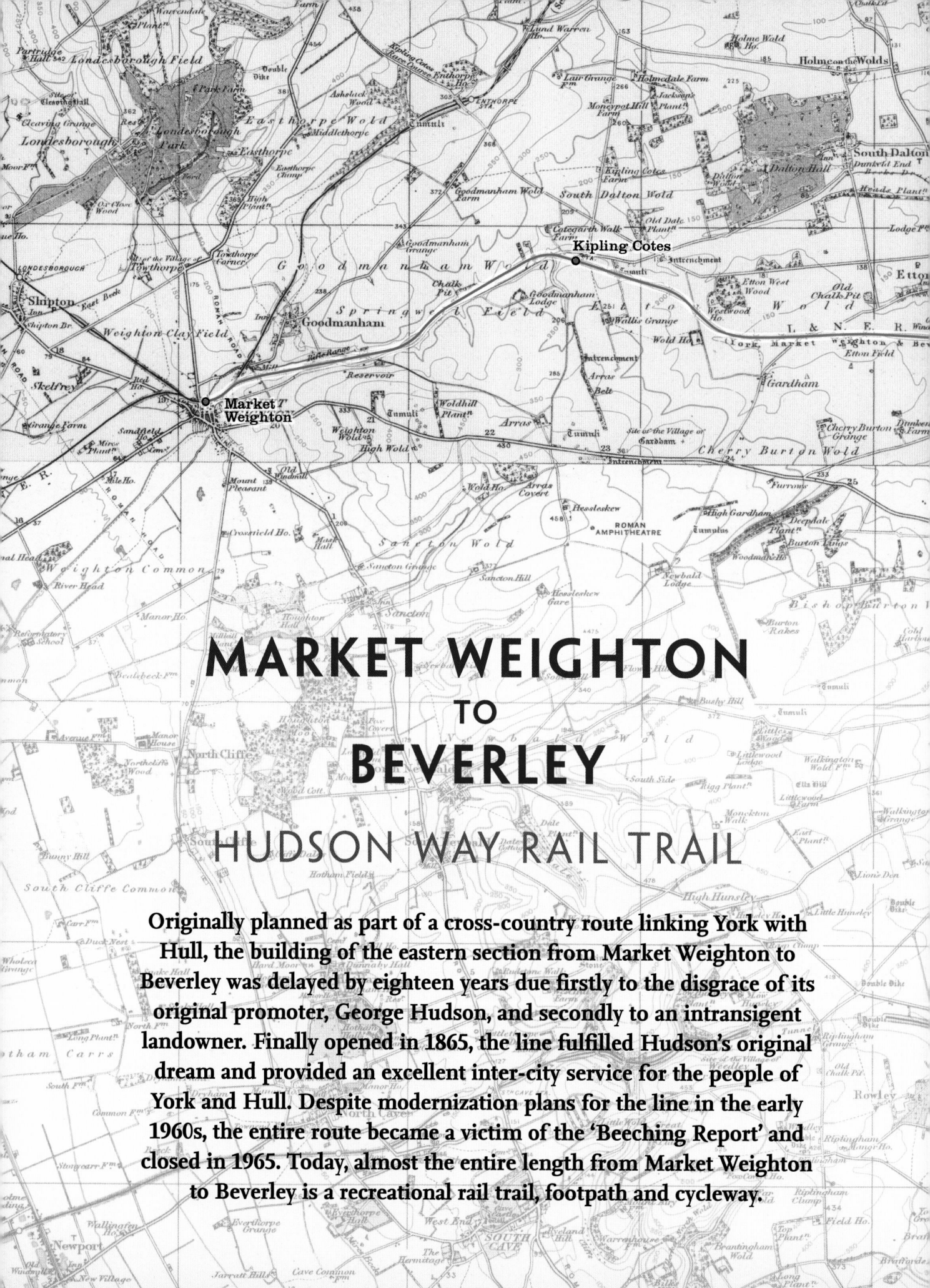

MARKET WEIGHTON
TO
BEVERLEY

HUDSON WAY RAIL TRAIL

Originally planned as part of a cross-country route linking York with Hull, the building of the eastern section from Market Weighton to Beverley was delayed by eighteen years due firstly to the disgrace of its original promoter, George Hudson, and secondly to an intransigent landowner. Finally opened in 1865, the line fulfilled Hudson's original dream and provided an excellent inter-city service for the people of York and Hull. Despite modernization plans for the line in the early 1960s, the entire route became a victim of the 'Beeching Report' and closed in 1965. Today, almost the entire length from Market Weighton to Beverley is a recreational rail trail, footpath and cycleway.

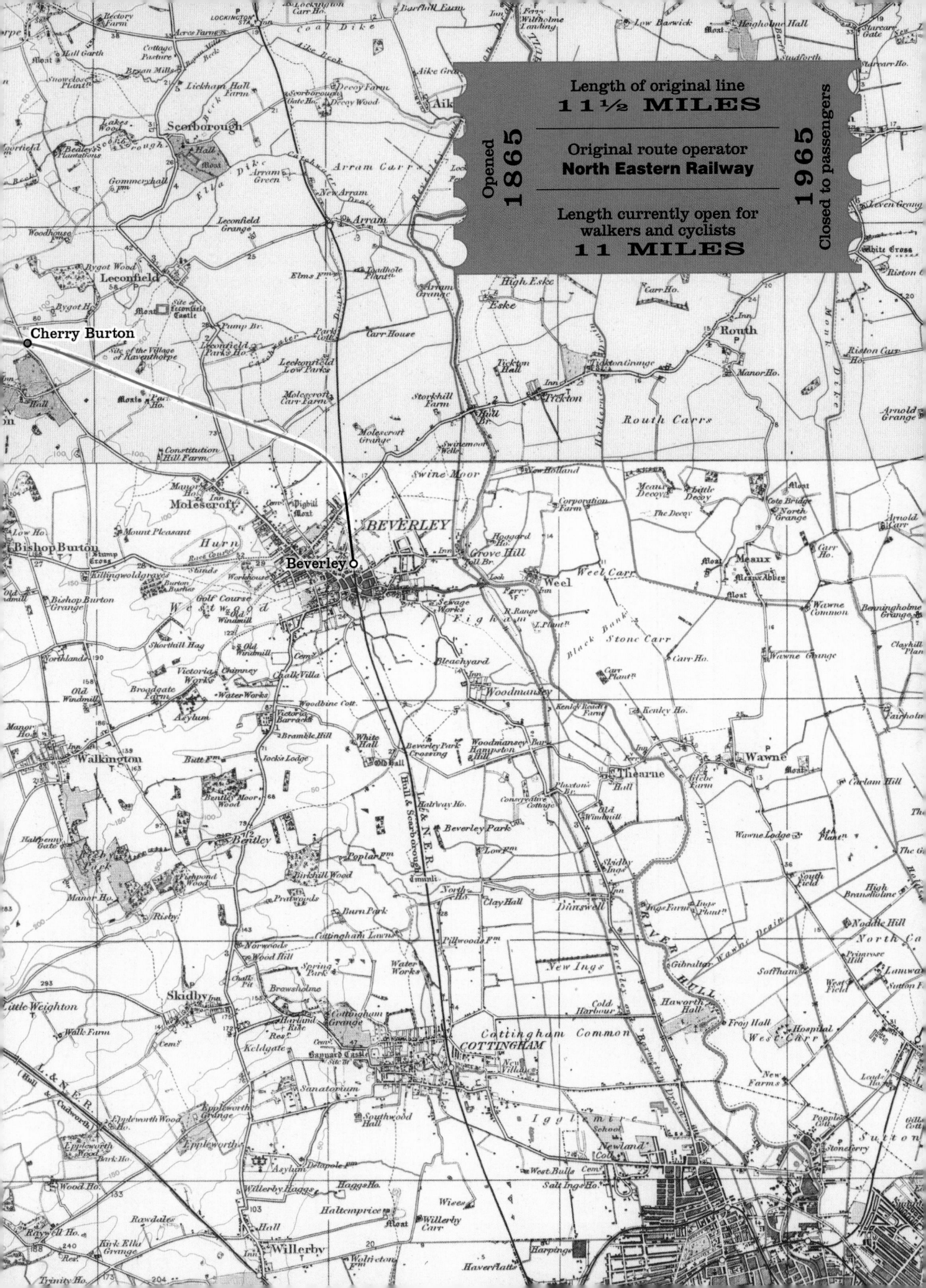

Cherry Burton

Beverley

The 11½-mile railway between Market Weighton and Beverley had begun life as a proposal by George Hudson's York & North Midland Railway Company for a railway linking York and Hull. The mercurial Hudson had already bought the Londesborough Estate near Market Weighton in 1845 and the proposed railway would pass through his grounds. Authorization for the 32-mile double-track line and the purchase of several canals between Bootham Junction, north of York, and Beverley, on the Y&NMR's line from Hull to Scarborough, came in 1846. With intermediate stations at Earstwick, Warthill, Stamford Bridge, Fangfoss, Pocklington, Nunburnholme and Londesborough, the 20½ miles of line between Bootham Junction and Market Weighton opened in 1847. A private station for George Hudson was also opened at Londesborough Park. The noted railway architect George Townsend Andrews (1804-1855) designed the stations along this route, as well as those at Beverley and Hull Paragon. The Y&NMR's single-line railway from Selby to Market Weighton opened in 1848 (see page 218).

Easterly progress beyond Market Weighton came to an abrupt halt however, owing to Hudson's disgrace amidst a financial scandal involving another of his railways. Hudson resigned in 1849 and the Y&NMR became part of the North Eastern Railway (NER) in 1854. With the NER in the driving seat, the single-line extension from Market Weighton to Beverley was next in line for construction but this was delayed by several years due to disputes with local MP and landowner, Lord Beaumont Hotham – after an army career, in which he fought at the Battle of Waterloo, he owned much of the land over which the railway was due to be built. A compromise was eventually reached between his lordship and the NER, with Hotham getting his own station at Kiplingcotes to serve the family seat at nearby Dalton Hall. The other part of the agreement was that trains would not run on the Sabbath.

With all the problems now resolved, and with intermediate stations at Kiplingcotes and Cherry Burton, the NER opened the Market Weighton line in 1865 and immediately started running through trains along the

A diesel multiple unit from Hull heads off towards York as the level crossing gates open at the west end of Market Weighton station on 1 May 1964. The station building at Market Weighton was designed by George Townsend Andrews. Following closure of the line to Beverley in 1965 it lay neglected until it was demolished in 1979. Apart from a few concrete gate posts nothing remains today.

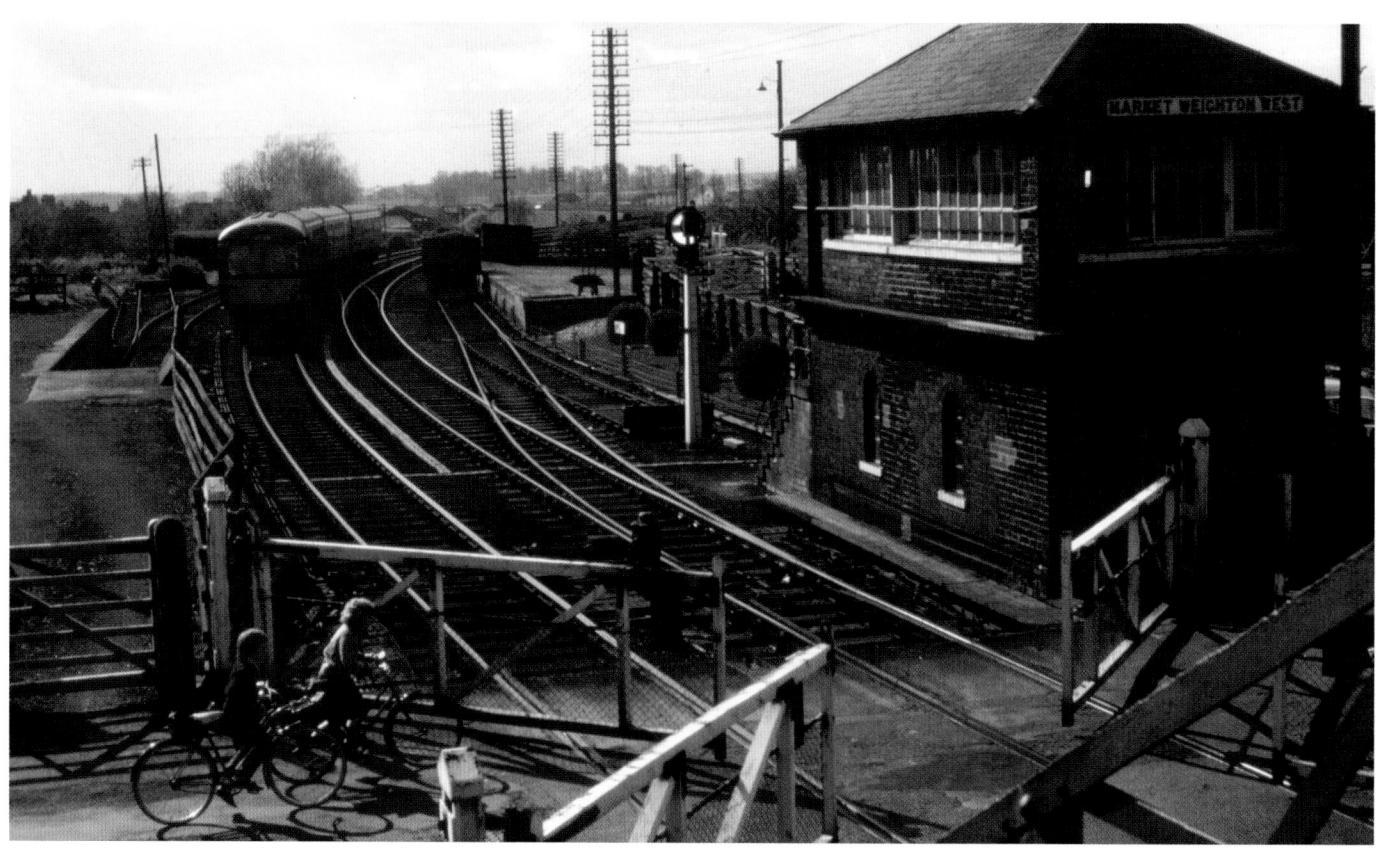

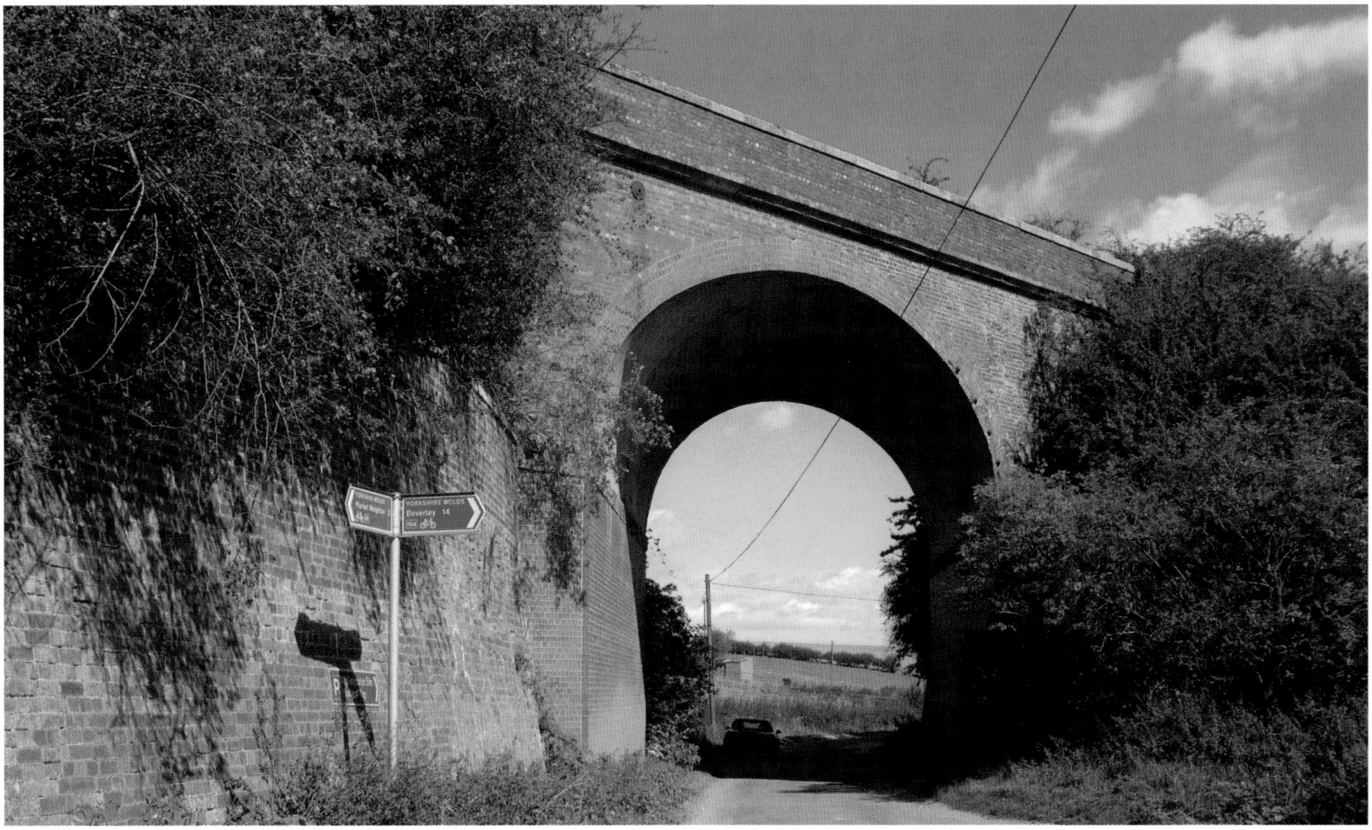

The Hudson Way Rail Trail approaches Kiplingcotes station over this graceful red-brick skewed arched bridge. Below, National Cycle Network Route 164 makes its way along quiet country roads on its route through the Yorkshire Wolds.

entire route between York and Hull. Meanwhile the ruined George Hudson had sold Londesborough Hall in 1849 to a banker who became the Earl of Londesborough. The private station serving the Hall had little use and was closed in 1867. The Market Weighton to Beverley line was doubled in 1889 and the former town became a railway crossroads in 1890 when a 13¼-mile line to Driffield was opened.

Apart from the closure of a few intermediate stations in 1959, the entire route still saw a healthy service of passenger trains into the 1960s. Diesel multiple units were introduced for some services and even in the summer of 1961 there were nine trains in each direction on weekdays. In that year the route was earmarked for Central Traffic Control, which involved singling of track, automatic level crossings and installing modern signalling. Contracts were signed and work had started when British Railways suddenly pulled the plug on the work at the beginning of 1962 – just over a year later all four railways converging on Market Weighton were listed for closure in the 'Beeching Report'. The argument made by BR for closure was that passengers travelling between York and Hull could still use the existing (albeit longer) route via Selby, and despite strong objections the line closed on 29 November 1965.

The station master and his wife pose for the camera in this early twentieth century photograph of Kiplingcotes station. This remote station was originally built for the use of local landowner Lord Hotham, who lived at nearby Dalton Hall, in exchange for allowing the railway to be built through his land. The platforms, station building, goods shed and signalbox all survive today alongside the Hudson Way Rail Trail.

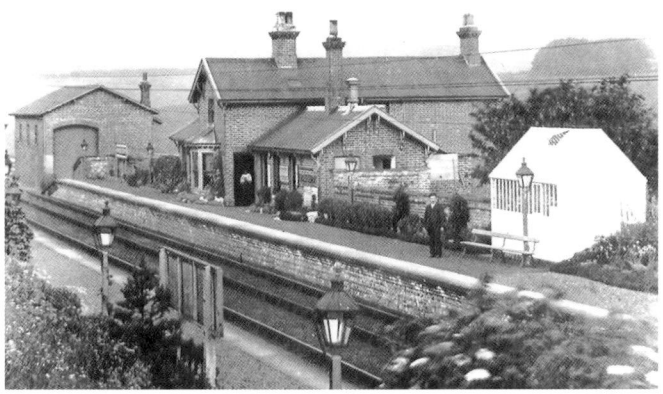

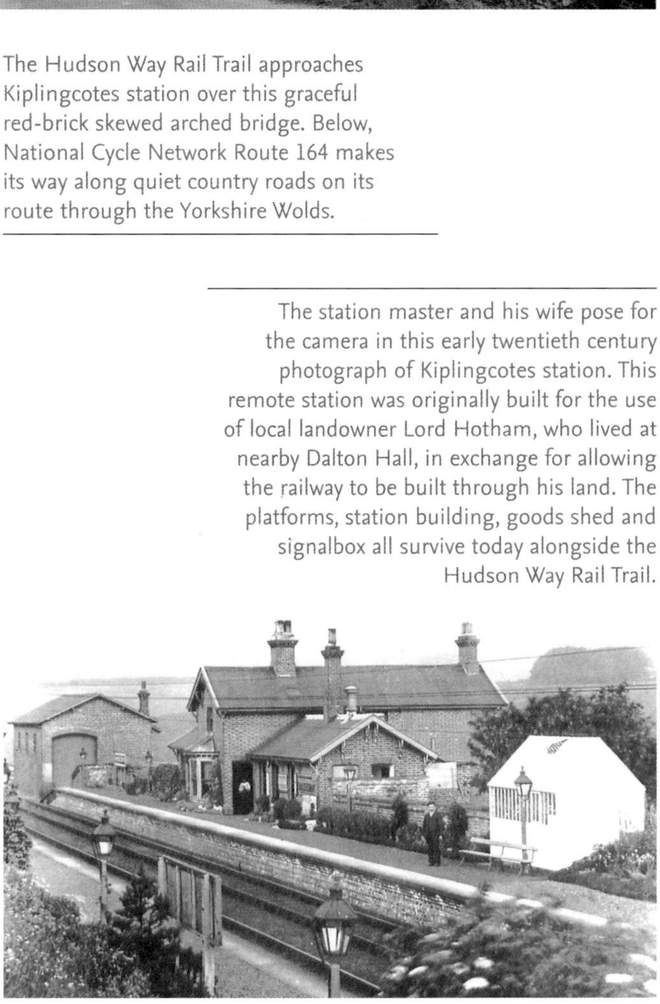

Following closure, East Riding County Council purchased the 11½ miles of railway trackbed between Market Weighton and Beverley in 1971 as a recreational nature trail. It has since been reopened as a footpath and cycleway known as the Hudson Way Rail Trail and it also forms part of the Wilberforce Way Long Distance Path.

The Trail starts at the site of Market Weighton station, which was demolished after years of neglect in 1979 – only two railway cottages remain although the concrete posts for the level crossing and pedestrian side gate have survived the developers! The nearly five-acre site is leased by Market Weighton Town Council and managed as an open space known as the Monkey Run.

Heading east, the Trail passes the former junction of the railway to Driffield before passing under a brick overbridge where a footpath leads to St Helen's Well, one of Yorkshire's most sacred wells. Two miles along the Trail from Market Weighton lies the Kiplingcotes Chalk Pit nature reserve which is administered by the Yorkshire Wildlife Trust and is a favourite haunt for bird watchers.

Heading through the gently undulating Yorkshire Wolds, the Trail passes over a graceful red-brick arched bridge before entering remote Kiplingcotes station, 3¾ miles from Market Weighton, where there is a car park. Built originally for Lord Hotham of nearby Dalton Hall, the station building, platforms, station nameboard, goods shed and signal box have all survived, albeit with different uses – the signal box is now an information centre run by the Yorkshire Wolds Heritage Trust. National Cycle Network Route 164 passes along country lanes half a mile to the west of the station.

Continuing eastwards for another four miles through the peaceful and unspoilt Wolds' landscape, the Trail alternately runs along the top of embankments and through cuttings spanned by road overbridges before reaching Cherry Burton station. Now a private residence,

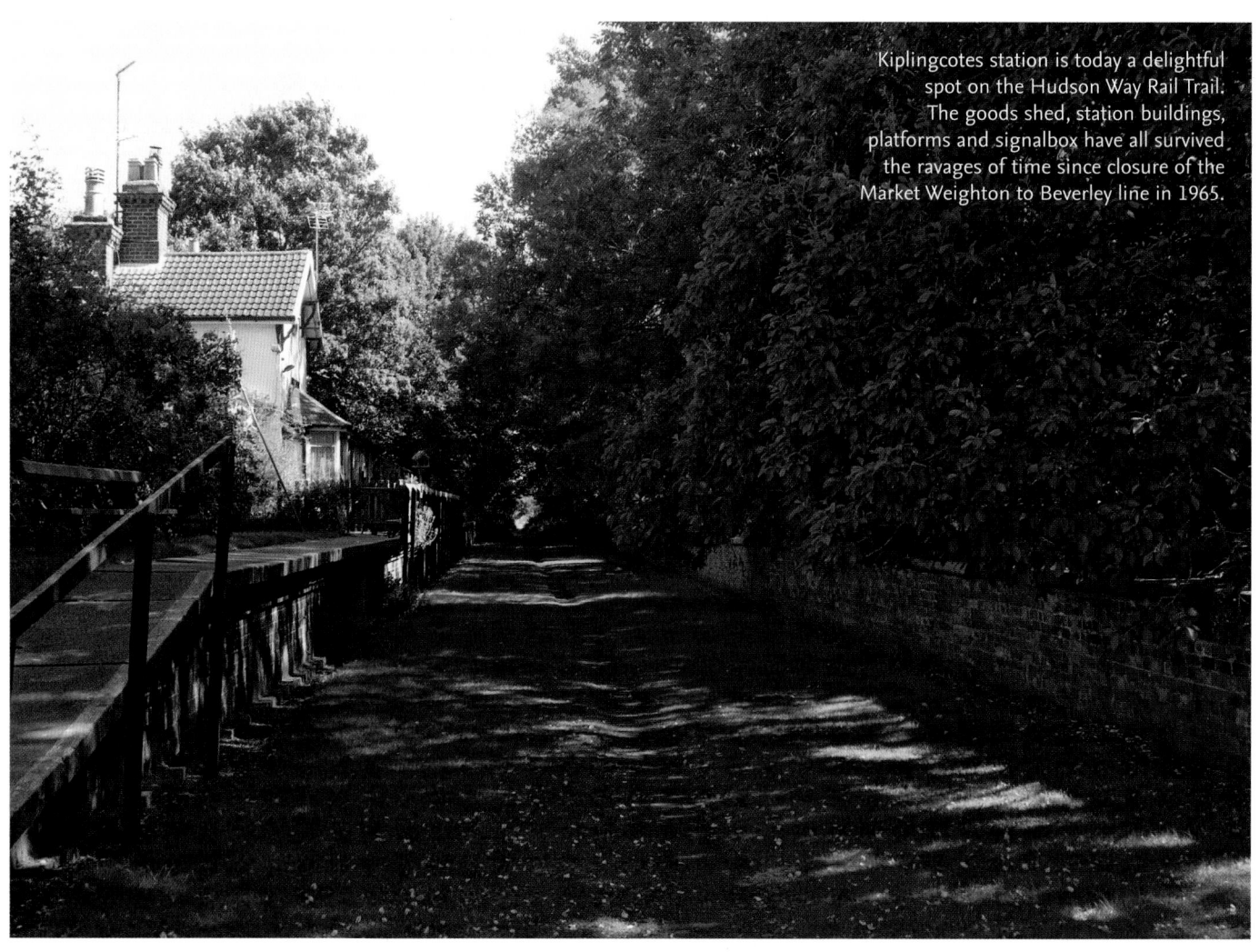

Kiplingcotes station is today a delightful spot on the Hudson Way Rail Trail. The goods shed, station buildings, platforms and signalbox have all survived the ravages of time since closure of the Market Weighton to Beverley line in 1965.

the station was closed in 1959 and is about half a mile north of the attractive village that it once served, which is also home to the Bay Horse pub.

From Cherry Burton the Trail runs in a straight line for nearly three miles to the outskirts of Beverley – here there is a car park for walkers and cyclists off the A1035 town bypass. Historic Beverley with its magnificent Minster, unspoilt town centre and plethora of real-ale pubs is well worth exploring, but the *pièce de résistance* must surely be the superbly restored railway station which is served by trains running between Hull and Bridlington. Now also home to a very upmarket restaurant, the station and its glorious train shed was designed by G T Andrews and opened by George Hudson's York & North Midland Railway in 1846. A visit to this Grade II listed building is a must!

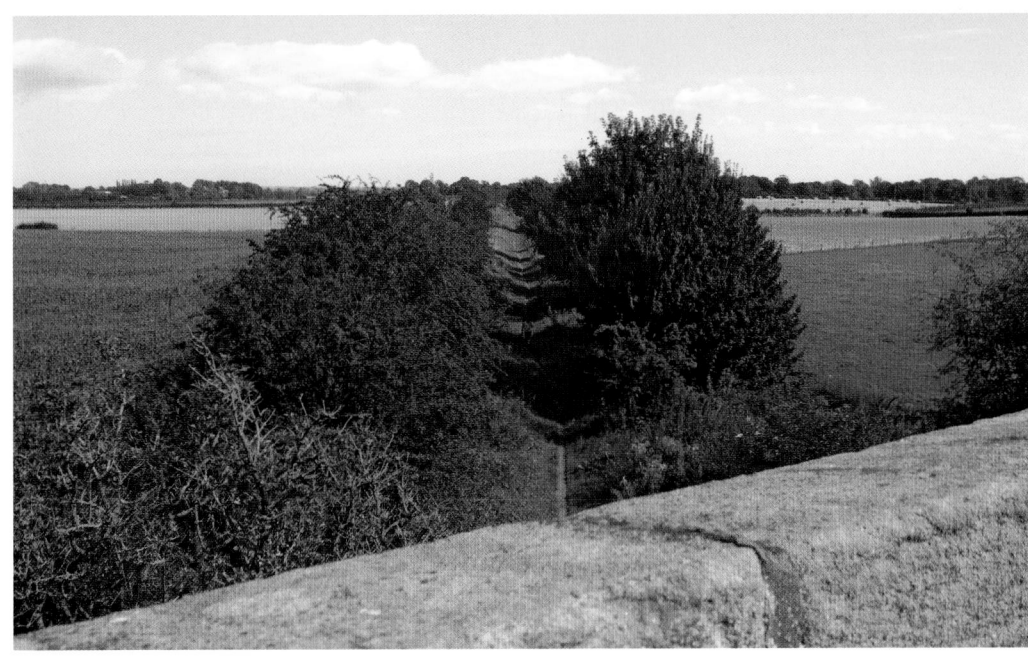

The Rail Trail continues eastward from Kiplingcotes station, passing through cuttings, along the top of embankments and under road overbridges towards Cherry Burton station.

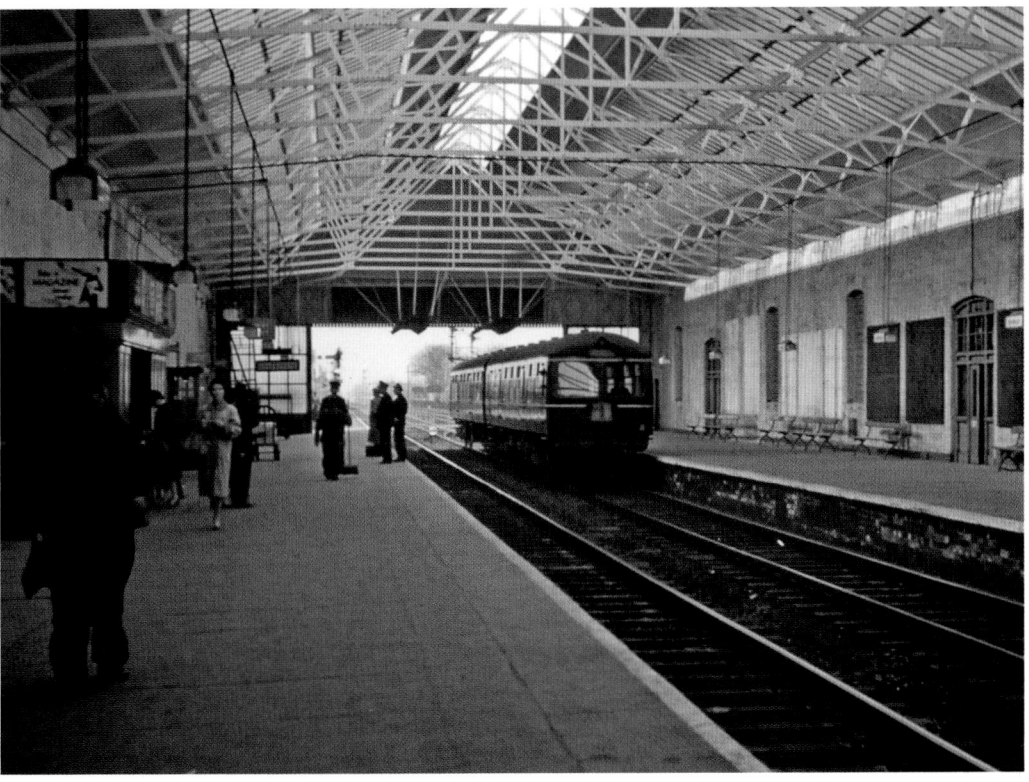

A diesel multiple unit bound for Hull calls at Beverley station in the early 1960s. The station is still open today and is served by trains running between Hull and Bridlington. Designed by George Townsend Andrews, the grand overall-roofed building has recently been superbly restored and is also home to an upmarket restaurant.

LOW MOOR
TO
DEWSBURY (THORNHILL)
SPEN VALLEY GREENWAY

The Lancashire & Yorkshire Railway's route along the heavily industrialized Spen Valley to the south of the 'wool capital' of Bradford remained an important artery for both passenger and freight traffic for over 100 years. Decline set in after the Second World War, with the southern section between Heckmondwike and Thornhill losing its passenger service at the beginning of 1962. The remaining section between Low Moor and Mirfield soldiered on until it, too, lost its passenger service in 1965. Freight services continued on the northern section from Low Moor to Heckmondwike until 1981 and at the southern end from Thornhill to Liversedge until 1990. Since closure almost the entire route has been reopened as a footpath and cycleway known as the Spen Valley Greenway.

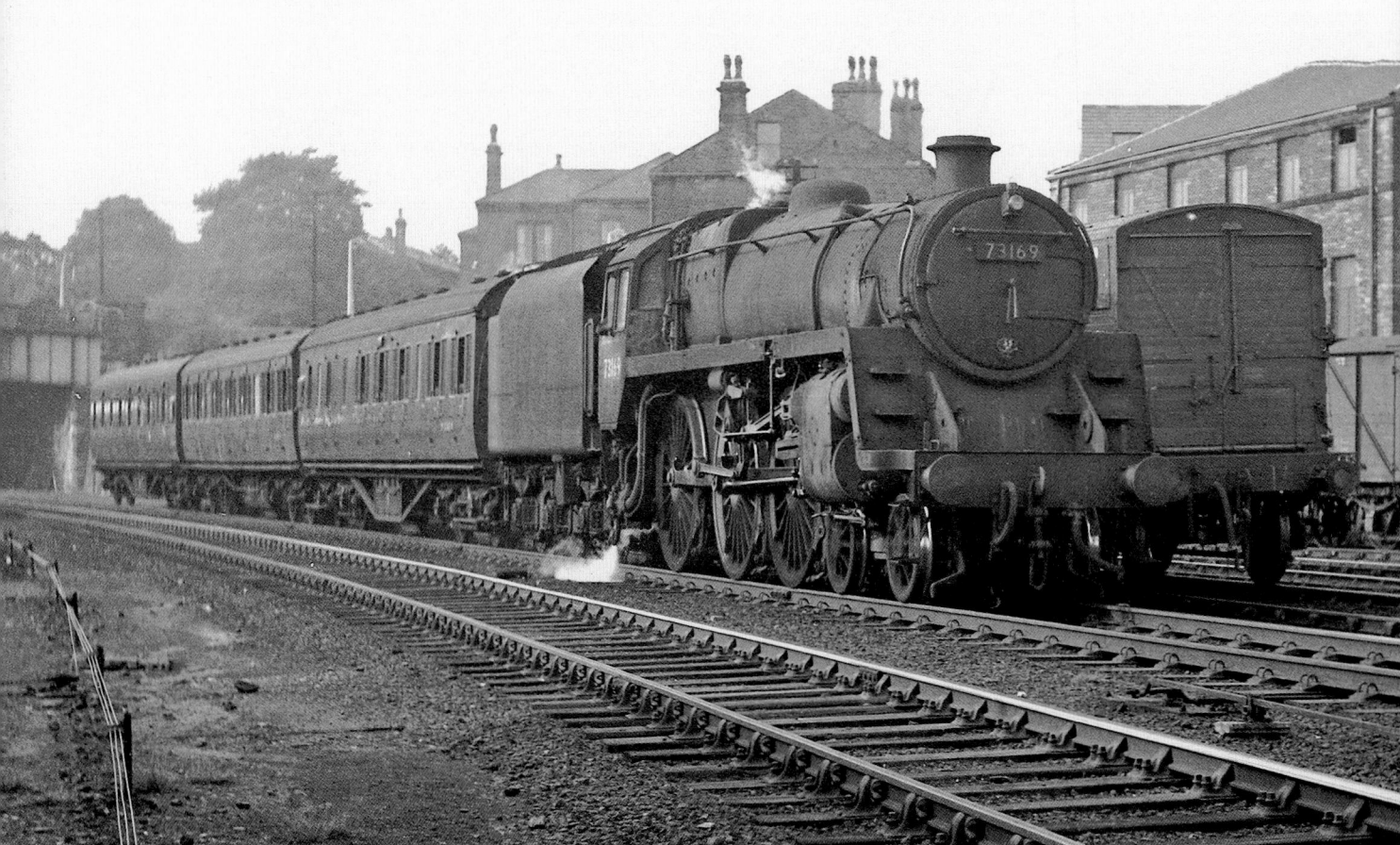

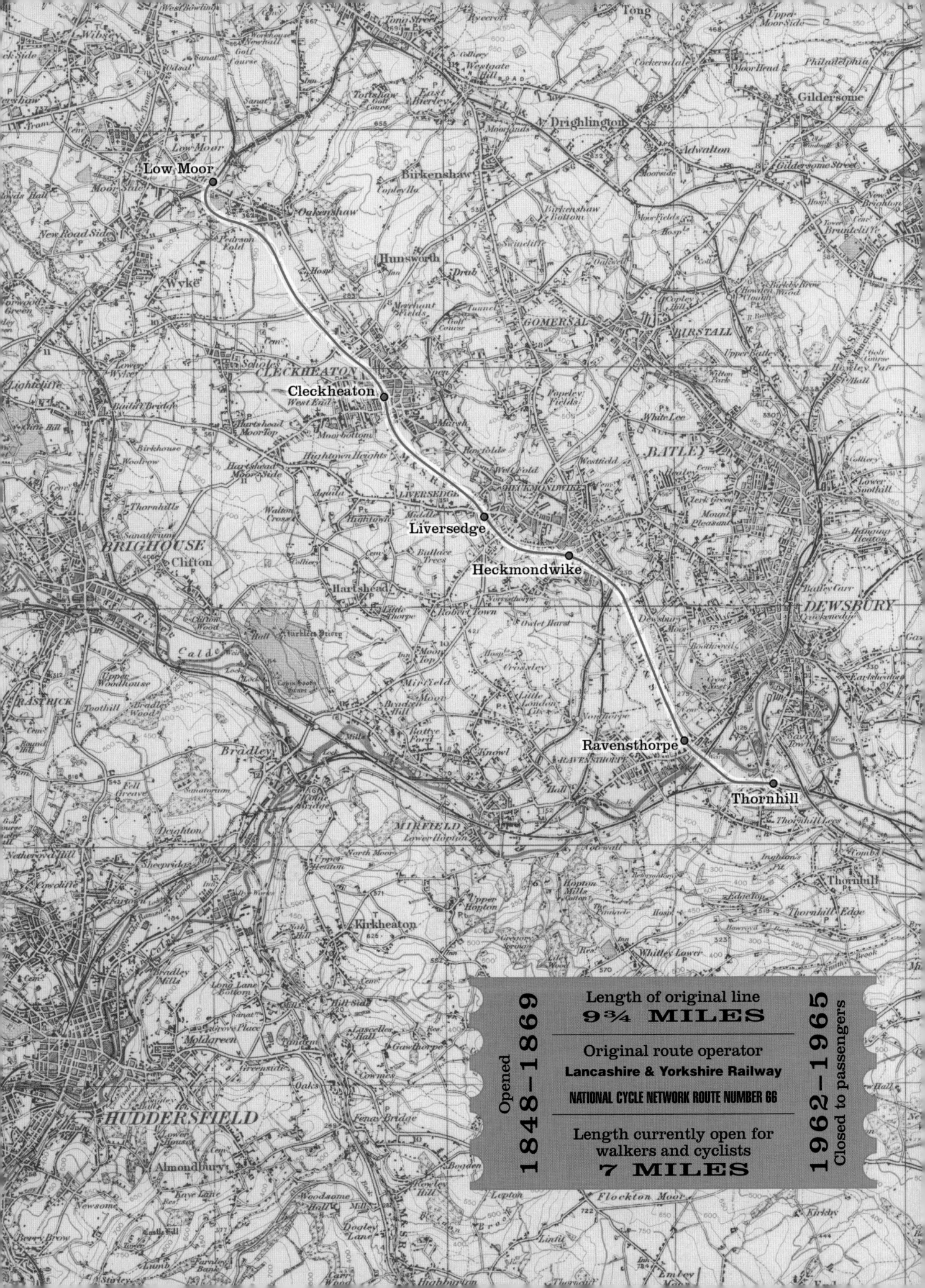

Low Moor

Cleckheaton

Liversedge

Heckmondwike

Ravensthorpe

Thornhill

Opened
1848–1869

Length of original line
9¾ MILES

Original route operator
Lancashire & Yorkshire Railway

NATIONAL CYCLE NETWORK ROUTE NUMBER 66

Length currently open for
walkers and cyclists
7 MILES

1962–1965
Closed to passengers

By the mid-nineteenth century the railways had reached the city of Bradford, which by then had become the 'wool capital' of the world. The easy access to coal, iron ore and soft water soon led to a massive population explosion, reaching 182,000 by 1850. In the city and surrounding valleys imported wool was woven into worsted cloth and exported around the world. In the wake of this a new recycling industry, called shoddy, grew up in the towns of the Spen Valley. Invented in 1813 by Benjamin Law, the process recovered wool from old clothes, which was then respun to make inferior clothing, and provided employment for thousands of workers in the towns of Cleckheaton, Heckmondwike, Liversedge and Dewsbury.

Originally proposed by the West Riding Union Railway, the Lancashire & Yorkshire Railway (L&YR) first reached Bradford from the south along the Spen Valley from Mirfield in 1848. Until the line from Halifax was completed this was the only rail approach from the south to the city. With intermediate stations at Heckmondwike, Liversedge, Cleckheaton and Low Moor, the line initially ended at a terminus at Adolphus Street in Bradford.

In the meantime the L&YR was still building its heavily engineered line from Sowerby Bridge, on the Calder Valley main line from Manchester, through Halifax and Low Moor, where it met the Spen Valley line. Involving the building of five tunnels, the line eventually opened up the Hebble Valley in 1852. In 1859 the London & North Western Railway (L&NWR) gained running powers over the Spen Valley line between Mirfield and Bradford although its trains (to and from Huddersfield) were not allowed to stop at intermediate stations until 1884. With all this extra traffic Adolphus Street station in Bradford soon proved inadequate so a new terminus, Bradford Exchange, was opened in 1867. A triangular junction was later provided at Low Moor.

The last section of the Spen Valley route from Heckmondwike to Thornhill (Dewsbury), with an intermediate station at Ravensthorpe, was opened by the L&YR in 1869 and involved the construction of a 12-arch viaduct over the Calder & Hebble Navigation.

At the southern end of the line, the town of Dewsbury had become a 'shoddy' boom town by the early 1870s and there was much competition between the railway companies to cash in on this business – by 1872 around 30,000 tons of rags were being brought to the town to convert into 'shoddy'. A wagon works was opened at Thornhill in 1878 and an extravagantly palatial station was opened at Northorpe, between Mirfield and Heckmondwike in 1891.

Serving such a heavily industrialized area, the Spen Valley line was kept very busy and in 1922 – the year when the

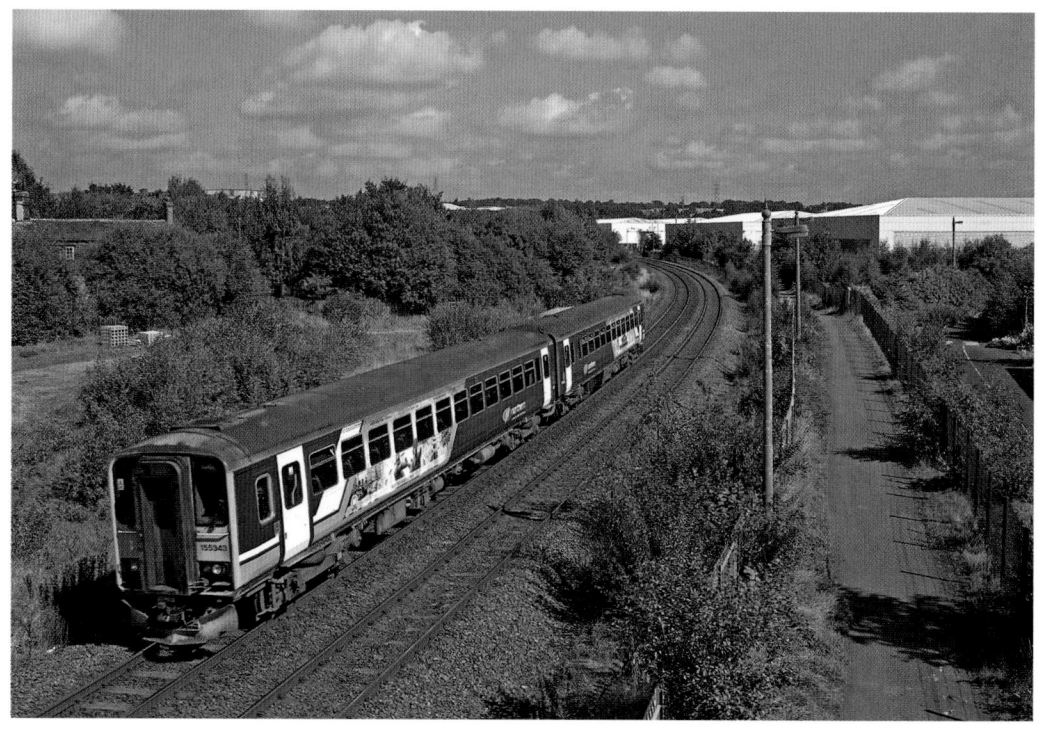

A Northern Rail Manchester to Leeds service heads towards Bradford at Low Moor. This was once an extensive railway complex with carriage sidings and engine shed and was the northern junction for the Spen Valley line. The Spen Valley Greenway can be seen on the right.

PREVIOUS SPREAD: A Mirfield to Bradford Exchange stopping train enters Cleckheaton station on 20 August 1959, hauled by Leeds Holbeck shed's BR Standard Class '5MT' 4-6-0 No. 73169. The locomotive was built at Doncaster Works in 1957 and after a short working life was withdrawn from Eastleigh shed in October 1966.

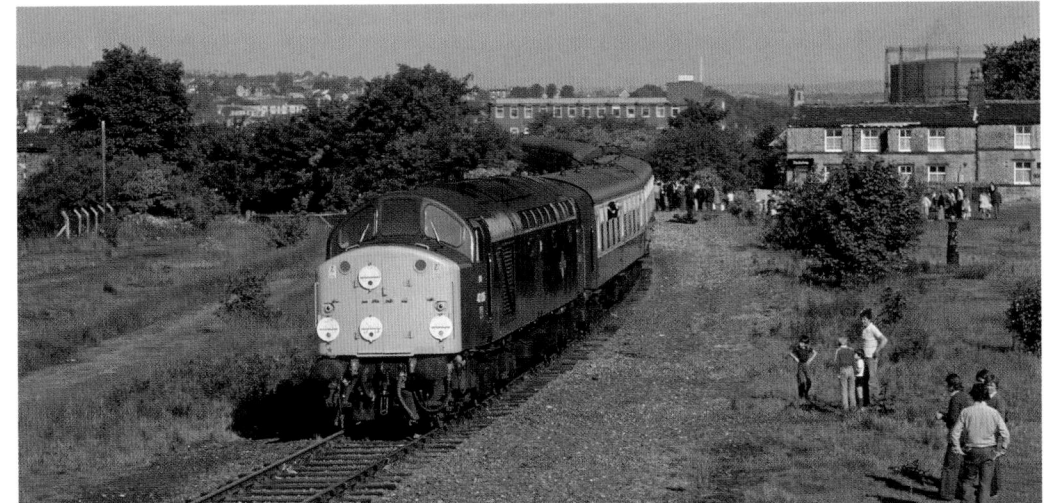

Headed by Class 40 diesel No. 40106, the Heckmondwike Working Men's Club annual outing to Morecambe stops at the site of Heckmondwike Central station on 17 June 1979 for passengers to board using steps and to take on a large quantity of beer.

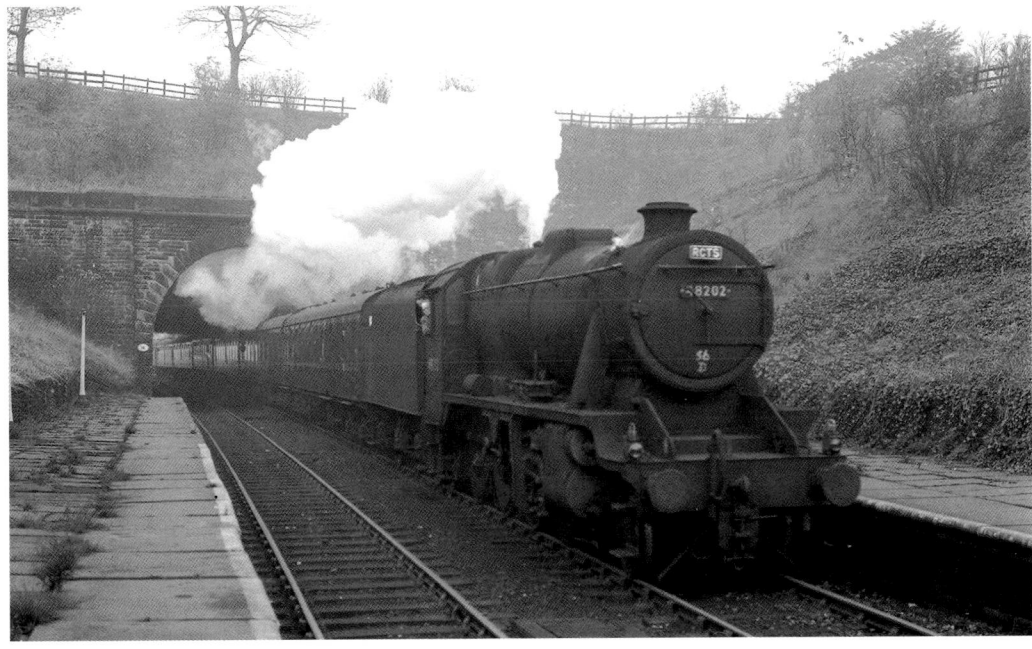

Ex-LMS Stanier Class '8F' 2-8-0 No. 48202 of Mirfield shed emerges from the short tunnel at the closed Heckmondwike station with the Railway Correspondence & Travel Society's 'South Yorks No. 5 Tour' on 23 October 1965.

L&YR amalgamated with the L&NWR – there were thirteen southbound trains (including two to St Pancras) and sixteen northbound (including two from St Pancras) on weekdays. There was just one local service in each direction on Sundays.

The first year of the British Railways era, 1948, saw a fairly healthy train service still running along the Spen Valley between Bradford and Mirfield – this included 'The South Yorkshireman' on weekdays to and from Marylebone until that train's demise on 2 January 1960. However, the Heckmondwike to Thornhill section was living on borrowed time with only six trains in each direction on weekdays, and closure to passengers came on 1 January 1962. Diesel multiple units were introduced

for the Bradford to Huddersfield via Heckmondwike and Mirfield service by the North Eastern Region of BR in 1959 but these cost-saving measures were not enough to save the line and it was listed for closure in the 1963 'Beeching Report'. Passenger services ceased on 14 June 1965 when the section from Mirfield to Heckmondwike was closed completely. The Spen Valley continued to be served by goods trains between Low Moor and Heckmondwike until 1981, although these were suspended during the building of the M62 across the route between 1970 and 1974. The southern section from Thornhill Junction to Liversedge Spen – via a spur linking the former L&YR and L&NWR lines which was opened in 1966 – was kept open for freight traffic until 1990.

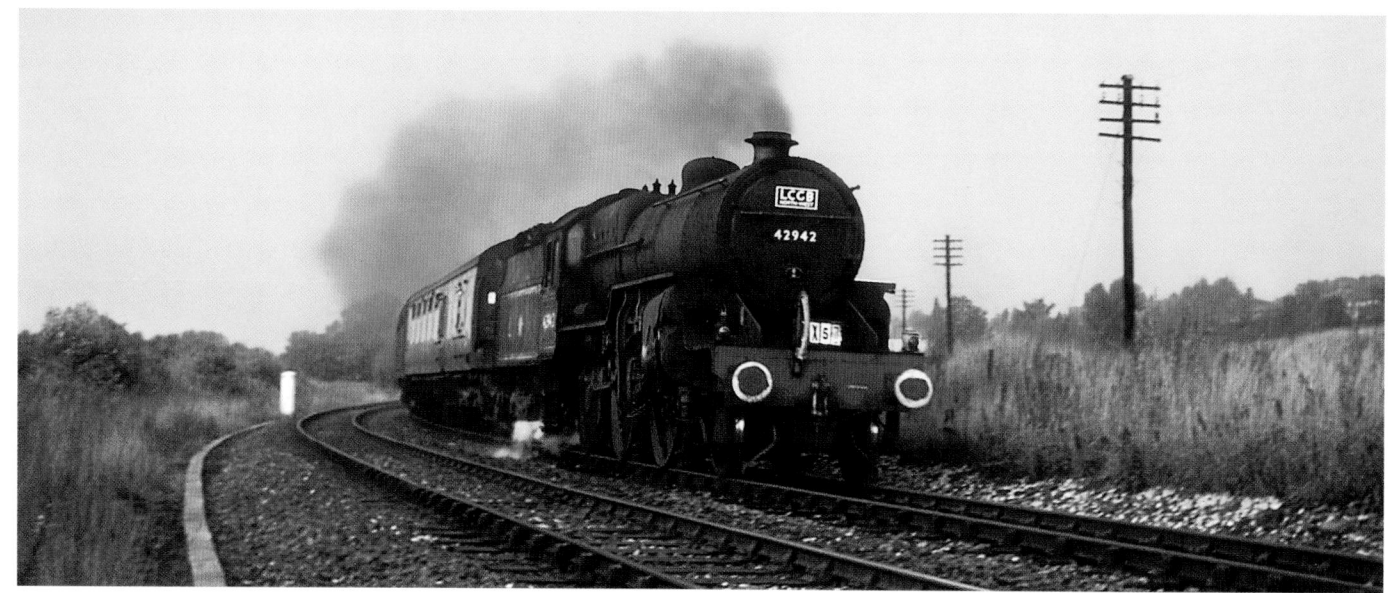

ABOVE: Ex-LMS 'Crab' Class '6P5F' 2-6-0
No. 42942 hauls the Locomotive Club of Great
Britain's 'Crab Commemorative Railtour' through
Ravensthorpe on 8 October 1966. The railtour
had started at Liverpool Exchange and travelled
to Goole via Manchester Victoria and the Low
Moor to Thornhill line to Wakefield Kirkgate.
The locomotive was built at Crewe in 1932 and
withdrawn from Birkenhead shed in January 1967.

BELOW: A Trans-Pennine Express train
crosses the southern end of the Spen Valley
Greenway near Thornhill. On the left is the
Calder & Hebble Navigation while in the
centre is the giant pedal and cycle seat by
sculptor Alan Evans.

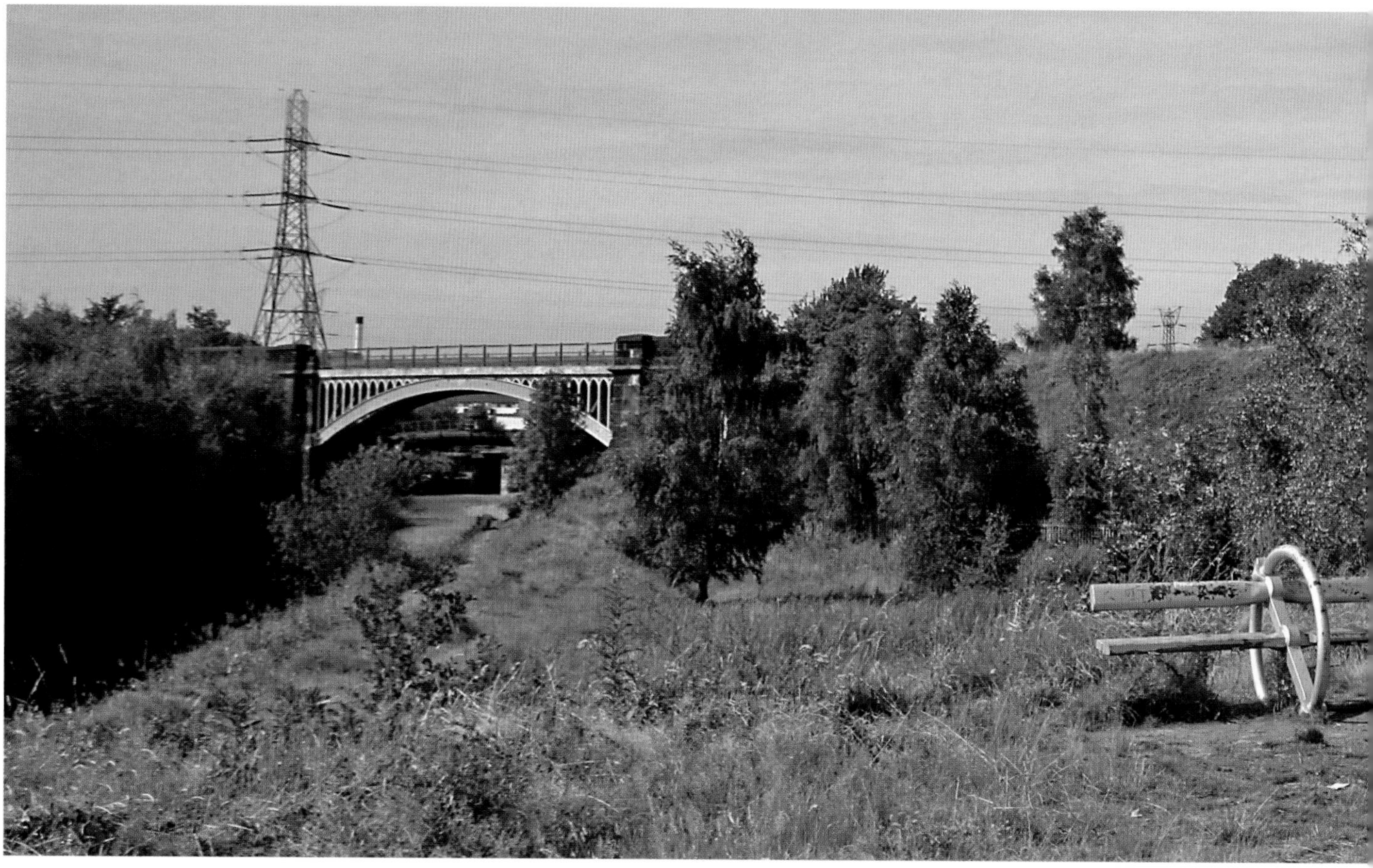

Since closure of the line the entire section between Low Moor and the Calder-Hebble Navigation at Thornhill has been reopened as a 7-mile footpath and cycleway known as the Spen Valley Greenway. Opened in 2001 it also forms part of National Cycle Network Route 66 and is essentially a green corridor running through a heavily populated urban area with distant views of moorland. Scattered along the trail is a collection of artworks including Sally Matthews' flock of Swaledale sheep, built from industrial scrap metal; Alan Evans' giant pedal and cycle seat; and Trudi Entwistle's forty giant steel hoops set in a circle.

The Greenway starts at Low Moor, which was once an extensive railway complex complete with carriage sidings and a 12-road engine shed, the latter closing in 1967. All this has long-since disappeared but the line from Sowerby Bridge and Halifax remains open through here for trains to and from Bradford. Heading south past Oakenshaw and into open country, the cycleway skirts a golf course before crossing the A58 on a high bridge and then immediately heading over the busy M62. The steel-girder bridge here was built in the early 1970s when the line was still open for goods traffic as far south as Heckmondwike.

One mile south of the motorway crossing the cycleway passes through the town of Cleckheaton, where the station site is now occupied by a supermarket. Liversedge is reached after a further mile – there is no trace of the station today – and continues through the urban landscape to Heckmondwike, where one of the station platforms has surprisingly survived.

Continuing south along the Spen Valley, the cycleway becomes sandwiched between a sewage works and the western outskirts of Dewsbury to reach the site of Ravensthorpe station, where the old stone goods shed is a remarkable survivor. Nearing the end of its 7-mile route, the cycleway crosses the A644 Huddersfield Road at Scout Hill on a new purpose-built arched bridge opened in 2009. Immediately south of this bridge the cycleway crosses the Calder & Hebble Navigation on the original 12-arch stone viaduct built in 1867. The cycleway ends alongside the Calder & Hebble Navigation after diving under the Leeds to Manchester Trans-Pennine main line – nearby, an abandoned 4-aspect-colour light-railway signal is a solitary reminder of this lost railway.

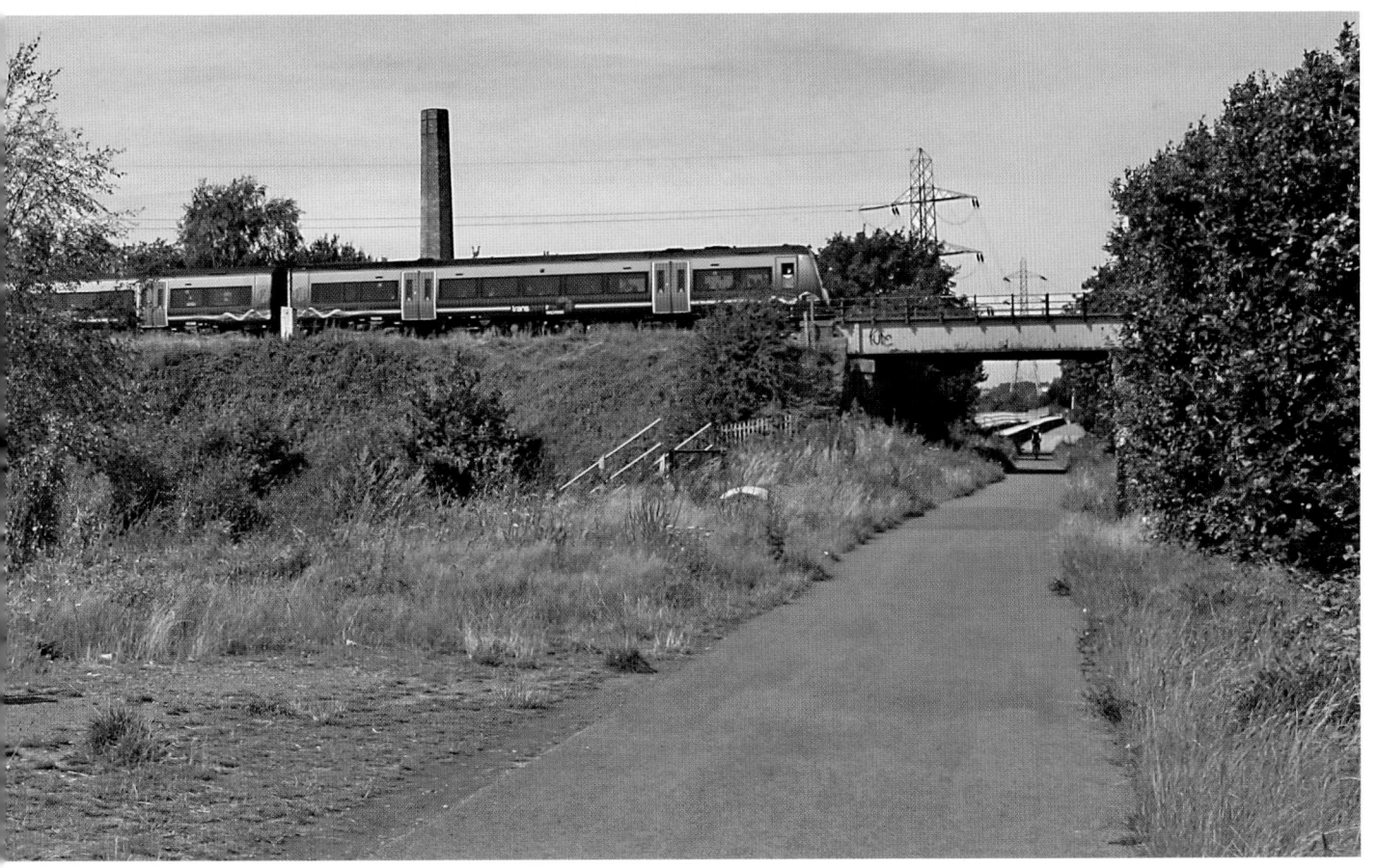

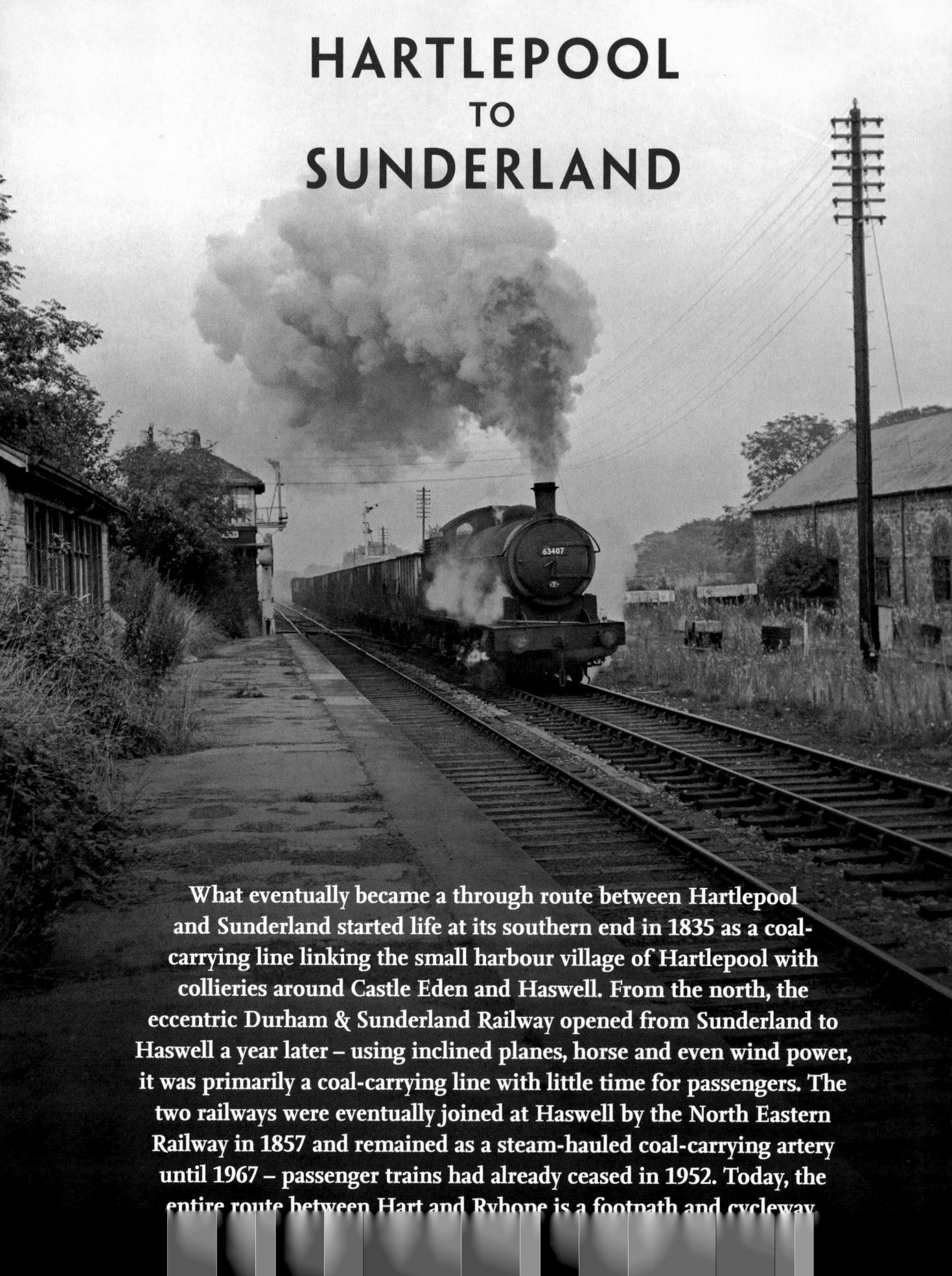

HARTLEPOOL
TO
SUNDERLAND

What eventually became a through route between Hartlepool
and Sunderland started life at its southern end in 1835 as a coal-
carrying line linking the small harbour village of Hartlepool with
collieries around Castle Eden and Haswell. From the north, the
eccentric Durham & Sunderland Railway opened from Sunderland to
Haswell a year later – using inclined planes, horse and even wind power,
it was primarily a coal-carrying line with little time for passengers. The
two railways were eventually joined at Haswell by the North Eastern
Railway in 1857 and remained as a steam-hauled coal-carrying artery
until 1967 – passenger trains had already ceased in 1952. Today, the
entire route between Hart and Ryhope is a footpath and cycleway.

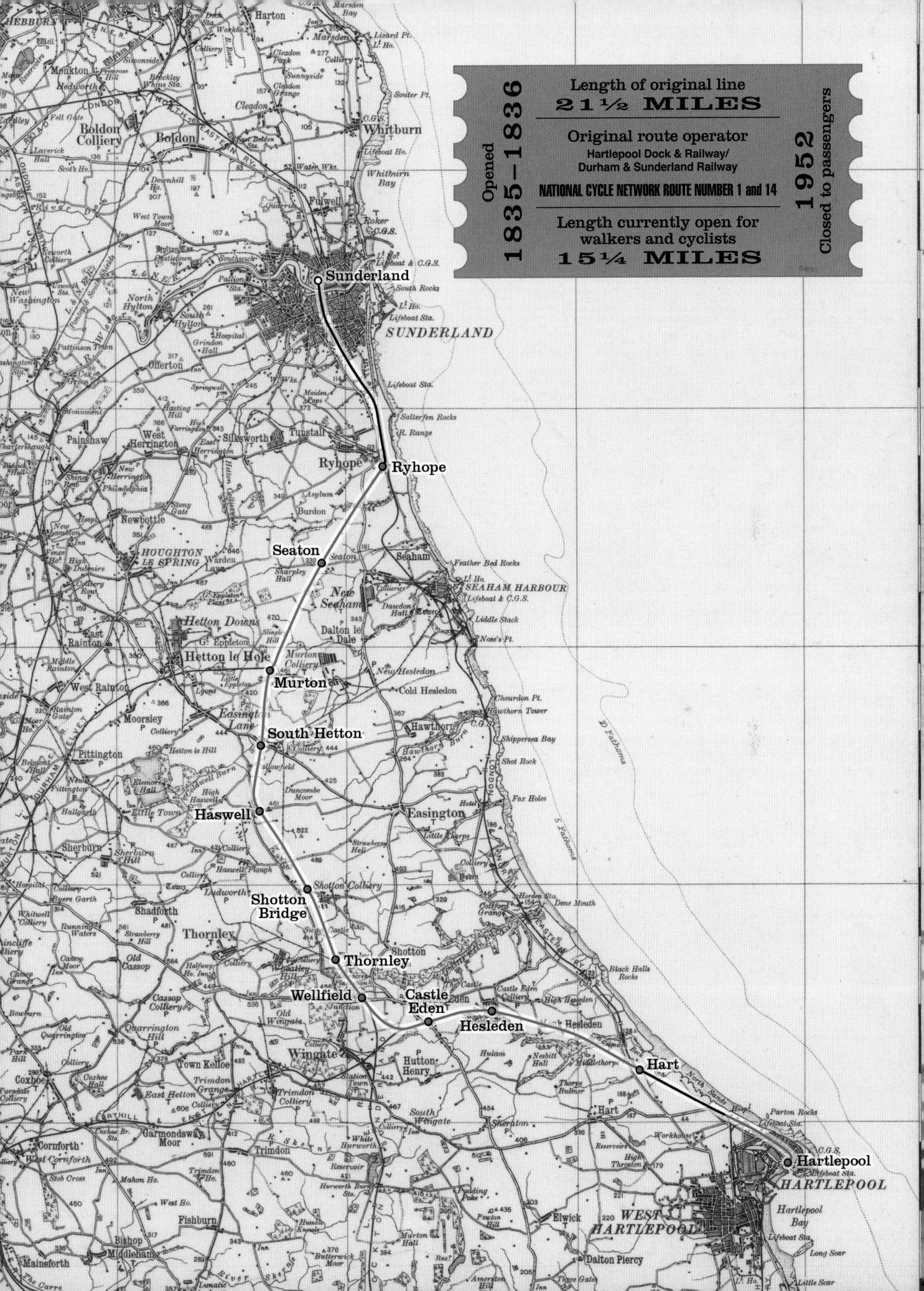

Opened **1835–1836**

Length of original line
21½ MILES

Original route operator
Hartlepool Dock & Railway/
Durham & Sunderland Railway

NATIONAL CYCLE NETWORK ROUTE NUMBER 1 and 14

Length currently open for walkers and cyclists
15¼ MILES

1952 Closed to passengers

Sunderland

Ryhope

Seaton

Murton

South Hetton

Haswell

Shotton Bridge

Thornley

Wellfield

Castle Eden

Hesleden

Hart

Hartlepool

The earliest railways in East Durham were simple horse-drawn waggonways built to link collieries with staithes on the River Wear. The first waggonway in the region was opened as early as 1693 and by the end of the eighteenth century there was a whole network of these primitive railways carrying coal across hilly country by way of gravity, inclined planes and horse power.

The first use of steam power came in 1822 when the Hetton Coal Company bought locomotives from George Stephenson to haul coal trains between Hetton and Sunderland – progress was slow as the line included inclined planes, some of which were self-acting while others were operated by stationary steam engines, with the intermediate level sections worked by the new steam locomotives. Another early railway in the area was opened between South Hetton Colliery and Seaham Harbour in 1833 and, from 1835, was operated by steam locomotives supplied by Timothy Hackworth. The line was later extended to collieries at Haswell and Shotton.

Meanwhile the Hartlepool Dock & Railway was seeking to develop what was then a small fishing harbour into a major coal shipment port by building a railway to link it with inland collieries. Although various branches and new docks at Hartlepool were authorized in 1832, only one of

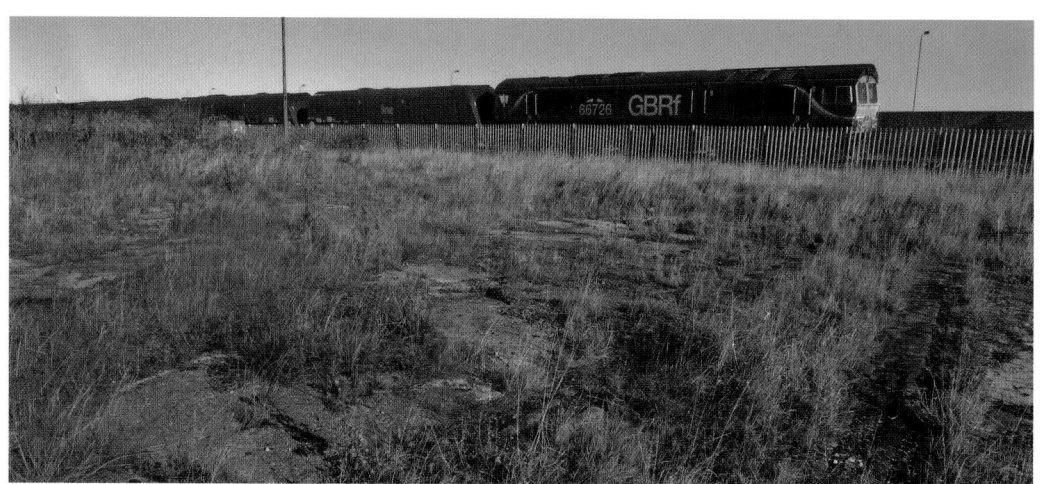

Class 66 diesel No 66726 hauls a train of hopper wagons past the site of one of two roundhouses at West Hartlepool engine shed. The shed was closed on 17 September 1967 and its allocation of ex-NER 'Q6' 0-8-0s and ex-WD 2-8-0s were sent for scrap.

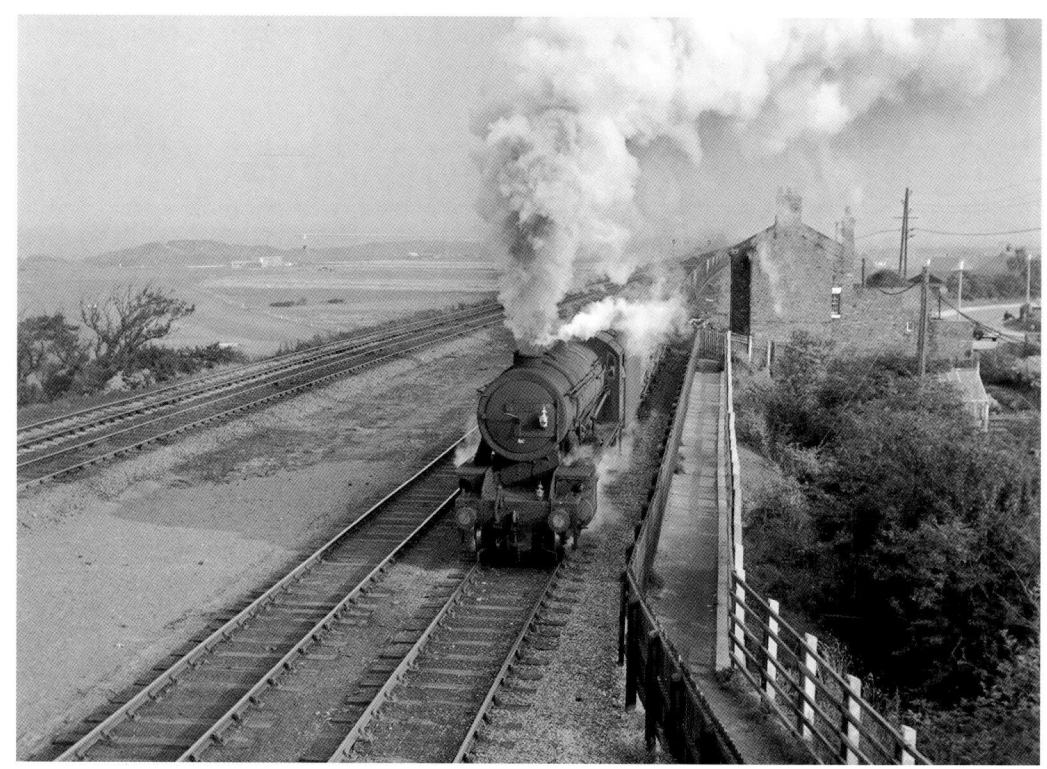

West Hartlepool shed's former War Department Class '8F' 2-8-0 No. 90339 passes Hart with a train of empty wagons for Hawthorn Colliery at Hesleden on 30 September 1966. The Hartlepool to Sunderland coastal route is on the left while in the distance is the North Sea. The Hart to Haswell Countryside Path along the trackbed starts near here.

PREVIOUS SPREAD:
Ex-NER Class 'Q6' 0-8-0 No. 63407 passes Hesleden with a train of empty wagons bound for nearby Hawthorn Colliery on 30 September 1966. The locomotive was built at Darlington in 1919 and was withdrawn from West Hartlepool shed in July 1967.

the lines, from Hartlepool to Haswell, was ever completed. Engineered by George Stephenson this 12¼-mile 'main line' opened via Hesleden and Castle Eden in 1835.

From the north, the Durham & Sunderland Railway opened its 9¾-mile line from Sunderland to Haswell via Seaton and South Hetton in 1836. The railway was run in an eccentric manner using horse power and stationary steam engines for the inclined planes, and even experimented with wind power using sails. The passenger service did not appear in Bradshaw until 1858 and prior to that can only be described as chronically slow! Although both railways terminated at Haswell there was no physical connection between the two stations until the companies were amalgamated with the North Eastern Railway (NER) in 1857. At 462 ft above sea level Haswell

was the summit of the line and was approached from the south up the gruelling Hesleden Bank and from the north by the equally taxing Seaton Bank.

Through passenger services between West Hartlepool and Sunderland were introduced only after the NER had taken over the route, and this remained the only rail link between the towns until the shorter, coastal railway was finally completed in 1905. After this date the route via Haswell was relegated to secondary status. Coal was the lifeblood of the line and steam-hauled coal trains battled up Seaton Bank until 1967, however British Railways withdrew passenger services on 9 June 1952. In its final years the line was served by only two return services each weekday with an extra three on Saturdays. There was just one return service on Sundays during the summer months. Steam hauled by NER 'Q6' 0-8-0s and ex-WD 2-8-0s to the end, coal trains continued to use the line until September 1967, by which time most of the collieries had also closed – one of the last to close was at Shotton in 1972.

The Railway Crossings pub in the former pit village of Wingate is a convenient watering hole for walkers and cyclists on the Hart to Haswell Countryside Path. One of the level crossing gates still survives nearby.

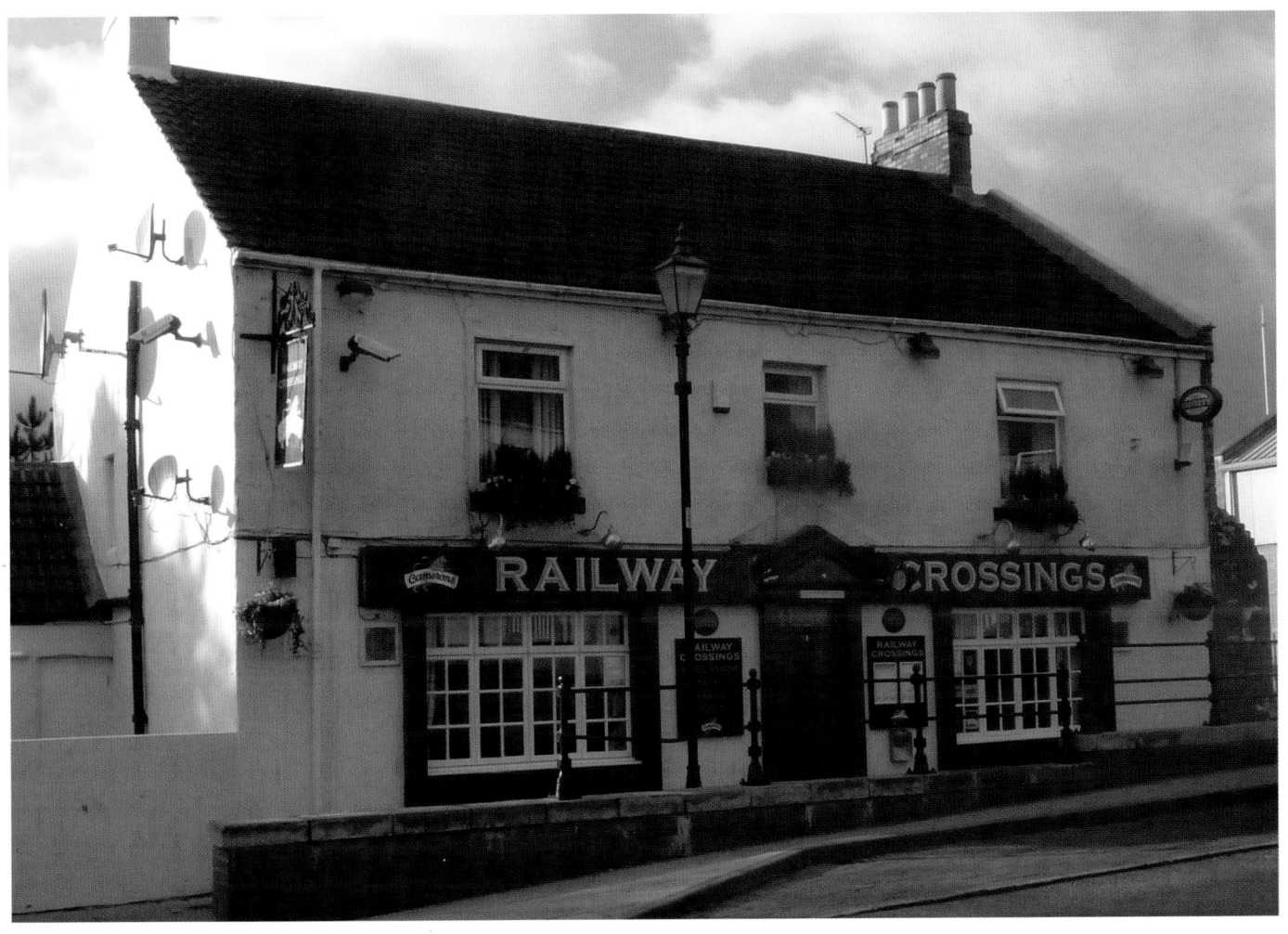

Since closure, almost the entire length (apart from a few short diversions) of the Hartlepool to Ryhope (three miles south of Sunderland) via Haswell railway route has been reopened as a footpath and cycleway. Between Hart and Haswell it is known as the Hart to Haswell Countryside Path. It also forms part of National Cycle Network Route 14 as far as Wingate, where it joins NCN Route 1 to Ryhope and Sunderland.

The railway path starts at the site of Cemetery North Junction on the Hartlepool to Sunderland coastal railway, and is reached on foot or by bicycle along a sign-posted route from the centre of Hartlepool. The town is still served by trains operating between Stockton-on-Tees and Sunderland.

From Cemetery North Junction, where only an iron footbridge remains of Hart station, the railway path heads northwest in a long cutting for 2½ miles to reach the former mining village of Hesleden – on the path's approach to the village a high embankment offers fine views of the Cleveland Hills. There is a car park for walkers and cyclists at Hesleden. One mile west from here the railway path reaches Castle Eden where there is another car park opposite the Castle Eden Inn.

From Castle Eden the path dives under the A19 dual carriageway before entering a cutting near the former railway junction at Wingate. Refreshments can be taken at the nearby Railway Crossings pub. Here the path links up with the Castle Eden Walkway (NCN Route 1) that has

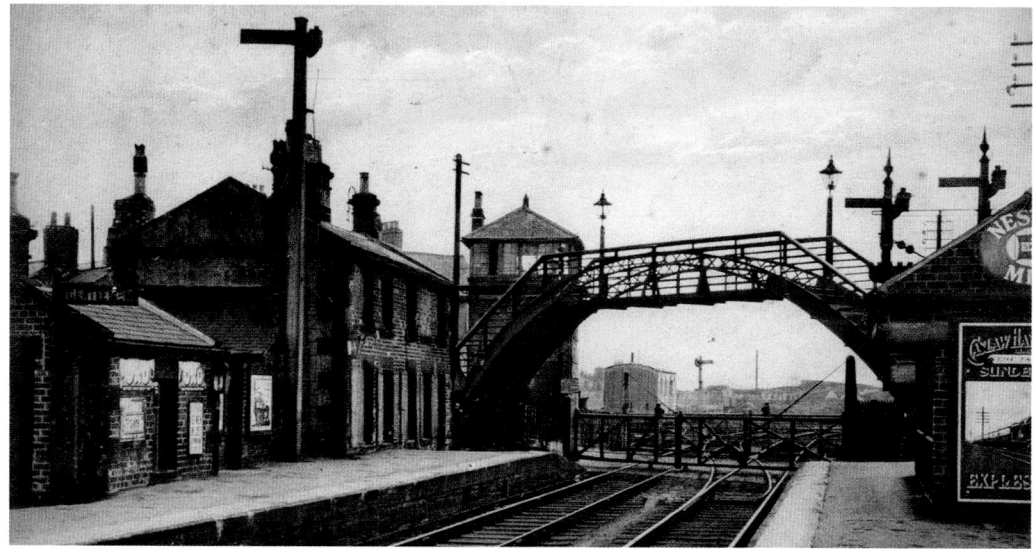

This colour postcard view of Haswell station dates from around 1910. Passenger services were withdrawn in 1952 but steam-hauled coal trains continued to pass through here until 1967.

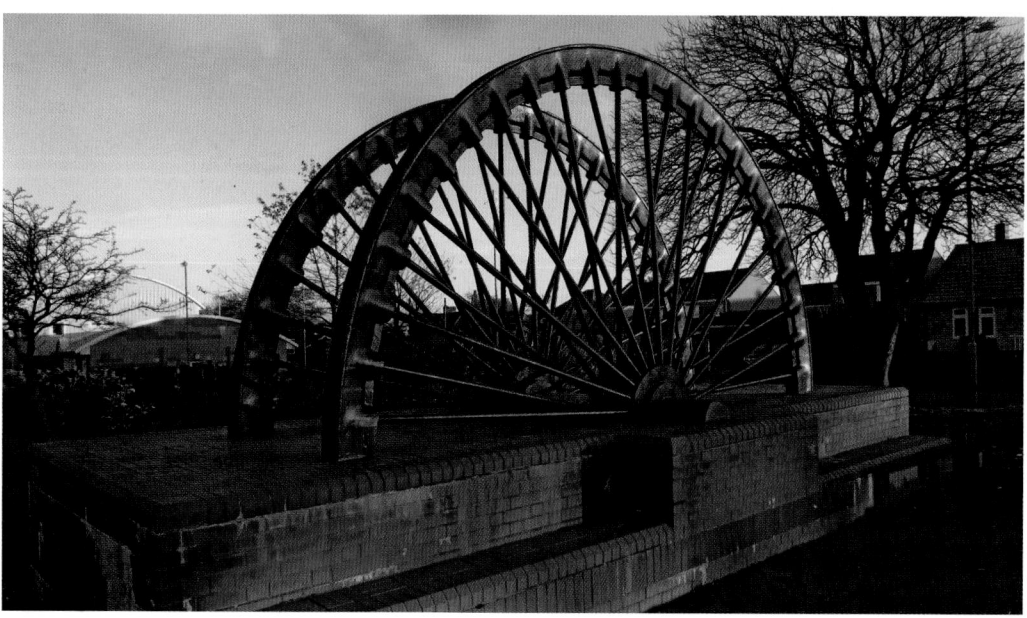

The only reminder of the once-important coal mining industry in the former pit village of South Hetton is this large semi-circular sculpture made of pit winding gear.

followed an old railway route from Stockton-on-Tees – some eight miles south of this junction there is a visitor centre and tearoom at Thorp Thewles station, where an old railway carriage serves as a classroom for visiting school parties.

Now designated as NCN Route 1, the railway path continues northwards away from Wingate – an old semaphore railway signal is a remarkable survivor here – through Edderacres Plantation before entering a long cutting near the site of Shotton Colliery, where the station platform and road overbridge are almost all that survive from the days of the railway. Nearby are two stone pillars, the only remains of an early waggonway bridge. The Hart to Haswell Countryside Path ends at the former mining village of Haswell where there is a car park between the Oddfellows Arms and The Wayfarers pubs. From here NCN Route 14 heads off west to Durham while the railway path and NCN Route 1 continue northwards

for one mile to South Hetton, where the Station Hotel is now the only evidence of the railway.

At South Hetton the Yellow Brick Road (also used as an alternative route by NCN Route 1) railway path heads east to follow the route of the early nineteenth-century wagonway to Seaham. The main railway path continues northwards for another mile to Murton, where the colliery remained in operation until 1991 – amazingly this large mining village once had an Olympic-size open-air swimming pool heated by water from the colliery's main compressors. The only reminder today of this once-important industry is a large semi-circular sculpture made of pit winding gear.

The railway path heads off towards the northeast from Murton before passing through a long cutting to emerge at the top of Seaton Bank. From here, where the NER's 'Q6' locomotives once struggled uphill in the opposite direction with their long trains of coal empties, the walker and cyclist follow the railway route downhill through Seaton and across the A19 to Ryhope. The cycle route continues from here via designated tracks and side roads to the centre of Sunderland.

Ex-NER Class 'J27' 0-6-0 No. 65833 takes its snaking rake of coal empties under the superb signal gantry at Ryhope. This locomotive was built by Robert Stephenson & Co in 1909 and withdrawn from Sunderland South Dock shed in May 1967.

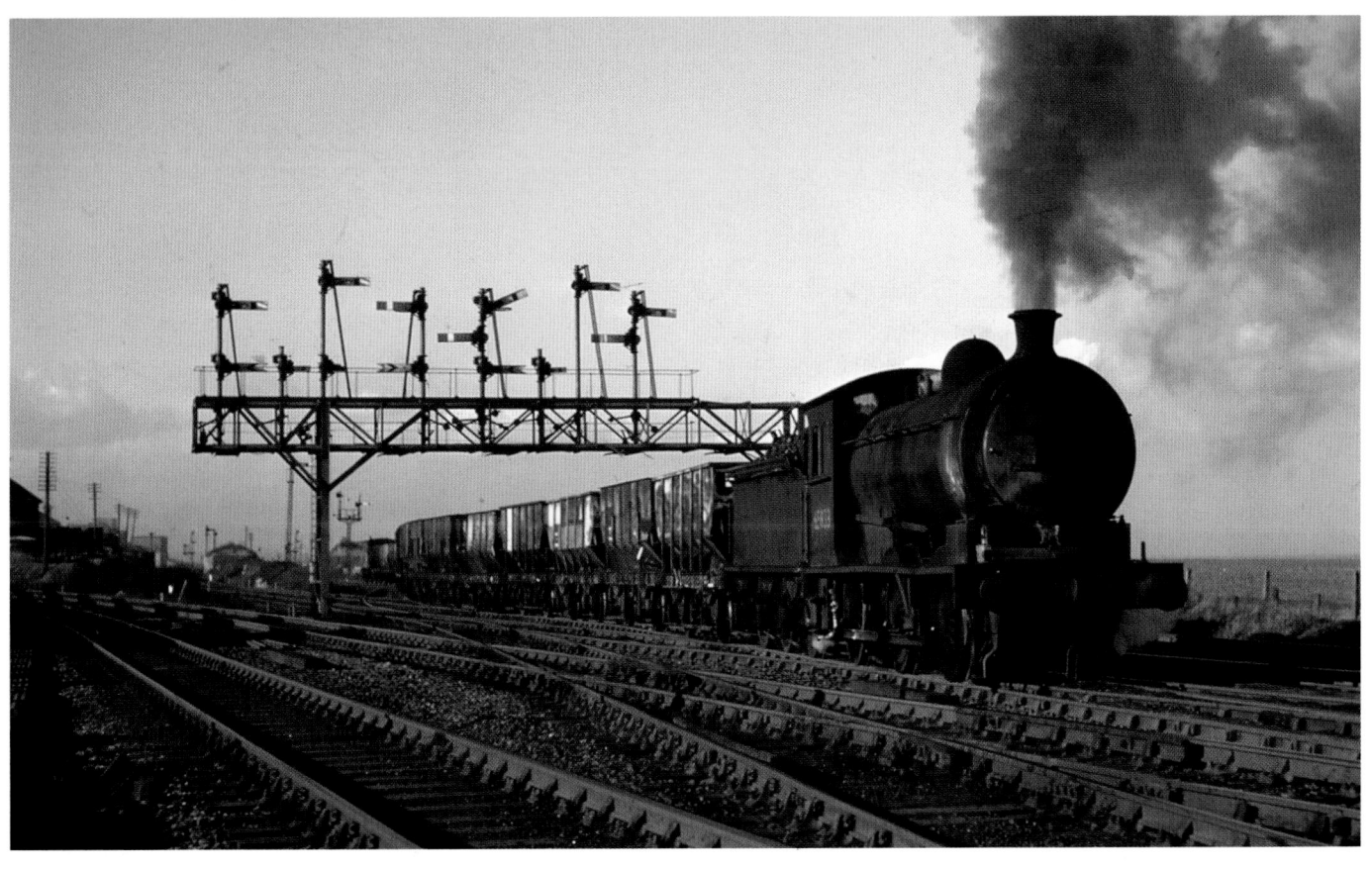

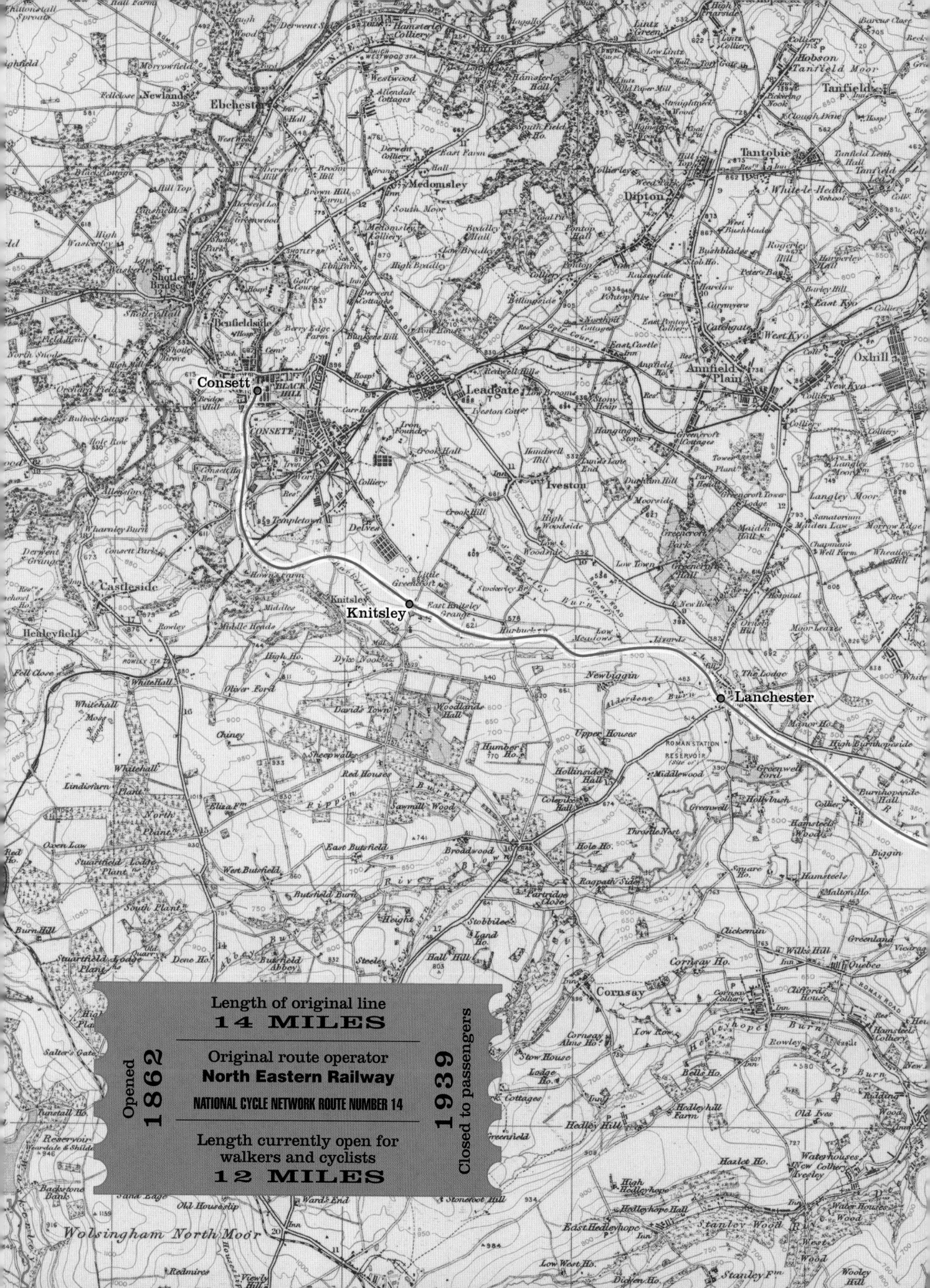

Consett

Knitsley

Lanchester

Length of original line
14 MILES

Original route operator
North Eastern Railway

NATIONAL CYCLE NETWORK ROUTE NUMBER 14

Length currently open for
walkers and cyclists
12 MILES

Opened
1862

1939
Closed to passengers

CONSETT (BLACKHILL)
TO
DURHAM

LANCHESTER VALLEY RAILWAY PATH

Built to transport iron ore from the Cleveland Hills to Consett's iron works, the 14-mile railway between Consett and Durham featured a rickety wooden viaduct at Knitsley, which was infilled with colliery waste in 1915 to form an embankment. Passenger traffic was of secondary importance, with trains being withdrawn in 1939. The line remained open for mineral traffic until 1966 when it closed completely. Nearly the entire length, including the famous Knitsley Embankment, has since been reopened as a footpath and cycleway known as the Lanchester Valley Railway Path.

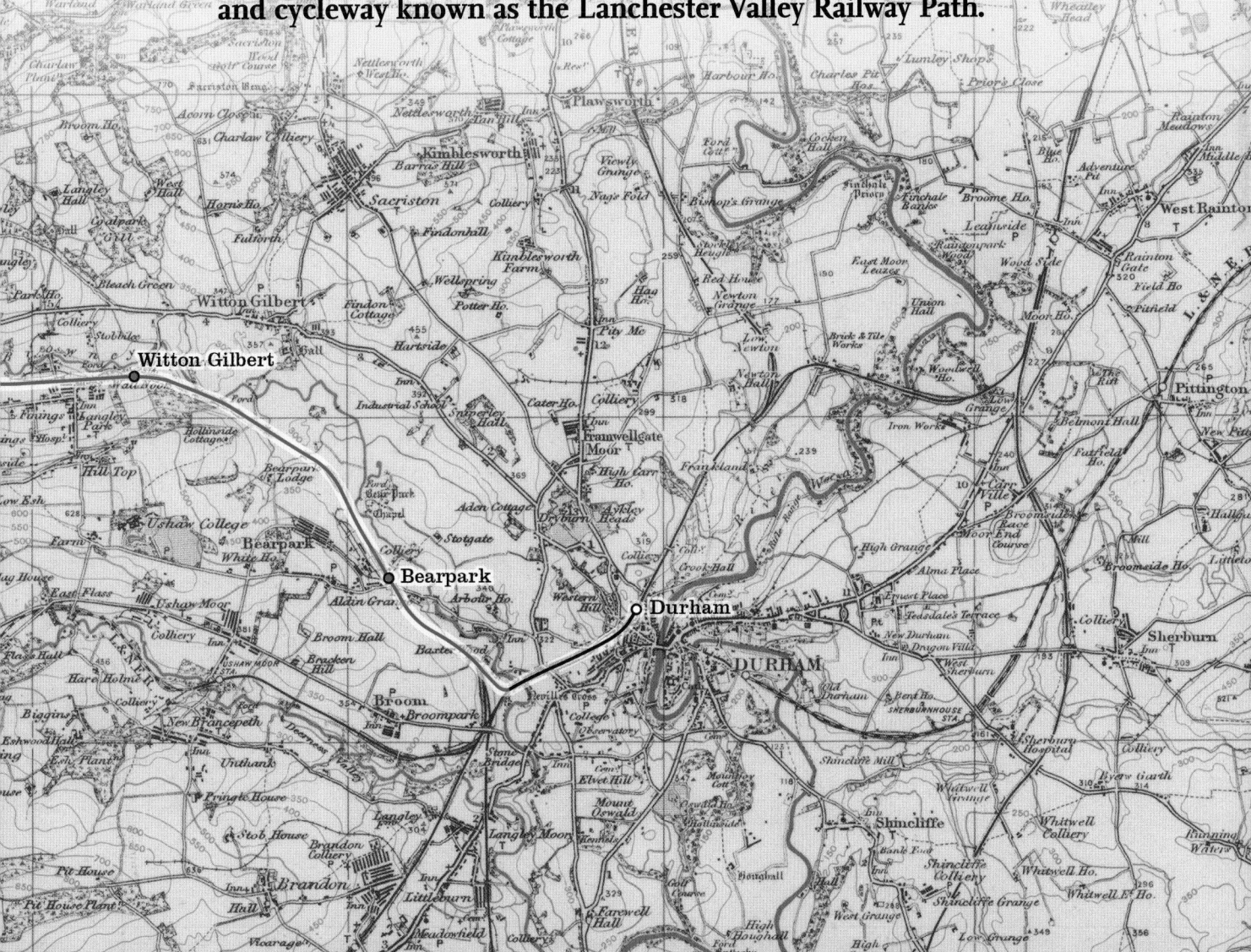

With local supplies of ironstone, coal and limestone readily available, the Derwent Iron Company's ironworks were established at Consett in 1840. A network of local tramways, railways and inclined planes sufficed for transporting the raw materials to the steelworks but by 1850 the local supplies of ironstone were running out and the company had to look further afield for materials. Thirty miles southeast of Consett, the Cleveland Hills – a rich source of ironstone – and the Teesside town of Middlesbrough were soon to play an important part in keeping the blast furnaces running at Consett.

Transporting the iron ore from Middlesbrough to Consett via the existing circuitous railway routes was time consuming and expensive. What was needed was a more direct route and so the North Eastern Railway started construction of a 14-mile single-track line along the Browney Valley between Durham and Consett (Blackhill). The main engineering features were three stone bridges over the River Browney between Durham and Lanchester and a 700-ft-long timber viaduct that carried the line 70 ft above Backgill Burn to the east of Knitsley station. Other intermediate stations were provided at Lanchester and Witton Gilbert. The line opened in 1862 and within a few years had been doubled to serve four new collieries that had sprung up along the valley. A new station was opened at Aldin Grange in 1883 (later renamed Bearpark). Nearing the end of its useful life, the timber viaduct near Knitsley was infilled by an embankment made of colliery waste and ballast in 1915.

While coal and ironstone were the lifeblood of the line, passengers were also catered for by an infrequent train service operating between Newcastle and Durham. This ran via the Browney Valley to Consett and then up to Newcastle via Ebchester and Rowlands Gill. Passenger traffic was light and was served by five return trains on weekdays, with an extra working on Saturdays.

Meanwhile the Derwent Iron Company's successor, the Consett Iron Company, had been established in 1864. With eighteen blast furnaces the company went from strength to strength, supplying steel plates for shipbuilders on the Tyne and Tees from 1882, and by the 1890s employing 6,000 workers in Consett. By the Second World War the company was employing 12,000 workers but, with a declining shipbuilding industry in northeast England, the post-war years brought contraction and nationalization.

In the meantime the Browney Valley line between Durham and Consett had lost its passenger service on 1 May 1939, although Durham Miners' Gala excursion trains continued to call at the stations during each July until 1954. Local goods traffic carried on until 5 July 1965, although mineral traffic to Consett continued until complete closure of the line on 20 June 1966. The by-now uneconomic and outdated steel works at Consett received iron ore by train from Tyne Dock via South Pelaw and Annfield Plain until complete closure of the works in 1980.

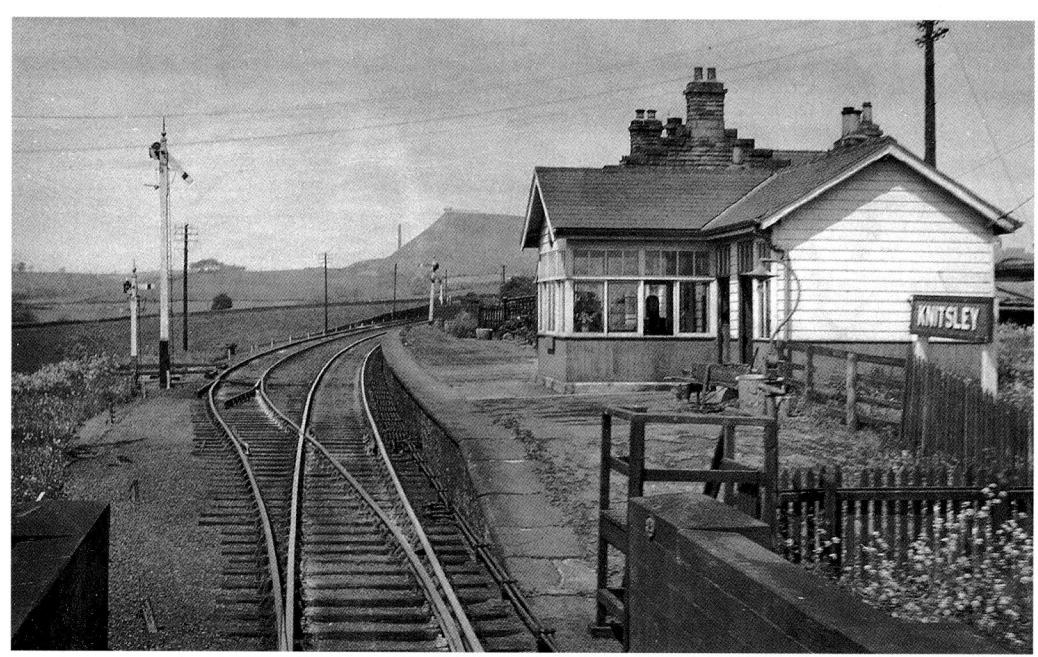

A fine array of NER lower quadrant signals guard the approach to Knitsley station on a sunny day, c.1920. While the Consett to Durham line lost its passenger service in 1939 the line remained open for mineral traffic until 1966. Today, the station house and platform survive as a private residence alongside the Lanchester Valley Railway Path.

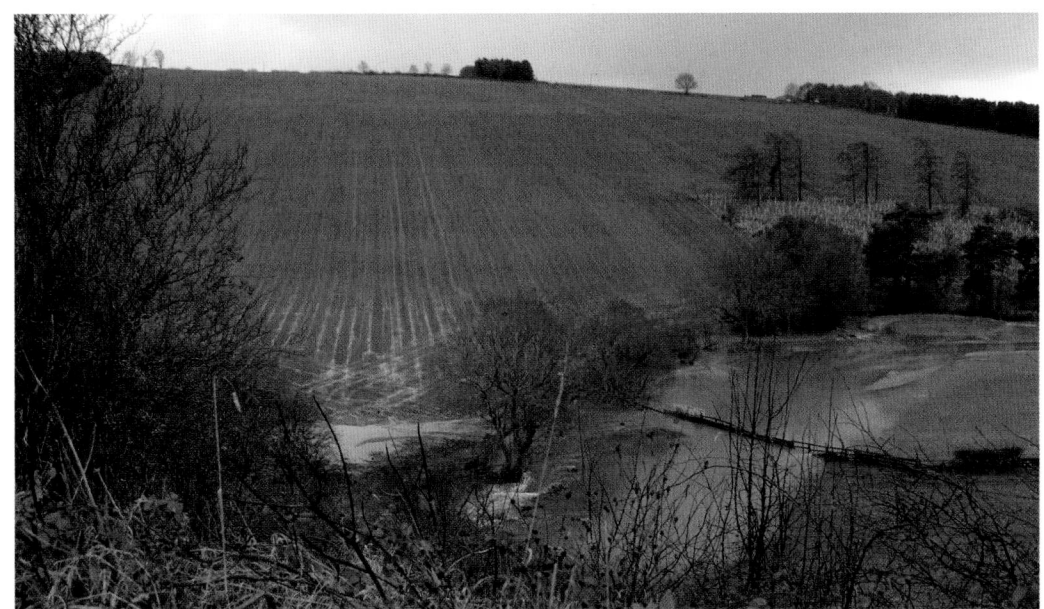

Walkers and cyclists along the Lanchester Valley Railway Path are treated to this fine view from the top of Knitsley Embankment, which was built to replace a 70-ft-high timber trestle bridge in 1915.

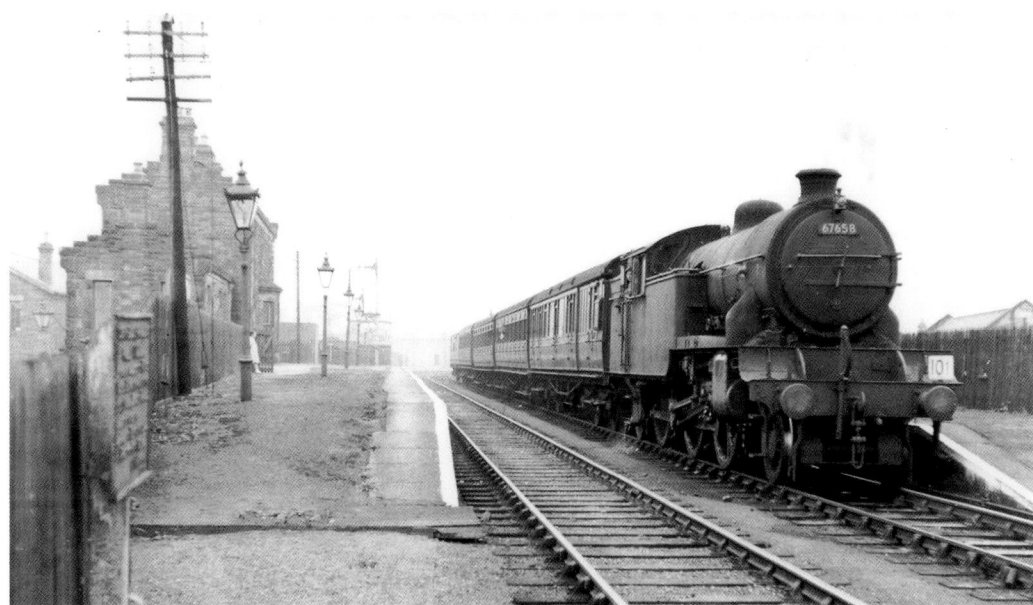

Headed by ex-LNER Class 'V3' 2-6-2T No. 67658, a Durham Miners' Gala excursion train stops at Lanchester's closed station on 1 July 1951. These special trains continued to operate each July until 1954. Today, the attractive stone station building with stepped gable ends is a private residence alongside the Lanchester Valley Railway Path.

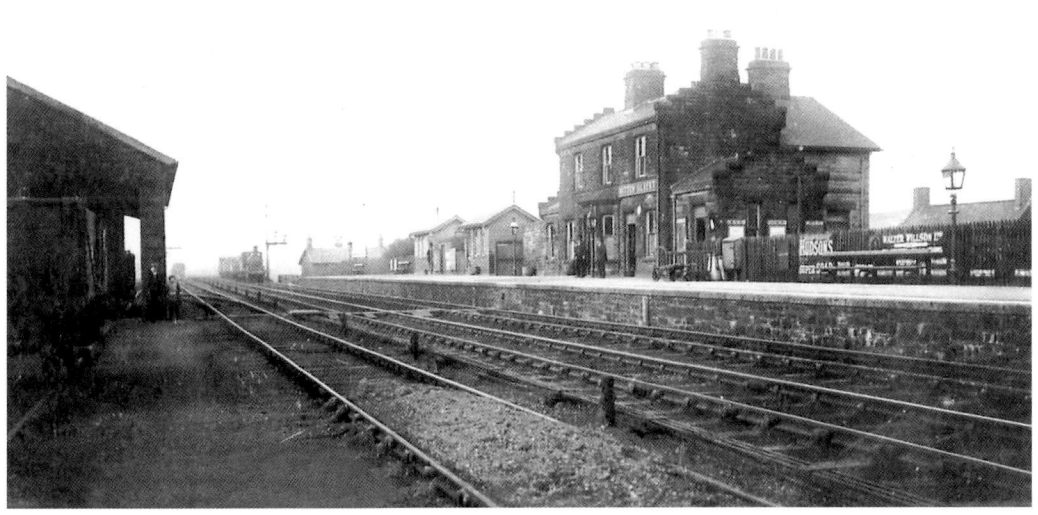

Station staff pose for the camera at Witton Gilbert station in the early twentieth century. This attractive building is now a private residence alongside the Lanchester Valley Railway Path.

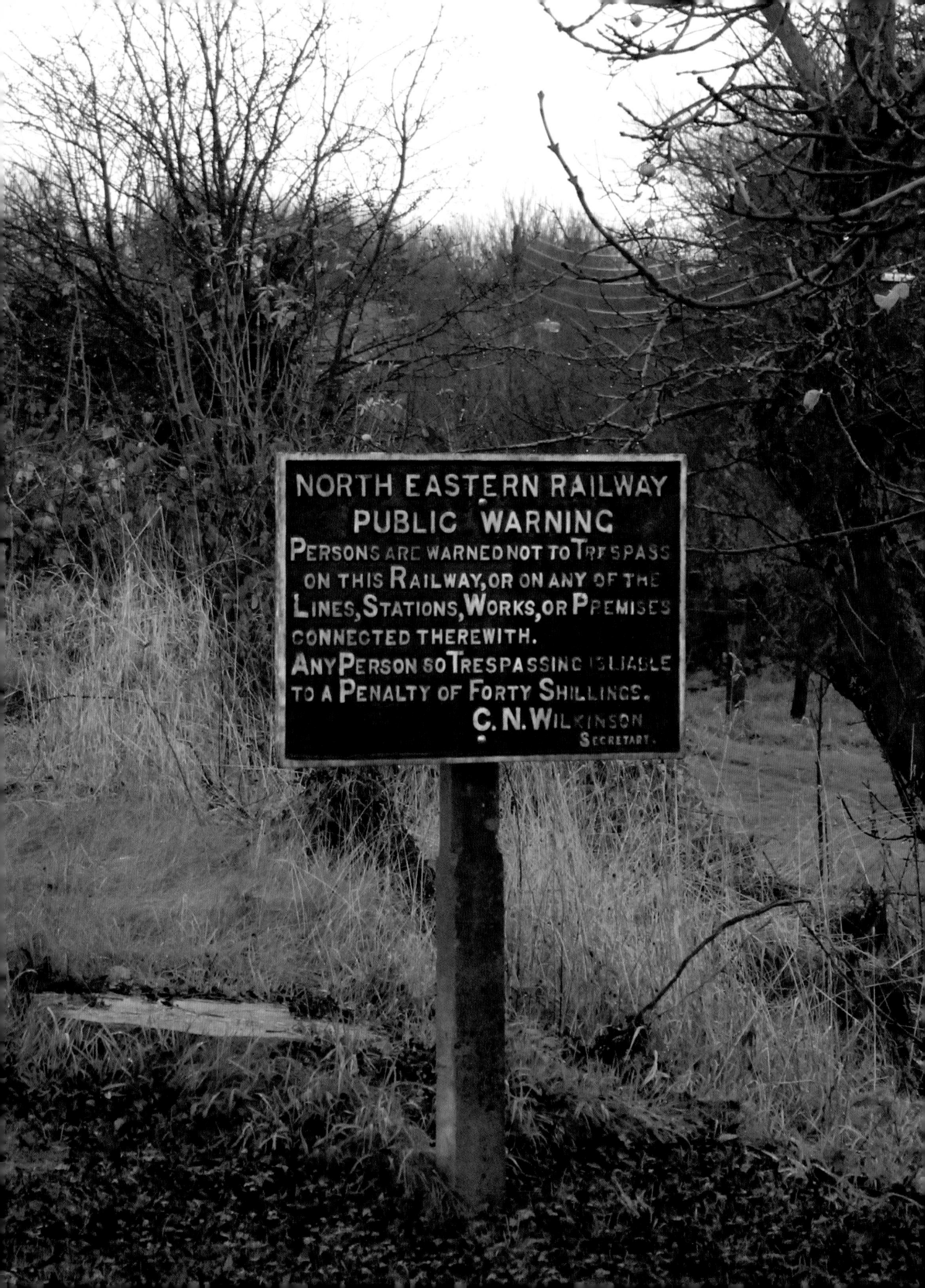

Since closure, around twelve miles of the Consett to Durham railway line has been opened as a footpath and cycleway known as the Lanchester Valley Railway Path. It also forms part of National Cycle Network Route 14.

At its western end the path starts at Lydgetts Junction, south of Consett, where there is a car park and picnic site. This is a crossroads of railway paths, with NCN Route 14 continuing northwards through Consett along the route of the old railway and down the Derwent Valley through Rowlands Gill, to end near Newcastle's Metro Centre on the south bank of the Tyne.

National Cycle Network Route 7 heads northeast from Lydgetts Junction along the old railway route through Annfield Plain, Stanley and Washington to Sunderland, while in the opposite direction it makes use of the railway route to Rowley on the long-closed line to Tow Law and Crook.

The Lanchester Valley Railway Path heads due east from Lydgetts Junction along the valley of Backgill Burn for 1½ miles to Knitsley station where the North Eastern Railway (NER) station building and eastbound platform survive as a private residence. Another 1½ miles west the path heads along the 70-ft embankment that was built in 1915 to replace a timber viaduct – the structure still lies buried beneath thousands of tons of colliery waste that was dumped here nearly 100 years ago.

After another 1½ miles the path reaches the village of Lanchester where refreshments can be taken at the Kings Head pub in Station Road. The eastbound platform and station building – built in a typical NER style with stepped gable ends – is also a private residence. One mile southeast of the village the path passes a car park and picnic site alongside the River Browney before crossing the river on a substantial stone bridge. Railway path and river keep close company down the valley for another three miles to reach Witton Gilbert station, where the substantial NER building is easily identified by an original NER cast-iron trespass notice at the bottom of its drive. While Witton Gilbert village is one mile away to the northeast, the village of Langley Park is much nearer and has the Rams Head pub as well as a car park for walkers and cyclists.

From Witton Gilbert station the railway path turns southeast and soon crosses the River Browney twice in quick succession on substantial stone bridges, followed by another two miles to the site of the long-demolished Bearpark (formerly Aldin Grange) station. The path then heads south for a further mile – after half a mile NCN Route 14 heads off east into Durham – before reaching the B6302 at the Broompark picnic site adjacent to the former Deerness Valley Junction on the East Coast Main Line south of Durham. From here the railway path continues southwards as NCN Route 20 to Bishop Auckland (see page 250).

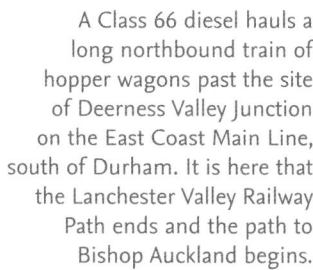

LEFT: This cast-iron North Eastern Railway sign warning of the penalty for trespassing still stands on the approach to Witton Gilbert station.

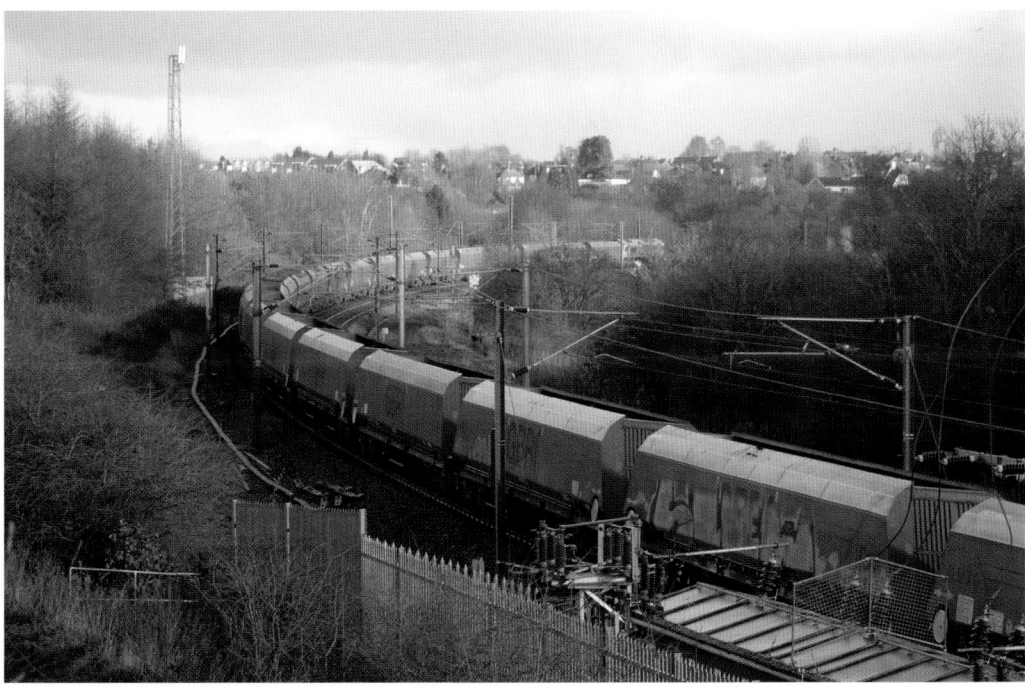

A Class 66 diesel hauls a long northbound train of hopper wagons past the site of Deerness Valley Junction on the East Coast Main Line, south of Durham. It is here that the Lanchester Valley Railway Path ends and the path to Bishop Auckland begins.

DURHAM
TO
BISHOP AUCKLAND

BRANDON TO BISHOP AUCKLAND RAILWAY PATH

Built to serve numerous collieries and brickworks, the 10-mile railway between Durham and the railway crossroads of Bishop Auckland was opened by the North Eastern Railway in 1857. In addition to local traffic the line was used by long-distance mineral and summer-only passenger trains that travelled via Barnard Castle and Stainmore Summit to and from destinations in northwest England until 1961. With declining coal and passenger traffic, the line then became a victim of the 'Beeching Report' and lost its passenger service in 1964, although it was kept open for coal traffic until 1968. Since then almost the entire length has been reopened as a footpath and cycleway.

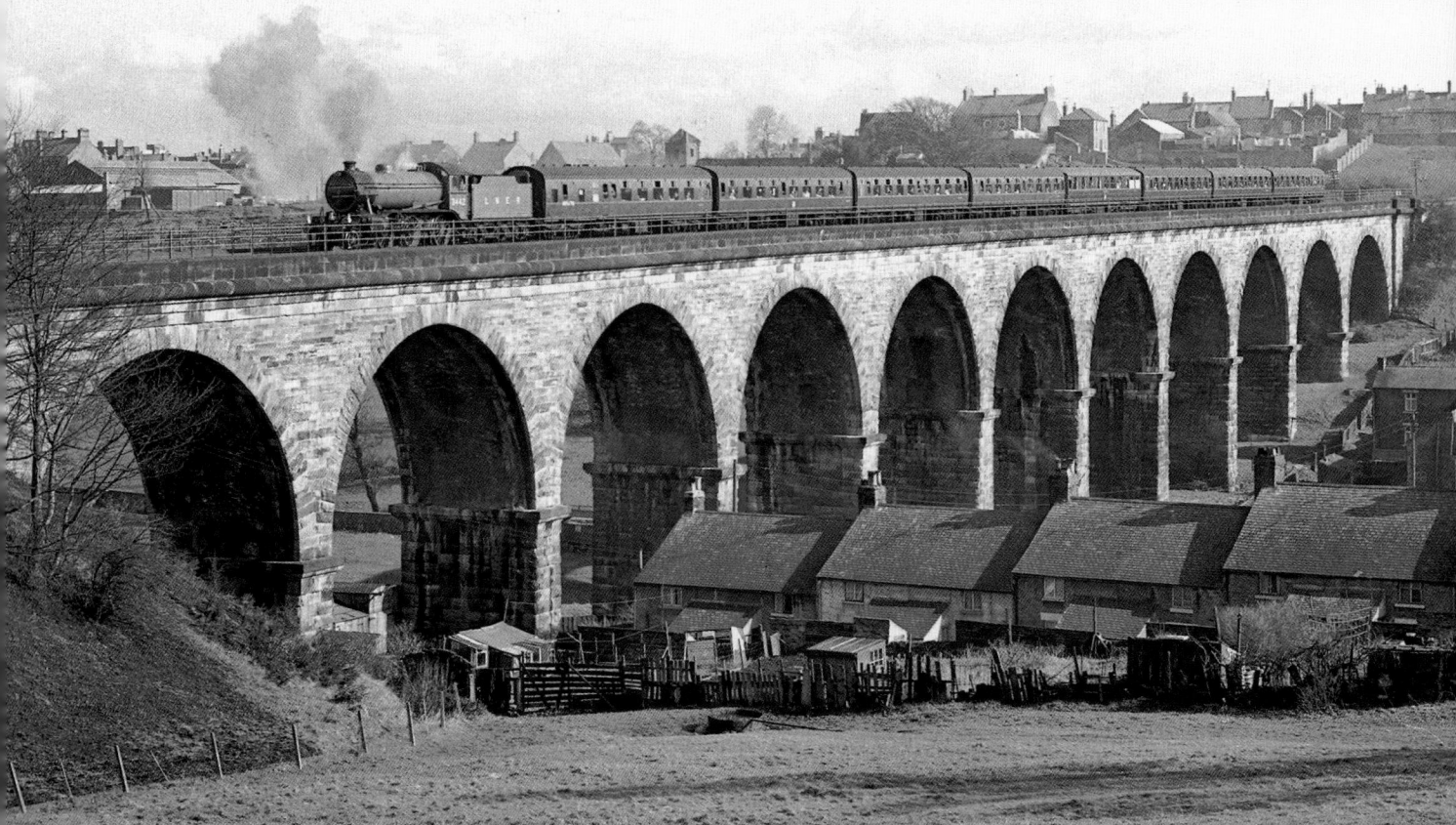

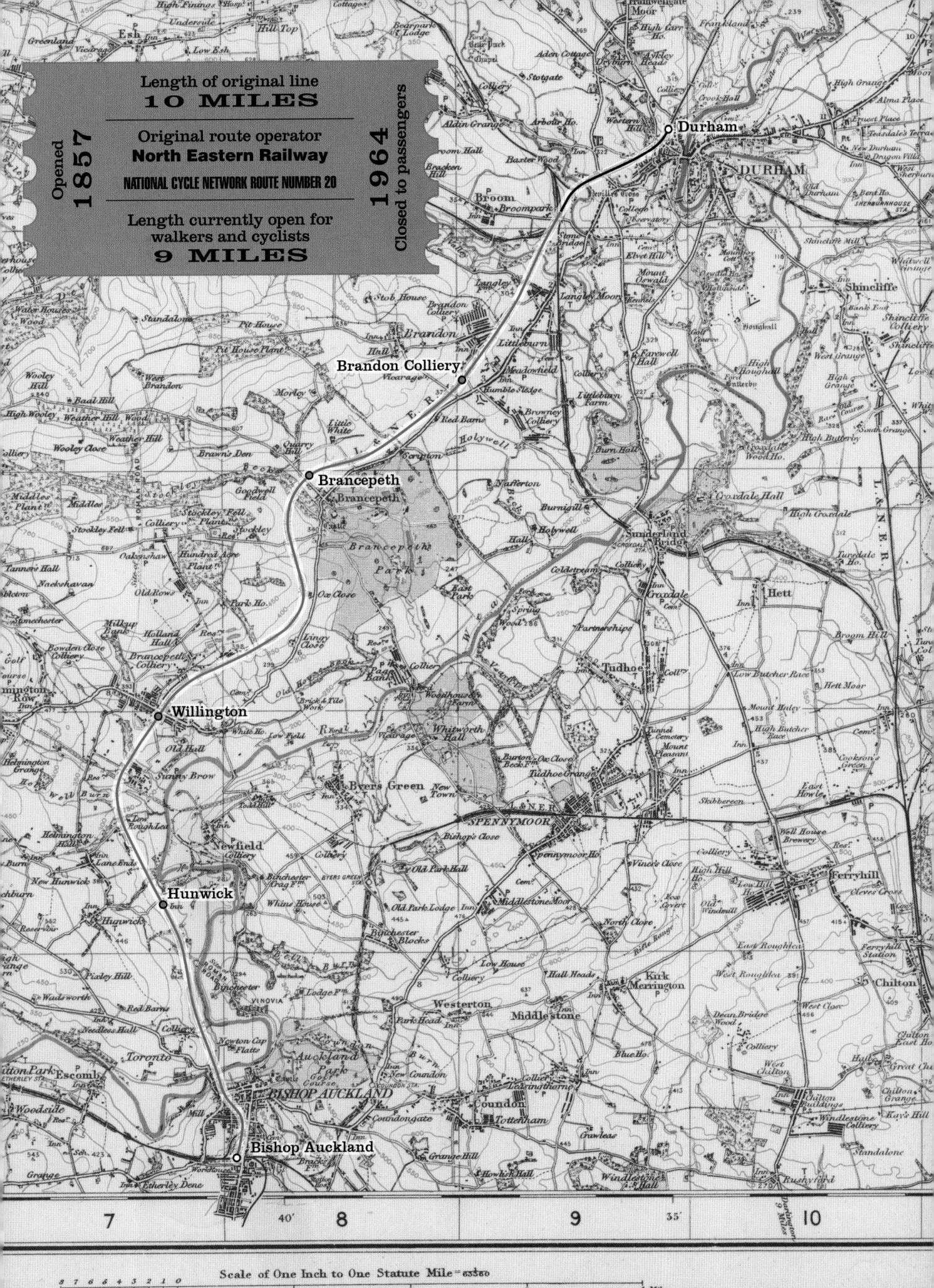

Durham

DURHAM

Shincliffe

Brandon Colliery

Brancepeth

Willington

Hunwick

BISHOP AUCKLAND

Bishop Auckland

Scale of One Inch to One Statute Mile = 63360

Located amidst a once-important coal-mining and limestone-quarrying region, the market town of Bishop Auckland has links with some of the earliest railways. The world's first publicly subscribed railway, the Stockton & Darlington Railway (S&DR), opened between collieries near Bishop Auckland and Stockton-on-Tees in 1825 – it was a great success and sparked a worldwide revolution in transport. By the 1880s Bishop Auckland was a major railway crossroads, with routes radiating out to Ferryhill, Stockton, Darlington, Barnard Castle, Weardale, Consett and Durham.

In 1854, four railway companies – York, Newcastle & Berwick, York & North Midland, Leeds Northern and Malton & Driffield Junction – had merged to form the North Eastern Railway (NER). The NER eventually went on to swallow up all the railway companies in northeast England, including the S&DR in 1863, and at its peak in 1922 controlled nearly 5,000 miles of railway.

One of the earliest railways to be built by the newly formed NER was the 10-mile line between Bishop Auckland and Durham, which opened to goods in 1857 and to passengers a year later. Intermediate stations were provided at Hunwick, Willington and Brancepeth and the line joined the East Coast Main Line one mile south of Durham at Deerness Valley Junction. The major engineering feature was the 11-arch Newton Cap Viaduct north of Bishop Auckland, which carried the railway 100 ft above the Wear Valley.

Serving numerous collieries and brickworks along its route, this primarily coal-carrying line also provided a link to the outside world for the coal miners and their families. A fourth intermediate station was opened at Brandon Colliery, north of Brancepeth, in 1861. In addition to locally generated passenger traffic the line was used in the summer months by through trains that operated between Newcastle, South Shields and Blackpool (North) via Barnard Castle, Stainmore and Tebay. Other traffic

Seen here at the end of the nineteenth century, the unusual station at Brandon Colliery was opened in 1861 and was originally named Brandon Siding. Trains only stopped here on Saturdays until 1878. The nearby Brandon Pit House Colliery closed in 1968. Since closure of the line, Brandon Colliery station has been demolished and the cutting has been infilled. It is used by walkers and cyclists on the Brandon to Bishop Auckland Railway Path.

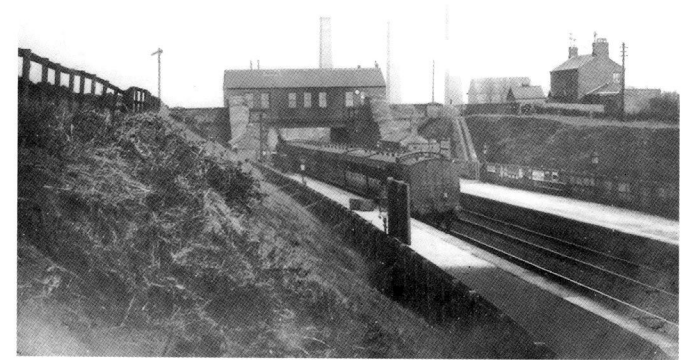

Three smartly dressed station staff strike a pose for the camera at Brancepeth station in the late nineteenth century. The attractive station building is now a well-screened private residence, while a nearby car park is provided for walkers and cyclists using the Brandon to Bishop Auckland Cycle Path.

PREVIOUS SPREAD: Preserved ex-LNER Class 'K4' No. 3442 'The Great Marquess' hauls a Railway Correspondence & Travel Society enthusiasts' special across Newton Cap Viaduct north of Bishop Auckland on 10 April 1965. The viaduct was converted into a road bridge with a pre-cast concrete deck in 1995.

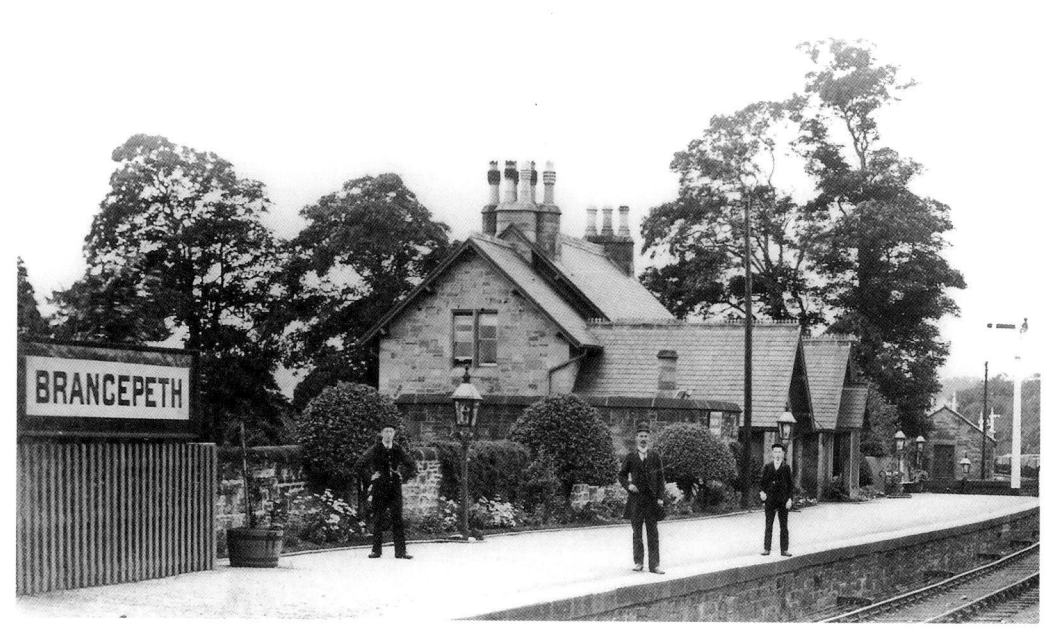

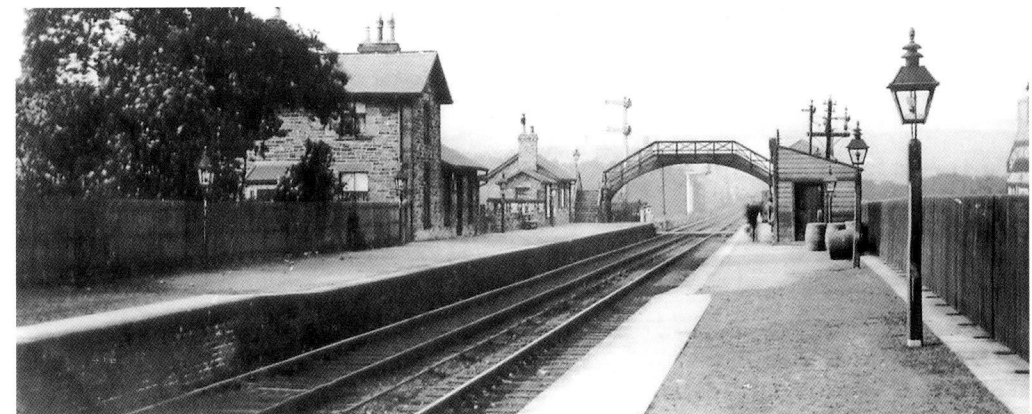

The sturdy stone station building at Hunwick, seen on the left in the early twentieth century and below today, is now a private residence alongside the Brandon to Bishop Auckland Railway Path. Nearby Hunwick Colliery closed in 1921 and the station lost its passenger service in May 1964.

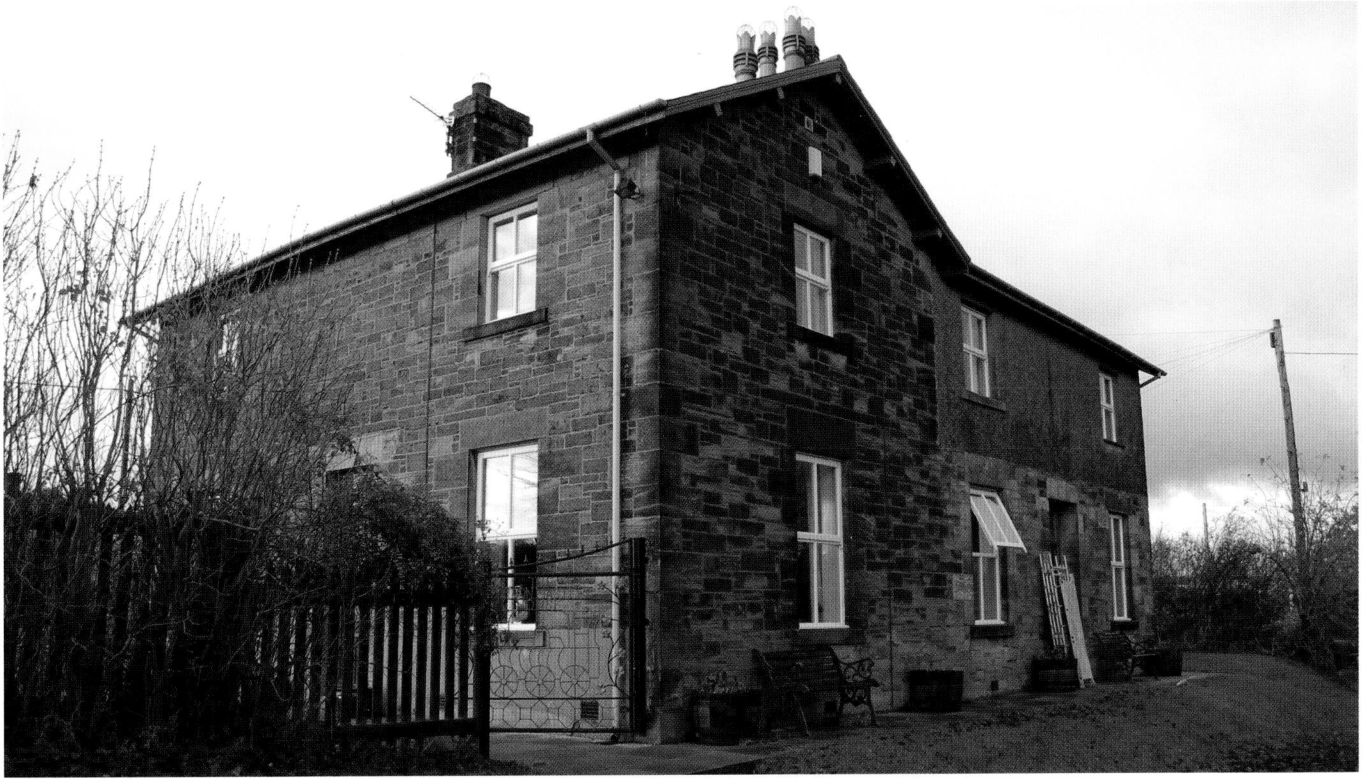

included Anglo-Scottish expresses that were diverted away from the East Coast Main Line during periods of engineering work at weekends. Most local services to and from Bishop Auckland were extended beyond Durham, beginning or ending their journeys at Sunderland. From 1871 the annual highlight was the second Saturday in July, when thousands of miners travelled by train from their local stations to the Durham Miners' Gala.

The austerity years following the Second World War brought in their wake a major contraction in County Durham's coal and coke industry, coupled with increased competition for the railways from road transport. Amidst declining coal traffic and falling passenger numbers,

British Railways introduced cost-effective diesel multiple units on the line in 1959. The through holiday trains to Blackpool (steam hauled to the end) made their last journey in September 1961 and the Stainmore route via Barnard Castle closed at the beginning of 1962.

The 1963 'Beeching Report' sounded the death knell for many railways in northeast England and the Bishops Auckland to Durham line was no exception. Closure to passengers came on 4 May 1964 and local goods facilities at the intermediate stations were withdrawn three months later. Despite this the line remained open for through freight trains and coal traffic until 1968 – the last coal mine, at Brandon, closed in that year.

The coal mines have long-since closed but nine miles of the Durham to Bishop Auckland railway route have been reopened as a footpath, cycleway and wildlife corridor known as the Brandon to Bishop Auckland Railway Path. It also forms part of National Cycle Network Route 20.

At its northern end, the path starts at the Broompark picnic site (only disabled parking here) on the B6302, about one mile to the southwest of Durham and on the site of the former Deerness Valley Junction adjacent to the East Coast Main Line. The Lanchester Valley Path from Consett joins it from the north (see page 240).

Heading southwards, the path soon reaches the urban sprawl of Brandon where the railway cutting has been infilled and the station demolished. This former coal-mining village once boasted three collieries, with the last one closing in 1968. One mile southwest of Brandon the path reaches the small village of Brancepeth, where there is a car park for walkers and cyclists. Nearby Brancepeth Castle, considerably rebuilt in the nineteenth century, was once the headquarters of the Durham Light Infantry but is now privately owned. The station building here has survived as a private residence.

From Brancepeth the path enters open country and winds around the contours for two miles before reaching the former coal-mining village of Willington. While the last coal mine closed in 1967, the village is still home to six pubs and a microbrewery – there is now no sign of the station or platforms. The path then heads south for 1½ miles into the valley of the meandering River Wear to reach the village of Hunwick – a car park for walkers and cyclists is located here while the station building is now a private residence.

From Hunwick the path edges ever closer to the River Wear for about one mile before ending at the magnificent Newton Cap Viaduct on the northern outskirts of Bishop Auckland. The path once crossed this Grade II structure, 100 ft above the River Wear, but in 1995 it was converted into a road bridge and widened with a pre-cast concrete top deck by 13 ft. After crossing the bridge it is but a short walk into the town.

Bishop Auckland is still served by trains from Darlington and is also the eastern terminus of the Weardale Railway from Stanhope.

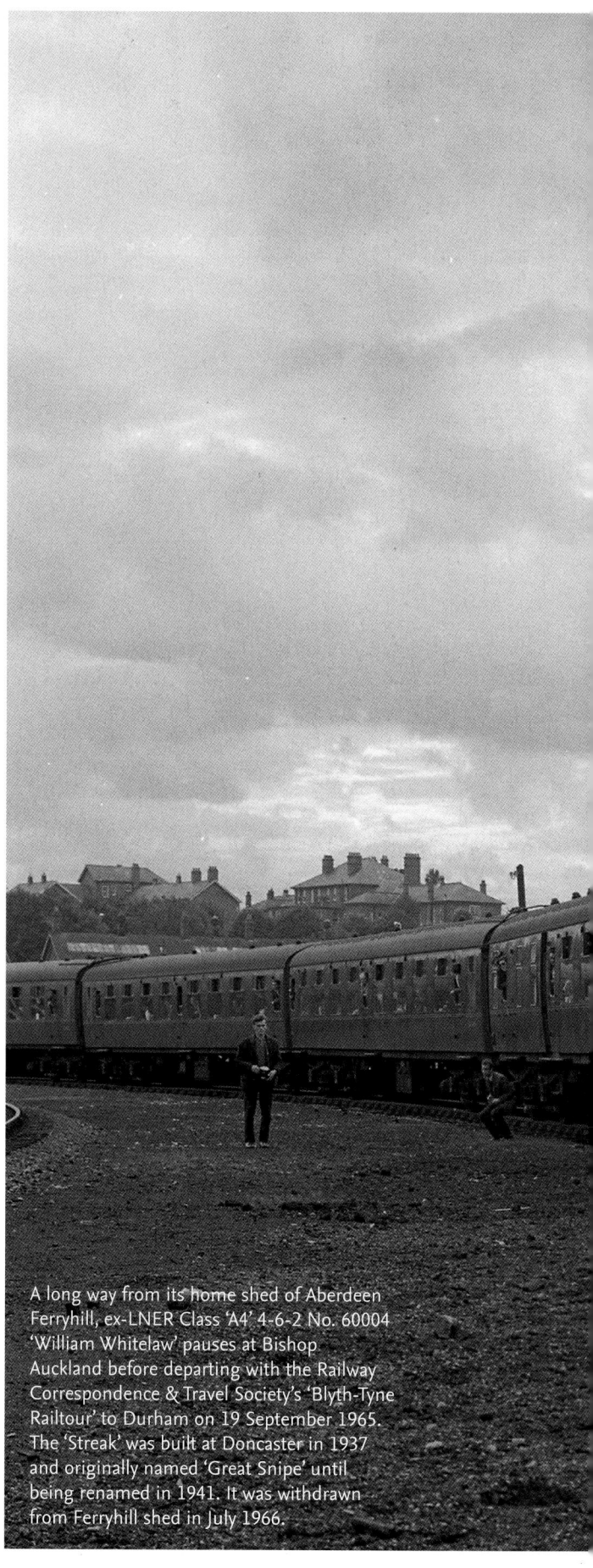

A long way from its home shed of Aberdeen Ferryhill, ex-LNER Class 'A4' 4-6-2 No. 60004 'William Whitelaw' pauses at Bishop Auckland before departing with the Railway Correspondence & Travel Society's 'Blyth-Tyne Railtour' to Durham on 19 September 1965. The 'Streak' was built at Doncaster in 1937 and originally named 'Great Snipe' until being renamed in 1941. It was withdrawn from Ferryhill shed in July 1966.

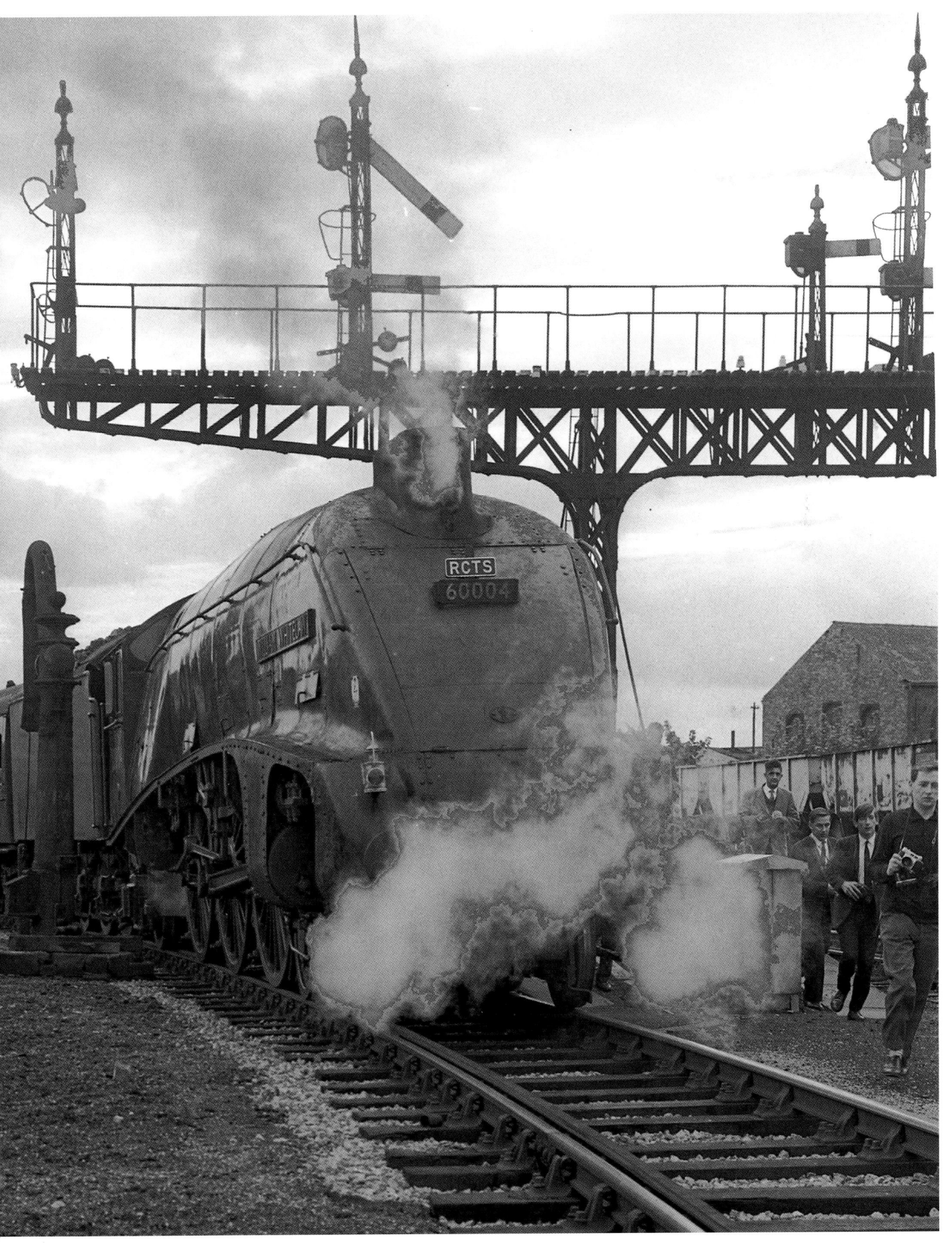

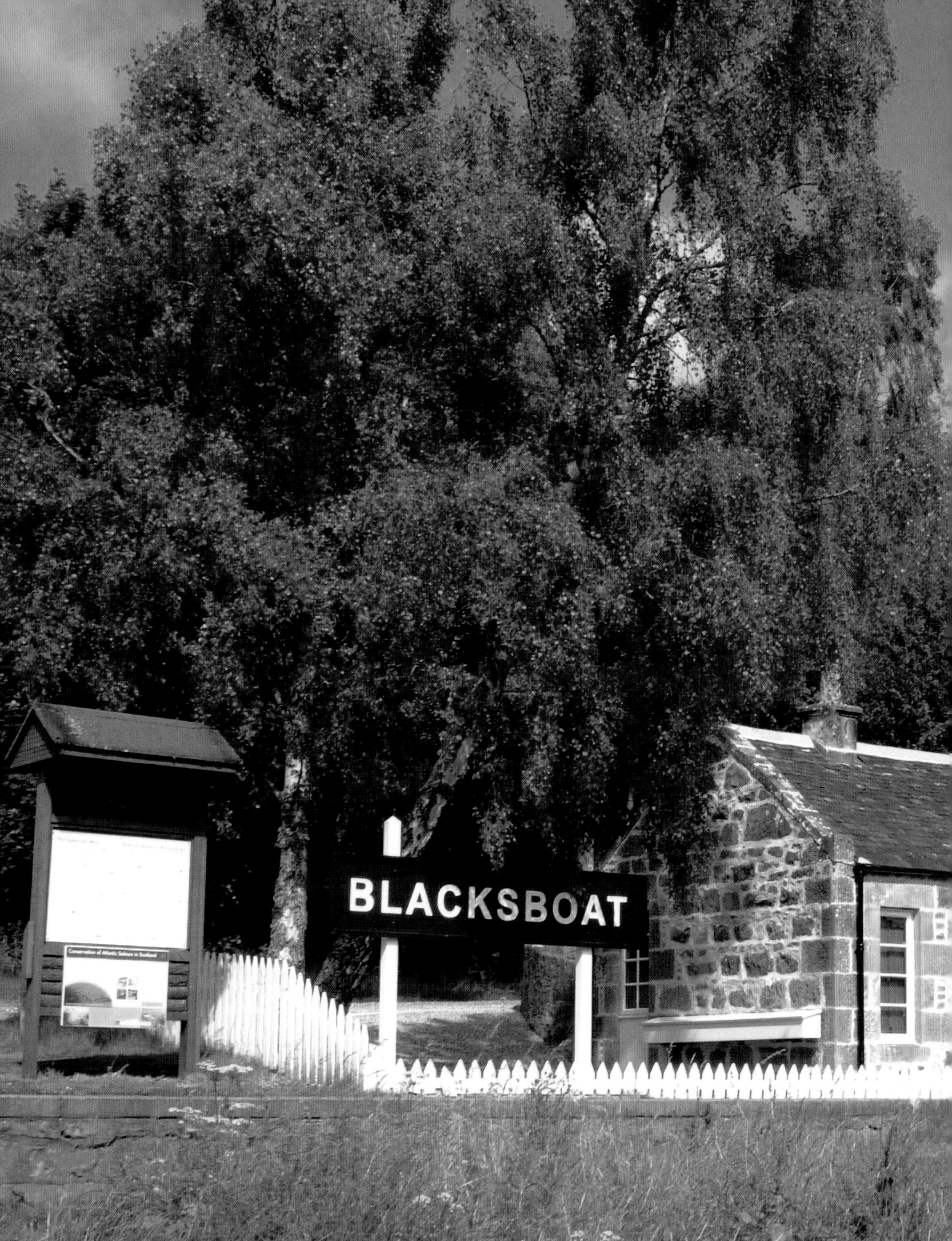

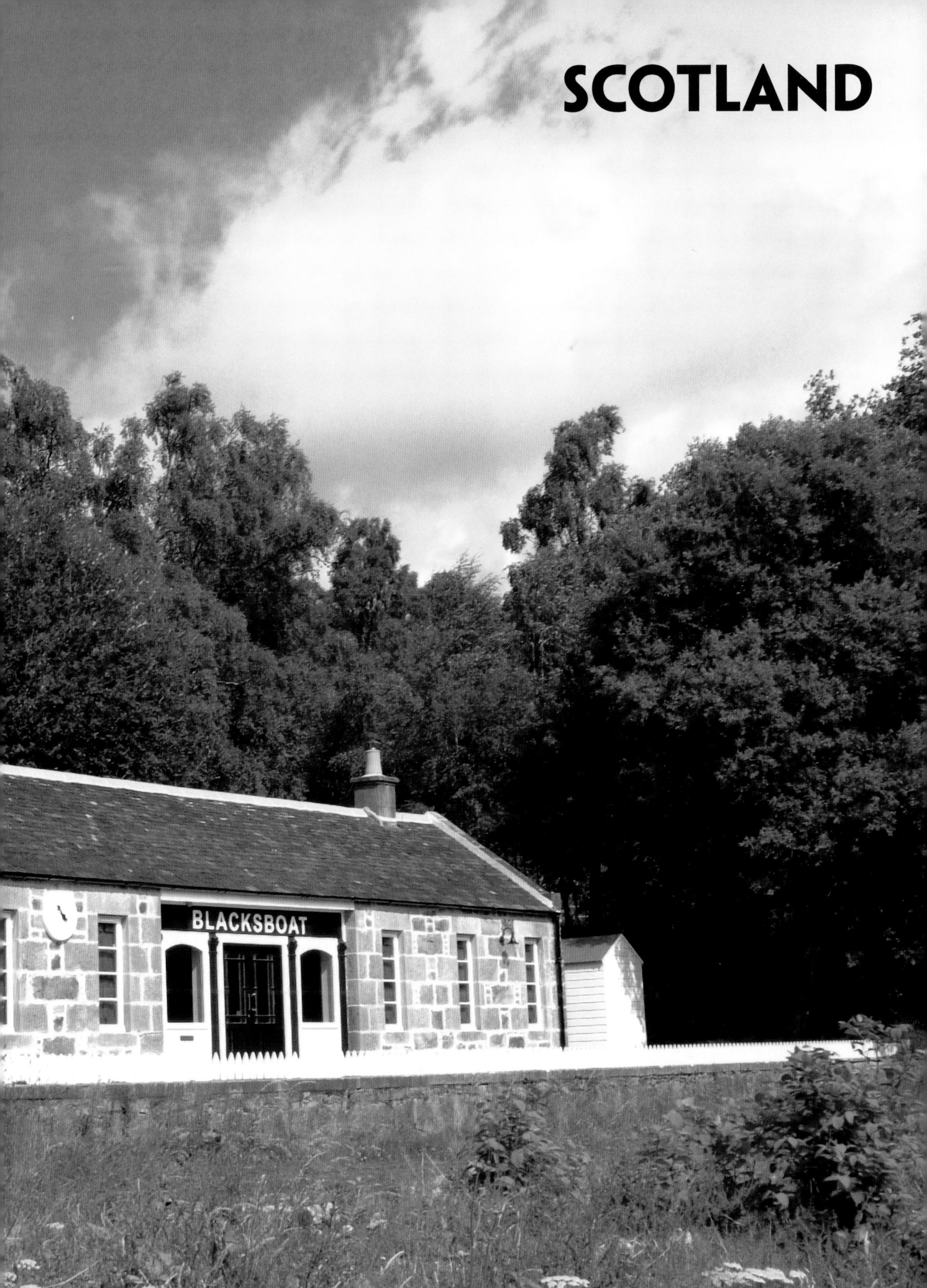

SCOTLAND

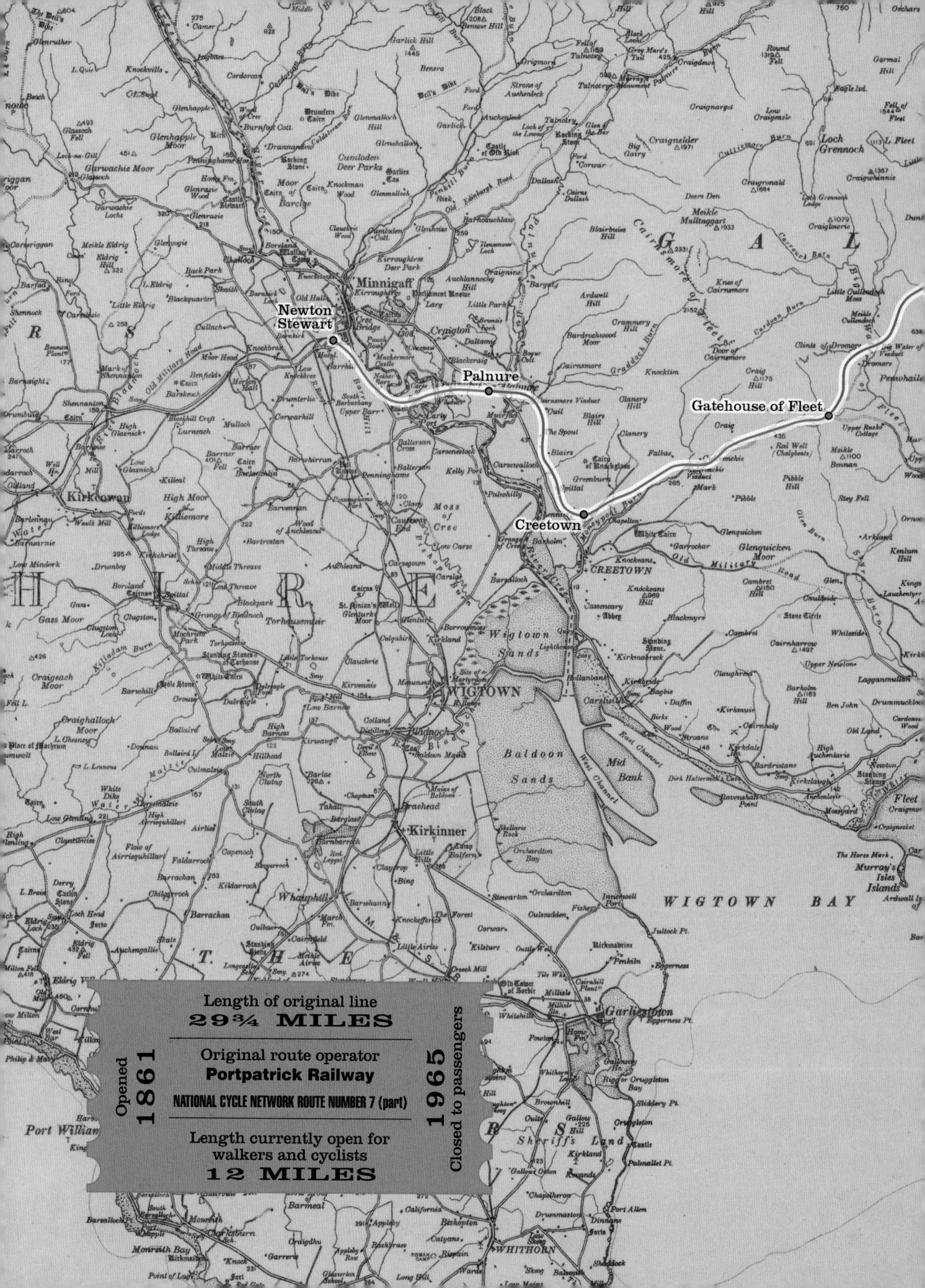

Newton
Stewart

Minnigaff

Palnure

Creetown

CREETOWN

Gatehouse of Fleet

WIGTOWN

Bladnoch

Kirkinner

WIGTOWN BAY

Garliestown

Port William

WHITHORN

Length of original line
29¾ MILES

Original route operator
Portpatrick Railway

NATIONAL CYCLE NETWORK ROUTE NUMBER 7 (part)

Length currently open for
walkers and cyclists
12 MILES

Opened **1861**

1965 Closed to passengers

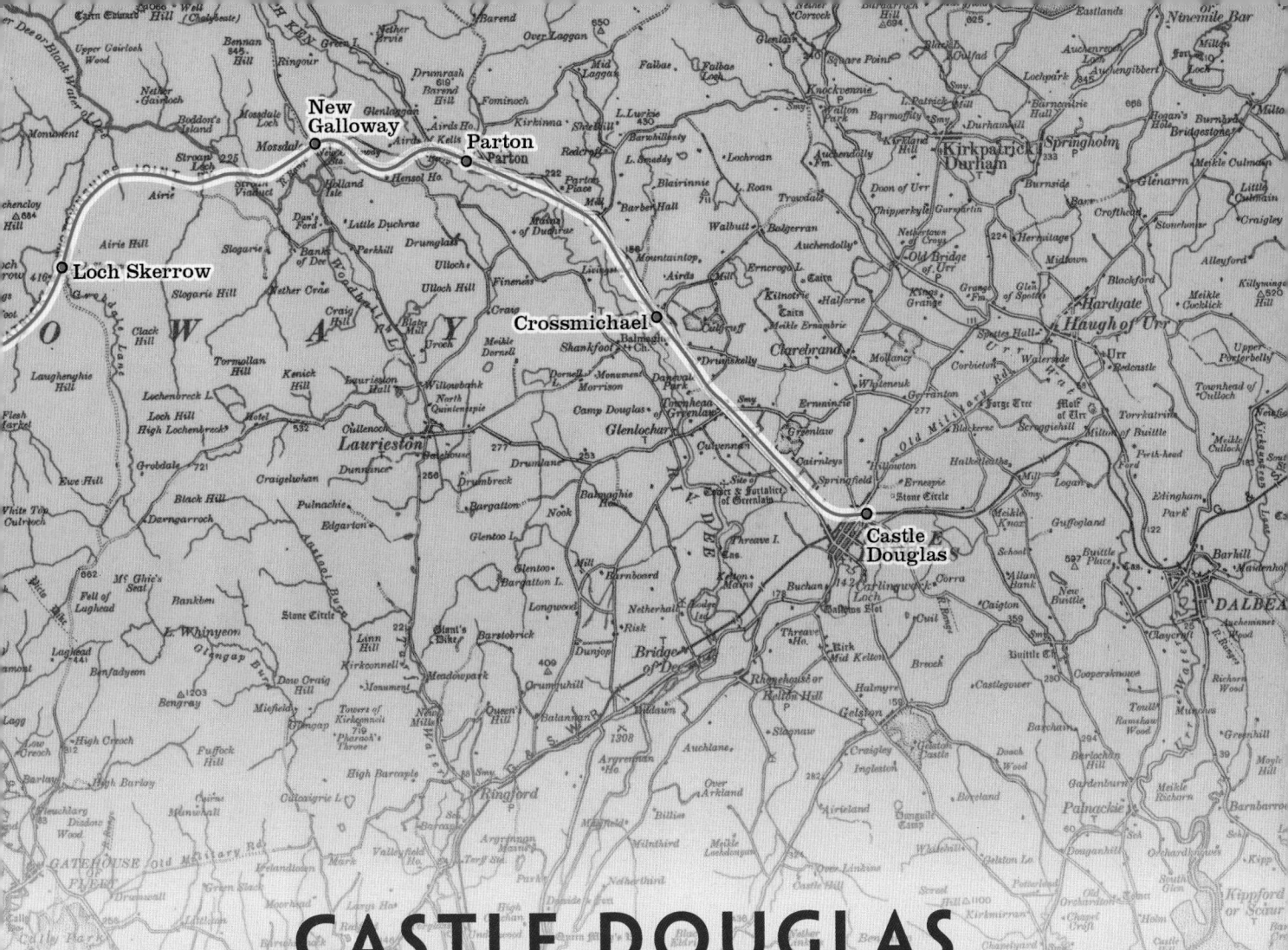

CASTLE DOUGLAS
TO
NEWTON STEWART

Known as the 'Port Road', the single-track railway through the remote hills of Galloway was once an important route for passenger and freight traffic to and from Northern Ireland via the port of Stranraer. Also served by an overnight sleeper train to and from Euston, the line featured several imposing viaducts and an attractive 3-arch bowstring bridge over Loch Ken. The years following the Second World War saw traffic in terminal decline and, steam-worked until the end, the entire route from Dumfries to Challoch Junction, east of Stranraer, closed in 1965. Today, a 10-mile stretch through remote forests between New Galloway and Gatehouse of Fleet, along with a 2-mile section north of Creetown, can be followed on foot or by mountain bike.

For centuries the shortest commercial sea crossing between Britain and Ireland was the twenty-one miles from Portpatrick in southwest Scotland to Donaghdee in County Down. This route had been used by sailing ships to carry soldiers, mail and livestock but the narrow harbour at Portpatrick was far from ideal for this purpose – from the land it was approached by a steep slope down through the cliffs and from the sea, it was open to southwesterly storms. Despite its unsuitability the Government poured taxpayers' money into improving the harbour during the nineteenth century, but all to no avail.

Portpatrick lost its Irish Mail traffic in 1850 when the Chester & Holyhead Railway was completely opened along the North Wales coast – despite the longer sea crossing between Holyhead and Dun Laoghaire, the introduction of new steam packets on this route provided a much faster service for Anglo-Irish traffic than via Portpatrick.

However, local railway promoters chose to ignore Portpatrick's unsuitability and were soon proposing various railways across the wilds of Galloway and Ayrshire to resuscitate the declining Irish traffic. The Castle Douglas & Dumfries Railway (CD&DR) opened the first 19¾-mile section of what became known as the 'Port Road' in 1859. A 53¼-mile single-track westward extension across the desolate wilds of Galloway, from Castle Douglas to Stranraer via Newton Stewart, was opened by the Portpatrick Railway (PR) in 1861 – this was extended by a further 7½ miles on a steeply graded route down to Portpatrick the following year. Involving the construction of numerous viaducts across river valleys and serving only a few small communities, the single-track railway across Galloway was costly to build and operate.

With the coming of the railway to Portpatrick more money was lavished on improvements to the harbour but, again, to no avail and it was abandoned as a steam packet

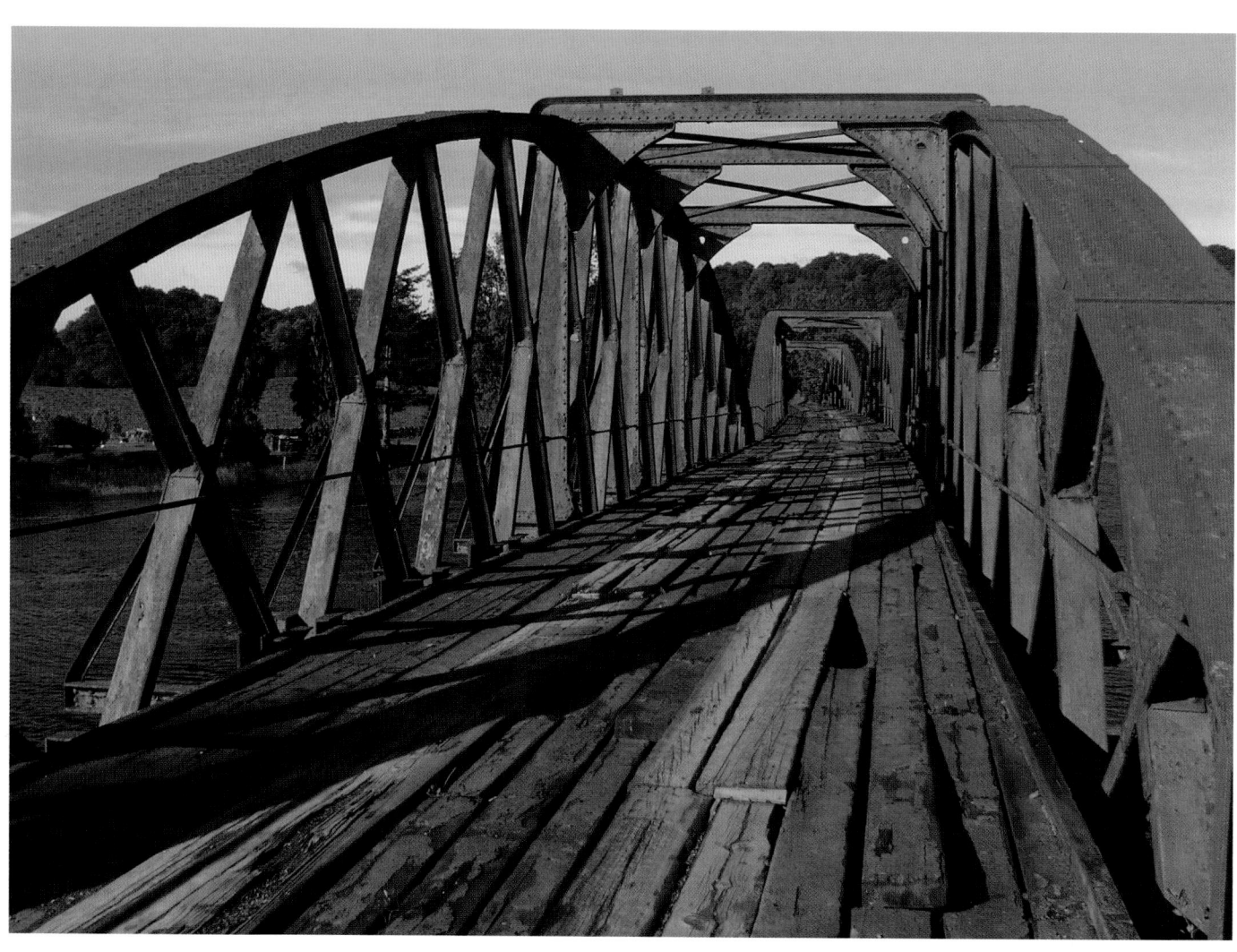

station in 1874 when a new harbour was built in the more sheltered waters of Loch Ryan at Stranraer. The Portpatrick branch line continued to be served by passenger trains until its closure in 1950. A second railway reached Stranraer from the north when the Girvan & Portpatrick Junction Railway opened in 1877 – the two lines met at Challoch Junction between Dunragit and Glenluce.

In 1877 the Wigtownshire Railway (WR) opened a branch line from Newton Stewart, on the 'Port Road', to the Isle of Whithorn but by 1885 both it and the PR were facing financial ruin. They were saved by their amalgamation as the Portpatrick & Wigtownshire Joint Railway (P&WJR) under the auspices of other interested parties: London & North Western Railway, Midland Railway, Caledonian Railway and Glasgow & South Western Railway. The latter had already taken over the CD&DR in 1865 and, in 1885, became jointly responsible for working the P&WJR with the Caledonian.

The 'Port Road' between Dumfries and Stranraer became part of the newly formed London Midland & Scottish Railway in 1923. While locally generated goods traffic in this sparsely populated region was always light, the line was heavily used during both World Wars and also by troop trains for the garrisons in Northern Ireland. Livestock traffic from Northern Ireland was also an important ingredient, with long cattle trains a common sight departing from Stranraer Harbour for distant markets around Britain.

While local passenger traffic was light, the 'Port Road' had seen a sleeping car train introduced by the Midland Railway between St Pancras and Stranraer Harbour in the early twentieth century. Affectionately known as 'The Paddy', the train connected with sailings to and from Larne in Northern Ireland. Euston station became the London terminus of the train in 1923 and it continued to run throughout the Second World War before receiving its official name, 'The Northern Irishman', in 1952. Passengers on the overnight train saw little of the Galloway landscape as this part of their journey, apart from during the long daylight hours in June, was covered at night. In summer months a through train also operated between Newcastle and Stranraer.

With increasing competition from road transport by the late 1950s however, both passenger and freight traffic on the 'Port Road' were in serious decline. Listed for closure in the 1963 'Beeching Report' the entire route from Dumfries to Challoch Junction closed on 14 June 1965 – beyond Challoch Junction the line remains open for passenger trains from Glasgow, Ayr and Girvan despite also being listed for closure by Beeching.

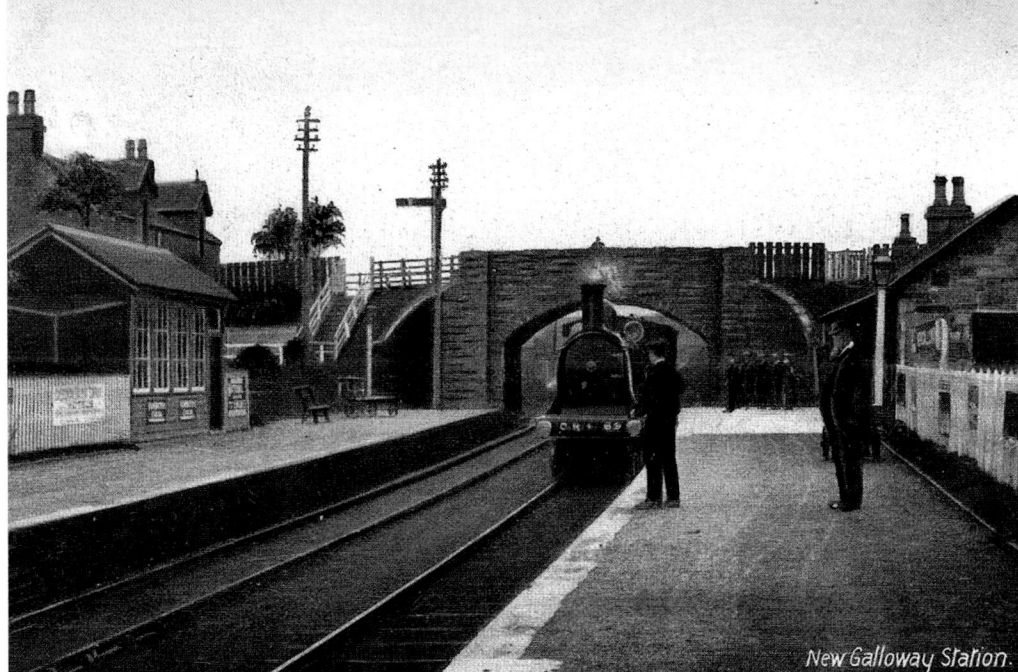

LEFT: Access to the magnificent 3-span bowstring bridge across Lock Ken is not permitted owing to its poor state of repair. The alternative route to the other side is a 10-mile road journey via the village of New Galloway.

This pre-1907 postcard depicts a Caledonian Railway locomotive arriving at New Galloway station with a Stranraer to Dumfries train. The station building survives today as a private house while the trackbed can be followed westwards under the road bridge to remote Loch Skerrow and Gatehouse of Fleet.

New Galloway Station.

Since closure two sections of the 'Port Road' between Castle Douglas and Newton Stewart have been reopened as footpaths and cycleways. While Castle Douglas station has long since disappeared, the substantial goods shed here still survives in its new guise as a building supply shop. Heading northwestwards out of Castle Douglas the A713 closely parallels, and in some places uses, the railway trackbed. Running alongside the east shore of Loch Ken for four miles, the road and old railway reach the village of Parton where the former station building is now a private residence. Half a mile west of the village the railway swung west across Loch Ken on a magnificent 3-span bowstring bridge – a padlocked gate blocks access to the rusting bridge but it can be viewed from a nearby car park. The road journey to the other side is a 10-mile detour via the village of New Galloway.

New Galloway station is actually five miles south of the village it purported to serve, in a settlement known as Mossdale where, alongside the A762, there is a car park. The station building and platform survive as a private residence. One mile to the east, the western end of the Loch Ken Bridge can be reached along a narrow lane. From the car park the trackbed of the 'Port Road' can be followed westwards on foot or mountain bike for ten

miles to Gatehouse of Fleet station. Much of the trackbed is also used for forestry operations so care should be taken when embarking on this journey – refreshments and a stout pair of walking boots are essential.

One mile west of New Galloway station, the track crosses the Black Water of Dee on the well-preserved Stroan Viaduct before continuing for another three miles around the lower slopes of Airie Hill to reach Loch Skerrow. Although not mentioned in timetables, trains once stopped here to fill up with water fed from the nearby loch – there was also a passing loop, signal box and platform in what must have been one of the loneliest outposts on Britain's railways. All that remains today are the slowly disintegrating westbound platform, concrete posts, fencing and cast-iron water pipes.

Heading southwest from Loch Skerrow, the trail sweeps through a vast area of forest for the next four miles. En route it passes the site of the Little Water of Fleet Viaduct, which was blown up by the Army as a training exercise following closure of the line. Fortunately the next viaduct across the Big Water of Fleet escaped the Army's attentions and still stands in all its glory. This imposing 20-arch structure was strengthened with ugly brick casing in 1924 following heavy use during

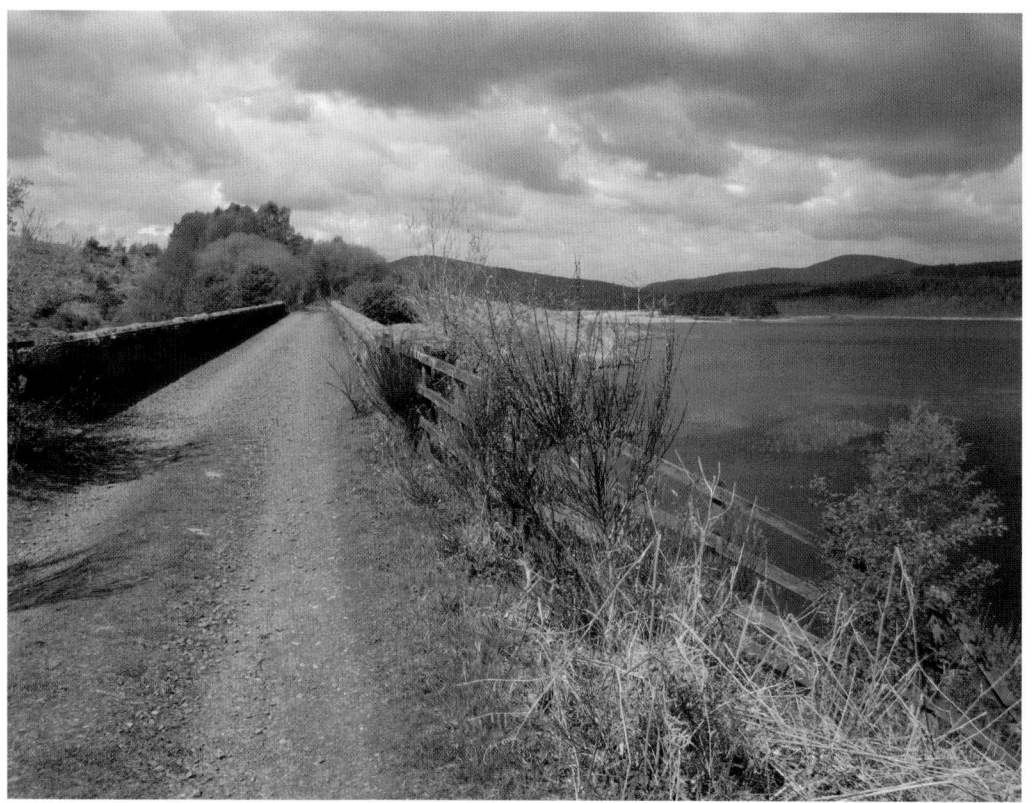

One mile west of New Galloway station, the 4-arch Stroan Viaduct once carried the 'Port Road' over the Black Water of Dee, where it flows out of Stroan Loch. Walkers and mountain bikers can now enjoy this remote route through the hills of Galloway.

RIGHT: Now owned by the cycling charity Sustrans, the impressive 20-arch viaduct across the Big Water of Fleet fortunately escaped the attention of the Army, which demolished its near neighbour across the Little Water of Fleet following closure of the line.

the First World War and is now owned by the charity Sustrans – National Cycle Network Route 7 passes beneath. Continuing over the viaduct, the old railway route can be followed along a forestry track for nearly two miles to Gatehouse of Fleet station – at 495 ft above sea level it was the summit of the line and was once home to a church housed in a grounded old clerestory railway coach! Now a private residence, the station was twelve miles north of the village it served.

The old railway route west of Gatehouse of Fleet is not passable but National Cycle Network Route 7 makes its journey through here along a country road and down the valley of Moneypool Burn to the village of Creetown. The former station and goods shed survive here as a private residence, their railway origins kept alive by an old BR goods van incongruously parked in the grounds. NCN Route 7 heads north out of Creetown along a country road for one mile before rejoining the old railway route up the valley of the River Cree to Palnure where the former station is now a private residence.

From Palnure the railway once headed west to cross the River Cree but the bridge no longer exists. Newton Stewart can only be reached from here by bike along NCN Route 7 via country roads or along the 'improved' A75.

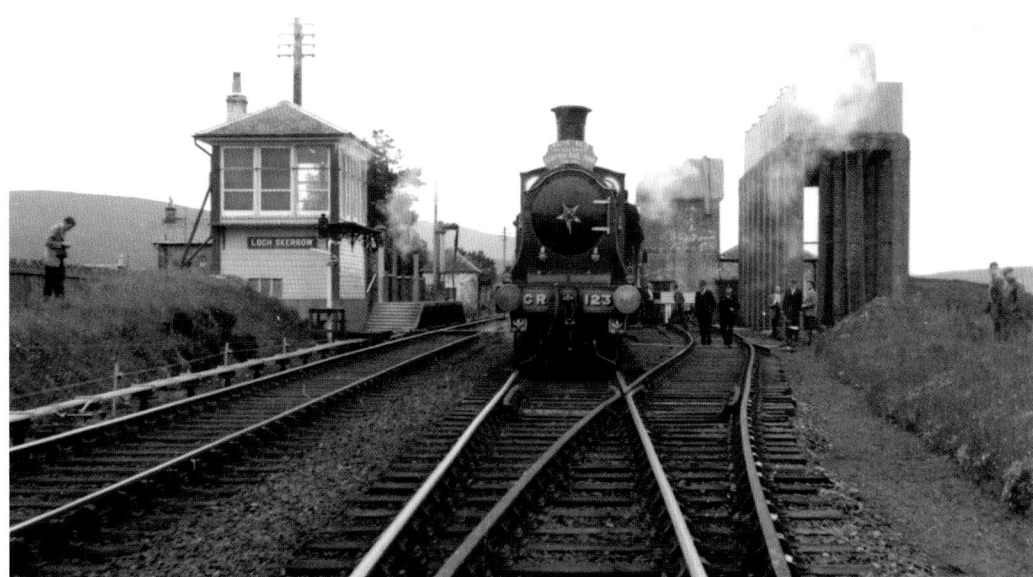

Inaccessible by road and never appearing in railway timetables, remote Loch Skerrow was one of the loneliest railway outposts in Britain. With snow fences, a passing loop, staff platform and signal box, it was a stopping place for engines to take on water fed from the nearby loch into a water tower. It is seen here during a visit by a Railway Correspondence & Travel Society/Stephenson Locomotive Society enthusiasts' special on 23 June 1962. The locomotive is preserved Caledonian Railway 4-2-2 No. 123.

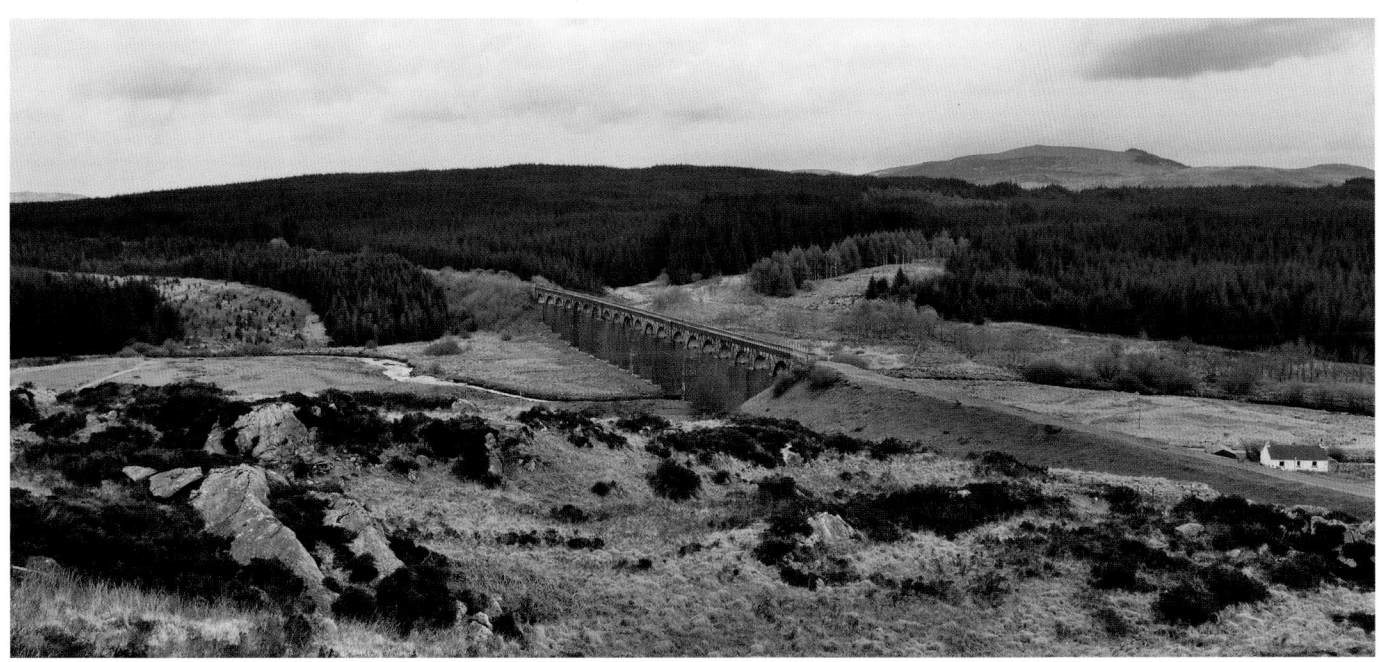

ELVANFOOT
TO
WANLOCKHEAD

Built as a Light Railway by 'Concrete Bob' McAlpine, the Leadhills &
Wanlockhead Light Railway served a once-thriving lead-mining industry
in the Lowther Hills. The main engineering feature was a concrete,
curving, 8-arch viaduct that was faced with terracotta bricks. With
the highest standard-gauge station in Britain, the line had only a short
life due to the ending of mining operations in 1934 and was closed
in 1939. Today, the trackbed can still be followed on foot or by mountain
bike up the Elvan Water Valley to Leadhills. Beyond here a passenger-
carrying narrow-gauge railway has opened along the trackbed to
the outskirts of Wanlockhead.

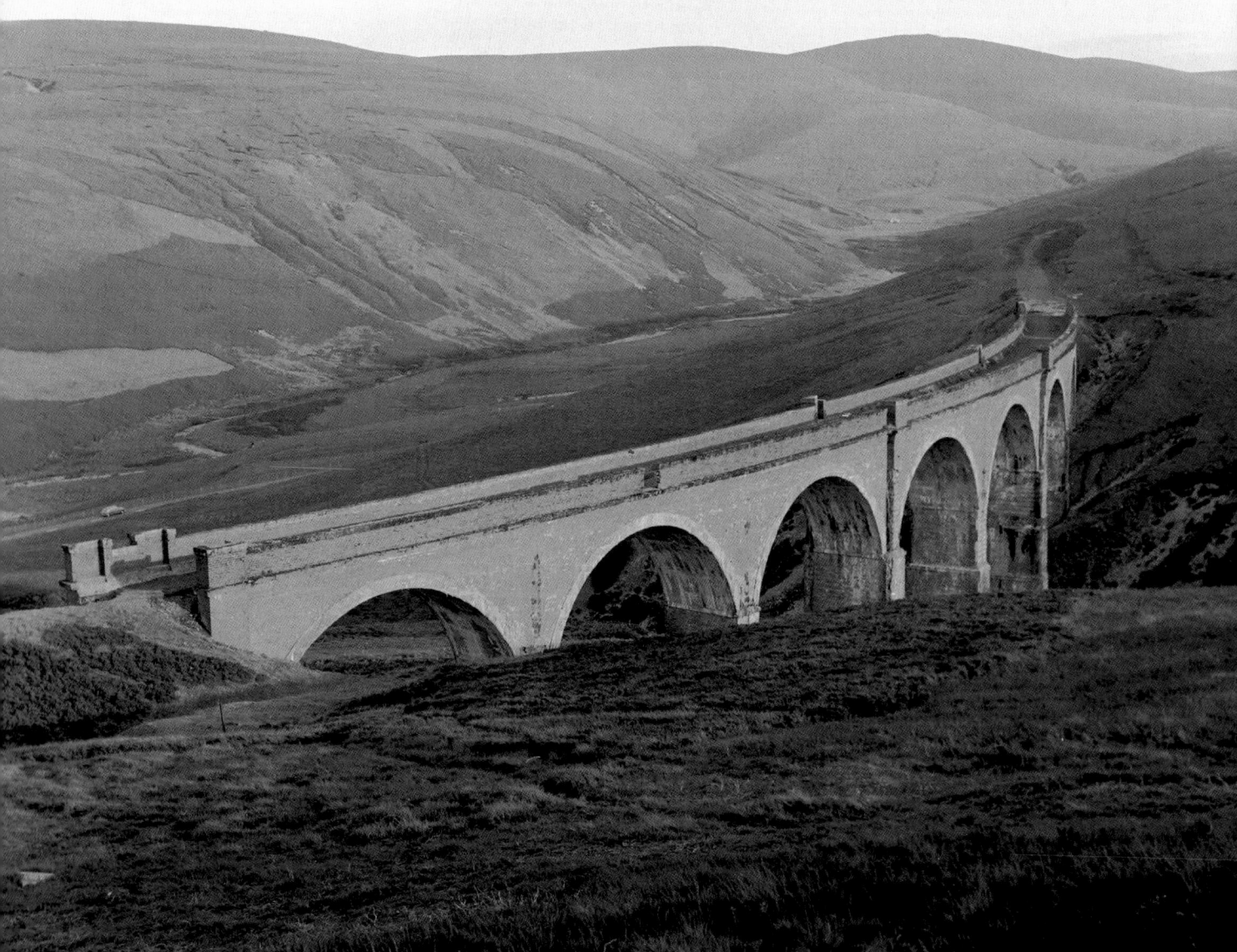

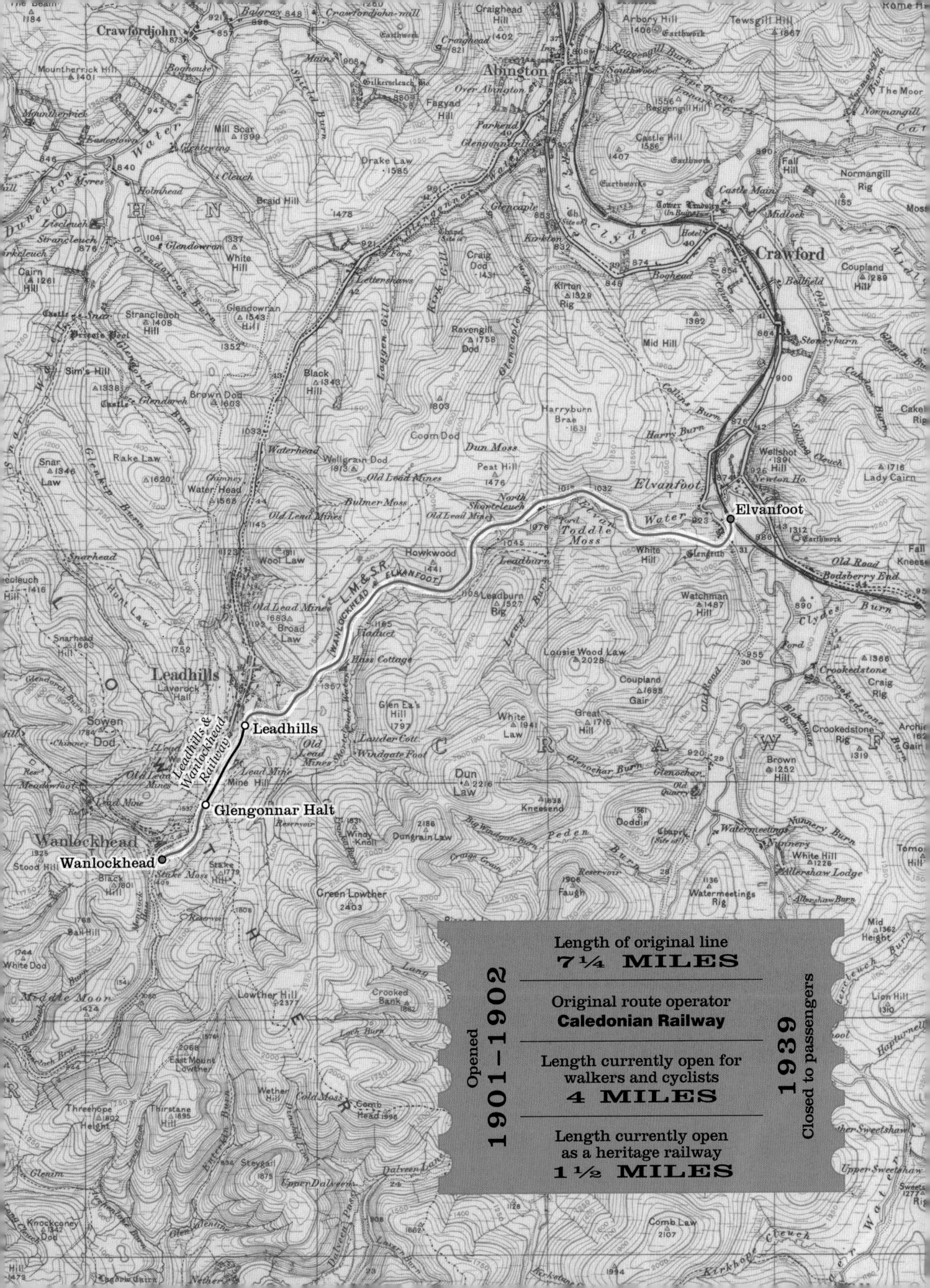

Leadhills & Wanlockhead Railway

Leadhills

Glengonnar Halt

Wanlockhead

Elvanfoot

Opened
1901–1902

Length of original line
7¼ MILES
————————————
Original route operator
Caledonian Railway
————————————
Length currently open for
walkers and cyclists
4 MILES
————————————
Length currently open
as a heritage railway
1½ MILES

1939
Closed to passengers

Set in Scotland's Southern Uplands, the bleak and remote Lowther Hills had been an important centre for the mining of lead and other mineral deposits since Roman times. By the late seventeenth century the local landowner, the Duke of Buccleuch, had built a lead-smelting plant and workers' cottages in the village of Wanlockhead and by the eighteenth century not only

lead but also zinc, silver, and copper were being mined in the surrounding hills, making Wanlockhead and its neighbouring village of Leadhills one of the richest sources of minerals in Scotland. Wanlockhead was also at the forefront of mining technology when a steam-powered beam engine with water buckets was introduced in the mid-eighteenth century to pump water out of one of the mines. The education of the miners and their families was not forgotten either, as the Duke of Buccleuch set up libraries for them in the villages – Wanlockhead Miners' Library is the second-oldest subscription library in Europe.

For centuries, transporting the mined minerals from the Lowther Hills involved long overland journeys by pack

PREVIOUS SPREAD: Built by 'Concrete Bob' McAlpine, the curving viaduct at Rispin Cleugh was the major engineering feature of the Leadhills branch. Seen here in 1974, its eight arches were faced with terracotta bricks but, sadly, the structure was demolished due to its poor state of repair in a controlled explosion in 1991.

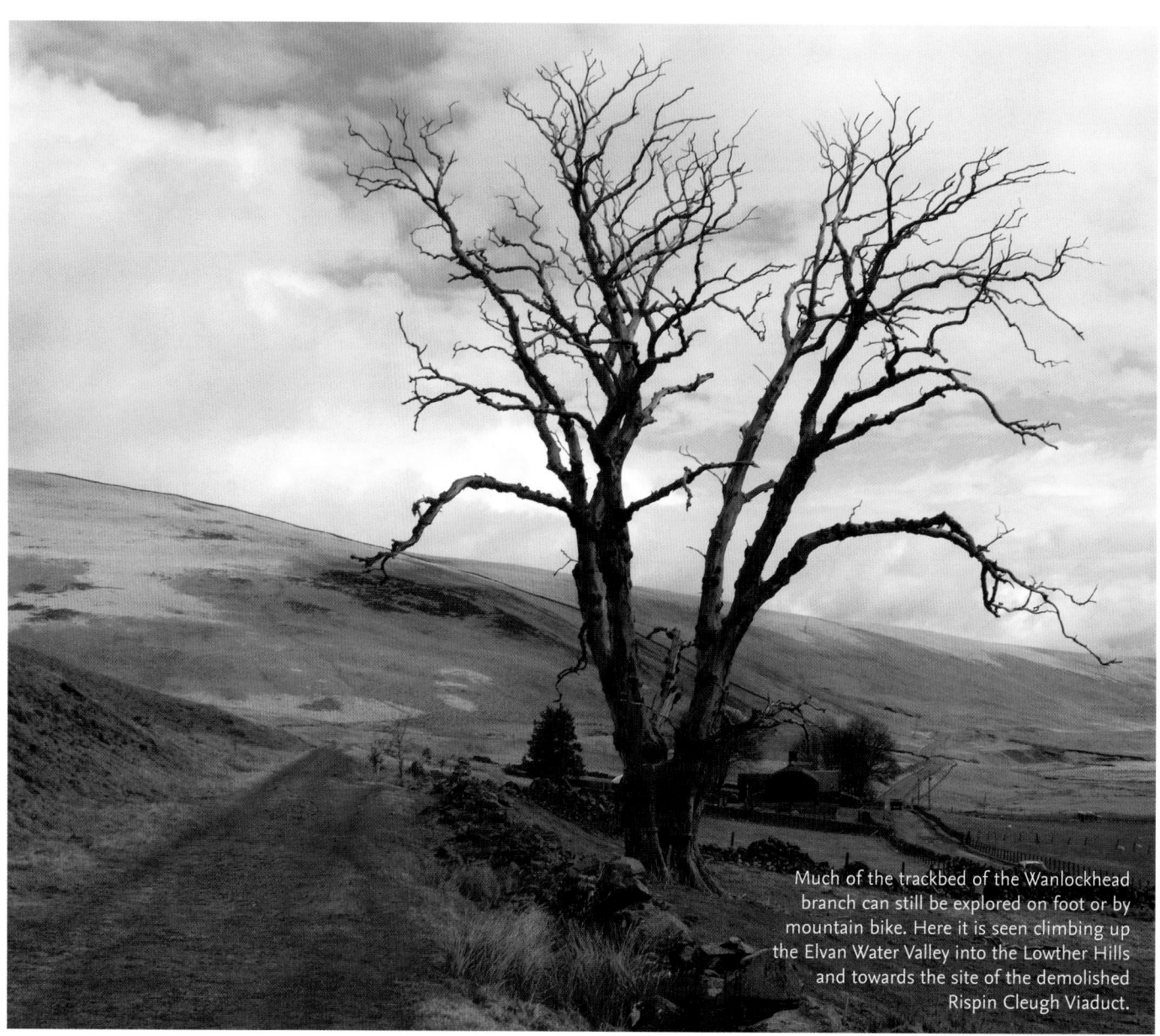

Much of the trackbed of the Wanlockhead branch can still be explored on foot or by mountain bike. Here it is seen climbing up the Elvan Water Valley into the Lowther Hills and towards the site of the demolished Rispin Cleugh Viaduct.

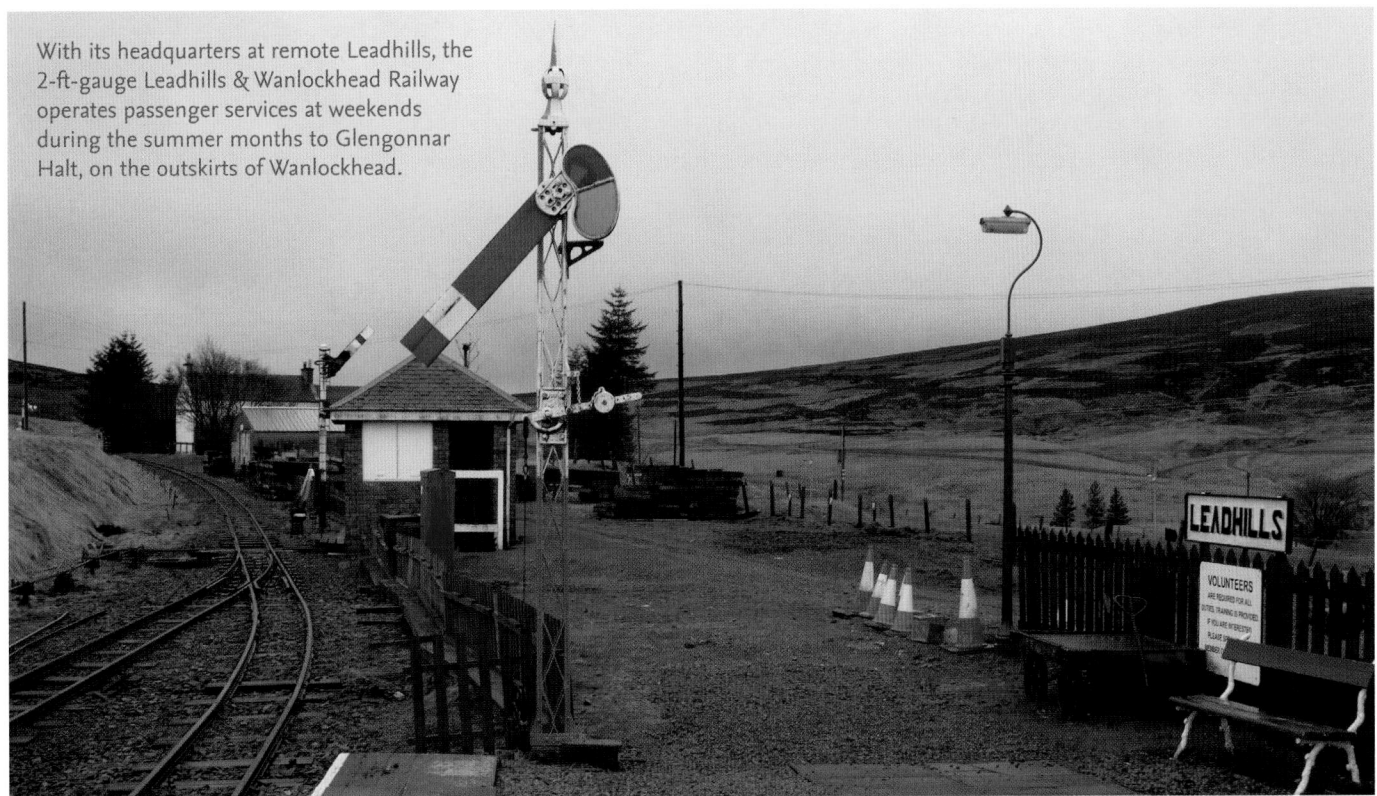

With its headquarters at remote Leadhills, the 2-ft-gauge Leadhills & Wanlockhead Railway operates passenger services at weekends during the summer months to Glengonnar Halt, on the outskirts of Wanlockhead.

horse or horse and cart to the nearest port. However, the opening of Elvanfoot station on the Caledonian Railway's (CR) main line between Carlisle and Glasgow in 1848 soon led to demands from the mining companies for a branch line to be built to the Lowther Hills – the CR considered the costs too prohibitive until 1896 when the Light Railways Act was passed by Parliament. Despite this, a local network of narrow-gauge lines had already been built to connect mines with smelters in Leadhills and Wanlockhead.

The Light Railways Act allowed lines to be built in sparsely populated rural areas to a much cheaper specification than before, without fencing, signalling, level crossing gates or station platforms, although weight and speed restrictions were imposed. One of the first of these Light Railways to be built was the CR-promoted Leadhills & Wanlockhead Light Railway, which was given permission for a 7¼-mile steeply graded single-track branch line from Elvanfoot up the Elvan Water Valley to Leadhills and Wanlockhead in 1898. The engineer for the line was Robert McAlpine, famous for his use of concrete, which earned him the nickname Concrete Bob. The only major engineering feature was the curving 8-arch Rispin Cleugh Viaduct, which was naturally built of concrete but faced with terracotta bricks.

Worked from the outset by the CR, the branch line opened to Leadhills in 1901 and to Wanlockhead the following year – at 1,498ft above sea level, the latter was the highest standard-gauge station in Britain. Passenger traffic was always light and one coach usually sufficed for the service, which consisted of four down trains on weekdays and three in the opposite direction (plus an extra working on Saturdays). In later years a balconied passenger coach from the closed Garstang & Knott End Railway in Lancashire was drafted in for this service. The leisurely journey was often interrupted to pick up passengers waiting at the trackside or for the guard to chase sheep off the line. Closure following heavy snowfall in the winter months was another regular feature of travel along this exposed railway.

Although the railway was built primarily to serve the mining industry at Leadhills and Wanlockhead, this *raison d'être* was not to last very long. The lead smelter at Wanlockhead closed in 1928 and by 1934 all the mines had followed suit. With little passenger traffic the line struggled on for a few more years until closure on 2 January 1939. Elvanfoot station closed in 1965 and the communities of the Lowther Hills were once again cut off from the outside world. Even Rispin Cleugh Viaduct was demolished in 1991.

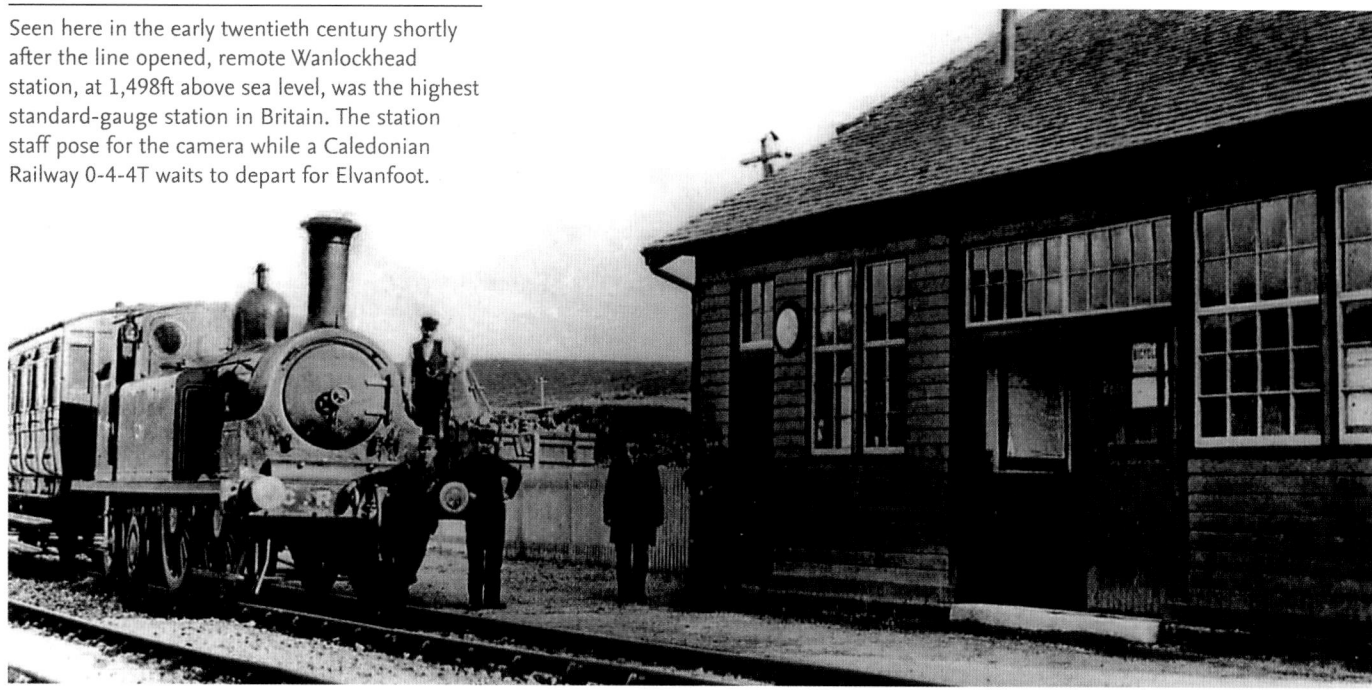

Seen here in the early twentieth century shortly after the line opened, remote Wanlockhead station, at 1,498ft above sea level, was the highest standard-gauge station in Britain. The station staff pose for the camera while a Caledonian Railway 0-4-4T waits to depart for Elvanfoot.

Despite closure nearly 75 years ago, much of the trackbed of the Leadhills & Wanlockhead Light Railway can still be traced today. While electric Pendolino trains glide effortlessly through Elvanfoot at 110mph and traffic roars along the M74 at breakneck speeds, a short diversion from this major trunk route through upper Strath Clyde will bring the intrepid explorer of lost railways to the hidden delights of the Lowther Hills.

Much of the railway's route up the Elvan Water Valley can be followed on foot – the best starting point is one mile west of Elvanfoot on the B7040, where the railway once crossed the road on the level. From here the old trackbed can be seen winding back down the valley to Elvanfoot, where its course is now blocked by a large electricity sub-station.

With the original ballast still visible the trackbed can be followed up the valley on foot to Leadhills, a distance of four miles. En route there are magnificent views of the surrounding Lowther Hills although it is sad that the railway's *pièce de résistance*, Rispin Cleugh Viaduct, was demolished several years ago – the only reminder is a small plaque on the roadside.

The small village of Leadhills provides basic amenities such as a shop and the Hopetoun Arms, but pride of place must surely go to the 2-ft-gauge Leadhills & Wanlockhead Railway which carries passengers along the old railway

trackbed for 1½ miles southwards as far as Glengonnar Halt. The railway opened in 1988 and has since been gradually extended to its current length. Future plans include extending southwards to a new terminus at Wanlockhead and also eastwards for half-a-mile from Leadhills station to the B7040. Trains are usually hauled by diminutive diesel locos and normally operate on weekends and Bank Holidays from May to September.

At 1,531 ft above sea level, Wanlockhead is Scotland's highest village (it also has the highest pub) and consequently has a much higher than average rainfall. The station has long gone, with its site now covered by agricultural buildings, but there are traces everywhere of old mine workings and the narrow-gauge feeder lines that once transported ore to the village. One such line can be followed up the Wanlock Water Valley, where there are still visible remains of the workings of the mines and their associated buildings. The village features a lead-mining museum, located in the Miners' Library, and a restored beam engine that once pumped water from a nearby mine.

RIGHT: At Wanlockhead, Scotland's highest village, there are reminders of its industrial past everywhere. Here the trackbed of a narrow-gauge feeder tramway can be followed up the Wanlock Water Valley past spoil heaps to old mine workings.

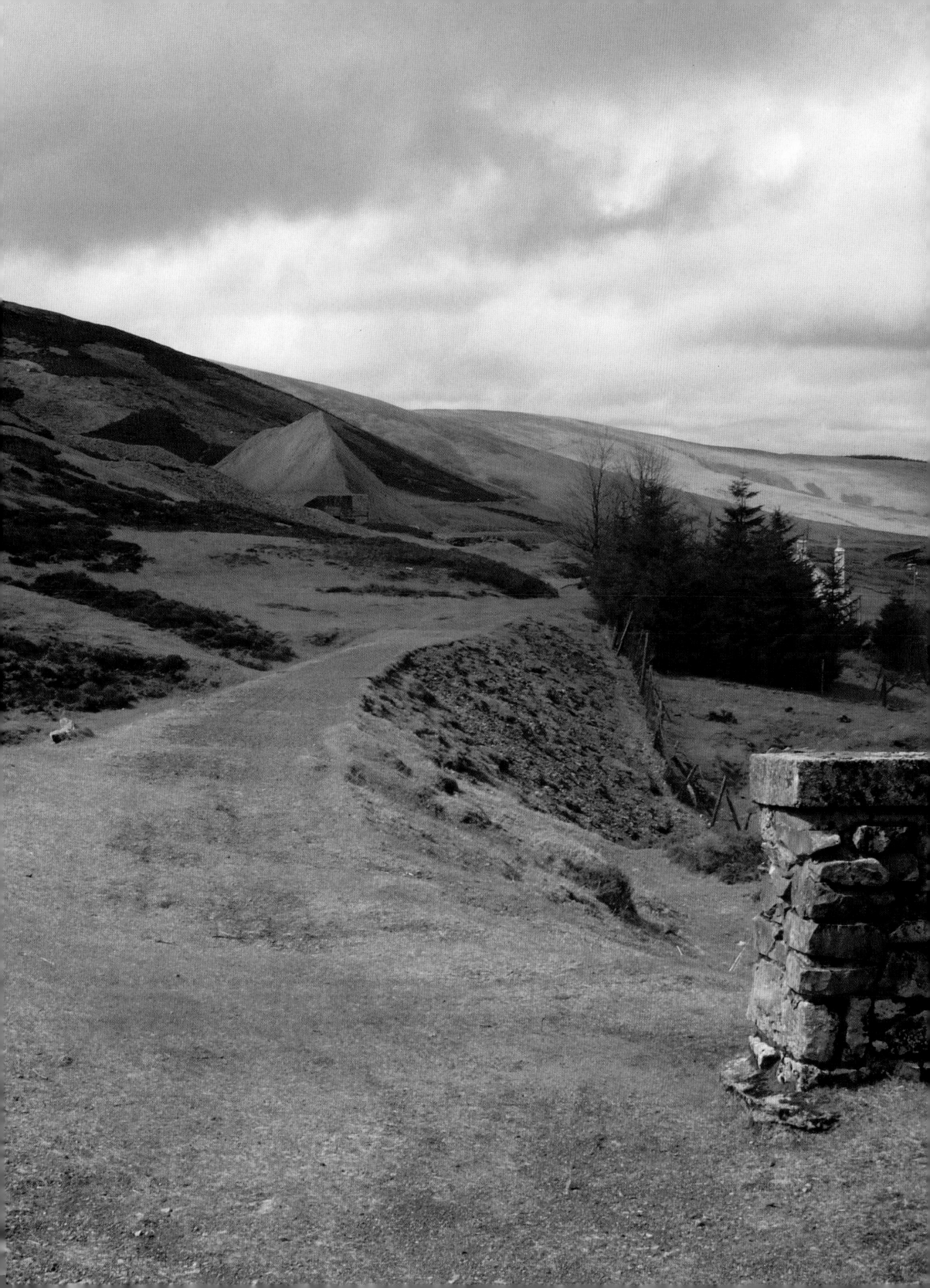

THE ST LEONARDS BRANCH, EDINBURGH

INNOCENT RAILWAY PATH

One of Scotland's first railways, the Edinburgh & Dalkeith Railway, was a horse-drawn affair until purchased by the North British Railway in 1845. It was then rebuilt and steam power introduced, although the steeply graded branch up to St Leonards lost its passenger service. Featuring Scotland's first railway tunnel, the branch continued to be used by goods trains until 1968. It has since been reopened as a footpath and cycleway known as the Innocent Railway Path.

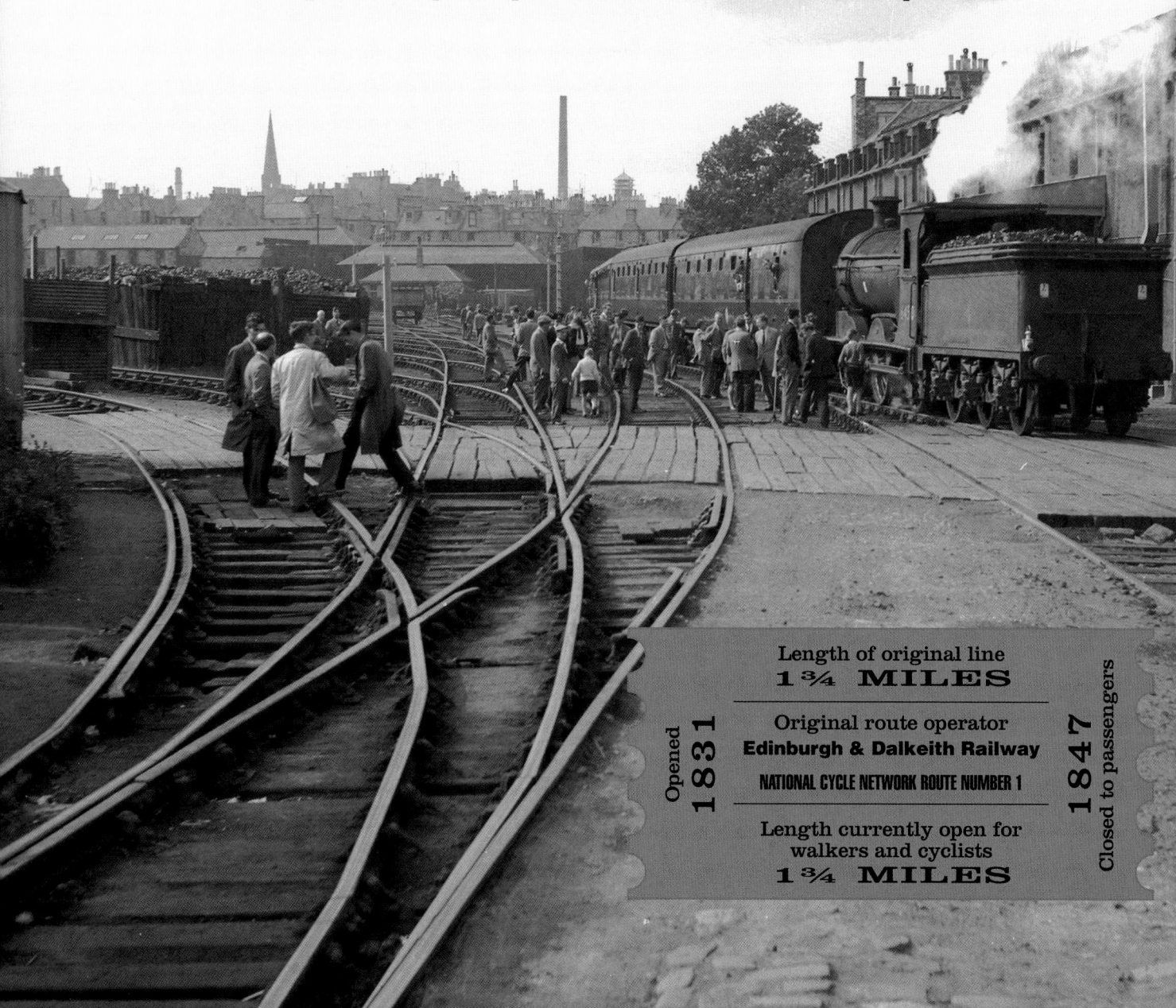

Opened **1831**

Length of original line
1 ¾ MILES

Original route operator
Edinburgh & Dalkeith Railway

NATIONAL CYCLE NETWORK ROUTE NUMBER 1

Length currently open for walkers and cyclists
1 ¾ MILES

Closed to passengers **1847**

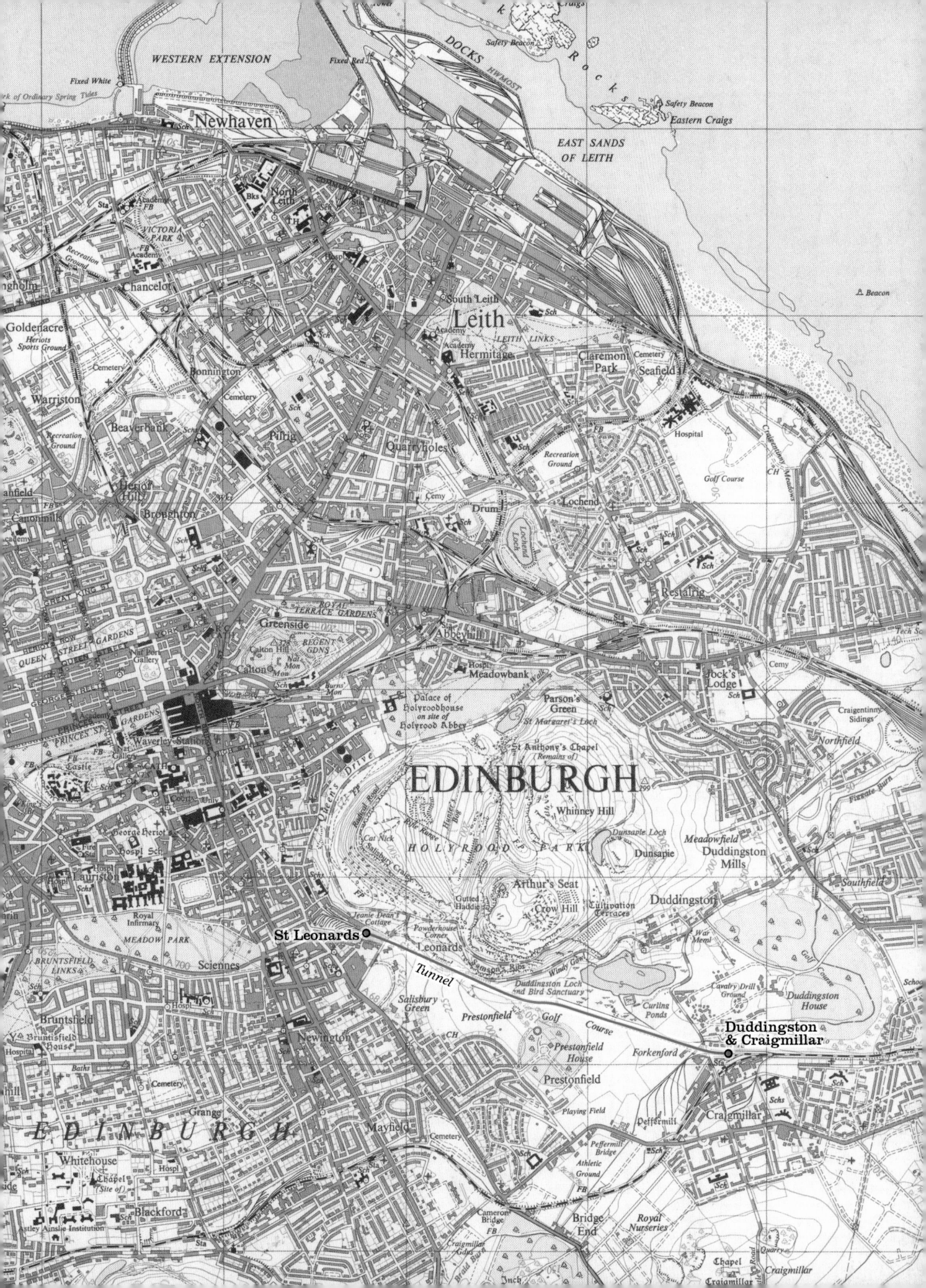

While coal had been mined in the Dalkeith area south of Edinburgh for centuries, the cost of transporting it to the city's inhabitants by horse and cart over poorly made roads was high. By the early nineteenth century the increasing demand for coal led the Duke of Buccleuch, who owned coal mines in Dalkeith, to propose a horse-drawn tramway linking the pits to Edinburgh, with branch lines to the coast at Fisherrow and Leith. Thus was the Edinburgh & Dalkeith Railway (E&DR) born.

Built to a gauge of 4 ft 6 in, the double-track line from Dalhousie Main to St Leonards in Edinburgh and the single-track branch from Niddrie to Fisherrow were opened in 1831. The main engineering feature was the 556-yd St Leonards Tunnel, which carried the line under Arthur's Seat and was excavated from volcanic rock. The 1-in-30 inclined plane up through the tunnel to the terminus at St Leonards was initially rope worked by a stationary steam engine. Other features along the route were a cast iron bridge over Braid Burn at Duddingston and the 65-ft-high stone-arched Glenesk Bridge over the River North Esk at Dalkeith – all these features from one of Scotland's earliest railways survive today.

Passengers were catered for in a converted horse-drawn stage coach laid on by an enterprising local businessman in 1832. The service proved such a success that around 150,000 passengers were carried in its first year of operation. The E&DR took over the service in 1836 and although still horse drawn, it carried more passengers than the Liverpool & Manchester Railway. Meanwhile the company had opened a branch from Niddrie to Leith Docks in 1835 and to Seafield in 1838.

The E&DR was a highly successful operation carrying over 100,000 tons of coal and over a million passengers a year by 1845. That year it was absorbed by the newly established North British Railway (NBR), which paid an eye-watering sum of £11 million at today's prices for what was basically a 12-mile antiquated system. In 1846 the railway was rebuilt to the standard gauge of 4 ft 8½ in, steam power was introduced and a connecting line opened from the NBR's new station at Waverley to Niddrie. While passenger services were then introduced from Waverley to Dalkeith, the St Leonards line, now effectively a branch line from Niddrie, lost its passenger service in 1847. Of course, the NBR had bought the E&DR as the first step in building a through route from Edinburgh to Carlisle – later known as the Waverley Route this 'third main line to England' opened throughout in 1862.

Despite losing its passenger service in 1847 the St Leonards branch continued in use for coal and goods traffic (including casked whisky) for another 121 years – the original rope-worked incline on the final approach through the tunnel to the terminus became

PREVIOUS SPREAD: Ex-NBR Class 'J35' 0-6-0 No. 64510 visited the St Leonards branch with an enthusiasts' special on 25 August 1962. The assembled all-male crowd wander round the goods yard before rejoining their train to depart down the 1-in-30 gradient through St Leonards Tunnel.

The Innocent Railway Path descends from St Leonards through Scotland's first railway tunnel. Opened in 1831, the 556-yd sandstone-lined tunnel carried the line under Arthur's Seat and was excavated from volcanic rock. Trains were initially rope-worked by a stationary steam engine until 1846 when steam locomotives were introduced.

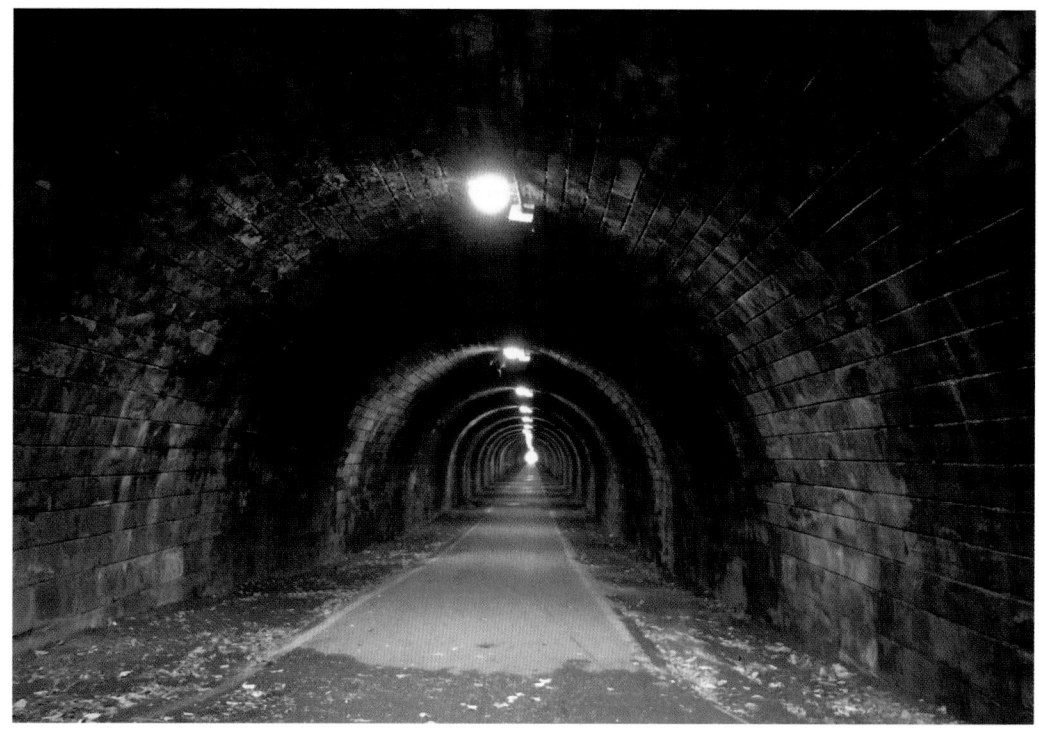

redundant with the introduction of steam power. Working a coal train up the 1-in-30 gradient through the tunnel under Arthur's Seat taxed locomotive drivers and firemen to the limit until the end of steam in the 1960s.

The E&DR was nicknamed the 'Innocent Railway' not because of its safety record but because the horse-drawn journeys that were once a feature of the line harked back to a golden age of leisurely travel that had been usurped by modern (considered by some as dangerous) steam locomotives.

The 1¾-mile branch line from Duddingston Junction, on the Edinburgh outer suburban line, to St Leonards remained steam-worked until the early 1960s, with ancient ex-NBR Class 'J35' 0-6-0 goods locos from St Margarets' shed manfully struggling up the 1-in-30 gradient through St Leonards Tunnel with their trains of coal. If they avoided asphyxiation in the hell hole, the crew were rewarded with a good 'dram' from the bonded warehouse on Fridays! The branch finally closed to all traffic on 5 August 1968.

Watched by a small group of children, ex-NBR Class 'J35' 0-6-0 No. 64479 slowly negotiates Cairntows level crossing with a train of empty coal wagons from St Leonards on 12 August 1961. Built in 1908, this locomotive was withdrawn from St Margarets shed in December 1961.

Since closure, the 1¾ miles of trackbed belonging to this pioneering railway between St Leonards and Duddingston has been reopened as a footpath and cycleway known as the Innocent Railway Path. Forming part of National Cycle Network Route 1, the path continues beyond Duddingston along paths to Brunstane, where there are rail connections to both Waverley station and Newcraighall. Trains will also serve this line on the Waverley Route to Galashiels, which is due to be reopened in 2014/15.

Accessed from St Leonards Lane in Edinburgh, the original 1830-built goods shed in St Leonards goods yard is a remarkable survivor and is now used as a vegetarian restaurant. From here the railway path dives into the well-lit sandstone-lined tunnel on a downhill gradient of 1-in-30 before emerging into a green corridor through the pleasant surroundings of Holyrood Park and the Bawsinch Nature Reserve. Immediately to the north looms the 823-ft peak of Arthur's Seat and its ancient fort, while nestling below is the natural freshwater Duddingston Loch, once used for ice skating and curling and now owned by the Scottish Wildlife Trust as an important breeding site for overwintering wildfowl. At Duddingston the railway path uses the original E&DR cast-iron bridge, made by the Shotts Iron Company in 1831, to cross over the Braid Burn.

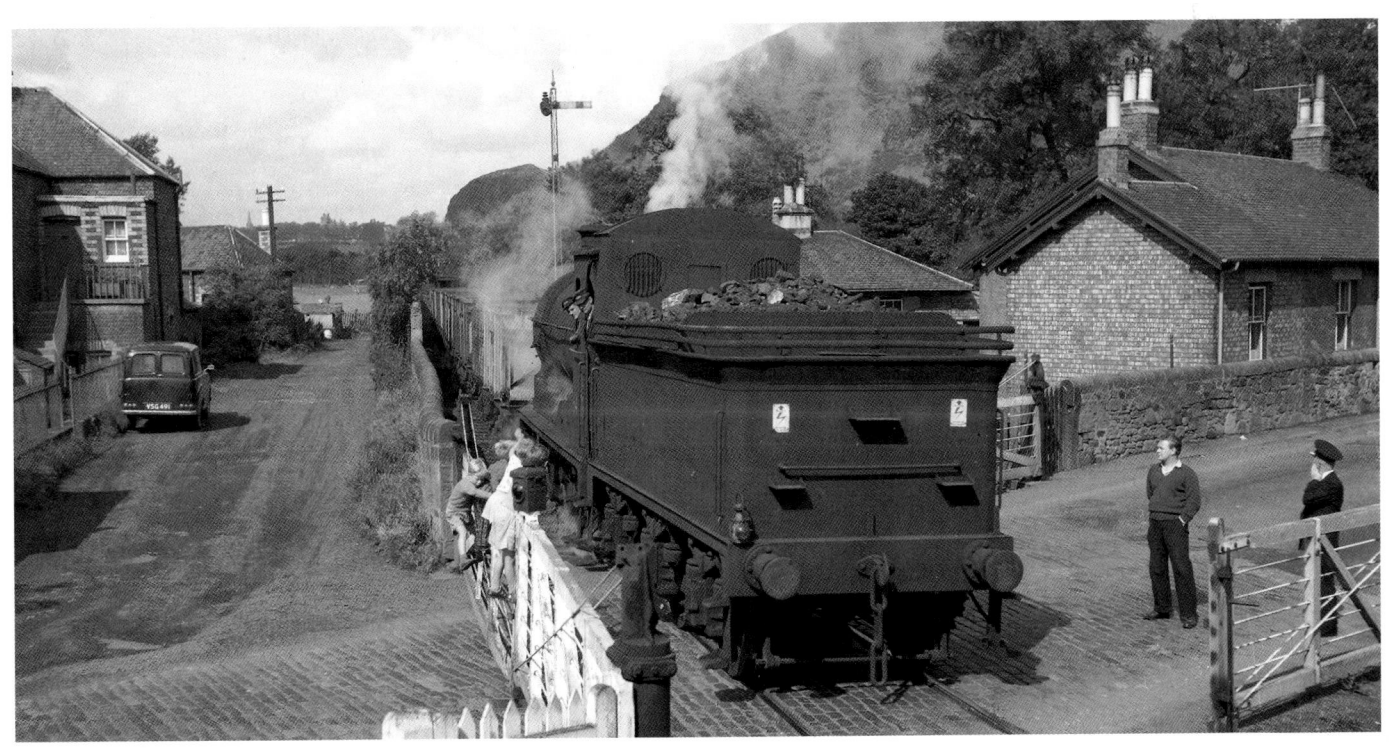

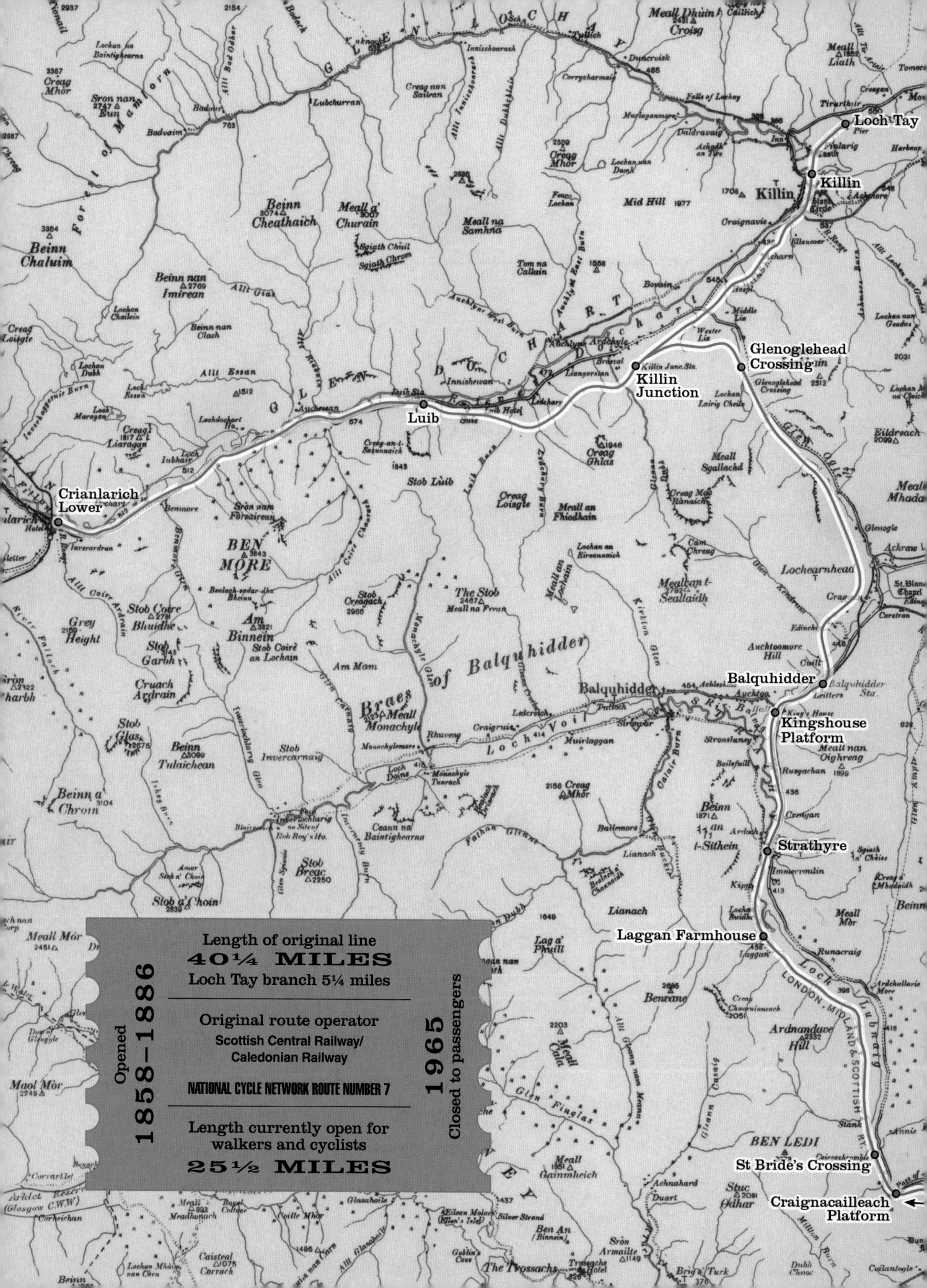

Loch Tay

Killin

Glenoglehead
Crossing

Killin
Junction

Luib

Crianlarich
Lower

Balquhidder

Kingshouse
Platform

Strathyre

Laggan Farmhouse

St Bride's Crossing

Craignacailleach
Platform

Opened
1858–1886

Length of original line
40¼ MILES
Loch Tay branch 5¼ miles

Original route operator
**Scottish Central Railway/
Caledonian Railway**

NATIONAL CYCLE NETWORK ROUTE NUMBER 7

Length currently open for
walkers and cyclists
25½ MILES

1965
Closed to passengers

DUNBLANE
TO
CRIANLARICH AND KILLIN

What was to become the Caledonian Railway's route to Oban started life in 1858 with the opening of the Dunblane, Doune & Callander Railway. The Callander & Oban Railway then took over and opened its complete route up through Glen Ogle to Crianlarich and then through the Pass of Brander in 1880. A branch line was opened from Killin Junction to Loch Tay in 1886. All these lines were worked by the Caledonian Railway. Although the Dunblane to Crianlarich section and the Killin branch were listed for closure in the 'Beeching Report', the end came sooner than expected after a rock fall in Glen Ogle and the line was never reopened. Today, isolated sections of the trackbed at Doune and to the east of Callander, together with nearly the entire route from Callander to Killin, have been reopened as a footpath and cycleway.

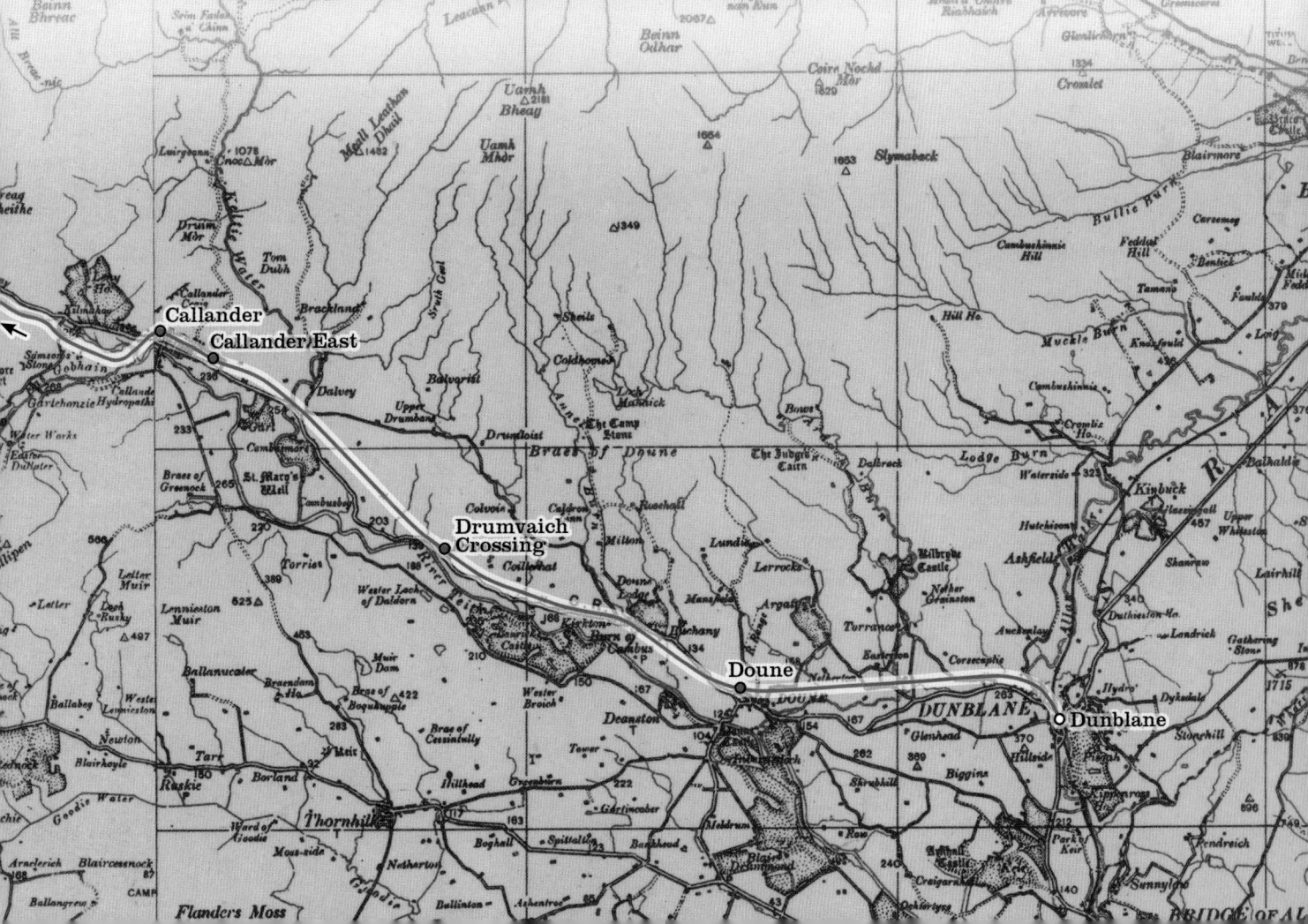

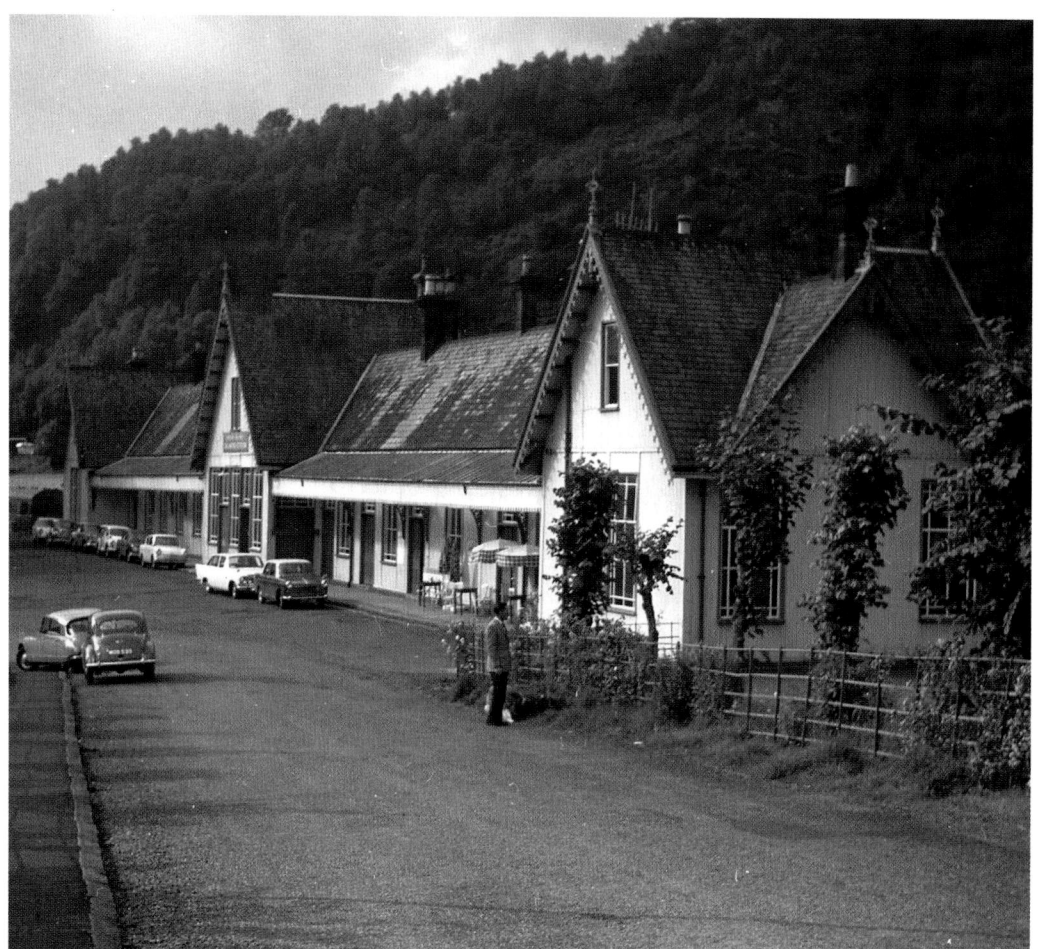

Taking the dog for a walk at Callander station. A fine array of post-war British cars and a Citroen DS grace the forecourt of this attractive building in the summer of 1965, only a few months before the premature closure of this highly scenic railway.

RIGHT: The train journey through the Pass of Leny, alongside Loch Lubnaig (seen here on the right) and up through Glen Ogle, must have rated as one of the most scenic in Britain. The trackbed now forms part of National Cycle Network Route 7.

The town of Dunblane received its first railway service when the Scottish Central Railway (SCR) opened its main line between Stirling and Perth in 1848. In anticipation of this historic event the Dunblane, Doune & Callander Railway (DD&CR) had first received authorization in 1846 to build an 11¼-mile single-track line between the three towns. However, no work was carried out and the powers lapsed until the company was re-authorized in 1856.

The line finally opened in 1858 and was leased to the SCR until 1865, when the Caledonian Railway absorbed both the SCR and the DD&CR.

Another important event occurred in 1865 when the Callander & Oban Railway (C&OR) was incorporated to build a 70¾-mile single-track railway northwards from Callander to the west coast at Oban. This was a massive undertaking, with major engineering work necessary to take the line up through Glen Ogle and further west through the Pass of Brander. Fortunately the C&OR was financially backed by the Caledonian Railway, which had

also undertaken to work it on completion of twenty route miles.

Construction of the line north of Callander was heavy going, with earthworks and viaducts climbing inexorably up the side of Glen Ogle to the summit. By 1870 the line had only reached Glenoglehead Crossing, north of Balquhidder and about 15 miles from Callander – the small station at Glenoglehead was originally named Killin despite the fact that it was miles away from the village it purported to serve. It took another three years before the railway reached Crianlarich and a temporary terminus at Tyndrum, 34 miles from Callander, and here it stopped until the CR injected more funds into the project. Dalmally, 46¼ miles from Callander, was reached in 1877 and Oban finally in 1880. The arrival of the railway transformed the town into a thriving resort for Victorian tourists and a gateway to the Western Isles. Crianlarich was also served by the North British Railway's West Highland Line that opened from Glasgow (Queen Street) to Fort William in 1894, when the C&OR line station was renamed Lower and that of the Fort William line was

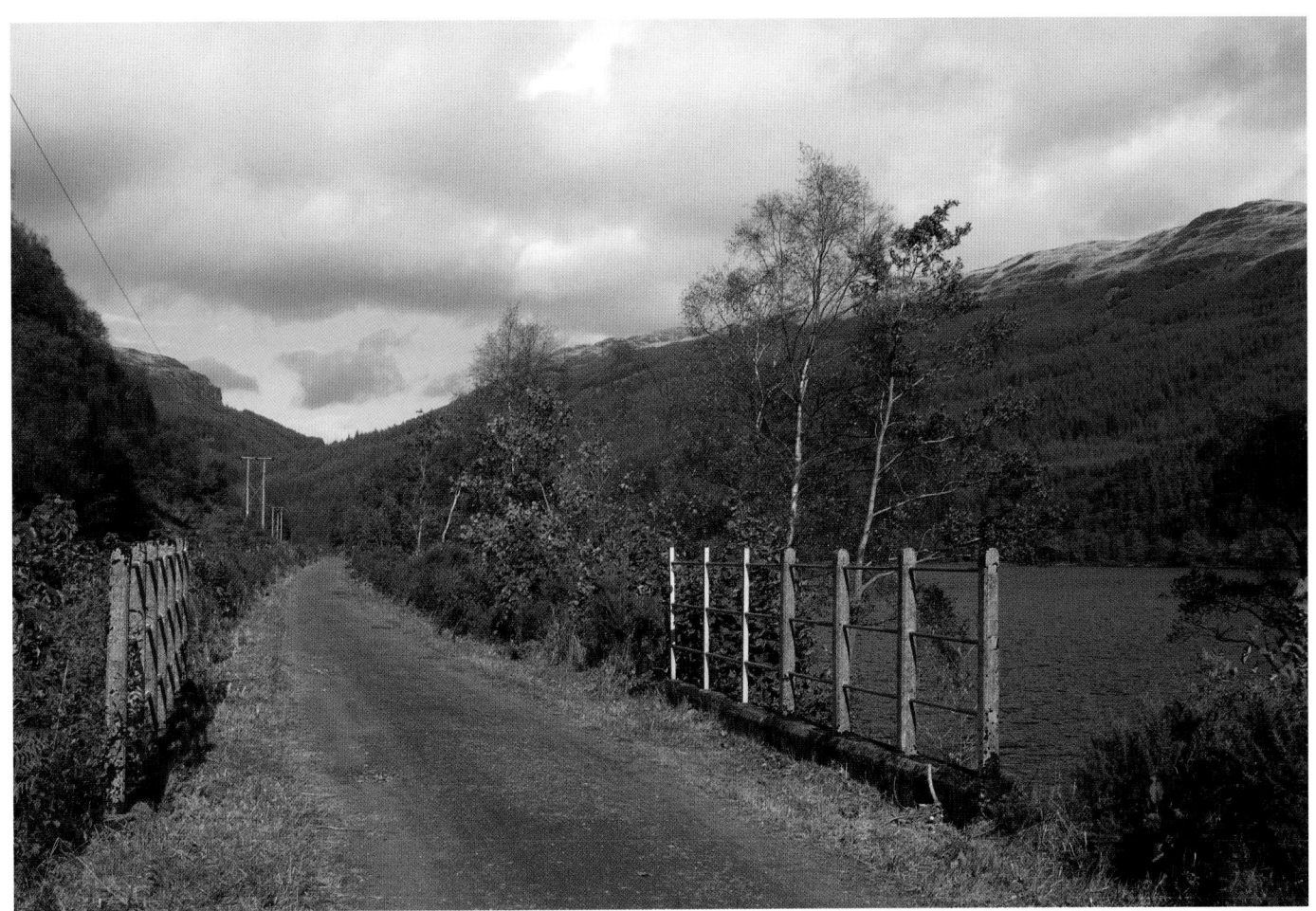

named Upper. The Dunblane to Doune section was doubled in 1902.

Tourism was the key to the success of the C&OR but unfortunately for the Earl of Breadalbane, the line passed five miles to the west of his ancestral lands around Loch Tay. The Earl, eager to promote Loch Tay for its scenic beauty, was the driving force behind the 5-mile Killin Railway, which opened from a new station at Killin Junction on the C&OR to the village of Killin and a pier on Loch Tay in 1886. By the end of the nineteenth century tourists were able to travel on a grand circular tour by train from Glasgow to Killin, followed by a cruise and lunch on the 'Lady of the Lake' paddle steamer before being taken by charabanc to Aberfeldy station for their return trip to Glasgow. The passenger service was truncated to end at Killin in 1939 although the diminutive engine shed at the Loch Tay terminus remained in use until closure.

Although worked by the Caledonian Railway from opening, the C&OR remained independent until the

'Big Four Grouping' of 1923 when it became part of the newly formed London Midland & Scottish Railway. Passenger services remained fairly constant well into the British Railways' era – on weekdays there were five trains from Glasgow to Oban and four in the opposite direction. Most of these also conveyed through coaches from and to Edinburgh, while one conveyed sleeping cars to and from London. Apart from the sleeping cars, which were attached or detached at Stirling, all other Oban line trains used Buchanan Street station in Glasgow. Callander was also the terminus of stopping trains to or from Glasgow or Edinburgh. Trains on the Killin branch connected with the Oban line services at Killin Junction.

Steam reigned supreme on the line until the early 1960s when the short-lived North British Locomotive Company's Type 2 diesels took over along with the more reliable Birmingham Railway Carriage & Wagon Company's Type 2s. While Oban engine shed closed in May 1963, the Killin branch trains continued to be steam hauled – in latter years by BR Standard Class 4 2-6-4Ts – until closure.

Seeking to rationalize train services between Glasgow and Oban/Fort William the 1963 'Beeching Report' recommended closure of the line between Dunblane and Crianlarich Lower, with Oban-line trains being diverted to run on the shorter route from Glasgow Queen Street to Crianlarich Upper via the West Highland Line, and the Killin branch was also to be closed. This was planned for 1 November 1965 but a major rockfall on the line in Glen Ogle on 27 September brought this date forward. From 28 September all services ceased between Callander and Crianlarich and on the Killin branch, although the Dunblane to Callander section remained open until the planned closure date. With hindsight, and if the line had not been closed, the train journey up through Glen Ogle today would surely have rated as one of the most scenic in Britain.

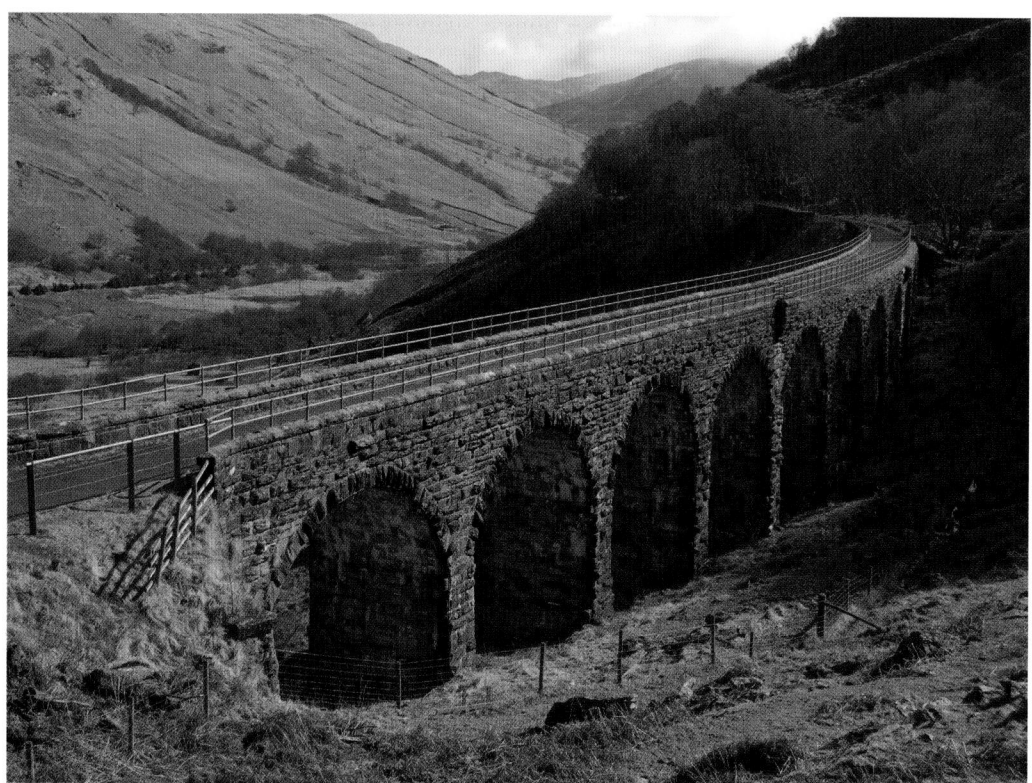

The Callander & Oban Railway's climb up Glen Ogle is the most spectacular part of this cycle route. Here the railway viaduct clings to the side of the glen which was once described by Queen Victoria as 'Scotland's Khyber Pass'.

RIGHT:
Built at Brighton Works in 1955, BR Standard Class '4MT' 2-6-4T No. 80126 heads a short branch-line train from Killin towards Killin Junction on a sunny 14 August 1962. The locomotive was withdrawn from Perth shed in November 1966.

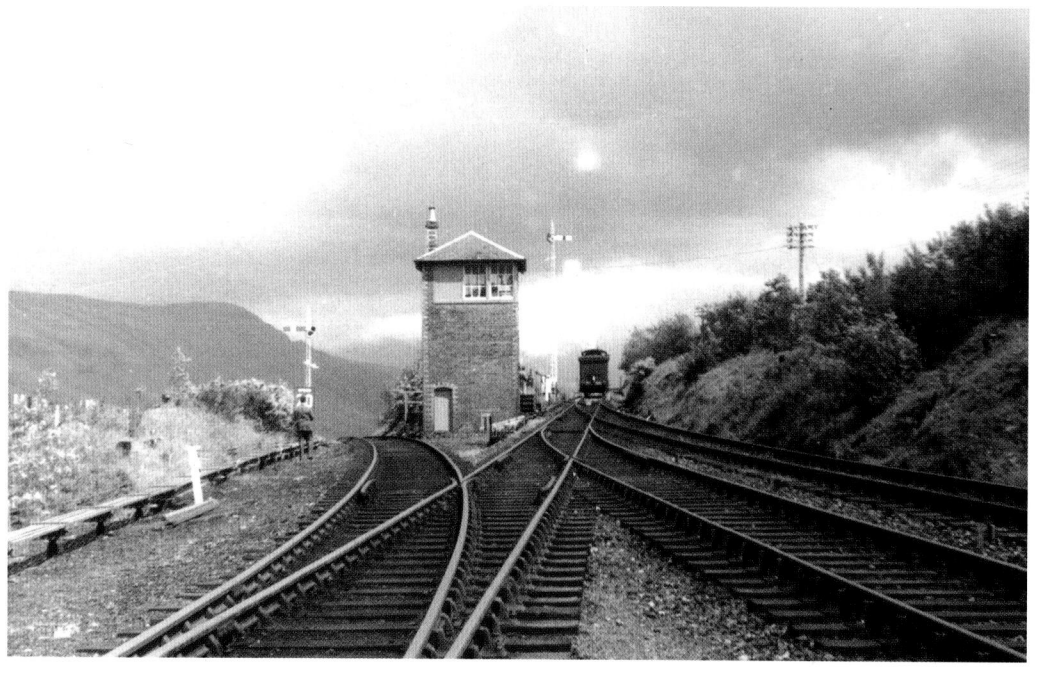

Guarded by ex-Caledonian Railway lower quadrant signals, Killin Junction featured a lofty signal box that gave signalmen a good view along both lines. Seen here on 18 June 1962, the Killin branch falls away to the left while the 'main line' to Callander and Dunblane is straight ahead. The locomotive in the distance is preserved ex-NBR 4-4-0 'Glen Douglas' which had just arrived with an enthusiasts' special.

Since closure much of the route of this scenic railway has been reopened as a footpath and cycleway, and forms part of National Cycle Network Route 7 between Callander and Killin. At its southern end Dunblane station is still open for trains operating between Glasgow, Perth, Aberdeen and Inverness, while trains between Glasgow and Oban/Fort William/Mallaig serve Crianlarich Upper station.

The old railway route immediately to the west of Dunblane has disappeared beneath housing development and has been severed by the A9 dual carriageway but there are plans to completely reopen it as a footpath and cycleway beyond here to Doune and Callander. In the meantime a 1-mile section to the east of Doune now forms a footpath and cycleway known as the Doune Trail. Doune station was demolished in 1968 and the site has since disappeared beneath housing development.

West of Doune the old railway route closely follows the A84 and for the last three miles from Drumvaich into Callander it has been reopened as a well-surfaced footpath and cycleway. Passing through forestry plantations, the dead-straight route includes a few surviving road overbridges and the railway bridge over the Keltie Water. Modern housing now covers the last half a mile into Callander while the station site in the town is now a car park.

North of Callander, National Cycle Network Route 7 follows much of the old railway route to Killin – the total distance is 23 miles but it can be divided into three sections: Callander to Strathyre; Strathyre to Lochearnhead; and Lochearnhead to Killin. There are car parks at the beginning and end of each section.

The railway path starts at Callander Meadows and soon heads west into the Pass of Leny where there is a small car park. The nearby Falls of Leny are a popular tourist attraction and this section of the path, with occasional detours away from the old railway route, can often be busy in the summer and muddy in the winter. North of here the railway path follows the tranquil west shore of Loch Lubnaig for five miles before arriving at the village of Strathyre where refreshments are available at the Inn & Bistro.

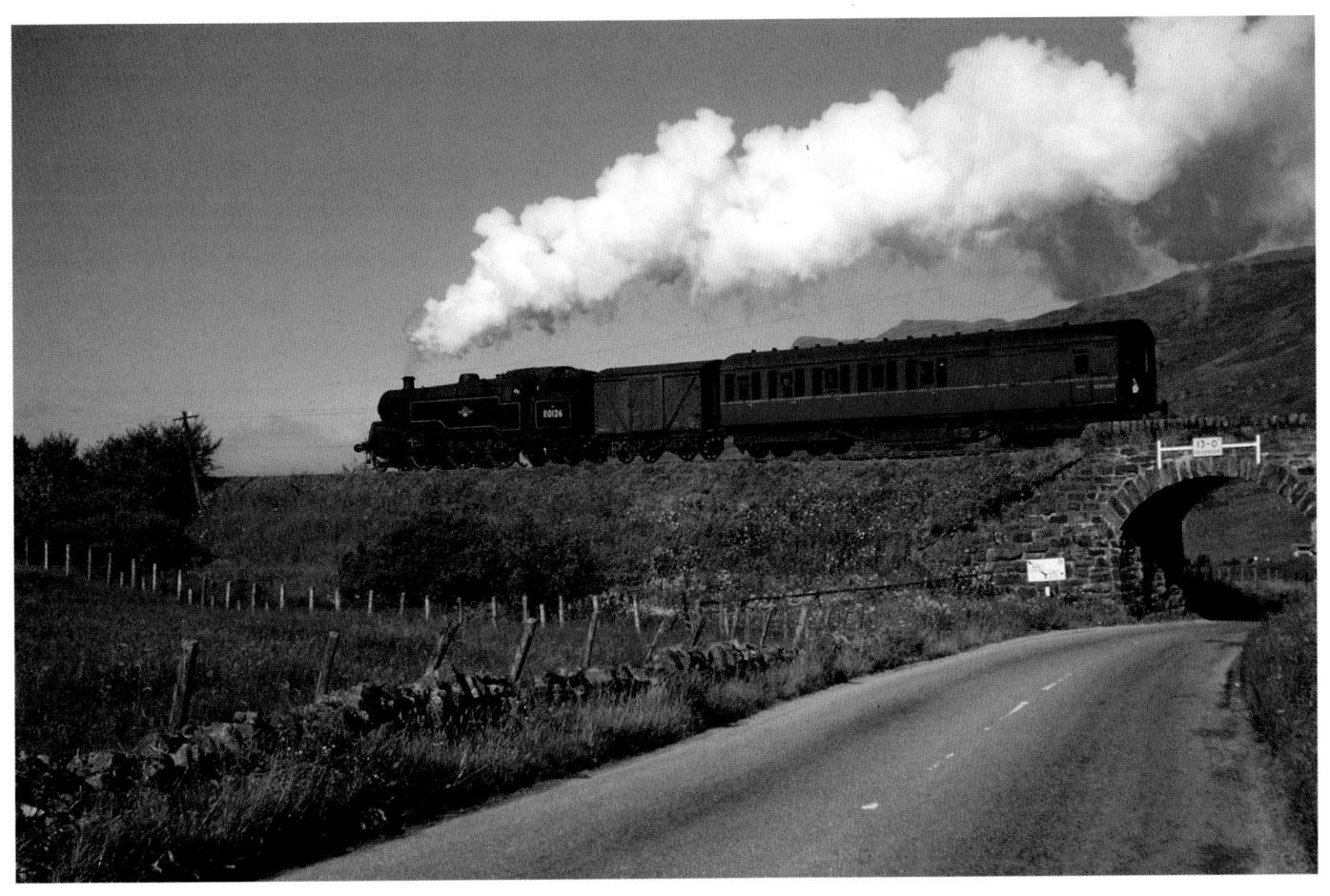

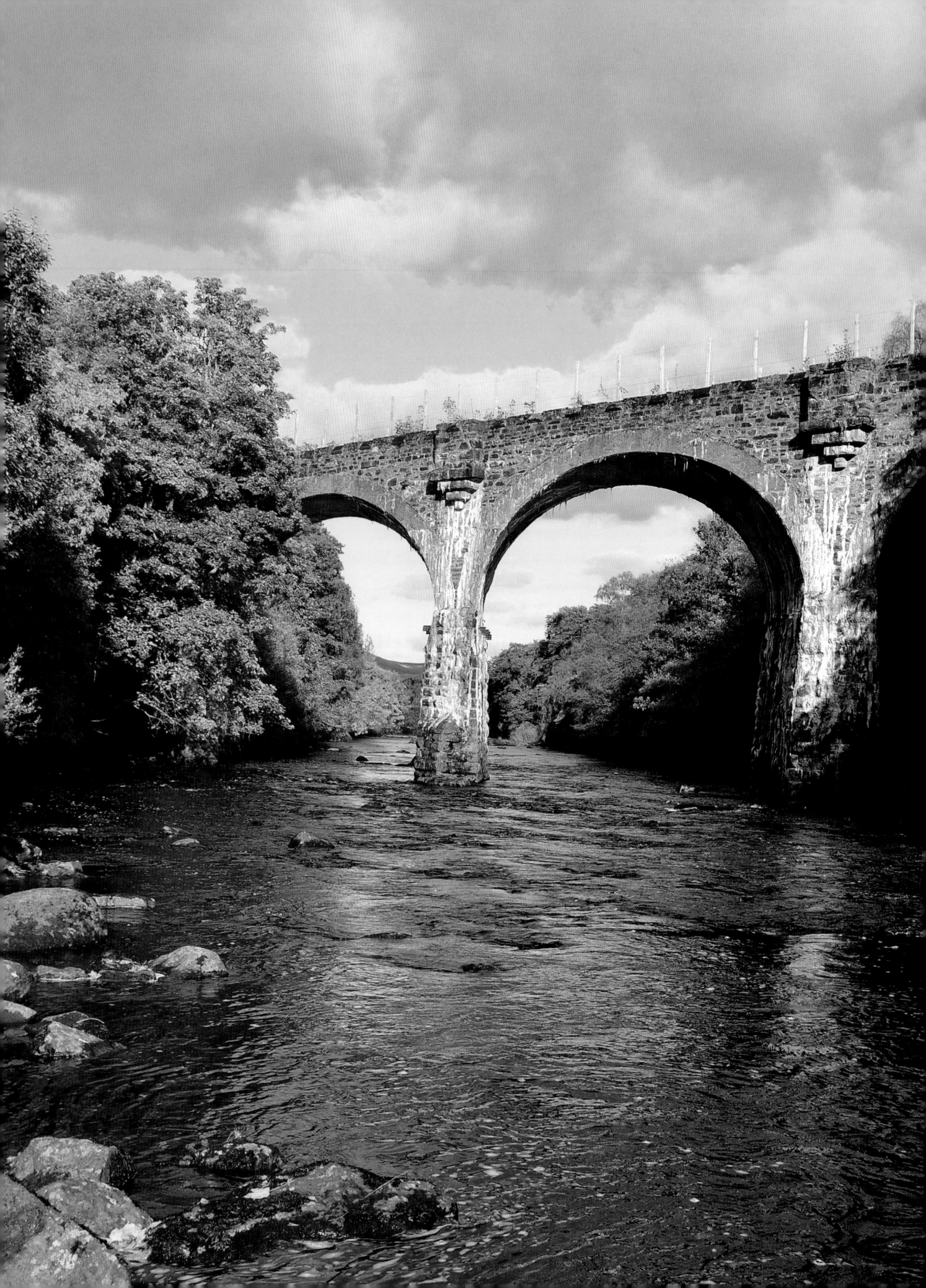

North of Strathyre the cycle route departs from the old railway, following a country lane through the forest to the village of Balquhidder where it crosses the River Balvag to head east to Kingshouse Hotel on the A84. Half a mile further north, the site of Balquhidder station is now a caravan park although the steps and subway to the station's platforms still survive alongside the road. The cycle route continues north, following for a small distance the trackbed of the short-lived Lochearnhead, St Fillans & Comrie Railway, which opened in 1905 and closed in 1951. The cycle route rejoins the route of the C&OR via a steep zig-zag at Craggan, half a mile south of Lochearnhead – the climb is well rewarded with far-reaching views over Strathyre and Loch Earn.

From Craggan the C&OR's dramatic climb up Glen Ogle is the most spectacular part of this cycle route, with magnificent views of what Queen Victoria called 'Scotland's Khyber Pass' and General Wade's eighteenth-century military road from the viaduct about two miles way up the glen. A further mile northwards the railway path ends alongside Lochan Lairig Cheile, where there is a car park and refreshment van alongside the A85 – from here the railway route can be followed along a forest track for 1½ miles to the site of Killin Junction station. Leaving the A85 the cycle route makes a detour away from the C&OR's main line by following forest tracks for a mile before joining the trackbed of the Killin branch line in Glen Dochart.

The route of the Killin branch is followed for two miles to the attractive village of Killin, passing over the River Dochart near the Falls of Dochart on a 3-arch stone viaduct. Car parking and refreshments are available in Killin while a footpath continues along the last section of railway, via an old rusting girder bridge over the River Lochay, to Loch Tay. Here the station and platform that once witnessed day trippers transferring to or from loch steamers is now a private residence.

For those lovers of lost railways who like to get away from it all, a pilgrimage to Killin Junction along the forest track from the A85 is well worthwhile. Here the overgrown island platform and derelict railway workers' cottages stand silently amidst the forest, while the trackbed can still be followed west as far as the viaduct over Gleann Dubh. Further west, on the lower northern slopes of Ben More, much of the route of the railway along Glen Dochart has disappeared beneath improvements to the A85 and the stations at Luib and Crianlarich Lower have long gone – the only crumb of comfort is the excellent station café at Crianlarich station, where you can still board trains for the wonderful journey across Rannoch Moor to Fort William, and on to Mallaig!

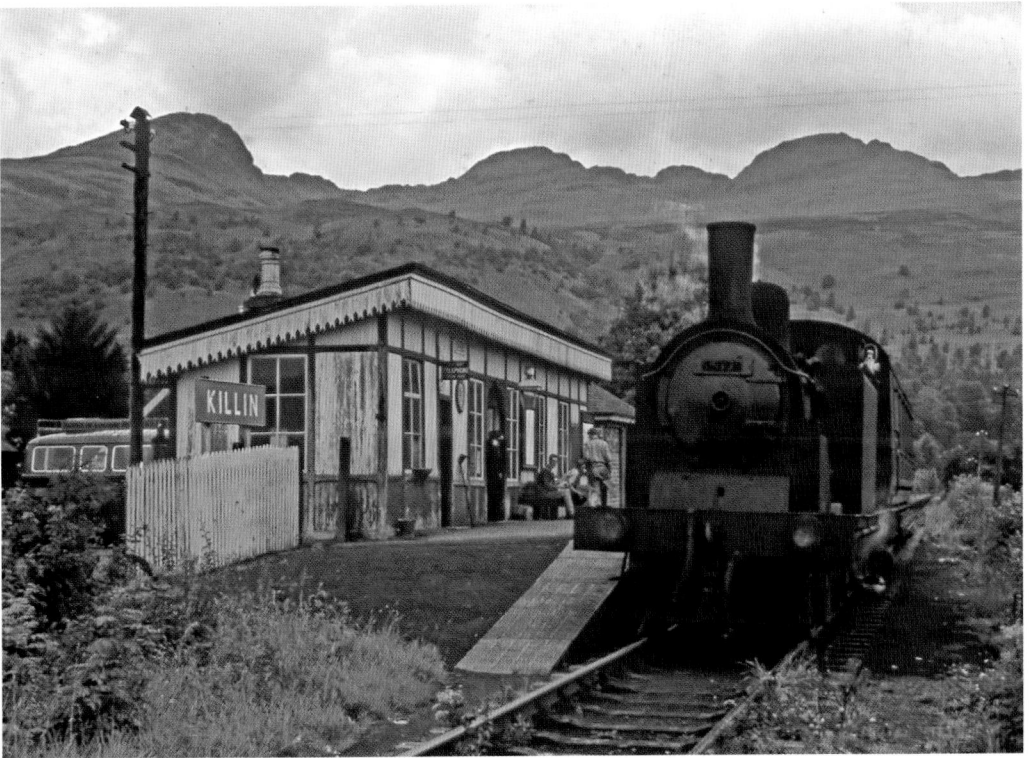

LEFT: The Killin branch crossed the River Dochart close to the Falls of Dochart on this 3-arch stone viaduct. Today, the structure forms part of National Cycle Network Route 7 which continues on around the southern shore of Loch Tay towards Pitlochry.

Set in glorious Highland scenery, ex-Caledonian Railway 0-4-4T No. 55173 is seen here on 10 August 1960 waiting to depart from the tiny station at Killin with a 1-coach train to Killin Junction. Built at St Rollox Works in 1900, this veteran locomotive was withdrawn from Forfar shed in January 1962.

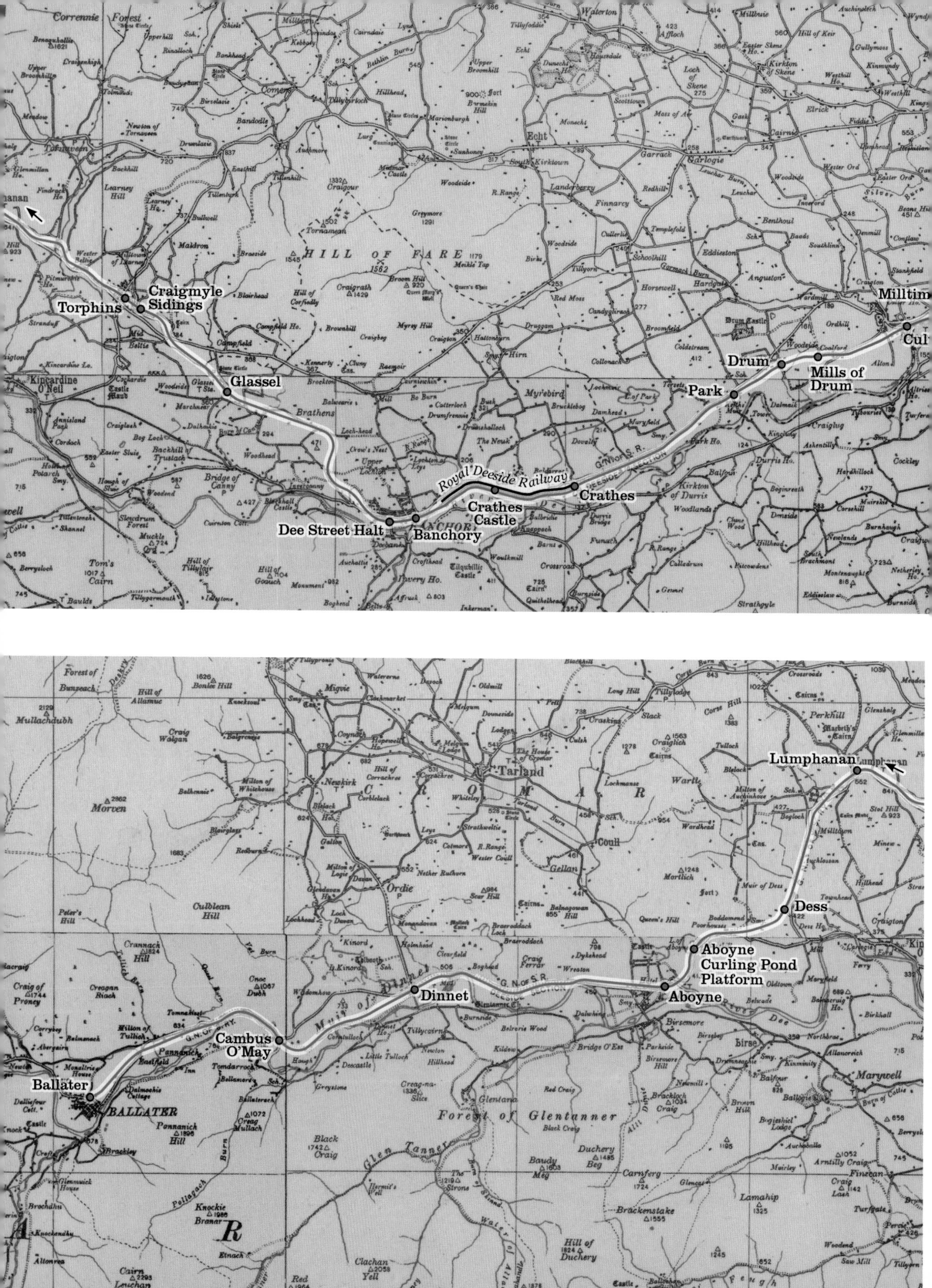

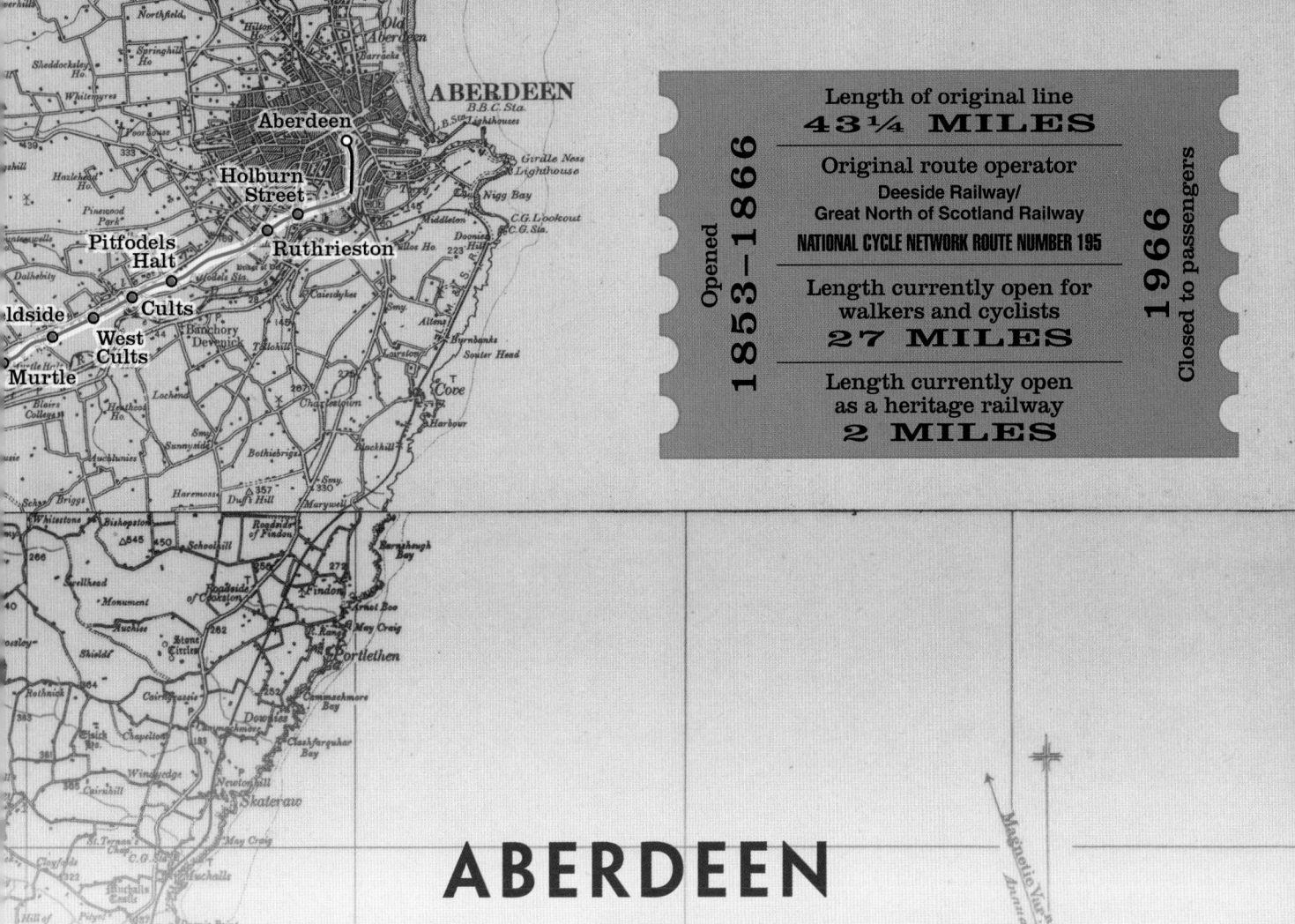

Length of original line
43¼ MILES

Opened 1853–1866

Original route operator
**Deeside Railway/
Great North of Scotland Railway**

NATIONAL CYCLE NETWORK ROUTE NUMBER 195

Length currently open for
walkers and cyclists
27 MILES

Length currently open
as a heritage railway
2 MILES

1966 Closed to passengers

ABERDEEN
TO
BALLATER

DEESIDE WAY

Patronized by royalty visiting nearby Balmoral Castle, the 43¼-mile railway along the Dee Valley from Aberdeen to Ballater was opened in three stages but Queen Victoria thwarted a planned extension to Braemar. The eastern section also featured an intensive suburban commuter service that was introduced at the end of the nineteenth century. Despite the regular passage of royal trains and the introduction of a unique battery-operated railcar in 1958, the line became a victim of Dr Beeching's Axe and closed in 1966. Today, two long sections of the trackbed form part of the Deeside Way footpath and cycleway while the Royal Deeside Railway operates heritage trains between Milton of Crathes and the outskirts of Banchory.

The 43¼-mile branch line up the Dee Valley from Aberdeen to Ballater was built in three distinct phases. First on the scene was the Deeside Railway (DR), which was incorporated in 1846 to build a railway as far as Aboyne. In the event the railway ended at Banchory and was opened in 1853. A private station was also opened at Crathes to serve the owner of nearby Crathes Castle although it became a public station in 1863. The second section to open was the Deeside Extension Railway, which was promoted by the DR and opened from Banchory to Aboyne in 1859. Also sponsored by the DR, the final section was built by the Aboyne & Braemar Railway and was opened between Aboyne and Ballater in 1866 – it deviated to the north of the Dee Valley between Banchory and Aboyne to serve the village of Lumphanan. All three railways were leased for 999 years by the Great North of Scotland Railway in the same year and absorbed by the company in 1875. Trains for Ballater originally departed from Guild Street station in Aberdeen until the new Joint station was opened in the city in 1867.

While the railway ended at Ballater, plans to extend it to Braemar were scuppered by Queen Victoria who had been given the Balmoral Estate by her Consort, Prince Albert, in 1852. Earthworks for a railway to serve forestry operations had been completed as far as the Water of Gairn in 1868 but the Queen, probably fearing hordes of day trippers descending on her idyllic hideaway, halted it in its tracks. The earthworks for this unfinished line can still be seen today west of Ballater.

As well as serving the various towns and villages scattered along the Dee Valley, the railway also introduced a frequent service of suburban trains for commuters between Aberdeen and Culter in 1894. This served eight intermediate stations but was withdrawn in the 1930s. Originally single track, the line had been doubled as far as Cults in 1884 and had been extended to Park by 1899. In the early twentieth century Ballater was also served by a limited-stop express service that carried, uniquely for a British single line, a slip coach for Banchory.

Mention should be made here of the bus services that were also operated by the Great North of Scotland Railway. The company was one of Britain's leading proponents of railway feeder bus services and operated

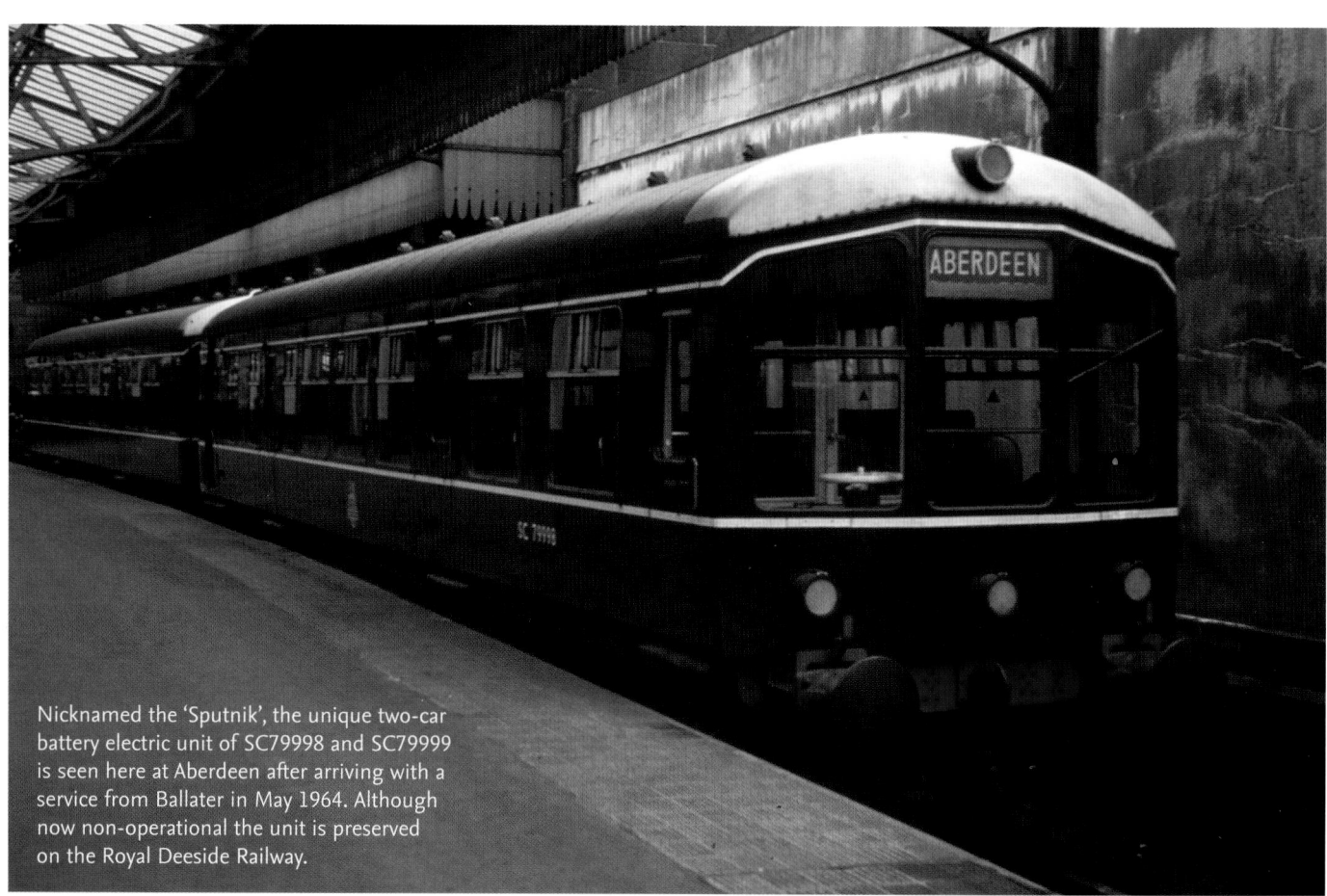

Nicknamed the 'Sputnik', the unique two-car battery electric unit of SC79998 and SC79999 is seen here at Aberdeen after arriving with a service from Ballater in May 1964. Although now non-operational the unit is preserved on the Royal Deeside Railway.

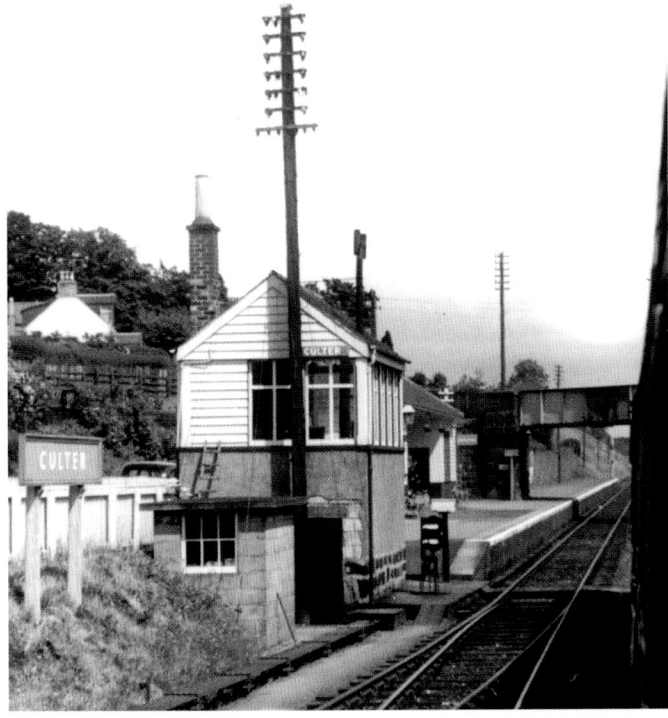

Culter station, seen from an Aberdeen to Ballater train on 9 July 1957. The platform and bridge abutments have survived alongside the Deeside Way.

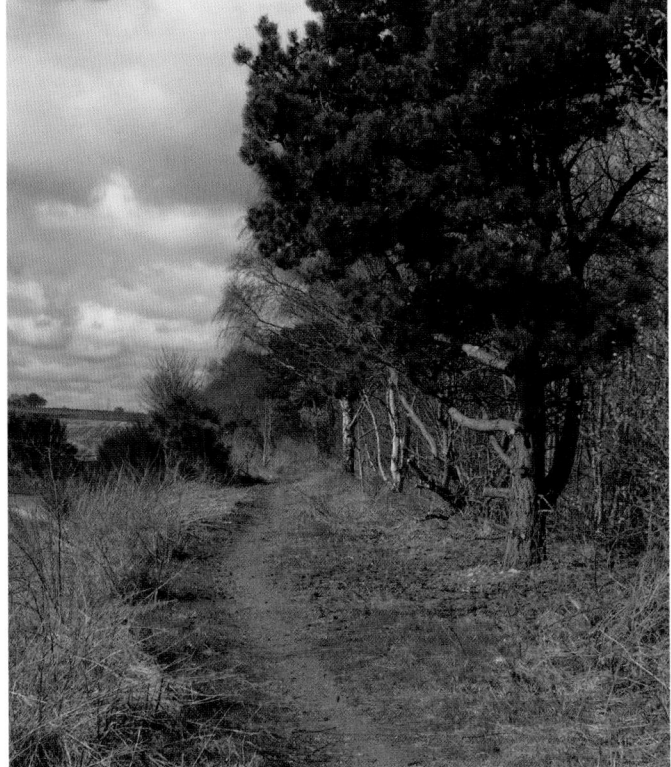

Seen here to the west of Culter, the Deeside Way heads towards Crathes and Banchory along a tree-lined embankment.

several in conjunction with the Dee Valley Line: Ballater to Braemar (16½ miles; 1904-1930); Culter to Midmar (12½ miles; 1905-1906); Ballater to Cockbridge (29 miles; summer only 1907-1925). From 1923 these services were operated by the newly formed London & North Eastern Railway before being taken over by private bus operators from 1930.

With the private royal residence of Balmoral only 8½ miles to the west of Ballater, royalty were the most important passengers on the Deeside line. The first recorded use of the railway by a reigning monarch came in 1853 when Queen Victoria and Prince Albert boarded a train at Banchory for their journey to London. Carrying the Prince and Priness of Wales, the first royal train to reach Ballater arrived in September 1866, before the station had officially opened. Many other reigning monarchs visited Balmoral by train including the Tsar of Russia in 1896, when electric lights were specially installed at Ballater for his visit. Never publicized, the passage of a royal train along the line – preceded by a pilot engine – involved tight security, with all other traffic being stopped and station platforms cleared of passengers. The last royal train to use the line carried our present Queen on her journey south on 15 October 1965, a few months before the line's closure. Unadvertised Royal Messenger Trains were also run every day until 1937 while the monarch was in residence at Balmoral.

By the 1950s both passenger and goods traffic were in decline, the bus service along the Dee Valley proving more convenient to the travelling public. The austerity post-war years and nationalization of the railways saw services drastically reduced – the autumn 1948 timetable shows only four services in each direction on weekdays with a journey time of around 1hr 40min. Cost-saving measures were introduced in 1958, with steam traction being replaced by diesel multiple units and the unique two-coach battery railcar nicknamed the 'Sputnik'. The timetabled service was also improved, with six return journeys each weekday and a faster journey time of between 1hr 12min and 1hr 27min, but all to no avail, as the line was listed for closure in the 1963 'Beeching Report'. The end came for passenger services on 28 February 1966, although Ballater continued to be served by goods trains for another five months until the line was cut back to Culter. Still served by goods trains from Aberdeen, this section of line was finally closed on 2 January 1967.

Aberdeenshire Council has reopened much of the Deeside line from Aberdeen to Ballater as a footpath and cycleway known as the Deeside Way. It also forms part of National Cycle Network Route 195. With a few deviations en route, the first section of the Deeside Way uses the trackbed of the railway from Guthrie Park, close to the site of the former Ferryhill engine shed, to Banchory, a distance of around sixteen miles. From Banchory the Deeside Way temporarily leaves the old railway route, which loops northwards through Lumphanan, following a route instead through Blackhall Forest to the south of the Dee. The old railway route is rejoined at Aboyne for the next eleven miles before terminating at Ballater station.

Car parking and refreshments can be found en route at Peterculter, Drumoak, Banchory, Kincardine O'Neil, Aboyne and Dinnet. There is much to interest lovers of lost railways along this long route, most of which is closely paralleled by the A93 to the north and the River Dee to the south. The first significant remains can be found at Culter station, where the eastbound platform has been graced by a reproduction station name board mounted on original concrete posts. At Milton of Crathes the Deeside Way runs alongside the Royal Deeside Railway, which has relaid nearly two miles of track to the eastern outskirts of Banchory. Steam and diesel trains operate from their base at Milton of Crathes on most weekends from April to September – pride of place on the railway is the original two-car battery railcar that once worked on the line. The Deeside Way ends its first section at Banchory where only the former engine shed has survived and is used as a garden machinery and equipment centre.

The Deeside Way then leaves the old railway route, rejoining it in the town of Aboyne where the former station building has been well preserved and is now used by a range of shops. Continuing westwards for 4½ miles, the Way reaches Dinnet station where both platforms have somehow survived, albeit hidden in the encroaching woodland, while the station building is now used as an

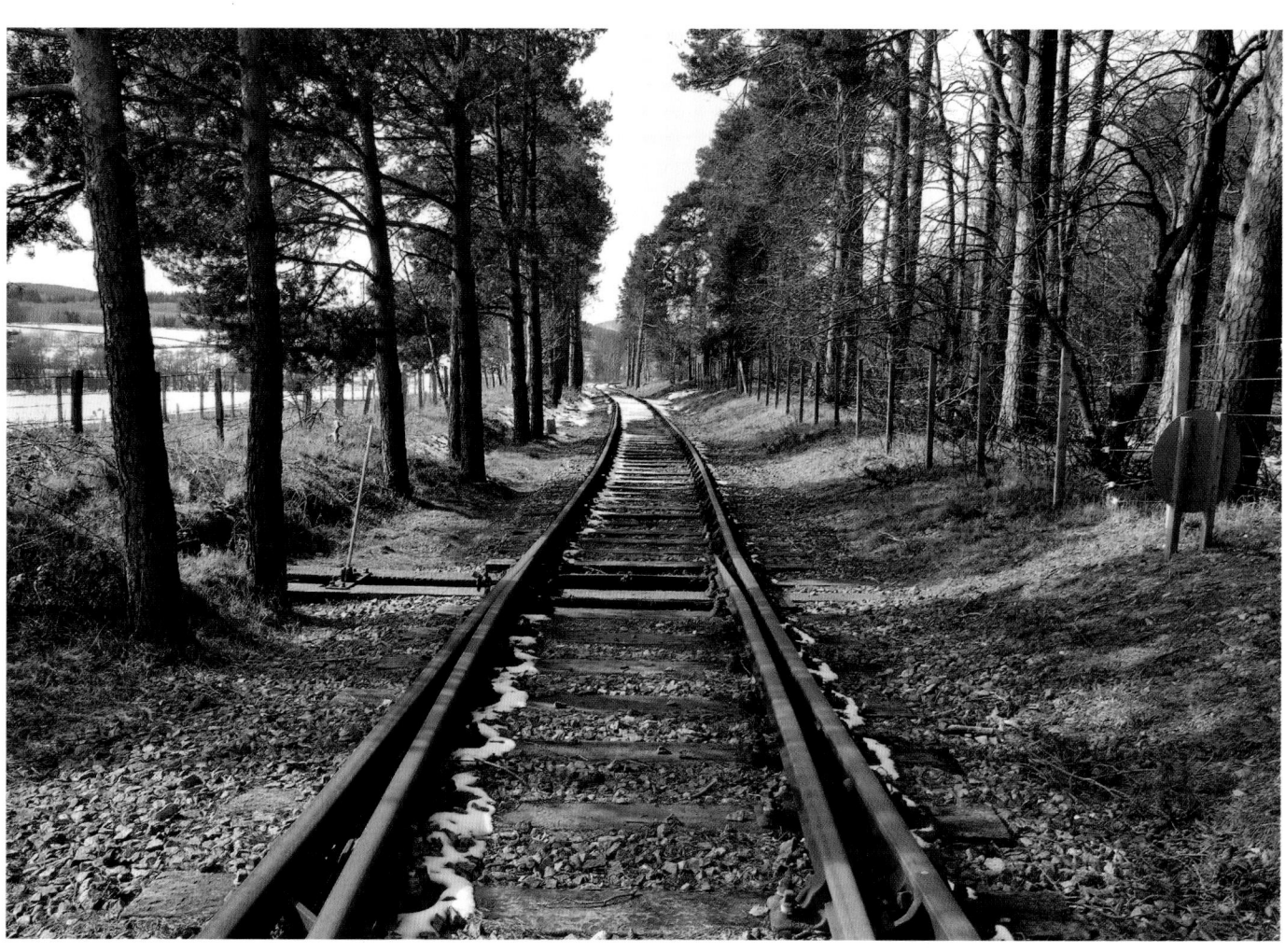

estate office – opposite, the level crossing gate still hangs on its sturdy concrete posts.

The Deeside Way continues westwards along the heavily wooded Dee Valley for another 2½ miles to reach the beautifully restored and secluded station of Cambus O'May, where road, rail and river converge through a narrow pass. Complete with platform this remote station is now used as a holiday cottage while a graceful suspension pedestrian bridge, built across the river in 1905, gains access to a riverbank path. Nearby is a hotel and car park alongside the A93.

Leaving Cambus O'May behind, the Deeside Way continues its westward journey for another four miles before ending at the beautifully preserved station at Ballater. The station building is home to a royalty exhibition, café and tourist information centre, while the attractive town is host to several hotels, cafés, a bicycle hire shop, a second-hand bookshop and a cake shop supposedly frequented by royalty!

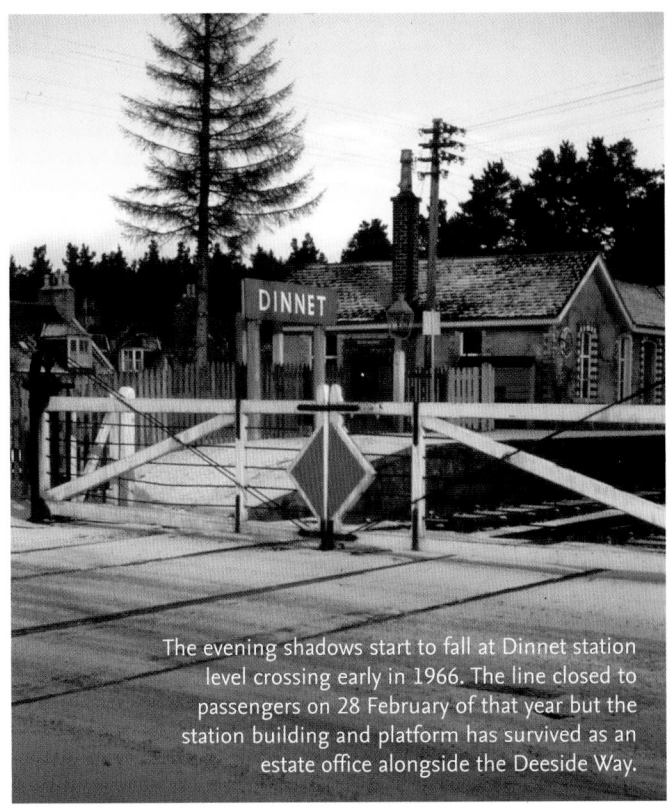

The evening shadows start to fall at Dinnet station level crossing early in 1966. The line closed to passengers on 28 February of that year but the station building and platform has survived as an estate office alongside the Deeside Way.

Set alongside the Deeside Way, Cambus O'May station has been restored on its platform as a holiday cottage. A nearby pedestrian suspension bridge over the River Dee gives walkers access to footpaths along the south bank of the river.

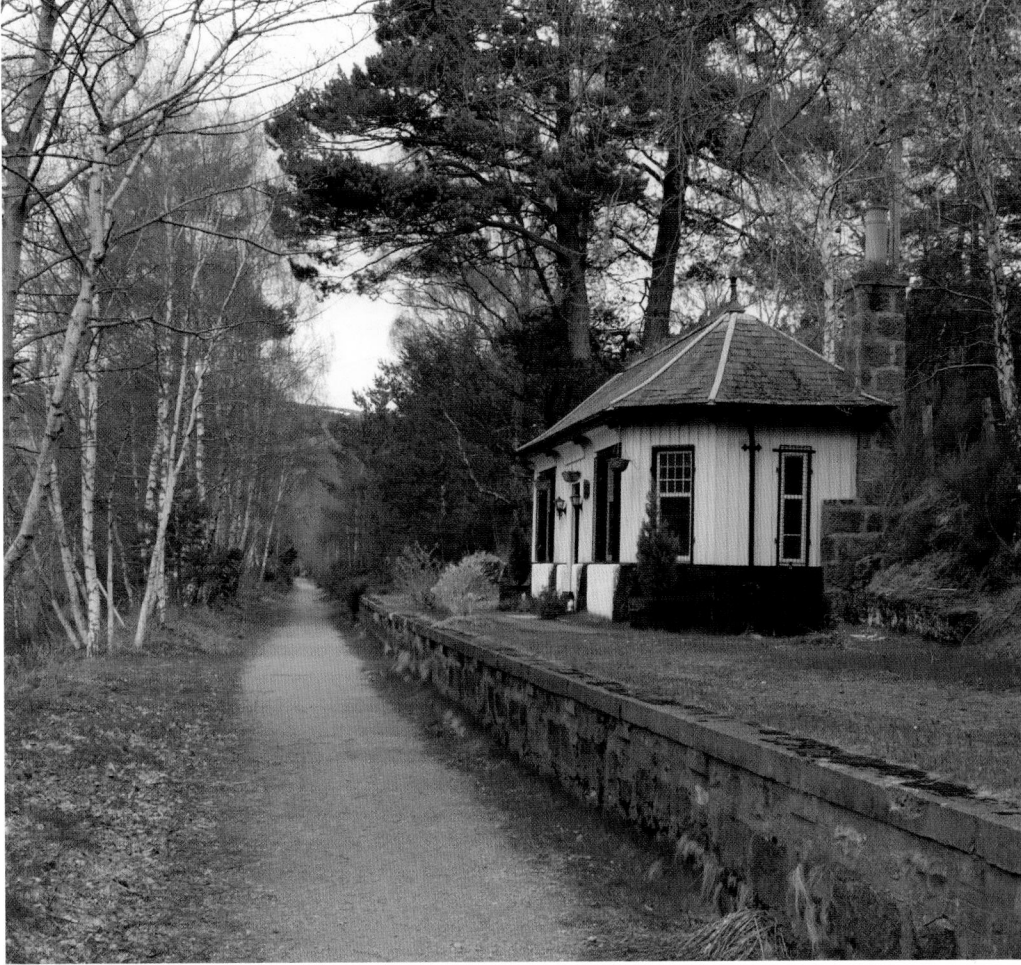

LEFT: The Royal Deeside Railway has laid around two miles of track from its headquarters at Milton of Crathes to the eastern outskirts of Banchory. Walkers and cyclists on this section of the Deeside Way use a parallel path separated by a fence.

BOAT OF GARTEN
TO
CRAIGELLACHIE

SPEYSIDE WAY

Serving numerous distilleries along its 33½-mile route up the
picturesque Spey Valley, the Strathspey Railway initially had problems
achieving its goal of reaching Boat of Garten. Worked from the outset
by the Great North of Scotland Railway, the single-track line led a
fairly quiet life and despite the introduction of cost-cutting railbuses
and the opening of new halts in the late 1950s it was listed for closure
in the 'Beeching Report'. It was closed to passengers in 1965 although
parts of the line remained open to serve whisky distilleries until 1971.
Since then many of the stations have been restored and several
long sections have been reopened as part of the Speyside Way
Long Distance Path.

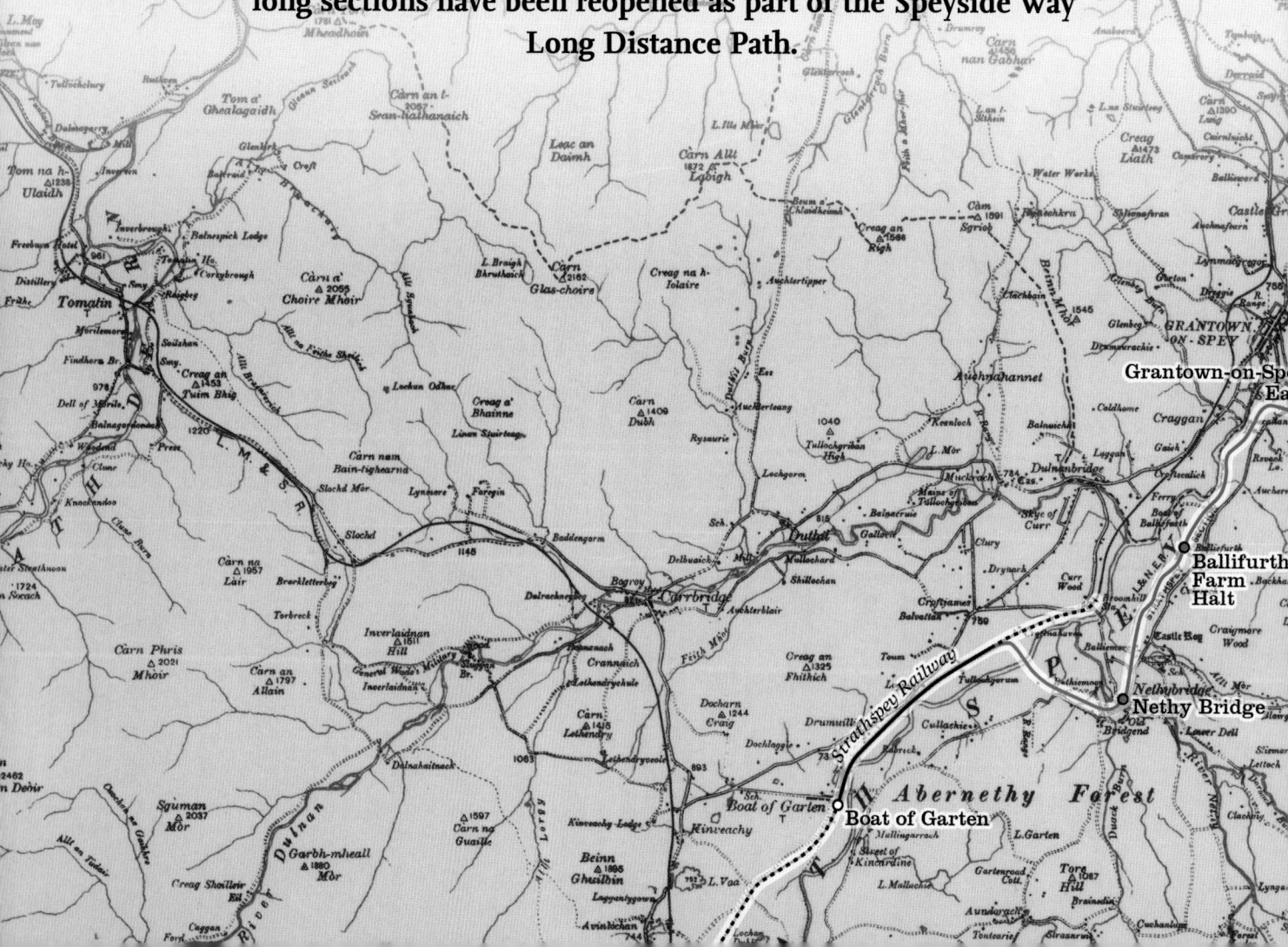

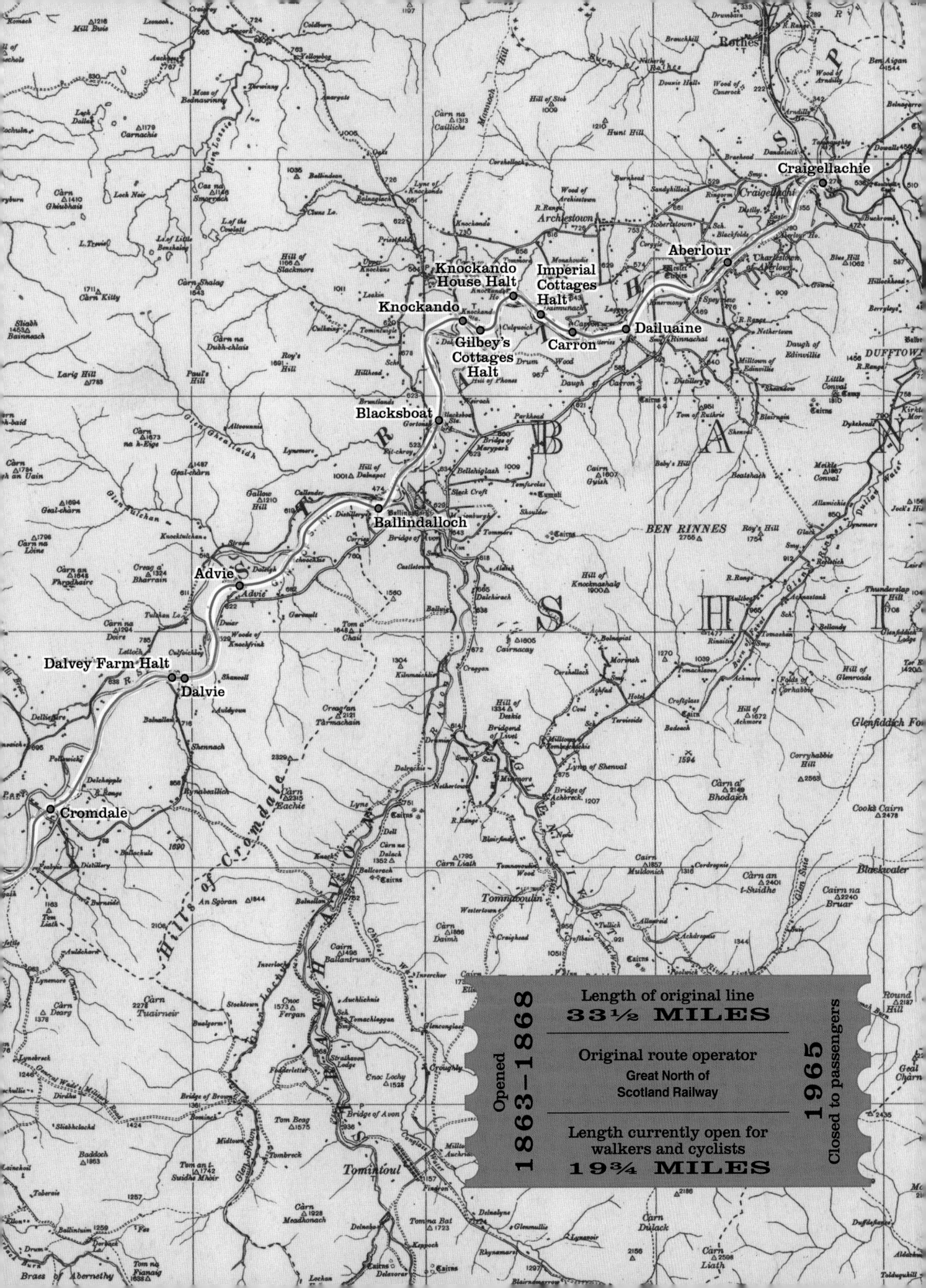

Craigellachie

Aberlour

Dailuaine

Imperial
Cottages
Halt

Knockando
House Halt

Carron

Knockando

Gilbey's
Cottages
Halt

Blacksboat

Ballindalloch

Advie

Dalvey Farm Halt

Dalvie

Cromdale

BEN RINNES
2755 △

Glenfiddich For

Tomintoul

Opened
1863–1868

Length of original line
33½ MILES

Original route operator
Great North of
Scotland Railway

Length currently open for
walkers and cyclists
19¾ MILES

1965
Closed to passengers

ncorporated in 1846, the Great North of Scotland Railway (GNoSR) eventually went on to operate over 300 miles of railway to the north and west of Aberdeen. The company's main line from Aberdeen to Keith was opened throughout in 1856 and in the following year the Keith & Dufftown Railway was incorporated to build an 8½-mile single-track line to Dufftown. This railway was backed by the GNoSR who saw it as the first step in a railway extending westward to serve the whisky industry in the Spey Valley. Money was tight and progress was slow, with the planned route being revised in favour of a cheaper but longer alternative. It eventually opened in 1862 and was worked by the GNoSR from the outset.

Meanwhile the Strathspey Railway had received authorization in 1861 to build a single-track line westwards from Dufftown to Craigellachie and then along the Spey Valley to Abernethy. Again this railway was backed by the GNoSR, who worked it from its opening in 1863. The railway met the Morayshire Railway (MR) from Elgin at Craigellachie, where the MR's original terminus was renamed Dandaleith in 1864.

Abernethy (renamed Nethy Bridge in 1867) was only a temporary terminus however, as the Strathspey Railway's

ultimate goal was to link up with the Inverness & Perth Junction Railway's (I&PJR) main line which had also opened from Forres through Boat of Garten and Aviemore in 1863 – two years later the I&PJR was one of two companies that formed the Highland Railway.

In 1866 the Strathspey Railway was extended from Abernethy across the River Spey to a junction with the newly formed Highland Railway at Tullochgorum, three miles north of Boat of Garten. Prolonged wranglings over the cost of signalling at this junction delayed the opening of the Strathspey's extension however, and in the meantime the railway, along with the K&DR, was amalgamated with the GNoSR in 1866, with the MR being absorbed in 1880.

With no positive outcome for the junction at Tullochgorum, the new owners of the Strathspey Railway eventually built their own single-track line parallel to the HR's line into Boat of Garten station. Trains finally started running along the Speyside line to Boat of Garten in 1868. While passenger traffic was always light the railway served numerous whisky distilleries, two of which, Dailuaine and Cromdale, had their own internal railway systems operated by diminutive 0-4-0 tank locomotives,

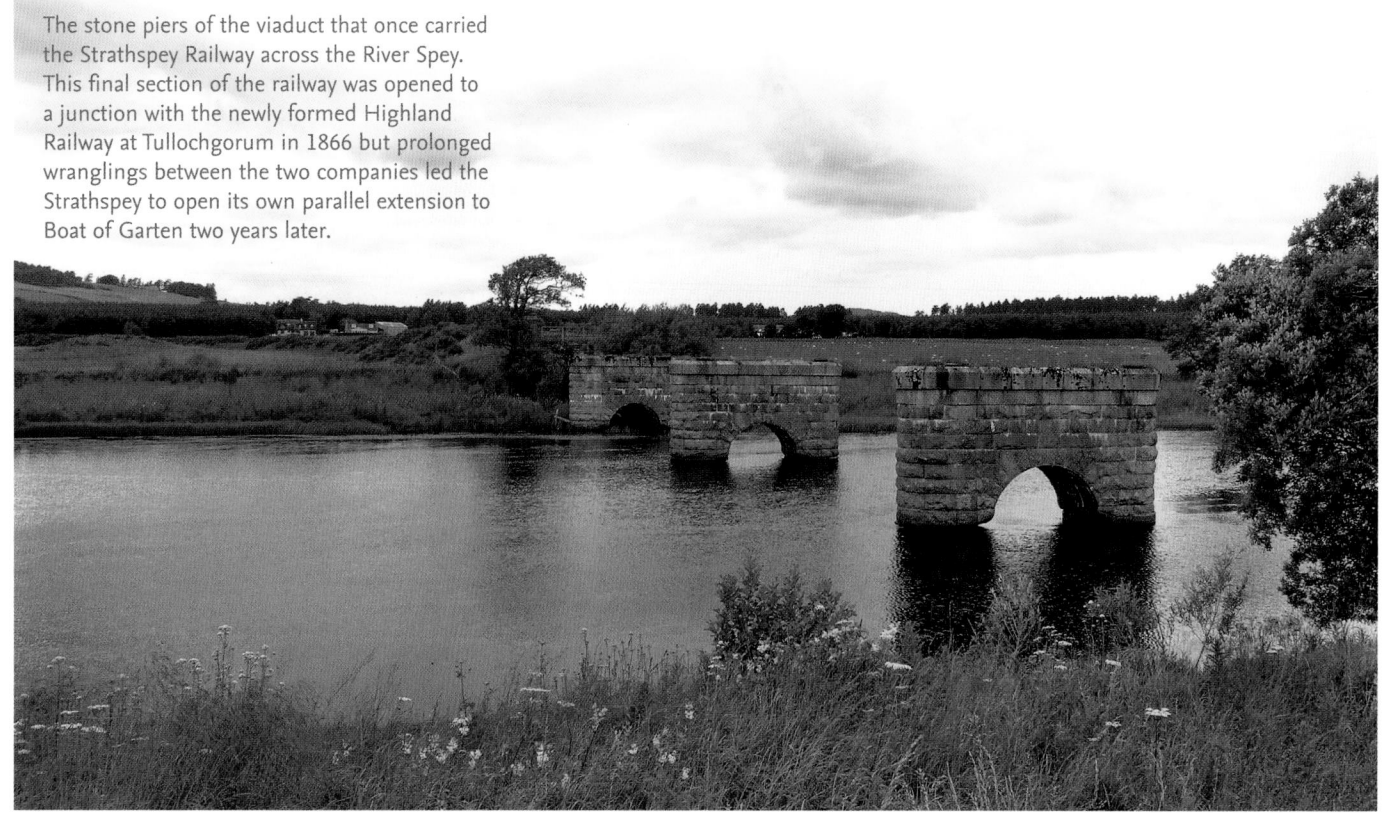

The stone piers of the viaduct that once carried the Strathspey Railway across the River Spey. This final section of the railway was opened to a junction with the newly formed Highland Railway at Tullochgorum in 1866 but prolonged wranglings between the two companies led the Strathspey to open its own parallel extension to Boat of Garten two years later.

affectionately known locally as 'puggies'. Timber traffic was also important, especially during the Second World War when the Canadian Forestry Corps was based at Knockando and Nethybridge.

The GNoSR, keen to promote the line's scenic attractions, introduced excursion trains from Aberdeen to Boat of Garten as early as 1905. The most ambitious of these was the Three Rivers Tour, which not only took in the River Spey but also the Dee and the Don, with railway-owned buses conveying passengers between the various routes. The GNoSR became part of the newly formed London & North Eastern Railway (LNER) in 1923. In addition to the existing intermediate stations at Aberlour, Carron, Knockando House Halt, Knockando, Blacksboat, Ballindalloch, Advie, Cromdale, Grantown-on-Spey (East) and Nethy Bridge the LNER opened a new halt at Dailuaine in 1933.

In an effort to cut running costs, British Railways introduced four-wheel diesel railcars on the line in 1958 and at the same time some trains were extended to Elgin in the north and Aviemore in the south – the 52¾ miles between Elgin and Aviemore via Craigellachie taking nearly two hours. Additional halts (just basic short platforms built from sleepers) were opened at Ballifurth Farm, Dalvey Farm, Gilbey's Cottages and Imperial Cottages in the summer of 1959. Sadly these measures failed to save the Speyside line, which was listed for closure along with the former HR main line from

Aviemore to Forres and all the other ex-GNoSR routes in northeast Scotland – apart from the Aberdeen to Keith main line – in the 1963 'Beeching Report'.

The 33 miles of railway between Boat of Garten and Craigellachie closed to passengers on 18 October 1965, as did the 36 miles between Aviemore and Forres. Craigellachie continued to be served by passenger trains running between Keith and Elgin until 6 May 1968. Meanwhile the whisky distilleries along the Spey Valley were served by goods trains until 4 November of that year, when the line between Aviemore, Boat of Garten and Aberlour was closed completely. Dufftown to Aberlour followed on 15 November 1971 although the 'whisky capital' of Dufftown continued to be rail served by luxury charter trains until 1985.

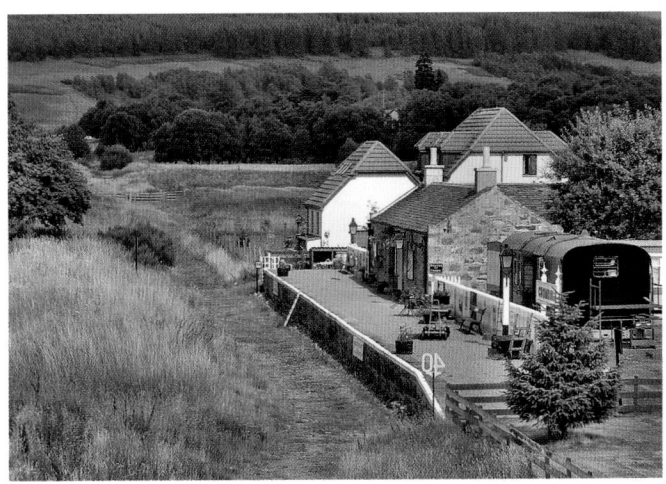

A deserted Cromdale station, looking north, on a sunny 22 June 1957. On the right is the stationmaster's allotment while beyond are sidings for the Balmenach distillery, which were worked by the company's own 'Puggie' engine. Today (above-right), the distillery is still in business while the superbly restored station and its platform survive, alongside the Speyside Way.

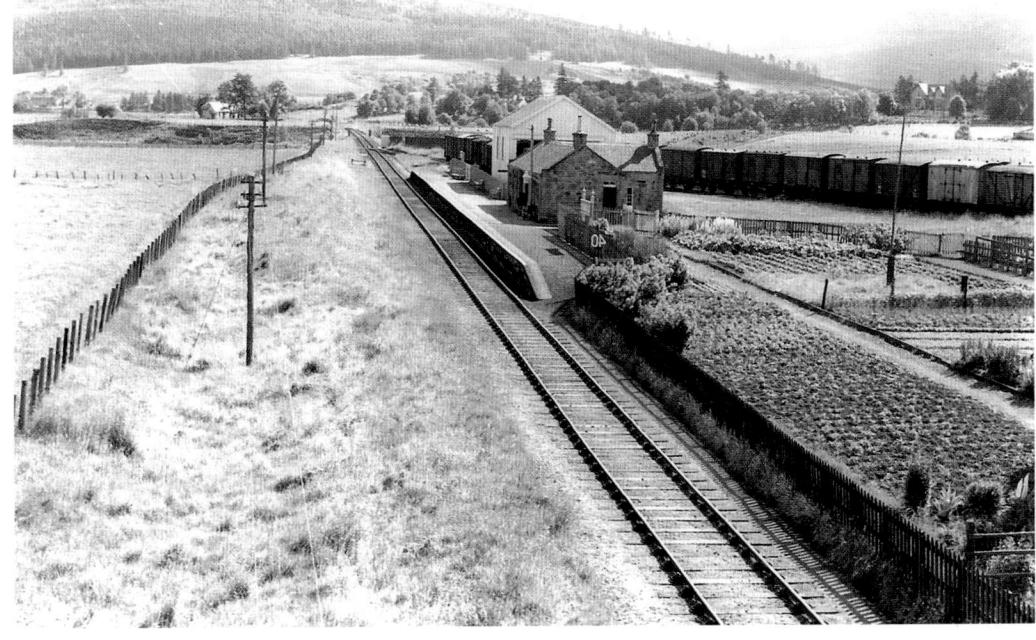

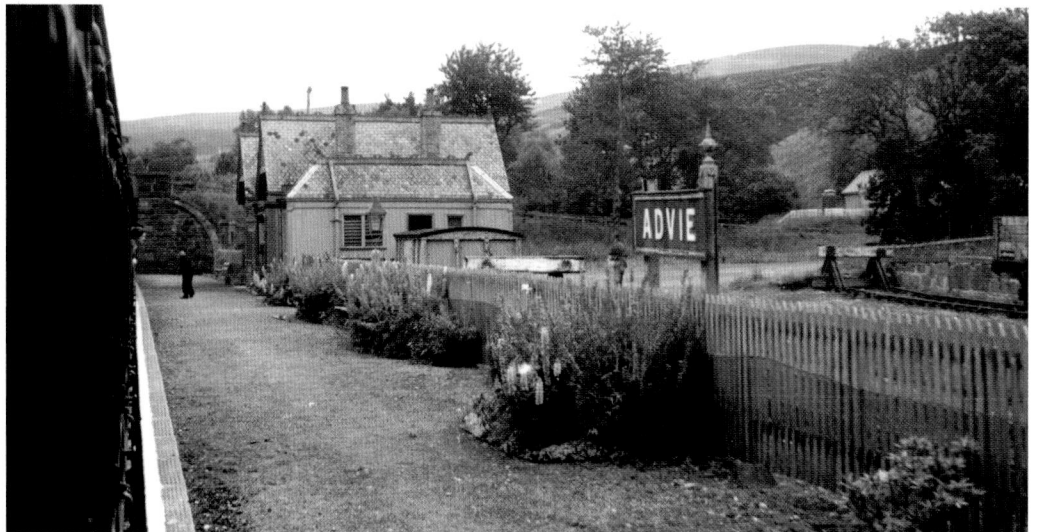

Henry Casserley took this photograph of Advie station from the 10.10am train from Craigellachie to Boat of Garten on 11 July 1957. The lupins are flowering, a few wagons sit in the goods yard and the stationmaster has a chat with the guard on this serene summer's day.

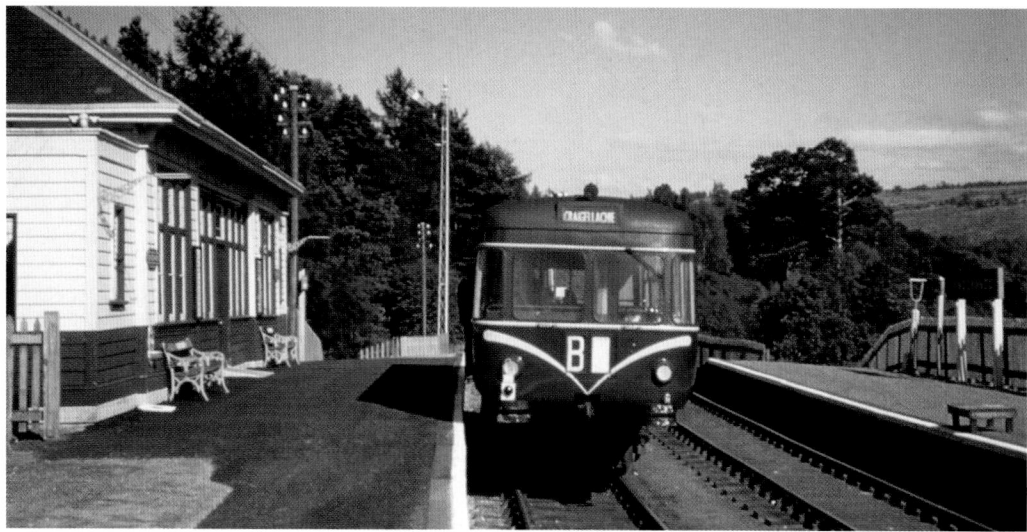

Bound for Boat of Garten, Park Royal Vehicles' railbus No. Sc79970 gets ready to leave Knockando station with a service from Craigellachie on 14 July 1959. Since closure of the line, Knockando station, its platforms and its signal box have been restored by the adjacent Tamdhu Distillery.

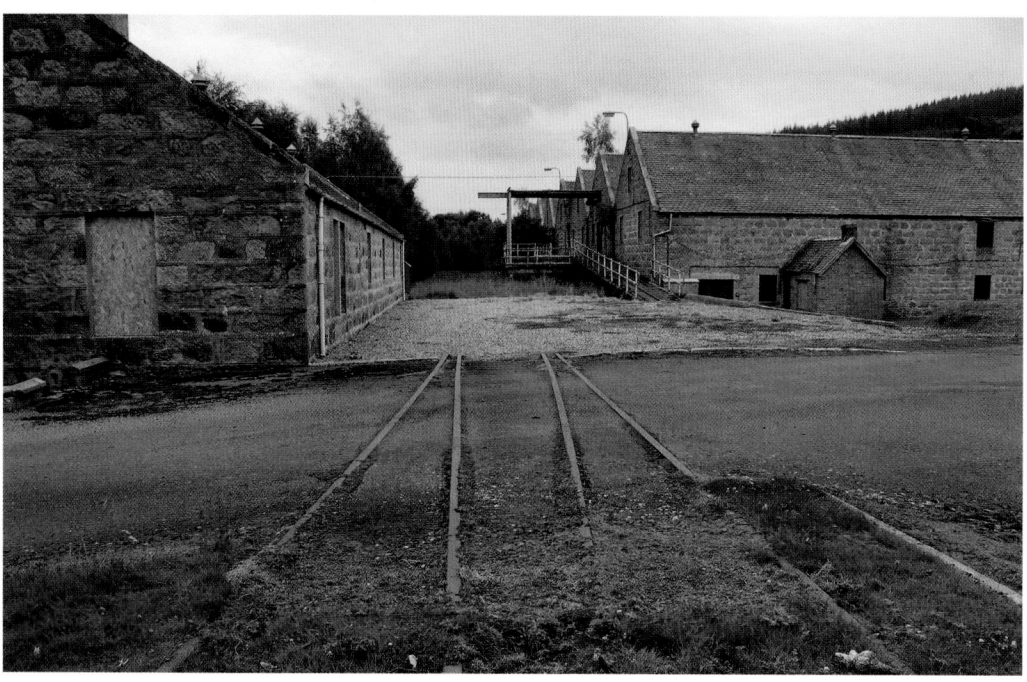

A set of points and a length of track can still be seen within the mothballed Imperial Distillery at Carron. Despite closure to passengers nearly fifty years ago, the nearby station building has survived along with its rusty clock and cast-iron drinking water fountain.

FAR RIGHT: Beyond Aberlour station, the Speyside Way is sandwiched between road and river and passes through the short Taminurie Tunnel, the only one to be encountered along the entire route.

Since closure several sections of the railway along the Spey Valley have been reopened as a footpath and cycleway, forming part of the Speyside Way Long Distance Path. The latter was opened in stages from 1981 onwards and currently extends from Buckie on the Banffshire coast to Aviemore, a distance of sixty-five miles. There is also a 4-mile branch that follows the old railway route from Craigellachie to Dufftown.

The present-day Strathspey Railway operates steam and diesel trains for 8½ miles between Aviemore, Boat of Garten and Broomhill while work is progressing on a northward extension to Grantown-on-Spey. To the east, the Keith & Dufftown Heritage Railway operates diesel trains at weekends along the eleven miles of line between Keith and Dufftown.

Walkers or cyclists wishing to follow the route of the old railway along the Spey Valley can join the Speyside Way at Nethy Bridge, where the former station building now provides bunkhouse accommodation. From here the trackbed of the railway is followed northwards, passing the site of Ballifurth Farm Halt to Grantown-on-Spey, where the Speyside Way diverts across the river before rejoining the railway route further on at Cromdale station. Following the course of the Grantown to Forres railway, the 24-mile Dava Way footpath and cycleway can also be joined at Grantown – here, East station and its platforms survive although their future seems uncertain. The situation at Cromdale however is completely different – here, the station building has been superbly restored by its new owner as a private residence. Plenty of railway ephemera and a restored carriage built at Inverurie Works complete this idyllic scene.

From Cromdale station the Speyside Way continues to follow the old railway route for about a mile before diverting along forest tracks and side roads to rejoin it about a mile to the west of Ballindalloch. Although not on the Speyside Way, the platform and road overbridge still survive at the site of the intermediate Advie station where the trackbed is also accessible to walkers. Ballindalloch station is now a hostel and from here the Speyside Way follows the old railway route right through to Craigellachie.

Immediately north of Ballindalloch station the Way crosses the River Spey on a fine steel lattice-work girder bridge before continuing northward down the valley to Blacksboat station. Popular amongst fishermen in this beautiful riverside location, the goods shed, platform and station building have been lovingly restored, the latter being used as holiday accommodation. Following the meandering river down the wooded valley, the railway route and Speyside Way reach Knockando station, which has been superbly restored as a visitor centre by the adjacent Tamdhu Distillery – only the track is missing from this delightful station with its two platforms and signal box. Shadowing the bends of the river, the Way passes the sites of Gilbey's Cottages Halt and Imperial Cottages Halt to arrive at Carron station, adjacent to the once rail-served but now mothballed Imperial Distillery. The station building survives here, complete with rusty clock and cast-iron drinking water fountain.

From Carron the Way and railway route cross over the Spey again and follow the river for 3½ miles to Aberlour, passing the lovingly restored but diminutive railway halt at Dailuaine en route. Aberlour is a good place to have a rest or find accommodation in the town – the restored station and platform now house a café, while the former station site and goods yard have been landscaped as a riverside park.

Beyond Aberlour the Way passes through the 68-yd Taminurie Tunnel, the only tunnel on the Speyside line, before reaching Craigellachie – here all that remains of the junction station is one platform and a road overbridge, while the station site is now a car park for users of the Speyside Way. Refreshments can be taken at the Highlander Inn or the Fiddichside Inn in the nearby village. From Craigellachie the 4-mile railway route southwards along the valley of the River Fiddich to Dufftown is also a footpath and cycleway.

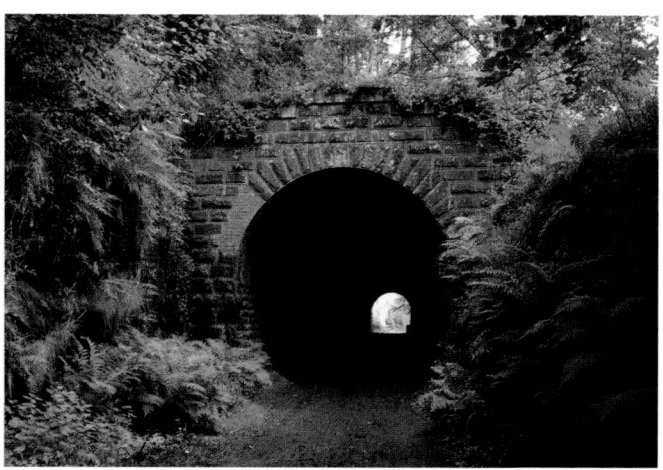

ELGIN
TO
LOSSIEMOUTH

Serving the harbour town of Lossiemouth and with no intermediate stations, the branch line from Elgin was built in a more-or-less straight line across low-lying land, crossing the Spynie Canal en route. Once served by a through sleeping car to and from London King's Cross, the railway fell on hard times in the years following the Second World War and lost its passenger service in 1964. Since complete closure in 1966, a long section south of Lossiemouth has been reopened as a footpath and cycleway while the grand terminus station at Elgin East has been beautifully restored as a business centre.

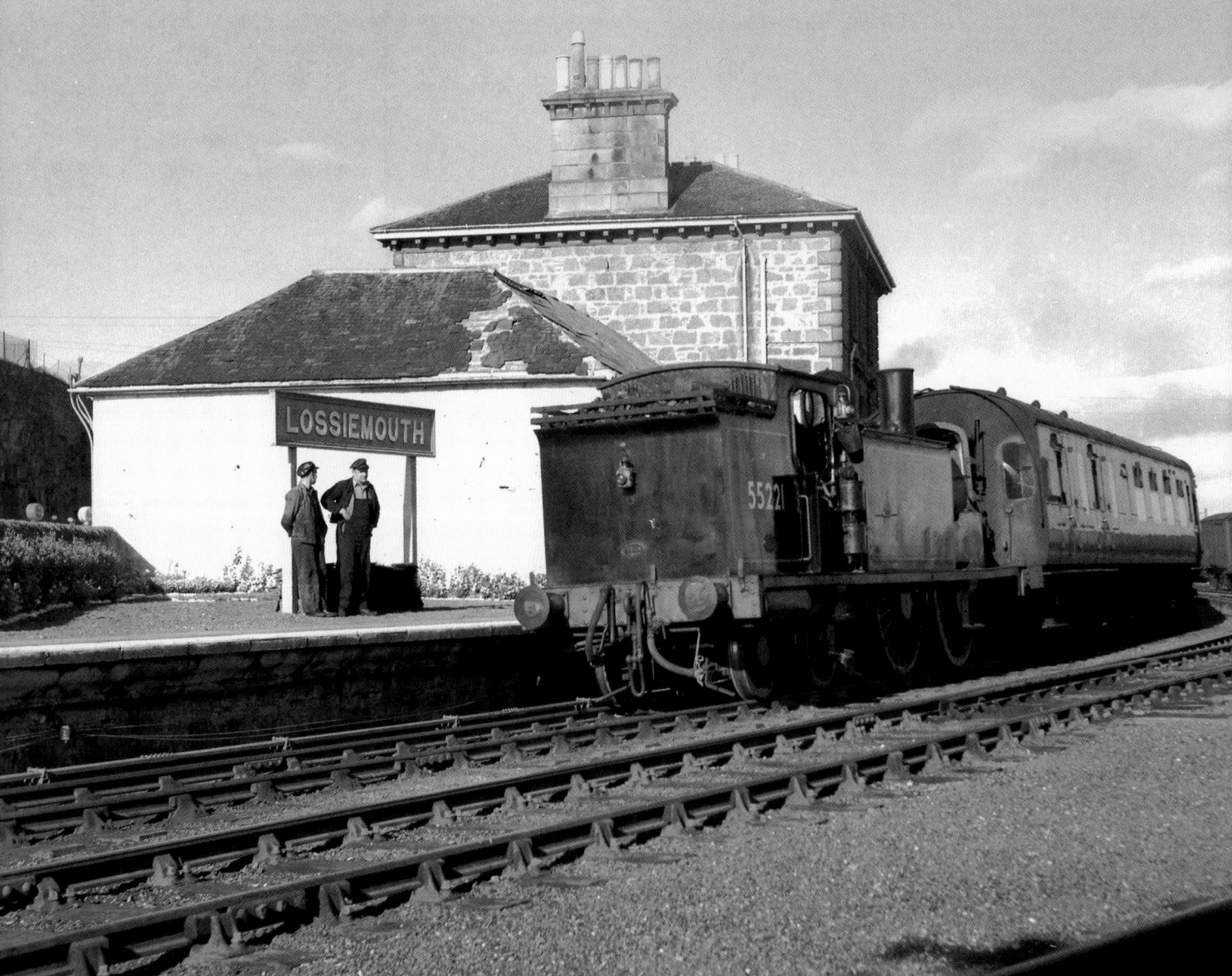

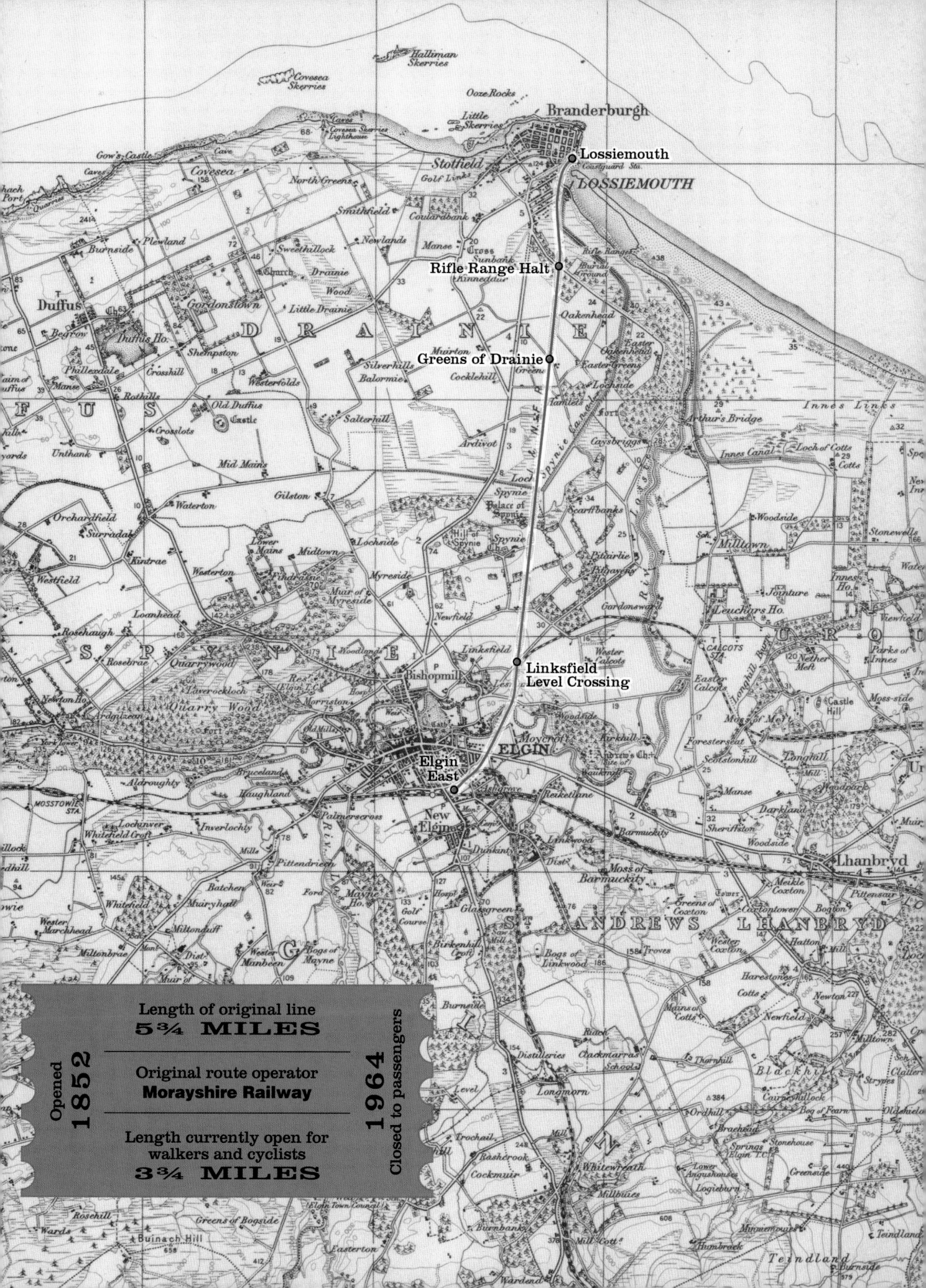

Branderburgh

Lossiemouth

LOSSIEMOUTH

Rifle Range Halt

Greens of Drainie

Linksfield
Level Crossing

Elgin
East

ELGIN

Opened **1852**

Length of original line
5¾ MILES

Original route operator
Morayshire Railway

Length currently open for
walkers and cyclists
3¾ MILES

1964 Closed to passengers

First proposed in 1841 by the owners of the Glen Grant distillery at Rothes, the 5¾-mile single-track railway from Elgin to the harbour town of Lossiemouth was opened by the Morayshire Railway (MR) in 1852. Built in a more-or-less dead-straight line across low-lying land, the only major engineering features on the railway were a deep cutting and the bridge over the River Lossie near Elgin. The railway also crossed the Spynie Canal near the ruined twelfth-century Spynie Palace two miles north of Elgin, and a short branch from Lossiemouth station to the harbour was also built. Opening day on 10 August 1852 was a close-run thing as the two locomotives needed to run the line were delivered to Lossiemouth by sea from Glasgow only ten days before the event. The railway was a great success and carried several thousand passengers on the first day.

The company also had plans to reach Rothes and Craigellachie in the south and opened a branch line from Orton, on the Inverness & Aberdeen Junction Railway's main line from Elgin to Keith, to Rothes and Craigellachie in 1858. With one intermediate station between Orton and Rothes at Sourden, this 3½-mile section of line had closed by 1866 – one of the earliest railway closures in Britain – although Sourden continued to be served by goods trains until 1880, with the track being lifted in 1907. The company opened the direct line from Elgin to Rothes and Craigellachie throughout in 1862.

By now the Morayshire Railway (MR) was deep in debt, not only to several banks but also to its bigger neighbour, the Great North of Scotland Railway (GNoSR). Approaches for a takeover by the rival Highland Railway in 1867 came to nothing but gradually matters improved for the MR with increased use of the Lossiemouth branch both by visitors to the newly opened public baths in the town and by the booming herring fishing industry – reduced fares were introduced for fisherwomen so they could take their catch by train to Craigellachie and further afield. By 1880 the MR was financially sound and the company was amalgamated retrospectively with the GNoSR in 1881.

Although it coped with traffic to Lossiemouth and Craigellachie, the original station at Elgin East became overstretched with the opening of the GNoSR's coastal route to Cairnie Junction via Buckie and Cullen in 1886 (see pages 294-299). A much-enlarged station was opened in 1902 to deal with the traffic and this magnificent building, recently restored, has fortunately survived the closure of all these railways.

While the GNoSR unsuccessfully experimented with steam railcars on the Lossiemouth branch in the early twentieth century, the scenic attractions of the Morayshire coast were heavily promoted to attract holidaymakers, with the company dubbing it the Scottish Riviera. Sand dunes along the east beach at Lossiemouth were created artificially in the early 1900s by placing disused railway carriages behind the beach! In 1923 the company was absorbed into the newly formed London & North Eastern Railway which introduced a through sleeping car service

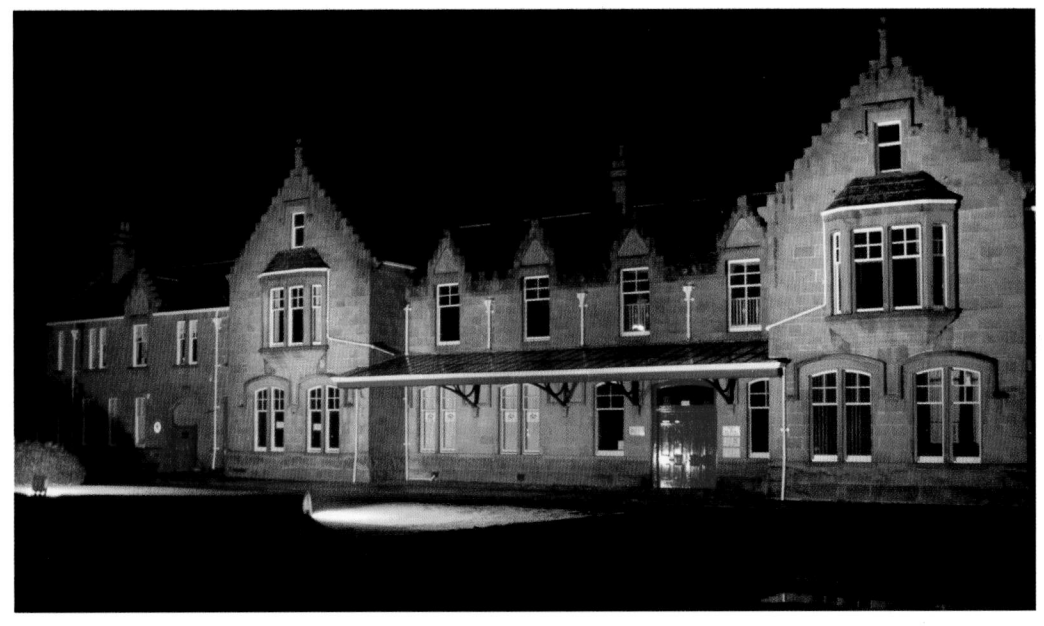

PREVIOUS SPREAD:
The driver and fireman of No. 55221 breathe in the sea air and relax in the autumn sunshine at Lossiemouth station before returning with their train to Elgin East on 9 October 1958.

Once the grand terminus for Great North of Scotland Railway trains to Craigellachie, Lossiemouth and the Morayshire coastal route via Cullen, the station at Elgin East was opened in 1902. Since closure it has been restored to its former glory and is now a business centre.

from King's Cross to Lossiemouth – one of the longest through coach workings in Britain. The Second World War put an end to holidays on the Morayshire coast but the Lossiemouth branch was kept busy serving the new RAF base that had grown up near the town.

With increasing competition from road transport the post-war years saw a rapid decline in both passenger and freight traffic on the branch. In an effort to reduce running costs diesel multiple units were introduced in the late 1950s but this move failed to stop the branch being listed for closure in the 1963 'Beeching Report'. Passenger services were withdrawn on 6 April 1964 and goods traffic on 28 March 1966. Elgin East remained open until 6 May 1968 when the remaining former GNoSR lines to Cairnie Junction via Cullen and Craigellachie were closed.

IIIIIIIIIIIIIIIIII

Since closure 3¾ miles of the northern section of the Lossiemouth branch line have been reopened as a footpath and cycleway. The harbour town of Lossiemouth – the birthplace of Britain's first Labour Prime Minister, Ramsay MacDonald – is once again a popular resort, with fine sandy beaches, bracing sea air and a championship golf course, although it is still heavily dependent on the nearby RAF station, which contributes millions of pounds to the local economy.

The railway station in the town has been demolished to make way for a leisure park but a short section of line can still be seen embedded in the nearby harbour quayside, where an old warehouse has taken on a new life as café and bar. The railway path starts close to the Mercat Cross, from where a tarmac path leads south out of the town before crossing the B9103. From here the unsurfaced railway path, which can be muddy in winter, heads south for three miles in a dead-straight line, crossing the Spynie Canal and skirting the ruins of Spynie Castle en route. When open to the public, the castle roof offers a good view of the railway's imprint on the landscape. The railway path proper ends about one mile south of the castle where there is a minor road into Elgin. Beyond here the trackbed is a very muddy farm track and is not recommended for walkers or cyclists.

The railway's approach to Elgin via a bridge over the River Lossie and a long embankment has survived the ravages of time and it is hoped that these will one day be incorporated into the railway path. Floodlit at night, Elgin East station building, with its magnificent booking hall, has been superbly restored and is now a business centre.

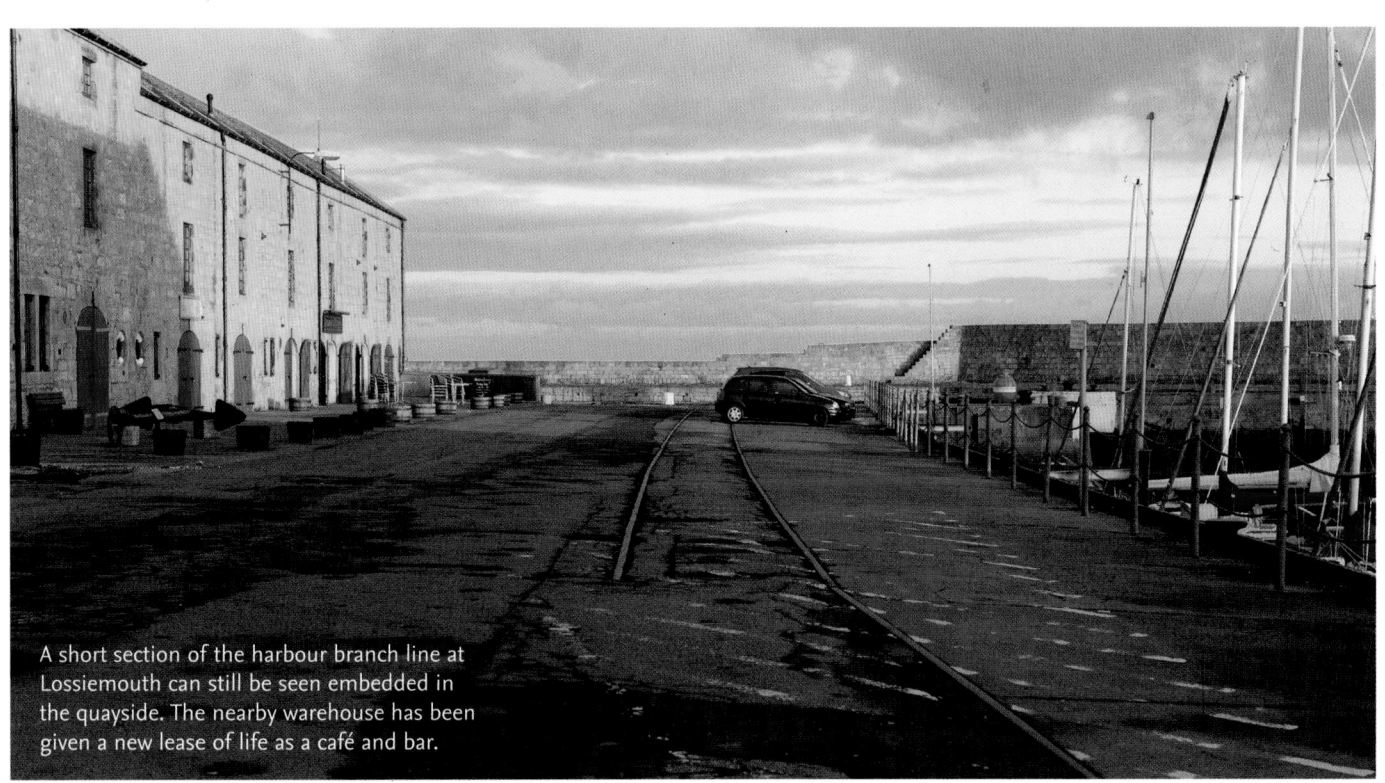

A short section of the harbour branch line at Lossiemouth can still be seen embedded in the quayside. The nearby warehouse has been given a new lease of life as a café and bar.

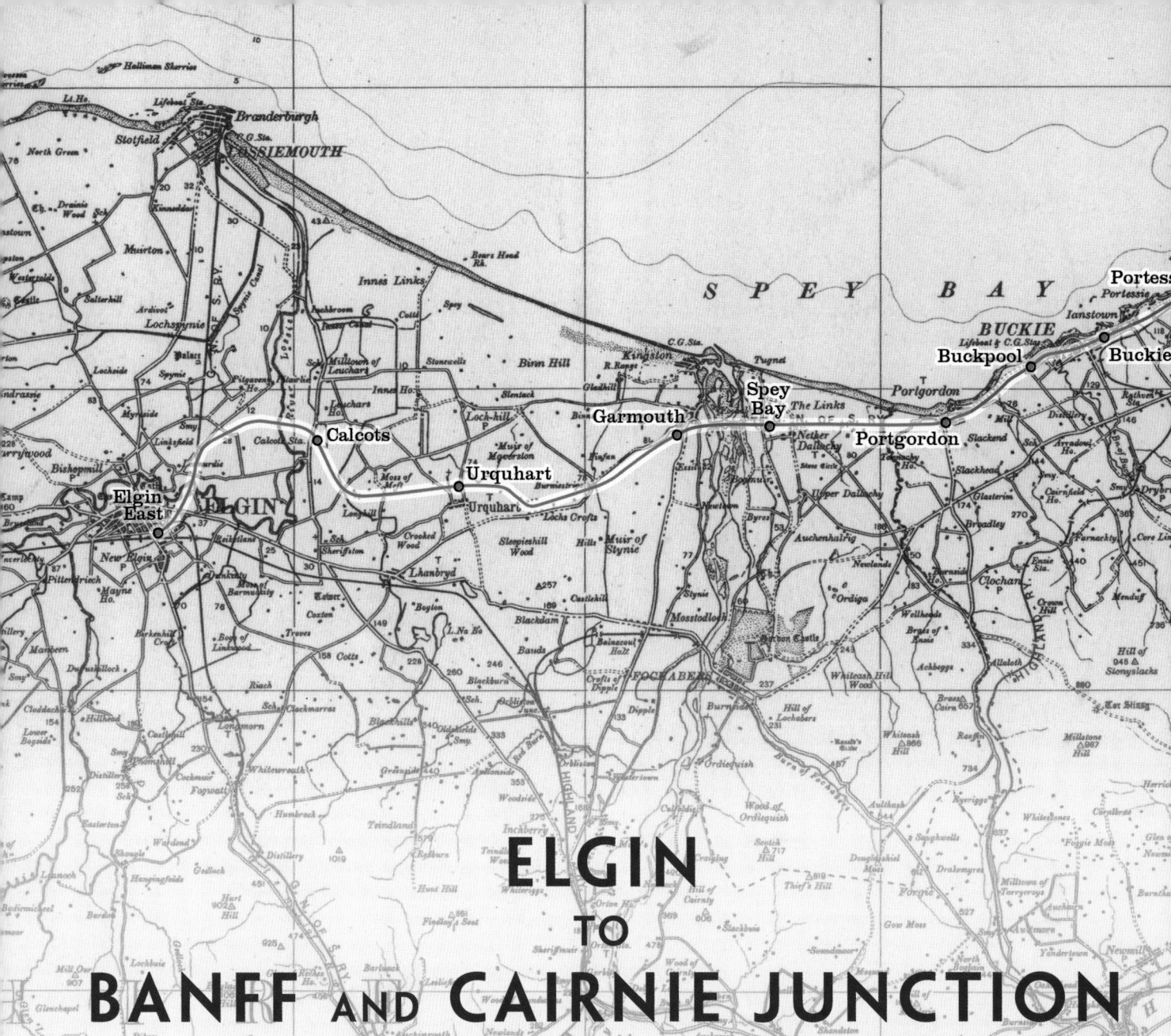

ELGIN
TO
BANFF AND CAIRNIE JUNCTION

A latecomer to the railway scene in northeast Scotland, the Great North of Scotland Railway's coastal route was finally completed in 1886. Featuring some fine viaducts on the coast at Cullen and a magnificent bridge across the River Spey, the line offered speedy transport for fish catches from the many coastal villages and an alternative route for passenger trains running between Elgin and Aberdeen. The branch line to Banff was served by a shuttle service of trains connecting with the 'main line' at Tillynaught. Passenger services to Banff ended in 1964 with complete closure for both lines coming in 1968. Since then much of the coastal route from Garmouth to Cullen, along with a short section on the coast near Banff, has been reopened as a footpath and cycleway.

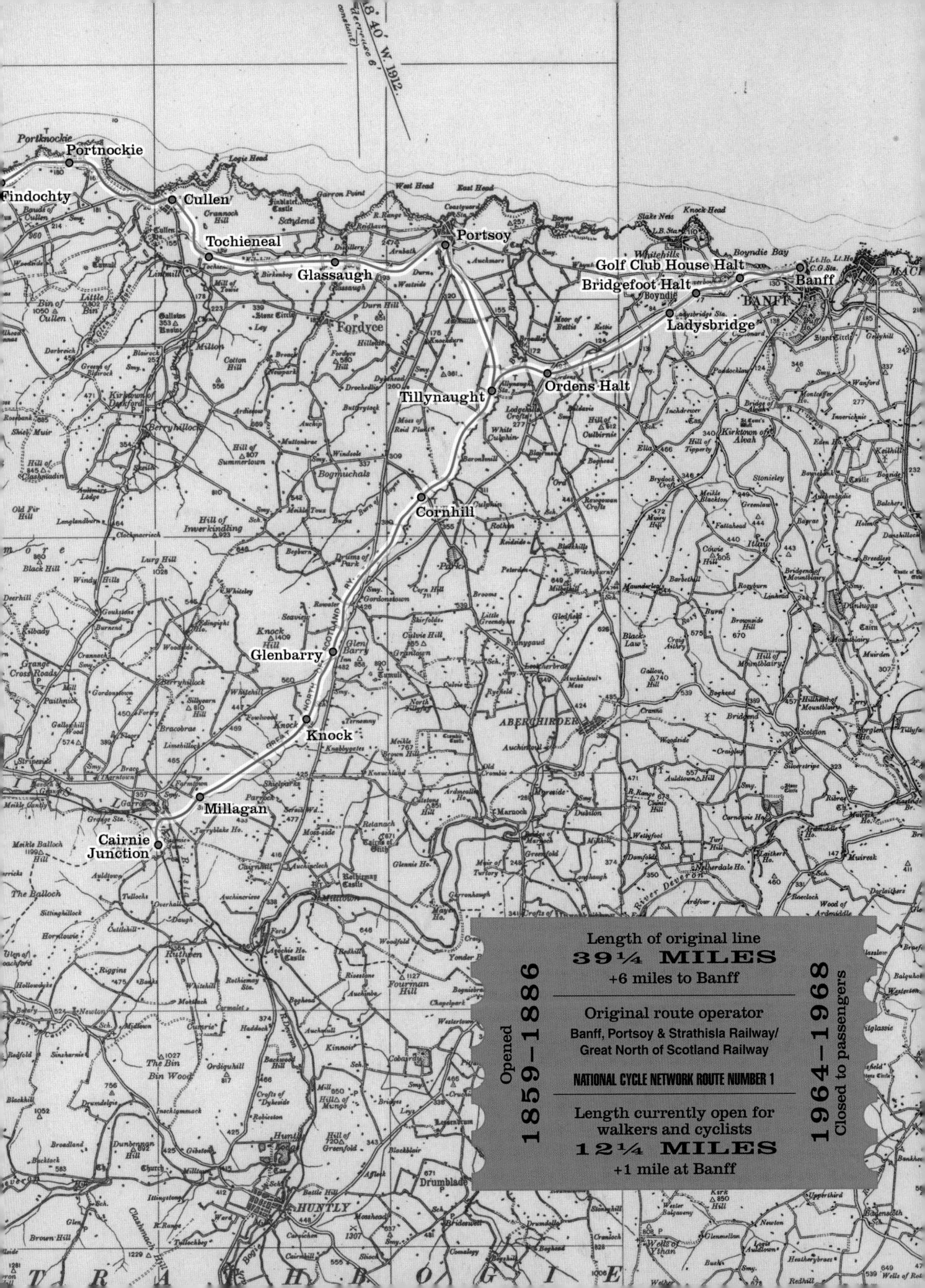

Portknockie
Portnockie
Findochty
Cullen
Tochieneal
Glassaugh
Fordyce
Portsoy
Golf Club House Halt
Bridgefoot Halt
Banff
Ladysbridge
Ordens Halt
Tillynaught
Cornhill
Glenbarry
Knock
Millagan
Cairnie Junction
ABERCHIRDER
HUNTLY

By 1856 the Great North of Scotland Railway (GNoSR) had extended its main line from Aberdeen as far as Keith. The penultimate station on this line was at Grange, just 4¼ miles east of Keith, and it was from here that the Banff, Portsoy & Strathisla Railway (BP&SR) was authorized in 1857 to build a 16¼-mile branch line to the harbour town of Banff, with a 2¾-mile branch from Tillynaught to Portsoy. The villages and towns along this stretch of coastline had long been important centres of the fishing industry and it was hoped that the railway would bring great benefits by transporting catches quickly to more distant markets.

The railway opened in 1859 but soon ran into operational difficulties and sought assistance from the GNoSR, which eventually took over the working of the line in 1863. In the same year the BP&SR changed its name to the Banffshire Railway and received authorization to extend the short Portsoy branch line westwards along the coast to the fishing village of Portgordon. However this was beyond the means of the company, which was finally absorbed by the GNoSR in 1867, and the extension quietly forgotten for a further fourteen years.

In 1882 the GNoSR received authorization to build a 26½-mile extension westward along the Morayshire coastline from Portsoy to Elgin. The new line met the company's existing branch line from Lossiemouth to Elgin (see pages 290-293) at Lossie Junction. The main engineering features were massive embankments and three viaducts at Cullen – built at great expense to avoid land owned by the Earl of Seafield (a director of the Highland Railway!) – and a long bridge over the River Spey at Spey Bay. The line was eventually completed in 1886 and, with the south facing spur at Cairnie Junction (three-quarters of a mile south of Grange), provided the GNoSR with a second 'main line' between Aberdeen and Elgin. The opening of this new route led to the Banff line becoming a branch served by trains from Tillynaught.

The new coastal route was a godsend to the local fishing industry which by then was enjoying boom times from herring catches – the railway duly obliged by building steeply graded branch lines down to the harbours at Banff, Portsoy and Buckie. At that time the latter was already a thriving fishing and shipbuilding port and by 1913 had the largest steam drifter fleet in Scotland. Vast amounts

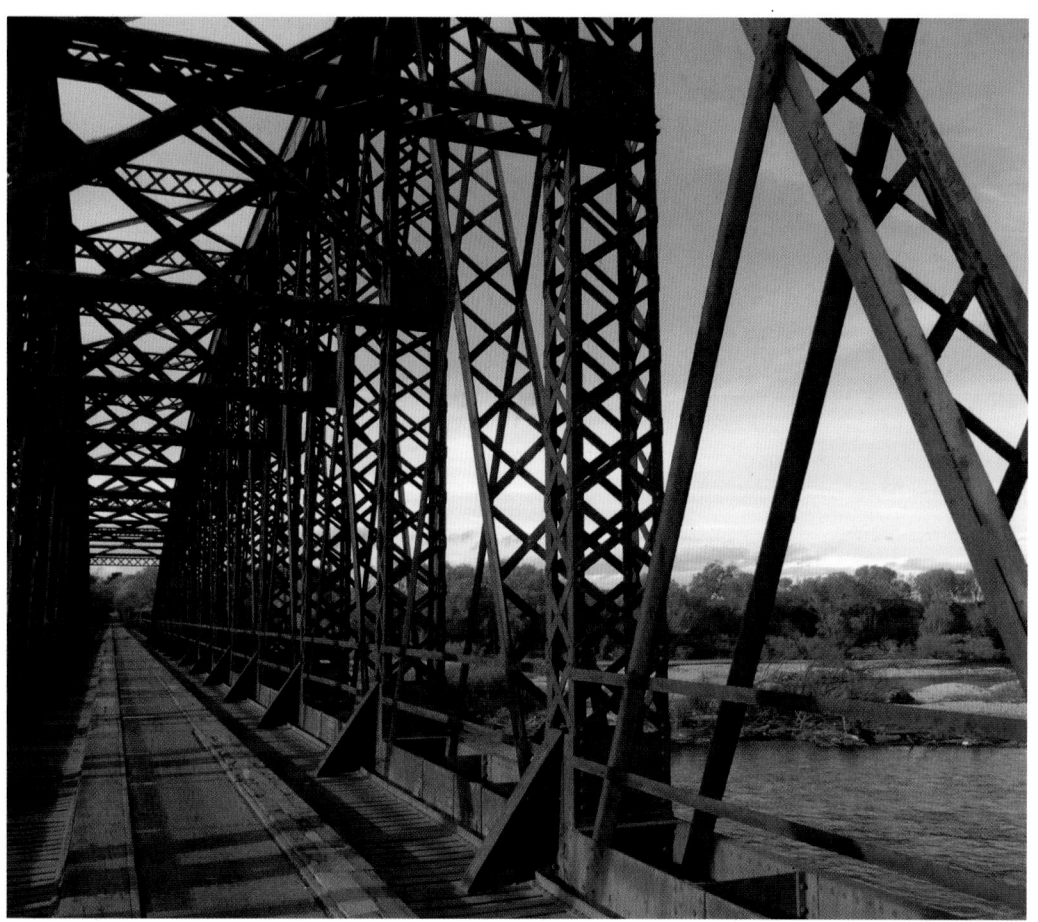

East of Garmouth the coastal railway path immediately crosses the River Spey on this impressive steel latticework bridge. Opened in 1886, the central bowstring span is reached from both sides by long approach viaducts, each with three steel spans.

RIGHT: A BRC&W Type 2 (Class 26) diesel halts at Spey Bay station with an Elgin to Aberdeen train on a sunny 13 April 1968. The eastbound track had already been lifted in anticipation of the line's closure on 6 May.

of fish were once transported from here by train to Aberdeen for overnight dispatch by rail to distant markets in London.

The GNoSR used its two circuitous 'main line' routes between Aberdeen and Elgin for all its traffic until 1897 when it came to an agreement with the Highland Railway, obtaining running powers over its more direct line between Keith and Elgin. The coastal route was then relegated to secondary status although it was still served by a few through trains between Elgin and Aberdeen until closure. The Banff branch was also served by a frequent service of trains shuttling to and from Tillynaught until closure.

The GNoSR became part of the newly formed London & North Eastern Railway in 1923 but increasing competition from road transport had started a decline in both passenger and goods traffic along the coastal route by the 1930s – the all important fish traffic from the coastal

harbours, so long the preserve of rail transport, was also being lost to lorries. The years following the Second World War saw further decline, and the introduction of unreliable North British Locomotive Company Type 2 diesels in the late 1950s and early 1960s probably made the situation worse rather than better.

The 1963 'Beeching Report' brought bad news for the vast majority of the former GNoSR lines in northeast Scotland including the Elgin to Cairnie Junction route and the Banff branch. Both were listed for closure with the Tillynaught to Banff passenger service – steam hauled until the end – being withdrawn on 6 July 1964. The coastal route and goods traffic to Banff continued operating until 6 May 1968 when both these lines were closed completely. In 1984 Banff station became the terminus of the short-lived 15-in-gauge West Buchan Railway, which ran westwards along the trackbed for one mile to Swordanes – the last train ran on 31 August 1985 and the company went into liquidation.

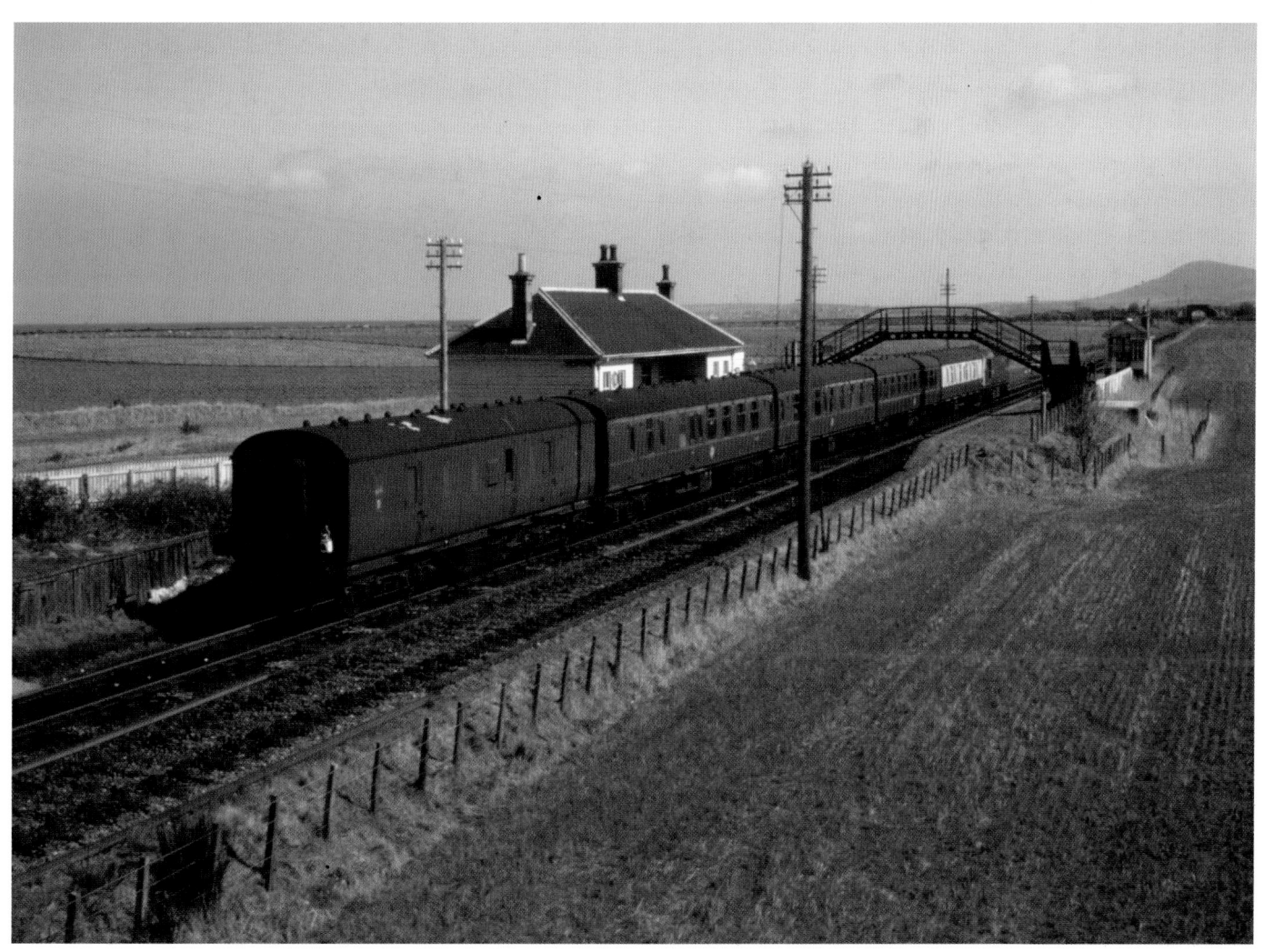

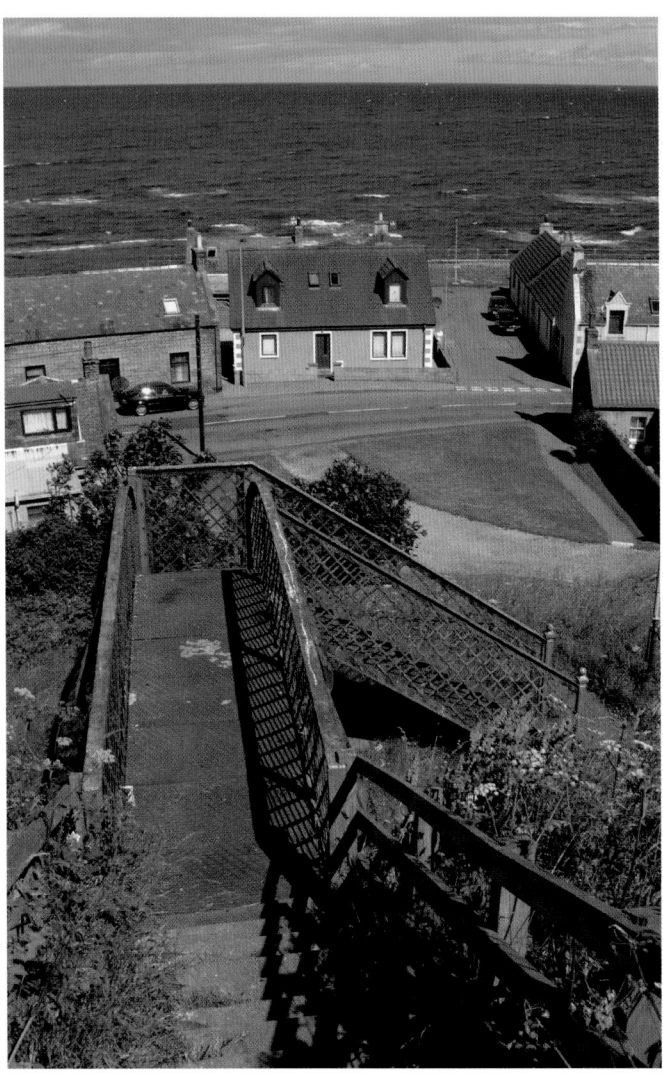

Despite closure over forty-five years ago, there are several scenic coastal sections of this railway that have been reopened as footpaths and cycleways. Between Garmouth and Cullen much of the trackbed now forms part of National Cycle Network Route 1 and the Speyside Way Long Distance Path (as far as Buckie).

West of Garmouth much of the old railway route to Elgin has long disappeared beneath farmland although a few forlorn bridges, such as one near Urquhart, still stand totally isolated in the middle of ploughed fields. The station buildings at Urquhart and Garmouth are now private residences.

The railway path starts at Garmouth, where there is a car park for walkers and cyclists. Heading east the path soon crosses the River Spey on an enormous steel latticework bridge – the daunting bowstring central span is reached from both sides by 300-ft-long approach viaducts, each with three steel latticework spans. Saved from demolition, the bridge was reopened by Moray District Council in 1981. On the east bank of the Spey, the station and platforms at Spey Bay survive as a private residence. From here NCN Route 1 diverts away from the old railway to follow side roads into Portgordon. The Speyside Way takes a different diversion towards the coast however, and later rejoins NCN Route 1 about one mile west of the village.

ABOVE: This steel latticework footbridge across the overgrown trackbed at Buckpool is still open for pedestrians.

One of several viaducts close to the coastline at Cullen that were built at great expense by the Great North of Scotland Railway to avoid land owned by the Earl of Seafield. Today, walkers and cyclists crossing it are treated to magnificent views of the sea and the rooftops of the village far below.

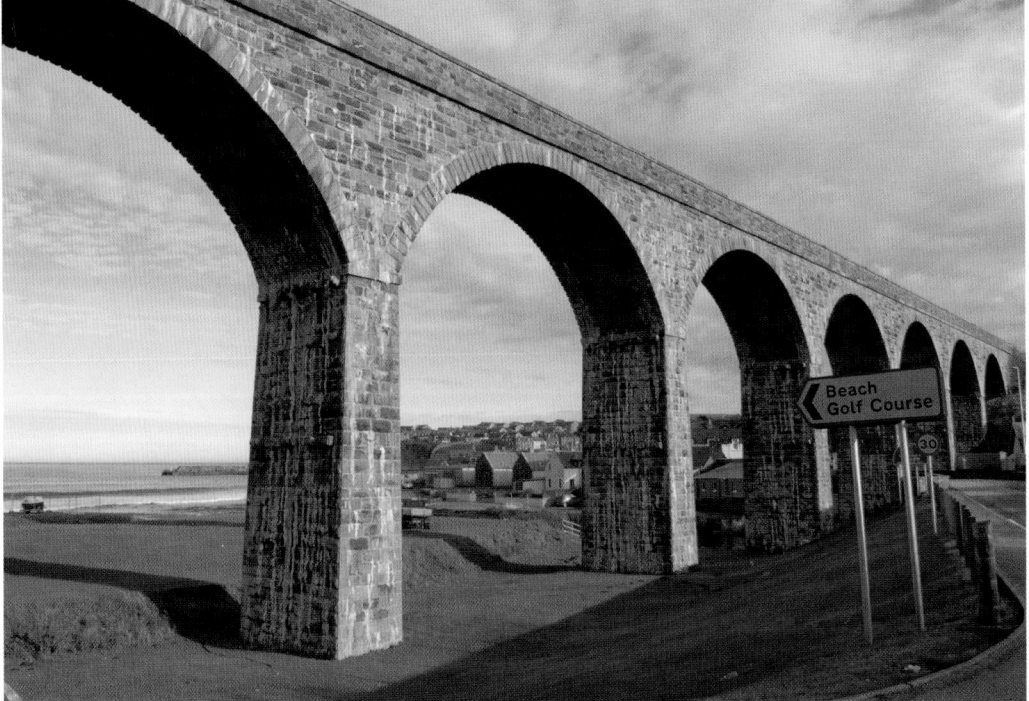

The station site at Portgordon is now occupied by a bowling club and the railway route is rejoined east of the village. The following 1-mile straight stretch along the coastline offers magnificent views across Spey Bay before there is another diversion away from the old railway route east of Buckie. Despite this there are still reminders of the railway at Buckpool, where a magnificent steel latticework footbridge across the overgrown trackbed is still open to pedestrians. Buckie station has been demolished but the old railway route is once again rejoined to the east of the town to follow it in a straight line to the village of Findochty. After a short diversion through the village, the railway route is rejoined again for 1½ miles to Portnockie. The stations at Findochty and Portnockie have been demolished to make way for housing.

The final, glorious 2-mile stretch from Portnockie to Cullen is the highlight of this coastal route. For a mile the path passes through a cutting before emerging high above the coast on an embankment to sweep over the rooftops of Cullen on a series of magnificent curving viaducts, offering breathtaking views of the sea and of the citizens of this famous fishing village far below, preparing their next pots of Cullen Skink!

At the moment, Cullen is the end of the road for walkers and cyclists along this superb railway coastal route. Further west at Banff the last mile or so of the railway route behind rows of former fishermen's cottages is also a footpath. The attractive overall-roofed station building at Banff was demolished in the 1980s.

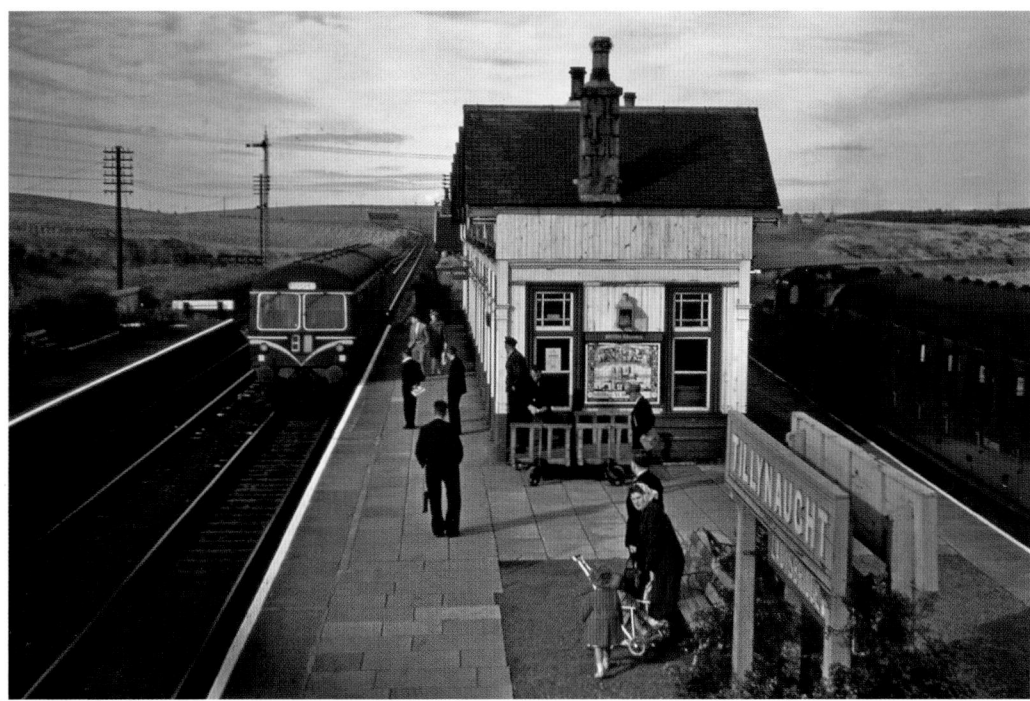

A wonderfully animated scene at Tillynaught station in 1964 as a 2-car diesel multiple unit arrives with a train from Elgin. On the right is the connecting branch line train to Banff headed by a BR Standard Class '2MT' 2-6-0. The Banff branch lost its passenger service on 6 July of that year.

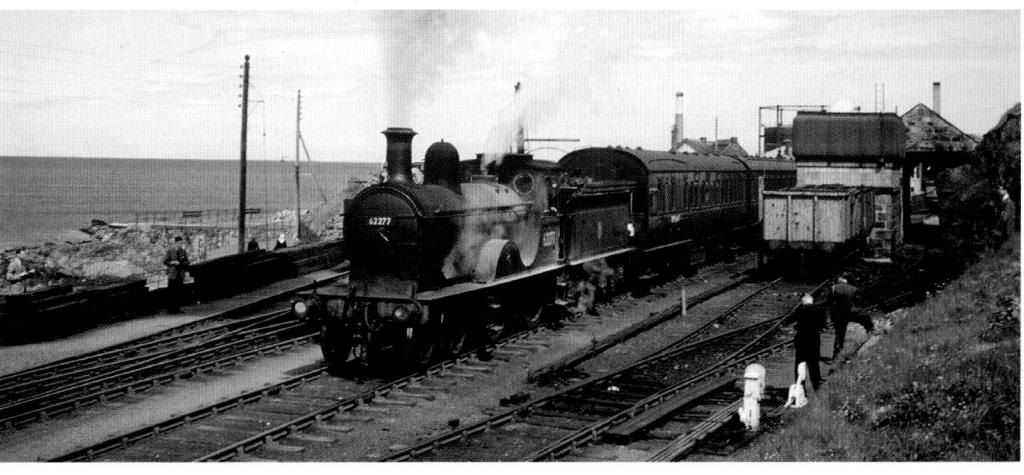

With the blue sea in the distance, ex-GNoSR Class 'D40' 4-4-0 No. 62277 'Gordon Highlander' gets ready to depart from Banff station with an enthusiasts' special on a sunny 2 August 1954. While scenes such as this have been confined to the dustbin of history by the likes of Mr Ernest Marples and Dr Richard Beeching, the locomotive lives on in preservation and can be seen at the Scottish Railway Exhibition in Bo'ness.

INDEX

ACKNOWLEDGEMENTS

Photo credits:
l = left; r = right; t = top; b = bottom; m = middle

Ben Ashworth: 133, 135
Mark Bartlett: 243t, 244, 245, 249m
Jack Boskett: 138, 139tr
Henry Casserley: 10/11, 18, 42, 54b, 55, 69, 90, 121m, 124b, 144, 146, 150, 152, 160, 163m,
    164t, 197t, 210, 212b, 274b, 281t, 288t
Richard Casserley: 4/5, 47b, 48/49, 89m, 93, 106, 109b, 116, 128/129, 170bl, 191t, 196, 259t
Colour-Rail: front cover (T B Owen), 17t, 17b, 20b, 21b, 26 (T B Owen), 52, 54t (John Sutton),
    60 (S C Townroe), 77, 81b (T B Owen), 89b, 96, 107t (M H Yardy), 113 (G W Powell), 127m,
    127b (P J Hughes), 139b, 147b (Tommy Tomalin), 149b (Tommy Tomalin), 155t, 158, 168,
    171b, 185t, 186 (Tony Cooke), 192, 193b, 199b (T B Owen), 227 (David Lawrence), 239
    (T B Owen), 275, 280 (R Hill), 283tr, 288m, 299m, 299b
Ewan Crawford: 292
Gordon Edgar: 200/201, 204, 205m, 207tr
Andrew Elliott: 236m, 237, 238b, back endpaper
Mike Esau: 38t, 39, 64, 101, 207b
John Furnevel: 6, 258
John Gilks: 206, 224, 297
John Goss: 22, 27b, 62, 72, 76, 78, 94, 134t, 234, 236b, 260
John Gray: 259b, 276, 282, 286, 287br, 288b, 289, 293
Tony Harden: 46bl, 46br, 66, 67m, 92bl, 117b, 174, 175mr, 178, 179b, 190, 211b, 216, 225b,
    238m, 242, 243m, 243b, 248mr, 248b, 249t, 257, 264, 287bl
Julian Holland: 7br, 8bl, 8br, 14, 15, 16, 17m, 21t, 24, 27t, 27m, 30, 31b, 32, 33t, 34, 37, 38b,
    43b, 43b, 47tr, 53t, 53b, 57, 58, 61t, 61br, 63, 67t, 68, 73b, 79, 81t, 85, 88, 92br, 97m, 97b,
    100, 102/103, 107m, 108, 109t, 112, 117t, 118, 120/121b, 132, 134b, 142, 147t, 148, 149t,
    153, 154, 155b, 156, 159, 162, 164b, 166/167, 170br, 171t, 172, 175b, 176, 179t, 180, 181t,

181b, 184, 185b, 187, 188, 191b, 193t, 197br, 198, 199t, 211t, 212t, 213, 217, 220, 225t, 226,
    227m, 252/253, 256, 262, 263, 265, 273, 281b, 283b, 298t
Mike Jones: 28, 31t, 33m, 33b
Colin Miller: 272
Michael Mensing: 143
Milepost 92½: 25, 36, 84
Gavin Morrison: 56, 73m, 205b, 221, 228, 231t, 231m, 246, 250/251, 277
David Panton: 268
Real Photos: front endpaper
Bill Roberton: 274m
Dave Rodgers: 7bl, 230, 232t, 232/233b
Stuart Sellar: 266, 269, 290
Brian Sharpe: 124tr, 125, 126, 163b, 165, 296, 298b

Maps courtesy of:
© Collins Bartholomew (UK map): 4
National Library of Scotland (Ordnance Survey Half-Inch, One-Inch and 1:25,000 Series):
    cover, 12/13, 19, 23, 29, 35, 40/41, 44/45, 50/51, 59, 65, 70/71, 74/75, 82/83, 86/87, 91, 95,
    98/99, 104/105, 110/111, 114/115, 119, 122/123, 130/131, 136/137, 140/141, 145, 151, 157,
    161, 169, 173, 177, 182/183, 189, 194/195, 202/203, 208/209, 214/215, 218/219, 222/223,
    229, 235, 240/241, 247, 254/255, 261, 267, 270/271, 278/279, 284/285, 291, 294/295

With thanks for research assistance/advice to:
Chris Fleet, Keith Farr.

PHOTO CAPTIONS

Cover image:
BR Standard Class 4MT 2-6-4T No. 80005 has just deposited its trainload of happy day trippers at Banff Golf Club House Halt on 8 July 1957. The wide sweeping bay, blue sea and bracing sea air beckon this crowd of hardy Scots. Scenes such as this are now fading memories as the Banff branch was closed to passenger traffic seven years later.

Front endpaper:
Frozen in time. A deserted Barnstaple Town station on the branch line to Ilfracombe, pre-1935, with the Taw Estuary on the right and the bay platform for the narrow-gauge Lynton & Barnstaple Railway on the left. The station building has survived and is now a school.

Contents (p4/5):
End of the line at Ilfracombe on 29 September 1956. Ex-Southern Railway 'N' Class 2-6-0 No. 31841 busies itself in the extensive carriage sidings at Ilfracombe while an unrebuilt Bulleid Light Pacific waits in the bay platform with a train for Barnstaple. After years of decline the Ilfracombe branch succumbed to Dr Beeching's 'Axe' on 5 October 1970.

West Country (p10/11):
Peace at last! With the Second World War having ended just twelve days before, Southern Railway 'N' Class 2-6-0 No. 1856 hauls a heavy westbound train over Meldon Viaduct on 27 August 1945. Based at Exmouth Junction shed, this loco was built in 1925 and withdrawn in September 1964. The viaduct still stands and is used by walkers and cyclists on the Granite Way from Okehampton to Lydford (see pages 18-21).

Southern England (p48/49):
Preserved Great Northern Railway Class 'J52' 0-6-0ST No. 1247 pauses at Ayot with a Stephenson Locomotive Society's special for Dunstable on 14 April 1962. Built in 1900 by Sharp Stewart, this locomotive was privately preserved by Captain Bill Smith in 1959 – the first private preservation of a BR loco – and donated to the National Railway Museum in 1980. Walkers and cyclists can now enjoy following the trackbed of this railway to Wheathampstead (see pages 86-89).

Eastern England (p102/103):
A victim of Dr Beeching's 'Axe', the branch line from Wivenhoe to Brightlingsea closed in 1964. The trackbed along the former railway embankment beside the Colne Estuary can now be enjoyed by walkers and cyclists between Brightlingsea and Alresford Creek (see pages 118-121).

Central England (p128/129):
Ex-Midland Railway Class '1F' 0-6-0T No. 41748 has just arrived at the closed Stroud Wallgate station with an enthusiasts' special from Gloucester on 25 August 1956. A sister engine waits at the other end to haul the train back down the short branch line to Dudbridge. The branch line from Stonehouse to Dudbridge and Nailsworth closed in 1966 and much of its route is now a footpath and cycleway known as the Stroud Valleys Trail (see pages 130-135).

Wales (p166/167):
The Prestatyn to Dyserth branch line closed completely in 1973 and its trackbed is now a footpath and cycleway. Seen here from the summit of Greig Fawr, the route of the railway is marked by an avenue of trees as it winds its way up the valley from distant Prestatyn (see pages 172-175).

Northern England (p200/201):
One of two fine railway bridges that once carried the Morecambe to Wennington railway over the meandering River Lune at Crook o'Lune. While the route closed in 1966, the section from Morecambe to Caton via Lancaster is now a footpath and cycleway (see pages 202-207).

Scotland (p252/253):
The Boat of Garten to Craigellachie railway along the picturesque Spey Valley closed to passengers in 1965. Seen here at the restored Blacksboat station, much of its route between Nethy Bridge and Craigellachie now forms part of the Speyside Way Long Distance Path (see pages 284-289).

Back endpaper:
A scene that was soon to disappear forever. Ex-NER Class 'Q6' 0-8-0 No. 63458 makes a fine sight climbing Seaton Bank with a train of coal empties for South Hetton in late March 1967. This locomotive was built by Armstrong Whitworth in 1921 and withdrawn from Tyne Dock shed in July 1967.

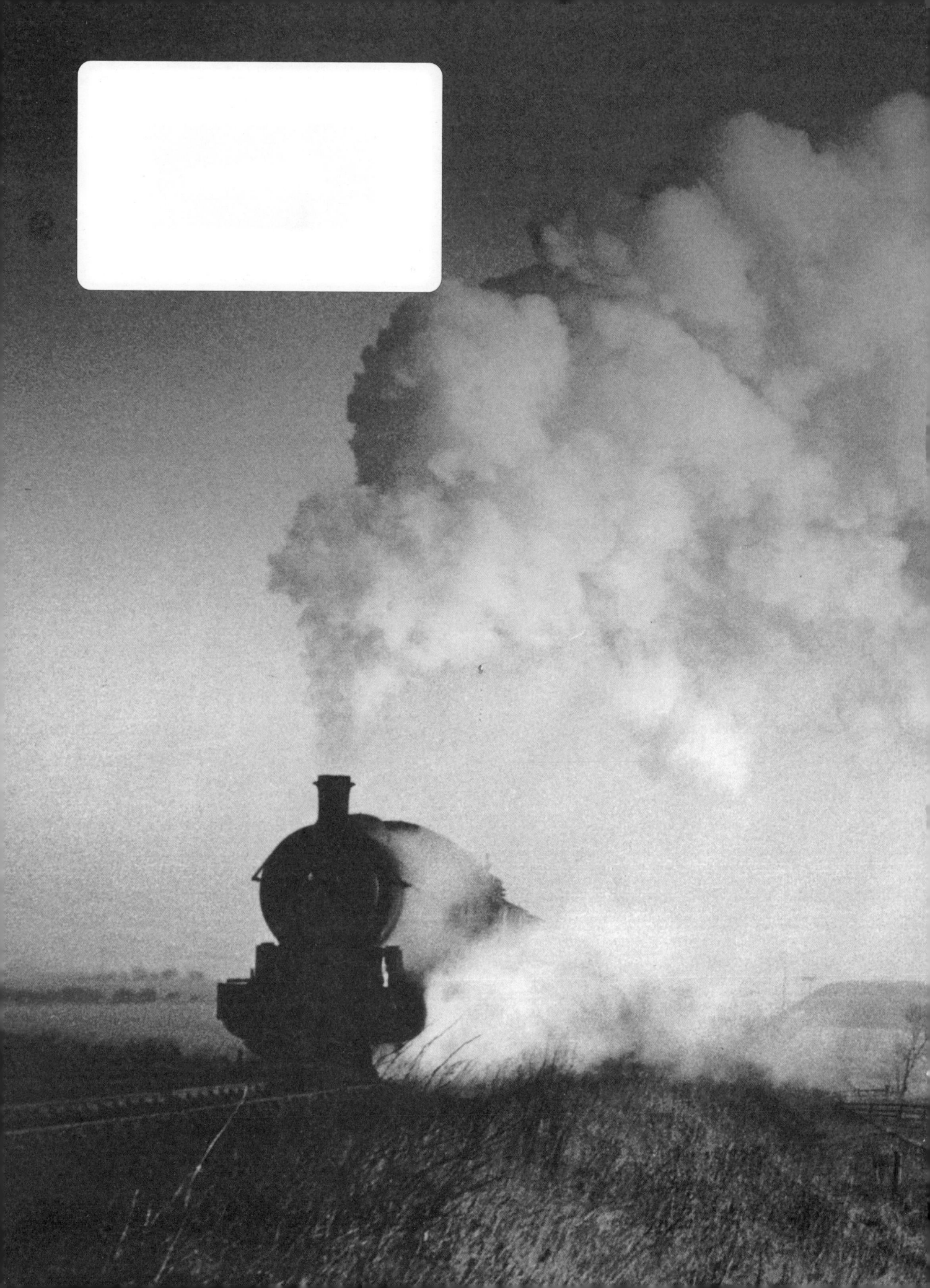